Land Legislation in
Mandate Palestine

Land Legislation in Mandate Palestine

VOLUME 3

STANDARD REFERENCE WORKS,
PART III

Editor: Martin Bunton

CAMBRIDGE UNIVERSITY PRESS

Cambridge, New York, Melbourne, Madrid, Cape Town, Singapore, São Paulo

Cambridge University Press
The Edinburgh Building, Cambridge CB2 2RU, UK

Published in the United States of America by Cambridge University Press,
New York

www.cambridge.org
Information on this title: www.archiveeditions.co.uk

© Copyright in this edition including research, selection of documents, arrangement,
contents lists and descriptions: Cambridge Archive Editions Ltd 2009

Cambridge Archive Editions is an imprint of Cambridge University Press.

Facsimiles of original documents including Crown copyright material are published
under licence from The National Archives, London, England. Images may be used only
for purposes of research, private study or education. Applications for any other use
should be made to The National Archives Image Library, Kew, Richmond, Surrey
TW9 4DU. Infringement of the above condition may result in legal action.

Subject to statutory exception and to the provisions of relevant collective licensing
agreements, no reproduction of other parts of the work may take place without written
permission of Cambridge University Press.

Every reasonable effort has been made to contact all copyright holders; in the event of
any omission please contact the publisher.

First published 2009

Printed and bound by CPI Group (UK) Ltd, Croydon, CR0 4YY

British Library Cataloguing in Publication Data
Land Legislation in Mandate Palestine.
 1. Land tenure–Law and legislation–Palestine–History–
 20th century. 2. Land tenure–Law and legislation–
 Palestine–History–20th century–Sources. 3. Palestine–
 Politics and government–1917-1948.
 I. Bunton, Martin P.
 346.5'6940432-dc22

ISBN-13: 978-1-84097-260-3 (set) (hardback)
          978-1-84097-259-7 (volume 3)

Land Legislation in Mandate Palestine

CONTENTS

VOLUME 3:

STANDARD REFERENCE WORKS, PART III

Section 1: *The Civil Law of Palestine and Trans-Jordan,* C.A. Hooper.   1
Volume 1.
(First published, Jerusalem, Azriel Printing Works, 1933. Reprinted,
London, Sweet & Maxwell Limited, 1934)

Section 2: *The Civil Law of Palestine and Trans-Jordan,* C.A. Hooper.   533
Volume 2.
(First published, Jerusalem, Azriel Printing Works, 1933. Reprinted,
London, Sweet & Maxwell Limited, 1934)

Section 1: *The Civil Law of Palestine and Trans-Jordan,* C.A. Hooper. Volume 1

THE CIVIL LAW
OF
PALESTINE
AND
TRANS-JORDAN

BY

C. A. HOOPER

of the Inner Temple, Barrister-at-Law,
Judicial Adviser to the Government of Transjordan.

(Gilchrist Memorial Scholar in Turkish; Ouseley Memorial Scholar in Arabic, in the University of London, 1913—1914).

VOLUME 1.

LONDON:
SWEET & MAXWELL LIMITED
2 & 3, CHANCERY LANE, W.C.2

First Published, Jerusalem - 1933
Reprinted, London - - - 1934

PRINTED OFFSET IN GREAT BRITAIN
BY HENDERSON AND SPALDING LTD., SYLVAN GROVE, LONDON, S.E.15

To Lieutenant General Sir
ARTHUR GRENFELL WAUCHOPE,
K.C.B., C.M.G., C.I.E., D.S.O.,
His Majesty's High Commissioner for Palestine and Trans-Jordan.

PREFACE.

In placing this work before the public in Palestine I believe I am meeting an actual want. The translations into English which have appeared of the Ottoman Civil Code, one by Dr. Grigsby and the other by Sir Charles Tyser have long since been out of print and are now unobtainable. The break-up of the Ottoman Empire as a result of the war left Palestine under a British Mandate, and with English as one of the three official languages. British judges and magistrates and occasionally administrative officials now preside in the Courts, and there is an increasing number of advocates practising in Palestine who carry on their legal work and plead in English. My object is to place at their disposal, in a separate volume, a complete English version of the Turkish text. The second volume will contain an exposition of the whole subject.

The Ottoman Civil Code became part of the law of Palestine, together with many other Ottoman enactments, in virtue of the terms of Article 46 of the Palestine Order-in-Council, 1922, and of Transjordan, in virtue of the terms of Article 58 of the Organic Law of the 16th April, 1928.

I have naturally endeavoured to obtain complete accuracy in the translation. With this object in view, I first wrote out by hand a complete translation from a reliable Turkish text published by authority in Constantinople in 1308 A. H. I then checked this translation with the two Arabic versions which are most commonly in use in the Arabic speaking territories of the former Ottoman Empire. Where any divergence was found, I referred again to the Turkish text to settle the point. This check revealed the existence of certain errors in these translations. The first of these Arabic versions is that of *Baz* published in Beyrouth (3rd Edition) in 1923, which is the version most commonly used in Palestine; the second is that of *Hawawini* published at Damascus in 1923, and which has been adopted as an official translation by the State of Syria.

In this connection I am happy to acknowledge the invaluable help of Abdullah Nusseir, Superintendent of the Ministry of Justice, Amman, who willingly gave up many hours of his spare time to the tedious task of hearing me read over my English translation, while he watched for any divergencies between this and the two Arabic versions referred to above. Fuad Ghanma, clerk in the Ministry of Justice, Amman, has also helped in the same way.

I also wish to acknowledge the kindly help and interest of Mr. Henry Kantrovitch, Junior Government Advocate, Governmet of Palestine, whose assistance has been invaluable in seeing this Volume through the press in Jerusalem.

C. A. HOOPER.

Amman, Transjordan

TABLE OF CONTENTS.

	page
REPORT OF THE COMMISSION APPOINTED TO DRAFT THE MEJELLE	1
INTRODUCTION	15
Part I. Definition and classification of Muhammadan jurisprudence	15
Part II. Maxims of Muhammadan jurisprudence	17

BOOK I. SALE

	page
Introduction. Terms of Muhammadan jurisprudence relating to sale	31
Chapter I. The contract of sale	37
Section I. The fundamental basis of sale	37
Section II. Agreement of acceptance with offer	40
Section III. The place where the sale is concluded	42
Section IV. Sale subject to a condition	44
Section V. Rescission of the sale	45
Chapter II. The subject matter of the sale	46
Section I. Conditions affecting the subject matter of the sale and description thereof	46
Section II. Things which may and may not be sold	47
Section III. Procedure at the sale	49
Section IV. Matters included but not explicitly mentioned in the sale	54
Chapter III. Matters relating to price	57
Section I. Nature of and circumstances affecting price	57
Section II. Sale subject to payment at a future date	58

II

	page
Chapter IV. Power to deal with the price and the thing sold after the sale	60
Section I. Right of the vendor to dispose of the price and of the purchaser to dispose of the thing sold after the conclusion of the contract and prior to delivery ...	60
Section II. Increase and decrease in the price and in the thing sold after the conclusion of the contract ...	60
Chapter V. Giving and taking delivery ...	64
Section I. Procedure on giving and taking delivery	64
Section II. Right of retention over the thing sold	66
Section III. The place of delivery ...	67
Section IV. Expenses connected with delivery	68
Section V. Destruction of the thing sold	69
Section VI. Sale on approval and subject to inspection	70
Chapter VI. Options	71
Section I. Contractual options ...	71
Section II. Option for misdescription ...	72
Section III. Option as to payment ...	73
Section IV. Option as to selection ...	74
Section V. Option as to inspection ...	74
Section VI. Option for defect	77
Section VII. Misrepresentation and deceit	83
Chapter VII. Various categories of things sold and the effect thereof	84
Section I. Types of sale	84
Section II. Effect of various kinds of sale	85
Section III. Sale by immediate payment against future delivery ...	87
Section IV. Contract for manufacture and sale	88
Section V. Sale by a person suffering from a mortal sickness ...	90
Section VI. Sale subject to a right of redemption	91

III

	page
BOOK II. HIRE	
Introduction. Terms of Muhammadan jurisprudence relating to hire	95
Chapter I. General	97
Chapter II. Questions relating to the contract of hire	100
Section I. The fundamental basis of the contract of hire	100
Section II. Conditions relating to the conclusion and execution of the contract of hire ...	103
Section III. Essentials to the validity of a contract of hire ...	103
Section IV. Nullity or voidability of the contract of hire	105
Chapter III. Questions affecting the amount of the hire	106
Section I. Rent	106
Section II. Necessity for rent: right of the person giving on hire to take rent	107
Section III. Right of lien of a person to whom a thing has been entrusted to work upon ...	111
Chapter IV. The period of hire	112
Chapter V. Options	114
Section I. Contractual options ...	114
Section II. Option of inspection ...	117
Section III. Option for defect	118
Chapter VI. Type of thing hired and matters relating thereto	120
Section I. Matters relating to the hire of real property	120
Section II. Hire of merchandise. ...	123
Section III. Hire of animals.	123
Section IV. Hire of personal services ...	128
Chapter VII. Rights and obligations of the person giving and the person taking on hire after the conclusion of the contract ...	132
Section I. Delivery of the thing hired...	132
Section II. Right of the contracting parties	

	page
to deal with the thing hired after the conclusion of the contract.	133
Section III. Return of the thing hired ...	134
Chapter VIII. Compensation	135
Section I. Compensation in respect to use	135
Section II. Compensation by the person taking the thing on hire ...	137
Section III. Loss caused by employees ..	139

BOOK III. GUARANTEE.

Introduction. Terms of Muhammadan jurisprudence relating to guarantee	143
Chapter I. The contract of guarantee	144
Section I. Fundamental basis of a contract of guarantee	144
Section II. Conditions attaching to a contract of guarantee	145
Chapter II. The contract of guarantee	148
Section I. Unconditional, conditional and future contracts of guarantee	148
Section II. Guarantee for the production of a particular person ...	151
Section III. Guarantee of property ...	151
Chapter III. Release from the contract of guarantee	156
Section I. General	156
Section II. Release from a contract of guarantee to produce a particular person	156
Section III. Release from a contract of guarantee of property ...	157

BOOK IV. TRANSFER OF DEBT.

Introduction. Terms of Muhammadan jurisprudence relating to transfer of debt	161
Chapter I. The contract of transfer of debt ...	161
Section I. The fundamental basis of a transfer of debt	161
Section II. Conditions relating to transfer of debt	163
Chapter II. Effect of a contract for the transfer of debt	164

V

	page
BOOK V. PLEDGES.	
Introduction. Terms of Muhammadan jurisprudence relating to pledges ...	171
Chapter I. Matters relating to the contract of pledge	171
Section I. Fundamental basis of the contract of pledge	171
Section II. Conditions incidental to a contract of pledge	172
Section III. Matters attached to the pledge: change and increase	173
Chapter II. Pledgor and pledgee	174
Chapter III. The pledge	174
Section I. Preservation of the pledge and expenses connected therewith	174
Section II. Pledge of borrowed articles ...	175
Chapter IV. Fundamental rules relating to a pledge	176
Section I. General ...	176
Section II. Rights of pledgor and pledgee over the pledge ...	178
Section III. Deposit of the pledge with a bailee	180
Section IV. Sale of the pledge...	181
BOOK VI. TRUSTS AND TRUSTEESHIP.	
Introduction. Terms of Muhammadan jurisprudence relating to trusts and trusteeship	185
Chapter I. General ...	186
Chapter II. Deposit for safe-keeping ...	188
Section I. Conclusion of the contract of deposit for safe-keeping and conditions relating thereto ...	188
Section II. Effect of making a deposit for safe-keeping and of making good any loss arising therefrom ...	189
Chapter III. Property lent for use	199
Section I. The contract of loan for use and conditions relating thereto ...	199
Section II. Effect of a contract of loan for use and compensation for loss sustained in connection therewith	200

BOOK VII. GIFT.

	page
Introduction. Terms of Muhammadan jurisprudence relating to gift	211
Chapter I. Matters relating to the contract of gift	211
Section I. Fundamental basis and receipt of a gift	211
Section II. Conditions attaching to a gift	215
Chapter II. Fundamental rules relating to gift ...	216
Section I. Revocation of a gift ...	216
Section II. Gifts made during the course of a mortal sickness ...	219

BOOK VIII.
WRONGFUL APPROPRIATION AND DESTRUCTION.

Introduction. Terms of Muhammadan jurisprudence	223
Chapter I. Wrongful appropriation	224
Section I. Wrongful appropriation in general	224
Section II. Wrongful appropriation of real property	229
Section III. Wrongful appropriation from a a person who has already wrongfully appropriated property	231
Chapter II. Destruction of property	232
Section I. Direct destruction of property	232
Section II. Indirect destruction of property	235
Section III. Matters occurring in the public highway	236
Section IV. Injury caused by animals ...	238

BOOK IX.
INTERDICTION, CONSTRAINT AND PRE-EMPTION.

Introduction. Terms of Muhammadan jurisprudence relating to interdiction, constraint and pre-emption	245
Chapter I. Matters relating to interdiction ...	247
Section I. Classes of interdicted persons and matters relating thereto	247
Section II. Matters relating to minors, lunatics and imbeciles ...	248

VII

		page
Section III. Interdicted prodigals	...	254
Section IV. Interdiction of debtors	...	255

Chapter II. Constraint 257
Chapter III. Pre-emption 258
    Section I. Degrees of pre-emption ... 258
    Section II. Conditions attaching to the
        right of pre-emption ... 262
    Section III. The claim of pre-emption ... 264
    Section IV. The effect of pre-emption ... 267

BOOK X. JOINT OWNERSHIP.

Introduction. Terms of Muhammadan jurisprudence   273
Chapter I. Joint ownership of property owned in
    absolute ownership 275
    Section I. Description and classification of
        joint ownership of property
        owned in absolute ownership   275
    Section II. The manner of dealing with
        specific property jointly owned   277
    Section III. Jointly owned debts ... 283
Chapter II. Partition 289
    Section I. Nature and categories of partition   289
    Section II. Conditions attaching to partition   292
    Section III. Partition by units ... 295
    Section IV. Partition by allotment ... 297
    Section V. Method of partition ... 299
    Section VI. Options 301
    Section VII. Cancellation and rescission of
        partition 302
    Section VIII. Effect of partition ... 303
    Section IX. Partition of usufruct ... 306
Chapter III. Walls and neighbours 311
    Section I. Rules of law relating to property
        owned in absolute ownership   311
    Section II. Relations of one neighbour to
        another. 312
    Section III. Roads 317
    Section IV. Right of way; right of acqueduct;
        right of flow 319

VIII

		page
Chapter IV. Jointly owned property which is free		321
Section I.	Things which are free and things which are not free ...	321
Section II.	Acquisition of ownership of things which are free ...	323
Section III.	General conditions attaching to things that are free ...	325
Section IV.	Right of taking water and right of drinking water... ...	326
Section V.	Vivification of dead land ...	328
Section VI.	Ownership of land surrounding wells sunk, water brought, and trees planted with Imperial permission in dead land ...	330
Section VII	Fundamental conditions affecting hunting	332
Chapter V. Joint Expenses		335
Section I.	Repairs to jointly owned property and expenses connected therewith ...	335
Section II.	The cleaning and improvement of rivers and water courses	339
Chapter VI. Partnership		341
Section I.	Definition and classification of partnership	341
Section II.	General conditions affecting a contractual partnership ...	343
Section III.	Conditions affecting a partnership in property ...	344
Section IV.	Rules relating to a contractual partnership	345
Section V.	Partnership with equal shares	349
Section VI.	Partnership with unequal shares	351
	(Sub-Section I.) Partnership in property	351
	(Sub-Section II.) Partnership for work ...	357
	(Sub-Section III.) Partnership on credit	360

	page
Chapter VII. Partnership of capital and labour ...	362
Section I. Definition and classification of partnership of capital and labour	362
Section II. Conditions affecting a partnership of capital and labour	363
Section III. Effect of a partnership of capital and labour	364
Chapter VIII. Partnership in land and work and partnership in trees and work	369
Section 1. Partnership in land and work	369
Section II. Partnership in trees and work	370

BOOK XI. AGENCY

Introduction. Terms of Muhammadan jurisprudence	375
Chapter I. Fundamental basis and classification of agency	375
Chapter II. Conditions attaching to agency	378
Chapter III. Essential elements of agency	379
Section I. General	379
Section II. Agency for purchase	382
Section III. Agency for sale	388
Section IV. Instructions given by one person to another	390
Section V. Agency for litigation	394
Section VI. Dismissal of agents	395

BOOK XII. SETTLEMENT AND RELEASE

Introduction. Terms of Muhammadan jurisprudence	399
Chapter I. Conclusion of a contract of settlement and release...	400
Chapter II. The consideration and subject matter of the settlement	403
Chapter III. The subject matter of the settlement	404
Section I. Settlement in respect to specific property ...	404
Section II. Settlement with regard to debt and other matters...	406

	page
Chapter IV. Fundamental conditions governing settlement and release	407
Section I. Fundamental conditions governing settlement	407
Section II. Fundamental conditions governing release ...	408

BOOK XIII. ADMISSIONS

Chapter I. Conditions governing admissions ...	413
Chapter II. Validity of an admission	415
Chapter III. Effect of an admission	417
Section I. General	417
Section II. Denial of ownership and title to a thing lent	419
Section III. Admission by a person suffering from a mortal sickness ...	421
Chapter IV. Admissions in writing	426

BOOK XIV. ACTIONS

Introduction. Terms of Muhammadan jurisprudence	431
Chapter I. Conditions and fundamental rules relating to an action and the defence thereto ...	431
Section I. Conditions for the validity of an action	431
Section II. The defence to an action ...	436
Section III. Parties to an action ...	437
Section IV. Estoppel...	443
Chapter II. Limitation	449

BOOK XV.
EVIDENCE AND ADMINISTRATION OF OATH.

Introduction. Terms of Muhammadan jurisprudence	457
Chapter I. Nature of evidence	458
Section I. Definition of evidence and number of witnesses ...	458
Section II. The manner of giving evidence	458
Section III. Fundamental conditions as to the giving of evidence ...	461

XI

		page
Section IV. Relevancy of evidence to the point at issue in the action		464
Section V. Contradictory evidence	...	467
Section VI. Inquiry into the credibility of witnesses	... ...	469
Section VII. Withdrawal of evidence	...	473
Section VIII. Conclusively substantiated evidence...	... ...	474
Chapter II. Documentary evidence and presumptive evidence		474
Section I. Documentary evidence	...	474
Section II. Presumptive evidence	...	475
Chapter III. Administering the oath	... ...	475
Chapter IV. Preferred evidence and administration of the oath to both parties	...	478
Section I. Actions regarding possession		478
Section II. Preferred evidence	...	480
Section III. Persons whose evidence is preferred. Judgment based on circumstantial evidence	...	484
Section IV. Administration of the oath to both parties	... ...	487

BOOK XVI.
ADMINISTRATION OF JUSTICE BY THE COURT.

Introduction: Terms of Muhammadan jurisprudence		493
Chapter I. Judges		494
Section I. Qualities requisite in a judge		494
Section II. Conduct of judges...	...	495
Section III. Duties of judges ...	...	495
Section IV. The hearing of an action	...	499
Chapter II. Judgments		501
Section I. Conditions attaching to a judgment		501
Section II. Judgment by default	...	502
Chapter III. Retrial		503
Chapter IV. Arbitration		504

REPORT OF THE COMMISSION APPOINTED TO DRAFT THE MEJELLE.

The science of Muhammadan jurisprudence in its relation to temporal matters is divided into sections dealing with domestic relations, civil obligations and punishments. The fundamental laws of civilized nations are also divided into these three sections, the section dealing with civil obligations being called civil law. In recent times, however, commercial transactions have extended considerably, and for this reason a large number of exceptions to the original law have been created, such as bills of exchange and bankruptcy, and a separate Commercial Code has been drawn up containing these exceptions. This Code is applied in commercial matters, but in other respects recourse must be had to the civil law. For example, in a case dealt with in the Commercial Court in accordance with the terms of the Commercial Code, recourse must be had to the original law in respect to such various matters as pledge, guarantee and agency. Similar procedure is adopted in actions brought in respect to civil rights arising out of criminal offences. Many laws and regulations corresponding to the civil law have been promulgated both in former times and recently in the Ottoman Empire; but although these laws and regulations are not sufficient for the settlement of all civil obligations, that branch of Muhammadan jurisprudence relating to civil obligations is amply sufficient for such purpose. It is true that the reference of actions to *Sharia* and civil law is the cause of certain difficulties. *Sharia* matters, however, are settled in accordance with Muhammadan

Law by the Civil Courts of Cassation presided over by *Sharia* judges, who also deal with civil matters, the difficulty being overcome in this manner, since the science of Muhammadan jurisprudence is the origin and source of the civil laws and regulations, a number of subsidiary matters dealt with by the Civil Courts being settled by applying the rules of Muhammadan jurisprudence. The members of the Courts of Cassation, however, have no knowledge of these rules, and this has given rise to a considerable amount of suspicion and gossip that the *Sharia* judges, when dealing with matters other than those comprised within the laws and regulations promulgated by the State, conduct the proceedings in whatever way they wish.

The Commercial Code is also applied in the Commercial Courts of the Ottoman Empire, but the various matters which have no relation to commercial actions are a source of great difficulty. If recourse is had to the laws of Europe, no judgment can be based thereon in the Courts of the Ottoman Empire, since these laws have not been promulgated by Royal Irada. If they are referred to the *Sharia*, however, the *Sharia* Courts are bound to treat such various matters on the basis of an original action. The rules of procedure of the two Courts, in fact, are fundamentally divergent and for this reason confusion is bound to occur. The result is that no reference can be made from the Commercial Courts to the *Sharia* Courts. If it is argued that the members of the Commercial Courts should refer to the treatises on Muhammadan Law, such argument is untenable, since these persons are in the same position in matters relating to Muhammadan jurisprudence as members of the Courts of Cassation.

The resources of the science of Muhammadan jurisprudence, however, are inexhaustible and it is possible to find therein the answer to all questions necessary to solve the difficulties which are dependent upon expert knowledge thereof. In particular, a large number of interpreters of all ranks of the Hanifite school have arisen, the result being a large number of divergencies of opinion. In spite of this fact, however, the *Hanifite* school did not crystallize as was the case of the *Shafi* school, but on the contrary has split up into innumerable sections and opposing sub-divisions. The result is that great difficulty has been occasioned in distinguishing the truth among these conflicting views, and applying the same to any given set of facts.

At the same time, questions of Muhammadan jurisprudence which were based upon custom have changed with the change in the times. For example, Muhammadan jurists in former times held that it was sufficient to inspect one room of a house which it was proposed to buy. Subsequent jurists, however, have held that it is necessary to inspect every room. This, however, is not a fundamental change in regard to evidence, but has arisen out of custom regarding building construction, the effect of which was that in former times every room of a house was built to a standard pattern and the inspection of one room was equivalent to an inspection of all. In later times, however, it became the custom to construct houses with rooms differing from each other, and consequently it became necessary to inspect each room. In fact, the essential point was to obtain sufficient knowledge with regard to the contemplated purchase. Consequently, the original rule of Muhammadan jurisprudence has not been changed, but the method of applying this rule to any given set of facts has changed with the change in the times. A great deal of attention is also required to dis-

4   REPORT OF COMMISSION

tinguish between the change in the times in such matters and a change in respect to proof.

It is a matter of great difficulty to obtain a knowledge of the principles of Muhammadan jurisprudence, and although at one period the jurists and learned men of the time assembled together and compiled treatises such as the *Tatarkhanieh* and the *Fatavai Jihangerieh* embracing the questions of Muhammadan jurisprudence according to the Hanifite school, they were not able to deal with the whole of the details thereof, nor of the divergencies of the school.

By *Fetwa* books is meant those compilations which contain *fetwas* issued regarding the application of the rules of Muhammadan jurisprudence to any given set of facts. There is, perhaps, no necessity to state how difficult it is to collect together the *fetwas* which have been issued by Hanifite jurists in respect to such matters during the course of the centuries. For this reason, *Ibn Nujaim* collected together a number of rules and questions and included thereunder in compendious form the details of Muhammadan jurisprudence. Succeeding centuries, however, were not so favourable to studies in Muhammadan jurisprudence as was formerly the case. People were content with the labours of *Ibn Nujaim* and no attempt was made to work on the ground which he had prepared.

At the present time, owing to the scarcity in any given locality of persons versed in Muhammadan jurisprudence, it is a matter of difficulty to find even a sufficient number of judges in the *Sharia* Courts of the Ottoman Empire, not to mention the question of finding members of the Civil Courts who, in case of need, could refer to the treatises on Muhammadan jurisprudence for the solution of any doubtful question. Consequently, if a work were compiled devoid of divergencies and including only accepted opinion with regard to civil obligations in Muhammadan Law and which is easy to refer to, all persons could easily study the same and apply the contents thereof to civil obligations. In the event of a book being in existence compiled in this manner, it would be of immense value to the judges of the Sharia Courts, members of the Civil Courts, and administrative officials who, by studying the same, could, if necessary, conduct their business in accordance with the precepts of Muhammadan jurisprudence. Such a book would be in force in the *Sharia* Courts and there would be no need to enact a law for civil actions in the Civil Courts. These are considerations which, for some time past, has made it desirable to produce an authoritative work of this nature. With this object in view, a Committee of jurists was set up in the office of the Legislative Council and a large number of questions were dealt with. The labours of this Committee, unfortunately, did not reach fruition, which, like many other beneficial matters, had to be adjourned until the time of His Majesty the present Sultan.

In accordance with the orders of His Majesty the Sultan to produce a work of this nature, sufficient for the application of the doctrines of Muhammadan jurisprudence to the daily civil obligations of the people, we met in the office of the High Court and collected together those matters of Muhammadan jurisprudence, according to the Hanifite school, which relate to civil obligations and are of frequent occurrence and of the greatest necessity at the present day. We then began to arrange them in the form of a Code, divided into Books and called *Ahkam-i-Adlieh* (rules of justice). When the Introduction and Book I were finished, we sent a copy to the *Sheikh-al-Islam*. Copies were also sent to persons skilled and learned in Muhammadan jurisprudence, and modifications were incor-

6 REPORT OF COMMISSION

porated therein according to their recommendations, whereupon a corrected copy was sent to the Grand Vizier. The translation of this work into Arabic was put in hand, and the other books are being composed.

Upon a perusal of the Introduction you will see that the second section thereof consists of the rules of Muhammadan jurisprudence collected together by *Ibn Nujaim* and jurists of his school. Although these rules alone are not sufficient to enable the *Sharia* judges to give a judgment in the absence of any more explicit authority, they are, nevertheless, of great value in connecting together the various questions of Muhammadan jurisprudence; and persons who have studied these questions are able to settle them by means of proofs.

In addition, other officials can refer to them in any matter whatsoever. By means of them a man can make his conduct conform to the *Sharia* law as far as possible. For this reason they have been included in an Introduction and not given the title of Book or Chapter. Although in treatises on Muhammadan jurisprudence details are mixed with principles, in this Code the terms of Muhammadan jurisprudence relating to each Book have been set forth in an Introduction to that Book and the details have been arranged in sequence. In order to explain the fundamental points, however, a large number of questions have been added by way of illustration taken from the *fetwa* books.

Commercial transactions at the present day are generally carried on subject to certain conditions. The most important part of the Book on Sale is the Section relating to sale subject to a condition. Owing to the Hanifite school holding that the majority of the conditions stipulated upon the conclusion of a contract of sale subject to a condition render the sale invalid, your Committee have examined the question with great care and have thought fit to set forth a summary of their discussions below.

The majority of the interpreters of Muhammadan law express conflicting opinions regarding sale subject to a condition. According to the Malikite School the vendor can stipulate to have some special advantage for himself in the thing sold for a limited period; and according to the Hanbalite school for an unlimited period. It seems, however, that to give the vendor this option and not to give it to the purchaser is contrary to opinion and to legal analogy. The Great Imam and the two interpreters of Muhammadan law, *Ibn Abu Leila* and *Ibn Shibrima*, who lived during the same period, and whose followers subsequently disappeared, are also completely opposed to one another in this respect. Thus, according to *Ibn Abu Leila*, in every case both sale and condition are voidable; but in the opinion of *Ibn Shibrima* both sale and condition are absolutely valid.

The school of *Ibn Abu Leila* seems to be contrary to the tradition of the Prophet which states "let the Muslims keep to their conditions". The school of *Ibn Shibrima* is in entire agreement with the doctrine of the Prophet: but should vendor or purchaser make any condition, whether legal or illegal, or whether capable of execution or not, it is a point agreed upon by all Muhammadan jurists that the observance of a condition shall only take place so far as that is possible.

Consequently, the question of observance of a condition is a rule which admits of limitation and exception. For this reason a middle course has been adopted in the Hanifite school and conditions have been divided into three categories: a valid condition, a voidable condition and a condition which is null and void. Thus, any condition stipulated in favour of one of the contracting parties and which is not of the very essence of the contract, or which does not serve to assure one of the essential elements thereof, is voidable and

REPORT OF COMMISSION

renders the sale voidable. A condition which brings no advantage to either of the parties, is regarded as null and void, the sale being valid, since the object of buying and selling is to confer and obtain ownership, that is to say, to enable the purchaser to obtain ownership of the thing sold and the vendor to obtain ownership of the price, without any let or hindrance. But if a condition existed in favour of one of the contracting parties alone, who insisted on the execution of such condition, and the other party sought to escape therefrom, such conduct would give rise to disputes, and it could not be claimed in such circumstances that the sale was complete. Sale subject to a condition of this nature, however, is permissible when it is allowed by custom, because in such a case the dispute itself would be finally settled by custom.

Commercial transactions in themselves are exceptional, as has been stated above. The majority of trade guilds have decided upon a procedure which is sanctioned by custom. There is consequently no need to deal with them, subject, however, to those conditions made without reference to custom, by persons undertaking some special piece of business. These are not numerous, however, and do not justify special treatment. It has consequently not been thought right to depart from the Hanifite school in their favour and to adopt the school of *Ibn Shibrima*. For this reason we have contented ourselves with mentioning in Section IV of Chapter I, the conditions which do not make a sale voidable according to the Hanifite school, a procedure adopted in the other Sections.

Finally, in view of the fact that the majority of the matters dealt with in this Code do not depart from the doctrines of the Hanifite school and are applied in the *Fatwakhana* at the present day, there is no need to discuss them here. But since the opinions of certain of the jurists of the Hanifite school who are accepted as authoritative owing to their being convenient for the people and suitable to the affairs of the moment are included, the sources of these persons and the reasons therefor are set out below.

In accordance with the terms of Articles 197 and 205 the sale of a thing not in existence is invalid. In view of the fact, however, that the produce of flowers such as roses and artichokes and of vegetables and fruits appear in succession, certain parts thereof maturing before the other parts, it has become the custom generally to sell the produce of such things which have appeared and which have yet to appear *en bloc*. The Imam *Muhammad Ibn Hassan al Shaibani* has, by applying the Muhammadan doctrine of equity, authorized the sale *en bloc* of things not yet in existence, together with the produce of things already in existence. Moreover, the Imam *Fasli, al-Halwani* and *Abu Bekr Ibn Fazl* have issued *fetwas* in conformity with this opinion. Consequently, the terms of Article 207 have been drawn up in conformity with the opinion of *Muhammad*, which is preferred in this Code, since it is not possible to disregard customs of this nature and since it is preferable to facilitate civil transactions as far as possible rather than to hinder them.

As regards sale *en bloc* such as the sale of a heap of corn at so much per *kilé*, the Great Imam holds that the sale of one *kilé* only is valid. The two Imams, however, hold that the price must be paid according to the total number of *kilés* comprised in that heap when it has been entirely sold. The terms of Article 220 have been drawn up in accordance with this opinion with a view to facilitating the transaction of civil business, more particularly since this view is shared by a large number of Muslim jurists such as the author of the *Hedaya*.

10 REPORT OF COMMISSION

According to the Great Imam, the period of an option conferred by contract may not exceed three days. According to the two Imams, however, the contract is valid, according to the number of days agreed upon in the contract. In view of this fact, the opinion of the latter has been deemed to be more in accordance with the needs of the people and an unlimited period has been inserted in Article 300.

These divergencies of opinion are also apparent as regards the option as to payment. The Imam *Muhammad* is alone in prescribing an unlimited period for the exercise of this option. Nevertheless, since this option is deemed to be most suitable to the needs of the people, the period was left to the contracting parties when drafting the terms of Article 313.

According to the Great Imam, when a contract for manufacture and sale is concluded, the contractor for manufacture can go back on the sale. According to the Imam *Abu Yusif,* however, he may not go back on the sale if the manufactured article is up to description. In these days, however, a large number of manufactories have been established and among other things guns, rifles and steamships are built to contract to such an extent that the contract for manufacture and sale has now become of very great importance. Consequently, if the contractor for sale had an option to denounce the contract for manufacture and sale, a large number of important interests would be ruined. Moreover, the contract for manufacture and sale, which is based upon the custom of the people, has a close resemblance to sale by immediate payment against future delivery, which is sanctioned by Muhammadan equity, although the latter is contrary to legal analogy. Therefore, in view of the needs of the time, it has been deemed essential to prefer the view of the Imam *Abu Yusif* and the terms of Article 392 have been drafted accordingly.

In questions which have been the subject of legal interpretation it has been found necessary to act in accordance with whatever order has been issued by the Sultan. If you approve, we request you to obtain Imperial sanction for this Code.

Dated 18 Zil Hijja 1285: 10th. March 1285.

INTRODUCTION

INTRODUCTION

PART I.

DEFINITION AND CLASSIFICATION OF MUHAMMADAN JURISPRUDENCE.

Article 1. The science of Muhammadan jurisprudence consists of a knowledge of the precepts of the Divine Legislator in their relation to human affairs.

The questions of Muhammadan jurisprudence either concern the next world, being known as rules relating to worship, or to this world, being divided into sections dealing with[1] domestic relations,[2] civil obligations and[3] punishments. Thus God decreed the continuation of the world until the appointed time. This, however, can only occur by mankind being perpetuated which is dependent upon marriage of male and female with a view to procreation. Moreover, the continuation of the human species is assured by individuals associating together. Man, however, in view of the weakness of his nature is dependent upon food, clothing, housing and the industries for his subsistence. In other words, in view of the fact that man is a civilized being, he cannot live in solitude like the other animals, but is in need of co-operation and association in work with his fellow men in order to live in a state of civilization. Every person, however, asks for the things which he likes and avoids things which are disagreable to him. As a result, it has been necessary to establish laws of a nature likely to maintain order and justice as regards marriage, mutual help and social relations, which are the basis of all civilization.

The first division of Muhammadan jurisprudence is the section dealing with domestic relations. The second is the section dealing with civil obligations. In view of the fact that the continuance of civilization on this basis necessitates the drawing up of certain matters relating to punishment, the third section of Muhammadan jurisprudence deals with punishments.

As regards the section dealing with civil obligations, the questions which are of the most frequent occurrence have been collected together from reliable works and set out in this Code in the form of Books. These Books have been divided into Chapters and the Chapters into Sections. The questions of detail which will be applied in the Courts are those questions which are set out in the following Chapters and Sections. Muslim jurists, however, have grouped questions of Muhammadan jurisprudence under certain general rules, each one of which embraces a large number of questions and which, in the treatises on Muhammadan jurisprudence, are taken as justification to prove these questions. The preliminary study of these rules facilitates the comprehension of the questions and serves to fix them in the mind. Consequently, ninety nine rules of Muhammadan jurisprudence have been collected together as follows, before commencing on the main work and form Part II.

Although a few of them, taken alone, admit of certain exceptions, their general application is in no way invalidated thereby, since they are closely interrelated.

PART II.

MAXIMS OF MUHAMMADAN JURISPRUDENCE.

Article 2. A matter is determined according to intention; that is to say, the effect to be given to any particular transaction must conform to the object of such transaction.

Article 3. In contracts effect is given to intention and meaning and not to words and phrases. Consequently, a contract for sale subject to a right of redemption has the force of a pledge.

Article 4. Certainty is not dispelled by doubt.

Article 5. It is a fundamental principle that a thing shall remain as it was originally.

Article 6. Things which have been in existence from time immemorial shall be left as they were.

Article 7. Injury cannot exist from time immemorial.

Article 8. Freedom from liability is a fundamental principle.

Therefore, if one person destroys the property of another, and a dispute arises as to the amount thereof, the statement of the person causing such destruction shall be heard, and the onus of proof as to any amount in excess thereof is upon the owner of such property.

Article 9. Non-existence is a fundamental principle which applies to all rights which may subsequently accrue.

Example :-
> In a case of partnership of capital and labour, a dispute arises as to whether profit has been made or not. The statement of the person supplying the labour is heard, and the owner of the capital must prove that profit has in fact been made, since the fundamental principle is the non-existence of the profit.

Article 10. Judgment shall be given in respect to any matter which has been proved at any particular time, unless the contrary is proved.

Consequently, if it is proved at any particular time that a particular thing is owned by a particular person in absolute ownership, the ownership thereof shall be held to be valid unless circumstances arise which invalidate such ownership.

Article 11. It is a fundamental principle that any new occurrence shall be regarded as happening at the time nearest to the present. That is to say, if a dispute arises regarding the cause of some new event and the time at which it occurred, such event shall be considered with reference to the time nearest to the present, unless it is proved that it relates to some remoter period.

Article 12. It is a fundamental principle that words shall be construed literally.

Article 13. No attention shall be paid to inferences in the face of obvious facts.

Article 14. Where the text is clear, there is no room for interpretation.

Article 15. A matter which has been proved contrary to legal analogy cannot be cited by way of analogy in respect to any other matter.

Article 16. One legal interpretation does not destroy another.

Article 17. Difficulty begets facility; that is to say, difficulty is the cause of facility and in time of hardship consideration must be shown. Very many subjects of Muhammadan jurisprudence, such as loans, transfer of debts and interdiction are derived from this principle, and the latitude and indulgence shown by Muhammadan jurists in their rulings are all based upon this rule.

Article 18. Latitude should be afforded in the case of difficulty, that is to say, upon the appearance of hardship in any particular matter, latitude and indulgence must be shown.

Article 19. Injury may not be met by injury.

Article 20. Injury is removed.

Article 21. Necessity renders prohibited things permissible.

Article 22. Necessity is estimated by the extent thereof.

Article 23. A thing which is permissible by reason of the existence of some excuse therefor, ceases to be permissible with the disappearance of that excuse.

Article 24. When a prohibition is removed, the thing to which such prohibition attaches reverts to its former status of legality.

Article 25. An injury cannot be removed by the commission of a similar injury.

Article 26. A private injury is tolerated in order to ward off a public injury. The prohibition from practice of an incompetent physician is derived from this principle.

Article 27. Severe injury is removed by lesser injury.

Article 28. In the presence of two evils, the greater is avoided by the commission of the lesser.

Article 29. The lesser of two evils is preferred.

Article 30. Repelling an evil is preferable to securing a benefit.

Article 31. Injury is removed as far as possible.

Article 32. Any want, whether of a public or private nature, is so dealt with as to meet the exigencies of the case. The validity of sale subject to a right of redemption is of this nature. The inhabitants of Bokhara having fallen badly into debt, this procedure was put into operation in order to meet the exigencies of the case.

Article 33. Necessity does not invalidate the right of another. Consequently, if a hungry person eats bread belonging to another, such person must later pay the value thereof.

Article 34. A thing which may not be taken may also not be given.

Article 35. It is forbidden to request the performance of a prohibited act.

Article 36. Custom is an arbitrator; that is to say, custom, whether public or private, may be invoked to justify the giving of judgment.

Article 37. Public usage is conclusive evidence and action must be taken in accordance therewith.

Article 38. A thing which it is customary to regard as impossible is considered to be impossible in fact.

Article 39. It is an accepted fact that the terms of law vary with the change in the times.

Article 40. In the presence of custom no regard is paid to the literal meaning of a thing.

Article 41. Effect is only given to custom where it is of regular occurrence or when universally prevailing.

Article 42. Effect is given to what is of common occurrence; not to what happens infrequently.

Article 43. A matter recognized by custom is regarded as though it were a contractual obligation.

MAXIMS

Article 44. A matter recognized by merchants is regarded as being a contractual obligation between them.

Article 45. A matter established by custom is like a matter established by law.

Article 46. When prohibition and necessity conflict, preference is given to the prohibition.

Consequently, a person may not sell to another a thing which he has given to his creditor as security for debt.

Article 47. An accessory which is attached to an object in fact is also attached to it in law.

Consequently, when a pregnant animal is sold, the young in its womb is sold with it.

Article 48. An accessory to an object cannot be dealt with separately.

Example :
The young in an animal's womb cannot be sold separately.

Article 49. The owner of a thing held in absolute ownership is also the owner of the things indispensable to the enjoyment of such thing.

Example:
A person who buys a house is also owner of the road leading to it.

Article 50. If the principal fails, the accessory also fails.

Article 51. A thing which fails is not restored; that is to say, that which goes does not return.

Article 52. When a thing becomes void, the thing contained in it also becomes void.

Article 53. When the original undertaking cannot be carried out, the equivalent thereof is carried out.

Article 54. A thing which is not permissible in itself, may be permissible as an accessory.

Example :-

It is not permissible for a purchaser to make the vendor his agent to receive the thing sold; but if he gives a sack to the vendor to measure and put therein the provisions which he has bought and the vendor puts the provisions into the sack, the purchaser thereby receives them impliedly and as an accessory.

Article 55. A thing which is not permissible at the outset may become permissible at some later period.

Example :-

The disposal of a share of undivided jointly owned property by way of gift is invalid, but if a person entitled to a share of undivided jointly owned property which has been bestowed by way of gift appears and takes possession thereof, the gift does not become void, but the remaining share becomes the property of the recipient of the gift.

Article 56. Continuance is easier than commencement.

Article 57. A gift becomes absolute only when delivery thereof is taken.

Example :-

A person bestows a thing upon another person by way of gift. Such gift is not binding until delivery thereof has been taken.

Article 58. The exercise of control over subjects is dependent upon the public welfare.

Article 59. Private guardianship is more effective than public guardianship.

Example :-

The guardianship exercised by the trustee of a pious foundation is more effective than the guardianship of the Court.

Article 60. A word should be construed as having some meaning, rather than passed over in silence. That is to say, if any particular meaning can be attributed to a word, it may not be passed over as devoid of meaning.

Article 61. When the literal meaning cannot be applied, the metaphorical sense may be used.

Article 62. If no meaning can be attached to a word it is disregarded altogether. That is to say, if a word cannot be construed in either a literal or metaphorical sense it is passed over in silence as being devoid of meaning.

Article 63. A reference to part of an indivisible thing is regarded as a reference to the whole.

Article 64. The absolute is construed in its absolute sense, provided that there is no proof of a restricted meaning either in the text of the law or by implication.

Article 65. A description with reference to a thing present is of no effect, but the contrary is the case if such thing is not present.

Example :-
> When a vendor who is about to sell a grey horse, such grey horse being present at the meeting where the sale took place, states that he is selling a brown horse for so many thousand piastres, his offer is held to be good and the word brown is of no effect. But if he sells a grey horse which is not present and he describes it as brown, the description is held to be good but the sale is not concluded.

Article 66. A question is considered to have been repeated in the answer. That is to say, in the event of a question being answered in the affirmative, the person answering the question is considered to have repeated the question.

MAXIMS

Article 67. No statement is imputed to a man who keeps silence, but silence is tantamount to a statement where there is an absolute necessity for speech. That is to say, it may not be said that a person who keeps silence has made such and such a statement, but if he keeps silence where he ought to have made a statement, such silence is regarded as an admission and a statement.

Article 68. In obscure matters the proof of a thing stands in the place of such thing. That is to say, obscure matters concerning which it is hard to discover the truth are judged according to the obvious proof concerning them.

Article 69. Correspondence takes the place of an exchange of conversation.

Article 70. The signs of a dumb person which are generally recognized take the place of a statement by word of mouth.

Article 71. The word of an interpreter is accepted in every respect.

Article 72. No validity is attached to conjecture which is obviously tainted by error.

Article 73. Probability, even though based upon evidence, is not proof.

Example:-

If a person admits while suffering from a mortal sickness that he owes a certain sum of money to one of his heirs, such admission is not proof unless confirmed by the other heirs, since the probability of such person defrauding the other heirs of their property is based upon the mortal sickness. If the statement, however, is made while in a state of good health, such admission is considered to be valid. The probability in that case is mere supposition and consequently there is no objection to the validity of the admission.

Article 74. No weight is attached to mere supposition.

Article 75. A thing established by proof is equivalent to a thing established by ocular inspection.

Article 76. Evidence is for him who affirms; the oath for him who denies.

Article 77. The object of evidence is to prove what is contrary to appearance; the object of the oath is to ensure the continuance of the original state.

Article 78. Evidence is proof affecting third persons; admission is proof affecting the person making such admission only.

Article 79. A person is bound by his own admission.

Article 80. Contradiction and proof are incompatible; but this does not invalidate a judgment given against the person contradicting.

Example :-
Witnesses contradict themselves by going back upon the evidence they have given. Such evidence is not proof; but if the Court has already given judgment based upon the original evidence, such judgment may not be set aside, but the witnesses must pay the value of the subject matter of the judgment to the persons against whom judgment has been given.

Article 81. Failure to establish the principal claim does not imply failure to establish a claim subsidiary thereto.

Example :-
A person states that A owes a sum of money to B and that he is the surety of A. Such person will be obliged to pay the sum in question if A repudiates the debt and B demands payment.

Article 82. If the validity of a condition is established, the validity of anything dependent thereon must also be established.

Article 83. A condition must be observed as far as possible.

Article 84. Any promise dependent upon a condition is irrevocable upon such condition being fulfilled.

Example :-
> A person tells A to sell a certain thing to B and informs A that he will pay him in the event of B failing to do so, and B does in fact fail so to do. The person making the promise is obliged to pay the money.

Article 85. The enjoyment of a thing is the compensating factor for any liability attaching thereto; that is to say, in the event of a thing being destroyed, the person to whom such thing belongs must suffer the loss and conversely may enjoy any advantages attaching thereto.

Example:-
> An animal is returned by reason of an option for defect. The vendor may not charge any fee on account of the use of the animal, because if it had been destroyed before being returned, the loss would have fallen upon the purchaser.

Article 86. Remuneration and liability to make good loss do not run together.

Article 87. Disadvantage is an obligation accompanying enjoyment. That is to say, a person who enjoys a thing must submit to the disadvantages attaching thereto.

Article 88. The burden is in proportion to the benefit and the benefit to the burden.

Article 89. The responsibility for an act falls upon the author thereof; it does not fall upon the person ordering such act to be performed, provided that such person does not compel the commission thereof.

Article 90. If a person performs any act personally and is implicated therein with the person who is the cause thereof, the person performing such act is responsible therefor.

Example:-
A digs a well in the public highway and B causes C's animal to fall therein and to be destroyed. B is responsible therefor and no liability rests with the person who dug the well.

Article 91. An act allowed by law cannot be made the subject of a claim to compensation.

Example:-
An animal belonging to A falls into a well which B has dug on his own property held in absolute ownership and such animal is destroyed. No compensation can be claimed.

Article 92. A person who performs an act, even though not intentionally, is liable to make good any loss caused thereby.

Article 93. A person who is the cause of an act being performed is not liable to make good any loss caused by such act unless he has acted intentionally.

Article 94. No liability attaches in connection with offences of or damage caused by animals of their own accord.

Article 95. Any order given for dealing with the property of any other person held in absolute ownership is void.

Article 96. No person may deal with the property of another held in absolute ownership without such person's permission.

Article 97. No person may take another person's property without some legal reason.

MAXIMS

Article 98. Any change in the cause of the ownership of a thing held in absolute ownership is equivalent to a change in that thing itself.

Article 99. Any person who hastens the accomplishment of a thing before its due time, is punished by being deprived thereof.

Article 100. If any person seeks to disavow any act performed by himself, such attempt is entirely disregarded.

BOOK I.

SALE

BOOK I.

SALE.

INTRODUCTION.

TERMS OF MUHAMMADAN JURISPRUDENCE RELATING TO SALE.

Article 101. Offer is the statement made in the first place with a view to making a disposition of property and such disposition is proved thereby.

Article 102. Acceptance is the statement made in the second place with a view to making a disposition of property. The contract becomes completed thereby.

Article 103. Contract is what the parties bind themselves and undertake to do with reference to a particular matter. It is composed of the combination of offer and acceptance.

Article 104. The conclusion of a contract consists of connecting offer and acceptance together legally in such a manner that the result may be perfectly clear.

Article 105. Sale consists of exchanging property for property. It may be concluded or non-concluded.

Article 106. A concluded sale is a sale in which there is a concluded contract. Such sales are divided into valid, voidable, executory, and conditional.

Article 107. A non-concluded sale is a sale which is void.

Article 108. A valid sale, or a sale which is permitted, is a sale which is lawful both in itself and as regards matters incidental thereto.

Article 109. A voidable sale is a sale which, while valid in itself, is invalid as regards matters incidental thereto. That is to say, it is a concluded sale in itself, but is illegal as regards certain external particulars. (See Chapter VII.)

Article 110. A void sale is a sale which is invalid in itself.

Article 111. A conditional sale is a sale which is dependent upon the rights of some third party, such as a sale by an unauthorized person.

Article 112. An unauthorized person is a person who, without any legal permission, deals with the property of some other person.

Article 113. An executory sale is a sale not dependent upon the rights of any third person. Such sales are divided into irrevocable and revocable sales.

Article 114. An irrevocable sale is an executory sale to which no options are attached.

Article 115. A revocable sale is an executory sale to which an option is attached.

Article 116. An option means having the power to choose, as will be explained in the relevant Chapter.

Article 117. An absolute sale is a final sale.

Article 118. A sale subject to a right of redemption is a sale in which one person sells property to another for a certain sum of money, subject to the right of redeeming such property, upon the price thereof being returned. Such a sale is considered to be permissible in view of the fact that the purchaser has a right to enjoyment of the property sold. It is also in the nature of a voidable sale inasmuch as the two parties have the right of cancelling the sale. Again, it is in the nature of a pledge, in view of the fact that the purchaser cannot sell the property sold to any third party.

Article 119. A sale with a right of usufruct is a sale subject to a right of redemption, the vendor having a right to take the property sold on hire.

Article 120. Sales are also divided into four categories with reference to the thing sold: 1) Sale of property to another person for a price. This is the commonest category of sale and is consequently specifically called sale; '2) Sale by exchange of money for money; 3) Sale by barter; 4) Sale by immediate payment against future delivery.

Article 121. Exchange of money for money consists of selling cash for cash.

Article 122. Sale by barter consists of exchanging one specific object for some other specific object, that is to say, of exchanging property for property other than money.

Article 123. Sale by immediate payment against future delivery consists of paying in advance for something to be delivered later, that is to say, to purchase something with money paid in advance, thereby giving credit.

Article 124. A contract for manufacture and sale consists of making a contract with any skilled person for the manufacture of any particular thing. The person making the article is called the manufacturer; the person causing the article to be made is called the contractor for manufacture, and the object made is called the manufactured article.

Article 125. Property held in absolute ownership is anything owned absolutely by man and may consist either of some specific object or of an interest therein.

34   SALE

Article 126. Property consists of something desired by human nature and which can be put aside against time of necessity. It comprises movable and immovable property.

Article 127. Property of some specific value is spoken of in two senses. (1) It is a thing the benefit of which it is lawful to enjoy; (2) The other is acquired property.

Example :
> A fish while in the sea is not of any specific value. When it is caught and taken, it becomes property of some specific value.

Article 128. Movable property consists of property which can be transferred from one place to another. This includes cash, merchandise, animals, things estimated by measure of capacity and things estimated by weight.

Article 129. Immovable property consists of property such as houses and land which are called real property and which cannot be transferred to another place.

Article 130. Cash consist of gold and silver coins.

Article 131. Merchandise consists of things such as goods and piece-goods other than cash, animals, things estimated by measure of capacity and things estimated by weight.

Article 132. Things estimated by quantity are those things the amount of which is determined by any measure of capacity or of weight, or of number, or of length.

Articles 133-6. These Articles repeat the measures of capacity etc. given in Articles 131 and 132 above.

Article 137. The expression 'possessing defined boundaries' refers to real property the boundaries and limits of which can be fixed.

Article 138. Undivided jointly owned property is property which contains undivided jointly owned shares.

Article 139. An undivided jointly owned share is a share which extends to and includes every part of the jointly-owned property.

Article 140. By a particular species of thing is meant a thing in respect to which there is no disproportionate difference in so far as the component elements thereof are concerned.

Article 141. A wholesale contract is a contract for sale *en bloc.*

Article 142. Right of way is the right of passing over real property held in absolute ownership belonging to another.

Article 143. The right of taking water is the right of taking a clearly defined and ascertained share of water from a river.

Article 144. The right of flow is the right of discharging water and of letting water drip from a house to some place outside.

Article 145. A common article is a thing the like of which can be found in the market without any difference of price.

Article 146. A rare article is an article the like of which cannot be found in the market, or, if it can be found, is different in price.

Article 147. Articles measured by enumeration and which closely resemble each other are those things in respect to which there is no difference as regards the price of each particular object. They are all in the nature of common articles.

Article 148. Articles measured by enumeration and

which are dissimilar from each other are those things in respect to which a difference in price exists as regards each particular article. They are all regarded as rare articles.

Article 149. The fundamental basis or essence of sale consists of one piece of property being exchanged for another. Offer and acceptance are also referred to as the fundamental basis of sale, since they imply exchange.

Article 150. The subject of sale is the thing sold.

Article 151. The thing sold is the property disposed of, that is, the specific object specified at the sale and which constitutes the original object thereof, because enjoyment can only be had of specific objects, price being the means of exchanging property.

Article 152. The price is the amount to be paid for the article sold, and entails liability to make payment.

Article 153. A fixed price is a price mutually named and agreed upon by the two contracting parties whether corresponding to the real value or whether more or less

Article 154. The value is the real price of an article.

Article 155. A priced article is a thing which is sold for a price.

Article 156. A postponement of payment consists of putting off a debt to a definite date.

Article 157. Payment by instalments consists of a postponement of payment of a debt in order that it may be paid at different and definite periods.

Article 158. A debt is the thing which is proved to be owing.

Examples :-

(1) A certain sum of money lent to A and owed by him ;

(2) A sum of money not immediately available;
(3) A definite sum of money now available;
(4) An ascertained share of a heap of corn prior to division. All these are in the nature of debts.

Article 159. A specific object is any object which is definite and identified.

Examples:-
A house; a horse; a chair; a heap of corn in existence; a sum of money. All these are specific objects.

Article 160. The vendor is a person who sells property.

Article 161. The purchaser is a person who buys.

Article 162. The two parties to the sale are the vendor and the purchaser. They are also called the two contracting parties.

Article 163. Rescission is setting aside and stopping a contract of sale.

Article 164. Deceit is cheating.

Article 165. Flagrant misrepresentation is misrepresentation which is practised with regard to no less than one twentieth in the case of merchandise; one tenth in the case of animals; and one fifth in the case of real property.

Article 166. Time immemorial refers to that thing the origin of which is unknown to any person.

CHAPTER I.

THE CONTRACT OF SALE.

SECTION I.

Fundamental basis of sale.

Article 167. Sale is concluded by offer and acceptance.

Article 168. In sale, offer and acceptance is made

38 SALE

by the use of words commonly employed in the particular locality in making a contract of sale*

Article 169. The past tense is usually employed in offer and acceptance.

Examples:-

(1) A vendor informs a purchaser that he has sold him a certain thing for one hundred piastres and the purchaser states that he has purchased it; or the purchaser states that he has bought a certain thing and the vendor afterwards states that he has sold such thing. The sale is concluded. In the first case the offer consists of the words "I have sold" and the acceptance of the words "I have purchased". In the second case the words "I have purchased" constitute the offer and the words "I have sold" the acceptance.

(2) The vendor, instead of stating that he has sold, states that he has given a person something or has transferred the property in it to him, and the purchaser instead of stating that he has purchased states that he has agreed thereto or has accepted. A valid contract of sale is concluded.

Article 170. A contract of sale may be concluded by employing the aorist tense if it imports the present: but if the future is meant, no sale is concluded.

Article 171. If the future tense is used in the sense of a mere promise, such as the statement "I will buy" or "I will sell" no sale is concluded.

Article 172. No sale is concluded by the use of the imperative mood, such as the expression "Sell" or "Buy". But when the present tense is necessarily meant a sale may also be concluded by the use of the imperative mood.

---

* An explanation of a Turkish word is not translated here as being of no significance to the English reader.

Example:-

A purchaser says to a vendor: "Sell me this article for so much money." The vendor replies "I have sold it to you". No sale is concluded. But if the vendor says: "Take this article for so much money" and the purchaser replies saying: "I have taken it"; or if the purchaser says "I have taken it", and the vendor says, "take it" or "you may enjoy the benefit of it," a valid sale is concluded, the expressions "take" or "enjoy the benefit of it" being equivalent to "I have sold" and "take it".

Article 173. Offer and acceptance may be made by writing as well as by word of mouth.

Article 174. A dumb person may make a valid contract of sale by making use of generally recognized signs.

Article 175. The fundamental object of offer and acceptance being the mutual agreement of the parties, a sale may also be concluded by any conduct of the parties which is evidence of offer and acceptance. This is called sale by conduct of the parties.

Examples:-

(1) A purchaser without bargaining and without making any statement gives money to a baker and the baker delivers bread to the purchaser. A contract of sale is concluded.

(2) A purchaser tenders money and takes a melon. The vendor remains silent. A contract of sale is concluded.

(3) A purchaser wishes to buy corn. With this object in view he tenders five pounds to a corn merchant asking the latter to tell him at what price he sells corn. The corn merchant replies that he sells corn at one pound per *kilé*. The purchaser thereupon remains silent, and later asks for the corn and the corn merchant states that on the following day he will deliver it to him. In this case a contract of sale has been concluded, although there has been no offer and

acceptence by the parties. So much so that if on the following day corn has gone up half a pound in price per *kilé*, the vendor is bound to deliver at one pound. If, on the other hand, the price of corn has gone down, the purchaser cannot refuse for this reason to accept delivery at the original price.

(4) A purchaser asks a butcher to weigh him so much money's worth of meat from such and such a part. The butcher cuts the meat up and weighs it. A contract of sale has been concluded, and the purchaser cannot refuse to accept the meat.

Article 176. If as a result of fresh bargaining after the conclusion of the contract, the price is changed, increased or decreased, the second contract is valid.

Example :-

A contract is concluded for the purchase of an article for one hundred piastres. Later on fresh bargaining takes place and as a result the original hundred piastres is substituted for a gold piece of one hundred piastres, or for one hundred and ten piastres or for ninety piastres. The second contract is valid.

SECTION II.

Agreement of acceptance with offer.

Article 177. The acceptance of one of the two contracting parties must agree exactly with the offer of the other contracting party as regards the price or subject matter. Such party has no power to separate or divide either the price or the subject matter.

Examples: -

(1) A vendor tells a purchaser that he has sold him certain cloth for one hundred piastres and the purchaser agrees thereto. He is then obliged to take the whole of such cloth for one hundred piastres. He cannot claim to take the cloth or a half thereof for fifty piastres.

(2) A tells B that he has sold him two horses for three thousand piastres and B accepts. B must take the two for three thousand piastres. He cannot take one of them for one thousand five hundred piastres.

Article 178. It is sufficient if the acceptance agrees with the offer by implication.

Examples :-
(1) A vendor informs a purchaser that he has sold him certain property for a thousand piastres. The purchaser tells the vendor that he accepts for one thousand five hundred piastres. The contract of sale is for one thousand piastres. If the vendor, however, agrees to the increase of price at the time it is mentioned, the purchaser is bound to pay the additional five hundred piastres.
(2) A purchaser states that he has bought certain property for one thousand piastres. The vendor states that he has sold it for eight hundred piastres. A contract of sale has been concluded, and the two hundred piastres must be deducted.

Article 179. If one of two parties to a sale enumerates the prices of various articles, and proposes the sale of such articles *en bloc* and the other party accepts such offer, the latter may buy the whole lot for the whole price. If he does not do so, he may not divide up the lot and agree to buy any article he wishes at the fixed price.

Examples :-
(1) A vendor states that he has sold two particular horses for three thousand piastres. The first one for one thousand piastres and the second for two thousand piastres; or each of them for one thousand five hundred piastres. The purchaser can take the two for three thousand piastres. He cannot, however, take the one he prefers of the two for the fixed price.
(2) A vendor states that he has sold three pieces of cloth for one hundred piastres. The purchaser states

that he has bought one piece for one hundred piastres, or two pieces for two hundred piastres. No sale is concluded.

Article 180. If one of the two parties to a sale enumerates the prices of the various articles, and offers them for sale separately and the other party accepts the article he desires, at the fixed price, a contract of sale is concluded.

Example :-

A vendor enumerates the prices of various articles for sale and repeats that he has sold them, this one for a thousand piastres and that one for two thousand piastres. In that case, the purchaser may accept one of the two for the fixed price and buy the same.

SECTION III

The place where the sale is concluded.

Article 181. The place where the sale is concluded is the place where the parties meet together with a view to the conclusion of the sale.

Article 182. Both parties possess an option during the meeting at the place of sale, after the offer has been made, up to the termination of the meeting.

Example :-

One of the two parties to the sale makes an offer at the meeting place of the parties to the sale by stating that he has sold such and such property for a certain sum of money, or that he has bought such property, and the other party fails to state immediately afterwards that he has bought or has sold and some time later accepts at the same meeting. The sale is concluded, no matter how long the meeting may have lasted or how long the period between offer and acceptance may have been.

SALE 43

Article 183. If one of the parties gives any indication of dissent after the offer and prior to acceptance, either by word or by deed, the offer becomes void and there is no longer any reason for acceptance.

Example:-
One of the two parties to the sale, after stating that he has bought or that he has sold, occupies himself with some other matter, or discusses some other question. The offer becomes void, and thereafter the sale cannot be concluded by acceptance.

Article 184. If one of the two parties to the sale makes an offer, but revokes such offer before the other party has accepted, the offer becomes void, and thereafter the sale cannot be concluded by acceptance.

Example :-
A vendor states that he has sold such and such goods for so much money, but revokes such offer before the purchaser has accepted, and the purchaser later states that he has accepted such offer. No sale is concluded.

Article 185. A renewal of the offer before acceptance cancels the first offer and its place is taken by the second offer.

Example :-
The vendor states that he has sold such and such property for one hundred piastres, but before the purchaser has accepted, revokes the offer, and states that he has sold for one hundred and twenty piastres, and the purchaser accepts such offer. The first offer is of no effect, and a sale is concluded on the basis of one hundred and twenty piastres.

SECTION IV.

Sale subject to a condition.

Article 186. If a contract of sale is concluded with an essential condition attached, both sale and condition are valid.

Example:-

A vendor sells subject to a right of retaining the thing sold until he has received payment of the price. This condition in no way prejudices the sale, but on the contrary is an essential condition of the contract.

Article 187. In the case of a sale concluded subject to a condition the object of which is to assure the due performance of the contract, both sale and condition are valid.

Example :-

A certain thing is sold subject to the condition that some other thing shall be pledged or that a certain individual shall become a surety. Both sale and condition are valid. Moreover, should the purchaser fail to observe the condition, the vendor may cancel the sale. The reason for this is that these conditions assure the handing over of the price, which is an essential condition of the contract.

Article 188. In the case of a sale concluded subject to a condition sanctioned by custom established and recognized in a particular locality, both sale and condition are valid.

Example :-

The sale of a fur subject to a condition that it shall be lined; or of a lock subject to a condition that it shall be nailed to its place; or of a suit of clothes subject to the condition that they shall be repaired. In these cases the condition must be observed in carrying out the sale.

SALE 45

Article 189. In the case of sale subject to a condition which is not to the benefit of either party, the sale is valid, but the condition is voidable.

Example :-
The sale of an animal subject to a condition that it shall not be sold to a third party, or that it shall be put out to graze. In such a case the sale is valid, but the condition is of no effect.

SECTION V.

Rescission of the sale.

Article 190. The two contracting parties may, by mutual agreement, rescind the sale after the conclusion of the contract.

Article 191. As in the case of sale, rescission is carried out by means of offer and acceptance.

Example :-
One of the two contracting parties states that he has rescinded or cancelled a sale and the other states that he has agreed thereto; or one of the parties tells the other to rescind the sale and the latter states that he has done so. The rescission is valid and the sale cancelled.

Article 192. A valid rescission may also be effected by any conduct which takes the place of offer and acceptance.

Article 193. As in the case of sale, a meeting of the parties must take place in the case of rescission. That is to say, acceptance must be made known at the place where the offer is made. If this is not done, and one of the contracting parties states that he has rescinded the sale, and the other party leaves without expressing his concurrence, or if one of the parties does anything which indicates dissent, the subsequent acceptance by the other is of no effect.

Article 194. It is an essential condition that the thing sold should be in the possession of the purchaser at the time of the rescission. Consequently, if the thing sold is destroyed, the rescission is invalid.

Article 195. If a portion of the thing sold is destroyed, rescission is valid as regards the remainder.

Example :-
A vendor sells land he owns in absolute ownership, together with growing crops. After the crops have been reaped by the purchaser, the parties rescind the contract. The rescission is valid in so far as that part of the price concerning the land is concerned.

Article 196. The loss of the price does not affect the validity of the rescission.

CHAPTER II.

THE SUBJECT MATTER OF THE SALE.

SECTION I.

Conditions affecting the subject matter of the sale and description thereof.

Article 197. The thing sold must be in existence.

Article 198. The thing sold must be capable of delivery.

Article 199. The thing sold must be property of some specific value.

Article 200. The thing sold must be known to the purchaser.

Article 201. The fact that the thing sold is known is ascertained by referring to its state and description which distinguish it from other things.

SALE

Example :-

A specific quantity of red corn, or a piece of land bounded by specific boundaries. If these are sold, the nature thereof is known and the sale is valid.

Article 202. If the thing sold is present at the meeting place of the parties to the sale, it is sufficient if such thing is pointed out by signs.

Example :-

The vendor states that he has sold a particular animal. The purchaser sees that animal and accepts it. The sale is valid.

Article 203. Since it is enough for the nature of the thing sold to be known to the purchaser, there is no need for any other sort of description or particularisation.

Article 204. The thing sold must be the particular thing with reference to which the contract is concluded.

Example :-

A vendor, pointing to a particular watch, states that he has sold it. Upon the purchaser accepting, the vendor is bound to deliver that identical watch. He cannot put that particular watch on one side and deliver another of the same sort.

SECTION II.

Things which may and may not be sold.

Article 205. The sale of a thing not in existence is void.

Example :-

The sale of the fruit of a tree which has not yet appeared is void.

Article 206. The sale of fruit which is completely visible while on a tree is valid, whether it is fit for consumption or not.

SALE

Article 207. The sale at one and the same time of dependent parts which are connected together is valid. For example, in the case of fruit, flowers, leaves and vegetables, which do not arrive at maturity simultaneously, a portion thereof only having come out, that portion which has not yet arrived at maturity may be sold together with the rest.

Article 208. If the species of the thing sold has been stated, and the thing sold turns out to be of another species, the sale is void.

Example :-
    The vendor sells a piece of glass stating that it is a diamond. The sale is void.

Article 209. The sale of a thing which is not capable of delivery is void.

Example :-
    The sale of a rowing-boat which has sunk in the sea and cannot be raised, or of a runaway animal which cannot be caught and delivered.

Article 210. The sale of a thing which is not generally recognized as property or the purchase of property therewith is void.

Example :-
    The sale of a corpse or of a free man, or the purchase of property in exchange for them is void.

Article 211. The sale of things which do not possess any specific value is void.

Article 212. The purchase of property with property which does not possess any specific value is voidable.

Article 213. The sale of a thing the nature of which is not known is voidable.

Example :-
> A vendor tells a purchaser that he has sold him the whole of the property he owns for a certain sum of money, and the purchaser states that he has bought the same. The nature of the things bought by the purchaser, however, is unknown. The sale is voidable.

Article 214. The sale of an ascertained, jointly owned undivided share in a piece of real property owned in absolute ownership prior to division, such as a half, a third or a tenth, is valid.

Article 215. A person may sell his undivided jointly owned share to some other person without obtaining the permission of his partner.

Article 216. The sale of a right of way, and of a right of taking water and of a right of flow attached to land and of water attached to canals is valid.

SECTION III.

Procedure at the sale.

Article 217. The sale of things estimated by measure of capacity, or by weight, or by enumeration, or by length, may be sold individually or *en bloc*.

Example :-
> A vendor sells a heap of corn, or a barn full of straw, or a load of bricks, or a bale of merchandise *en bloc*. The sale is valid.

Article 218. If grain is sold in a specified vessel or measured in a measure, or by weighing it according to a fixed weight, the sale is valid, although the capacity of the vessel or measure, or the heaviness of the weight may not be known.

Article 219. A thing which may be sold separately may validly be separated from the thing sold.

SALE

Example:-
The vendor stipulates to retain a certain number of *okes* of the fruit of a tree that he has sold. The stipulation is valid.

Article 220. The sale *en bloc* of things estimated by quantity on the basis of the price of each thing or part thereof is valid.

Example:-
The sale of a heap of corn, a ship-load of wood, a flock of sheep, and a roll of cloth, on the basis of the price of each *kilé,* or measure, or *oke,* or herd of sheep, or yard, is valid.

Article 221. Real property may be sold by defining the boundaries thereof. In cases where the boundaries have already been defined, it may be sold by the yard or the donum.

Article 222. The contract of sale is only valid in respect to the amount stipulated in the contract.

Article 223. The sale of things estimated by measure of capacity, or by enumeration and which closely resemble each other and things estimated by weight, and which do not suffer damage by being separated from the whole, may be sold *en bloc* if the amount thereof is made known, whether the price is named in respect to the whole amount, or in respect to each individual unit. If on delivery the amount is found to be correct, the sale is irrevocable. If it is found to be short, however, the purchaser has the option of cancelling the sale, or of purchasing the amount actually delivered for the proportionate part of the price. If more than the stipulated amount is delivered, the excess belongs to the vendor.

Examples:
(1) A vendor sells a heap of corn said to be fifty *kilés,* at five hundred piastres, or, on the basis of fifty *kilés,*

at ten piastres a *kilé*. If the amount delivered is correct, the sale is irrevocable. If forty-five *kilés* only are delivered, the purchaser has an option of cancelling the sale, or of taking forty-five *kilés* for four hundred and fifty piastres. If fifty-five *kilés* are delivered, the five *kilés* in excess belong to the vendor.

(2) A basket of eggs said to contain one hundred is sold for fifty piastres, or at twenty *paras* for each egg. If it turns out on delivery that there are only ninety eggs, the purchaser has an option of cancelling the sale or of taking the ninety eggs for forty-five piastres. If one hundred and ten are delivered, the ten eggs remaining over belong to the vendor.

(3) A barrel of oil is sold as containing one hundred *okes* The principle explained above applies.

Article 224. In the case of the sale of a whole amount of things estimated by weight which suffer by being separated from the whole, the price of the whole amount only being named, the purchaser has the option of cancelling the sale on delivery, if the amount proves to be short, or of taking the portion delivered for the price fixed for the whole. If more than the amount is delivered, it belongs to the purchaser and the vendor has no option in the matter.

Example :-

A diamond stated to be five carat is sold for twenty thousand piastres. It turns out to be four and a half carat. The purchaser has the option of rejecting the diamond, or of taking the stone for twenty thousand piastres. If it turns out to be five and a half carat, the purchaser can have it for twenty thousand piastres, the vendor having no option in the matter.

Article 225. In the case of the sale of a whole amount of things estimated by weight which suffer damage by being separated from the whole, stating the amount thereof and the price fixed for parts or portions thereof, the purchaser has an option on delivery, if the amount delivered turns out to be less or more, of cancelling the sale, or of taking the amount delivered on the basis of the price fixed for the parts and portions thereof.

Example :-

A copper brazier said to weigh five *okes* is sold at the rate of forty piastres per *oke*. If it turns out to weigh either four and a half or five and a half *okes*, the purchaser has two options. He can either decline to accept the brazier, or, if it weighs four and a half *okes* he can purchase it for one hundred and eighty piastres, and if it weighs five and a half *okes*, he can purchase it for two hundred and twenty piastres.

Article 226. In the case of the sale of a whole amount of things estimated by measure of length, whether land, goods, or similar things on the basis of the price for the whole amount, or of the price per yard, they are dealt with in both cases as in the case of things estimated by weight which suffer damage by being separated from the whole. Goods and articles such as linens and woollens which do not suffer damage by being cut and separated, are treated in the same manner as things estimated by measure of capacity.

Examples :-

(1) A piece of land said to measure one hundred yards is sold for one thousand piastres. It turns out to measure ninety-five yards only. The purchaser has an option of leaving it or of buying it for one thousand piastres. If it turns out to be larger, the purchaser can take the whole piece for one thousand piastres.

(2) A piece of cloth said to measure eight yards is sold for four hundred piastres with a view to being made up into a suit of clothes. It turns out to measure seven yards only. The purchaser has an option of leaving it or of buying it for four hundred piastres.

If it turns out to measure nine yards, the purchaser can take the whole piece for four hundred piastres.

(3) A piece of land said to measure one hundred yards is sold at the rate of ten piastres per yard. If it turns out to measure ninety-five or one hundred and five yards, the purchaser has an option of leaving it, or, if it turns out to be ninety-five yards, of buying it for nine hundred and fifty piastres, or, if it turns out to be one hundred and five yards, of buying it for one thousand and fifty piastres.

(4) Some cloth said to measure eight yards is sold at the rate of fifty piastres per yard with a view to being made up into a suit of clothes. If it turns out to measure seven or nine yards, the purchaser has an option of either rejecting it or, if it turns out to be seven yards, of buying it for three hundred and fifty piastres, and if it turns out to be nine yards of buying it for four hundred and fifty piastres.

(5) If a whole piece of cloth, however, said to measure one hundred and fifty yards is sold for seven thousand five hundred piastres, or at the rate of fifty piastres per yard, turns out to measure one hundred and forty yards, the purchaser has the option of cancelling the sale or of taking the hundred and forty yards for seven thousand piastres. If it turns out to be more, the balance belongs to the vendor.

Article 227. In the event of the sale of things estimated by enumeration and which are dissimilar from each other, the price of the whole amount only being named and the number of such things is found to be exact on delivery, the sale is valid and irrevocable. If the number is greater or smaller, however, the sale is voidable in both cases.

Example :-
A flock of sheep said to contain fifty head of sheep is sold for two thousand five hundred piastres. If on delivery the flock is found to consist of forty-five or fifty-five sheep, the sale is voidable.

SALE

Article 228. In the event of the sale of a portion of a whole amount of things estimated by enumeration, and which are dissimilar from each other, stating the amount thereof, and at a price calculated at so much per piece or per unit, and on delivery the number is found to be exact, the sale is irrevocable. If the number is found to be smaller, the purchaser has the option of leaving the things or of taking them for the proportionate share of the fixed price. If more than the stated number are delivered, the sale is voidable.

Example :-

A flock of sheep said to consist of fifty is sold at the rate of fifty piastres per head. If it turns out to consist of forty-five head of sheep, the purchaser has the option of leaving them or of buying the forty-five head of sheep for two thousand two hundred and fifty piastres. If it turns out to be fifty-five head of sheep, the sale is voidable.

Article 229. The purchaser, after having taken delivery of the thing sold, loses the option of cancelling the sale conferred upon him by the preceding Articles, if he knew that less than the stipulated amount had in fact been delivered.

SECTION IV.

Matters included but not explicitly mentioned in the sale.

Article 230. The sale includes everything which by local custom is included in the thing sold, even though not specifically mentioned.

Example :-

In the case of the sale of a house, the kitchen and the cellar are included ; and in the event of the sale of an olive grove, the olive trees are included, even though not specifically mentioned. The reason for this is that the kitchen and cellar are appurtenances of the house, and the olive grove is so called because it is a piece of land containing olive trees. A mere piece of land, on the other hand, is not called an olive grove.

Article 231. Things which are considered to be part of the thing sold, that is to say, things which cannot be separated from the thing sold, having regard to the object of the purchase, are included in the sale without being specifically mentioned.

Example :-

In the case of the sale of a lock, the key is included; and in the case of the sale of a milch cow, the sucking calf of such cow is included in the sale without being specifically mentioned.

Article 232. Fixtures attached to the thing sold are included in the sale, even though not specifically mentioned.

Example :-

In the event of the sale of a large country house, things which have been fixed or constructed permanently, such as locks which have been nailed, and fixed cupboards and divans, are included in the sale. Similarly, the garden included in the boundaries of the house, together with the paths leading to the public road or to a blind alley are included. Again, in the event of the sale of a garden and of a piece of land, trees planted as fixtures are included in the sale, even though this was not specifically stated at the time the bargain was concluded.

Article 233. Things which are neither appurtenances nor permanent fixtures attached to the thing sold, and things which are not considered to be part of the thing sold, or things which are not by reason of custom included in the thing sold, are not included in the sale unless they are specifically mentioned at the time the sale was concluded. But things which by reason of local custom go with the thing sold, are included in the sale without being specifically mentioned.

Example :-
In the case of the sale of a house, things which are not fixtures, but have been placed so that they may be removed, such as cupboards, sofas and chairs, are not included in the sale unless specifically mentioned. And in the event of the sale of an orchard or a garden, flower pots, and pots for lemons and young plants which have been planted with a view to their removal elsewhere, are not included in the sale, unless specifically mentioned. Similarly, when land is sold, the growing crops, and when trees are sold, the fruit thereof, are not included in the sale, unless some special stipulation to that effect was made at the time the bargain was concluded. But the bridle of a riding horse and the halter of a draught horse are included in the sale although not specifically mentioned, in places where such is the custom.

Article 234. The thing included in the sale as being attached thereto is not a part of the price of such sale.

Example :-
If the halters of draught horses are stolen before the delivery thereof, there is no necessity to deduct anything from the fixed price.

Article 235. Things comprised in any general expressions added at the time of the sale are included in the sale.

Example :-
The vendor states that he has sold a particular house "with all rights". Any right of way, or right of taking water, or right of flow attaching to the house are included in the sale.

Article 236. Any fruits or increase occuring after the conclusion of the contract and before delivery of the thing sold belong to the purchaser.

Examples :-

(1) In the case of the sale of a garden, any fruit or vegetables that are produced before delivery belong to the purchaser.

(2) Where a cow has been sold, a calf born before delivery of the cow becomes the property of the purchaser.

CHAPTER III.

MATTERS RELATING TO PRICE.

SECTION I.

Nature of and circumstances affecting price.

Article 237. The price must be named at the time of the sale. Consequently, if the price of the thing sold is not mentioned, the sale is voidable.

Article 238. The price must be ascertained.

Article 239. The price is ascertained by being seen, if it is visible. If not, it is ascertained by stating the amount and description thereof.

Article 240. If the price is stated to be so many gold coins in a locality in which different types of gold coins are in circulation, without stating the particular type of gold coin, the sale is voidable. The same rule applies to silver coins.

Article 241. If the price is stated in piastres, the purchaser can give any type of coin he likes, provided that the circulation thereof is not forbidden.

Article 242. When a contract is drawn up expressing the nature of the price, payment must be made in whatever kind of currency is mentioned.

SALE

Example :-

A contract is made for payment in Turkish, English, or French pounds, or in pieces of twenty *medjidies* each, or in dollars. Payment must be made in whatever currency is stipulated.

Article 243. Anything produced at the time of the conclusion of the contract cannot be regarded as determining the nature of the price.

Example :-

A purchaser shows a gold piece of one hundred piastres which he has in his hand, and states that he has bought such and such a piece of property with that particular gold coin. The vendor agrees to sell. The purchaser is not obliged to give that particular gold coin itself, but may substitute for it another gold piece of one hundred piastres of the same type.

Article 244. Fractions of coins may be given instead of a particular type of coinage. In this case, however, local custom must be followed.

Example :-

A bargain is concluded for payment by *medjidies* of twenty piastres. Payment may also be made with pieces of ten and five. But in view of custom now prevailing in Constantinople, fractions of pieces of forty and of two may not be given instead of pieces of twenty.

SECTION II:

Sale subject to payment at a future date.

Article 245. A valid sale may be concluded in which payment of the price is deferred and is made by instalments.

Article 246. In the event of deferment and payment of the price by instalments, the period thereof must be definitely ascertained and fixed.

Article 247. If a bargain is concluded with a promise for payment at some definite future date which is fixed by the two contracting parties, such as in so many days, or months, or years time, or the 26th October next, the sale is valid.

Article 248. If a bargain is concluded stipulating for payment at a time which is not clearly fixed, such as "when it rains" the sale is voidable.

Article 249. If a bargain is concluded whereby credit is given for an undefined period, payment becomes due within one month.

Article 250. The time agreed upon for deferred payment, or payment by instalments, begins to run from the time the thing sold is delivered.

Example :-
Goods are sold to be paid for in a year's time. The vendor after keeping them for a year, delivers them to the purchaser. The money must be paid after a period of one year from the date of delivery, that is, upon the expiration of precisely two years from the time of the sale.

Article 251. An unconditional sale is concluded with a view to payment forthwith. But in places where by custom an unconditional sale is concluded for payment by some definite future date, or by instalments, payment becomes due on the date or dates in question.

Example :-
A purchases a thing from the market without stipulating as to whether payment is to be made forthwith or whether purchased on credit. Payment must be made forthwith. But where by local custom the whole or a part of the price is payable at the end of a week or month, such custom must be observed.

CHAPTER IV.

POWER TO DEAL WITH THE PRICE AND THE THING SOLD AFTER THE SALE.

SECTION I.

Right of the vendor to dispose of the price and of the purchaser to dispose of the thing sold after the conclusion of the contract and prior to delivery.

Article 252. The vendor has a right to dispose of the price of the thing sold before receiving the same.

Example :-

A person who has sold property of his own can transfer the price thereof to meet a debt.

Article 253. If the thing sold is real property, the purchaser can sell such real property to another person before taking delivery thereof. He may not, however, sell movable property.

SECTION II.

Increase and decrease in the price and in the thing sold after the conclusion of the contract.

Article 254. The vendor may increase the amount of the thing sold after the conclusion of the contract. If the purchaser agrees to such increase at the meeting place of the parties, he has a right to insist upon such increase and the vendor may not go back upon his offer. An acceptance by the purchaser after the meeting, however, is invalid.

Example :-

A bargain is concluded for the purchase of twenty melons at twenty piastres. The vendor states that he has given five more. If the purchaser accepts at the meeting, he has the right of taking twenty-five melons for twenty piasters. If he fails to accept at the meeting however, but seeks to accept subsequently, the vendor cannot be obliged to give the additional number.

Article 255. The purchaser may increase the fixed price after the conclusion of the sale. If the vendor accepts such increase at the meeting where the offer is made, he has the right to insist upon such increase and the purchaser may not go back upon his offer. If the vendor accepts after the meeting, however, such acceptance is invalid.

Example :-
A bargain is concluded for the sale of an animal for one thousand piastres. After the conclusion of the sale, the purchaser states that he has added an additional two hundred piastres. If the vendor accepts at the meeting where the offer is made, he must pay one thousand two hundred piastres for the animal. If the vendor fails to accept at the meeting, however, but signifies his acceptance later, the purchaser cannot be forced to pay the additional two hundred piastres which he has undertaken to give.

Article 256. The vendor may validly deduct a portion of the fixed price after the conclusion of the contract.

Example :-
A bargain is concluded for the sale of certain property for one hundred piastres. Later, the vendor states that he has deducted twenty piastres. He can only obtain eighty piastres for the property in question.

Article 257. Any increase made by the vendor in the thing sold and by the purchaser in the fixed price, or any decrease on the part of the vendor of the fixed price after the conclusion of the contract becomes a part of the original contract. That is to say, such increase or decrease is contemplated as having been part of the original contract at the time such contract was concluded.

Article 258. If the vendor increases the thing sold after the conclusion of the contract, the increase becomes part of the fixed price.

Examples:-

(1) A vendor adds two water melons to the eight water melons which he has sold for ten piastres. The purchaser agrees and the ten water melons are sold for ten piastres. If the two water melons are destroyed before delivery, the price thereof is deducted from the total price and the vendor can only demand eight piastres for the eight water melons.

(2) A vendor sells a piece of land measuring one thousand yards for ten thousand piastres. After the sale he adds one hundred yards, to which the purchaser agrees. If a person claiming a right of pre-emption comes forward, he can take the whole amount represented by the ten thousand piastres, that is to say, one thousand one hundred yards.

Article 259. If the purchaser increases the fixed price after the conclusion of the contract, the sum total of the fixed price together with the increase becomes the corresponding value of the thing sold in respect to the two contracting parties.

Example :-

A purchaser buys a piece of real property held in absolute ownership for ten thousand piastres. Before taking delivery he adds five hundred piastres, to which the vendor agrees. The price of the real property in question is ten thousand five hundred piastres. If a person who is entitled to such property comes forward, proves his case, obtains judgment, and takes possession of the real property in question, the purchaser is entitled to claim the sum of ten thousand five hundred piastres from the vendor. If a person claiming a right of pre-emption to such real property comes forward, such person can take the real property in question for ten thousand piastres, but the vendor cannot claim the five hundred piastres subsequently added from the person claiming the right of pre-emption, because such person's right is based upon the fixed price in the original contract, the subsequent increase to the original contract affecting the contracting parties only and in no way invalidating such person's claim.

Article 260. If the vendor reduces the price of the thing sold after the conclusion of the contract, the remainder of the fixed price is the corresponding value of the whole of the thing sold.

Example :-
A piece of real property held in absolute ownership is bought for ten thousand piastres. The vendor deducts one thousand piastres. The price of the real property in question is nine thousand piastres. Consequently, if a person claiming a right of pre-emption comes forward, he may take such property for nine thousand piastres.

Article 261. The vendor may deduct the whole of the price of the thing sold before delivery, but this is not part of the original contract.

Example :-
The vendor sells a piece of real property held in absolute ownership for ten thousand piastres. Prior to delivery he forgoes the price thereof altogether. A person claiming to have a right of pre-emption may take such real property for ten thousand piastres. He may not claim to take it for nothing.

CHAPTER V.

GIVING AND TAKING DELIVERY.

SECTION I.

Procedure on giving and taking delivery.

Article 262. Taking delivery is not an essential condition of sale. After the conclusion of the contract, however, the purchaser must first deliver the price to the vendor, and the vendor is then bound to deliver the thing sold to the purchaser.

Article 263. The thing sold must be delivered in such a way that the purchaser may take delivery thereof without hindrance. The vendor must give permission for such delivery.

Article 264. As soon as the thing sold has been delivered, the purchaser is considered to have taken delivery thereof.

Article 265. The method of delivery differs, according to the nature of the thing sold.

Article 266. If the purchaser is on a piece of land, or in any field, or if the purchaser sees such land or fields from near by, any permission given by the vendor to take delivery thereof, is considered to be delivery.

Article 267. If land is sold upon which crops are growing, the vendor must clear the land of such crops by reaping them or by pasturing animals thereon.

Article 268. In the event of the delivery of a tree bearing fruit, such fruit must first be gathered and the tree then handed over by the vendor.

Article 269. If fruit is sold while upon a tree, and the vendor gives permission to the purchaser to pick such fruit, delivery thereof has been effected.

SALE 65

Article 270. If the purchaser is within any real property, such as a house or an orchard, which can be closed by locking, and is informed by the vendor that the latter has delivered such real property to him, delivery thereof has been effected. If he is outside such property, and the purchaser is so near thereto that he could immediately lock the same, delivery thereof is effected by the vendor merely stating that he has made delivery. If he is not in such close proximity to such property, however, delivery is effected after the expiration of such time as is necessary for him to arrive and enter therein.

Article 271. Delivery of real property which can be locked is effected by handing over the key.

Article 272. Delivery of an animal is taken by seizing it by the head or by the ear or by the halter. Delivery of such animals may also be given by the vendor merely pointing to them and giving permission for them to be taken, if they are in such a place that the purchaser can take delivery thereof without inconvenience.

Article 273. Delivery of things estimated by measure of capacity, or by weight, may be given by placing them in a cover or receptacle prepared by order of the purchaser.

Article 274. Delivery of articles of merchandise is effected by placing them in the hands of the purchaser or by placing them beside him, or, if they are exposed to view, by pointing to them and giving him permission to take them.

Article 275. Delivery of things sold *en bloc* and kept in a locked place, such as a store or box, is effected by giving the key to the purchaser and giving him permission to take them.

Example :-

A store full of corn or a box of books is sold *en bloc*. Delivery of the things sold is effected by handing over the key.

Article 276. If the purchaser takes delivery of the things sold and the vendor, seeing this, makes no objection, permission to take delivery is given.

Article 277. If the purchaser takes delivery of the thing sold without paying the price and without the permission of the vendor, such taking delivery is invalid. But if the thing sold is taken by the purchaser without permission and is destroyed or damaged while in his possession, such taking delivery is valid.

SECTION II.

Right of retention over the thing sold.

Article 278. In the case of a sale for immediate payment, the vendor has a right of retaining the thing sold until the price is fully paid by the purchaser.

Article 279. If the vendor sells various articles *en bloc,* the whole of the things sold may be retained until the full price has been paid, even though a separate price has been stated for each article.

Article 280. The fact that a pledge or a guarantor has been furnished by the purchaser does not invalidate the vendor's right of retention.

Article 281. If the vendor gives delivery of the thing sold without receiving the price, he loses his right of retention. He cannot ask for the return of the thing sold in order to hold it until payment of the price is made.

Article 282. If the vendor transfers the right of receiving the price of the thing sold from the purchaser to some other person, he loses his right of retention. In this case, the thing sold must be delivered to the purchaser forthwith.

Article 283. In the case of a sale on credit, there is no right of retention on the part of the vendor. He must deliver the thing sold to the purchaser forthwith in order to receive payment on due date.

Article 284. Should the vendor postpone payment of the price after having sold for immediate payment, he loses his right of retention. He must hand the thing sold to the purchaser forthwith in order to receive payment on due date.

SECTION III.

The place of delivery.

Article 285. In an unconditional contract the thing sold must be delivered at the place where it was when the sale was concluded.

Example :-
> A sells wheat at *Tekfur Dagh* to B in Constantinople. A delivers the wheat in *Tekfur Dagh*. He cannot be forced to deliver the wheat in Constantinople.

Article 286. If at the time of the sale the purchaser did not know where the thing sold was, but received information thereof after the conclusion of the contract, he has an option. He may either cancel the sale, or take delivery of the thing sold at the place where it was at the time the sale was concluded.

Article 287. Property sold with a condition for delivery at a given place must be delivered at that place.

SALE

SECTION IV.

Expenses connected with delivery.

Article 288. Expenses connected with the price fall upon the purchaser.

Example :-
> Fees in connection with money-changing, such as counting and weighing the money, fall upon the purchaser.

Article 289. Expenses connected with the delivery of the thing sold fall upon the vendor.

Example :-
> Fees of measurers and weighers must be borne by the vendor.

Article 290. Any charges connected with things sold *en bloc* must be borne by the purchaser.

Examples :-
> (1) If grapes in an orchard are sold *en bloc,* the purchaser must gather them.
>
> (2) If a store full of corn is sold *en bloc,* the purchaser must take such corn away from the store.

Article 291. In the case of things sold which are loaded upon animals, such as wood and charcoal, the question of transport to the house of the purchaser is decided in accordance with local custom.

Article 292. The cost of drawing up contracts and written instruments falls upon the purchaser. The vendor, however, must declare the sale and attest the same in Court.

SECTION V.

Destruction of the thing sold.

Article 293. If the thing sold is destroyed while in the possession of the vendor prior to delivery, no liability attaches to the purchaser, and the loss must be borne by the vendor.

Article 294. If the thing sold is destroyed after delivery, no liability attaches to the vendor, and the loss must be borne by the purchaser.

Article 295. If the purchaser dies bankrupt after having taken delivery of the thing sold, but without having paid the price, the vendor cannot demand the return of the thing sold, but becomes one of the creditors.

Article 296. If the purchaser dies bankrupt before the delivery of the thing sold and payment of the price, the vendor has a right of retaining the thing sold until payment has been made from the estate of the purchaser. Thus, the thing sold is disposed of by the Court and if the sum realized is sufficient, the amount due to the vendor is paid in full, any surplus being paid to the other creditors. If less than the sum due to the vendor is realized, the full amount thereof is paid to the vendor, and the balance still remaining due is deducted from the estate of the purchaser.

Article 297. If the vendor dies bankrupt after having received the price, but without having delivered the thing sold to the purchaser, such thing remains in the possession of the vendor on trust. Thus, the purchaser takes the thing sold, and the other creditors cannot intervene.

SECTION VI.

Sale on approval and subject to inspection.

Article 298. If property bought on approval as to price, that is to say, property the price of which has been fixed, is delivered to the purchaser and while in his possession is destroyed or lost, the price thereof must be paid to the vendor, if it is in the nature of a thing the like of which cannot be found in the market. If it is a thing the like of which can be found in the market, a similar article must be given to the vendor. If the price has not been fixed, however, it is considered to be in the possession of the purchaser on trust, and if it is destroyed or lost without any fault of the purchaser, there is no need to make good the loss.

Example :-
> A vendor offers an animal for one thousand piastres, asking the purchaser to buy it if he is pleased with it. If the purchaser takes it with a view to buying it and the animal is destroyed while in his possession, the purchaser must pay the price to the vendor. But if the price is not stated and the vendor asks the purchaser to buy the animal if he is pleased with it, and the purchaser, being satisfied with it, later enters into negotiations with a view to purchase, and the animal is destroyed without any fault of the purchaser, while in the latter's possession, the purchaser is not obliged to make good the loss.

Article 299. If delivery is taken of property on approval subject to inspection, that is to say, to be examined or shown, and such property is destroyed or lost while in the possession of the prospective purchaser without any fault on his part, such purchaser is considered to have held the property on trust and there is no need to make good the loss, whether the price has been stated or not.

CHAPTER VI.

OPTIONS

SECTION I.

Contractual Options.

Article 300. The vendor, or the purchaser, or both, may insert a condition in the contract of sale giving them an option, within a fixed period, to cancel the sale or to ratify it by carrying out the terms thereof.

Article 301. The person in the enjoyment of an option conferred by the contract is empowered either to cancel or to ratify the contract within the period of the validity of the option.

Article 302. Both cancellation and ratification of the contract may be by word of mouth or by conduct.

Article 303. Words importing ratification are words implying satisfaction, such as, "I ratify", or "I am pleased". Words importing cancellation are words implying dissatisfaction, such as, "I have cancelled" or, "I have gone back".

Article 304. Acts importing ratification are those acts implying satisfaction and acts importing cancellation are those acts implying dissatisfaction.

Example:-
> A purchaser having a right to an option performs some act within the period during which the option is valid, indicative of a right of ownership in such property, such as putting it up for sale, or pledging it, or letting it on hire. Such act is an act of ratification by conduct. If the vendor has an option and deals with the property in the same way, it is an act of cancellation by conduct.

Article 305. If the person possessing the option allows the period during which the option is valid to expire without either cancelling the sale or ratifying it, the sale becomes irrevocable.

Article 306. An option conferred by contract is not transmissible by way of inheritance. Thus, if the person possessing the option is the vendor, the purchaser becomes the owner of the thing sold upon the death of the vendor. If the purchaser is the person having the option and dies, his heirs become owners of the thing sold without any option.

Article 307. If both vendor and purchaser have an option, the sale can be cancelled by whichever party so desires. If one party only ratifies, that party loses his option, the other retaining his.

Article 308. If the vendor alone has an option, he does not lose his title in the thing sold, which is still considered to be a part of his own property. If the thing sold is destroyed while in the possession of the purchaser after delivery thereof, the fixed price does not become due, but the purchaser must pay the value thereof on the day he took delivery.

Article 309. If the purchaser alone has an option he acquires a title in the thing sold, which is considered to be a part of his own property. If the thing sold is destroyed while in the possession of the purchaser after delivery thereof, the fixed price must be paid.

SECTION II.

Option for misdescription.

Article 310. If the vendor sells property as possessing a certain desirable quality and such property proves to be devoid of such quality, the purchaser has the option of either cancelling the sale, or of accepting the thing sold for the whole of the fixed price. This is called option for misdescription.

Examples :-

(1) If a cow is sold described as giving milk and it proves that she has ceased to give milk, the purchaser acquires an option.

(2) If a stone sold at night-time as a red ruby proves to be a yellow ruby, the purchaser acquires an option.

Article 311. The option for misdescription is transmissible by way of inheritance. That is to say, that if on the death of the purchaser who has an option for misdescription, it turns out that the thing sold does not conform to the description given, the heir also has the power of cancelling the sale.

Article 312. If the purchaser having an option for misdescription deals with the thing sold in a manner indicative of a right of ownership over such thing, he loses his option thereby.

SECTION III.

Option as to payment.

Article 313. Vendor and purchaser may validly conclude a bargain whereby payment of the price is to be made by a certain time and in the event of payment not being made, the sale is not to take place. This option is called an option as to payment.

Article 314. If the purchaser does not pay the price within the stipulated period, a sale concluded subject to an option as to payment is voidable.

Article 315. If a purchaser having an option as to payment dies within the prescribed period, the sale is void.

SALE

SECTION IV.

Option as to selection.

Article 316. A stipulation may validly be made in a sale whereby the purchaser may take whichever he likes of two or three things at different prices the like of which cannot be found in the market, or the vendor may give whichever one he pleases. This is called an option as to selection.

Article 317. A period must be fixed during which the option as to selection is valid.

Article 318. A person having an option as to selection is bound to choose the thing he has bought on the expiration of the prescribed period.

Article 319. An option as to selection is transmissible by way of inheritance.

Example :-
> If the vendor sells three pieces of cloth all being of one type and consisting of superior, medium and inferior quality, the purchaser to take the piece he prefers within a period of three or four days, and such purchaser agrees thereto, a valid sale is concluded, and on the expiration of the stipulated period, the purchaser must choose one and pay the fixed price thereof. If he dies before exercising his option, his heir must choose one in the same manner.

SECTION V.

Option as to inspection.

Article 320. If a person buys a piece of property without seeing such property, he has an option upon inspection thereof of either cancelling the sale or of ratifying it. This is called the option of inspection.

SALE

Article 321. The option of inspection is not transmissible by way of inheritance. Consequently, if the purchaser dies without having seen the property which he has bought, his heir becomes owner of the property without having any option in the matter.

Article 322. No option of inspection accrues to the vendor who sells property without seeing it.

Example :-
> A sells property which he has not seen and which has come to him by way of inheritance. The sale is concluded without any right of option.

Article 323. The object of the option of inspection is to ascertain the nature of the thing sold and the whereabouts thereof.

Example :-
> A person who examines the outside of a plain piece of cloth which is the same on both sides; or a piece of cloth marked with stripes or flowers; or the teat of a sheep bought for breeding; or the back of a sheep bought for killing; or who tries the taste of things for eating and drinking and who later makes a purchase, has no option of inspection.

Article 324. It is sufficient to see a sample produced of things sold by sample.

Article 325. If the thing sold proves to be inferior to the sample, the purchaser has an option of taking or rejecting it.

Example :-
> If such things as corn or oil, and linen or wool manufactured so as to conform to a set standard of excellence are bought after inspecting a sample thereof, and are later found not to come up to sample, the purchaser has an option.

Article 326. In the purchase of real property such as an inn or a house, every room must be inspected. If the rooms are all of one type, however, it is sufficient to inspect one of the rooms.

Article 327. When things which are dissimilar to each other are purchased *en bloc*, each one must be inspected separately.

Article 328. If the purchaser buys things which are dissimilar from each other *en bloc* and inspects some of them and fails to inspect the rest, and, upon inspection of the latter, is dissatisfied therewith, he has the option of accepting or rejecting the whole lot. He may not take those with which he is satisfied and reject the rest.

Article 329. A blind person may validly buy and sell, but if he buys property the description of which is unknown to him, he has an option.

Example :-
If he buys a house the description of which is unknown to him, he has an option, upon learning the description thereof, of accepting or rejecting.

Article 330. A blind person has no option if he purchases a thing which has been described to him beforehand.

Article 331. If a blind person touches anything the nature of which can be ascertained by means of the sense of touch, and smells things the nature of which can be ascertained by means of the sense of smell, and tastes things the nature of which can be ascertained by means of the sense of taste, his right of option is destroyed. That is to say, if he touches or smells such things and afterwards purchases them, the sale is valid and irrevocable.

Article 332. If a person who has inspected a piece of property with a view to purchase later buys such property knowing it is the property in question, such person has no option of inspection. Should any change have been made in such property, however, such person has an option.

Article 333. Inspection by an agent authorized to buy or receive the thing sold, is equivalent to inspection by the principal.

Article 334. Inspection by a messenger, that is to say, a person sent, who merely has the power of collecting and despatching the thing sold, does not destroy the purchaser's option of inspection.

Article 335. If the purchaser deals with the thing sold in any way indicative of a right of ownership, his option of inspection is destroyed.

SECTION VI.

Option for defect.

Article 336. In an unconditional sale, the thing sold must be free from any defect. That is to say, although property is sold without stipulating that it shall be free from faults, and without stating whether it is sound, or bad, or defective, or free from fault, such property nevertheless must be sound and free from defect.

Article 337. If some defect of long standing is revealed upon the unconditional sale of any piece of property, the purchaser has the option of rejecting it or accepting it for the fixed price. He cannot keep the property and reduce the price on account of the defect. This is called option for defect.

Article 338. A defect consists of any faults which, in the opinion of persons competent to judge, cause a depreciation in the price of the property.

Article 339. A defect of long standing is a fault which existed while the thing sold was in the possession of the vendor.

Article 340. Any defect which occurs in the thing sold after sale and before delivery, while in the possession of the vendor, is considered a defect of long standing and justifies rejection.

Article 341. If the vendor declares at the time of the sale that there is a defect in the thing sold, and the purchaser accepts the thing sold with the defect, he has no option on account of such defect.

Article 342. If the vendor sells property subject to the condition that he shall be free from any claim on account of any defect, the purchaser has no option on account of defect found therein.

Article 343. If a purchaser buys property, including all defects, he cannot make any claim on account of any defect found therein.

Example :-
If a purchaser buys an animal with all faults of any description whatsoever whether blind, lame, or worthless, he cannot return such animal asserting that it had a defect of long standing.

Article 344. If the purchaser after becoming aware of a defect in the thing sold performs any act indicative of the exercise of a right of ownership, he loses his option for defect.

Example :-
The purchaser, after becoming aware of the existence of a defect of long standing in the thing sold, offers

such thing for sale. He is taken to have acquiesced therein and cannot reject the thing sold.

Article 345. If a defect appears in the thing sold while in the possession of the purchaser, and it proves to be a defect of long standing, the purchaser has no right to return the thing sold to the vendor, but has a right to claim a reduction in the price.

Example :-
If the purchaser discovers a defect of long standing in the thing he has purchased, such as a piece of cloth which after being cut up and measured is found to be rotten and frayed, he cannot return the same, because by cutting it he caused a fresh defect. He can, however, claim a reduction in the price on account of the defect.

Article 346. The amount of the reduction in the price is ascertained by a report drawn up by impartial experts. With this object in view, the value of the thing sold when sound and also when defective is ascertained, and a reduction is made from the fixed price on the basis of the difference between the two prices.

Example :-
A purchaser after buying a roll of cloth for sixty piastres and cutting it up and measuring it becomes aware of a defect of long standing. Experts estimate the value of such property at sixty piastres when sound and with the defect of long standing at forty-five piastres. The reduction to be made in the price is fifteen piastres, and the purchaser has a right to make a claim for that amount. If the experts report that the value of such property when sound was eighty piastres and with the defect sixty piastres, the difference of' twenty piastres between the two prices, that is to say a fourth of eighty piastres or a quarter of the fixed price may be claimed by the purchaser. If the value of the cloth when sound is reported to be fifty piastres

and with the defect forty piastres, the difference of ten piastres between the two, that is to say, one fifth of the fixed price, is considered to be the amount to be deducted from the price.

Article 347. If a defect of recent origin disappears, a defect of long standing still justifies rejection.

Example :-
A horse is purchased and falls sick while in the possession of the purchaser. Thereupon a defect of long standing is revealed. The purchaser is unable to return the horse, but can obtain a reduction in the price. If the animal recovers from the illness, the purchaser can return the horse to the vendor on account of the defect of long standing.

Article 348. If the vendor agrees to take back the thing sold after the occurrence of a defect while in the possession of the purchaser which reveals a defect of long standing, and should there be nothing to prevent its return, the purchaser cannot claim a reduction in price, but must either return the thing sold or keep it and pay the full price. Should the purchaser sell the property to some third person after becoming aware of the existence of the defect of long standing, he is in no way entitled to claim a reduction of price.

Example :-
A purchaser buys a roll of linen and cuts it up to make shirts. He then finds it to be defective and sells it. He cannot claim any reduction of the price from the vendor. The reason for this is that while the vendor may state that he would take back the stuff with the defect of recent origin, that is to say, cut up, the sale thereof by the purchaser is tantamount to an adoption of the defect.

Article 349. Any increase, that is to say, any addition of property belonging to the purchaser to the thing sold makes any return thereof impossible.

Example :-
A purchaser adds certain sewing or dyeing with his own thread or colour to a piece of cloth; or the purchaser of a piece of land plants trees therein. Such acts prevent the return of the thing sold.

Article 350. If there is anything to prevent the return of the thing sold, the vendor cannot receive back the defective thing sold, even though he is willing to do so, but must make a reduction in price. If the purchaser becomes aware of the existence of a defect of long standing in the property in question and sells the same, he can demand a reduction in price from the vendor.

Example :-
A purchaser buys a roll of linen to make into shirts. After measuring them and sewing them, he finds that the linen is defective. He cannot ask for the linen to be taken back, even though the vendor is prepared to do so. The vendor is obliged to make a reduction in the price. If the purchaser sells the shirts, he can recover the reduction in the price from the vendor. The reason for this is that the thread belonging to the purchaser has been added to the thing sold and prevents its return. The vendor cannot say that he will take the thing back after it has been cut up and sewn, and the purchaser is not considered to have kept back the thing sold from the vendor.

Article 351. Before taking delivery, the purchaser may reject the whole of a number of things bought *en bloc,* if some of them prove to be defective, or he may elect to take them for the fixed price. He cannot reject the things which are defective and keep the rest. If the defect becomes apparent after delivery, and no loss is incurred by separation, he can return that portion in which the defect has appeared, against a proportionate share of the fixed price when sound. He cannot return the whole unless the vendor agrees thereto. If any loss is caused by the separation, however, he may return or keep the whole amount at the fixed price.

Example :-
If one of two fezzes bought for forty piastres proves to be defective before delivery, both can be rejected together. If one of them proves to be defective after delivery, he can return that fez, deducting the value of such fez when sound from the forty piastres. If he has bought a pair of shoes, however, and after delivery, one of them turns out to be defective, he can return them both and can demand the return of the whole of his money.

Article 352. If a person who has bought and taken delivery of a definite number of things estimated by measure of capacity or weight and which are of one type, finds a portion thereof to be defective, he has the option of accepting or rejecting the whole number.

Article 353. If cereals such as wheat prove to be earthy, though to an extent considered by custom to be negligible, the sale is valid and irrevocable. If, however, such cereals are considered by local opinion to be positively defective, the purchaser has an option.

Article 354. If such things as eggs and nuts prove to be bad and defective but not to a greater extent than that sanctioned by custom, such as three per cent, the sale is valid. If the defect is considerable, however, such as ten per cent, the sale is invalid and the purchaser can return the whole amount to the vendor and recover the entire price.

Article 355. If the thing sold appears to be in such a state that no benefit can ever be derived therefrom, the sale is void and the purchaser can recover the whole of the price.

Example:-
> If eggs which have been bought prove to be so bad that they are useless, the purchaser can recover the whole of his money.

SECTION VII.

Misrepresentation and Deceit.

Article 356. The existence of flagrant misrepresentation in a sale, but without actual deceit, does not enable the person who has been the victim of such misrepresentation to cancel the sale. But if the sale of the property of orphans is tainted by flagrant misrepresentation, although there is no actual deceit, such sale is invalid. Property belonging to a pious foundation and to the Treasury is treated on the same basis as the property of orphans.

Article 357. If one of the two parties to the sale deceives the other, and flagrant misrepresentation is also proved to be present in the sale, the person so deceived can cancel the sale.

Article 358. If the person who is the victim of flagrant misrepresentation dies, no right to an action for deceit is transmitted to his heirs.

Article 359. If the purchaser who is the victim of deceit becomes aware that the sale is tainted by flagrant misrepresentation and deals with the thing sold in any manner indicative of a right of ownership, he has no right whatsoever to cancel such sale.

SALE

Article 360. If a thing sold which has been bought as a result of deceit or flagrant misrepresentation is destroyed, or perishes, or becomes defective, or if something new is added, such as a building to a piece of land, the victim of such misrepresentation has no right to cancel the sale.

CHAPTER VII.

VARIOUS CATEGORIES OF THINGS SOLD AND THE EFFECT THEREOF.

SECTION I.

Types of Sale.

Article 361. It is a condition precedent to the conclusion of the sale that the parties thereto should be of sound mind and perfect understanding and that the sale should be made with reference to some thing which may properly be the subject of sale.

Article 362. A sale which is defective in any essential condition, such as sale by a lunatic, is void.

Article 363. In order that any object may properly be the subject of sale, such object must be in existence, must be capable of delivery, and must be of some specific value. Consequently, the sale of a thing which is not in existence, or is incapable of delivery, or is not of any specific value, is void.

Article 364. If a sale is concluded validly, but is not legal as regards certain subsidiary matters, such as the thing sold being unknown, or defective as regards the price, the sale is voidable.

Article 365. For a sale to be executory, the vendor must be the owner of the thing sold, or the agent of the owner, or his tutor or guardian, and no other person must be entitled thereto.

Article 366. A voidable sale becomes executory on taking delivery. That is to say, the purchaser may deal with the thing sold.

Article 367. If one of the options attaches to the sale, such sale is not irrevocable.

Article 368. A sale dependent upon the right of some third person may validly be concluded if the permission of such person is obtained, as in the case of a sale by an unauthorized person, or the sale of property given as a pledge.

SECTION II.

Effect of various kinds of sale.

Article 369. The effect of the conclusion of a sale is ownership, that is to say, the purchaser becomes the owner of the thing sold and the vendor becomes the owner of the price.

Article 370. A sale which is void is of no effect whatsoever. Consequently, if in the case of a sale which is void, the purchaser has taken delivery of the thing sold with the permission of the vendor, and such thing is destroyed without the fault of the purchaser while in his possession, there is no necessity for the purchaser to make good the loss, the thing sold being in the nature of a thing deposited on trust.

Article 371. A voidable sale, on delivery, is effective, that is to say, if the purchaser takes possession of the thing sold with the permission of the vendor, he becomes

86 SALE

the owner thereof. Consequently, if a thing bought as the result of a voidable sale is destroyed while in the possession of the purchaser, the purchaser must make good the loss. If the thing sold is one the like of which can be found in the market, a like thing must be given by the purchaser to the vendor, or if it is a thing the like of which cannot be found in the market, the value thereof on the day of delivery must be paid.

Article 372. In the case of a voidable sale, each of the contracting parties has the right of cancelling the sale. But if the thing sold is destroyed while in the possession of the purchaser, or if the purchaser disposes of it in any way, such as consuming it, or selling it validly to some other person, or bestowing it upon someone by way of gift, or if the thing sold being a house, the purchaser adds to it in any way, such as repairing it, or, if it is a piece of land, planting trees on it, or, if it is corn, changes it by grinding it into flour, so that its name is changed, there is no right of cancellation.

Article 373. In the case of cancellation of a voidable sale, if the price has been received, the purchaser has the right of retaining the thing sold until the vendor has returned the price.

Article 374. An executory sale becomes effective forthwith.

Article 375. An executory sale is irrevocable, and neither of the two parties to the sale may go back thereon.

Article 376. In the case of a revocable sale, a person possessing an option can cancel such sale.

Article 377. A conditional sale becomes effective when the necessary permission is given.

Article 378. In the event of a sale by an unauthorized person, such sale is executory if the owner of the property, or his agent, or his tutor, or his guardian give their permission. Otherwise it is of no effect. For the permission to be effective, however, it is necessary for the vendor, the purchaser, the person giving permission and the thing sold to be in existence. If any of these is absent, the permission is invalid.

Article 379. In the case of sale by barter, the conditions applicable to a thing sold also apply, since the value of the two things exchanged is considered to constitute a thing sold. If a dispute arises as to delivery, however, the two parties to the sale must respectively give and take delivery simultaneously.

SECTION III.

Sale by immediate payment against future delivery.

Article 380. A contract of sale by immediate payment against future delivery is concluded by offer and acceptance, as in the case of sale.

Example :-
A purchaser tells a vendor that he has paid a thousand piastres immediately against future delivery of one hundred *kilés* of corn. The vendor agrees. A contract of sale by immediate payment against future delivery has been concluded.

Article 381. A sale by immediate payment against future delivery can only be concluded validly with reference to things the quantity and quality of which can be determined; for example, the highest or lowest.

Article 382. The amount of things estimated by measure of capacity or by weight or by length is fixed by the *kilé,* the weight, or the yard.

Article 383. The amount of things estimated by enumeration and which closely resemble each other may be measured by counting, and also by the *kilé* and by weight.

Article 384. In the case of things estimated by enumeration, such as burnt bricks and sundried bricks, the mould thereof must be made known.

Article 385. The length, breadth and thickness of things measured by length, such as linen and woollens, the material they are made from, and the place in which they were made, must be stated.

Article 386. It is essential to the validity of a sale by immediate payment against future delivery that the type of thing sold should be stated; for instance, corn, rice or dates: and the particular variety; for example, whether produced by rain or by irrigation: and the quality; for example, the highest or the lowest: the amount of the price of the thing sold, and the time and place of delivery thereof must also be stated.

Article 387. It is essential to the validity of a sale by immediate payment against future delivery that the price should be paid at the meeting where the contract is concluded. If the two contracting parties separate before the price is handed over, the contract is cancelled.

SECTION IV.

Contract for manufacture and sale.

Article 388. If a person requests a skilled workman to make a certain thing for a certain sum of money and the latter undertakes to do so, a contract for manufacture and sale has been concluded.

Examples :-

(1) A purchaser displays his foot to a boot-maker and asks him to make a pair of boots from such and such leather for so many piastres and the latter agrees to do so; or a bargain is struck with a ship's carpenter for the building of a rowing boat or ship, after describing the length, breadth and essential qualities thereof. A contract for manufacture and sale has been concluded.

(2) A bargain is concluded with a manufacturer for the production of a certain number of needle guns at so much per gun, after describing the length and size thereof, and other requirements. A contract for manufacture and sale has been concluded.

Article 389. A contract for manufacture and sale is generally valid if it is customary to conclude such a contract. If a period is prescribed, however, in respect to things to which no such custom applies, the conditions applicable in the case of immediate payment against future delivery are in force. If no period is prescribed, however, the contract is in the nature of a contract for manufacture and sale.

Article 390. In the case of contract for manufacture and sale, an identification and description of the article must be given as required.

Article 391. It is not essential to a contract for manufacture and sale, that the money should be paid immediately.

Article 392. After the conclusion of a contract for manufacture and sale, neither party can go back on the bargain they have struck. If, however, the object manufactured is not in accordance with the specification, the person who has given the order may exercise an option.

SECTION V.

Sale by a person suffering from a mortal sickness.

Article 393. If a person suffering from a mortal sickness sells a thing to one of his heirs, such sale is dependent upon the permission of the other heirs. If such heirs give their permission after the death of the person suffering from the mortal sickness, such sale becomes executory. If they do not so give their permission, it is not executory.

Article 394. If a person suffering from a mortal sickness sells a thing to a person who is not one of his heirs at the time of his death for a price equal to the value of such thing, such sale is valid. If he gives favourable terms, that is to say, sells such thing for less than its value and gives delivery thereof, and one third of his property allows thereof, and thereafter dies, the sale is valid. If a third of his property is insufficient to allow of such favourable terms, the purchaser must make good such deficiency. If he does not do so, the heirs can cancel the sale.

Examples:-

(1) A person suffering from a mortal sickness, and who owns nothing but a house worth one thousand five hundred piastres, sells and delivers such house to a person who is not one of his heirs for one thousand piastres. Such sale is valid, since the five hundred piastres which he has made a subject of his generosity do not exceed a third of his property, and the heir cannot cancel the sale.

(2) If a person suffering from a mortal sickness sells and delivers the house for five hundred piastres, the purchaser is obliged to increase the price to two thirds, upon being requested to do so by the heirs, since the thousand piastres which he has made the subject of his generosity is twice as much as one third of his

property. If he does so, the heir cannot cancel the sale. If he fails to do so, the heirs can cancel the sale and demand the return of the house.

Article 395. If a person whose estate is overwhelmed by debts and who is suffering from a mortal sickness sells his property for a price less than the true value and then dies, the creditors can oblige the purchaser to make good the balance of the price. If he does not do so, the creditors can cancel the sale.

SECTION VI.

Sale subject to a right of redemption.

Article 396. In sale subject to a right of redemption the vendor may return the price and claim back the thing sold. The purchaser likewise can return the thing sold and claim back the price.

Article 397. A thing sold subject to a right of redemption may not be sold to any other person by either the vendor or the purchaser.

Article 398. A condition may validly be made that a portion of the profits of the thing sold shall be for the purchaser.

Example :-
If it is mutually agreed to make a contract that the grapes of a vineyard sold subject to a right of redemption shall be equally divided between vendor and purchaser, the contract must be carried out.

Article 399. If property sold subject to a right of redemption is equal to the amount of the debt and perishes while in the possession of the purchaser, the debt which it secures is cancelled.

92	SALE

Article 400. If the value of the property sold subject to a right of redemption is less than the debt and perishes while in the possession of the purchaser, a sum equivalent to the amount of the debt is deducted, and the purchaser can claim the return of the balance from the vendor.

Article 401. If the value of the property sold subject to a right of redemption is greater than the amount of the debt and perishes while in the possession of the purchaser, a sum equivalent to the amount of the debt is deducted. If the purchaser has been guilty of some wrongful act, he must make good the balance. If he has not been guilty of any wrongful act, and the property has been destroyed, the purchaser is not obliged to make good the balance.

Article 402. If one of the two parties to a sale subject to a right of redemption dies, the right of cancellation is transmitted to his heirs by way of inheritance.

Article 403. No other creditors of the vendor have the right of interfering with property sold subject to a right of redemption, until the purchaser thereof has recovered payment of what is due to him.

Promulgated by Royal Iradah, 8th. Muharram, 1286.

BOOK II.

HIRE.

BOOK II

HIRE.

INTRODUCTION.

TERMS OF MUHAMMADAN JURISPRUDENCE RELATING TO HIRE.

Article 404. Rent is hire, that is to say, the price paid for the use of a thing; letting is giving on hire, and hiring is taking on hire.

Article 405. *Has no meaning for the English reader.*

Article 406. An irrevocable contract of hire is any valid contract of hire which is not burdened by a contractual option, or by an option for defect or by an option for inspection, and which neither of the parties may cancel without some lawful excuse.

Article 407. An immediate contract of hire is a contract of hire which comes into force immediately upon the conclusion of the contract.

Article 408. A future contract of hire is a contract of hire which comes into force as from some definite future date.

Example :-
> A house is given on hire as from the beginning of some future month for a certain period and for a certain sum of money. A future contract of hire has been concluded.

Article 409. The lessor is the person who gives on hire.

96	HIRE

Article 410. The lessee is the person who takes on hire.

Article 411. The thing hired is the thing which is given on hire.

Article 412. Property given to work upon is property handed to a person employed by the employer, so that the person employed may do the work which has been entrusted to him, such as stuff given to a tailor to make into clothes, or a load given to a porter to carry.

Article 413. The employee is the person giving his services on hire.

Article 414. Estimated rent is the rent fixed by disinterested experts.

Article 415. Fixed rent is the rent mentioned and fixed at the time of the conclusion of the contract.

Article 416. Indemnification consists of giving a similar thing if it is a thing the like of which can be found in the market, or the value thereof, if it is a thing the like of which cannot be found.

Article 417. Prepared for hire is said of any thing designed and prepared to be let on hire. It relates to real property such as inns, houses, baths and shops originally built or bought in order to be let on hire, and also such things as carriages and horses let on hire. If a thing is let continuously on hire for a period of three years, it is a proof that it is prepared for hire. If a person has a thing made for himself and tells people that it is prepared for hire, such thing is deemed to be prepared for hire.

Article 418. A hirer of a wet nurse is a person who hires a nurse to give milk to a baby.

Article 419. Partition of usufruct consists of a division of benefit.

Example :-
Two persons who are joint owners of a house agree to take the benefit arising therefrom separately in alternate years.

CHAPTER I.

GENERAL.

Article 420. In a contract of hire, the subject matter of the contract consists of some advantage to be derived from such contract.

Article 421. Hire in relation to the subject matter of the contract is of two categories. The first is a contract for hire made with reference to an interest in specific things. The thing which is the subject of hire is called both the object given on hire and the object taken on hire. The first category is divided into three classes.

The first class relates to the lease of real property, such as the hire of houses and lands.

The second class relates to the hire of merchandise such as the hire of clothes and utensils.

The third class relates to the hire of animals.

The second category is a contract of hire with regard to labour. In this category, the person hired is called the employee, as in the case of workmen and servants employed for a wage. Hiring the services of craftsmen and artisans is also included in this category.

Example :-
A contract for manufacture and sale is concluded when clothes are ordered to be made by a tailor who supplies the cloth. If the cloth is given to the tailor in

order that he should make the clothes, such person's labour has been hired.

Article 422. Employees are of two classes.

The first class comprises private employees, that is, persons whose services are retained by one employer only, as in the case of a servant paid a monthly wage.

The second class comprises public employees, that is persons who are not bound by an undertaking not to work for more than one employer.

Example :-

Porters, brokers, tailors, clock-makers, jewellers, harbour boatmen, cab-drivers, and village shepherds are all public employees; that is, persons who are not employed specially by one particular individual, but work for anyone. But if any one of such persons undertakes to give his services on hire to one employer only for a specific period, he becomes during that period a private employee. Again, a porter, or a cab-driver, or a boatman who gives his services on hire to one employer alone to take such employer to a certain place, and who works for no other person is, until he arrives at his destination, a private employee.

Article 423. The person employing a private employee may be one single individual or several persons contemplated as one individual only. Consequently, when the inhabitants of a village hire the services of a shepherd for themselves alone by means of a single contract, such shepherd becomes a private employee. But should those persons permit the shepherd to tend some other person's animals, such shepherd becomes a public employee.

Article 424. The wages of a public employee are due when the work is done.

HIRE

Article 425. The wages of a private employee are due if he is ready to work during the period for which his services were hired. It is not essential that he should actually have performed the work. He cannot, however, decline to do the work. If he does so, he is not entitled to his wages.

Article 426. A person who is entitled to a definite advantage arising out of a contract of hire may obtain enjoyment of such advantage or the equivalent thereof, or of some lesser advantage. He cannot, however, obtain any greater advantage.

Examples :-

(1) A blacksmith hires a shop in order to carry on his trade there. He can carry on any other trade there which causes no greater injury to the lessor, or a trade causing a lesser degree of injury.

(2) If a person does not live in a house which he has hired for purposes of habitation, he may store goods therein. But he may not carry on trade as a blacksmith in a shop which he has hired as a grocer's shop.

Article 427. Anything which becomes altered by any change in the person using it may validly be made the subject of a restriction.

Example :-

A person hires a horse to ride himself. No other person may ride it.

Article 428. Any restriction imposed in connection with any thing which does not become altered by any change in the person using it is inoperative.

Example :-

A hires a house to dwell in. B can also dwell in it.

Article 429. The owner of a share of undivided jointly owned property may let such share to his co-owner whether such share is capable of division or not. He may not let it to any other person. He may, however, after a partition of the usufruct has been made, let his share to some other person.

Article 430. The existence of undivided shares of jointly owned property after the conclusion of a contract of hire does not invalidate such contract.

Example :-
A lets his house and after doing so a half share is seized by a person entitled thereto. The lease relating to the other undivided share remains in force.

Article 431. Two joint owners may simultaneously let property jointly owned to some other person.

Article 432. One particular thing may be let to two particular persons. Each one must pay the amount of the rent which falls to his own share. The share of one may not be obtained from the other unless they are guarantors of one another.

CHAPTER II

QUESTIONS RELATING TO THE CONTRACT OF HIRE.

SECTION I.

The fundamental basis of the contract of hire.

Article 433. As in the case of sale, the contract of hire is concluded by offer and acceptance.

Article 434. In a contract of hire, statements made indicative of offer and acceptance are such expressions as "I have given on hire", "I have let", "I have taken on hire" and "I have accepted".

Article 435. As in the case of sale, the contract of hire is concluded by the use of the past tense. It cannot be concluded by the use of the future tense.

Example:-
A says "I will give on hire" and B says "I have taken on hire"; or A says "hire" and B says "I have hired". In both cases no contract of hire has been concluded.

Article 436. A contract of hire may be concluded by word of mouth, or by writing, or by the use of generally recognized signs by dumb persons.

Article 437. A contract of hire may also be concluded by conduct. Thus, if a traveller boards a steam boat or a harbour rowing boat or rides a hired pony, the rate of hire of which is well known, without concluding any oral contract, the amount of hire involved must be paid. If such rate is not known, an estimated rate must be paid.

Article 438. In a contract of hire, silence is considered to indicate assent and acceptance.

Examples :-
(1) A leases a shop at a monthly rent of fifty piastres. After staying there for a few months, the lessor informs him that if he agrees to pay sixty piastres on the first of the month he can remain, but if not, he must leave. A refuses to pay sixty piastres and remains in the shop. He is only obliged to pay fifty piastres as hitherto. If, however, he remains silent and continues to reside in the shop without interruption, he must pay a monthly rent of sixty piastres.

(2) An owner of a shop proposes a rent of one hundred piastres and the lessee a rent of eighty piastres. The owner leaves the lessee, who remains in the shop. The rent is eighty piastres. If the two parties persist in their contention, and the lessee remains in possession, an estimated rent must be paid.

Article 439. If fresh negotiations are commenced after the conclusion of the contract with regard to any change, increase or decrease of the rent, the second contract takes the place of the first.

Article 440. A contract of hire may validly be concluded to take effect at some future date. It is irrevocable, although it may not yet have come into force. Consequently, neither of the contracting parties may cancel such contract merely on the ground that it has not yet come into force.

Article 441. If after the conclusion of a valid contract of hire, some other person offers a higher rent, the contract of hire may not be cancelled by the lessor by reason of that fact alone. If a guardian or trustee of a pious foundation, however, lets the real property of an orphan or of a pious foundation for a rent which is less than the estimated rent, the contract of hire is voidable and the rent must be increased to the estimated rent.

Article 442. If the person taking the property on hire becomes owner of the hired property in any manner, such as by way of inheritance or gift, such property loses its quality of hired property.

Article 443. If any event happens whereby the reason for the conclusion of the contract disappears, so that the contract cannot be carried out, such contract is cancelled.

Examples :-

(1) A cook is hired for a wedding feast. One of the spouses dies. The contract of hire is cancelled.

(2) A person suffering from toothache makes a contract with a dentist to extract his tooth for a certain fee. The pain ceases. The contract of hire is cancelled.

(3) A person seeking a wet-nurse dies. The contract of hire is not cancelled. But upon the death of the child or the wet-nurse, such contract is cancelled.

SECTION II.

Conditions relating to the conclusion and execution of the contract of hire.

Article 444. To conclude a contract of hire, the two contracting parties must possess the requisite capacity, that is to say, they must be of sound mind and perfect understanding.

Article 445. In a contract of hire offer and acceptance must agree and the parties must meet together at the same time and place, as in the case of sale.

Article 446. The person letting a thing on hire must be the owner of the thing he lets on hire, or the agent of the owner, or his tutor or guardian.

Article 447. If any unauthorized person lets anything on hire, such letting is dependent upon the ratification of the owner, and if the owner is a minor or is mad, and a contract of letting on hire has been concluded for an estimated rent, such contract is dependent upon the ratification of the tutor or guardian. There are four essentials to the validity of such permission, which remain constant: the two contracting parties; the property; the subject matter of the contract; and the rent, should it be payable from merchandise. If one of these essentials is lacking, the permission is invalid.

SECTION III.

Essentials to the validity of a contract of hire.

Article 448. The consent of the two contracting parties is essential to the validity of a contract of hire.

HIRE

Article 449. The subject matter of the contract of hire must be specified. Consequently, if one of two shops is let on hire, without the particular shop in question being specified, and the lessee being given an option as to which one he will take, such contract is invalid.

Article 450. The rent must be clearly ascertained.

Article 451. In a contract of hire, the advantage to be derived from the subject matter of the contract must be specified in such a manner as to avoid any possibility of dispute.

Article 452. In the case of the hire of such things as houses, shops and a wet-nurse, the advantage to be derived therefrom is defined by stating the period of hire.

Article 453. In the case of hire of a horse, it must be stated whether such horse is to be used as a draught horse, or a riding horse, and if so, who is to ride it: or it may be stated in general terms that whosoever wishes may ride such horse, and the period for which the contract is concluded, or the distance, must also be stated.

Article 454. In the case of hire of land, the period of hire must be stated; the purpose for which such land is to be used; and, if it is to be used for cultivation, the nature of the things to be planted; or, if the person taking such land on hire so desires, a statement in general terms must be made to the effect that he may plant whatever he likes.

Article 455. In the case of hire of the services of skilled workmen, the advantage to be derived from the services of such workmen may be specified by stating the nature of the work, that is to say, what work is to be done and how it is to be performed.

Example :-

> When clothes are to be dyed, they must be shown to the dyer, the texture thereof must be specified, and the colour stated.

Article 456. In the case of transport of goods, the advantage to be derived therefrom is specified by indicating them, and by stating the place to which they are to be transported.

Example :-

> A instructs B to carry a certain load to a certain place. The advantage to be derived therefrom is specified by such load being inspected and the distance being made known.

Article 457. The advantage to be derived from the thing hired must be capable of enjoyment. Consequently, a contract of hire in respect to a runaway animal is invalid.

SECTION IV.

Nullity or voidability of the contract of hire.

Article 458. If one of the conditions essential to the conclusion of a contract of hire is absent, such contract is void.

Example :-

> A contract of letting or taking on hire entered into by a madman or by a minor of imperfect understanding is void. But if the person giving or letting on hire becomes mad after the conclusion of the contract, such contract is not cancelled.

Article 459. If a contract of hire which is void is carried out the amount of the hire need not be paid. But if the property is dedicated to pious purposes, or belongs to orphans, an estimated rent must be paid. A madman is treated on the same basis as an orphan.

Article 460. If the conditions requisite for the conclusion of a contract of hire are present, but one of the conditions essential to the validity of the contract is absent, the contract of hire is voidable.

Article 461. A voidable contract of hire is executory. But in a voidable contract of hire, the person giving on hire is not entitled to the fixed rent, but to the estimated rent only.

Article 462. The voidability of a contract of hire sometimes arises from the amount of the hire not being known and sometimes owing to the absence of other conditions essential to the validity of the contract. In the first case, the estimated rent must be paid, whatever the amount thereof may be. In the second case, the estimated rent is payable, provided that it does not exceed the fixed rent.

CHAPTER III.

QUESTIONS AFFECTING THE AMOUNT OF THE HIRE.

SECTION I.

Rent.

Article 463. A thing which is valid as the price in a contract of sale, may be the rent in a contract of hire. On the other hand, a thing which is not valid as the price in a contract of sale may nevertheless be valid as the rent in a contract of hire.

Example :-
> A garden may be taken on hire in exchange for an animal, or in exchange for the right of dwelling in a house.

HIRE

Article 464. If the rent is cash, the amount thereof must be clearly ascertained, as in the case of the price of a thing sold.

Article 465. If the rent consists of merchandise, or things estimated by measure of capacity, or by measure of weight, or things estimated by enumeration and which closely resemble each other, such rent must be made known by stating both the amount and description thereof.

In the case of things which require loading and entail expense on account of transport such things must be delivered at the place agreed upon for delivery. If no place has been designated for delivery and the thing hired consists of real property, delivery of such real property must be given at the place where such real property is situated, and if it consists of labour, delivery thereof must be given at the place where the person hired performs his work; if it consists of loading, delivery thereof must be given in the place where the hire becomes payable.

In the case of things which do not require loading and do not entail expense on account of transport, however, delivery thereof must be given at any place that may be required.

SECTION II.

Necessity for rent: right of the person giving on hire to take rent.

Article 466. Rent does not become payable irrevocably by the conclusion of an unconditional contract: that is to say, there is no necessity to hand over the rent immediately, owing to the mere conclusion of a contract of hire.

HIRE

Article 467. Rent which is payable immediately is irrevocable : that is to say, if the person taking the thing on hire pays the rent in advance, the person letting the thing on hire becomes the owner thereof, and the person taking the thing on hire cannot demand the return thereof.

Article 468. Rent with a condition for immediate payment is irrevocable; that is to say, if it is stipulated that rent must be paid in advance, the person taking the thing on hire is bound in any case and first of all to hand over the rent, whether the contract of hire is for the use of some specific thing, or for the performance of any piece of work.

In the first case, the person letting the thing on hire may refuse to hand over the thing hired until the rent has been paid. In the second case, the person giving his services on hire may refuse to perform the work until his wages have been paid.

In both cases, if the person letting the thing on hire demands payment of the rent in advance and the person taking the thing on hire refuses, the contract of hire may be cancelled.

Article 469. Rent becomes payable when the thing is put to the use for which it is hired.

Example :-

A the owner of a horse, lets such horse on hire to B in order that he may ride it to a certain place. Upon arrival at that place, A is entitled to the amount of the hire.

Article 470. In a valid contract of hire, the rent is also payable when there is ability to put the thing to the use for which it was hired.

Example:-
>A takes possession of a house which he has taken on hire by means of a valid contract of hire. A is obliged to pay the rent, even though he does not inhabit such house.

Article 471. In a voidable contract of hire, mere ability to put the thing to the use for which it was hired is not enough. The rent is not payable unless the thing is actually put to the use for which it was hired.

Article 472. If a person uses the property of another person without the conclusion of a contract and without such person's permission, and if it is property prepared for hire, an estimated rent must be paid, but not otherwise. But if the owner of the property has previously demanded payment of rent, and such person uses such property, rent is payable, even though no benefit can be derived from such property. The reason for this is that by using the property, such person is deemed to have agreed to pay the rent.

Article 473. Effect is given to any condition agreed upon by the two contracting parties regarding immediate or deferred payment of the rent.

Article 474. If a stipulation is made for a deferred payment of the price of the hire, the person giving the thing on hire must first of all deliver such thing; and a person giving his services on hire, must perform his work. The price of the contract of hire is not payable until after the expiration of the period agreed upon.

Article 475. If an unconditional contract of hire is concluded for the use of some specific object, or for the performance of any piece of work, and no stipulation is made as to immediate or deferred payment, the person giving the thing on hire must in any case first of all give

110	HIRE

delivery of the thing hired, and the person giving his services on hire must perform the work.

Article 476. If the rent is payable by some specified period, such as monthly or yearly, such rent must be paid at the expiration of that period.

Example :-
>Rent payble monthly must be paid at the end of the month. Rent payable yearly must be paid at the end of the year.

Article 477. When the rent falls due, delivery must be given of the thing hired; that is to say, rent falls due as from the time of delivery. Thus, the person giving the thing on hire is not entitled to rent in respect to the period expiring prior to delivery. If the period of hire terminates prior to delivery, no part of the rent is payable.

Article 478. If the benefit to be obtained from the thing hired is entirely lost, no rent is payable.

Examples:-
>(1) A bath is in need of repairs. If it cannot be used during that period, the portion of the rent corresponding to such period is deducted.
>
>(2) The water of a mill is cut off and the mill remains idle. No rent is payable from the time at which the water was cut off. But if the person hiring the mill uses it for any purpose other than that of grinding corn, such person is bound to pay a portion of the rent corresponding thereto.

Article 479. If a person takes a shop on hire and is given delivery thereof and alleges that on account of slackness of business his trade has stopped and his shop has been shut, such person cannot refuse to pay rent for that period.

Article 480. If a boat is taken on hire for a certain period, and the period of such hire expires while on the journey, the period of hire is extended until the shore is reached. The person taking the boat on hire must pay an estimated rent in respect to such excess period.

Article 481. If one person gives his house to another person in order that the latter may repair it and live in it rent free, and such person does in fact effect such repairs himself and dwells in such house for a certain period, the expenses occasioned by such repairs fall upon such person, since the giving of the house is in the nature of a loan for use. The owner of the house cannot claim anything from him by way of rent in respect to such period.

SECTION III.

Right of lien of a person to whom a thing has been entrusted to work upon.

Article 482. A person hired to do work, and whose work causes a change in the thing given to him to work upon, such as a tailor, a dyer, or a cleaner, and who has made no contract whereby his work is to be done on a credit basis, has a right of retention over the thing entrusted to him to work upon, for payment of his wage. If he exercises such right of retention and the property is destroyed while in his possession, he cannot be called upon to make good the loss. He cannot, however, claim his wages in addition.

Article 483. A person hired to do work, and whose work causes no change in the thing upon which he works, such as a porter or a sailor, has no right of retention over the thing upon which he is working, for payment of his wage. Thus, if he exercises a right of retention and the property is destroyed while in his possession, he is liable to make good the value thereof.

The owner of the property has an option either of claiming compensation on the basis of the value of the thing destroyed, plus cost of transport and of paying the wages, or of merely claiming the value of the thing destroyed, without paying the wages.

CHAPTER IV.

THE PERIOD OF HIRE.

Article 484. A person may give his property on hire, whatever the form of ownership, for a fixed period, whether of short duration, such as a day, or whether of long duration, such as a period of years.

Article 485. The commencement of the period of hire is deemed to be the time named when the contract was concluded.

Article 486. If no time is mentioned as the commencement of the period of hire when the contract is concluded, such time is deemed to be the time when the contract was concluded.

Article 487. Real property may validly be let on hire for a period of a year, either at a rent of so much per month, or of so much for the year, without stating the rent per month.

Article 488. If a contract of hire is made at the beginning of the month for a period of one month, or for any period in excess thereof, such contract is a monthly contract. In such a case, if the month is less than thirty days, a full month's rent must be paid.

Article 489. If a contract is made for a period of one month and a portion thereof has expired, the period of one month is considered to consist of thirty days.

Article 490. If a portion of the month has expired and a contract has been concluded for a period of months and the first month is not complete, such month is completed by the payment of rent at so much per day, from days taken from the last month, so as to make thirty days. The intervening months are calculated as from the first day of each lunar month.

Article 491. If a portion of the month has expired and the number of months is not expressed, and a certain sum is agreed upon as being payable as rent for each month, the first incomplete month is considered to consist of thirty days in the same manner as the other months.

Article 492. If a contract of hire is concluded for a period of one year at the beginning of the month, the year is considered to consist of twelve months.

Article 493. If a portion of the month has expired and a contract of hire has been concluded for a period of one year, the first month is calculated according to days, and the other eleven months as from the first of the lunar month.

Article 494. If real property is hired at a rent of so much per month and the number of months is not mentioned, a valid contract has been concluded. Upon the completion of the first month, however, both the person giving and the person taking such real property on hire may cancel the contract of hire on the first night and day of the second and subsequent months. If the first night and day, however, have expired, such contract cannot be cancelled. If one of the two contracting parties alleges that he has cancelled the contract during the course of the month, such contract is cancelled as from the end of the month. If during the course of the month one of the parties states that he has cancelled the contract as from the beginning of the following month, such contract is cancelled as from the beginning of the following month. If payment is made in advance for two or more months, neither party may cancel the contract of hire in respect to those months.

Article 495. If a person hires another to work for a day from sunrise to the time of evening prayer or till sunset, the conditions prescribed by local custom must be observed as regards the performance of the work.

Article 496. If a person is hired to work for a period of days, as for example, a carpenter for a period of ten days, the contract is presumed to be concluded with reference to the days following. If he is hired to do ten days work during the summer, the contract of employment is invalid unless the month is stated and the day from which the work is to commence.

CHAPTER V.

OPTIONS.

SECTION I.

Contractual options.

Article 497. A contractual option exists in the case of hire, as in the case of sale. Either or both of the parties may give or take on hire, subject to an option of a certain number of days.

Article 498. The person having the option may cancel the contract of hire during the period of the option or may ratify such contract.

Article 499. Both cancellation and ratification may be by word of mouth, or in writing, or by conduct, as is set forth in Articles 302, 303 and 304. Consequently, if

HIRE

the person giving on hire possesses an option and performs any act with regard to the thing hired indicative of the exercise of a right of ownership, the contract of hire is cancelled by conduct. If the person taking on hire possesses an option and performs any act with regard to the thing hired indicative of the exercise of the right of a lessee, the contract of hire is ratified by conduct.

Article 500. If the person possessing an option allows the period of the option to expire without cancelling or carrying out the contract, the option is lost and the contract of hire becomes irrevocable.

Article 501. The period of option is presumed to run from the time of the conclusion of the contract.

Article 502. The commencement of the contract of hire is presumed to run from the time when the option was lost.

Article 503. If a piece of land taken on hire and said to consist of so many yards or donums proves to be of greater or smaller extent, the contract of hire is valid and the fixed rent becomes payable. Should it prove to be smaller, however, the person taking the land on hire has the option of cancelling the contract of hire.

Article 504. If a piece of land is taken on hire at so much per donum the rent is payable at so much per donum.

Article 505. If a wage is fixed as payment for work to be performed by a given period, the contract of hire is valid and the condition effective.

Examples:-
(1) A gives cloth to a tailor to be cut up and made into a shirt to be ready on the same day.

(2) A hires a camel from B to carry him to Mecca in so many days.

In both cases the contract of hire is executory, and if the person giving the thing on hire fulfils the condition, he can claim the fixed wage. If he fails to do so, however, he is entitled to an estimated wage, provided such wage does not exceed the fixed wage.

Article 506. The wages may validly be fixed alternatively in two or three ways as regards the work, the workman, the load, the distance, the place and the time, and the wages must be paid according to whichever way the work is carried out.

Examples:-

(1) A contract is made for back-stitching a thing for so much, and for over-stitching it for so much. The wages must be paid according to the way in which it is sewn.

(2) A contract is concluded for so much in respect to a shop to be used as a perfumery and for so much as a forge. The person taking the thing on hire must pay the fixed rent according to the way in which he uses the shop.

(3) A contract is concluded to load corn on a draught animal for so much and iron for so much. The hire agreed upon must be paid according to the load used.

(4) A muleteer states that he has let a particular animal on hire to go to *Chorlu* for one hundred piastres and to *Adrianople* for two hundred piastres and to *Philipolis* for three hundred piastres. The person taking the animal on hire must pay a sum corresponding to the place to which he goes.

(5) A states that he has let one particular house on hire for one hundred piastres and another house for two hundred piastres. The person taking the house on hire agrees. Such person must then pay the fixed rent according to whichever house he lives in.

HIRE 117

(6) A hands a cloak to a tailor stating that he will pay fifty piastres if it is stitched on the same day, and thirty piastres if it is stitched on the following day. The contract is executory and the condition is valid.

SECTION II.

Option of inspection.

Article 507. The person taking the thing on hire has an option of inspection.

Article 508. An inspection of the thing hired is equivalent to an inspection of the advantage to be derived therefrom.

Article 509. If a person takes a piece of real property on hire without seeing it, he may exercise an option as soon as he sees it.

Article 510. If a person takes on hire a house which he has seen previously, he has no option of inspection in respect to such house. However, if the place is dilapidated and unfit for habitation to such an extent that its original form is changed, such person may exercise an option.

Article 511. A person hired to do a piece of work which changes in accordance with any change in the subject-matter of such work, has an option of inspection.

Example :-
> An agreement is concluded with a tailor to stitch a cloak. Upon seeing the cloth or the cloak, the tailor may exercise an option.

Article 512. There is no option of inspection attaching to a thing which is not changed in accordance with any change in the subject-matter of such work.

Example :-

A contract is made to clean a certain amount of cotton seed for a certain sum of money. Although the person so employed has not seen the cotton seed, he has no option of inspection.

SECTION III.

Option for defect.

Article 513. There is an option for defect in the case of a contract of hire, as in a contract of sale.

Article 514. In a contract of hire, the circumstance which creates an option on account of defect is something which causes the complete loss of or interference with the benefits sought to be obtained.

Example :-

A house is entirely destroyed; the utility of a mill is negatived by the water being cut off; the frame of the roof of a house sinks; a place is knocked down so as to be unsuitable for habitation; the back of a horse which is hired is injured by galling. In all these cases there is an option for defect if they are taken on hire, on account of the benefits sought to be obtained being destroyed. But defects which do not interfere with the benefits sought to be obtained give no right to an option for defect in the case of a contract of hire, as where the plaster of a house falls off, but not to such an extent that rain and cold can enter; or where the mane or tail of a horse is cut.

Article 515. If a defect occurs in the thing hired before such thing has been put to the use for which it was hired, such defect is considered to have existed at the time the contract was concluded.

Article 516. If a defect occurs in the thing hired, the person taking the thing on hire may exercise an option. He may either put the thing hired to the use

HIRE

for which it was hired in spite of the defect, in which case he must pay the whole of the rent, or he may cancel the contract of hire.

Article 517. If the person giving a thing on hire removes a defect of recent origin before the cancellation of the contract of hire by the person taking such thing on hire, the latter has no right of cancellation. And if the person taking the thing on hire wishes to take possession thereof for the remainder of the period, the person giving such thing on hire cannot prevent him from doing so.

Article 518. If the person taking a thing on hire wishes to cancel the contract of hire prior to the removal of a defect of recent origin which prevents the thing hired being put to the use for which it was hired, such person may cancel the contract in the presence of the person giving the thing on hire. He may not do so in his absence. If he cancels the contract in the absence of the person giving the thing on hire, that is to say, without giving him notice thereof, such cancellation is of no effect, and the rent continues to be payable as heretofore.

If the benefits sought to be obtained are entirely lost, however, the contract may be cancelled in the absence of the person giving the thing on hire.

Whether the contract is cancelled or not the rent is not due, as is set forth in Article 478.

Example:-
> A place collapses and destroys the use to which a house taken on hire can be put. The person taking the house on hire may cancel the contract of hire. The cancellation, however, must take place in the presence of the person letting the house on hire. If he fails to give notice and leaves the house, he is bound to pay rent as though he had not left the

house. If the house is entirely destroyed, however, the person taking the house on hire may cancel the contract without the necessity of doing so in the presence of the person giving the house on hire. In any case the rent is not due.

Article 519. If a room or a wall of a house collapses and the person taking the house on hire does not cancel the contract of hire, but dwells in the rest of the house, no portion of the rent is remitted.

Article 520. If a person takes two houses on hire together for a certain sum of money and one of them collapses, he may leave both of them together.

Article 521. If a house taken on hire as containing so many rooms proves to contain fewer rooms than the stipulated number, the person taking the house on hire has the option of cancelling the contract of hire or of agreeing to the contract of hire and of paying the fixed rent. If he carries out the terms of the contract of hire, however, he is not entitled to any reduction in the rent.

CHAPTER VI.

TYPE OF THING HIRED AND MATTERS RELATING THERETO.

SECTION 1.

Matters relating to the hire of real property.

Article 522. A person may validly take a house or shop on hire without stating who is to live therein.

Article 523. If a person lets his house or shop on hire containing his goods or effects, the contract of hire is valid, but the person letting such house or shop on hire is bound to deliver the house or shop after taking out the goods or effects.

HIRE

Article 524. If a person takes a piece of land on hire without stating what he will sow therein or without making a stipulation of a general nature to the effect that he may sow whatever he likes, the contract of hire is voidable. But if such matter is defined before cancellation, and the person giving the land on hire agrees thereto, such contract becomes a valid contract of hire.

Article 525. If a person takes a piece of land on hire with a right of sowing what he likes, he may cultivate such land more than once in a year with a view to winter and summer crops.

Article 526. If the period of the contract of hire expires before the crops are ripe, such crops may remain on the land until they are ripe, the person taking such land on hire paying an estimated rent.

Article 527. A person may validly conclude a contract of hire for a shop or house without stating the use to which it is to be put, which matter is settled according to custom.

Article 528. A person who takes a house on hire without stating the use to which it is to be put, may dwell in it himself or let some other person dwell therein, and may place his effects therein. He may perform any kind of work therein, provided it is not of such a nature as to weaken or damage the building. He may not perform any work of such a nature as to damage the building unless he receives the permission of the owner. Local custom is followed as regards the tethering of animals. The same stipulations are in force as regards shops.

Article 529. The person giving the thing on hire must put right anything likely to interfere with the benefits sought to be obtained from the thing hired.

Examples :-

(1) The owner must clean the water channel of a mill.

(2) Repairs and improvements to the house and water courses and pipes, the repair of things detrimental to habitation and other matters relating to the building must all be performed by the owner. If the owner refuses to do these, the person taking the house on hire may leave the same. If, however, such person was aware that the house was in that state when he took it on hire, he is considered to have agreed to the defect. He cannot later make this a pretext for leaving the house. If the person taking the house on hire does these things himself, such act is in the nature of a gift and he cannot claim the expenses incurred thereby from the person giving the house on hire.

Article 530. If the person taking property on hire does repairs with the consent of the person giving such property on hire, and such repairs are for the improvement of the property, such as changing the tiles of the roof, or preventing any harm being done thereto, the person taking the property on hire may call upon the person giving the property on hire to make good the expenses incurred by such repairs, even though no stipulation has been made to that effect. However, if such repairs are purely in the interest of the person taking the property on hire, such as repairing the oven of the house, the person taking the house on hire cannot claim the expenses from the person giving the house on hire, unless a stipulation has been made to that effect.

Article 531. If the person taking real property on hire erects buildings or plants trees thereon, the person giving such real property on hire has the option, on the expiration of the period of hire, either of having such building pulled down, or of having such trees uprooted, or of keeping them upon payment of the value thereof, whatever that may be.

Article 532. Dust, earth and sweepings which have accumulated during the period of the contract of hire must be cleaned and removed by the person taking the thing on hire.

Article 533. In the event of the person taking the thing on hire damaging such thing, the person giving such thing on hire, may, if he is unable to prevent such damage, apply to the Court for an order cancelling the contract of hire.

SECTION II.

Hire of merchandise.

Article 534. A valid contract of hire may be concluded for a definite period and for a definite rent with regard to movable property such as clothing, weapons and tents.

Article 535. If a person takes clothing on hire to go to any particular place, and fails to go to such place and wears them in his house, or does not wear them at all, he must nevertheless pay the hire thereof.

Article 536. A person who takes clothes on hire to wear himself may not give such clothing to another person to wear.

Article 537. Jewellery is treated on the same basis as clothing.

SECTION III.

Hire of animals.

Article 538. A contract may validly be made to take a specific animal on hire and a valid contract may also be made with an owner of animals to be carried to a specific place.

HIRE

Article 539. If a specific animal is taken on hire to proceed to a certain place, and such animal becomes fatigued and stops on the way, the person taking such animal on hire has the option either of waiting till the animal gets better or of avoiding the contract of hire, in which case he is obliged to pay a portion of the fixed hire proportionate to the distance he has been carried.

Article 540. If a bargain has been struck to carry a certain load to a certain place and the animal becomes fatigued and stops on the way, the owner of the animal is bound to charge such load on to another animal and carry it to the place in question.

Article 541. A contract to take an unspecified animal on hire is of no effect. If such animal is specified after the conclusion of the contract, however, and the person taking such animal on hire agrees thereto, such contract is valid. But if it is customary to take an animal of no particular type on hire, such hire is valid, and is governed by such custom.

Example :-
A horse is hired from a horse-owner to take a person as far as a particular place, in accordance with custom. The owner is obliged to transport that person to such place by horse in accordance with the particular custom.

Article 542. In a contract of hire it is not enough to designate the end of a journey by mentioning the name of a particular territory, such as a *sanjak* or vilayet. On the other hand, this may validly be done if by custom the name of such territory is applied to a town.

Example :-
A valid contract of hire cannot be concluded to take an animal on hire to go to Bosnia or Arabia. The name of the town, township or village to which such person is going must be mentioned. The word *Sham,*

however, the name of a certain territory, is by custom applied to the town of Damascus, and therefore a valid contract may be concluded to hire an animal to go as far as *Sham*.

Article 543. If an animal is taken on hire to proceed to a certain place, and it so happens that there are two places of that name, an estimated sum by way of hire must be paid in respect to whichever place the person taking the animal on hire goes.

Example :-
An animal is taken on hire to proceed from Constantinople to *Chekmeje,* and it is not specified as to whether the animal is to go to Greater or Lesser *Chekmeje.* An estimated sum by way of hire must be paid according to the distance to the place in question.

Article 544. If an animal is taken on hire to proceed to a certain town, the person taking such animal on hire must be taken to his house in such town.

Article 545. A person who takes an animal on hire to proceed to a specified place may not go beyond that place without the permission of the owner. If he does in fact go beyond such place, the person taking such animal on hire is responsible for handing over the animal safe and sound, and if such animal is destroyed either on the outward or return journey, he must make good the loss.

Article 546. If an animal is taken on hire to go to a specified place, the person taking such animal on hire cannot go with him to another place. If he does so and the animal is destroyed, he must make good the loss.

Example :-
If an animal is taken on hire to go to *Tekfur Dagh* but instead goes to *Islimiyeh* and the animal is destroyed, the loss must be made good.

HIRE

Article 547. If an animal is taken on hire to go to a specified place, and there are several roads leading thereto, the person taking such animal on hire may proceed by whichever road he prefers which is commonly used by the public. If the owner of the animal prescribes the road which is to be taken, and the person taking such animal on hire proceeds by another road and the animal is destroyed, the loss must be made good if the road taken is more winding or difficult than that prescribed by the owner of the animal. But if it is of equal length or easier, the loss need not be made good.

Article 548. The person taking the animal on hire for a specified period may not use it for longer than that period. If he does so, and the animal is destroyed while in his possession, he must make good the loss.

Article 549. A valid contract may be made to take an animal on hire to be ridden by a specified person. A valid contract may also be made in general terms to take an animal on hire to be ridden by anyone.

Article 550. An animal which is taken on hire for riding may not be used as a draught animal. If it is so used and the animal is destroyed, the loss must be made good. In this case, however, no hire need be paid. (See Article 86).

Article 551. If an animal is hired to be ridden by a certain person, no other person may ride such animal. If he does so, and the animal is destroyed, the loss must be made good.

Article 552. A person who has taken an animal on hire in order that it may be ridden by any person he likes, may either ride such animal himself, or allow some other person to do so. But whether he rides it himself or allows some other person to ride it, once the particular person to ride such animal is known, no other person may ride it.

Article 553. If an animal is taken on hire for riding and it is not stated who is to ride it, nor laid down in general terms that any particular person who wishes may ride it, the contract of hire is voidable.

But if this is made clear before the contract is cancelled, such contract becomes valid. In this case also, once a particular person has been named no other person may be allowed to ride the animal.

Article 554. If an animal is taken on hire as a draught animal, local custom is binding as regards the saddle, rope and sack.

Article 555. If the amount of the load is not stated or made clear by signs, the amount of such load is determined by custom when an animal is taken on hire.

Article 556. The person taking an animal on hire may not beat such animal without the owner's permission. If he does so, and the animal is destroyed as a result thereof, he must make good the loss.

Article 557. If the owner gives his permission for an animal taken on hire to be beaten, the person taking the animal on hire may only beat such animal on a place where it is usual to do so. If he beats him on any other place, as for example, on the head, instead of the quarter, and the animal is destroyed as a result thereof, such loss must be made good.

Article 558. An animal hired to carry loads may also be used for riding purposes.

Article 559. When an animal is taken on hire and the nature and quantity of the load is stated, a load of another nature equal to or lesser than such load may also be placed upon such animal. But no greater load may be placed thereon.

Examples :-

(1) A takes a horse on hire to carry five *kilés* of wheat. A may load five *kilés* of his own wheat, or of anybody else's wheat of whatsoever sort upon such horse. He may also load five *kilés* of barley. But he may not load five *kilés* of wheat on an animal hired to carry five *kilés* of barley.

(2) A hundred *okes* of iron may not be loaded upon an animal hired to carry a hundred *okes* of cotton.

Article 560. The owner of the animal taken on hire must unload such animal.

Article 561. The person giving the animal on hire is responsible for feeding such animal.

Example :-

The feeding and watering of an animal taken on hire fall upon the owner. If the person taking the animal on hire, however, feeds it without the permission of the owner, such feeding, is an involuntary gift and the value thereof cannot later be claimed from the owner.

SECTION IV.

Hire of personal services.

Article 562. A contract may validly be made for the hire of personal services or the performance of skilled labour for a specified period or in some other way, as by specifying the nature of the work, as is set forth in Section III of Chapter II.

Article 563. If a person works for some other person at the latter's request without entering into any contract in regard to the wage to be paid, he is entitled to receive an estimated wage if he is of the class of persons who work for a wage. If he is not of such class, however, he is not entitled to receive anything.

Article 564. If a person requests some other person to do a certain piece of work for him and promises him something in return without mentioning the amount thereof, and such person does that work, he is entitled to an estimated wage.

Article 565. If a person employs workmen without fixing the amount of the wage to be paid, and if the daily wage of such workmen is known, they are entitled to receive the daily wage. If it is not known, they are entitled to an estimated wage.

The work performed by skilled workmen is also of this type.

Article 566. If a contract of hire is entered into with an employee whereby payment is to be made by giving a thing the like of which cannot be found in the market, and the nature of which has not been defined, an estimated wage must be paid.

Example :-

> A calls B and asks B to work for him for a certain number of days in return for which A promises to give B a pair of oxen. There is no need to give the pair of oxen, but an estimated wage must be paid. It is customary, however, when a wet nurse is taken on hire for clothes to be made for her. If the nature of the clothes has not been defined beforehand, they are to be of medium quality.

Article 567. Tips given to servants from outside cannot be included in wages.

Article 568. If a teacher is employed to teach any science or art and the period is defined, the contract of employment is concluded in respect to that particular period. Such person is entitled to his fee if he is ready and willing to teach, whether the pupil studies or not. If the period is not defined, the contract of hire is voidable. If the pupil studies under these circumstances, the teacher is entitled to his fee. If not, he is not entitled to his fee.

Article 569. If a person sends his son to a master to learn a trade and no agreement is made between the two as to the fee to be paid, and they both claim a fee after the boy has learnt the trade, the question is decided in accordance with local custom.

Article 570. If the inhabitants of a village hire the services of a *khoja* or an *imam* or a *muezzin,* and such persons perform their duties, they are entitled to receive their wages from the inhabitants of that village.

Article 571. When a person has been employed to do work personally, he may not employ anyone to do the work in his place.

Example :-
A contracts with B for B to sew him a cloak with his own hand for so many piastres. The tailor may not have it sewn by any other person. It must be sewn by B himself. If B has it sewn by any other person and it is destroyed, he must make good the loss.

Article 572. If an unconditional contract has been made, the employee may employ another person in his place.

Article 573. If the employer gives a definite order to the employee to do a certain piece of work, such order is unconditional.

Example :-
A instructs a tailor to sew a cloak for so much money without binding him to do the work personally.

HIRE 131

After the conclusion of the contract, the tailor has the cloak sewn by his assistant or by another tailor. The tailor is entitled to the fixed price. If the cloak is destroyed without his fault, he may not be called upon to make good the loss.

Article 574. Matters connected with the work done are settled in accordance with local custom when there is no specific condition binding the person employed. Thus, custom has it that the thread shall be the tailor's thread.

Article 575. A porter must carry the load inside the house, but he is not bound to put it in position.

Example: -

It is not the duty of the porter to take the load up to the top floor; nor to put grain into a barn.

Article 576. The employer is not bound to feed the employee unless local custom is to that effect.

Article 577. If a broker hawks property round but cannot sell it, and the owner sells it at some later date, the broker is not entitled to a fee. If another broker sells such property, such second broker takes the whole of the fee, and the first broker is not entitled to anything.

Article 578. If a person gives his property to a broker, instructing him to sell it for so many piastres, and such broker sells it for more than the stipulated sum, the owner of the property is entitled to the whole of such sum in excess, and the broker is not entitled to anything more than the brokerage fee.

Article 579. In the case of a sale, where the broker has received his fee, and some person appears who is entitled to the thing sold and takes possession of the same, or if the thing sold is returned on account of some defect, the return of the brokerage fee cannot be claimed.

Article 580. If a person employs reapers to reap crops in his field for a certain sum of money, and after such reapers have reaped a portion thereof, the rest is destroyed by a fall of hail or by some other accident, the reapers are entitled to a share of the fixed wage proportionate to the quantity reaped, but not to the balance.

Article 581. If a wet nurse falls sick she is entitled to cancel the contract of employment. The employer may also cancel the contract of employment if she becomes sick or pregnant, or if the child refuses to take her breasts, or if it brings up the milk.

CHAPTER VII.

RIGHTS AND OBLIGATIONS OF THE PERSON GIVING AND THE PERSON TAKING ON HIRE AFTER THE CONCLUSION OF THE CONTRACT.

SECTION I.

Delivery of the thing hired.

Article 582. Delivery of the thing hired consists of permission being given by the person giving the thing on hire to the person taking the thing on hire to enjoy such thing without let or hindrance.

Article 583. Upon the conclusion of a valid contract of hire for a particular time or for a particular journey, the thing hired must be delivered to the person taking the thing on hire to be continuously in his possession until the expiration of such period, or the end of such journey.

Example :-

A takes a cart on hire for a certain period, or in order to go to a certain place. A can use the cart during such period or until he has arrived at his destination. The owner may not use it for his own purposes during that period.

Article 584. If a person who owns real property in absolute ownership containing other property of his own, gives such real property on hire, no rent is payable until it is delivered free from all such encumbrances, unless they have been sold to the person taking the property on hire.

Article 585. When the lessor of a house hands the house over minus a room in which he has stored his goods, the proportion of the rent represented by such room must be deducted. As regards the rest of the house the lessee may exercise an option. If the lessor evacuates the house entirely and hands it over before cancellation of the contract, such contract is irrevocable; that is to say, the right of the lessee to cancel the contract is lost.

SECTION II.

Right of the contracting parties to deal with the thing hired after the conclusion of the contract.

Article 586. If the thing hired consists of real property, the person taking such real property on hire may give it on hire to some third person before taking delivery thereof. He may not do so, however, if it is movable property.

Article 587. The person taking the thing on hire may let such thing on hire to some third person if it is not changed by use or enjoyment.

Article 588. In the case of a voidable contract of hire the person taking the thing on hire may validly give it on hire to some third person after taking delivery thereof.

134   HIRE

Article 589. If a person who has given his property on hire to some other person for a definite period in accordance with the terms of an irrevocable contract of hire, again gives such property on hire to some third person, the second contract of hire is ineffective.

Article 590. If the person giving the thing on hire sells the thing hired without the permission of the person taking the thing on hire, the sale is not executory as regards the latter, but is executory as regards the vendor and the purchaser, and on the expiration of the period of hire, the sale is irrevocable as regards the purchaser and he may not refuse to take delivery thereof. However, if before the expiration of the period of hire the purchaser asks the vendor to hand over the thing sold, and it is impossible to do so, the Court shall cancel the contract of sale. If the person taking the property on hire ratifies the sale, the sale becomes executory in respect to each party. If the person taking the thing on hire, however, has made payment in advance, the thing hired cannot be taken from him until he has received payment of the amount of the rent paid by him in respect to the unexpired portion of the lease. If the person taking the thing on hire hands it over without receiving payment, he loses his right of retention.

SECTION III.

Return of the thing hired.

Article 591. On the termination of the contract of hire, the person taking the thing on hire must give up the thing hired.

Article 592. The person taking the thing on hire may not use the thing hired after the termination of the contract of hire.

HIRE

Article 593. If the person giving the thing on hire asks for the return of his property upon the termination of the contract of hire, the person taking the thing on hire is bound to return it to him.

Article 594. The person taking the thing on hire is not bound to return the thing hired, but the person giving the thing on hire is bound to take over the thing hired on the expiration of the contract of hire.

Examples :-

(1) Upon the termination of the lease of a house the owner must come and take delivery thereof.

(2) An animal is taken on hire to go to a certain place. If the owner is in that place, he must take over his animal. If he arrives and does not take it over, and it is destroyed while in the possession of the person hiring the animal without such person's fault, or neglect, such person may not be called upon to make good the loss. If, however, the animal is hired to leave and return to a definite place, it must be brought to that place. If it is not brought to such place, but is brought to the house of the person taking the animal on hire and is destroyed while there, the loss must be made good by such person.

Article 595. If the return of the thing hired involves expenditure for transport, such expenses fall upon the person giving the thing on hire.

CHAPTER VIII.

COMPENSATION

SECTION I.

Compensation in respect to use.

Article 596. If a person uses any property without the permission of the owner thereof, this amounts to wrongful appropriation, and he is not obliged to pay for the use thereof. If, however, the property has been dedicated to pious purposes, or is the property of a minor, an estimated rent must be paid in any case. If it is property prepared for hire and is not claimed to be property owned in absolute ownership, nor as a result of contract, payment for use must be made; that is, an estimated rent must be paid.

Examples :-

(1) A lives in B's house for a certain period without concluding a contract of hire. He is not obliged to pay rent. But if the house has been dedicated to pious purposes or is the property of a minor, an estimated rent must be paid in respect to the period during which it has been inhabited, whether it is claimed to be property held in absolute ownership, or as a result of contract.

(2) In the case of a house for hire, an estimated rent must be paid if it is not claimed to be property held in absolute ownership nor as a result of contract.

(3) A takes B's horse, which B lets out on hire, and uses it for a certain period without the permission of B. An estimated sum by way of hire must be paid.

Article 597. If property is used which is claimed to be property owned in absolute ownership, even though it is prepared for hire, nothing need be paid in respect to such use.

Example :-

One of the joint owners of a piece of jointly owned property uses such property for a certain period independently and without the consent of the other joint owner, asserting that it is his own property owned in absolute ownership. The other joint owner cannot claim rent in respect to his share, even though it is property prepared for hire.

Article 598. If use is made of property which is claimed to be owned as a result of contract, even though it is prepared for hire, nothing need be paid in respect to such use.

Examples:-

(1) A is joint owner of a shop and sells such shop to B without the permission of the other joint-owner. B holds such shop for a certain period. The other joint-owner does not give his assent to the sale and seizes his share. He cannot claim rent in respect to his share, however much the shop may have been prepared for giving on hire, because the purchaser, having asserted that he has used it as an owner, his ownership being claimed to be based upon a contract, that is to say, upon a contract of sale, is not obliged to pay for the benefit received.

(2) A sells and delivers his mill to B which he asserts is his own property held in absolute ownership. After having held it for a certain period, another person appears claiming the mill and after proving his case and obtaining judgment, takes it from the purchaser. Such person cannot claim anything from B in the way of rent in respect to that period, since this is claimed to be based on a contract.

Article 599. If any person employs a minor without the consent of his tutor, such minor is entitled to receive an estimated wage for his services upon his reaching the age of puberty. If the minor dies, his heirs may claim an estimated wage from the employer in respect to the period of the employment.

SECTION II.

Compensation by the person taking the thing on hire.

Article 600. Whether the contract of hire is valid or not, the thing taken on hire is on trust while in the possession of the person taking such thing on hire.

Article 601. If the thing taken on hire is destroyed while in the possession of the person taking such thing on hire, the latter may not be called upon to make good the loss, unless he has committed some wrongful act, or negligence, or performed any act which he is not authorized to do.

Article 602. If the thing hired is destroyed by reason of the wrongful act of the person taking the thing on hire, or the value thereof is diminished, such person must make good the loss.

Example :-

The person taking an animal on hire beats it and it dies, or is destroyed by reason of his brutal and violent driving. Such person must make good the loss.

Article 603. If the person taking the thing on hire acts in a way contrary to what is customary, such act is wrongful and he must make good any damage or loss resulting therefrom.

Examples :-

(1) Clothes which are taken on hire are used in a way contrary to what is customary and become tattered. The loss must be made good.

(2) A fire breaks out in a house which has been hired by reason of a fire being lighted which is larger than what is customary and the house is burnt. The loss must be made good.

Article 604. If the thing hired is destroyed owing to the failure of the person taking the thing on hire to take proper care, or the value thereof is decreased, the loss must be made good.

Example :-

A person takes an animal on hire and drives it into a deserted place so that it is lost. He must make good the loss.

Article 605. If the person taking the thing on hire goes beyond what he has agreed to do, acting in contravention of what he has been authorized to do, he must make good any loss caused thereby. But if his act in contravention results in something equivalent to or less than what he has agreed to do, he incurs no liability.

Example :-

A takes an animal on hire to load so many *okes* of oil and instead loads the same number of *okes* of iron upon it and the animal is destroyed. A must make good the loss. But if a load equal to or lighter than oil is loaded and the animal is destroyed, there is no liability to make good the loss.

Article 606. On the expiration of the contract of hire, the thing hired remains on trust in the possession of the person taking the thing on hire for safe keeping. Consequently, if the person taking the thing on hire uses such thing on the expiration of the period of hire and such thing is destroyed, he must make good the loss. Again, if the person giving the thing on hire asks for his property to be returned on the termination of the contract of hire, and the person taking the thing on hire fails to do so, he must make good the loss if such property is destroyed.

SECTION III.

Loss caused by employees.

Article 607. If the thing entrusted to an employee to work upon is destroyed by the wrongful act or negligence of such person, the latter must make good the loss.

Article 608. A wrongful act of an employee consists of any act or conduct contrary to the express or implied order of his employer.

HIRE

Examples:-

(1) A instructs his shepherd who is his private employee to pasture his flock in a certain place and no other. The shepherd takes the flock to another place. He has committed a wrongful act, and if the animals are destroyed while in that place, the shepherd must make good the loss.

(2) A hands cloth to a tailor instructing him to cut it and make him a long coat therefrom, if the cloth is sufficient. The tailor tells him that it is sufficient. If it turns out after the cloth is cut up that it is not sufficient for the purpose, A can claim to have the loss made good by the tailor.

Article 609. Negligence of the employee consists of any fault of his of which he is guilty without excuse in the preservation of the thing entrusted to him on account of his employment.

Example:-

An animal strays from the flock and is lost purely on account of the neglect of the shepherd to come and catch such animal. The shepherd must make good the loss. He is not liable, however, if his failure to go after the animal arose out of the probability that in so doing he would lose the other animals.

Article 610. A private employee is a trustee. Consequently, he is under no obligation to make good any loss arising out of the destruction of property in his possession not caused by any act of his. Similarly, if property is destroyed by his own act without his fault he is not liable to make good the loss.

Article 611. A public employee is liable to make good any damage or loss incurred by his own act, whether resulting from any wrongful act or negligence of his or not.

Promulgated by Royal Iradah 6th. Zil Qada, 1286.

BOOK III
GUARANTEE

BOOK III.

GUARANTEE.

INTRODUCTION.

TERMS OF MUHAMMADAN JURISPRUDENCE RELATING TO GUARANTEE.

Article 612. A guarantee consists of the addition of an obligation to an obligation in respect to a demand for a particular thing. That is to say, it consists of one person joining himself to another person, and binding himself also to meet the obligation which accrues to that other person.

Article 613. A personal guarantee is constituted by a person becoming a guarantor for another man personally.

Article 614. A guarantee of property is constituted by a person becoming guarantor for the payment of something.

Article 615. A guarantee for delivery is constituted by a person becoming guarantor for the delivery of something.

Article 616. A contingent guarantee is constituted by a person becoming guarantor for the payment of the price of the property sold, in the event of its being appropriated by a person having a right thereto, or for the vendor personally.

Article 617. An unconditional guarantee is a guarantee constituted independently of any condition or of any future time.

GUARANTEE

Article 618. A guarantor is a person who adds an obligation of his own to that of some other person. In other words, a person who undertakes to do a thing which some other person has undertaken to do. The latter person is called the principal, or the person guaranteed.

Article 619. The person in whose favour the guarantee is made is the person demanding the guarantee and who is the creditor.

Article 620. The subject matter of the guarantee is the thing which the gurantor undertakes to hand over or pay. In the case of a personal guarantee the person guaranteed and the subject matter of the guarantee are one and the same thing.

CHAPTER I.

THE CONTRACT OF GUARANTEE.

SECTION I.

Fundamental basis of a contract of guarantee.

Article 621. A guarantee may be concluded and become executory by the mere offer of the guarantor. The person in whose favour the guarantee is made may decline to accept such guarantee. Until such time as he does so, however, the guarantee is valid. Thus, if in the absence of the person in whose favour the guarantee is made, a person stands security for the latter recovering any amount due to him, and the creditor dies without receiving information that such person has stood security, the guarantor is bound thereby.

Article 622. The offer of the guarantor, that is, words used importing guarantee, are any words which by custom are evidence of an undertaking to be bound.

GUARANTEE

Example:-
A states that he has stood security, or that he is a guarantor, or that he is ready to indemnify someone. A valid contract of guarantee is thereby concluded.

Article 623. A contract of guarantee may also be concluded by means of a promise dependent on a condition. (see Article 84).

Example:-
A tells B that he will stand security for the payment of any sum due to B in the event of B not receiving payment thereof. A valid contract of guarantee is thereby concluded, and if the person in whose favour the guarantee is made claims the sum due to him, and the debtor fails to pay, such person may demand payment from the guarantor.

Article 624. Should a person undertake to be a guarantor for any limited period of time, a contract of guarantee of limited duration is thereby concluded independently of any condition or of any future time.

Article 625. In addition to the conclusion of an unconditional contract of guarantee, a contract of guarantee subject to a condition for immediate or future performance may also be concluded. That is to say, a guarantee may be concluded for payment forthwith or at some future date.

Article 626. A person may validly be a guarantor of a guarantor.

Article 627. There may also be more than one guarantor.

SECTION II.

Conditions attaching to a contract of Guarantee.

Article 628. In order to be able to make a contract of guarantee, a surety must be of sound mind and must have arrived at the age of puberty. Consequently, a

GUARANTEE

madman, an imbecile and a minor cannot make a valid contract of guarantee. If a minor becomes a guarantor while a minor and after arriving at the age of puberty ratifies the contract of guarantee, he cannot be made to abide thereby.

Article 629. It is not essential for the person guaranteed to be of sound mind, nor to have arrived at the age of puberty. Consequently, a valid contract of guarantee may be entered into in respect of the debt of a madman or a minor.

Article 630. If the subject matter of the guarantee is a person, the identity of such person must be clearly established. If it is property, however, there is no need for such property to be identified. Consequently, if a person becomes guarantor for the debt of another owing to some third person, the amount of such debt being unknown, a valid contract of guarantee is concluded.

Article 631. In the case of a guarantee of property, the obligation must fall upon the principal debtor, that is to say, the performance of such obligation must be binding on the principal debtor. Consequently, a valid contract of guarantee may be concluded with regard to the price of a thing sold, rent and other proved debts. Similarly, a valid contract of guarantee may be concluded with regard to property which has been wrongfully appropriated, and on demand, the guarantor is bound to make good the same in kind or in cash. Again, a valid contract of guarantee may be concluded with regard to property bought on approval as to price, provided the price has been fixed. But a valid contract of guarantee cannot be made with regard to any actual property sold before the receipt thereof, because if the property sold perishes while in possession of the vendor, there is no obligation upon him to deliver the actual property sold, since the sale is cancelled, he being merely obliged to return the price thereof if he has received the same. Likewise, a valid contract of guarantee cannot be concluded with regard to property pledged or lent for use, or let on hire or in other cases where property has been entrusted to some third party, the responsibility for which does not fall upon the principal. But a person may validly undertake to be guarantor for the person guaranteed if such things are wasted or destroyed. A valid contract of guarantee may also be concluded in respect to both the property sold and the delivery thereof. Upon demand, the guarantor is bound to deliver such goods, provided there is no right of retention. If they are destroyed, however, the guarantor is in no way liable, just as the death of the person with regard to whom a contract of guarantee has been concluded frees the guarantor from liability.

Article 632. No substitution is permissible in criminal punishment. Consequently, no valid contract of guarantee can be concluded in respect to capital punishment and other criminal matters and punishments of a personal nature. But a valid contract of guarantee may be concluded with reference to indemnities for personal injury payable by persons who may have inflicted bodily injury, including blood money payable by a murderer.

Article 633. It is not a condition that the person guaranteed should be solvent, since a valid contract of guarantee may be concluded with regard to a bankrupt also.

CHAPTER II.

THE CONTRACT OF GUARANTEE.

SECTION I.

Unconditional, conditional and future contracts of guarantee.

Article 634. The effect of a contract of guarantee is a claim. That is to say, it consists of the right of the person in whose favour the guarantee is made to claim the subject matter of the guarantee from the guarantor.

Article 635. In an unconditional contract of guarantee, the sum guaranteed may be claimed forthwith if the debt is payable immediately by the principal debtor, and at the expiration of the period prescribed for payment, if payable at some future date.

Example:-

> A states that he guarantees the debt of B. If the debt is payable forthwith, payment may be demanded by the creditor at once from the guarantor, and if it is payable at some future date, then upon the expiration of the prescribed period.

Article 636. Where a contract of guarantee is concluded subject to a condition, or is to take effect at some future date, the guarantor may not be called upon to make payment until the condition has been fulfilled, and the time has arrived.

Examples:-

> (1) A tells B that if C does not pay his debt to B, he will stand security for the debt. A conditional contract of guarantee has been concluded, and if C does not pay his debt when it falls due, payment may be demanded from the guarantor. But no claim may be made against the guarantor until the principal debtor has been asked to pay.

GUARANTEE

(2) A tells B that if C steals his property he will make good the loss. A valid contract of guarantee has been concluded, and if B is robbed by C, payment may be demanded from the guarantor.

(3) A becomes guarantor on condition that when the person in whose favour the guarantee is made makes a claim for payment he shall be given so many days grace. The person in whose favour the guarantee is made is entitled to ask for payment at any time whatsoever after the expiration of the period of grace as from the time at which the demand for payment was made. The guarantor has no right of asking for the same period of grace a second time.

(4) A tells B that he is guarantor for any sum that may be due to him, or for any sum that may be lent by him, or in respect to anything that may be wrongfully appropriated from him, or in respect to the price of anything that he may sell. The guarantor is only liable in the circumstances contemplated, that is to say, when the debt falls due, or when the money is lent, or wrongful appropriation is proved, or when the property is sold and delivery thereof is given.

(5) A stands security for the appearance of B upon a certain day. No claim may be made upon the guarantor to produce the person guaranteed before the day in question.

Article 637. Upon the fulfilment of a condition, all matters in amplification or restriction thereof must also be fulfilled.

Example :-

A undertakes to be guarantor of B for the payment of any sum which may be given in judgment against him. B admits that he is in debt for a certain sum of money. The guarantor is not liable to pay the sum of money in question, until judgment has been given by the Court.

GUARANTEE

Article 638. In the case of a contingent guarantee, the guarantor may not be called upon for payment should any person prove that he is entitled to the thing sold, until the Court has given judgment for the return of the price by the vendor.

Article 639. In cases of guarantee of limited duration, no demand may be made from the guarantor except during the period of the guarantee.

Example:-

> A states that he is guarantor for B for a period of one month as from to-day. A is only liable during that period, and thereafter is discharged from the guarantee.

Article 640. After the conclusion of a contract of guarantee, the guarantor cannot withdraw from the guarantee. In the case of a conditional or future contract of guarantee, however, the guarantor can withdraw from the guarantee before the debtor has become liable in respect to any debt.

Example:-

> A becomes guarantor absolutely for B, either personally or in respect to a debt. A cannot withdraw from the contract. Nor can he withdraw if he states that he will make good any sum which may be owing to C from D, because the debt came into existence before the conclusion of the contract of guarantee, notwithstanding the fact that it was proved after the conclusion of the contract. But if A undertakes to be guarantor for anything which B may sell to C, or for the price of any goods which he may sell, A is responsible to the person in whose favour the guarantee is made for anything sold to C. He may, however, withdraw from the contract of guarantee prior to the sale. And if A states that he has withdrawn from the contract and requests B not to sell to C and B nevertheless does sell to C, A is not bound as guarantor for the price.

Article 641. A person who is guarantor for the return and delivery of property wrongfully appropriated or lent for use and who delivers such property to the owner, may claim indemnification for the cost of transport from the person wrongfully appropriating or borrowing such property for use.

SECTION II.

Guarantee for the production of a particular person.

Article 642. A personal guarantee consists of producing the person guaranteed. Thus, the guarantor must produce the person guaranteed at any time stipulated, in the event of his being called upon to do so. If he produces such person, he is discharged from his obligation. If he fails, he shall be compelled to produce him.

SECTION III.

Guarantee of property.

Article 643. A guarantor is obliged to make good the loss suffered.

Article 644. The person claiming under the guarantee has the option of claiming either against the guarantor or against the principal debtor. The exercise of his right against the one in no way destroys his right of claiming from the other. He may claim first from the one and then from the other or from both simultaneously.

Article 645. If a person who is guarantor of property has been guaranteed by some third person for any sum for which he may become liable by reason of his guarantee, the creditor may have recourse against whichever one of them he wishes.

Article 646. If persons who are jointly indebted on one particular account guarantee each other, action may be taken against any one of them for the whole amount.

GUARANTEE

Article 647. If there are several guarantors of one debt who have become guarantors for such debt separately, action may be taken against any one of them for the whole amount of the debt.

If they become guarantors at one and the same time, action shall be taken against each one for his share of the debt. But if they have also each guaranteed the amount to be paid by the others, each of them is liable for the whole amount of the debt.

Example :-

A is guarantor for a debt of one thousand piastres contracted by B. C also becomes a guarantor for the thousand piastres. The creditor can demand payment of his sum from whichever of the two guarantors he wishes. But if the two guarantors jointly guarantee the debt, they are each liable for the half of this sum only. If they each guarantee the amount for which the other is liable, however, they can both be called upon to pay the whole amount of one thousand piastres.

Article 648. If there is a condition in the contract of guarantee whereby the principal debtor becomes freed from his liability, the contract is changed into a transfer of debt.

Article 649. A transfer of debt subject to a condition that the debtor shall not be freed from liability is a contract of guarantee. Consequently, if a creditor instructs his debtor to transfer the sum he is owing to some other person on condition that the debtor is to guarantee payment, and he does so, such person may demand payment from whichever of the two he wishes.

Article 650. A person who holds property belonging to some other person on trust may validly become the guarantor of that person for the payment of a debt owing by him, on condition that payment shall be made out of such property and the guarantor is then obliged to make payment from such property. If the property is destroyed, the guarantor is not obliged to pay anything. If he returns the property to the owner thereof after becoming guarantor, he is then personally liable.

Article 651. If any person guarantees to produce another at a given time and in the event of his failing to do so, guarantees to pay the debt of such person, and fails to produce such person at the appointed time, the guarantor is obliged to pay such debt. In the event of the death of the guarantor, the heirs must produce the person whose appearance is guaranteed at the time agreed upon, or if such person surrenders himself in accordance with the contract of guarantee, the guarantor's property is freed from all liability. If they fail to produce the person guaranteed, or if such person fails to surrender himself, the estate of the guarantor becomes liable for payment of the debt. In the event of the death of the person in whose favour the guarantee is given, his heirs may claim the sum in question.

If the guarantor produces the person guaranteed at the time agreed upon and the person is whose favour the guarantee has been given cannot be found, the guarantor may make application to the Court for the appointment of a representative of such person and for the person guaranteed to be handed over to him.

Article 652. In the case of an absolute contract of guarantee, if the debt is payable forthwith by the principal debtor, payment thereof may also be demanded forthwith from the guarantor. If the principal debtor is to make payment at some future definite date, however, payment may only be demanded from the guarantor on that date.

154 GUARANTEE

Article 653. In the case of a restricted contract of guarantee, payment may be demanded from the guarantor in accordance with the nature of the guarantee, that is to say, whether for immediate payment, or for payment at some future definite date.

Article 654. A contract of guarantee may validly be concluded in respect to a debt payable at some future definite date for a period to coincide with such date, and also for a period beyond that date.

Article 655. If the creditor postpones his claim in respect to the principal debtor, he is considered to have postponed his claim both in respect to the guarantor and any person guaranteeing him. Any postponement in respect to a first guarantor acts as a postponement of the second guarantor. A postponement in respect to the guarantor, however, does not act as a postponement in respect to the principal debtor.

Article 656. If a person who has contracted debts repayable at some future definite date wishes to leave for some other country before such debts fall due for payment, such person must find a guarantor upon the creditor applying to the Court to that effect.

Article 657. If a person requests another to guarantee a debt which he owes to some third person and such person agrees, and pays the debt, and wishes to exercise his right of recourse against the debtor, he may do so, in respect to what he has guaranteed and not what he has paid. But if he has paid a portion of the debt as a result of a settlement with the creditor, he has a right of recourse in respect to that amount only, and not to the whole debt.

Examples:-

(1) A is a guarantor for sound coin. He pays with base coin. He is entitled to receive sound coin from the principal debtor. On the other hand, if he is guarantor in respect to base coin and pays in sound coin, he is only entitled to receive base coin from the principal debtor.

(2) A is a guarantor for so many piastres and as the result of a settlement pays with goods. A recovers from the principal debtor in cash the amount that he has guaranteed. But if A is guarantor in respect to one thousand piastres and as the result of a settlement pays five hundred piastres, A can only recover five hundred piastres from the principal debtor.

Article 658. If any party to a contract based upon consideration deceives another party thereto, such party must make good any loss caused to the other.

Examples:-

(1) A buys a piece of land and erects a building thereon. Thereupon, a person appears who proves to be entitled to such land and takes possession thereof. A is entitled to recover the value of the land from the vendor and in addition the value of the building at the time of handing it over.

(2) A requests certain merchants to sell certain goods to his son, who is a minor, stating that he has given him permission to engage in trade. It is later proved that the boy is the son of some other person. The merchants are entitled to recover the value of the goods which they have sold to the boy from A.

GUARANTEE

CHAPTER III.

RELEASE FROM THE CONTRACT OF GUARANTEE.

SECTION I.

General.

Article 659. When the subject matter of the guarantee is made over to the person in whose favour the guarantee was made, whether by the principal debtor or the guarantor the guarantor is released from the contract of guarantee.

Article 660. If the person in whose favour the guarantee is made informs the guarantor that he has released him from the contract of guarantee, or that he has renounced any rights he may have against him, the guarantor is freed from all liability.

Article 661. The release of the guarantor does not bring about the release of the principal debtor.

Article 662. The release of the principal debtor from liability brings about the release of the guarantor.

SECTION II.

Release from a contract of guarantee to produce a particular person.

Article 663. Upon the guarantor producing the person whose appearance was guaranteed to the person in whose favour the guarantee was given in a place where it is possible to take legal proceedings, such as a town or township, he is released from the contract of guarantee, whether such person agrees or not. If it has been stipulated that he shall deliver him in some specified town, however, and delivers him elsewhere, he is not released from the contract of guarantee. If he has agreed to produce him in Court, but hands him over in the street, he is not freed from the contract of guarantee. If he hands him over in the presence of a police officer, however, he is released from the guarantee.

Article 664. The guarantor is released from the contract of guarantee by simply handing over the person guaranteed when requested to do so. But if he hands over the person guaranteed without being requested to do so, he is not released from the contract unless he states that he is handing him over in pursuance of the contract of guarantee.

Article 665. If a person who has guaranteed to produce a certain person on a certain day produces such person before that day, he is released from the contract of guarantee, even though the person in whose favour the contract is given does not agree thereto.

Article 666. If the person whose appearance is guaranteed dies, the guarantor is released from the contract of guarantee, and if there is any person guaranteeing the guarantor, he also is released. Again, if the guarantor dies, he is released from the contract of guarantee and any person guaranteeing him is also released from the contract. Should the person in whose favour the guarantee is given die, however, the guarantor is not released from the contract of guarantee, and a claim may be made by such person's heirs.

SECTION III.

Release from a contract of guarantee of property.

Article 667. In the event of the death of the creditor, the guarantor is released from the contract of guarantee, should the debtor be the sole heir of the creditor. Should there be some other heir of the debtor, however, the guarantor is only released from the share of the debtor, and not from the share of the other heir.

GUARANTEE

Article 668. In the event of the guarantor or of the principal debtor coming to a settlement with the creditor in respect to a portion of the debt, both of them are released from the contract of guarantee, if a stipulation has been inserted to the effect that both of them or the principal debtor are to be released, or if no condition has been inserted at all. If a condition has been inserted stipulating for the release of the guarantor only, the guarantor alone is freed, and the creditor has the option of claiming the whole of the debt from the principal debtor or of claiming the amount covered by the settlement from the guarantor and the balance from the principal debtor.

Article 669. If the guarantor transfers liability in respect to the person in whose favour he has concluded the contract of guarantee to some other person, and both such persons agree thereto, the guarantor and the principal debtor are released from liability.

Article 670. In the event of the death of a guarantor of property, the property guaranteed may be claimed from the guarantor's estate.

Article 671. If a person becomes guarantor for the price of a thing sold and the contract of sale is cancelled or the thing sold is claimed by some person who is entitled thereto or is returned on account of some defect, the guarantor is released from the contract of guarantee.

Article 672. If property is taken on hire for a fixed period and some person becomes guarantor for the rent to be paid in respect thereto, the contract of guarantee terminates at the end of such period. Should a fresh contract of hire be concluded in respect to that property, such contract does not include the contract of guarantee.

Promulgated by Royal Iradah, 18th. Muharram, 1287.

BOOK IV.

TRANSFER OF DEBT

BOOK IV.

TRANSFER OF DEBT.

INTRODUCTION.

TERMS OF MUHAMMADAN JURISPRUDENCE RELATING TO TRANSFER OF DEBT.

Article 673. By transfer of debt is meant transferring a debt from the account of one person to that of another.

Article 674. The transferor is the debtor who makes the transfer.

Article 675. The person in whose favour the debt is transferred is the creditor.

Article 676. The transferee is the person who agrees to the transfer of the debt to himself.

Article 677. The subject matter of the transfer is the property transferred.

Article 678. A restricted transfer of debt is a transfer of debt whereby the transferor limits the payment by the transferee to property of his owing by the transferee or in his possession.

Article 679. An absolute transfer of debt is a transfer of debt whereby the transferor does not limit the payment to property of his in the possession of the transferee.

CHAPTER I.

THE CONTRACT OF TRANSFER OF DEBT.

SECTION I.

The fundamental basis of a transfer of debt.

Article 680. A contract for the transfer of a debt is concluded by the transferor informing his creditor that he has transferred his debt to some other person, and by the agreement thereto of the creditor and such other person.

TRANSFER OF DEBT

Article 681. A contract for the transfer of a debt may be concluded between the person in whose favour the transfer is made and the transferee alone.

Example :-

A informs B that he has transferred to him a certain sum of money owing to him by C, and B agrees thereto; or A tells B to transfer to him a sum of money owing to him by C and B agrees thereto. In both cases a valid contract for the transfer of debt has been concluded and the transferee may not thereafter go back on the transaction.

Article 682. A contract for the transfer of a debt may validly be concluded between the transferor and the person in whose favour the transfer is made alone, provided the transferee, on being informed thereof, agrees thereto.

Example :-

A transfers a debt which he owes B, to C, who is resident in some other country. B agrees thereto. If the transferee, on being informed thereof, agrees thereto, a valid contract for the transfer of the debt is concluded.

Article 683. A contract for the transfer of a debt may be concluded between the transferor and the transferee only, subject to the agreement of the person in whose favour the transfer is made.

Example :-

A transfers a debt owing to him by B to C. C agrees. The contract for the transfer of a debt has been concluded, subject to the consent of the person in whose favour the transfer has been made, and if the latter agrees thereto, such transfer becomes executory.

SECTION II.

Conditions relating to transfer of debt.

Article 684. To conclude a contract for the transfer of a debt, the transferor and the person in whose favour the transfer is made must be of sound mind, and the transferee must be of sound mind and have reached the age of puberty. Consequently, any transfer or acceptance of the transfer of a debt by a minor of imperfect understanding is void, and any acceptance of the transfer of a debt by a minor whether of perfect or imperfect understanding, or whether permitted by his tutor to undertake business, or whether interdicted, is void.

Article 685. For the contract of transfer of debt to be executory, the transferor and the person in whose favour the transfer is made must have reached the age of puberty. Consequently, the transfer or acceptance of the transfer of a debt by a minor of perfect understanding is dependent upon ratification by the tutor. If the tutor ratifies, the contract becomes executory. Moreover, if the minor accepts the transfer of a debt and the tutor gives his permission, the transferee must be wealthier than the transferor.

Article 686. It is not essential to the validity of a contract for the transfer of a debt that the transferee should be indebted to the transferor, nor that the transferor should be entitled to receive something from him.

Article 687. A contract for the transfer of a debt in respect to which a valid contract of guarantee cannot be concluded, is invalid.

Article 688. Any contract for the transfer of a debt in respect to which a valid contract of guarantee can be

164 TRANSFER OF DEBT

concluded, is valid. The subject matter of the contract must, however, be clearly ascertained. Consequently, any contract for the transfer of a debt which is unknown is invalid.

Example:-
> A agrees to accept the transfer by B of some debt which may be proved in the future to be due to him. The contract is invalid.

Article 689. A contract for the transfer of a debt incurred by reason of a guarantee or arising out of a contract for the transfer of a debt may be validly concluded, in the same way as a contract for the transfer of debts which have been incurred directly.

CHAPTER II.

EFFECT OF A CONTRACT FOR THE TRANSFER OF DEBT.

Article 690. The effect of a contract for the transfer of a debt is that the transferor, and his guarantor, if any, are liberated from all responsibility for the debt. The person in whose favour the contract is made then has the right of demanding payment thereof from the transferee. A pledgee who transfers his right to claim the debt from the pledgor to some third person loses all right of retention over the pledge.

Article 691. If any person who makes an absolute transfer of a debt has no claim against the transferee, the latter may have recourse against the former, after he has paid his debt. If such person has a claim against the transferee, the amount of the claim is set off against the debt after payment has been made.

Article 692. In the case of a restricted contract for the transfer of a debt, the transferor loses his right to claim on account of the subject matter of the transfer. The transferee is under no obligation whatsover to give the subject matter of the transfer to the transferor. If he does so, he is liable to make good any loss resulting therefrom. Upon making good such loss, he has a right of recourse against the transferor. If the transferor dies before making payment, his debts being greater than the value of his estate, the other creditors have no right to touch the subject matter of the transfer.

Article 693. If a restricted contract for the transfer of a debt is concluded whereby payment is to be made from the sum to be received in respect to the price of a thing sold due to the vendor from the purchaser, and the thing sold is destroyed before delivery, the price in consequence being no longer due, or if the thing sold is returned by virtue of a contractual option, or by reason of an option of inspection or an option for defect, or if the sale is rescinded, such transfer is not void and the transferee has a right of recourse against the transferor after payment. That is to say, he may obtain what he has given from the transferor. But if any person appears who is entitled to the thing sold and takes possession of the same whereby it is proved that the transferee is free from the debt, the contract of transfer is void.

Article 694. If a restricted contract for the transfer of a debt is concluded whereby payment is to be made from a sum of money deposited on trust by the transferor with the transferee, and some person appears who is entitled to such money and takes possession of the same, the contract of transfer is void, and the debt reverts to the transferor.

TRANSFER OF DEBT

Article 695. If a restricted contract for the transfer of a debt is concluded whereby payment is to be made from a sum of money belonging to the transferor in the possession of the transferee, and such sum of money is not subject to compensation, the contract is void and the debt reverts to the transferor. If it is subject to compensation, however, the contract continues in force.

Example:-

A transfers to C a debt which is due to B, to be paid from money which he has deposited with C on trust, and such money is lost without any fault being attributable, before payment is made. The transfer is void and the sum due to the creditor reverts to the transferor. If such money has been wrongfully appropriated, or if, being deposited on trust, it has been lost by the act of C and must be repaid by him, the contract is not void.

Article 696. If any person transfers a debt to some other person and provides that payment is to be made from the price realized on the sale of some specific property of his, and such person agrees to the transfer on that condition, the contract is valid, and the transferee is bound to sell the property and pay the debt from the price realized.

Article 697. In the case of a vague transfer of debt, that is to say, in the case of a transfer of debt where it is not stipulated whether the subject matter of the transfer is payable forthwith, or at some future definite date, the transfer is one payable forthwith, if the debt is likewise payable forthwith by the transferor. If the debt is payable at some future definite date, the transfer is of the same nature, and payment must be made when the debt falls due.

Article 698. There is no right of recourse against the transferor until the transferee has paid the debt; and when recourse is made, the subject matter of the transfer may be claimed. That is to say, the transferee takes from the transferor exactly the same type of money that was the subject of the transfer. He cannot, however, claim the identical money which has been paid.

Examples :-

(1) Silver money is transferred. Payment is made in gold. Silver money may be claimed from the transferor and not gold.

(2) Payment is made with goods and effects. The money which was the subject of the transfer may be claimed.

Article 699. If the subject matter of the transfer is paid, or it is transferred to some other person, or the person in whose favour the transfer is made liberates the transferee from the debt, or the person in whose favour the transfer is made makes a gift of the subject matter of the transfer or disposes of it as alms and the transferee accepts, he is liberated from the debt.

Article 700. In the event of the death of the person in whose favour the transfer is made, and of the transferee becoming his heir, the transfer becomes devoid of effect.

Promulgated by Royal Iradah, 25 Sefer, 1288

BOOK V.
PLEDGES

BOOK V.

PLEDGES.

INTRODUCTION.

TERMS OF MUHAMMADAN JURISPRUDENCE RELATING TO PLEDGES.

Article 701. A pledge consists of setting aside property from which it is possible to obtain payment or satisfaction of some claim. Such property is then said to be pledged, or given in pledge.

Article 702. The act of accepting property as a pledge is called taking on pledge.

Article 703. The person who gives his property as security is called the pledgor.

Article 704. The person who accepts property as security is called the pledgee.

Article 705. The person with whom the pledgor and the pledgee deposit the pledge on trust is called the bailee.

CHAPTER I.

MATTERS RELATING TO THE CONTRACT OF PLEDGE.

SECTION I.

Fundamental basis of the contract of pledge.

Article 706. A contract of pledge is concluded by the offer and acceptance of the pledgor and the pledgee. If the pledge is not transferred to the effective possession of the pledgee, however, such contract is incomplete and revocable. The pledgor may, therefore, denounce such contract before delivery of the pledge.

Article 707. In a contract of pledge, offer and acceptance is made by words purporting to imply agreement, as where the pledgor states that he has given such and such property as security for his debt to the pledgee, or similar words to that effect, and where the pledgee states that he has accepted such pledge or has assented thereto, or words indicating consent. It is not an essential condition that the word pledge should be mentioned.

Example: -
> A person having purchased an article for so much, hands the vendor certain of his property, telling him to keep it until the price is paid. Such property is then validly given in pledge.

SECTION II.

Conditions incidental to a contract of pledge.

Article 708. The pledgor and pledgee must be of sound mind. They need not have reached the age of puberty. Consequently, a minor of perfect understanding may be either pledgor or pledgee.

Article 709. The subject matter of the pledge must be something which may be validly sold. Consequently, it must be in existence at the time of the contract, must have some specific value, and also be capable of delivery.

Article 710. The property in respect of which the pledge is given must be capable of sustaining a claim in respect to such pledge. Consequently, a pledge may be taken in respect to property wrongfully appropriated. But a pledge taken in respect to property held on trust is invalid.

SECTION III.

Matters attached to the pledge: change and increase.

Article 711. Things which are implicitly included in sale are also included in pledge. Thus, when a piece of land is pledged, all trees growing thereon, together with the fruits thereof and all plants and growing crops are included therein even though not explicitly mentioned.

Article 712. A pledge may be exchanged for another pledge.

Example :-

A person who has pledged his watch for so many piastres may ask the pledgee to take a sword instead of the watch and if the pledgee returns the watch and accepts the sword, such sword thereupon becomes the pledge for the debt in question.

Article 713. The subject matter of the pledge may be increased by the pledgor after the conclusion of the contract. That is to say, a second piece of property may be added to the first after the contract relating thereto has been concluded, the first pledge remaining intact. The additional pledge is added to the pledge of the original contract, as though the original contract had been concluded with reference to the two pledges, both becoming one pledge for the debt as it stood at the time the pledge was increased.

Article 714. The debt secured by the pledge may be validly increased in respect to the same pledge.

Example :-

A person pledges a watch worth two thousands piastres to secure a debt of one thousand piastres. If such person contracts a further loan from the creditor of five hundred piastres, the watch becomes a pledge for one thousand five hundred piastres.

174	PLEDGES

Article 715. Any increase arising out of the pledge is part of the original pledge.

CHAPTER II.

PLEDGOR AND PLEDGEE.

Article 716. The pledgee may of his own accord cancel the contract of pledge.

Article 717. The pledgor may not cancel the contract of pledge without the consent of the pledgee.

Article 718. The pledgor and pledgee may cancel the contract of pledge by agreement. The pledgee, however, may retain the pledge after the cancellation of the contract, until the sum secured by such pledge has been paid.

Article 719. A principal debtor may validly give a pledge to his guarantor.

Article 720. A pledge may be validly taken from a debtor by two creditors, whether such creditors are partners or not, such pledge securing both debts.

Article 721. A creditor may validly take a pledge in respect to sums due from two persons, such pledge securing both debts.

CHAPTER III.

THE PLEDGE.

SECTION I.

Preservation of the pledge and expenses connected therewith.

Article 722. The pledgee may keep the pledge himself or may have it kept by some person in whom he has confidence, such as members of his family, or a partner, or a servant.

PLEDGES

Article 723. The pledgee is responsible for expenses incurred in connection with the preservation of the pledge, such as rent of the premises and wages of the watchman.

Article 724. If the pledge consists of an animal, the cost of forage and the wages of the keeper must be paid by the pledgor. If the pledge consists of immovable property, all expenses incurred in connection with the improvement and maintenance thereof, such as repairs, irrigation, grafting, weeding, and the cleansing of watercourses must be borne by the pledgor.

Article 725. Should either the pledgor or the pledgee of their own accord defray expenses which should rightly be met by the other, such payment is in the nature of a gift, with regard to which no subsequent claim may be made.

SECTION II.

Pledge of borrowed articles.

Article 726. A person may make a valid pledge of property borrowed from some third person, provided he has received the permission of that person. This is known as a pledge of a borrowed article.

Article 727. Should the owner of property give his permission unconditionally, the borrower may pledge such property in any way whatsoever.

Article 728. Should the owner of such property have given permission subject to a condition as to the amount of money, or the nature of the property to be secured, or that the pledge is to be made to a certain person, or in a certain town, the borrower must strictly observe such condition.

CHAPTER IV.

FUNDAMENTAL RULES RELATING TO A PLEDGE.

SECTION I.

General.

Article 729. It is a fundamental rule that the pledgee has the right of retaining possession of the pledge until the redemption thereof. In the event of the death of the pledgor, the pledgee has a prior right over other creditors and may obtain payment of the debt from the pledge.

Article 730. The pledge does not extinguish the right to claim the debt. The pledgee after taking possession of the pledge preserves intact his right to demand payment from the pledgor.

Article 731. Upon part payment of the debt there is no necessity to return a portion of the pledge equivalent to such part payment, the pledgee having a right to retain the entire pledge until the whole debt is repaid. When two things have been pledged, however, each one in respect to a specified portion of the debt, and the sum relating to one such specified portion has been repaid, the pledgor may claim the return of such thing only.

Article 732. The owner of borrowed property which has been pledged may call upon the pledgor to redeem the pledge and return it to him. Should the borrower of such property be unable to repay his debt by reason of lack of funds, the person lending such property may himself pay the debt and thus redeem the property pledged.

Article 733. In the event of the death of either the pledgor or the pledgee, the pledge remains intact.

Article 734. Upon the death of the pledgor, his heirs of age stand in his stead. They must redeem the

PLEDGES

pledge by payment of the debt from the estate of the deceased person. If the heirs are minors, however, or if, being of age, they are absent, that is to say, they are elsewhere in the course of a long journey, the guardian of such heirs may sell the pledge subject to the permission of the pledgee, and repay the debt from the sum realised.

Article 735. The lender of property which has been given as security for a debt may not claim such property from the pledgee until the debt in respect to which it has been given as security has been repaid, and this whether the pledgor of the borrowed property be alive or has died before the redemption of the pledge.

Article 736. In the event of the death in a state of bankruptcy of a person who has pledged borrowed property, such borrowed property continues as a pledge in the possession of the pledgee and cannot be sold without the consent of the lender. Should the lender of the pledge seek to repay the debt by means of the sale of the pledge, such pledge shall be sold independently of the consent of the pledgee, provided the value thereof is sufficient to meet the debt. If the value of the pledge is not sufficient to meet the debt, however, such pledge may not be sold without the consent of the pledgee.

Article 737. In the event of the death of the lender of a pledge and of his debts being greater than his estate, the pledgor shall be called upon personally to pay his debt and to redeem the pledge which he has borrowed. Should he be unable to do so, however, by reason of lack of means, the borrowed property continues as a pledge in the possession of the pledgee. The heirs of the lender of the pledge may redeem such pledge by repaying the debt. In the event of the creditors of the lender of the pledge claiming the sale of such pledge, the pledge, if the value thereof is sufficient to repay the debt, shall be sold regardless of the consent of the pledgee. If it is insufficient to repay the debt, such pledge may only be sold with the consent of the pledgee.

Article 738. Upon the death of the pledgee, the pledge devolves upon his heirs.

Article 739. Should a pledgor give a pledge in respect to debts due to two persons, and repay the debt of one of them, such pledgor may not demand the return of half of the pledge, having no right to redeem the pledge until he has repaid in full the debt due to both creditors.

Article 740. A person taking a pledge from two debtors may retain such pledge until the debt of both has been paid in full.

Article 741. In the event of a pledgor destroying or damaging the pledge, he must make good such destruction or damage. Should a pledgee destroy or damage the pledge, a sum corresponding to the amount of such destruction or damage shall be deducted from the debt.

Article 742. In the event of a third person destroying the pledge, such person shall make good the value thereof as on the day it was destroyed. The sum in question shall be held as a pledge by the pledgee.

SECTION II.

Rights of pledgor and pledgee over the pledge.

Article 743. A pledge by either pledgor or pledgee of the original pledge to some third person is null and void, unless the permission of either the pledgor or pledgee has been obtained.

PLEDGES

Article 744. In the event of a pledge of the original pledge being made by the pledgor to some third person with the permission of the pledgee, the second pledge stands in the place of the first pledge, which becomes null and void.

Article 745. In the event of a pledge of the original pledge being made by the pledgee, with the permission of the pledgor, the first pledge becomes null and void, and the second pledge is valid, being in the nature of a pledge made of a borrowed object.

Article 746. In the event of the pledgee selling the pledge without the permission of the pledgor, the pledgor may either adopt or cancel such sale.

Article 747. In the event of the pledgor selling the pledge without the permission of the pledgee, such sale is invalid and the pledgee may retain possession of the pledge. If the debt is repaid, however, such sale is valid. Moreover, if the pledgee adopts such sale it is valid, the sale acting as a release of the pledge, the debt being unaffected. The price realised by the sale becomes the pledge for the thing sold. Should the pledgee not agree, however, the purchaser may either wait until the pledge has been redeemed, or apply to the Court for an order cancelling the sale.

Article 748. Provided permission is mutually given, both the pledgor and the pledgee may lend the pledge to a third person. Either of them may afterwards restore it to a state of pledge.

Article 749. The pledgee may lend the pledge to the pledgor. If he does so and the pledgor dies, the pledgee has a right of preference over other creditors of the pledgor in respect to the pledge.

PLEDGES

Article 750. The pledgee may not make use of the pledge without the permission of the pledgor. The pledgee, however, may use the pledge with the permission of the pledgor and may take the produce thereof, such as fruit and milk. In such case there is no reduction of the debt in consideration thereof.

Article 751. The pledgee, upon removing to another place may take the pledge with him, provided the road is safe.

SECTION III.

Deposit of the pledge with a bailee.

Article 752. Possession by a bailee is equivalent to possession by the pledgee. That is to say, should the pledgor and pledgee agree to deposit the pledge with some person in whom they have confidence, and such person agrees to take possession thereof, the pledge becomes irrevocable. The bailee then stands in the place of the pledgee.

Article 753. In cases where at the time of the conclusion of the contract it has been agreed that the pledgee shall take possession of the pledge, the pledgor and the pledgee may by mutual consent deposit the pledge with a bailee.

Article 754. The bailee may not give the pledge to either the pledgor or the pledgee during the continuance of the debt without the consent of the other. Should he do so, the return thereof may be demanded. Should the pledge be destroyed before it is returned, the bailee must make good the value thereof.

Article 755. In the event of the death of the bailee, the pledge may, subject to the consent of the two contracting parties, be deposited with some other bailee, and in the event of their failing to agree, the pledge shall be deposited with a bailee appointed by the Court.

PLEDGES

SECTION IV.

Sale of the pledge.

Article 756. Neither the pledgor nor the pledgee may sell the pledge without the consent of the other.

Article 757. Should the pledgor refuse to make payment when the debt falls due, he shall be directed by the Court to sell the pledge and pay the debt. Should he still persist in his refusal, the pledge shall be sold by the Court and the debt repaid.

Article 758. Should the pledgor be absent and should it be uncertain whether he is alive or dead, the pledgee may apply to the Court for an order for the sale of the pledge and the satisfaction of the debt from the proceeds.

Article 759. If there is good ground for believing that the pledge is likely to deteriorate, the pledgee may apply to the Court for an order directing him to sell the pledge and he thereupon holds the proceeds of the sale as the pledge. Should the pledgee sell the pledge without having obtained an order from the Court, he becomes responsible therefor. Thus, if there is good ground for believing that the ripe fruit and vegetables of an orchard and garden which have been pledged are likely to perish, they may be sold by order of the Court. Should the pledgee, however, sell them on his own initiative, he is liable to make good any loss which may be incurred thereby.

Article 760. The pledgor may validly appoint the pledgee or the bailee, or some third person his agent for the sale of the pledge when the debt falls due for payment. The pledgor may not thereafter revoke the power of such agent, nor can he be removed in the event of the death of either the pledgor or the pledgee.

Article 761. An agent for the sale of a pledge shall, when the debt falls due for payment, sell such pledge and hand the proceeds to the pledgee. Should he refuse to do so, the pledgor shall be forced to sell the pledge himself. In the event of the pledgor likewise refusing to sell, such pledge shall be sold by the Court. Should either the pledgor or his heirs be absent, the agent shall be obliged to sell the pledge. Should he refuse to do so, such pledge shall be sold by the Court.

Promulgated by Royal Iradah, 25 Sefer, 1288

BOOK VI.

TRUSTS AND TRUSTEESHIP.

BOOK VI.

TRUSTS AND TRUSTEESHIP.

INTRODUCTION.

TERMS OF MUHAMMADAN JURISPRUDENCE RELATING TO TRUSTS AND TRUSTEESHIP.

Article 762. The subject matter of the trust is the thing entrusted to the person who is responsible for the safe keeping thereof, whether placed on trust for safe keeping in pursuance of an express contract, such as a contract of deposit for safe keeping, or by implication, as in the case of a thing taken on hire or borrowed, or whether entrusted to someone without any contract or intention, as where wind blows into the house of a certain person the property of such person's neighbour. Such property does not become property deposited for safe keeping with the owner of the house, since there is no contract to that effect, but is held by him on trust.

Article 763. By deposit for safe keeping is meant handing property to any particular person in order that it may be kept safely.

Article 764. By delivery for safe keeping is meant handing over one's own property to some other person for safe keeping. The person handing over such property is called the person delivering and the person accepting such property is called the custodian or keeper.

Article 765. By loan for use is meant conferring upon somebody the usufruct of a thing gratuitously, that is to say, without payment.

Article 766. By loaning for use is meant giving on loan in order that the usufruct of the loan may be enjoyed.

Article 767. By taking a loan for use is meant accepting a loan in order that the usufruct of the thing borrowed may be enjoyed.

CHAPTER I.

GENERAL.

Article 768. A trust is not subject to compensation. That is to say, if the trustee is not guilty of any wrongful act or negligence and the subject of the trust is destroyed or lost, the trustee is not obliged to make good the loss.

Article 769. If any person finds anything in the highway or in any other place and keeps such thing as his own, he is considered to be a person wrongfully appropriating property. Consequently, if such property is destroyed or lost, even without such person's wrongful act or negligence, he is obliged to make good the loss. But if he takes it with the intention of restoring it to the owner thereof, and it is known who such person is, such property is held on trust while in his possession and must be restored to its rightful owner. If the owner thereof is unknown, such property is lost property and is held in trust by the finder.

Article 770. The finder of lost property must make known the fact that he has found such property, and must keep it in his possession on trust until such time as the owner appears. If any person appears and proves that such property is his, the property in question must be handed over to him.

Article 771. In the event of property belonging to one person being destroyed accidentally while in the possession of another, and such person has taken such property without the permission of the owner, the loss must in any case be made good by the former. If such property is taken with the permission of the owner thereof, the person so taking the property is under no obligation to make good the loss, since he held such property on trust. But in the case of property purchased on approval as to price, the price of which has been fixed, the loss must be made good.

Examples: -

(1) A takes a cup from a china shop of his own accord. The cup falls from his hand and is broken. A must make good the loss. If he takes it with the permission of the owner, and it is accidentally destroyed by falling from A's hand while in the act of inspecting the cup, A is not obliged to make good the loss. But if such cup falls upon a number of other cups and the latter are also broken, the loss thereof must be made good. As regards the first cup, however, there is no need to make good the loss, since it was held on trust. If A enquires the price of the cup, however, and the shopkeeper informs him of the price thereof, and tells him to take it, and A does in fact take it in his hand and it falls to the ground and is broken, A must make good the loss.

(2) A is drinking sherbet and while doing so drops the glass belonging to the sherbet vendor, and it is broken. A is not obliged to make good the loss, since the glass is in his possession on trust as a loan for use. But if the glass was dropped as a result of some improper use, A is obliged to make good the loss.

Article 772. Permission given by implication is the same as permission given explicitly. But in the presence of an express prohibition, any permission given by implication is of no effect.

Example :-

A enters B's house with the latter's permission. A is permitted by implication to drink water by means of a glass which he finds in the house. If the glass falls from A's hand while he is drinking the water and it is broken, A need not make good the loss. But if the owner of the house tells A not to touch the glass and A does so in spite of the prohibition, and the glass falls and is broken, A must make good the loss.

CHAPTER II.

DEPOSIT FOR SAFE KEEPING.

SECTION I.

Conclusion of the contract of deposit for safe keeping and conditions relating thereto.

Article 773. A contract of deposit for safe keeping may be concluded by offer and acceptance either expressly or by implication.

Examples :-

(1) A informs B that he has deposited with him for safe keeping certain property of which he is the owner, or that he has placed such property with him on trust, and the person with whom such property is deposited agrees thereto. An express contract for the deposit of a thing for safe keeping has been concluded.

(2) A enters an inn and asks the inn-keeper where he should tie up his animal. The latter shows him a certain place and A ties his animal up there. A contract for deposit for safe keeping has been concluded by implication.

(3) A leaves certain property with a shopkeeper. The shopkeeper is aware thereof, and keeps silence. The property in question is deposited for safe keeping with the shopkeeper. If the shopkeeper, however, declines to keep the property, no contract for safe keeping is concluded.

(4) A leaves property of his with certain persons for safe keeping. The latter are aware thereof, but keep silence. The property in question is deposited for safe keeping with all of such persons. But if such persons leave the place in question one by one, such property is deposited for safe keeping with the last remaining person, who is responsible for its preservation.

Article 774. The person making the deposit for safe keeping and the person so receiving it may either of them cancel the contract of deposit for safe keeping at any time they wish.

Article 775. The thing deposited for safe keeping must be capable of possession and delivery. Consequently, a deposit for safe keeping of a bird in the air is invalid.

Article 776. The person making the deposit for safe keeping and the person so receiving it must be of sound mind and perfect understanding, though they need not have arrived at the age of puberty. Consequently, a madman or a minor of imperfect understanding cannot validly make or receive a deposit for safe keeping. A deposit for safe keeping or the receipt thereof by a minor of perfect understanding, however, who has been duly authorized thereunto, is valid.

SECTION II.

Effect of making a deposit for safe keeping and of making good any loss arising therefrom.

Article 777. The thing deposited for safe keeping is a trust in the possession of the person receiving such thing. Consequently, if it is destroyed or lost without the fault or negligence of the person keeping such thing, there is no necessity to make good the loss. But if such thing has been deposited for safe keeping in consideration of payment of a fee, and the thing has been destroyed or lost owing to some cause which might have been avoided, the loss must be made good.

Examples:-

(1) A watch is entrusted to A for safe keeping, and A accidently drops and breaks it. A cannot be called upon to make good the loss. But if A treads on the watch or drops something on it and it is broken, A must make good the loss.

(2) A entrusts certain property to B for safe keeping and pays him a fee for so doing. Later, the property is stolen. The person receiving such property must make good the loss, since it arose from a cause which could have been avoided.

Article 778. If the servant of the person receiving property for safe keeping drops something on to such property and it is destroyed, the servant must make good the loss.

Article 779. The person receiving the property for safe keeping may not perform any act with regard to such property which he is not authorised to do by the owner thereof.

Article 780. The person receiving property for safe keeping must keep such property personally and as though it were his own property, or cause it to be kept by some person in whom he has confidence. If such property is destroyed or lost while in the possession of the latter without any default or negligence on his part, neither he nor the person receiving the property for safe keeping may be called upon to make good the loss.

Article 781. The person receiving property for safe keeping may keep such property in the place where he keeps his own property.

Article 782. The property entrusted for safe keeping must be kept in the same way as articles similar thereto are kept. Consequently, placing property such as cash and jewels in such places as stables and barns amounts to negligence, and if they are destroyed or lost while there, the loss must be made good.

Article 783. If the persons receiving property for safe keeping are several, and the property deposited for safe keeping is not capable of division, one of them may keep such property with the permission of the others, or they may keep it in turn. If the property entrusted for safe keeping in these circumstances is destroyed without any fault or negligence, none of them may be called upon to make good the loss. If the property deposited for safe keeping, however, is capable of division, the persons receiving such property may divide it among themselves equally, each person keeping his own share. No one of them may give his share to any other person for safe keeping unless he obtains the permission of the person who has deposited his property with him. If he does so, and it is destroyed or lost without fault or negligence while in such other person's possession, the latter is not liable to make good the loss, but the former may be called upon to do so in respect to his share.

Article 784. If any condition contained in the contract of deposit for safe keeping is capable of execution and beneficial, such condition is valid. If not, it is null and void.

Examples: -

(1) A contract of deposit for the safe keeping of certain property is drawn up subject to the condition that such property is to be kept in the house of the person receiving such property. A fire breaks out, and the property has to be transferred to another place. The condition becomes invalid; and if the property after having been transferred to such other place is destroyed

or lost without any fault or negligence, there is no obligation to make good the loss.

(2) A person entrusts property to another for safe keeping, instructing the latter to keep such property, and forbids him to entrust it to his wife or his son, or to a servant, or to a person to whom he has entrusted his own property, and such person is forced to disobey his instructions. The prohibition becomes invalid. If the property entrusted to such person in these circumstances is destroyed or lost, without any fault or negligence, there is no need to make good the loss. If he was under no necessity to do so, however, the loss must be made good.

(3) A contract of deposit for safe keeping is concluded subject to the condition that the property shall be kept in a particular room of the house. The person receiving such property stores it in another room. If such rooms are identical the one with the other, as regards safety, the condition is invalid; and if the property entrusted for safe keeping is destroyed in these circumstances, there is no need to make good the loss. But if one room differs from the other, as where one is made of stone and the other of wood, the condition is valid and the person to whom the property is entrusted is bound to store the property in the room agreed upon: and if he puts such property in a room which is inferior to the room agreed upon as regards safety, and the property is destroyed, the loss must be made good.

Article 785. If the owner of the property deposited for safe keeping is absent, and it is unknown whether he is alive or dead, the person receiving such thing must keep it until such time as it is proved that he is dead. If the property is of such a nature, however, that it would spoil by being kept, it may be sold by order of the Court, and such person may then keep the proceeds on trust. If the property is not sold and is ruined, there is no need to make good the loss.

Article 786. The owner of a thing deposited for safe keeping which requires maintenance, such as a horse or a cow, is responsible for the maintenance thereof. In the event of the absence of the owner, the person receiving such thing for safe keeping may apply to the Court, which will decide upon the most suitable and useful manner for the owner in which to deal with the matter. Thus, if the property can be let on hire, the person receiving the property may let it on hire, subject to the approval of the Court, and may provide for its maintenance out of the proceeds, or may sell it for an estimated price. If it is not capable of being let on hire, he may, subject to the approval of the Court, sell such thing for an estimated price forthwith, or after having provided for the maintenance thereof from his own property for a period of three days, the expenses incurred in connection with the three days upkeep being charged to the owner. If he incurs such expenditure without the sanction of the Court, however, he cannot recover it from the person depositing the property for safe keeping.

Article 787. If the property deposited for safe keeping is destroyed or the value thereof diminished by the fault or negligence of the person entrusted therewith, such person must make good the loss.

Examples :-
(1) The person to whom money is entrusted for safe keeping uses such money for his own purposes. He must make good the loss. If he spends a purse of money in this manner which has been left with him on trust, and afterwards replaces it with money of his own, and it is later lost without any fault or negligence on his part, he is nevertheless liable to make good the loss.

(2) A person to whom an animal has been entrusted for safe keeping rides the animal without the permission of the owner, and such animal is destroyed either by riding it in some unusual manner, or for some other reason, or for no reason at all, or such animal is stolen while on the road. Such person must make good the loss.

(3) A person to whom property has been entrusted for safe keeping fails to transport the property entrusted to him to some other place upon the outbreak of a fire, although able to do so, and such property is destroyed by the fire. Such person must make good the loss.

Article 788. If the person to whom property has been entrusted for safe keeping mixes such property without the permission of the owner with other property in such a manner that it cannot be distinguished therefrom, such person is guilty of negligence. Consequently, if the person to whom a quantity of gold pounds have been entrusted for safe keeping mixes them without permission with gold pounds of his own, or with gold pounds delivered to him for safe keeping by some other person, and they are lost or stolen, he must make good the loss. Again, if any other than the person to whom they have been entrusted for safe keeping so mixes them, such person must make good the loss.

Article 789. If the person to whom property has been entrusted for safe keeping mixes such property with the permission of the owner thereof with other property as is stated in the preceding Article, or if, without any fault on his part two pieces of property are mixed together in such a way that they cannot be distinguished the one from the other, as, for example, where a purse of money which is delivered for safe keeping is put in a box and the purse is torn and the gold coins therein are mixed with other gold coins, the person to whom they have been entrusted for safe keeping and the owner become joint owners of the total amount of such coins in proportion to their shares. In these circumstances, if the coins are destroyed or lost without fault or negligence, there is no need to make good the loss.

Article 790. The person to whom property has been entrusted for safe keeping may not transfer such property for safe keeping to any other person without permission. If he does so, and the property is destroyed, he must make good the loss. If the property is destroyed owing to the fault or negligence of the second person, the owner of the property may at his option claim to have the loss made good from either the second or the first. If he recovers from the first person, the latter has a right of recourse against the second.

Article 791. If the person to whom property has been entrusted for safe keeping deposits such property with some other person, and the owner of the property adopts the transaction, the first person is replaced by the second.

Article 792. The person to whom property has been entrusted for safe keeping may, with the permission of the owner thereof, use such property or let it on hire, or lend it, or give it on pledge. If he does so without the permission of the owner, however, and such property is destroyed or lost while in the possession of the person taking it on hire, or the borrower, or the pledgee, or the value thereof is decreased, the person to whom the property has been entrusted for safe keeping must make good the loss.

Article 793. If the person to whom money has been delivered on trust lends and delivers such money to some other person without permission, and the owner

TRUSTS AND TRUSTEESHIP

thereof does not adopt such transaction, the person to whom the money has been entrusted must make good any loss incurred. Again, if he repays a debt owing to some other person by the person who has entrusted money to him out of such money, and the owner does not agree, he must make good the loss.

Article 794. Upon the owner of the property entrusted for safe keeping asking for the return thereof, such property must be restored to him. Any charges and expenses occasioned thereby must be borne by the owner of the property. If the owner asks for the return of his property and the person to whom it has been entrusted fails to restore it to him, and the property is destroyed or lost, such person must make good the loss. But if the property is not restored by reason of some lawful excuse, as for example where the property is in some remote place when its return is asked for and it is destroyed or lost, there is then no liability to make good the loss.

Article 795. The person to whom property has been entrusted for safe keeping may restore such property himself or by means of some person on whom he relies. If he returns the property through the latter, and before delivery to the owner, such property is destroyed or lost without any fault or negligence, there is no liability to make good the loss.

Article 796. If two persons who are joint owners of various pieces of property deposit such property with any person for safekeeping, and one of the joint owners, in the absence of the other, requests delivery of his share from such person, the latter may restore to such joint owner his share of the property, providing they are things the like of which can be found in the market, but not otherwise.

TRUSTS AND TRUSTEESHIP

Article 797. The property delivered for safe keeping must be returned at the place where it was handed over for safe keeping.

Example :-
   Goods handed over for safe keeping at Constantinople must be returned in Constantinople. The person to whom they have been entrusted cannot be obliged to hand them over at Adrianople.

Article 798. Any usufruct of the property deposited for safe keeping belongs to the owner.

Example:-
   The young, or the milk, or the wool of an animal handed over for safe keeping belongs to the owner of such animal.

Article 799. If a person who has deposited money for safe keeping is absent, any person dependent upon such person for support may apply to the Court for an order that a certain sum may be set aside therefrom for him; and if the person with whom such money has been so deposited pays such sum to him by way of maintenance, he is in no way liable. He is liable, however, if he does so without the order of the Court.

Article 800. If the person to whom property is entrusted for safe keeping goes mad, and there is little hope of his recovery, and if the thing deposited for safe keeping prior to such person's madness is itself no longer in existence, the owner of such property may, upon producing a reliable guarantor, have the loss made good from the mad person's property. Should he recover from his madness, however, and allege that the property deposited has been returned to the owner thereof, or that such property has been destroyed or lost without any fault or negligence on his part, and should such statement be confirmed on oath, the money which has been taken must be returned.

TRUSTS AND TRUSTEESHIP

Article 801. If upon the death of the person to whom a thing has been entrusted for safe keeping such thing is found among the estate of the deceased, it is held on trust by the heir, and must be returned to the owner. If it cannot be found in the estate of the deceased person, however, and the heirs are able to prove that such person during his lifetime had stated that he had returned such thing to the owner thereof, or that it had been lost without any wrongful act on his part, there is no need to make good the loss. Again, if the heirs state that they know the thing that was handed over for safe keeping, and describe it, and allege that it was lost after the death of the person to whom it had been entrusted, without any fault or negligence on their part, and such statement is confirmed on oath, there is no need to make good the loss. If the person to whom the thing has been entrusted dies without making any statement as to the condition of the property entrusted to him, the value thereof must be paid out of the estate, in the same manner as other debts. Similarly, if the heirs fail to describe the thing which has been entrusted for safe keeping and merely state that they know of such thing and that it was lost, such statement, unless proved, is of no effect, and the value of such thing must be paid from the estate.

Article 802. Upon the death of the person who has entrusted a thing for safe keeping, such thing must be handed to the heirs. If the estate is overwhelmed with debts, however, the matter must be referred to the Court. If the matter is not so referred, and the person to whom such thing has been entrusted hands it over to the heirs, who consume the same, the person to whom it has been entrusted for safe keeping must make good the loss.

Article 803. Should it be necessary to make good the loss of the thing entrusted for safe keeping, and such thing is one the like of which can be found in the market, a similar thing must be given. If it is a thing the like of which cannot be found in the market, the value of such thing at the time it was lost must be made good.

CHAPTER III.

PROPERTY LENT FOR USE.

SECTION I.

The contract of loan for use and conditions relating thereto.

Article 804. A contract of loan for use is concluded by offer and acceptance and by conduct.

Example :-
> A tells B that he has lent him certain property for use or that he has made him a loan for use and B accepts, or without making any statement takes such thing. A contract has been concluded for a loan for use. Again, A asks B to lend him certain property to use and B lends him such property. A contract of loan for use is concluded.

Article 805. The silence of the person giving the loan is not considered to be acceptance. Consequently, if one person asks another to lend him a thing for use, and the owner of such thing keeps silence, and the other takes it, such person becomes a person wrongfully appropriating property.

Article 806. The person lending the thing for use may at any time withdraw from the contract.

Article 807. A contract of loan for use is cancelled upon the death of either the person giving or the person taking the thing on loan for use.

200 TRUSTS AND TRUSTEESHIP

Article 808. The thing given on loan for use must be capable of enjoyment. Consequently, the giving or taking of a runaway animal on loan for use is invalid.

Article 809. The person giving and the person taking a thing on loan for use must be of sound mind and perfect understanding. They need not have arrived at the age of puberty. Consequently, a madman or a minor of imperfect understanding cannot conclude a valid contract for giving or taking a thing on loan for use. A minor who has received permission from his tutor, however, may do so.

Article 810. Taking delivery is essential to the validity of a contract of loan for use. The contract is devoid of effect before delivery.

Article 811. The thing given on loan for use must be clearly defined.

Example :-
> A contract is concluded for a loan for the use of one of two horses without stating which one or without giving an option for selection. The contract is invalid The person making the loan must state which one he gives on loan. But if he gives the person taking the horse on loan the option of selecting whichever one he likes, the contract is valid.

SECTION II.

Effect of a contract of loan for use and compensation for loss sustained in connection therewith.

Article 812. The person to whom a thing has been lent for use becomes owner of the usufruct thereof without giving anything in return. Consequently, the person giving the thing on loan cannot demand any payment from the person taking such thing on loan after he has used it.

Article 813. The thing lent for use is on trust while in the possession of the person to whom it has been lent. If it is destroyed without any fault or negligence, or if the value thereof is decreased, there is no need to make good the loss.

Examples:-

(1) A person to whom a mirror has been lent for use accidentally drops it or slips and knocks it with his foot and it is broken. There is no need to make good the loss.

(2) A carpet lent for use is accidentally stained by something dropping on it so that its value is decreased. There is no need to make good the loss.

Article 814. If the thing lent for use is destroyed or the value thereof decreased owing to any fault or negligence, or for any reason whatsoever on the part of the person receiving such thing, the loss must be made good.

Examples:-

(1) An animal is lent to A to go to a certain place with the proviso that he shall take two days to reach that place. He arrives there in one day and the animal is destroyed or is rendered so weak that its value is diminished. A must make good the loss.

(2) A borrows an animal to go to a certain place. On arrival there he continues his journey on the animal and it dies a natural death. A must make good the loss.

(3) A borrows a necklace and puts it round the neck of a child. A leaves the child without anyone to look after it and the necklace is stolen. If the child is able to look after the thing which it is wearing, there is no need to make good the loss. If the child is incapable of doing so, the loss must be made good.

Article 815. Expenses occasioned by the upkeep of the thing lent must be borne by the person to whom it is lent. Consequently, if the person who borrows an animal fails to provide fodder for such animal and it dies, such person must make good the loss.

Article 816. In the case of an absolute contract of loan for use, that is to say, when the person granting the loan makes no stipulation as to time or place or the use to which the thing lent is to be put, the person borrowing the thing may use such thing at any time or in any place he wishes, subject, however, to custom.

Examples:-

(1) A lends B his horse absolutely as stated above. B can ride the horse whenever he likes, and to whichever place he likes. He may not ride it to a place in one hour, however, which by custom takes two hours to reach.

(2) A lends B the room of an inn absolutely. B may, if he wishes, live in it or store goods in it. But he may not, contrary to custom, carry on the trade of a blacksmith therein.

Article 817. If the loan for use is restricted as to time and place, the restriction is valid and the person to whom the loan is made may not act in contravention thereof.

Example:-

An animal borrowed for riding for a period of three hours, may not be ridden for four; and an animal borrowed to go to a specific place may not be taken to some other place.

Article 818. If the loan for use is restricted as to the use to which it may be put, the person to whom it is lent may not put it to any more exacting use. But if it is put to a similar or less exacting use, the breach of the restriction is valid.

Examples:-

(1) An animal is borrowed to carry a load of corn. Iron or stone may not be loaded on him. A load equal to or lighter than the weight of corn may, however, be loaded on him.

(2) A load may not be placed upon an animal which has been borrowed for riding. An animal which has been borrowed to carry loads, however, may be used for riding.

Article 819. If the person making the loan makes it absolutely, without specifying the person who is to enjoy the benefit thereof, the person to whom it is lent may use it as he likes. That is to say, he may use it himself or he may lend it to another person to use, and this, whether the thing lent is one which is not changed by the person using it, such as a room, or one that is so changed, such as a horse for riding.

Examples :-

(1) A tells B that he has lent him his room. The person to whom the room is lent may either live in the room himself or let some other person live therein.

(2) A tells B that he has lent him a certain horse. B may either ride the horse himself or let some other person ride him.

Article 820. The person who is to enjoy the benefit of the loan may validly be specified in the case of things which change with the change of persons using such things. This is not the case with things which do not so change. If the person making the loan, however, states that it is not to be given to any other person, the person to whom such thing is loaned may not under any circumstances cause it to be used by another.

Example :-

A tells B that he has lent him a certain horse to ride. The person to whom it is lent may not give it to his servant to ride. But if A tells B that he has lent him a room in which to live, B can live in it himself or let some other person live in it. He may not do so, however, if A has told him not to allow any other person to live there.

Article 821. If an animal is borrowed to go to a certain place, and there are several roads leading thereto, the borrower can proceed along whichever of the roads he likes in accordance with custom. But if he proceeds along a road which it is not customary to use, and the animal is destroyed, he must make good the loss. Again, if the borrower uses a road other than that prescribed by the lender and the animal is destroyed, the borrower must make good the loss if the road used by him is longer or less secure than that prescribed by the lender, or not customarily used.

Article 822. If a person asks a woman to make him a loan for use of a thing which is the property of her husband, and she gives such thing on loan without her husband's permission, and it is lost, there is no need for either the woman or the borrower to make good the loss, if it is one of those things which are found in the women's quarter of the house, and which by custom is in the possession of the wife. If the thing borrowed is not one of such things, however, but is a thing which is not in the possession of women, such as a horse, the husband may, at his option, have the loss made good by the wife or the borrower.

Article 823. The borrower may not give the thing borrowed on hire, nor pledge it without the permission of the lender, nor may the borrower pledge a piece of property which has been lent to secure a loan in one town as security for a loan in another town. If he does so, and the thing lent for use is destroyed or lost, the loss must be made good.

Article 824. The borrower may deposit the thing borrowed for safe keeping with some other person. If it is destroyed without any fault or negligence while in the possession of the latter, there is no need to make good the loss.

Example :-
A borrows a horse from B for the purpose of going to and returning from a certain place. Upon arrival at that place, the horse is found to be tired and unable to proceed, and B entrusts the horse to C to mind. Later the horse dies a natural death. A need not make good the loss.

Article 825. Upon the lender asking the borrower to return the thing lent, the latter must do so forthwith. If he keeps it and delays returning it without any valid excuse and it is destroyed or lost, or there is a decrease in the value thereof, the borrower must make good the loss.

Article 826. A thing which has been lent for use for a definite period of time, whether express or implied, must be returned to the lender on the expiration of such period. But any delay which is sanctioned by custom is excused.

Examples :-
(1) Ornaments are borrowed to be used on a certain day until the afternoon. When that time arrives they must be returned.

(2) Ornaments are borrowed to be used at a certain person's wedding. When the wedding is over the ornaments must be returned. But the time ordinarily necessary for the return of the ornaments is allowed.

TRUSTS AND TRUSTEESHIP

Article 827. If a thing is borrowed for use in connection with any particular piece of work, such thing, on the completion of such work is regarded as property entrusted for safe keeping to the borrower. He may not use it in any way whatsoever and may not retain it for any period longer than is allowed by custom. If he does so and such property is destroyed, he must make good the loss.

Article 828. The borrower must return the thing borrowed to the lender either personally or through some reliable person. If he returns such thing through a person who is not reliable, and it is destroyed or lost, he must make good the loss.

Article 829. Things borrowed for use which are of great value, such as jewels, must be returned to the lender personally. In other cases, however, it is sufficient to return them at the place where it is customary to do so, or to deliver them to the servant of the lender.

Example :-
> Return of an animal borrowed for use may be effected by delivering it at the stable of the lender or by handing it over to his groom.

Article 830. Upon the return of a thing borrowed for use which is in the possession of the borrower, all expenses occasioned thereby, including cost of transport, must be borne by the borrower.

Article 831. A piece of land may validly be lent for use for the purpose of erecting buildings or planting trees. The lender, however, may at any time go back on the loan and oblige the borrower to pull down the buildings or uproot the trees. However, if the loan is for a definite period, the lender must make good the difference between the value of the buildings and trees at the time they were pulled down or uprooted and what would have been the value thereof at the end of the period, had they remained standing.

Example:-

Should the pulled down and uprooted value of buildings and trees which are pulled down and uprooted forthwith be twelve gold pounds, and the value thereof if left standing up to the end of the period be twenty gold pounds, and should the lender cause them to be pulled down or uprooted forthwith, he is obliged to pay a sum of eight gold pounds.

Article 832. If land is lent for cultivation, whether for a fixed period or not, the lender cannot withdraw from the contract and demand the return of the land from the borrower before the harvest.

Promulgated by Royal Iradah, 24 Zil Hijja, 1288.

BOOK VII.

GIFT.

BOOK VII.

GIFT.

INTRODUCTION.

TERMS OF MUHAMMADAN JURISPRUDENCE RELATING TO GIFT.

Article 833. A gift consists of bestowing the ownership of property upon some other person without receiving anything in return. The person giving is called the donor; the property given is called the property bestowed by way of gift; and the person who receives such property is called the recipient.

Article 834. A present is property brought or sent to someone by way of gratification.

Article 835. Alms consists of property given for some charitable object.

Article 836. Allowing another person to eat and drink without receiving anything in exchange is called gratuitous feeding.

CHAPTER I.

MATTERS RELATING TO THE CONTRACT OF GIFT

SECTION I.

Fundamental basis and receipt of a gift.

Article 837. A contract of gift is concluded by offer and acceptance. Upon taking delivery the contract becomes complete.

Article 838. Offer, as regards donation, consists of the employment of words importing the gratuitous transfer of ownership in property, such as "I have given for nothing": "I have given by way of gift": "I have given as a present". An offer of a gift is also made by the use of expressions importing the intention of transferring ownership in property gratuitously, as where a husband hands a pair of earrings or some other jewel to his wife, telling her to take such thing and wear it.

Article 839. A contract of gift may also be concluded by conduct.

Article 840. The despatch and receipt of a gift and of alms are tantamount to verbal offer and acceptance.

Article 841. Receipt in the case of gift is like acceptance in the case of sale. Consequently, if the donor makes his offer by stating that he has given the thing by way of gift or by using some similar expression, and the recipient, without signifying his acceptance, merely takes delivery of the thing given, at the time it was offered, the gift thereupon becomes complete.

Article 842. The recipient may not take delivery of the thing given by way of gift, unless he has received the permission, express or implied, of the donor.

Article 843. The donor, by his offer, is considered by implication to have authorized the recipient to take delivery of the thing given. There is an express authority, however, when the donor makes use of formal words, as when he states that he has given something to someone and invites that person to take it, in the event of the gift being present when the parties meet, or that he has given something to someone and invites him to go and get it, should the gift itself not be there when the parties meet.

Article 844. When the donor has given his express authority, the recipient may take delivery of the property bestowed by way of gift either at the meeting place of the parties, or after they have separated. If the authority is merely implied, however, it is only valid so long as the parties are present together. After they have separated, the recipient may not validly take delivery of such property.

Example:-
> The donor states that he has bestowed a certain thing by way of gift. The recipient may validly take delivery of the thing given so long as the parties remain present together, but he may not do so once they have separated. If the donor states that he has made a gift of something belonging to him which is in a certain place, without requesting the recipient to go and get it, the recipient may not validly go to the place where such thing is and take delivery thereof.

Article 845. A purchaser may make a valid gift to a third party of a thing he has purchased, even before having taken delivery thereof from the vendor.

Article 846. A gift made by the owner of a thing to a person who is already in possession thereof is complete by reason of the mere acceptance of the recipient, without the necessity of any further delivery.

Article 847. If a person to whom money is due makes a gift of such money to the person from whom the money is due, or releases the debtor from payment thereof, such gift or release is valid, and the debt is forthwith extinguished, provided that the debtor does not decline to agree thereto.

Article 848. Should a person to whom money is due make a gift of the sum due to him to some person other than the person who owes him such money, expressly authorizing the recipient to take payment from the latter, the gift is complete as soon as the recipient has received payment.

Article 849. The death of the donor or the recipient before the transfer of the gift makes such gift null and void.

Article 850. In the case of gift made by a father to a son who is of age, that is, who is of sound mind and who has arrived at the age of puberty, the thing bestowed by way of gift must be delivered by the donor, and delivery must be taken thereof by the recipient.

Article 851. A gift made to a minor by his tutor or by the person in charge of his upbringing and education, of such person's property is complete by reason only of the offer of the donor, and the minor becomes absolute owner thereof without any need for taking delivery, whether the thing given is in the possession of the donor, or in the safe keeping of some third person.

Article 852. A gift made by a person to a child is complete when the tutor or person in charge of the upbringing or education of the child takes delivery of such gift.

Article 853. If the recipient is a minor who is of perfect understanding, the gift becomes complete when the minor himself takes delivery thereof, even though he has a tutor.

Article 854. A gift which is to take effect in the future is invalid.

Example :-

A donor states that he has made a gift of a certain thing with effect as from the first of next month. The gift is invalid.

Article 855. The donor may validly demand some compensation in return for his gift. In such a case the contract is valid and the condition binding upon the recipient.

Examples:-

(1) The donor makes a condition that the recipient shall give him some particular thing in return, or that he shall pay his debt amounting to a certain sum. If the recipient fulfils the condition the gift becomes irrevocable; if not, the donor has the right of revoking it.

(2) A person makes a gift of his real property held in absolute ownership upon condition that the recipient shall make provision for his maintenance for the whole of his life time. If such person changes his mind, he cannot revoke his gift and claim the return of such property so long as the recipient continues to comply with the condition.

SECTION II.

Conditions attaching to a gift.

Article 856. The thing bestowed by way of gift must be in existence at the time the gift is made. Consequently, if a gift is made of grapes to be produced in a vineyard, or the foal of a mare not yet born, such gift is invalid.

Article 857. The thing bestowed by way of gift must be the property of the donor. Consequently, if a person makes a gift to some other person of property which is not his own, such gift is invalid. If the owner, however, thereafter ratifies the gift, such gift is valid.

Article 858. The thing bestowed by way of gift must be clearly ascertained and defined. Consequently, if the donor makes a gift of a certain portion of his property without specifying which, or if he makes a gift of one of two horses, such gift is invalid. If the donor makes a gift of a horse by telling the recipient that he may take whichever he likes of two horses, and the recipient at the time the gift is made states which one of the two he selects, such gift is valid. If the recipient selects the one he wants after the meeting at which the gift has been made, however, such selection is invalid.

Article 859. The donor must be of sound mind and must have arrived at the age of puberty. Consequently, a gift made by a minor, or a madman, or an imbecile is invalid. A gift however, may validly be bestowed upon such person.

Article 860. The donor must assent to the gift. Consequently, a gift made as a result of force or constraint is invalid.

CHAPTER II.

FUNDAMENTAL RULES RELATING TO GIFT.

SECTION I.

Revocation of a gift.

Article 861. The recipient becomes owner of the property bestowed by way of gift upon taking delivery thereof.

Article 862. The donor may revoke the gift of his own accord before delivery thereof is taken.

Article 863. If the donor forbids the recipient to take delivery after making an offer of the property, he revokes the gift.

Article 864. The donor may revoke the gift or present after delivery has been taken, provided the recipient agrees thereto. If the recipient does not agree, the owner may apply to the Court, and the Court may cancel the gift in the absence of any prohibition contained in the following Articles, but not otherwise.

GIFT

Article 865. If the donor takes back the gift after delivery has been taken thereof without the assent of the recipient, or of an order of the Court, he becomes a person wrongfully appropriating property; and if the gift is destroyed or lost while in his possession, he must make good the loss.

Article 866. If a person makes a gift of anything to his ascendants or descendants, or to his brother, sister, or to their children or to his uncle and aunt, he may not revoke such gift.

Article 867. If either husband or wife make a gift to each other during the subsistence of the marriage and hand such gift over, they may in no way revoke such gift.

Article 868. If something is given on account of the gift and is received by the donor, the donor may not revoke such gift. Consequently, if something is given to the donor on account of the gift, whether by the recipient or by some other person, and the donor takes delivery thereof, he may not revoke such gift.

Article 869. In cases where something is added to and becomes part of the gift, as where the property bestowed by way of gift consists of land, and the person in whose favour the gift is made erects buildings or plants trees thereon; or where the gift consists of a lean animal and the person in whose favour the gift is made fattens such animal; or where the gift is altered in such a way that its name is changed, as where corn is ground into flour, the gift may not validly be revoked. But an increase which is not part of the gift in no way prevents revocation. Consequently, if a mare which is bestowed by way of gift to a certain person becomes in foal, the gift may not be revoked. But after the mare has foaled, the gift may be revoked. In that case the foal belongs to the person in whose favour the gift has been made.

Article 870. If the person in whose favour the gift has been made divests himself of the ownership therein by selling such gift or making a gift thereof, and delivering the same, the donor has no right of revoking the gift.

Article 871. If the gift has been destroyed while in the possession of the person in whose favour the gift has been made, such gift may not be revoked.

Article 872. In the event of the death of either the donor or the person in whose favour the gift has been made, the gift may not be revoked. Consequently, if the person in whose favour the gift has been made dies, the donor may not revoke the gift; and if the donor dies his heirs cannot claim the return of the gift.

Article 873. If a creditor makes a gift of a sum owing to him by a person who is indebted to him, he can in no case revoke the gift. (See Articles 51 and 848).

Article 874. A gift made by way of alms cannot be revoked once delivery thereof has been taken.

Article 875. If a person allows some other person to consume certain food, the latter, after receiving it, may not deal with it in a manner indicative of a right of ownership, as by selling it, or by making a gift of it to some third person. He may, however, eat such food, and the owner cannot later claim the value thereof.

Example:-
A eats a quantity of grapes in a vineyard with the permission of the owner thereof. The owner may not later claim the value of such grapes.

Article 876. Presents made on the occasion of circumcision or marriage ceremonies belong to those persons for whom they were intended by the owners thereof, whether for the child, or the bride, or the father, or the mother. If they fail to state for whom they were brought and the point cannot be settled by inquiry from them, the question will be dealt with in accordance with local custom.

SECTION II.

Gifts made during the course of a mortal sickness.

Article 877. If a person who is without an heir makes a gift of the whole of his possessions to some other person during the course of a mortal sickness and delivers the same, such gift is valid, and the Treasury has no right of interfering with the estate after his decease.

Article 878. If a husband who has no heir apart from his wife, or a wife who has no heir other than her husband, makes a gift of the whole of his or her possessions to the wife or husband respectively during the course of a mortal sickness and delivers the same, such gift is valid, and the Treasury has no right of interfering with the estate of either of them after their decease.

Article 879. If any person makes a gift to one of his heirs during the course of a mortal sickness, and then dies, such gift is not valid unless ratified by the other heirs. If the gift, however, is made and delivered to some person other than an heir, and the gift does not exceed one third of the estate, such gift is valid. If it exceeds one third, however, and the heirs do not ratify the gift, such gift is valid in respect to one third of the estate, and the person in whose favour the gift is made must return the balance.

Article 880. If a person whose estate is overwhelmed by debts makes a gift of his property during the

220   GIFT

course of a mortal sickness to his heir, or to some other person, and delivers the same and then dies, the creditors may disregard the gift and may divide such property between them in proportion to their claims.

Promulgated by Royal Iradah 29th Muharram, 1289.

BOOK VIII.

WRONGFUL APPROPRIATION AND DESTRUCTION

BOOK VIII

WRONGFUL APPROPRIATION AND DESTRUCTION.

INTRODUCTION.

TERMS OF MUHAMMADAN JURISPRUDENCE.

Article 881. Wrongful appropriation consists of taking and keeping the property of another, without that person's permission. The person taking such property is called the person wrongfully appropriating property. The property itself is called the property wrongfully appropriated. The owner of such property is called the person whose property has been wrongfully appropriated.

Article 882. Standing value is the value of buildings and trees as they stand in the ground. The value of the land is estimated first together with the buildings and trees and then without the buildings and trees. The difference between the two valuations is called the standing value of the buildings and trees.

Article 883. The building value is the standing value of buildings.

Article 884. The pulled-down value is the value of the debris of the buildings after they have been pulled down and of the trees after they have been uprooted.

Article 885. The pulling-down value is the pulled-down value after deducting therefrom the cost of pulling down buildings or uprooting trees.

Article 886. The minus value of land consists of the difference between the rent of a piece of land before cultivation and after cultivation.

Article 887. Direct destruction consists of the destruction of a thing by a person himself. The person destroying the thing is called the actual doer of the act.

Article 888. Indirect destruction consists of being the cause of the destruction of a thing. That is to say, to do an act which causes the destruction of another thing in the normal course of events. The person performing such act is called the person causing the destruction.

Examples:-

(1) The cord of a hanging lamp is cut. The lamp falls to the ground and is broken. The person cutting the cord is the direct cause of the destruction of the cord and is the indirect cause of the destruction of the lamp.

(2) A person splits a water-skin in half and oil contained therein escapes and is lost. Such person is the direct cause of the destruction of the water-skin and the indirect cause of the destruction of the oil.

Article 889. Prior warning consists of giving warning and recommendation before taking action, with a view to preventing the occurrence of any probable injury.

CHAPTER I.
WRONGFUL APPROPRIATION
SECTION 1.
Wrongful appropriation in general.

Article 890. If the wrongfully appropriated property exists in its original state, such property must be restored to the owner thereof at the place where it was wrongfully taken. If the owner meets the person who has wrongfully appropriated the property in some other place, and the wrongfully appropriated property is with him, the owner may, if he wishes, demand the return of the property there. If he asks for the property to be handed over at the place where the wrongful appropriation occurred, the

WRONGFUL APPROPRIATION

expenses occasioned by handing over and transport fall upon the person who has wrongfully appropriated the property.

Article 891. If the person who has wrongfully appropriated property destroys the same, he must make good the loss occasioned thereby. He is also liable to make good the loss if such property is destroyed or lost with or without his fault. Thus, he must pay the value thereof if such property is of the sort the like of which cannot be found in the market, as at the time and place at which the wrongful appropriation occurred, and give a similar article if the like of it can be found in the market.

Article 892. If the person wrongfully appropriating property returns the identical property to the owner thereof at the place where the wrongful appropriation occurred, he is free from all liability to make compensation.

Article 893. If the person who has wrongfully appropriated property places such property before the owner thereof in such a way that he can take possession of it, the property in question is deemed to have been restored, even though the owner may not actually have taken delivery thereof.

If such person places the value of property which has been wrongfully appropriated and which has been destroyed before the owner thereof, he is not free from liability to make good the loss until the owner has taken delivery thereof.

Article 894. If the person who has wrongfully appropriated some specific piece of property delivers such property to the owner thereof in a dangerous place, the owner has the right of refusing to accept it. In such case, the person who has wrongfully appropriated the property is not freed from the liability of making good any loss.

226   WRONGFUL APPROPRIATION

Article 895. If the person who has wrongfully appropriated property which has been destroyed, tenders the value thereof to the owner, who refuses to accept the same, such person may apply to the Court for an order for acceptance.

Article 896. If the person whose property has been wrongfully appropriated is a minor, the person who has wrongfully appropriated may validly restore such property to the minor, provided the latter is of perfect understanding and capable of preserving the property, but not otherwise.

Article 897. If the property wrongfully appropriated consists of fruit and the condition thereof changes while in the possession of the person who has wrongfully appropriated such property, such as by becoming dry, the owner has the option either of claiming the return of the identical property wrongfully appropriated, or of asking for the value thereof to be paid.

Article 898. If the person wrongfully appropriating property in any way changes the nature of such property by adding thereto anything of his own, the person whose property has been wrongfully appropriated has the option either of claiming the value of such property, or of asking for the return of the identical property after paying the value of the increase.

Example :-
    A wrongfully appropriates cloth and dyes the same. The owner thereof has the option either of claiming the value of the cloth or of asking for the return of the cloth itself after paying the price of the dye.

Article 899. If the person wrongfully appropriating property alters such property in such a way that the name thereof is changed, he is bound to make good the loss and keep the property himself.

Examples :-

(1) A wrongfully appropriates certain wheat and grinds it into flour. He is obliged to make good the loss and the flour becomes his property.

(2) A wrongfully appropriates wheat and sows it in his own field. He is obliged to make good the loss and the crops become his property.

Article 900. If the price and value of a thing decrease after the wrongful appropriation thereof, the owner may not refuse to accept it and claim the value thereof at the time such thing was wrongfully appropriated. But if the value of such thing decreases by reason of the use thereof by the person who has wrongfully appropriated such property, such loss must be made good.

Examples :-

(1) A wrongfully appropriates an animal and restores such animal to its owner in a weakened condition. A is bound to make good the decrease in the value of the animal.

(2) A wrongfully appropriates clothes and tears them, thereby decreasing their value. If the decrease is of small amount, that is to say, if it does not amount to one fourth of the value of the property wrongfully appropriated, the person wrongfully appropriating such property is liable to make good the loss. But if the decrease in value is of great amount, that is to say, if it is equal to or exceeds one fourth of the value thereof, the person from whom such property has been wrongfully appropriated has the option either of claiming to have the amount of the decrease in value made good, or of abandoning the property to the person wrongfully appropriating it and claiming the full value thereof.

Article 901. Any act whereby a person is deprived of his power to deal with his own property and which results in a situation equivalent to that created by wrongful appropriation is considered to amount to wrongful

228   WRONGFUL APPROPRIATION

appropriation. Thus, if a person to whom property has been entrusted for safe keeping denies such trust, such act amounts to wrongful appropriation, and if thereafter the property entrusted to him is destroyed without his fault, he is liable to make good the loss.

Article 902. If any person is deprived of possession of his property held in absolute ownership without any intention of being so deprived, as where a garden situated upon a mountain subsides and falls upon another garden situated below it, the property which is of lesser value is subject to that which is of greater value. That is to say, the owner of property which is greater in value is bound to indemnify the owner of property which is of lesser value, and becomes owner of such property.

Examples :-
(1) If the value of the garden situated above is worth five hundred piastres and that of the garden situated below is worth one thousand piastres before the collapse of the mountain, the owner of the latter, by paying the owner of the former five hundred piastres, may take over the first garden.

(2) The owner of a pearl worth fifty piastres drops it and it is swallowed by a hen worth five piastres. The owner of the pearl may take the hen upon payment of five piastres. (See Articles 27, 28 and 29).

Article 903. Any increase in the property wrongfully appropriated belongs to the owner thereof. If the person wrongfully appropriating such property consumes such increase, he is bound to make good the loss.

Examples :-
(1) The milk and young of an animal wrongfully appropriated and which are produced while in the possession of the person wrongfully appropriating them, and the fruit produced in a garden while in the possession of a person who has wrongfully appropriated

such garden, are the property of the owner of the things wrongfully appropriated; and if the person wrongfully appropriating them consumes them, he is liable to make good the loss.

(2) A wrongfully appropriates a hive belonging to B together with the bees therein. The owner, when recovering the hive together with the bees, is also entitled to take the honey produced while in the possession of A.

Article 904. The honey of bees which make their home in a garden belongs to the owner of the garden. If any other person takes and consumes such honey, he is liable to make good the loss.

SECTION II.

Wrongful appropriation of real property.

Article 905. If the property wrongfully appropriated is real property, the person wrongfully appropriating such property is bound to restore it to the owner thereof without any change or decrease.

If the real property wrongfully appropriated is decreased in value by the act of the person wrongfully appropriating such property, he is bound to make good the decrease in value.

Examples :-

(1) A wrongfully appropriates a house and destroys a part thereof, or ruins it by living in it. If the value thereof is decreased, he is bound to make good the amount of such decrease.

(2) If a person wrongfully appropriating a house destroys it by lighting a fire therein, he is bound to make good the building value of such house.

Article 906. If the property wrongfully appropriated is land and the person wrongfully appropriating such

230 WRONGFUL APPROPRIATION

property constructs buildings or plants trees thereon, such person shall be ordered to restore such land after uprooting the trees or pulling down the buildings.

If the fact of pulling down the buildings or of uprooting the trees causes injury to the land, the person whose land has been wrongfully appropriated may take possession of such buildings or trees upon paying the pulling-down value thereof.

If the value of the buildings and trees is greater than that of the land, however, and such buildings or trees have been constructed or planted under the belief that there was some legal justification for so doing, the owner of the buildings or trees may claim to be vested with the ownership of the land, upon paying the price thereof.

Example :-
>A inherits a piece of land from his father and erects buildings thereon for a cash expenditure exceeding the value of the land. Thereupon, a person who has a right to that land appears and claims it. A is entitled to take possession of the land upon paying the price thereof.

Article 907. If a person wrongfully appropriates a piece of land belonging to another and cultivates it, and the owner obtains the return thereof, the latter is also entitled to be indemnified for any decrease in the value of the land arising out of such cultivation.

Similarly, if a person who is joint owner with another of a piece of land cultivates that land alone without the permission of the other, such person's co-owner is entitled, upon taking his share of the land, to be compensated, in respect to his share, for any decrease in the value of the land caused by the other co-owner's cultivation.

Article 908. If a person wrongfully appropriates a field belonging to another and clears it, and the owner thereafter retakes possession of such field, such person has no right of claiming the cost of clearing the land from the owner thereof.

Article 909. If any person occupies a piece of land belonging to another and places sweepings or similar refuse thereon, such person shall be obliged to remove such matter, and to evacuate the land.

SECTION III.

Wrongful appropriation from a person who has already wrongfully appropriated property.

Article 910. Any person who wrongfully appropriates property from a person who has already wrongfully appropriated such property is considered to be in the same position as the first person wrongfully appropriating the property. Consequently, if property already wrongfully appropriated is again wrongfully appropriated from the first person by some other person and is destroyed by him or while in his possession, the person from whom the property has been wrongfully appropriated has the option of claiming to have his loss made good either by the first or second person who has wrongfully appropriated such property. He also has the option of claiming a portion of the value of the property from the first and a portion from the second person wrongfully appropriating such property. If the first person wrongfully appropriating such property makes good the loss thereof, such person has a right of recourse against the second. If the second person, however, makes good the loss, such person has no right of recourse against the first.

Article 911. If the second person wrongfully appropriating property restores it to the first person who has wrongfully appropriated such property, the former alone is free from liability in connection therewith. If he returns it to the person from whom the property has been wrongfully appropriated, however, both persons are free from liability.

CHAPTER II.

DESTRUCTION OF PROPERTY.

SECTION I.

Direct destruction of property.

Article 912. If any person destroys property of another, whether intentionally or unintentionally, and whether in his own possession or in that of some person to whom it has been entrusted, such person must make good the loss occasioned thereby.

If any person destroys property which has been wrongfully appropriated while in the possession of the person who has wrongfully appropriated it, the owner of the property may claim to have the loss made good by the person who has wrongfully appropriated such property, who in turn has a right of recourse against the person who destroyed the property, or he can claim to have the loss made good by him. The latter, however, has no right of recourse against the person wrongfully appropriating the property.

Article 913. If a person slips and falls upon and destroys any property belonging to another, he is bound to make good the loss.

Article 914. If any person destroys the property of any other person under the mistaken belief that it is his own, he must make good the loss occasioned thereby.

Article 915. If any person drags the clothes of another and tears them, he must make good the full value

DESTRUCTION OF PROPERTY 233

thereof. If a person takes hold of the clothes of another, and the owner of such clothes drags them and tears them, however, such person is liable to make good half the value thereof.

Similarly, if any person sits upon the skirt of another, and the owner, unaware thereof, gets up, and tears his clothes, such person must make good half the value of the clothes.

Article 916. If a minor destroys the property of another, he must make good the loss thereof out of his own property. If he is not possessed of any property, payment may be postponed until he is in a position to pay. His tutor may not be called upon to make good the loss.

Article 917. If any person causes any diminution in value of the property of another, he must make good the amount of such loss.

Article 918. If any person without justification knocks down the real property of another, such as a house or a shop, the owner of such property has the option either of abandoning the *débris* of such real property to the person who has knocked it down and of claiming the building value thereof from him, or of deducting the value of the *débris* from the building value of such real property and of claiming the value of the remainder, keeping the *débris*. If the person wrongfully appropriating such property rebuilds the property and restores it to its original state, he is not liable to make conpensation.

Article 919. Should fire break out in any particular place and should any person pull down a house without the permission of the owner thereof, and the fire is stopped, such person is not liable to make good the loss occasioned thereby, provided he has pulled down the house

234   DESTRUCTION OF PROPERTY

by order of the authorities. If the pulls down the house on his own initiative, however, he must make good the loss.

Article 920. If any person without any justification cuts down the trees in the garden of another, the owner has the option of claiming the standing value of such trees and of abandoning them to the person who has cut them down, or of deducting the cut-down value from the standing value and of claiming the balance together with the trees cut down.

Example :-

If the value of the garden with the trees standing amounts to ten thousand piastres and without the trees to five thousand piastres, and the value of the trees when cut down to two thousand piastres, the owner has the option of leaving the trees cut down to the person who has felled them, and of taking five thousand piastres, or of taking three thousand piastres, keeping the trees cut down.

Article 921. The fact that a person has suffered an injury does not authorize that person to inflict an injury upon another person.

Examples :-

(1) A destroys the property of B. If B in turn destroys the property of A, both persons are liable to make good the loss they have caused.

(2) A member of one tribe destroys the property of a member of another tribe. The latter destroys the property of another member of the first tribe. Both persons are liable to make good the loss they have caused.

(3) A is given counterfeited money by B. B may not pass the money on to another person.

DESTRUCTION OF PROPERTY

SECTION II.

Indirect destruction of property.

Article 922. If a person is the cause of the destruction of the property of another, or of any decrease in the value thereof, that is to say, if his own act is the cause leading to the destruction or decrease in value of such property, such person must make good the loss.

Examples :-

(1) A quarrels with B. During the quarrel A seizes hold of B's clothes, and an object in B's clothes falls to the ground and is destroyed or damaged. A is bound to make good the loss.

(2) A without any justification cuts off the water in B's field or garden. If the crops and plantations dry up and are destroyed, or if A lets the water overflow into the garden of another and swamps his crops, causing them to be destroyed, A must make good the loss.

(3) A opens the door of B's stable. An animal therein runs away and is lost. A must make good the loss.

(4) A opens the door of a cage belonging to B. A bird therein flies away. A must make good the loss.

Article 923. If an animal takes fright at a particular person and runs away and is lost, such person is not obliged to make good the loss. But if such person intentionally frightens such animal, he is bound to make good the loss. Similarly, if an animal takes fright at the noise of a gun fired by a huntsman when hunting and runs away, and while doing so, falls and is killed or breaks its leg, the huntsman is not liable to make good the loss. But if the latter fires his gun with the intention of frightening the animal, he is bound to make good the loss. (See Article 93).

Article 924. The liability of a person who is the cause of an act, as referred to above, to make good any loss sustained thereby, depends upon such act being of a wrongful nature. That is to say, the liability of a person who causes an injury to be sustained to make good the loss caused thereby, is dependent upon the act which led to such injury being performed by him without any justification.

Example :-

A without permission from any public authority digs a well in the public highway. An animal belonging to B falls therein and is destroyed. A must make good the loss. But if A digs a well in his own land held in absolute ownership and B's animal falls therein and is destroyed, A is not liable to make good the loss.

Article 925. If a person performs any act which is the cause of the destruction of a thing and meanwhile some voluntary act supervenes, that is to say, if some other person directly destroys that thing, the author of such voluntary act is liable to make good the loss. (See Article 90).

SECTION III.

Matters occurring in the public highway.

Article 926. Every person has a right of way on the public highway, subject to the safety of others. That is to say, provided no harm is caused to others in circumstances which can be avoided.

Examples :-

(1) If a porter drops the load he is carrying on the public highway and destroys the property of another, the porter must make good the loss.

(2) If sparks fly from a blacksmith's shop while he is working iron and set fire to the clothes of a passer-

by in the public highway, the blacksmith must make good the loss.

Article 927. No person may set up in the public highway for the purpose of buying and selling without the permission of the public authorities, nor may he place or produce anything there without permission. If he does so, he is bound to make good any injury or loss which may be caused thereby.

Examples:-
(1) A piles up wood or stones in the public highway. B's animal treads thereon, slips and is destroyed. A must make good the loss.

(2) A drops a slippery substance such as oil on the public highway. B's animal slips thereon and is destroyed. A must make good the loss.

Article 928. If a wall belonging to a particular person falls down and causes damage to any other person, the owner of the wall is under no necessity to make good the loss. But if some other person has previously warned the owner to knock down the wall as it is likely to collapse, and sufficient time has elapsed for the wall to be knocked down, the owner is then obliged to make good the loss. Provided always that the person giving such warning has the right to do so. Thus, if the wall has collapsed on to a neighbour's house, the person giving the warning must be one of the inhabitants of that house. A warning given by a person outside is of no effect. If the wall collapses on to a private road, the person giving the warning must be a person having a right of way over such road. If it collapses on the public highway, any person whatsoever has the right of giving the warning.

INJURY BY ANIMALS

SECTION IV.

Injury caused by animals.

Article 929. The owner of an animal is not liable to make good any damage caused by the animal of its own volition. (See Article 94). But if an animal consumes the property of some other person and the owner of the animal is cognizant thereof and takes no steps to prevent the injury, the owner is bound to make good the loss. But if the owner of an animal known to be of a destructive character such as a bull which gores, or a dog which bites, is warned by one of the inhabitants of the district or village to tie up such animal, and the owner nevertheless lets him go loose and he destroys the animal or property of some other person, the owner is bound to make good the loss.

Article 930. If an animal, whether ridden by its owner or not, and while on land owned by him in absolute ownership, injures any other person by striking such person with his fore feet, or with his head, or tail, or by kicking with his hind legs, the owner of such animal is not liable to make good the loss.

Article 931. If any person causes any animal to enter the property held in absolute ownership belonging to another, having obtained the permission of the owner of such property to do so, such animal is regarded as being on such person's land, and the owner is not liable to make good the loss in respect to any injury caused by such animal, as set forth in the preceding Article. If the owner has caused the animal to enter without such permission, he is liable in any case to make good any damage caused, whether riding, leading or driving, or even when not near to such animal.

But if an animal breaks loose and enters the property of another held in absolute ownership and does damage thereon of its own accord, the owner is not liable to make good the loss.

Article 932. Every person has a right of way with his animal over the public highway. Consequently, if anyone rides his animal on the public highway, he is not liable to make good any injury or loss which he could not have avoided.

Example:
If dirt and mud are scattered about by the hoofs of an animal and another person's clothes are splashed therewith; or if such animal kicks with his hind legs or swishes his tail and inflicts injury thereby, there is no need to make good the loss. But a person riding an animal is responsible for collision or for blows inflicted by the fore feet or the head.

Article 933. Any person leading and any person driving an animal in the public highway is considered to be the same as a person riding such animal. That is to say, they are only obliged to make good any loss sustained to the extent that the person riding the animal is so obliged.

Article 934. No person has the right of stopping or of tying up his animal in the public highway. Consequently, if any person stops his animal or ties it up in the public highway and such animal kicks with his fore or hind legs, or inflicts injuries in any other way, such person is in every case obliged to make good the loss caused by such animal. An exception, however, is made in the case of places specially set aside for animals, such as horse-markets and places for animals sent out on hire.

Article 935. If any person turns his animal loose on the public highway he is responsible for any injury caused by such animal.

R

INJURY BY ANIMALS

Article 936. If an animal ridden by any person tramples upon anything with either his fore or hind legs, whether upon his own property or upon that of any other person and such thing is destroyed, such person is considered to have directly destroyed it and in every case is bound to make good the loss.

Article 937. If the animal does not take the bit, and the rider is unable to hold his head, and injury is caused by such animal, the rider is not responsible therefor.

Article 938. If any person ties his animal up in his own property and a second person arrives and likewise ties up his animal there without permission, and the animal belonging to the owner of the property kicks and destroys the animal belonging to such second person, the owner of the first animal need not make good the loss.

If the animal belonging to the second person destroys the animal of the owner of the property, the second person must make good the loss.

Article 939. If two persons have the right of tying up their animals in one place, and having done so, one of them destroys the other, there is no need to make good the loss.

Example :-

> Two persons who are joint owners of a house tie up their animals in a certain place in such house and while there the animal belonging to one of them destroys the animal belonging to the other. The owner of the animal inflicting the injury is not liable to make good the loss.

Article 940. If two persons tie up their animals in a place where they have no right to do so and the animal belonging to the first person who ties up his animal destroys the animal belonging to the second, the first person is not obliged to make good the loss. But if the animal belonging to the second person who so ties up his animal destroys the animal belonging to the first, the second person must make good the loss.

Promulgated by Royal Iradah, 23rd Rabi ul Akhra, 1289.

BOOK IX.

INTERDICTION, CONSTRAINT AND PRE-EMPTION.

BOOK IX.

INTERDICTION, CONSTRAINT AND PRE-EMPTION.

INTRODUCTION.

TERMS OF MUHAMMADAN JURISPRUDENCE RELATING TO INTERDICTION, CONSTRAINT AND PRE-EMPTION.

Article 941. Interdiction consists of prohibiting any particular person from dealing with his own property. After interdiction, such person is called an interdicted person.

Article 942. By permission is meant removing the interdiction and destroying the right of prohibition. The person to whom such permission is given is called the permitted person.

Article 943. A minor of imperfect understanding is a young person who does not understand selling and buying, that is to say, who does not understand that ownership is lost by sale and acquired by purchase, and who is unable to distinguish obvious flagrant misrepresentation, that is misrepresentation amounting to five in ten, from minor misrepresentation. A minor who can distinguish between these matters is called a young person of perfect understanding.

Article 944. Lunatics are divided into two classes, The first consists of persons who are continuously mad and whose madness lasts the whole time. The second class consists of persons whose madness is intermittent. that is to say, persons who are sometimes mad and sometimes sane.

246 INTERDICTION, CONSTRAINT, PRE-EMPTION

Article 945. An imbecile is a person whose mind is so deranged that his comprehension is extremely limited, his speech confused, and whose actions are imperfect.

Article 946. A prodigal person is a person who by reckless expenditure wastes and destroys his property to no purpose. Persons who are deceived in their business owing to their being stupid or simple-minded are also considered to be prodigal persons.

Article 947. A person of mature mind is a person who is able to take control of his own property and who does not waste it to no purpose.

Article 948. Constraint consists of wrongfully forcing a person through fear to do something without his own consent. (*)

Article 949. Constraint is divided into two classes. The first class consists of major constraint, whereby the death of a person or the loss of a limb is caused. The second consists of minor constraint whereby grief or pain alone is caused, such as assault or imprisonment.

Article 950. Pre-emption consists of acquiring possession of a piece of property held in absolute ownership which has been purchased, by paying the purchaser the amount he gave for it.

Article 951. The pre-emptor is the person enjoying the right of pre-emption.

Article 952. The subject of pre-emption is real property to which the right of pre-emption is attached.

Article 953. The subject matter of pre-emption is the property held in absolute ownership of the pre-emptor in virtue of which the right of pre-emption is exercised.

(*) The translation of certain technical terms in this Article has been omitted as having no meaning for the English reader.

Article 954. A joint owner of a servitude is a person who shares with another in rights over property held in absolute ownership, such as a share in water, or a share in a road.

Article 955. A private right of taking water is a right of taking water from some flowing water reserved for a limited number of persons. But the right of taking water from rivers used by the public does not belong to this class.

Article 956. A private road is a road from which there is no exit.

CHAPTER I.

MATTERS RELATING TO INTERDICTION.

SECTION I.

Classes of interdicted persons and matters relating thereto.

Article 957. Minors, lunatics and imbeciles are *ipso facto* interdicted.

Article 958. A person who is a prodigal may be interdicted by the Court.

Article 959. A person who is in debt may also be interdicted by the Court upon the application of the creditors.

Article 960. Any disposition of property such as sale and purchase on the part of interdicted persons referred to in the preceding Articles, is invalid. Such persons, moreover, must immediately make good any loss caused by their own acts.

Example :-
> If A, even though he be a young person of imperfect understanding, destroys property belonging to B, he must make good the loss.

Article 961. Upon the Court declaring a prodigal and a person in debt to be interdicted, the reason for such interdiction must be given, and announced in public.

Article 962. It is not essential that the person whom the Court intends to interdict should be present. He may validly be interdicted in his absence. Such person must, however, be informed of the interdiction; and the interdiction does not take effect until he has been so informed. Consequently, any contracts or admissions made by him up to that date are valid.

Article 963. Provided he has not squandered his property, a person of dissolute character may not be interdicted solely by reason of his dissolute conduct.

Article 964. Persons who cause injury to the public, such as an ignorant physician, may also be interdicted. In such cases, however, the object of the interdiction is to restrain them from practice, and not to prohibit them from dealing with their property.

Article 965. No person who carries on business or trade in the market may be restrained from carrying on the same by reason of the fact that other persons carrying on such business or trade allege that their work is being ruined thereby.

SECTION II.

Matters relating to minors, lunatics and imbeciles.

Article 966. A minor of imperfect understanding may not in any manner make any valid disposition of his property, even though his tutor assents thereto.

Article 967. Any disposition of property entered into by a minor of perfect understanding, which is purely for his own benefit, such as the acceptance of gifts and presents, is valid, even though his tutor does not assent thereto. Any disposition of property, however, which is purely to his own disadvantage, such as bestowing a thing upon another by way of gift, is invalid, even though the tutor assents thereto. But in the case of contracts where it is not certain whether they will be for his benefit or disadvantage, such contracts are concluded subject to the permission of the tutor. The tutor has the option of giving or withholding his consent. Thus, if he thinks that it is to the advantage of the minor, he will give his consent, and not otherwise.

Example :-
> A minor of perfect understanding sells certain property without permission. The execution of the sale is subject to the assent of his tutor, even though he has sold it for a price which is greater than the value thereof, the reason being that the contract of sale is one where it is not certain whether it will be for his advantage or disadvantage.

Article 968. A tutor may give a minor of perfect understanding a portion of his property on trial with which to engage in business, and if it turns out as a result that he is of mature mind, he may deliver him the balance of such property.

Article 969. The repeated conclusion of contracts from which the intention to make profit may be inferred, amounts to permission to engage in business.

Example :-
> A tutor tells a minor to engage in business, or to buy and sell property of a certain nature. This amounts to permission to engage in business. But if he merely authorizes him to conclude a single contract, as where he states that certain things are to be found in the

market and tells him to buy them, or tells him to sell a certain thing, such act does not amount to permission to engage in business, but the tutor is considered to have employed such minor as agent in accordance with custom.

Article 970. Permission given by the tutor may not be made subject to any condition as to time and place, or limited to any particular type of business.

Examples :-

(1) The tutor gives permission to a minor of perfect understanding for a period of one day or one month. The minor has full and absolute permission, and may act for all time, until the tutor makes him interdicted.

(2) The tutor tells the minor to engage in trade in a certain market. The minor may engage in trade anywhere.

(3) The tutor tells the minor to buy and sell property of a particular sort. The minor may buy and sell any sort of property.

Article 971. Permission may be given explicitly or by implication.

Example :-

A minor of perfect understanding engages in business with the knowledge of his tutor, who makes no comment thereon and does not prohibit him from so doing. The tutor has given his permission by implication.

Article 972. When permission is given to a minor by his tutor, such minor is considered to have arrived at the age of puberty in respect to the matters included in the permission. Contracts such as those relating to sale and hire are valid.

Article 973. A tutor who has given permission to a minor may later revoke such permission by making the minor interdicted, but the interdiction must take the same form as the permission.

INTERDICTION

Example:

A tutor gives a general permission to a minor to engage in business. After this permission has become known to people in the market, he wishes to make the minor interdicted. The interdiction must in the same way be made general, and must be made known to the majority of people in the market. It is not enough for him to be made interdicted in his own house in the presence of two or three persons.

Article 974. The tutor of a minor in this connection is:

(1) His father.

(2) If his father is dead, the guardian chosen, that is to say, the guardian chosen and appointed by the father during his lifetime.

(3) If the guardian chosen is dead, then the guardian appointed by him during his lifetime.

(4) The true ancestor, that is to say, the father of the father of the minor, or the father of the father of his father.

(5) The guardian chosen and appointed by such ancestor during his lifetime.

(6) The guardian appointed by such guardian.

(7) The Court, or the guardian appointed, that is to say, the guardian appointed by the Court.

Any permission given by a brother, or an uncle, or other relative who are not guardians, is invalid.

Article 975. If the Court deems it in the interest of a minor that he be allowed to dispose of property, and a senior tutor of such minor refuses to give permission, the Court may give the minor permission to do so, and no other tutor may under any circumstances make such minor interdicted.

Article 976. In the event of the death of a tutor who has given permission to a minor, the permission which he has given becomes void. But permission given by the Court does not become null and void by reason of the death or dismissal of the judge.

Article 977. A minor who has been granted permission by the Court may be interdicted by such Court or by the successor of the judge who granted such permission. The father, or any other tutor, however, may not make the minor interdicted after the death or dismissal of such judge.

Article 978. An imbecile is considered to be a minor of perfect understanding.

Article 979. Lunatics who are continuously mad are considered to be minors of imperfect understanding.

Article 980. Acts of disposition over property by lunatics who are not continuously mad, and performed during a lucid interval, are like acts of disposition over property performed by a sane person.

Article 981. When a young person arrives at the age of puberty, there should be no undue haste in handing his property to him, but his capacity should be put to the test, and if it turns out that he is of mature mind, his property should then be given to him.

Article 982. If a young person who is not of mature mind arrives at the age of puberty, his property should not be handed to him and he should be prohibited as previously from dealing therewith, until it has been proved that he is of mature mind.

Article 983. If property is handed by a guardian to a minor before it has been proved that he is of mature mind, and such property is lost while in the possession of the minor, or the minor destroys the same, the guardian must make good the loss.

INTERDICTION

Article 984. If property is handed to a minor upon his reaching the age of puberty, and it is later proved that he is a prodigal, such person shall be interdicted by the Court.

Article 985. Puberty is proved by the emission of seed during dreams, by the power to make pregnant, by menstruation, and by the capacity to conceive.

Article 986. The commencement of the age of puberty in the case of males is twelve years completed and in the case of females nine years completed. The termination of the age of puberty in both cases is fifteen years completed. If a male on reaching twelve years and a female on reaching nine years completed have not arrived at the age of puberty, they are said to be approaching puberty until such time as they do in fact arrive at the age of puberty.

Article 987. Any person who upon reaching the termination of the age of puberty, shows no signs of puberty, is considered in law to have arrived at the age of puberty.

Article 988. If any young person who has not arrived at the commencement of the age of puberty brings an action to prove that he has in fact arrived at the age of puberty, such action shall not be heard.

Article 989. If a male or female approaching the age of puberty admit in Court that they have arrived at the age of puberty, and the condition of their bodies shows that their admission is false, such admission shall not be confirmed. If, however, the condition of their bodies shows that their admission is true, their admission shall be confirmed, and their contracts and admissions are executory and valid. If such persons later state that at

254 INTERDICTION

the time they made the admission they had not arrived at the age of puberty, and seek to annul any disposition they may have made over their property, no attention shall be paid thereto.

SECTION III.

Interdicted prodigals.

Article 990. An interdicted prodigal is, as regards his civil transactions, like a minor of perfect understanding. The Court alone, however, may be the tutor of the prodigal. The father, ancestor and guardians have no right of tutorship over him.

Article 991. Any disposition of property by the prodigal after interdiction as regards his civil transactions are invalid. Any such dispositions made prior to the interdiction are the same as those of other people.

Article 992. Any expenditure necessary for the interdicted prodigal or for those dependent upon him for support may be made from his own property.

Article 993. If the interdicted prodigal sells property, such sale is not executory. If the Court thinks that any benefit may be derived therefrom, however, it may validate such sale.

Article 994. An admission made by an interdicted prodigal of a debt due to another is absolutely invalid, that is to say, any admission made in respect to property in existence at the time the interdiction was declared, or accruing thereafter, is without effect.

Article 995. Any claim which any person may have against an interdicted prodigal shall be paid from the prodigal's property.

Article 996. If an interdicted prodigal borrows money and uses it for his personal expenditure, and the amount thereof is not excessive, the Court shall repay such money from the prodigal's property. If it is excessive, however, the Court shall estimate the amount necessary for his maintenance and disallow the rest.

Article 997. If the interdicted prodigal reforms, the interdiction may be removed by the Court.

SECTION IV.

Interdiction of debtors.

Article 998. If it is clear to the Court that the debtor is putting off paying his creditors, although he is able to pay, and the creditors ask the Court to sell the property of the debtor and pay his debts therefrom, the Court shall prohibit the debtor from dealing with his property.

Should the debtor himself refuse to sell his property and pay his debts therefrom, the Court shall do so. The Court shall begin by selling those things which are most advantageous to the debtor

The Court shall first deal with the cash assets and if these are not sufficient the merchandise, and if that is not sufficient, the real property of the debtor.

Article 999. If the debtor is bankrupt, that is to say, if his debts are equal to or exceed his property, and the creditors fear that his property will be lost by trading, or that he will dispose of his property in fraud of his creditors, or that he will make it over to some other person, they may make application to the Court and ask for such person to be prohibited from dealing with his property or admitting a debt to some other person, and the Court shall then declare the debtor to be interdicted and shall sell his property and divide the proceeds among the creditors. One or two suits of clothes shall be left for the debtor. If the debtor's clothes, however, are expensive, and it is possible to do with less expensive clothes, such clothes shall be sold and a suit of cheap clothes shall be bought from the sum realized and the balance shall be paid to the creditors. Again, if the debtor has a large country house and a smaller one is sufficient for him, such country house shall be sold and a suitable dwelling purchased from the sum realized, and the balance given to the creditors.

Article 1000. Any expenditure necessary for the maintenance of an insolvent debtor during the period of his interdiction, or for persons dependent upon him for support, shall be paid from the debtor's property.

Article 1001. Interdiction on account of debt only applies to property of the debtor in existence at the time the interdiction was declared. It does not apply to any property accruing to the debtor after the interdiction.

Article 1002. The interdiction applies to anything likely to destroy the rights of creditors, such as making gifts and bestowing alms and selling property at less than the estimated value. Consequently, any contracts entered into by a bankrupt debtor which are prejudicial to the rights of creditors, and other dispositions of property and gifts, are invalid in respect to property which existed at the time the interdiction was pronounced. They are valid, however, in respect to property acquired after the interdiction was pronounced. Any admission made to any other person in respect to a debt relating to any property in existence at the time the interdiction was pronounced, is invalid. After the interdiction has been removed, however, the admission is valid, and he is liable to make payment thereof. If he acquires property after the interdiction has been pronounced, an admission that he will make payment therefrom is executory.

CHAPTER II.
CONSTRAINT.

Article 1003. The person who causes constraint must be capable of carrying out his threat. Consequently, the threat of any person who is unable to put such threat into execution, is considered to be of no effect.

Article 1004. The person who is the subject of the constraint must be afraid of the occurrence of the event with which he is threatened. That is to say, he must have become convinced that the person causing the constraint would carry out his threat in the event of his failing to do what he was being constrained to do.

Article 1005. Constraint is considered to be effective if the person who is the subject of such constraint performs the act he has been forced to do, in the presence of the person causing the constraint, or of his representative. But if he performs such act in the absence of the person causing the constraint or of his representative, such act is not considered to have been caused by constraint since he has performed the act freely after the cessation of the constraint.

Example :-
> A brings constraint to bear on B to oblige him to sell property to C. B sells the property to C. in the absence of A or of his representative. The sale is considered to be valid and the constraint ineffective.

Article 1006. Contracts of sale, purchase, hire, gift, transfer of real property, settlement in regard to property, admission, release, postponement of debt and renunciation of a right of pre-emption, if entered into as a result of effective constraint, are invalid, whether caused by major constraint or minor constraint. If the person subject to constraint ratifies the contract after the cessation of the constraint, such contract is valid.

Article 1007. Major constraint applies not only to cases of formal dispositions of property as referred to above, but also to dispositions of property by conduct. Minor constraint, however, only applies to formal dispositions of property and not to dispositions of property by conduct. Consequently, if a person tells another to destroy the property of a certain person or he will murder him, or destroy one of his limbs, and the person who is the subject of such constraint does destroy the property, the constraint is effective and the person responsible for the constraint alone may be called upon to make good the loss. But if a person tells another to destroy property of a certain person, or he will strike him or imprison him and he does destroy such property, the constraint is not effective, and the person destroying such property alone may be called upon to make good the loss.

CHAPTER III.

PRE-EMPTION.

SECTION I.

Degrees of pre-emption.

Article 1008. There are three causes of pre-emption.

(1) Where a person is the joint owner of the property sold itself. As where two persons jointly own an undivided share of real property.

(2) Where a person is part owner of a servitude in the thing sold. As where a person shares in a private right of taking water or in a private road.

Examples:-

(1) One of several gardens each having shares in a private right of taking water is sold. Each of the owners of the other gardens obtains a right of pre-emption, whether they are adjoining neighbours or not.

(2) A house opening on to a private road is sold. Each of the owners of the other houses giving on to the private road obtains a right of pre-emption, whether they are adjoining neighbours or not.

But if a house taking water from a river which is open to the use of the public or the doors of which give on to a public road is sold, the owners of the other houses taking water from such river, or which give on to the public road, do not possess any right of pre-emption.

(3) Where a person is adjoining neighbour to the thing sold.

Article 1009. The right of pre-emption belongs:

First, to the person who is a joint owner of the thing sold.

Second, to the person who is a joint owner of a servitude over the thing sold.

Third, to the adjoining neighbour.

If the first person claims his right of pre-emption, the others lose theirs. If the second person claims his right of pre-emption, the third person loses his.

Article 1010. If a person is not a joint owner of the thing sold, or if, being a joint owner, he has renounced his right of pre-emption, and there is a person who has a share in a servitude in the thing sold, such person possesses a right of pre-emption. Should there be no person having a servitude in the thing sold, or, should there be one, and such person renounces his right thereto, the right of pre-emption accrues to the adjoining neighbour.

Example:-

A sells real property which he owns in absolute ownership to the exclusion of any other person, or A, being a joint owner of real property, sells his undivided jointly owned share therein and his partner relinquishes his right of pre-emption to such real property, and there is a person enjoying a private right of taking water who is part owner in a servitude over a private road. The right of pre-emption belongs to such person. Should there be no such person, or, in the event of there being such a person, that person relinquishes his right thereto, the right of pre-emption accrues to the adjoining neighbour.

Article 1011. Where the upper portion, that is, the top storey belongs to one person and the lower portion, that is the lower storey of a building belongs to another, such persons are considered to be adjoining neighbours.

Article 1012. Where a person is joint owner of the wall of a house, he is considered to be joint owner of such house. And if, while not being joint owner of the wall, the beams of his own house rest upon his neighbour's wall, he is considered to be an adjoining neighbour. The mere fact, however, that such person enjoys the right of putting the ends of his beams upon such wall does not entitle him to be considered as a joint owner or as a person sharing in a servitude over such property.

Article 1013. Should there be several persons enjoying a right of pre-emption, they are dealt with according to their numbers and not according to the number of parts, that is shares, which they hold.

Example :-

A holds a half share in a house, and B and C hold a third and sixth share respectively. In the event of the owner of the half share selling such share to another person, and of B and C claiming the right of pre-emption, the half share is divided between them equally. B, the owner of the share of one third, may not claim to have a larger share granted to him on the basis of his prior holding.

Article 1014. Where two classes of persons having joint shares in a servitude come together, the particular take precedence over the general.

Examples :-

(1) Where a person who is the owner of a garden owned in absolute ownership, situated on land enjoying the right of taking water from a creek opening from a small river to which a right of taking water is also attached sells such garden, those persons having a right of taking water from the creek have a prior right of pre-emption. But if a person who is owner of a garden owned in absolute ownership situated on land enjoying the right of taking water from such river, sells his garden, all persons enjoying the right of taking water, whether from the river, or from the creek, possess a right of pre-emption.

(2) A person who is the owner of a house held in absolute ownership the door of which opens on to a blind alley which branches off from another blind alley, sells such house. Those persons the door of whose houses open on to the branch blind alley possess a right of pre-emption. But if the owner of a house the door of which opens on to the principal blind alley sells such house, all persons having a right of way, whether over the principal or the branch blind alley, possess a right of pre-emption.

Article 1015. If the owner of a garden possessing a private right of taking water sells such garden without the right of taking water, those persons who share in the right of taking water cannot claim a right of pre-emption. The same principle is applied in the case of a private road.

Article 1016. A right of taking water is preferred to a right of way. Therefore, if upon the sale of a garden in respect of which one person is the joint owner of a private right of taking water and another of a private right of way attaching thereto, the owner of the right of taking water is preferred to the owner of the right of way.

SECTION II.

Conditions attaching to the right of pre-emption.

Article 1017. The property to which the right of pre-emption attaches must be real property held in absolute ownership. Therefore, no right of pre-emption can attach to a ship or other movable property, nor to real property which has been dedicated to pious purposes, nor to state land.

Article 1018. The property on account of which the right of pre-emption is claimed must also be held in absolute ownership. Consequently, upon the sale of real property held in absolute ownership, the trustee or tenant of adjacent real property which has been dedicated to pious purposes cannot claim a right of pre-emption.

Article 1019. No right of pre-emption may be claimed in respect to trees and buildings held in absolute ownership and situated on land dedicated to pious purposes, or on state land, since these are regarded as movable property.

Article 1020. In the event of a piece of land held in absolute ownership being sold together with the trees and buildings standing thereon, such trees and buildings, since they follow the land, are also subject to the right of pre-emption. But if such trees and buildings alone are sold, no right of pre-emption can be claimed.

Article 1021. Pre-emption can only be established by a contract of sale.

Article 1022. A gift subject to compensation is regarded as a sale. Consequently, if a person who is the owner of a house in absolute ownership bestows such house upon another by way of gift subject to compensation and gives delivery thereof, his adjoining neighbour has a right of pre-emption.

Article 1023. No right of pre-emption attaches to real property given to others in absolute ownership without payment, as in cases of gift without right of compensation, inheritance, or bequest.

Article 1024. The person claiming the right of pre-emption must not have agreed to the sale which has been concluded, either expressly or by implication.

Examples :-

(1) If A, upon hearing of the conclusion of the sale expresses his concurrence therein, he loses his right of pre-emption, and he may not thereafter claim any such right.

(2) If A, after having heard of the conclusion of the sale, seeks to buy or to hire the property to which the right of pre-emption attaches from the purchaser, he loses his right of pre-emption.

Similarly, no right of pre-emption can be claimed by a person who has sold real property as agent for some other person. (see Article 100).

Article 1025. The price must consist of property the amount of which is clearly ascertained. Consequently, there is no right of pre-emption in respect of real property transferred in absolute ownership for a price which does not consist of property.

Examples :-
(1) A sells a house which he owns in absolute ownership for the rent accruing from the letting of a bath. No right of pre-emption can be claimed because in this case the price of the house is not clearly ascertained, but is rent which is in the nature of an interest.

(2) There is no right of pre-emption in respect to real property held in absolute ownership and which is given as a marriage portion.

Article 1026. The vendor must have divested himself of his absolute ownership in the thing sold. Consequently, in the case of a voidable sale, so long as the vendor retains the right to demand the return of the thing sold, there is no right of pre-emption. In the case of sale subject to an option, however, there is a right of pre-emption if the person possessing the option is the purchaser only. If the vendor has a right of option, however, there is no right of pre-emption until the vendor has divested himself of his right of option. But the existence of an option for defect or for inspection is no bar to the assertion of a right of pre-emption.

Article 1027. There is no right of pre-emption upon the division of real property.

Example :-
If the joint owners of a house jointly owned divide such house among themselves, the adjoining neighbour has no right of pre-emption.

SECTION III.

The claim of pre-emption.

Article 1028. Three claims must be made in cases of pre-emption.

(1) A claim made immediately upon hearing of the sale;

(2) A claim made formally and in the presence of witnesses;

(3) A claim that the person alleging the right of pre-emption is entitled to bring an action and to be granted absolute ownership of the property.

Article 1029. The person claiming the right of pre-emption must at the moment he heard of the conclusion of the sale, make a statement showing that he claims the right of pre-emption, as by saying that he is the person who has a right to the property sold subject to pre-emption, or that he claims the property by way of pre-emption. This claim is referred to as the claim made immediately upon hearing of the sale.

Article 1030. After having made a claim immediately upon hearing of the sale, the person claiming the right of pre-emption must make a claim formally and in the presence of witnesses.

Thus, such person must say in the presence of two witnesses, and by the side of the property sold, that such and such a person has bought the real property in question, or, being by the side of the purchaser, must say that such person has bought such and such a piece of real property or, if the property sold is still in the possession of the vendor, must say by the side of the vendor that the latter has sold the real property in question to such and such a person, but that he has a right of pre-emption thereto, and that he has made a claim by way of pre-emption and that he calls such person to witness that he has made a further claim at that moment.

If the person claiming the right of pre-emption is in some distant place and is not in a position personally to make a claim formally and in the presence of witnesses, he may appoint a person as his agent to do so. If he is unable to find an agent, he may send a letter.

Article 1031. After having made a claim formally and in the presence of witnesses, the person claiming the right of pre-emption must make a claim before the Court and bring an action. This is called a claim to bring an action and to be granted absolute ownership of the property.

Article 1032. If the person claiming the right of pre-emption delays in making his claim immediately upon hearing of the sale, he loses his right of pre-emption. Thus, if he fails to claim the right of pre-emption at the moment he hears of the sale, but behaves in a manner tending to show that he does not intend to pursue his claim such as dealing with some other matter, or engaging in conversation regarding a different subject, or if he goes away without making any claim to pre-emption whatsoever, such person loses his right of pre-emption.

Article 1033. If the person claiming the right of pre-emption delays in making his claim formally and in the presence of witnesses for any time longer than is necessary for him to act, even though it be by letter, such person loses his right of pre-emption.

Article 1034. If the person claiming the right of pre-emption delays without any legal excuse, as where he is in some other country, for more than one month in making a claim to bring an action, after having made his claim formally and in the presence of witnesses, such person loses his right of pre-emption.

Article 1035. The tutor of an interdicted person may claim the right of pre-emption on behalf of such person. If a tutor fails to claim a right of pre-emption on behalf of a minor, such minor is not entitled to claim by way of pre-emption after he has reached the age of puberty.

SECTION IV.

The effect of pre-emption.

Article 1036. The person who is entitled to a right of pre-emption becomes owner of the property to which such right attaches, either by the purchaser handing over such property as the result of mutual agreement, or by virtue of a judgment issued by the Court.

Article 1037. The act of taking over property held in absolute ownership, by way of pre-emption, is equivalent to buying such property in the first instance.

Consequently, rights which are valid in the case of an original purchase, such as the option of inspection and the option for defect, are also valid in the case of pre-emption.

Article 1038. If the person claiming the right of pre-emption dies after having made both the immediate and formal claims, but without becoming the owner of the property to which the right of pre-emption attaches owing to such property having been handed over by the purchaser either by way of mutual agreement or as the result of a judgment of the Court, the right of pre-emption is not transferred to his heirs.

Article 1039. If the person claiming the right of pre-emption sells the property by virtue of which he holds a right of pre-emption after having made the two claims as set out above, but without having become owner of the property to which the right of pre-emption attaches, such person loses his right of pre-emption.

Article 1040. If a piece of real property held in absolute ownership adjoining the property subject to the right of pre-emption is sold before the person claiming the right of pre-emption has become the owner of the property to which the right of pre-emption attaches as set out above, such person cannot claim a right of pre-emption in the second piece of real property.

Article 1041. Pre-emption does not admit of division. Consequently, the person claiming the right of pre-emption has no right to reject a portion of the property to which the right of pre-emption attaches and take the rest.

Article 1042. None of the holders of a right of pre-emption may bestow their right upon other holders by way of gift. If they do so, their right of pre-emption is lost.

Article 1043. If any holder of a right of pre-emption relinquishes such right prior to the judgment of the Court, any other person possessing a right of pre-emption may take the whole of the real property to which the right of pre-emption attaches. If any holder of a right of pre-emption relinquishes his right of pre-emption after judgment by the Court, such person's right does not accrue to any other person holding a right of pre-emption.

Article 1044. If the purchaser adds something to the building to which the right of pre-emption attaches, such as paint, the person possessing the right of pre-emption has the option either of leaving such building or of taking it and paying the price of such addition, together with the price of the building. If the purchaser has erected buildings upon the real property to which the right of pre-emption attaches, or has planted trees thereon, the

PRE-EMPTION 269

holder of the right of pre-emption has an option of leaving such real property, or of taking it and paying the price thereof together with the value of such buildings and trees. If he does not do so, he cannot force the purchaser to pull down the buildings and uproot the trees.

Promulgated by Royal Iradah, 16th Rebi ul Akhir, 1290.

BOOK X.
JOINT OWNERSHIP.

BOOK X.

JOINT OWNERSHIP.

INTRODUCTION.

TERMS OF MUHAMMADAN JURISPRUDENCE.

Article 1045. Joint ownership consists of a thing itself belonging absolutely to more than one person, so that such persons enjoy a special position in relation to such thing. It is also customary to apply this expression to the contract whereby the state of joint ownership is brought about, and it is used in this sense in technical legal phraseology. Consequently, joint ownership is generally divided into two classes. The first consists of joint ownership of property held in absolute ownership brought about by one of the modes of acquiring property, such as purchase, or the acceptance of a gift. The second consists of joint ownership as a result of contract brought about by the offer and acceptance of the joint owners, the details concerning both of which are dealt with in the relevant Chapters. Another class consists of gratuitous joint ownership which is brought about by the joint acquisition of ownership by the public of things which are free and themselves belong absolutely to no particular person, such as water.

Article 1046. Partition means to split up. The description and definition thereof will be given in the relevant Chapter.

Article 1047. By wall is meant any wall, or partition made of boards or a fence of brushwood.

JOINT OWNERSHIP

Article 1048. By passers by is meant generally those who pass along and cross the public highway.

Article 1049. By water channels is meant pipes and underground channels for conducting water.

Article 1050. By dam is meant any boundary or water dam and the sides of any water channel.

Article 1051. By vivification is meant cultivation whereby land is made fit for agriculture.

Article 1052. By fencing is meant putting stones and other matter round land in order that other persons may not take possession thereof.

Article 1053. By expenditure is meant disbursing property.

Article 1054. Maintenance consists of the expenditure of money, goods and provisions for upkeep and sustenance.

Article 1055. By accepting responsibility is meant undertaking to do and carry out any particular piece of work.

Article 1056. Partners with equal shares are those who form a partnership with equal shares.

Article 1057. By capital is meant money invested in anything.

Article 1058. Profit consists of interest and benefit.

Article 1059. Where one person supplies capital to another on condition that the whole of the profit is to belong to him, the capital is called the invested capital: the person supplying such capital is called the investor and the person taking such capital is called the person employing capital.

CHAPTER I.

JOINT OWNERSHIP OF PROPERTY OWNED IN ABSOLUTE OWNERSHIP.

SECTION I.

Description and classification of joint ownership of property owned in absolute ownership.

Article 1060. Joint ownership of property owned in absolute ownership is brought about when more than one person join in the ownership of any particular thing, that is to say, where such thing belongs to them, as where ownership therein is acquired by any of the causes of acquiring ownership such as purchase, or taking by way of gift, or by acceptance of a bequest, or inheritance or by mixing or causing to mix one property with another, that is to say, by uniting them in such a way that they cannot be distinguished or separated the one from the other.

Examples:-
(1) Two persons buy a piece of property, or a person bestows property upon them by way of gift or by bequest and they accept the same: or two persons take a piece of property by way of inheritance. Such property is jointly owned by them and they become joint owners in that property, and each one participates therein with the other.

(2) Two persons mix their corn together, or their corn becomes mixed together by reason of there being holes in the sacks. The corn mixed together in this way becomes their joint property.

Article 1061. If a gold coin belonging to one particular person is mixed with two other gold coins of the same type belonging to some other person in such

JOINT OWNERSHIP

a way that it cannot be distinguished from them, and two of them are lost, the remaining gold coin becomes the joint property of the two persons, in the proportion of one third and two thirds, the two thirds belonging to the owner of the two gold coins, the one third belonging to the owner of the one coin.

Article 1062. Joint ownership of property owned in absolute ownership is divided into voluntary and obligatory joint ownership.

Article 1063. Voluntary joint ownership is joint ownership brought about by the acts of the joint owners themselves, as where it arises through purchase, or acceptance of a gift, or by accepting a bequest, or mixing property together as referred to above.

Article 1064. Obligatory joint ownership is joint ownership brought about by some cause other than the acts of the joint owners, as where it arises through inheritance or through two properties being mixed together.

Article 1065. The joint responsibility of various persons to whom a thing has been entrusted for safe keeping is in the nature of voluntary joint ownership. But if a gust of wind carries away a person's garment, and it falls in a house which is jointly owned, the joint responsibility of the owners of the house for the preservation of the garment is in the nature of obligatory joint ownership.

Article 1066. Joint ownership of property owned in absolute ownership is also divided into joint ownership of specific property and joint ownership of debt.

Article 1067. Joint ownership of specific property consists of joint ownership of some specific property which is in existence, as where two persons have undivided joint ownership of a sheep or of a flock of sheep.

Article 1068. Joint ownership of debt consists of joint ownership of something to be received, as where two persons are joint owners of a certain sum of money owing to them by some other person.

SECTION II.

The manner of dealing with specific property jointly owned.

Article 1069. The joint owners of property held in absolute ownership may by agreement deal with their property in any way they wish, in the same way as a single owner of such property.

Article 1070. The joint owners of a house may dwell together in such house. If one of them, however, wishes to introduce a stranger into the house, the other can prevent him from so doing.

Article 1071. One of the joint owners of property held in absolute ownership may deal with such property alone, with the permission of the other. He may not, however, deal with it in such way as to cause injury to the other joint owner.

Article 1072. Neither of the joint owners may force the other to sell or purchase his share. If the property held in absolute ownership jointly by them is capable of division, and the other joint owner is not absent, such property may be divided. If it is not capable of division they may share the usufruct thereof. Details are given in Chapter II.

Article 1073. The produce of property jointly owned in absolute ownership may be divided among the owners in accordance with their shares. Consequently, any stipulation that the milk of an animal which is jointly owned, or the young thereof shall go to one of the joint owners in excess of his share is invalid.

Article 1074. The property in the young of animals follows the mother.

Examples:-

(1) A stallion belonging to A covers a mare belonging to B. The foal belongs to the owner of the mare.

(2) A owns male and B female pigeons. The young belong to the owner of the female pigeons.

Article 1075. The joint owners of property held in absolute ownership are strangers to one another as regards their shares. Neither is the agent of the other. Consequently, neither joint owner may deal with the share of the other without the latter's permission. But in the case of dwelling in a house which is jointly owned and as regards matters pertaining thereto, such as coming in and going out, each of the joint owners is considered to be an absolute owner of such property.

Examples :-

(1) One of the owners of a jointly owned horse lends or gives such horse on hire without the permission of the other, and it is destroyed while in the possession of the borrower or of the person taking it on hire. The second joint owner may claim to have the loss of his share made good by the first.

(2) One joint owner rides a jointly owned horse, or places a load upon him without the permission of the other, the horse is destroyed while being ridden or driven. The second joint owner may claim to have the loss of his share made good by the first.

(3) One joint owner uses a horse for a certain period so that it becomes weak and its value decreases. The other joint owner may claim to have the decrease in value which is represented by his share made good.

JOINT OWNERSHIP

(4) One of two joint owners of a house lives in such house for a certain period without obtaining the permission of the other. He is considered to be living in his own property held in absolute ownership, and he cannot be called upon by the other joint owner to pay rent corresponding to his share. If the house is burnt down by accident, he is likewise under no obligation to make good any loss.

Article 1076. If one of two joint owners of land cultivates such land, the other may not claim a share of the produce thereof in accordance with local custom, such as a third or a fourth. If the value of the land is decreased by reason of the cultivation, however, he may claim to have the amount of the decrease in value of his share made good by the joint owner cultivating the land.

Article 1077. If one of two joint owners of property lets such property on hire and receives the rent therefor, he is obliged to pay the other his share thereof.

Article 1078. If one of the joint owners of property owned in absolute ownership is absent, the one who is present may take the usufruct of such property to the extent of his share thereof, provided the consent of the other is given by implication, as is set forth in the following Articles.

Article 1079. The absent joint owner is considered to have given his consent by implication to enjoyment of the usufruct by the joint-owner who is present, if the latter causes no harm in so doing to the jointly owned property held in absolute ownership.

Article 1080. There can be no consent by implication to the enjoyment of the usufruct of jointly owned property held in absolute ownership where such property is changed by use by the particular person using it. Consequently,

JOINT OWNERSHIP

one of two joint owners of a piece of clothing cannot wear such clothing in the absence of the other. Again, one of two joint owners may not ride a jointly owned horse in the absence of the other. He may do so, however, up to the extent of his share in cases where there is no change by use of the particular person using it, such as carrying burdens, or ploughing land. Again, where one of two joint owners is absent, the other may, every other day, enjoy the services of a servant who has been taken into their joint service.

Article 1081. Habitation of a house is not changed by a change of persons dwelling therein. Consequently, if one of two joint owners of a house held in common in equal shares is absent, the other may use such house for a period of six months and leave it for six months. If the members of such person's household are numerous, however, their dwelling in the house is of such a nature as to change it by reason thereof, and the absent joint owner cannot be held to have assented thereto by implication.

Article 1082. In the event of the shares of a house jointly owned by two persons, one of whom is absent, being separated the one from the other, the joint owner who is present may not dwell in the part of the joint owner who is absent. If there is danger of the house falling into disrepair, however, by reason of its being left vacant, the Court may let such separate part on hire and keep the rent on behalf of the absent joint owner.

Article 1083. Partition of usufruct can only be had and is only valid after being settled by an action at law. Consequently, if one of the owners of a jointly owned house lives alone in such house for a certain period without paying any rent in respect to the share of the other, the latter cannot claim rent in respect to his share for that period, or claim that he will dwell in it for a corresponding period. He may, however, divide such house if it is capable of partition, or he may cause the usufruct thereof to be divided so that it may be valid thereafter. But if one of the joint owners is absent, and the other, as stated in the preceding Article, dwells therein for a certain period, and the absent joint owner returns, he may dwell in such house for a corresponding period.

Article 1084. One of the owners of a jointly owned house who is present may validly let such house on hire, taking his own share of the rent and keeping the share of the absent joint owner. On the return of the latter, he may obtain his share from the former.

Article 1085. Should one of the joint owners of land be absent, and it is known that cultivation will be beneficial to such land and will not result in any decrease in the value thereof, the joint owner who is present may cultivate the whole of such land. If the absent joint owner returns, he may cultivate the land for a corresponding period. If it is known that cultivation of the land will result in a diminution of the value thereof and that leaving the land fallow will be beneficial thereto and will result in the increased fertility thereof, the absent joint owner cannot be held to have agreed by implication to the cultivation of such land. Consequently, a joint owner who is present may only cultivate the amount of his own share of such land. For example, if such land is jointly owned in equal shares, he may cultivate a half thereof. Should he cultivate the land again in the following year, he may only cultivate his own half. He may not cultivate one half in one year and the other half in the following year. If he cultivates the whole of such land and the absent joint owner returns, he must make good to him the decrease in value of his share of the land.

The details as set out above apply, if the joint owner who is present does not make any application to the Court. Should he apply to the Court, however, the Court shall give permission for him to cultivate the whole of such land in order that the tithe and land tax shall not be lost. In such a case, should the absent joint owner return, he may not bring an action on account of any decrease in the value of the land.

Article 1086. If one of the joint owners of an orchard is absent, the owner who is present stands in the place of the absent joint owner, and when the fruit ripens may take and consume his own share. He may also sell the share of the absent joint owner and set aside the price thereof. The absent joint owner, on return, has the option of either ratifying the sale and taking the price set aside, or of rejecting the sale and claiming to be given the value of his share.

Article 1087. The share of one of the joint owners is considered to be deposited for safe keeping with the other. Consequently, if one of them, on his own initiative, deposits the jointly owned property with some other person for safe keeping and such property is destroyed, he must make good the loss of the share of the other joint owner. (See Article 790).

Article 1088. One of the joint owners may, if he wishes, sell his share to the other joint owner, or he may also sell it to some other person without the permission of the other joint owner. (See Article 215). In the case of mixed property, however, as mentioned in Section I, no person may sell his share of the mixed property to another unless he has obtained the permission of the other joint owner.

Article 1089. If some of a number of heirs to land which has devolved upon them by way of inheritance sow seed therein which is their joint property with the permission of the other heirs, or if such other heirs are minors, with the permission of their guardians, the whole of the resulting produce is jointly owned by all of them. If one of them sows his own seed, the resulting produce is his own. He must, however, make good any loss accruing to the share of the other heirs by reason of any decrease in the value of the land caused by the cultivation thereof. (See Article 907).

Article 1090. If one of a number of heirs, without the permission of the others, takes and uses a quantity of money belonging to the estate prior to the division thereof, he must bear any loss occasioned thereby, but is entitled to keep the profits obtained by such transaction.

SECTION III.

Jointly owned debts.

Article 1091. If two or more persons are owed a sum of money by some other person and that debt arises from a single cause, such debt is a debt jointly owned by the two creditors. If the debt does not arise from a single cause, it is not a joint debt. These matters will be dealt with in the following Articles.

Article 1092. Any specific property left by a deceased person is jointly owned by his heirs in proportion to their shares. In the same way, sums owing to him by any other person are jointly owned by the heirs in proportion to their shares.

Article 1093. A debt owed by a person and arising by reason of such person having to make good loss

JOINT OWNERSHIP

caused by the destruction by him of property jointly owned, is jointly owned by the owners of such property.

Article 1094. If two persons who jointly own a certain sum of money lend such money to some other person, the debt is jointly owned by such two persons. If two persons lend money separately to some other person, each one becomes a separate creditor, and the debts are not jointly owned by the two persons.

Article 1095. If property jointly owned is sold *en bloc,* and the share of none of the joint owners is mentioned at the time of the sale, the sum of money to be paid by the purchaser becomes a debt jointly owned. If the amount of the share of the price of the thing sold of each one of them is mentioned at the time of the sale, or the nature thereof, as for example, where it is stated that the share of one of them consists of so much money and the share of the other of so much, or where the share of one is said to consist of sound coin and the share of the other of base coin, whereby their shares are defined, the vendors do not jointly own the price of the thing sold, but each becomes a separate creditor. Similarly, if one of them sells his undivided share to some other person, and the other also sells his undivided share to that person separately, such persons do not jointly own the price of the thing sold, but each of them becomes a separate creditor.

Article 1096. If two persons each sell their property *en bloc* to some other person, as, for example, when one sells a horse and the other a mare at one and the same time, for a certain sum of money, the amount in question becomes a debt jointly owned by the vendors. If each one of them names the price of his own animal as being so much, they each become separate creditors, and the total value of their animals does not become a debt jointly owned. Again, if two persons each separately sell property to some other person, the total value of the things sold does not become jointly owned, but each one becomes a separate creditor.

Article 1097. If two persons in their capacity as guarantors pay the debt of some other person from property which they jointly own, the amount which they are entitled to recover from the principal debtor is a debt jointly owned.

Article 1098. If a person gives an order to two other persons to pay a debt amounting to a certain sum and the latter pay such debt from property which they jointly own, the sum which they are entitled to receive from such person is a debt jointly owned. If the money they have paid is not jointly owned by them, and the share of each of them is in fact clearly distinguished, the mere fact that they have paid at one and the same time does not make the amount they are entitled to claim from such person a debt jointly owned.

Article 1099. If the debt is not jointly owned, each of the creditors may demand payment separately from the debtor of the sum he is entitled to receive and whatever sum either of them receives, is credited to such person's account. The other creditor is not entitled to share therein.

Article 1100. If the debt is a joint one, each of the creditors may demand and receive payment of his own share from the debtor separately. If one of the creditors applies to the Court in the absence of another and asks for payment of his share from the debtor, the Court shall make an order to this effect.

Article 1101. Whatever sum is received by one of the creditors in respect to a joint debt is jointly owned by him and the other creditors who are entitled to receive their share therefrom. The creditor who receives such sum may not deduct it from his own share alone.

Article 1102. If one of the creditors receives his share of a joint debt and disposes of it, the other joint creditor may claim to have the loss he has suffered made good.

Example :-

> One of two persons who are joint creditors in equal shares for a sum of one thousand piastres receives his share of five hundred piastres from the debtor and disposes of it. The other joint creditor may claim from him the sum of two hundred and fifty piastres for the loss he has suffered. The five hundred piastres still remaining due continues to be jointly owned by the two creditors.

Article 1103. If one of the joint creditors while receiving nothing in respect to the joint debt buys goods from the debtor against his share, the other does not become a joint owner of the goods. He may, however, claim to have his share made good by the other creditor out of the price of the goods. If they come to an agreement as to their shares, the goods are held jointly between them.

Article 1104. If one of the joint creditors comes to a settlement with the debtor as to his share in the joint debt, as for example, where he agrees to accept from the debtor a certain quantity of cloth and does in fact do so, he may either hand to the other joint creditor an amount of cloth corresponding to the latter's share, out of the cloth he has received, or he may deliver him a sum of money corresponding to the amount of the share of the joint debt which he has forgone.

Article 1105. If one of the creditors, as mentioned above, receives a part of the whole of a joint debt, or if he buys property to the value of his share, or if he comes to a settlement with the debtor as to certain property against his claim, the other creditor in any case has the option of either adopting the transaction of the other joint creditor, when, as is set forth in the preceding Articles, he has the right of receiving his share from him, or of refusing to adopt the transaction and claiming his share from the debtor. If he fails to obtain anything from the debtor, he has a right of recourse against the creditor who has obtained his share, and the fact that he has not previously adopted the transaction is no bar to his right of recourse.

Article 1106. If one of the creditors receives his share of the joint debt from the debtor, and it is accidentally destroyed while in his possession, he is not liable to make good the loss to the other joint creditor in respect to the amount represented by such joint creditor's share therein. He is regarded as having received payment of his own share. The amount remaining to be paid by the debtor belongs to the joint creditor.

Article 1107. If one of the creditors employs the debtor for a wage to be reckoned against his share of the joint debt, the other joint creditor may call upon the former to make good to him the amount represented by his share therein.

Article 1108. If one of the joint creditors receives a pledge from the debtor in respect to his own share, and the pledge is destroyed while in his possession, the other joint creditor may call upon the former to make good to him the amount represented by his share therein.

Example :-

> The amount of the joint debt held in equal shares is one thousand piastres. One of the creditors receives a pledge in respect to his share of five hundred piastres. The pledge is destroyed while in his possession. The other creditor may call upon the former to make good to him a sum of two hundred and fifty piastres, since half the joint debt has been lost.

Article 1109. If one of the creditors obtains a guarantor from the debtor in respect to his share of the joint debt, or transfers his share to some other person, any sum obtained by such creditor from the guarantor or the person to whom the transfer has been made is shared by the other creditor.

Article 1110. If one of the debtors makes a gift of his share in the joint debt to the debtor or releases him therefrom, such gift or release is valid. He is not liable on that account to the other creditor in respect to his share.

Article 1111. If one of the joint creditors in respect to a joint debt is responsible for the destruction of the property of the debtor, and the sum represented thereby is set off against the debt, the other joint creditor has the right of receiving his share from him in respect thereto. But if one of the joint creditors was in the debt of the debtor in respect to a debt which came into existence prior to the joint debt in respect to which he has a claim, the two claims are set off one against the other and the other joint creditor cannot claim from him anything in respect thereto.

Article 1112. Neither of the joint creditors may extend the due date or postpone the joint debt without the permission of the other.

Supplement.

Article 1113. If any person sells any property to two other persons, he may claim his share from each one of them separately. He may not claim the amount owing by one of them from the other, unless they are guarantors of each other.

CHAPTER II.

PARTITION.

SECTION I.

Nature and categories of partition.

Article 1114. Partition consists of defining an undivided share. That is to say, to distinguish and separate shares from each other by means of some standard, such as a measure of capacity, or of weight, or of length.

Article 1115. Partition is effected in two ways. The first consists of specific objects owned jointly, that is, numerous and jointly owned things being separated into parts, the undivided shares belonging to each individual being united in one part. This is called partition by units, as where thirty sheep which are jointly owned between three persons are divided up into tens.

The second consists of dividing a specific thing owned jointly and of allotting a part in respect to the undivided shares relating to each portion. This is known as partition by allotment, or individual partition, as where a piece of land is divided into two parts.

Article 1116. Partition consists on the one hand of separation and on the other of exchange.

Examples :-

(1) Two persons own a *kilé* of corn jointly in equal shares. Each has a half share in each grain. When it is divided into two parts, the division is by partition by units, one part being given to one and the other part to the other joint owner. Each one is then considered to have separated his half share and to have exchanged his own half with the half share of the other.

(2) Two persons are joint owners of a piece of land which they hold in equal shares in respect to every part. The land is divided into two by partition by allotment, and a part is given to each one of them. Each one is considered to have separated his own half share and to have exchanged it with the half share of the other joint owner.

Article 1117. Separation is preferred in the case of things the like of which can be found in the market. Consequently, each joint owner of jointly owned things the like of which can be found in the market may take his own share in the absence of the other and without his permission. The division, however, is not complete until the share of the absent joint owner has been handed over to him. If the share of the absent joint owner is destroyed before being handed over, the share which has been received by the other joint owner is jointly owned between them.

Article 1118. In the case of things the like of which cannot be found in the market, exchange is preferred. Exchange may take place by agreement of the parties or may be made as the result of a judgment by the Court. Consequently, one of the joint owners may not take his share of any specific object the like of which cannot be found in the market, in the absence of the other and without his permission.

JOINT OWNERSHIP

Article 1119. Things estimated by measure of capacity, things estimated by weight and things measured by enumeration and which closely resemble one another, such as walnuts and eggs, are all things the like of which can be found in the market. But things estimated by weight and which change in accordance with the difference of craftsmanship, such as hand-made pottery, are things the like of which cannot be found in the market. Things which are similar to each other, though of a different nature, and which are mixed together in such a way that they cannot be distinguished and separated from each other, such as barley and corn, are things the like of which cannot be found in the market.

Things measured by length are also things the like of which cannot be found in the market. But things measured by length and sold at so much per yard, there being no difference between the undivided units thereof, such as cloth of a particular type, and linen goods produced by a process of manufacture, are things the like of which can be found in the market.

Things measured by enumeration and which are dissimilar from each other and in respect to which there is a difference in value as regards the undivided units thereof, such as animals, melons and water melons, are things the like of which cannot be found in the market.

Books written by hand are things the like of which cannot be found in the market. Printed books are things the like of which can be found in the market.

Article 1120. Partition by units and partition by allotment are each divided into two categories. The first is partition by consent. The second is partition by order of the Court.

JOINT OWNERSHIP

Article 1121. Partition by consent consists of a partition made by agreement of the two joint owners of property held in absolute ownership, whereby they mutually agree to a division between them, or whereby the Court makes a division with the assent of all parties.

Article 1122. Partition by order of the Court consists of a partition which is obligatory and has the force of law, and which is made upon the application of certain of the owners of the jointly owned property.

SECTION II.

Conditions attaching to partition.

Article 1123. The thing divided must be some specific object. Consequently, any partition of a debt jointly owned prior to being received is invalid.

Example :-

A deceased person has various sums of money owing to him. The allocation of so much money owing to him by A to one of his heirs and so much owing to him by B to another of his heirs is invalid. Should one of the heirs obtain any sum of money in this way, the other heirs become joint owners therein. (See Chapter I, Section IV).

Article 1124. No partition is valid until the shares have been identified and separated.

Example :-

One of the joint owners of a heap of corn requests the other joint owner to take one half of the heap, adding that he will take the other. The partition is invalid.

Article 1125. The thing divided must be the property of the joint owners held in absolute ownership at the time of partition. Consequently, if some person appears

JOINT OWNERSHIP

who is entitled to the whole of the property after the partition has been made, such partition becomes null and void. Similarly, if someone appears who is entitled to an undivided share therein such as a half or a third, the partition is invalid and the property must be divided again. Again, if someone appears who is entitled to the whole of a share, the partition is invalid, and the remainder is jointly owned by the other persons holding shares in the property. If someone appears who is entitled to some specific part of a share only, or an undivided part, the owner of such undivided share has the option of either cancelling the partition, or of agreeing thereto, and of exercising a right of recourse against the other joint owner in respect to the amount short.

Example :-
A piece of land measuring one hundred and sixty *arshuns* is divided into two equal shares. Someone appears who is entitled to a half of one share. The owner of such share may, at his option, cancel the partition, or may exercise a right of recourse against the other joint owner to the extent of a quarter of his share, that is to say, he may take from his share a portion measuring twenty *arshuns.* If someone appears who is entitled to a specific part of each share, the partition cannot be cancelled if it has been made in equal shares. If one has received less and the other more, the greater amount only is held to be valid, the matter being regarded as though only one person had appeared entitled to a fixed portion of one share. The person to whose share the greater amount is attributed as stated above has the option either of cancelling the partition, or of having recourse against the other joint owner in respect to the amount which he has lost.

Article 1126. Partition by an unauthorized person is subject to ratification, which may be oral, or in writing, or by conduct.

294 JOINT OWNERSHIP

Example :-

A divides jointly owned property on his own initiative. The partition is neither permissible nor executory. But if the owners ratify by signifying their assent, or if they deal with their separate shares by way of absolute ownership, that is to say, if they perform any act indicative of a right of ownership, such as sale or hire, the partition is valid and executory.

Article 1127. The partition must be equitable. That is to say, it must be made in accordance with the shares due to each joint owner, and no one may in any way be deprived of the full amount to which he is entitled. Consequently, an action for flagrant misrepresentation will lie in a case of partition. If the person in whose favour the partition has been made, however, admits that he has received what he is entitled to, his admission is a bar to an action for flagrant misrepresentation.

Article 1128. In partition by consent, the consent of each of the persons sharing in the partition must be given. Consequently, if one of them is absent, partition by consent is invalid. If one of them is a minor, the tutor or guardian stands in his place. In the absence of a tutor or guardian, the partition is subject to the order of the Court, which will appoint a guardian through whom the partition will be carried out.

Article 1129. Partition made by order of the Court is subject to a request being made to that effect. Any compulsory partition made by the Court in the absence of any request made by one of the parties is invalid.

Article 1130. If some of the joint owners apply for partition and others oppose such application, the Court shall make a compulsory partition if the property jointly owned is capable of partition, as is set forth in Section 3 and Section 4. Otherwise no partition shall be made.

JOINT OWNERSHIP

Article 1131. Capable of partition refers to jointly owned property which is fit for partition. Thus, the benefit to be derived from such property must not be lost by the partition.

SECTION III.

Partition by units.

Article 1132. Specific objects which are jointly owned and which are of one type, are subject to partition by order of the Court. That is to say, the Court will order the partition of such property upon the application of some only of the joint owners, whether the property in question consists of things the like of which can be found in the market or not.

Article 1133. In the case of partition of things the like of which can be found in the market, and which are of one type, each of the joint owners receives what he is entitled to and becomes absolute owner thereof, since there is no difference between the various undivided units thereof, and partition cannot injure any one of the joint owners. Thus, upon the partition of a quantity of corn jointly owned by two persons, in accordance with their shares, each of them receives what he is entitled to, and becomes the independent owner of the corn falling to his share. The same applies in the case of a number of *dirhems* of bar gold, or of a number of *okes* of bar silver, or of bar copper or iron, or of a number of pieces of woollen cloth of one type, or of a number of pieces of linen, or a quantity of eggs.

Article 1134. If a difference exists between things the like of which cannot be found in the market, and which are of one type, but such difference is so small that it may be said not to exist at all, such things are considered to be capable of partition as referred to above.

Example :-
> Five hundred sheep owned jointly by two persons are divided between them in accordance with their shares. Each one is considered to have received the identical things to which he is entitled. The same thing applies in the case of so many hundreds of camels and so many hundreds of cows.

Article 1135. Specific objects which are jointly owned and which are of different types, are not subject to partition by the Court, whether consisting of things the like of which can be found in the market or not. That is to say, the Court will not give an order for their compulsory division by units upon the application of one of the joint owners only.

Example :-
> An order of the Court for the partition of property whereby one of the joint owners receives so many *kilés* of corn, and another so many *kilés* of barley, as being equivalent thereto; to one so many sheep, to another so many camels or cows, as being equivalent thereto; to one a sword, to the other a set of saddlery; to one a country house, to the other a shop or a farm, is invalid. But if the joint owners agree thereto, a partition by order of the Court, as mentioned above, is valid.

Article 1136. Pots which differ in accordance with the craftsmanship are considered to be of different types, even though made from metal of one type.

Article 1137. Ornaments, large pearls and jewellery are also specific objects of different types. But small jewels not differing from each other in value, such as tiny pearls and small diamonds known as counting stones, are considered to be of the same type.

JOINT OWNERSHIP

Article 1138. A number of country houses, shops and farms, are also of different types and cannot be divided by partition by units.

Example :-

One of a number of country houses may not be given to one joint owner and another to a second in pursuance of an order for partition given by the Court. Each of them may be divided by partition by allotment as set out below.

SECTION IV.

Partition by allotment.

Article 1139. Any specific piece of property which is jointly owned is capable of partition, provided such partition does not injure any of the owners thereof.

Examples :-

(1) A piece of land is divided and buildings erected on each portion, trees are planted and wells sunk. In this way, the benefit to be derived from the land is preserved.

(2) A country house is divided into men's and women's quarters, so that it becomes two separate houses. The benefit to be derived from the country house, which was to dwell therein, is not lost. Each of the joint owners becomes the independent owner of a separate house. Consequently, both in the case of the land and of the country house, a division by order of the Court is valid. That is to say, if one of the owners desires partition and the other does not, the Court may give an order for compulsory partition.

Article 1140. Should the partition of some specific piece of property jointly owned be advantageous to one of the owners thereof, and disadvantageous to the other, that is to say, should the benefit to be derived therefrom be lost to him, and should the person deriving some advantage therefrom desire partition, the Court may give an order for partition.

Example :-

> A house is jointly owned and the share of one of the joint owners is so small that after partition he is unable to derive benefit therefrom by dwelling therein. The joint owner holding the greater share desires partition. The Court will give an order for partition.

Article 1141. Partition may not be ordered by the Court of some specific property which is jointly owned in cases where such partition would be injurious to each of the joint owners of such property.

Example :-

> If a mill is divided, it can no longer be used as a mill, and for this reason the benefit to be derived therefrom is lost. Consequently, the Court will not order the partition of the mill upon the application of one of the joint owners only. It may, however, be divided by consent. Baths, wells, water pipes, a small room, a wall between two houses, are of the same type. Merchandise such as a horse and a carriage, a saddle, a cloak, the stone for a ring, which must be broken or split, are also of this nature. In no case may division be ordered by the Court.

Article 1142. The partition of the pages of a book jointly owned is invalid: and the partition volume by volume of a book in several volumes is likewise invalid.

Article 1143. If one of the joint owners of a road owned by two or more person to which no other person has the right of access desires partition, and the others object, it must first be ascertained as to whether, if partition is effected, each of the joint owners will have a road. If so, the road will be divided. If not, no order will be made for compulsory partition. Nevertheless, if each one has a separate road and entrance, partition may be made.

Article 1144. A right of flow jointly owned is similar to a road jointly owned. If one of the owners desires partition and the other objects, and there is sufficient room for each one for the flow of water after partition, or there is some other place to which the water may flow, the partition may be made, but not otherwise.

Article 1145. A person may sell a road which he owns in absolute ownership, subject to his retaining a right of way thereover, in the same way that upon the partition of a piece of real property jointly owned by two persons, the absolute ownership of a road jointly owned may be retained by one, and the other may be given a right of way thereover only.

Article 1146. Upon the partition of a house, a wall separating the two shares may remain in the joint ownership of the owners thereof, or such house may be divided in such manner that the wall becomes the property in absolute ownership of one of them only.

SECTION V.

Method of partition.

Article 1147. If property jointly owned is estimated by measure of capacity, it is divided by such measure; if it is estimated by weight, it is divided by weight; if it is estimated by number, it is divided by number; if it is estimated by length, it is divided by length.

Article 1148. Land being measured by length, is divided by length. But trees and buildings situated thereon are divided by estimating the value thereof.

JOINT OWNERSHIP

Article 1149. Should it be found upon the partition of a country house that the building represented by one share is more valuable than the building of the other, land in addition is taken from the site of the other share, if this course is possible, equivalent to the difference in value, and added thereto. If this is not possible, a proportionate amount of money is added.

Article 1150. If two persons who are joint owners of a house desire partition thereof so that one receives the upper portion and the other the lower portion, both the upper and the lower portions are valued, and the partition is made on the basis of the value.

Article 1151. If a country house is to be divided, the person carrying out the partition must first make a plan thereof on paper, must measure the land upon which it is built, value the buildings thereof, and make a settlement and adjustment in accordance with the shares of the owners thereof. If possible he must divide any right of way, or right of taking water, or right of flow, so that they are completely independent the one from the other. They must be called share number one, two and three respectively. Afterwards, lots must be drawn. The first name turned up gets the first share, the second name gets the second share, and the third name gets the third share. If there are more than three, the same procedure is followed.

Article 1152. If taxes levied by the State are for the protection of the interests of the people, they must be levied in accordance with the amount of the population. Women and children are not included in the register. If they are levied for the protection of property, they are levied in accordance with the amount of such property, because, as is mentioned in Article 87, disadvantage is an obligation accompanying enjoyment.

SECTION VI.

Options.

Article 1153. An option conferred by contract, an option of inspection, and an option for defect are attached to the various types of partition, as in the case of sale.

Example: -

Property jointly owned is divided by agreement between the owners thereof. One receives so many *kilés* of corn and the other so many *kilés* of barley, or one of them receives so many sheep and the other so many cows. If one of the joint owners has a contractual option, he may, during that period, either agree to the partition, or cancel it. If one of them has not yet seen the divided property, he similarly has an option upon seeing it. If the share of one of them proves to be defective, he may either accept it or reject it.

Article 1154. An option conferred by contract, an option of inspection, and an option for defect are also attached to things the like of which cannot be found in the market, upon the partition thereof.

Example :-

Upon the partition of one hundred sheep among the owners thereof in proportion to their shares, one of the owners may, if he has stipulated therefor by contract, exercise an option of accepting or rejecting the partition within a period of so many days. If he has not yet seen the sheep, he similarly may exercise an option upon seeing them. If a defect of long standing is revealed in the sheep which fall to the share of one of them, he likewise has an option and may either accept them or reject them.

JOINT OWNERSHIP

Article 1155. Upon the division of things the like of which can be found in the market, and which are of the same type, no option is conferred by contract or upon inspection. An option, however, exists for defect.

Example :-

A heap of corn belonging to two persons jointly is divided. An option conferred by contract to be exercised within a certain number of days is invalid. If one of them has not seen the corn, he cannot exercise an option upon seeing it. But if one of them is given the upper part and the other the lower, and the lower portion proves to be rotten, the owner has the option of rejecting or accepting it.

SECTION VII.

Cancellation and rescission of partition.

Article 1156. When the lots have all been drawn, the partition is complete.

Article 1157. When the partition has been completed, there cannot be any withdrawal therefrom.

Article 1158. If one of the joint owners wishes to withdraw while the partition is being carried out, as for example, where the majority of the lots have been drawn and there remains one only, the withdrawal is valid if the partition is one made by consent. It is invalid, however, if it is made by order of the Court.

Article 1159. If the joint owners cancel and rescind the partition by agreement after such partition has been carried out, they may again become joint owners of the property as heretofore.

Article 1160. If flagrant misrepresentation is apparent during the partition, the partition is cancelled, and an equitable partition is made afresh.

Article 1161. If after the partition of an estate it proves that the deceased person was in debt, the partition is cancelled. Nevertheless, if the heirs pay the debt, or if the creditors relinquish their claims, or if there is other property belonging to the deceased and the debt is satisfied therefrom, the partition is not cancelled.

SECTION VIII.

Effect of partition.

Article 1162. Each of the joint owners becomes the independent owner of his own share after partition. No one has any further interest in the share of the other. Each one of them may deal with his own share precisely as he wishes, as will be set forth in Chapter III. So that if a house jointly owned by two persons is divided, one of them obtaining the buildings and the other the vacant land, the owner of the land may dig wells, or make a channel for water, or erect a building of any height he wishes, even to the extent of depriving the owner of the building of air or sun-light, and the latter is powerless to prevent the former from so doing.

Article 1163. Upon the partition of land, trees are included therein without being mentioned. Upon a farm being partitioned, trees and buildings are also included without being mentioned. That is to say, the trees and buildings belong to the person to whose share they fall. There is no need for the inclusion of any particular statement or of any general expressions, such as that the partition includes all rights or all appurtenances.

Article 1164. Upon the partition of either lands or farms, crops and fruits are not included therein unless specifically mentioned and they remain jointly owned as heretofore, and this, whether any general expression was used when the partition was carried out, such as that the partition includes all rights, or not.

Article 1165. Any right of way or of flow over adjoining lands attaching to the partitioned property is in every case included in the partition. That is to say, the rights in question belong to the person who obtains the share to which they are attached, and this, whether at the time the partition is carried out, the partition is stated to include all rights or not.

Article 1166. If at the time the partition is carried out, it is stipulated that there shall be a right of way or right of flow over another share, the stipulation is valid.

Article 1167. If the road belonging to one share exists in the other share, and no stipulation is made for the retention thereof at the time of the partition, and it is possible to place the road elsewhere, this shall be done, whether at the time of partition the partition was stated to include all rights or not. If the road cannot be placed elsewhere, however, and at the time of the partition, all rights were stated to be included, the road shall be included in the partition without any change. If no such expression of a general nature has been included, the partition shall be cancelled.

In this connection, the right of flow follows the same rule as the right of way.

Article 1168. If a person has a right of way through a house jointly owned by two other persons, and the two joint owners desire to partition such house, the owner of the right of way cannot prevent them from so doing. The two joint owners, however, upon carrying out the partition, must leave the road intact. If all three agree to sell the house together with the road and the road is jointly owned between the three, the price is divided between them. If the absolute ownership of the

JOINT OWNERSHIP

road belongs to the owners of the country house, and such person merely possesses a right of way, each one takes what he is entitled to receive. Thus, if the land is valued on one occasion with the right of way and on another without, the difference between the two belongs to the owner of the right of way. The balance belongs to the owners of the house.

The same rule applies in the case of a right of flow. That is to say, if one person has a right of flow over the house of another which is jointly owned and the owners of the house desire the partition of such house, the right of flow remains undisturbed.

Article 1169. If a person owns a dwelling situated in the courtyard of a country house, and possesses a right of way over the courtyard, and the owners of the country house desire to partition the same, the owner of the dwelling cannot prevent them from so doing. Upon carrying out the partition, however, they are obliged to leave him a road as wide as the breadth of the door of the dwelling.

Article 1170. If a country house is divided into two and there is a wall separating the two parts, and the ends of the beams of the wall of one part project on to the wall which is jointly owned, and at the time of the partition a stipulation has been made that the beams shall be removed, such beams shall be so removed, but not otherwise. The same rule applies when a partition is made subject to the condition that the wall separating the two parts shall belong to one joint owner in absolute ownership, and the beams the ends of which rest upon such wall belong to the other.

Article 1171. The branches of trees situated in one part and which project into the other part may not be

JOINT OWNERSHIP

cut off unless a condition has been made to that effect at the time the partition was made.

Article 1172. Upon the partition of a house jointly owned having a right of way over a private road, each of the joint owners may construct doors and open windows looking on to such road. The other owners of the road may not prevent them from so doing.

Article 1173. If one of the joint owners of a piece of property held in absolute ownership which is capable of partition erects a building for himself without the permission of the other, and the other joint owner asks for partition, such partition shall be made. If the building falls to the share of the person who built it, such building shall remain intact. If the building falls to the share of the other joint owner he may have such building pulled down.

SECTION IX.

Partition of usufruct.

Article 1174. Partition of usufruct consists of the division of benefits.

Article 1175. There can be no partition of usufruct in the case of things the like of which can be found in the market. Partition of usufruct may be had in the case of those things the like of which cannot be found in the market, the usufruct of which may be enjoyed, while the identical things remain intact.

Article 1176. Partition of usufruct is of two categories. The first category consists of a partition of usufruct limited by time.

Examples :-

(1) Two persons are joint owners of land which they hold subject to the condition that one shall cultivate such land one year, and the other the second year.

(2) Each of the joint owners of a country house own such house on the terms that they shall each dwell therein in turns for a period of one year.

The second category consists of a partition of usufruct limited as to place.

Examples :-
(1) Two persons are joint owners of land subject to the condition that one shall cultivate the first half and the other the second half.
(2) The joint owners of a country house agree to live one in one part and the other in the other part thereof, or one in the upper part and the other in the lower part thereof.
(3) Two persons own two houses jointly. They agree to live one in one house and the other in the other.

Article 1177. The joint owners of an animal may validly agree to share the usufruct thereof by using such animal in turns. They may also agree to share the usufruct of two animals by one using one of them and the other the other.

Article 1178. Partition of usufruct limited by time is in the nature of an exchange. Thus, one of the joint owners is considered to have exchanged his share of the benefit accruing to his turn for that of the share of the benefit accruing to the turn of the other. From this point of view, partition of usufruct limited by time is in the nature of hire. Consequently, in partition of usufruct limited by time, a period of time must be mentioned, such as so many days or months.

Article 1179. Partition of usufruct limited by place is in the nature of separation. Thus, the usufruct accruing to two joint owners of a country house is undivided, that is to say, it embraces every part of such house. Upon partition, the usufruct of one of the joint owners is considered to be concentrated in one part of such country house, and the usufruct of the second joint owner in the other part thereof. Consequently, there is no necessity to mention a period of time in the case of partition of usufruct limited as to place.

Article 1180. In the case of partition of usufruct limited as to time, the commencement of the period, that is to say, determining who of the joint owners is to enjoy the usufruct first, is decided by drawing lots. Similarly, in the case of a partition of usufruct limited as to place, the place is determined by drawing lots.

Article 1181. If one of the joint owners of several things jointly owned desires a partition of the usufruct thereof, and the other joint owner objects thereto, a partition will be enforced if the usufruct of the jointly owned property is of the same type. If the usufruct is of a different type, the partition will not be enforced.

Example :-

> One of the joint owners of two houses jointly owned desires a partition of the usufruct whereby he shall live in one and the other joint owner in the other; or in the case of two animals jointly owned, one of the joint owners desires a partition of the usufruct whereby one of them shall use one animal, and the other the other. If the other joint owner objects thereto the partition may be enforced. But if one of them desires partition whereby one is to live in one house and the other is to be let on hire as a bath, or whereby one is to live in one house and the other is to cultivate land, such partition is valid if it is by consent; but if one of the joint owners objects thereto, the division of the usufruct cannot be enforced.

Article 1182. If one of the joint owners of property which is capable of partition desires partition, and the other desires partition of the usufruct, the claim to partition will be upheld. If none of the joint owners desires partition, but one of them desires partition of the usufruct and the other objects, partition of the usufruct will be enforced.

Article 1183. If one of the joint owners of some specific object which is not capable of division desires partition of the usufruct and the other objects, partition of the usufruct will be enforced.

Article 1184. The rent of real property jointly owned, such as a ship, a mill, a coffee-shop, an inn, and a bath, which are let on hire to the public, is divided between the joint owners in accordance with their shares. If one of the joint owners objects to giving his share on hire, partition of the usufruct will be enforced. If the rent accruing to the share of one of the joint owners during his turn is disproportionately large, the amount in excess is divided among the joint owners.

Article 1185. Each joint owner may, after a partition of usufruct limited as to time has been carried out, make personal use of the real property jointly owned, when his turn comes, and in the case of a partition of usufruct limited as to place, may make personal use of the part falling to his own share. He may also obtain rent therefor by giving it on hire to some third party.

Article 1186. If after a partition of usufruct has been made, the joint owners give their respective shares on hire, and the revenue accruing thereby to one of them is greater than that of the other, the latter does not share in such excess.

But if a partition of usufruct arising out of profit is made, as, for example, whereby one of the joint owners receives the rent of a house for one month and the other for another month, any excess amount is jointly held. But if a partition of usufruct is made whereby the profit arising out of one of two houses is to go to one joint owner and the other to the other, and the profit arising out of one is greater than that of the other, the latter does not share therein.

Article 1187. There may be no partition of usufruct in the case of any specific property.

Example :-

The partition of the usufruct of the fruit of trees jointly owned, or of the milk or wool of animals jointly owned, on the terms that one joint owner shall gather the fruit of a certain number of such trees and the other the fruit of some other number of trees, or that one shall take the milk and wool of one flock of sheep, and the other the milk and wool of the other, is invalid, since they relate to specific property.

Article 1188. If the joint owners divide the usufruct of their shares by consent, one of them alone may subsequently cancel such partition. If one of them, however, has given his share on hire to some other person, the other cannot cancel the partition of usufruct until after the termination of the period of hire.

Article 1189. One of the joint owners alone may not cancel a partition of usufruct carried out by order of the Court. The whole of the joint owners, however, may cancel such partition by consent.

Article 1190. If one of the joint owners wishes to sell his share or to divide it, he may cancel the partition of usufruct. But any partition of usufruct which is sought to be cancelled without any due cause and whereby the jointly owned property will merely return to its former state, will be disallowed by the Court.

Article 1191. A partition of usufruct continues to be valid after the death of one or all of the joint owners.

CHAPTER III.

WALLS AND NEIGHBOURS.

SECTION I.

Rules of law relating to property owned in absolute ownership.

Article 1192. Any person may deal with his property owned in absolute ownership as he wishes. But if the rights of any other person are concerned therein, the owner of such property may not deal with it as though he were the independent owner thereof.

Example:-
The upper storey of a building is owned in absolute ownership by A and the lower storey similarly by B. A has a right of support from B and B has a right to be protected from sun and rain. Neither may perform any act which will prejudice the other without obtaining permission from him, and neither may pull down his part of the building.

Article 1193. If there is one door giving on to the street for both the upper and lower storeys, both owners may make use thereof. Neither may prevent the other from coming in or going out thereby.

Article 1194. Whoever owns a piece of land in absolute ownership is likewise owner of what is above it and what is below it. That is to say, he may deal with it as by erecting buildings on a piece of land he owns in absolute ownership, and raising it as high as he wishes. He may also dig the ground and make store-rooms therein and dig wells as deep as he wishes.

Article 1195. No person may extend the eaves of a room which he has constructed in his house, over his neighbour's house.

If he does so, the amount which so extends over his neighbour's house may be removed.

JOINT OWNERSHIP

Article 1196. If the branches of trees in any person's garden extend into the house or garden of his neighbour, the owner may be made by the neighbour to tie up such branches and thus bring them back into his own garden, or to cut them down and thus obtain a clear current of air. He may not, however, cut down the tree on the grounds that the shadow of such tree is injurious to the cultivation in his garden.

Article 1197. No person may be prevented from dealing with his property which he owns in absolute ownership. Nevertheless, if such person by so doing causes great injury to any other person, he may be prohibited therefrom, as will be set forth in Section II.

SECTION II.

Relations of one neighbour to another.

Article 1198. Any person may raise the wall of his property owned in absolute ownership to any extent he wishes, and may do anything he desires, and, providing that he does not cause his neighbour any great injury thereby, the latter cannot prevent him from doing so.

Article 1199. Great injury consists of anything which causes damage to a building, that is to say, which weakens it and causes it to collapse or makes it impossible for it to be put to the use for which it was originally intended, as in the case of a dwelling house.

Article 1200. Great injury, caused in any way whatsoever, must be removed.

Examples:-

(1) A forge or a mill is erected adjacent to a house The house is weakened by the hammering from the forge, or the turning of the mill wheel; or it becomes

impossible for the owner of such house to dwell therein by reason of the great quantity of smoke given off by a furnace or a linseed oil factory, erected in close proximity thereto. These acts amount to great injury, which must be removed.

(2) A constructs a water channel on a piece of land adjoining B's house. Water is brought along it to a mill and the walls of B's house are weakened: or A makes a rubbish heap at the foot of the neighbour's wall and throws sweepings there and the walls become rotten. The owner of the house may have the injury removed.

(3) A constructs a threshing floor near to B's house and the dust coming therefrom makes it impossible for B to dwell in his house. B may have the injury removed.

(4) A erects a high building near a threshing floor belonging to B and thereby cuts off the flow of air to the threshing floor. This act amounts to great injury and may be stopped.

(5) A opens a cook shop in the cloth merchants' market. The smoke therefrom is deposited on his neighbours goods and causes great injury thereto. The injury may be stopped.

(6) The sewer in A's house is broken and the sewage flows into his neighbour's house. This amounts to great injury, and upon the neighbour bringing an action, A must repair the sewer and put it in order.

Article 1201. Any interference with benefits which are not fundamental necessities, such as cutting off the air or the view of a house, or preventing the entrance of sunlight, does not amount to great injury. If light is entirely cut off, however, this amounts to great injury. Consequently, if a person erects a building and cuts off the light from the window of a room belonging to his neighbour, the room being darkened to such an extent that it is impossible to read anything written therein, the act amounts to great injury and may be stopped; and it may not be argued that light can come in through the door, since the door must be kept closed on account of the cold and for other reasons. If the room has two windows, however, and a building is erected and the light of one of them is cut off as mentioned above, such act does not amount to great injury.

Article 1202. The fact that places which are frequented by women, such as a kitchen, the head of a well, and the courtyard of a house are overlooked, is considered to amount to great injury. Consequently, if a person constructs a new window in his house whereby he overlooks quarters frequented by the women of an adjoining neighbour, or of the owner of a house on the other side of the street, or if he overlooks them from a window in a newly built house, an order shall be given for the removal of such injury. Such person may also be obliged to remove such injury by building a wall or constructing a partition in such a way that the women cannot be seen. He may not in any case, however, be forced to close up the window. If quarters occupied by women can be seen through the interstices of a wall made of brushwood, the owner of the wall may be ordered to close up such interstices. He may not, however, be obliged to tear the brushwood down and build a wall. (See Article 22).

Article 1203. If a window is constructed in a place which is of the same height as a man, a neighbour of the person constructing such window may not have it removed by alleging that it is probable that he will overlook the women's quarter of his neighbour by placing a ladder there. (See Article 74).

Article 1204. A garden is not considered to be women's quarters. Consequently, if a person is unable to see the women's quarters of his neighbour's house, but is able to see his garden, and consequently the women, but merely on the occasions when they go out into the garden, his neighbour may not demand that his view into the garden shall be stopped.

Article 1205. If a person climbs up the fruit trees in his garden, and thereby overlooks the women's quarters of his neighbour, such person must give information that he intends to climb such trees, in order that the women may cover themselves. Should he fail to give such information, the Court may forthwith prohibit him from climbing such trees.

Article 1206. If upon the partition of a country house jointly owned by two persons, the share falling to one overlooks the women's quarters of the other, the joint owners shall be ordered to construct a joint partition.

Article 1207. If any person deals with property owned in absolute ownership in some manner authorized by law, and some other person constructs a building by the side thereof whereby he suffers injury, he himself alone must remove such injury.

Examples:-

(1) The women's quarters in a house newly constructed are overlooked by the windows of an old house. The owner of the newly constructed house must himself remove the injury. He may not call upon the owner of the old house to do so.

(2) A person constructs a house on a piece of land adjoining a blacksmith's forge, and alleges that the hammering in the forge has caused great injury to his house. He cannot stop the forge from working.

(3) A person builds a house in a place where a threshing floor has been established for some time past and alleges that the dust is being deposited in his

house. He cannot call upon the owner of the threshing floor to stop work.

Article 1208. If a person who owns an old house with windows looking on to a piece of vacant land belonging to his neighbour has such house destroyed by fire, and the neighbour builds a house on the land in question, and thereafter the owner of the old house has it rebuilt in its former state and from the windows thereof overlooks the women's quarters of the new house, the injury must be removed by the owner of the new house himself. He cannot oblige the owner of the old house to remove the injury.

Article 1209. If a person constructs new windows in his house and is unable to overlook the women's quarters of his neighbour by reason of the latter having constructed a high room between, and the room is later pulled down by the neighbour with the result that the women's quarters of the latter can be seen, the neighbour cannot call upon such person to stop the view from the windows, or to close them up, but must remove the injury himself.

Article 1210. One of the joint owners of a wall may not raise such wall without the permission of the other, nor may he erect a kiosk thereon or any similar thing, whether causing injury to the other or not. But if one of them wishes to place beams on the ground in order to build a room, that is to say, if he wishes to place them upon the edges of the beams on the wall, he may not be prevented from doing so. The other joint owner, however, has the right of placing the same number of beams. He may not, however, put more than half the total number of beams which can be supported and may not exceed that number. If both of them originally had an equal

JOINT OWNERSHIP 317

number of beams upon such wall, and one of them increases his number of beams, the other may prevent him from so doing.

Article 1211. One of the joint owners of a wall may not have the position of the beams on such wall changed to the right or to the left or up or down. If the beams, however, are placed in an elevated part of the wall, he may put them on a lower part thereof.

Article 1212. If any person constructs a cesspit or a sewer near a well of water belonging to some other person, and contaminates the water thereof, he may be made to remove the injury. If it is impossible to remove the injury, he may be made to close up the cesspit or sewer. Again, if any person constructs a sewer near to a water channel, and the dirty water from such sewer flows into the channel and causes great injury thereto, and no other way can be found to remove such injury than by closing it, the sewer shall be closed.

SECTION III.

Roads.

Article 1213. If any person who owns a house on either side of a street wishes to construct a bridge from the one to the other, he shall be prevented from so doing. If he does so, and the bridge causes no injury to the passers by, such bridge shall not be pulled down. There is, however, no right to permanency in the case of bridges and resting places constructed over the public highway. Consequently, if after a bridge constructed over the public highway as mentioned above has been pulled down, and the owner wishes to construct another such bridge, he may again be prevented from so doing.

JOINT OWNERSHIP

Article 1214. Anything which causes great injury to passers by on the public highway may be removed, such as low projecting balconies and resting places, even though they have been there for a long period of time. (See Article 7).

Article 1215. Any person who wishes to repair his house may make mortar quickly on one side of the road for use on his building, provided that he does not thereby cause any injury to the passers by.

Article 1216. When necessary, the property of any person held in absolute ownership may be taken for its value by order of the authorities and made part of the road. He may not be deprived of ownership thereof, however, until he has been paid the price. (See Articles 251 and 262).

Article 1217. Provided no injury is done to passers by, any person may obtain any surplus land on the highway by paying its estimated price to the Government, and attach such land to his house.

Article 1218. Any person whatsoever may construct a door giving on to the public highway.

Article 1219. No person who is not the owner of a right of way in a private road may construct a door looking thereon.

Article 1220. A private road is like the jointly owned property held in absolute ownership of persons having a right of way. Consequently, none of the owners of a private road may make any fresh construction therein without the permission of the other, whether such construction is prejudicial or not.

Article 1221. One of the owners of a private road may not allow water to flow from a house which he has newly built, on to such road, without the permission of the other owners.

JOINT OWNERSHIP

Article 1222. If any person closes up a door giving on to a private road, he does not thereby lose his right of way thereover. Consequently, if he sells his house at some later date, the purchaser may again construct the door.

Article 1223. Persons passing along the public highway have the right, if there is a great crowd of people therein, of entering a private road. Consequently, the owners of a private road may not sell it by agreement among themselves, nor may they divide it among themselves, nor may they close up the entrance thereto.

SECTION IV.

Right of way, right of acqueduct, right of flow.

Article 1224. In case of right of way, right of acqueduct and right of flow, ancient rights shall be observed. That is to say, rights acquired in the remote past are left as they were, because, as is laid down in Article 6, things which have been in existence from time immemorial shall be left as they were; and until some proof to the contrary is produced, they shall not be changed. But anything existing from time immemorial which is contrary to law is invalid. That is to say, if any act which has been performed was originally illegal and has existed from time immemorial, such act is invalid, and, if it causes great injury, shall be removed (See Article 27).

Example :-
> If the dirty water of a house has flowed from time immemorial into the public highway, and causes injury to the passers by, the ancient rights are disregarded, and the injury must be removed.

Article 1225. If any person has a right of way over the land of another, the owner of the land cannot prevent him from passing and crossing over the land.

Article 1226. A person who has given something for nothing, to be consumed, has a right to revoke the gift. If injury is inflicted by consent, such consent may be withdrawn. Consequently, if a person who has no right of way over the land belonging to another exercises a right of way thereover for a certain period, with the permission of the owner of such land only, the latter may, whenever he wishes, prevent him from exercising the right.

Article 1227. If any person has a right of way over a defined pathway on the land of some other person, and the owner of the land erects a building on such pathway with the permission of the owner of the right of way, the latter loses his right of way, and has no right of disputing the matter with the owner of the land. (See Article 51)

Article 1228. If a cutting or a water channel belonging to one person runs by right across the land of another, the owner of the land may not endeavour to prevent the former from exercising his right in the future. If such cutting and water channel are in need of improvement and repair, the owner thereof shall be allowed access thereto, if this is possible, and may make such improvements and repairs. If it is not possible to make the improvements and repairs, however, without entering upon the land, and the owner of the land will not give the necessary permission, the Court shall oblige him either to grant permission for entry on the land, or to carry out the repairs.

Article 1229. If the rain water of a house has flowed on to the house of a neighbour from time immemorial, the latter may not thereafter seek to prevent such flow.

Article 1230. If water from a house situated in a road has flowed into such road from time immemorial and from there has flowed into a piece of land situated below such road, the owner of the land may not stop the flow by blocking it up. If he does so, the Court shall order the barrier to be removed and the former state of affairs to be restored.

Article 1231. No person may cause the water from a newly constructed room to flow into the house of some other person.

Article 1232. The owner of a house which is burdened by a right of sewage may not stop the right of flow, nor may any person who purchases such house.

Article 1233. The owner of a sewer the sewage of which flows through the house of some other person must, if the sewer becomes full, or breaks, thereby causing great injury to the owner of the house, remove such injury.

CHAPTER IV.

JOINTLY OWNED PROPERTY WHICH IS FREE.

SECTION I.

Things which are free and things which are not free.

Article 1234. Water, grass and fire are free. The public are joint owners of these three things.

Article 1235. Water flowing under ground is not the absolute property of any person.

Article 1236. Wells which have not been made by the labour of any particular person, the benefit of which may be enjoyed by the public, are the jointly owned and free property of the public.

Article 1237. Seas and large lakes are free.

Article 1238. Rivers which belong to the State and are not the property owned in absolute ownership of any person, are those rivers the bed of which does not pass through the property of a group of persons owned in absolute ownership. All such rivers are free. Examples of such rivers are the Nile, the Euphrates, the Danube and the Tonja.

Article 1239. Rivers which are the property of individuals owned in absolute ownership, that is to say, rivers which, as stated above, flow through the property of persons owned in absolute ownership are of two categories.

The first category consists of rivers the water of which is divided between the joint owners of the land through which they flow, but is not completely exhausted and continues its course through vacant land which is free to the public. Rivers of this class are called public rivers, since they are at the disposal of the public. No right of pre-emption attaches to these rivers.

The second category consists of private rivers, the waters of which are divided between the land belonging to a limited number of persons, and which, upon arriving at the limits of such land, disappear and do not flow in vacant land. A right of pre-emption attaches to such land.

Article 1240. Mud brought down by a river and deposited upon a person's land becomes such person's property owned in absolute ownership, and no other person may interfere therewith.

Article 1241. Grasses which grow wild in places having no owner are free. So also are grasses which grow in any person's property owned in absolute ownership, without being planted. But if such person is the indirect cause of their growing, as when he waters the land or digs a creek round it, thereby preparing it and making it fit for vegetation to grow in, the vegetation produced becomes his property and no other person has any right thereto. If any other person takes them and consumes the same, he must make good the loss.

Article 1242. Grasses consist of vegetation which has no trunk, and consequently does not include trees. Mushrooms are considered to be grasses.

Article 1243. Trees which grow wild on mountains which are free, that is to say, mountains which have not yet passed into the possession of anyone, are also free.

Article 1244. Trees which grow wild in property owned by anyone in absolute ownership belong to such person. No person may cut them down ♦for firewood without the owner's permission. If he does so, he must make good the loss.

Article 1245. If any person grafts a tree, the shoots coming from the graft are his property held in absolute ownership, including the fruit thereof.

Article 1246. All produce arising from seeds sown by any person for himself is such person's property, and no one may interfere therewith.

Article 1247. Game is free.

SECTION II.

Acquisition of ownership of things which are free.

Article 1248. There are three means of acquiring absolute ownership. The first consists of the transfer of property held in absolute ownership from one owner to another, such as sale or gift. The second consists of one person succeeding another, such as inheritance. The third consists of obtaining a thing which is free and which has no owner. The latter is either actual, as where someone in fact appropriates such thing, or constructive, as where someone puts out a receptacle to collect rain water, or sets a trap to catch game.

Article 1249. Any person who obtains possession of a thing which is free, becomes the independent owner thereof.

Example :-
> A, by means of a receptacle such as a jug or a can obtains water from a river and stores it therein. The water becomes the property of A. No other person may make use of it without A's permission. If any other person takes and consumes it without A's permission, he must make good the loss.

Article 1250. Taking possession must be coupled with intention. Consequently, if any person puts out a receptacle with the object of catching rain water, the rain water caught in the receptacle becomes that person's property. Again, water collected in a tank or cistern constructed for that purpose, becomes the property of the owner. But rain water collected in a receptacle not intentionally put in any particular place, does not become the property of the owner thereof. Any other person may take it and consume it. (See Article 2)

Article 1251 In taking possession of water, the flow thereof must be interrupted. Consequently, possession cannot be taken of water from a well which oozes out from the sides thereof and if a person takes and uses the water, he is not liable to make good the loss thereof, even though the owner has not made a free gift thereof for consumption. Similarly, possession cannot be taken of water the flow of which is regulated, that is to say, water which leaves one side of a tank in the same quantity as it enters the other side.

Article 1252. Possession may be taken of wild grasses by collecting them and by cutting them and making them into bunches.

Article 1253. Trees growing in a state of nature on mountains which are the property of no one, may be cut down for firewood by any person whatsoever. And by merely cutting them down such person becomes the owner thereof. There is no need to tie them into bunches.

SECTION III.

General conditions attaching to things that are free.

Article 1254. Any person may make use of any thing that is free provided that in doing so no injury is inflicted upon any other person.

Article 1255. No person may prevent any other person from taking and obtaining possession of anything that is free.

Article 1256. Any person may pasture his beasts on wild grasses growing in places that have no owner. He may take and obtain possession of as much thereof as he pleases.

Article 1257. Although wild grasses growing on the property of a person owned in absolute ownership, and of which such person is not the indirect cause, are free, the owner, nevertheless, may prevent any other person from entering on his property.

Article 1258. If any person gathers wood from mountains which are free, and leaves such wood there

JOINT OWNERSHIP

and some other person takes it, the former may demand the return thereof.

Article 1259. The fruit of trees having no owner and which are found in mountains that are free, and in valleys and pasture lands having no owner, may be gathered by any person whatsoever.

Article 1260. If any person hires any other person to gather wood or to catch game for him from uncultivated country, the wood gathered or game caught by such person belongs to the person employing him.

Article 1261. If a person lights a fire in his own property owned in absolute ownership, he may prevent any person from entering thereon and taking advantage thereof. But if any person lights a fire in a desert place belonging to no one, other persons may take advantage thereof. They may warm themselves by it, may sew by the light thereof, and may light their lamps therefrom. The owner of the fire may not prevent them from so doing. No one, however, may take a live coal from the fire without the owner's permission.

SECTION IV.

Right of taking water and right of drinking water.

Article 1262. By watering is meant taking one's turn in making use of water to water crops and animals.

Article 1263. The right of drinking consists of the right of drinking water.

Article 1264. Any person may make use of air and light and of seas and big lakes.

Article 1265. Any person may water his lands from rivers which are not owned in absolute ownership by any particular person, and, in order to irrigate them and to construct mills, may open a canal or water channels, provided that he does not thereby inflict injury on any other person. Consequently, if the water overflows and causes injury to the public, or the water of the river is entirely cut off, or boats cannot be navigated, such injury must be stopped.

Article 1266. All persons and animals have a right of drinking from water, possession of which has not been taken by any other person.

Article 1267. The right of taking water from rivers which are privately owned, that is to say, the course of which are privately owned, belongs to the owners thereof. Other persons have a right of drinking therefrom. Consequently, no person may, without permission, water his land from a river which is appropriated to a group of persons, or from a water course, or a water pipe, or a well. He may, however, drink water therefrom, since he has a right of drinking water. He may also water his animals, by reason of the large number thereof, from such river, water-course, or water-pipe, provided there is no danger of destroying the same. He may also bring the water to his house or to his garden by means of jugs or buckets.

Article 1268. Any person having in his property which he owns in absolute ownership a tank, a well, or a river, from which water alternatively enters and leaves, may prevent any person who wishes to drink water from entering his property. If however, there is no free water to be had in the neighbourhood, the owner of the property is obliged either to draw off water, or to give such person permission to enter his property and take it. If he does not draw off the water, such person has the right of entering and taking it, subject, however, to no injury being caused, that is to say, provided that no injury is done, such as destroying the edge of the tank, or of the well, or of the river.

Article 1269. A person who is joint owner of a river may not open up another river, that is to say, a canal or water channel leading therefrom, unless he has obtained the permission of the other joint owners. Neither may he alter the old established order in which he has his right of taking water. Nor may he divert his share of the water from such river on to other land not enjoying a right of taking water. If the other joint owners agree to such things, either they, or their heirs, may denounce such agreement at any subsequent date.

SECTION V.

The vivification of dead land.

Article 1270. Dead land consists of land which is not the property of anyone owned in absolute ownership, nor the grazing ground of any town or village, nor a place where wood can be gathered, and which is remote from civilization. That is to say, a place where the voice of a person who is shouting from the outskirts of a town or village cannot be heard.

Article 1271. Land which is near to civilization is left to the public for grazing grounds, threshing floors, and for cutting wood. Such land is called land left to the public.

Article 1272. If any person, after obtaining Imperial sanction vivifies and cultivates any place consisting of dead land, such person becomes the absolute owner thereof. If the Sultan or his representative gives permission to any person to vivify land on the terms that he shall merely make use of such land without becoming owner thereof, such person may deal with the land in the way he has been authorized to do, but does not become the absolute owner thereof.

Article 1273. If a person vivifies a piece of land and leaves the rest, he becomes the absolute owner of the part he vivifies, but not of the remainder. But if in the middle of the part he has cultivated he leaves a portion vacant, such portion becomes his.

Article 1274. If a person vivifies a piece of dead land and thereafter some other persons arrive and vivify the land situated on all four sides thereof, a road shall be made in the land of the last comer for the former. That is to say, there shall be a road for him there.

Article 1275. Vivification consists of sowing seed, planting trees, ploughing the land, watering it, or opening water-channels or canals, in order to irrigate it.

Article 1276. If any person builds walls round dead land, or with a view to protecting it from flooding, makes a dam round it by raising the sides thereof, such land is considered to have been vivified.

Article 1277. The placing of stones, or thorns, or the dead branches of trees so that they surround the four sides of land, or clearing away the grasses on such land, or burning the thorns on it, or sinking wells thereon, does not amount to vivification. This is enclosing land.

Article 1278. If any person cuts down the grasses or thorns on dead land, puts them round such land and puts earth thereon, but does not complete it in such a way that they form a dam preventing the flow of water, such act does not amount to vivification, but is considered to be enclosing the land.

JOINT OWNERSHIP

Article 1279. If any person encloses a piece of dead land, he possesses a stronger right to such land than any other person, for a period of three years. If he fails to vivify it during the period of three years, he loses such right. It may be given to some other person to vivify.

Article 1280. If any person digs a well in dead land with Imperial permission, such person becomes the absolute owner of such well.

SECTION VI.

Ownership of land surrounding wells sunk, water brought, and trees planted with Imperial permission in dead land.

Article 1281. The land attaching to the ownership in a well amounts to forty *arshins*.

Article 1282. The land attaching to springs of water is five hundred *arshins* from each side.

Article 1283. The land attaching to the two sides of a big river which does not require continually to be cleaned amounts to one half the breadth of the river. The amount of land attaching to both sides of the river is equal to the breadth of the whole river.

Article 1284. The land attaching to small rivers which continually require to be cleaned, that is to say water courses, canals and underground channels, consists of an amount large enough for the stones and mud to be thrown upon when being cleaned.

Article 1285. The land attaching to water in channels running along the surface of the ground amounts to five hundred *arshins*, as in the case of springs.

Article 1286. The land attaching to wells is the absolute property of the owner of the wells. No other person may deal therewith in any way whatsoever. If any other person sinks a well in such person's land, he can cause it to be closed. The same rule applies to land attaching to springs, rivers and water channels.

Article 1287. If any person, with Imperial sanction, digs a well in the vicinity of land attaching to some other well, the land attaching thereto on the other side amounts to forty *arshins*. He may not, however, trespass upon the land attaching to the first well.

Article 1288. If any person digs a well outside the land attaching to some other well, and the water from the first well flows into the second well, no liability is incurred. Similarly, if a person opens a shop next door to the shop of some other person and the business of the latter declines, the former cannot be obliged to shut his shop.

Article 1289. The land attaching to trees planted in dead land with Imperial sanction is five *arshins* on each side. No other person may plant trees within this distance.

Article 1290. The banks of a water channel, the water of which flows into the land of some other person, belong to the owner of such channel, on each side, to the amount necessary to hold the water. If the banks are raised on both sides, the raised land also belongs to the owner of the channel. If the banks are not raised, and there is no evidence to prove that either the owner of the land or of the water channel has taken possession thereof, as by planting trees therein, the banks belong to the owner of the land. The owner of the channel, however, has the right, when cleaning his channel, of throwing mud therefrom on both sides.

Article 1291. No land attaches to a well dug by a person in his own land owned in absolute ownership. His neighbour may dig a well next to it in his own land owned in absolute ownership and the former may not seek to prevent the latter from doing so by alleging that he is attracting water away from his well.

SECTION VII.

Fundamental conditions affecting hunting.

Article 1292. Game may be hunted with implements which inflict wounds, such as a lance or a gun, or with things such as a net or a trap, or with savage animals, such as a trained dog, or with birds of prey, such as a trained hawk.

Article 1293. Game consists of wild animals which are afraid of man.

Article 1294. Domestic animals may not be hunted, nor wild animals which have been tamed. Consequently, if any person catches a pigeon or a hawk with a ring on its leg, or a stag with a collar on its neck, from which it may be inferred that they are not wild, they are considered to be lost property, and the person who has taken them must make known that he will restore them to their owners upon application made by them.

Article 1295. Game must be in a position to flee from mankind. That is to say, must be able to get away and escape by means of its legs or its wings. If it is unable to escape and flee, as, for example, where a stag falls into a well, it loses its quality of game.

Article 1296. Any person who deprives game of its quality of game is considered to have caught it.

Article 1297. Game belongs to any person who catches it.

Examples:-

(1) A shoots at game and wounds it so that it cannot escape. The game becomes the property of A. But

JOINT OWNERSHIP

if A wounds it slightly so that it can escape, he does not become the owner thereof and if any other person hits or catches it in any other way, the latter becomes the owner thereof.

(2) A shoots at game and after it has fallen, it rises again, and while escaping is caught by B. B becomes the owner thereof.

Article 1298. If two persons shoot at game and both hit it, the game in question is divided in equal shares between the two.

Article 1299. If two persons each let trained dogs chase after game and both catch an animal, such animal similarly becomes the joint property of the owners of the dogs.

If each of them catch an animal, their masters become owners of such animal.

Again, if two persons each let trained dogs chase after game and one of them brings down the animal and the other kills it, the master of the first dog becomes owner of the animal, if the dog has so treated it that it could not get away and escape.

Article 1300. If any person catches fish found in a water channel or canal belonging to some other person, which cannot be caught without fishing for them, such person becomes the owner thereof.

Article 1301. If any person prepares a place for fishing by the water side, and a large number of fish come there, and on account of the water decreasing the fish can be taken without the need of fishing for them, such fish belong to that person. But if by reason of the large quantity of water in that place it is necessary to catch the fish, such fish do not become the property of that person, but, if fished for and caught by some other person, become the property of the latter.

JOINT OWNERSHIP

Article 1302. If game enters the house of any person, and such person closes the door and catches the game, the game becomes his property.

If he closes the door, however, but fails to obtain possession of the game, he does not become owner thereof, and if any other person catches it, such person becomes owner thereof.

Article 1303. If any person puts down anything such as a net or a trap in a particular place in order to trap game, and catches such game therewith, such person becomes the owner thereof. But if any person puts out a net in a particular place to dry and game is caught therewith, such game does not become his property. Again, if game falls into a hole in land belonging to a particular person, any other person may take it and thereby become the owner thereof. But if the owner of the land dug the hole for the purpose of catching game, he has a prior right over any other person to such game. (See Article 1250).

Article 1304. If a wild bird builds its nest in any person's garden and lays eggs therein, it does not become the property of such person. Any other person may take its eggs, or its young, and the owner of the garden may not demand their return. But if such person has prepared his garden so that a wild bird may lay its eggs, and bring forth its young there, such person may take the eggs and the young of such bird and becomes the owner thereof.

Article 1305. If bees select a place in any person's garden and make a hive there, the honey is considered to be one of the perquisites of the garden and becomes the property of such person, and no other person may interfere therewith. A tithe, however, must be paid to the Treasury.

Article 1306. Bees which gather in a hive belonging to any particular person are considered to be property of which he has obtained possession. The honey produced by them also becomes the property of that person.

Article 1307. If a swarm of bees leave the hive of one particular person and settle in the house of another and such person appropriates them, the owner can demand the return thereof.

CHAPTER V.

JOINT EXPENSES.

SECTION I.

Repairs to jointly owned property and expenses connected therewith.

Article 1308. If property jointly owned in absolute ownership is in need of repairs, the joint owners must jointly repair such property in proportion to their shares

Article 1309. If one of the joint owners spends a reasonable sum of his own money with the permission of the other on the repair of the jointly owned property, he may have recourse against the other joint owner for his share. That is to say, he may recover from the joint owner whatever part of the expenditure falls to his share.

Article 1310. If one of the owners of the property jointly held in absolute ownership which requires repairs is absent, the other may apply to the Court for permission to effect such repairs. Permission given by the Court is equivalent to permission given by the absent joint owner. That is to say, upon the joint owner who is present carrying out the repairs of the jointly owned property by order of the Court, he is considered to have obtained the

JOINT OWNERSHIP

permission of the absent joint owner and has a right of recourse against him for his share of the expenses.

Article 1311. If any person carries out repairs to property jointly owned in absolute ownership on his own initiative without obtaining the permission of the other joint owner, or of the Court, he is considered to have carried out such repairs free of charge. That is to say, he has no right to claim an amount corresponding to the share of the other joint owner, whether such jointly owned property is capable of partition or not.

Article 1312. If any person wishes to carry out repairs to property jointly owned in absolute ownership which is capable of partition, and the other joint owner objects thereto, and he carries out such repairs on his own initiative, such person is considered to have carried out the repairs free of charge. That is to say, he cannot have recourse against the other joint owner for his share. If upon the refusal of the joint owner in this manner, such person applies to the Court, no order can be made for repairs, in view of the terms of Article 25. An order may, however, be given for partition. After partition has been effected, such person may do what he likes with his share.

Article 1313. If property jointly owned in absolute ownership such as a mill or a bath, which is not capable of partition, is in need of repairs and one of the joint owners wishes to carry out such repairs and the other refuses to agree, the former, after obtaining an order from the Court, may expend a reasonable amount of money on such repairs. He becomes a creditor of the other joint owner for a portion of the expenses occasioned by the repairs corresponding to his share. He may obtain payment of the sum owing to him by letting the jointly owned property on hire and taking the rent. If he carries out the repairs without obtaining an order from the Court, he can only obtain payment of a sum, as laid down, corresponding to the value of the share of the other joint owner calculated according to the value of the building at the time the repairs were carried out, notwithstanding what he may actually have paid.

Article 1314. If things jointly owned in absolute ownership which are not capable of partition, such as a mill and a bath, are totally destroyed, so that only the land upon which they were erected remains, and one of the owners wishes to erect a building thereon and the other refuses to agree, the latter cannot be obliged to build, but the land shall be divided.

Article 1315. If a building owned in absolute ownership is destroyed or burnt, the upper storey belonging to one person and the lower storey to another, either of them may restore his portion of such building to its original state. Neither can prevent the other from so doing. If the owner of the upper storey requests the owner of the lower storey to repair his part so that he may build his portion thereon, and the owner of the lower storey refuses, the owner of the upper storey may apply to the Court for an order empowering him to reconstruct both lower and upper storeys and upon doing so, he may prevent the owner of the lower storey from dealing therewith until he has paid his share of the expenses.

Article 1316. If a wall jointly owned by two neighbours is destroyed and things are resting upon it, such as a kiosk or the ends of beams belonging to the two, and one of them rebuilds the wall and the other refuses to do so, the one who rebuilds can prevent the other from placing anything on such wall until he has paid his half of the expenses.

JOINT OWNERSHIP

Article 1317. If a wall separating two houses is destroyed, and the women's quarters of one of them can be overlooked from the other, and the owner of one of the houses wishes the wall to be rebuilt jointly and the owner of the other refuses, he may not be forced to do so. The Court, however, may order them to build jointly a screen made of wood or some other material.

Article 1318. If a wall jointly owned by two neighbours becomes weak and it is feared that it will collapse, and one of them wishes to knock it down and the other refuses to agree thereto, he shall be obliged to knock down such wall together with the other joint owner.

Article 1319. If real property jointly owned by two minors, or which is situated between two properties which have been dedicated to pious purposes, is in need of repair, and injury will result thereto if it is left in its present state, and one of the two guardians, or one of the two administrators of the pious foundations wishes to carry out the repairs and the other does not, the latter shall be obliged to do so.

Examples: -

(1) A jointly owned wall separates the houses of two minors and it is feared that it will collapse. One of the guardians wishes to repair the wall and the other refuses. The Court will then send a reliable person to investigate the matter. If as a result it proves that injury will result to the minor if the wall is left in its present state, the guardian who refuses shall be forced to repair such wall jointly with the other guardian from the property of the minor.

(2) A house which is the joint property of two pious foundations is in need of repairs. One of the administrators wishes to carry out the repairs and the other does not. The latter will be forced to do so by the Court from the property of the pious foundation.

JOINT OWNERSHIP

Article 1320. If two persons are joint owners of an animal, and one of them refuses to feed him and the other applies to the Court, the Court shall order the joint owner who refuses to feed him either to sell his share, or feed the animal jointly with the other owner.

SECTION II.

The cleaning and improvement of rivers and water courses.

Article 1321. The cleaning and improvement of rivers which do not belong to any particular person in absolute ownership is incumbent upon the Treasury. If it is not in the power of the Treasury to do so, the public may be forced to do so.

Article 1322. The cleaning of rivers jointly owned in absolute ownership is incumbent upon the owners thereof, that is to say, upon those who have the right of taking water therefrom. The owners of a right of drinking water may not be called upon to share in the expenses of cleaning and improvement.

Article 1323. If some of the owners of a right of taking water from a jointly owned river desire to clean such river and the others refuse to do so, the persons who refuse will be made to clean such river jointly with the others, if it is a public river. If it is a private river, those persons who wish to clean it may, by order of the Court, proceed to do so, and may prevent those who refuse from making use of the river until such time as they have paid the amount which falls to their share of the expenses.

Article 1324. Should all the owners of a right of taking water refuse to clean a river which is jointly owned, they may be forced to do so, if it is a public river, but not if it is a private river.

JOINT OWNERSHIP

Article 1325. If any person owns land on the banks of a public river, whether such river is owned in absolute ownership or not, and there is no other road for satisfying such needs as drinking water or improving the river, the public may pass over such land the owner cannot prevent them from so doing.

Article 1326. Expenses connected with the cleaning and improvement of a jointly owned river begin from above. First of all, the whole of the joint owners must share therein, beginning with the joint owner whose land comes first and ending with the joint owner whose land comes last, the reason being that disadvantage is an obligation accompanying enjoyment.

Example :-

A river jointly owned by ten persons is being cleaned. The expenses connected with the joint owner's land which is highest up must be borne by the whole of the joint owners and thereafter by the nine others. The same procedure is then followed in the case of the land of the second joint owner, the expenses being divided among the eight others. This procedure is then continued until the joint owner's land which is lowest down is reached, who shares in the expenses of all. The last joint owner does his share alone. In this way, the expenses of the joint owner who is highest up are the least of all, and the expenses of the joint owner who is lowest down are the greatest of all.

Article 1327. The expenses occasioned by the cleaning of a jointly owned sewer begin from below. Thus, all the joint owners contribute towards the payment of the expenses of the portion of the sewer which is situated on the land of the joint owner who is lowest. On proceeding higher up, the latter has no further expenses to pay, and so on until they have all paid their shares, the joint owner who is highest up paying the expenses connected with his share alone. In this way, the expenses of the joint owner who is lowest down are lower than those of any other, and the expenses of the joint owner who is highest up are greater than those of the rest.

Article 1328. The repair of a private road, like a sewer, begins from below. The entrance is considered to be the lowest part, and the termination the highest part. A joint owner who is at the entrance shares in the expenses of repairing connected with his share alone. The joint owner who is at the termination of the private road, besides sharing in the expenses attaching to the shares of all the joint owners, pays his own share alone.

CHAPTER VI.

PARTNERSHIP.

SECTION I.

Definition and classification of partnership.

Article 1329. A contract of partnership consists of a contract for joint ownership whereby two or more persons jointly share in capital and profit.

Article 1330. The basis of a contract of partnership consists of offer and acceptance, express or implied.

Examples :-

(1) A informs B that he has become his partner whereby they will carry on business with a certain amount of capital. B agrees. An express partnership has been formed by offer and acceptance.

(2) A gives a thousand piastres to B, requesting B to give a thousand piastres also and buy certain property. B does so. A partnership has been formed by his implied acceptance.

Article 1331. Contractual partnership is divided into two categories:

(1) Partnership with equal shares.

A partnership with equal shares is a partnership which is formed when the partners enter into a contract of partnership stipulating for complete equality between them, and, after they have contributed the property which is to form the capital of the partnership, they maintain equality in the amount of their capital, and their shares of the profit. Similarly, if a person dies, and his sons take over the whole of his property left to them and make it their capital on the terms that they may buy and sell property of all kinds and share the profit equally between them, they may thereby form a partnership with equal shares. Formation of a partnership of this type, where there is complete equality, however, is rare.

(2) Partnership with unequal shares.

A partnership with unequal shares is formed when a contractual partnership is concluded without stipulating for complete equality.

Article 1332. A partnership, whether one of equal or of unequal shares, is either a partnership in property, or a partnership in work, or a partnership on credit. Thus, if the partners contribute a quantity of property to be the capital either jointly, or separately, or absolutely, and form a partnership with a view to trading and sharing the profits between them, such partnership is a partnership in property. If they agree that their labour shall be their capital and that they shall undertake to do work for some other person, and that the remuneration they receive shall be divided between them and form a partnership to that effect, such partnership is a partnership of work. A partnership of this nature is also called a personal partnership, or an artisans partnership, or a partnership of wage-earners, as, for example, where one tailor goes into partnership with another tailor, or a tailor goes into partnership with a dyer. If a partnership is concluded in which there is no capital and the partners buy and sell on credit on the terms that they shall divide the profits, such partnership is a partnership on credit.

SECTION II.

General conditions affecting a contractual partnership.

Article 1333. Every contractual partnership includes a contract of agency. Thus, each of the partners is the agent of the other to deal with property, that is to say, to buy or sell, or to work for a wage for some other person. Consequently, in all partnerships there is a condition that the partners shall be of sound mind and perfect understanding, as in the case of agency.

Article 1334. A partnership with equal shares also includes a contract of guarantee. Consequently, the partners must be competent to conclude a contract of guarantee.

Article 1335. A partnership with unequal shares includes a contract of agency only and does not include a contract of guarantee. Consequently, if at the time of the conclusion of the contract there has been no mention of a guarantee, the partners are not guarantors of each other. Consequently, a minor who has received authority may also enter into a partnership with unequal shares. But if at the time of the conclusion of a partnership with unequal shares, the contract of guarantee has been mentioned, the partners are guarantors of each other.

Article 1336. It must be stated in what way the profit is to be divided among the partners. If this is vague or unknown, the partnership is voidable.

JOINT OWNERSHIP

Article 1337. The shares of the profit to be divided between the partners must consist of undivided parts such as a half, a third, or a quarter. If a contract is made whereby one of the partners is to receive a fixed amount of the profit, the partnership is null and void.

SECTION III.

Conditions affecting a partnership in property.

Article 1338. The capital must be some kind of cash.

Article 1339. Copper coins which are in current use are considered by custom to be cash.

Article 1340. If it is customary among people to transact business with gold and silver which has not been coined, such gold and silver is considered to be cash. If not, it is considered to be merchandise.

Article 1341. The capital must consist of some specific object. A debt, that is to say, a sum due to be received from anyone, cannot be the capital of a partnership.

Example:-

> Two persons cannot form a partnership with capital consisting of something due from some other person. If the capital of one consists of some specific property and of the other of a debt, the partnership is invalid.

Article 1342. A partnership may not be validly concluded with regard to property which is not considered to be cash, such as merchandise or real property. That is to say, it cannot be the capital of the partnership. Nevertheless, if two persons desire to make the capital of the partnership out of property which is not in the nature of cash, each of them may sell the half of his property to the other, and after they have become joint owners thereof, they may conclude a partnership in respect to the jointly owned property. Similarly, if two persons mix together property of theirs the like of which can be found in the market, as, for example, a quantity of wheat, they then become joint owners of property owned in absolute ownership, and they can conclude a partnership with the mixed property as their capital.

Article 1343. A partnership formed whereby one person provides a horse and the other the harness on the terms that the money obtained by letting the horse on hire is to be shared between them is voidable, and the money obtained belongs to the owner of the horse; and since the harness is a necessary of the horse, the owner thereof is not entitled to a share of the money received but may only claim an estimated sum for the harness.

Article 1344. If two persons enter into a partnership whereby one who is the owner of an animal loads the goods of the other on to such animal, on the terms that the animal shall be taken round and the goods sold, the profit being shared between them, such partnership is voidable, and the profit earned belongs to the owner of the goods. The owner of the animal is entitled to an estimated payment. The case of a shop is similar to that of an animal. If two persons enter into a partnership whereby one of them sells his goods in the shop of the other on the terms that the profit shall be shared between them, the partnership is voidable and the profit derived from the goods belong to the owner. The owner of the shop is entitled to receive an estimated rent for the shop.

SECTION IV.

Rules relating to a contractual partnership.

Article 1345. Work becomes possessed of specific value when the value thereof is estimated. That is to say, labour is valued when the worth thereof is assessed. The work of one person may be proportionately more valuable than the work of some other person.

Example :-
> Two persons are partners in a partnership of unequal shares. Their capital is subscribed in equal shares and it is stipulated that both of them shall work in the business. It may validly be agreed that one of them shall have a greater share of the profits than the other since the skill of one in trading may be greater and his output of work larger and more valuable.

Article 1346. A liability for work is in the nature of work. Consequently, a contract of partnership in work may validly be made whereby a person puts an artisan in his shop and has the work which he has undertaken to do performed by him on the terms that they are to divide the profit equally between them. The right of the owner of the shop to a half share accrues merely by reason of his having guaranteed and undertaken the work, and this includes his right to make use of the shop.

Article 1347. The right to profit may arise out of property, or work, or, as is shown in Article 85, by liability in respect thereto. Thus, in a case where one supplies the capital and the other the labour, profit is earned by property being supplied by the owner thereof and the labour furnished by the person who undertakes to work. An artisan may also engage an apprentice and validly cause such apprentice to perform work which he has undertaken to do for half the normal wages. The apprentice is entitled to half the wage received from the employers by reason of the work he has performed, and his master is entitled to the other half, since he is liable for the work being properly performed.

JOINT OWNERSHIP

Article 1348. If none of the three elements mentioned above, that is to say, property, work, and liability are present, there is no right to profit.

Example : -

A asks B to trade with his property and share the profit with him. No partnership is formed, and A cannot thereby take a share of the profit.

Article 1349. The right to profit is entirely limited by the terms of the contract of partnership. It is not in proportion to the business done. Consequently, even though the partner who is bound to do certain work fails to do so, he is presumed to have done such work.

Example :-

If it is stipulated in a valid partnership that the two partners shall both perform certain work and one of them does so and the other with some excuse, or without any excuse, fails to do so, the latter, by reason of his being the agent of the former, is considered to have performed the work, and the profit is divided between them in the manner agreed upon.

Article 1350. Partners are trustees the one for the other, and the property of the partnership in the possession of either is considered to be property entrusted for safe keeping. If the property of the partnership is destroyed while in the possession of one of them without any fault or negligence on his part, he is not liable to make good the loss to the share of his partner.

Article 1351. In a case of partnership in property, the capital may be subscribed in equal or unequal shares by the partners. But if in a case where one supplies the capital and the other the labour, it is agreed that the profit shall be shared jointly between them, the partnership is one where one partner subscribes the capital and the other furnishes the labour. This type of partnership

JOINT OWNERSHIP

will be dealt with in the relevant Chapter. Should the profit go entirely to the workman, it is a loan; and if it is stipulated that the profit shall go entirely to the owner of the capital, such capital, while in the possession of the workman, is called invested capital and the workman is called a person employing capital. If he is such, he is considered to be an agent working for nothing, and profit and loss fall upon the owner of the property.

Article 1352. The death of one of the partners, or his affliction by permanent madness, causes the dissolution of the partnership. But if there are three or more partners, the dissolution of the partnership only affects the one who dies or goes mad and the partnership subsists as regards the others.

Article 1353. The partnership may also be dissolved by one of the partners, provided the others are informed thereof. Cancellation by one without the knowledge of the others does not bring about the dissolution of the partnership.

Article 1354. If the partners dissolve the partnership on the terms that the cash in hand is to go to one of them and debts due to the other, the division is invalid; and any sums received in this way from cash in hand by one of them is jointly owned with the other. Debts due are jointly owned in the same way. (See Article 1123.)

Article 1355. If one of the partners receives a quantity of the partnership property and dies while dealing with it in a manner unknown to the other partner, the share of the latter shall be paid out of the estate of the deceased. (See Article 801.)

JOINT OWNERSHIP

SECTION V.

Partnership with equal shares.

Article 1356. As is stated in Section II, partners with equal shares are guarantors the one of the other. Consequently, an admission made by one of the partners has identically the same effect with regard to the other. If one of them makes an admission with regard to a debt, the person in whose favour the admission is made may demand payment from whichever of the partners he wishes. Any loan contracted, of any nature whatsoever, by one of the partners on account of the business transactions of the partnership, such as sale, purchase, or hire, is binding on the other also. Anything sold by one of them containing a defect may be returned to the other, and anything bought by one of them may be returned by the other on account of defect.

Article 1357. Any food, clothing and other necessaries bought by one of the partners with equal shares for himself and his family are his property and his partner has no right therein. The vendor, however, may claim the price thereof from the other partner by virtue of the guarantee also.

Article 1358. In partnerships in property with equal shares, the shares of the partners must be equal in respect to capital and to profit. Neither of the partners may introduce any property by way of capital, that is to say, cash or property in the nature of cash, in excess of the capital of the partnership. The equality of shares, however, is not affected if one of the partners introduces property which cannot become capital of the partnership in excess of the partnership capital, that is to say, merchandise, or real property, or debts due from some other person.

JOINT OWNERSHIP

Article 1359. If it is agreed in a partnership for work that each of the partners may undertake work of any nature whatsoever, and that they are liable for the work equally, and that they shall be equal as regards profit and loss, and that the one is the guarantor of the other for anything which may happen to the partnership, such partnership is a partnership with equal shares. Consequently, the wages of an employee and the hire of a shop may be claimed from any one of them, and if any person claims goods from them and one of them admits the claim, the admission is binding even though the other denies such claim.

Article 1360. If two persons conclude a partnership whereby they agree to buy and sell property on credit and that the property purchased and the price received and the profit shall be jointly owned by them in equal shares and that each one shall be the guarantor of the other, a partnership on credit is formed with equal shares.

Article 1361. Upon the formation of a partnership with equal shares, either the actual word denoting equal shares must be used, or the whole of the terms of such partnership must be enumerated. If a contract for partnership is made in general terms, such partnership is one with unequal shares.

Article 1362. If one of the conditions as mentioned above in this Section is absent, a partnership with equal shares is changed into a partnership with unequal shares.

Example :-

In the case of a partnership in property with equal shares, one of the partners acquires possession of property by way of inheritance or gift. If such property is capable of being used as the capital of the partnership, such as cash, the partnership is changed into a partnership with unequal shares. If it is property, however, which cannot become the capital of the partnership, such as merchandise or real property, no injury is caused to the partnership with equal shares.

Article 1363. Any condition essential to the validity of a partnership with unequal shares is also essential to the validity of a partnership with equal shares.

Article 1364. Any act performed by partners in a partnership with unequal shares may also be performed by partners in a partnership with equal shares.

SECTION VI.

Partnership with unequal shares.

SUB-SECTION I.

Partnership in property.

Article 1365. It is not essential to the validity of a partnership with unequal shares that the partners should subscribe the capital in equal shares.

The capital of one may be greater than the capital of another. None of them is obliged to subscribe the whole of his money to the capital fund, but may form a partnership with regard to the whole of their property or a portion thereof. For this reason, they may have property, as for example, money, apart from the capital of the partnership, and which may become capital of the partnership.

Article 1366. A contract of partnership may be entered into both with regard to commerce in general, and any particular branch of commerce, as, for example, the provision trade.

JOINT OWNERSHIP

Article 1367. Any condition which has been laid down with regard to the division of profit in a valid partnership must be observed.

Article 1368. In a voidable partnership, the profit must be divided in accordance with the amount of the shares of capital. If a stipulation has been made that more shall go to one than to the other, no effect shall be given thereto.

Article 1369. Any damage suffered without any fault or negligence shall in any case be divided in proportion to the amount of the shares of capital. If any stipulation has been made to the contrary, no effect shall be given thereto.

Article 1370. If the partners agree that the profit shall be divided among them in proportion to the amount of their shares of capital, such agreement is valid, whether the capital has been subscribed in equal or unequal shares, and the profit shall be divided between them in the manner agreed upon, in accordance with the amount of their shares of capital, and that, whether it has been agreed that both of them or only one of them shall work therein. If it is stipulated, however, that only one of them shall work therein, the capital of the other is considered to be invested capital in such person's possession.

Article 1371. If the capital subscribed by the partners is equal and it is stipulated that a larger share of the profit, for example, two thirds, shall go to one than to the other, and it is also stipulated that both shall work therein, both the partnership and the stipulation are valid. (See Article 1345). If it is stipulated that only one of them shall work therein, and it has been agreed that the work shall be performed by the partner whose share of the profits is greater, the partnership is valid and effect shall be given to the condition, the partner being entitled to a share of the profits arising out of the capital by reason of the amount he has subscribed to the business, and also to an additional amount on account of his work. The partnership, however, resembles a partnership where capital is furnished by one and labour by another, since the capital of the other partner in such person's possession is in the nature of capital subscribed to such a partnership. If it is stipulated that the work shall be performed by the partner whose share in the profits is smaller, such stipulation is invalid, and the profit shall be divided between them in proportion to the amount of capital, the reason being that if the profit is divided as agreed, the additional amount to be received by the partner who performs no work is not sufficient to compensate for property, work aud liability. If there is a right to profit it is only in respect to one of these three things. (See Articles 1347 and 1348.)

Article 1372. If the shares of the partners are unequal, for example, if the capital of one amounts to one hundred thousand piastres and of the other to one hundred and fifty thousand piastres, and it has been agreed that the profits shall be divided among them in equal shares, such agreement resembles the case of a partnership where the shares of the partners are equal, a stipulation having been made for a greater share of the profits to be given to one of them, the reason being that it has been agreed that the partner with the lesser capital shall have a share of the profit greater than the share in proportion to the capital. Consequently, if it has been stipulated that both the partners whose share of the profits is greater, that is to say, whose capital is greater, shall do the work, the partnership is valid and effect shall be given to the condition. If it has been stipulated that only the partner whose share of the profits is smaller, that is to say, whose

354 JOINT OWNERSHIP

capital is greater, shall perform the work, such stipulation is invalid, and the profit shall be divided among them in proportion to the amount of their shares of the capital.

Article 1373. Each of the partners may sell the partnership property for ready money or on credit, for any price he thinks fit.

Article 1374. Property may be bought for the partnership either with ready money or on credit by whomsoever of the partners is in possession of the capital of the partnership. But if he buys the property as the result of flagrant misrepresentation, such property becomes his own and is not the property of the partnership.

Article 1375. No partner who is not in possession of the capital of the partnership may buy property for the partnership. If he does so, such property becomes his own.

Article 1376. If one of the partners buys anything which is not of the type used in their branch of commerce with his own money, such property is his own and his partner cannot claim a share therein. But if one of the partners while in possession of the capital of the partnership buys property of the type used in their branch of commerce with his own money, it becomes the property of the partnership.

Example :-

One of two persons who have entered into a partnership to carry on the business of cloth merchants buys a horse with his own money. The horse becomes his own property, and his partner cannot claim a share in such horse. But if he buys cloth, it becomes the property of the partnership, and he has no right of maintaining that he has bought the cloth for himself and that his partner has no share therein. He owns the cloth jointly with his partner.

JOINT OWNERSHIP

Article 1377. Contractual rights belong to the contracting party only. Consequently, if one of the partners takes delivery of property he has purchased and pays the price thereof, the transaction is binding on him alone. Thus, any claim made by any person as to the price of the property purchased may be made against such partner only, and may not be claimed from the other partner. Again, if one of the partners sells property, he alone is entitled to receive the price thereof. Thus, if the purchaser gives the price to the other partner, he is only liberated in respect to the share of the partner who has received the price, but is not released in respect to the share of the partner with whom he contracted. Moreover, if the partner who has concluded the contract appoints some other person to be his agent to receive the price of the property sold, such person's partner cannot dismiss the agent. But the partner may remove an agent appointed by the other in respect to contracts of sale, purchase and hire.

Article 1378. The right of rejection on account of defect being a contractual right, one of the partners may not reject property purchased by one of the other partners on account of defect. Property sold by one may not be returned to another on account of defect.

Article 1379. Each of the partners may deposit the partnership property for safe keeping, may give it to some other person on condition that he obtains the whole of the profit, may place it in a business where one person supplies the capital and the other the labour, and may conclude contracts of hire, for example, he may take a shop on hire and pay wages to persons for the preservation of the partnership property. He may not, however, mix the partnership property with his own property or enter into a partnership with some other

356 JOINT OWNERSHIP

person without the consent of the other partner. If he does so and ths partnership property is lost, he must make good the loss suffered by his partner.

Article 1380. No partner may lend the partnership property to any other person without the permission of the other. He may, however, obtain property on loan on behalf of the partnership. Any sum of money borrowed by one partner is a debt for which the other is jointly liable.

Article 1381. If one of the partners leaves for some other country on behalf of the business of the partnership, the expenses are a charge on the partnership property.

Article 1382. If each of the partners authorises the other to act in accordance with his own judgment or to do as he likes, each of them may perform the work falling to his branch of commerce. Thus, each of them may pledge the partnership property, or take a pledge in respect thereto, or proceed to some other country with the partnership property, or mix it with his own property, or conclude a partnership with some other person. He, may not, however, destroy the partnership property or confer the absolute ownership therein upon some other person without consideration, unless he obtains the express permission of his partner.

Example:-
One partner may not lend or make a gift of the partnership property to any other person without the express permission of the other partner.

Article 1383. If one of the partners forbids the other to proceed to some other country with the partnership property, or to sell on credit, and the latter nevertheless does so, he is bound to make good any loss occasioned thereby.

Article 1384. Any admission of debt made by one of the partners in respect to the operations of a partnership with unequal shares does not bind the other. Thus, if he admits that the debt has arisen solely in connection with his own contracts and transactions, he himself is responsible for the whole of the debt. If he admits that the debt has arisen in connection with a transaction carried out in conjunction with his partner, he must pay half thereof. If he admits that the debt has been incurred solely on account of some transaction carried out by his partner, he is not obliged to pay anything.

SUB-SECTION II.

Partnership for work.

Article 1385. A partnership for work consists of the conclusion of a partnership with a view to undertaking work. Thus, the partners enter into a partnership whereby they undertake and hold themselves ready to perform any work which they may be commissioned to perform by those who employ them, and that, whether they are liable equally for the performance of the work or not. That is to say, whether they have concluded a partnership whereby they undertake to be responsible equally for the performance of the work, or whether, for example, one of them undertakes to be responsible for one third and the other for two thirds.

Article 1386. Each of the partners may obtain and perform work. One of them may obtain work and the other may perform it. One of two tailors who are partners in a partnership of skilled workmen may accept and cut the material and the other may sew it.

Article 1387. Each partner is the agent of the other for the purpose of undertaking work. Any work so undertaken by one of them must be performed both by him and by his partner. Consequently, the liability for the performance of work in the case of a partnership for work in unequal shares is considered to be that of a partnership in equal shares, since the employer may require the performance of the work by any one of the partners he selects, and each of the partners is obliged to perform such work. No partner may refuse to perform the work by alleging that his partner undertook to do it.

Article 1388. A partnership for work in unequal shares is like a partnership in equal shares as regards the right to wages. That is to say, each of the partners may claim the whole of the wages due from the employer and on paying any one of them the employer is discharged from all liability.

Article 1389. The partner who actually undertakes to do the work is not obliged personally to perform such work. He may perform such work himself if he so desires, or he may cause his partner or some other person to do so. If the employer, however, makes a condition that the partner shall perform the work himself, he must then perform the work personally. (See Article 571.)

Article 1390. The earnings of the partners are divided in the manner agreed. That is to say, if it has been agreed that the wages shall be divided in equal shares they shall be so divided. If it has been agreed that the wages shall be divided in unequal shares, for example, one third or two thirds, they shall be divided accordingly.

Article 1391. It may validly be agreed that work shall be in equal shares, but that the wages shall be unequal.

Example :-
> The partners may validly agree that the work shall be performed in equal shares and that the wages shall be divided in the proportion of two thirds and one third, the reason being that one may be more expert in his craft, and his work correspondingly better.

Article 1392. The partners are entitled to their wages by reason of their liability to perform the work. Consequently, if one of them performs no work, as, for example, if he falls sick, or has to proceed to some other place, or remains idle, and his partner alone performs such work, the earnings and wages must nevertheless be divided in the manner agreed upon.

Article 1393. If one of the partners causes the destruction or damage of property delivered to be worked upon, the other partner is jointly liable with him to make good the loss, and the employer may call upon whichever one he likes to make good the loss to his property, such loss being divided among the partners in accordance with the amount of the loss they have to make good.

Example :-
> The partners enter into a partnership whereby they undertake to perform the work in equal shares. They must make good any loss in equal shares. If they enter into a partnership whereby one undertakes to perform one third and the other two thirds, the loss also must be made good in the proportion of two thirds and one third.

Article 1394. Porters may validly agree to enter into a partnership whereby they undertake jointly to perform work.

Article 1395. Two persons, one of whom owns a shop and the other tools and implements, may validly enter into a partnership whereby they undertake to do work.

Article 1396. Two persons may validly enter into a partnership to do skilled work whereby one supplies the shop and the other the labour. (See Article 1346).

Article 1397. Two persons may validly enter into a partnership for work whereby they undertake on equal terms to transport property, one supplying a mule and the other a camel. The earnings and wages shall be divided equally between them. The fact that the load of the camel is the greater is of no importance, since in a partnership for work the partners are entitled to their wages by reason of their liability to perform the work. But if no partnership is concluded for undertaking work, but the partners agree to let their mule and camel on hire as such and to divide the earnings between them, the partnership is voidable and the amount of hire paid in respect to the hiring of either the mule or camel belongs to the owner thereof. If one of them helps the other in loading and transport, he is entitled to an estimated wage for his services.

Article 1398. Any person who, together with his son living in his household, carries on any skilled work, is entitled to the whole of the earnings. The son is considered to be an assistant. Again, if a person plants a tree and is assisted by his son, the trees belong to such person and the son has no right therein.

SUB-SECTION III.

Partnership on credit.

Article 1399. It is not essential that the partners should have equal shares in the property purchased.

Example:-

The property purchased may be divided between them in shares of one half, two thirds, and one third.

JOINT OWNERSHIP

Article 1400. In a partnership on credit, the right to profit arises out of the liability to make good any loss.

Article 1401. The liability to make good any loss in respect to the price of the property bought is in proportion to the share of the partners therein.

Article 1402. The share of the profit accruing to each of the partners is in proportion to their share of the property purchased.

If one of the partners makes a stipulation that he shall receive more than his share in the property purchased, such stipulation is void; and the profit shall be divided between them in proportion to their share in the property purchased

Example :-
An agreement is made that the property purchased shall be divided between them in equal shares. The profit must also be divided between them in equal shares. If they agree to divide the property purchased in the proportion of two thirds and one third, the profit shall also be in the same ratio. But if it is agreed that the property purchased shall be divided in equal shares and that the profits shall be divided in proportions of one third and two thirds, the latter condition is invalid, and the profit shall be divided between them equally.

Article 1403. Any loss shall be divided between the partners in any case in proportion to their shares in the property purchased and this whether the contract for purchase was made jointly, or by one of them alone.

Example :-
Two persons who are partners in a partnership on credit suffer loss in their business. The loss must be shared by them equally if they entered into the partnership on the terms that the property purchased should be divided between them equally. If the partnership

was concluded on the terms that they should share in the property purchased in the proportion of one third and two thirds, the loss must be divided between them in the same ratio, and this whether the property with regard to which the loss has been suffered was bought by the partners jointly or by one of them on behalf of the partnership.

CHAPTER VII.

PARTNERSHIP OF CAPITAL AND LABOUR.

SECTION I.

Definition and classification of partnership of capital and labour.

Article 1404. A partnership of capital and labour is a type of partnership where one party supplies the capital and the other the labour. The person who owns the capital is called the owner of the capital and the person who performs the work is called the workman.

Article 1405. The basis of a partnership of capital and labour is offer and acceptance.

Example:-

A person possessing capital asks some other person to take the capital and use it and to share the profits between them equally, or in the ratio of two thirds and one third, or says something indicative of an intention to form a partnership of Capital and Labour, as whem he asks such person to take so much money and use it as capital and share the profits with him in a certain ratio and the latter accepts. A partnership of capital and labour has been concluded.

Article 1406. Partnership of capital and labour are of two categories:

(1) Absolute partnerships of capital and labour;

(2) Limited partnerships of capital and labour.

Article 1407. An absolute partnership of capital and labour is one where there is no limitation as to time or place, or any particular type of commerce, or any particular vendor or purchaser. If there is any limitation in respect to any of these matters, the partnership is a limited partnership.

Example :-
It is stipulated that property shall be bought at a certain time, or a certain place, or shall be of a certain type, or that business shall be done with certain persons or with the inhabitants of a certain place. A limited partnership of capital and labour has been concluded.

SECTION II.

Conditions affecting a partnership of capital and labour.

Article 1408. The owner of the capital must possess the requisite capacity to appoint an agent. The person supplying the labour must possess the requisite capacity to be appointed an agent.

Article 1409. The capital must consist of property which can be made the capital of a partnership. (See Section III of the Chapter dealing with the contract of partnership). Consequently, merchandise, real property and debts due to be paid may not be used as capital in a partnership of capital and labour. But if the owner of the capital hands over to the person supplying the labour certain merchandise and asks him to sell the same and trade with the proceeds thereof by way of a partnership of capital and labour and the person supplying the labour accepts and takes delivery of the merchandise and sells the same, applying the proceeds thereof to the capital and trades therewith, the partnership of capital and labour

JOINT OWNERSHIP

is valid. Likewise, if the owner of the capital asks the person supplying the labour to receive a sum due by a certain person and use the same in the partnership business and the person supplying the labour agrees, the partnership is valid.

Article 1410. The capital must be delivered to the person supplying the labour.

Article 1411. In a partnership of capital and labour the capital must be definitely stated, as in the case of a contractual partnership, and an undivided part must be fixed of the shares in the profits of the two contracting parties, such as a half or a third. If the partnership is defined in general terms, however, as, for example, that the profit shall be shared between the partners, such partnership is regarded as being in equal shares. The profit is divided by halves between the owner of the capital and person supplying the labour.

Article 1412. If any of the conditions mentioned above is absent, as, for example, where the shares of the two contracting parties, being in undivided parts, are not mentioned, and one of them has been given a certain sum of money from the profits, the partnership is voidable.

SECTION III.

Effect of a partnership of capital and labour.

Article 1413. The person supplying the labour is a trustee. While in his possession, the capital is considered to be entrusted to him for safe keeping. He is the agent of the owner of the capital in respect to any dealing with the capital. If he makes any profit, he is the joint owner thereof.

JOINT OWNERSHIP

Article 1414. In an absolute partnership of capital and labour, the person supplying the labour is authorized to perform any act connected with the partnership, whether fundamental or accessory, solely by virtue of the contract. Thus, he may perform the following acts:

(1) He may buy property with a view to selling it at a profit. But if he buys property as a result of flagrant misrepresentation, he is considered to have bought it for himself. It is not entered to the account of the partnership;

(2) He may sell at high or low prices, whether for cash or on credit, but he must give a period for payment which is customary among merchants. He may not sell for a long period of time not recognized by merchants;

(3) He may accept payment of the price of the goods by means of a transfer of debt;

(4) He may authorize some other person to act as his agent for buying and selling;

(5) He may deposit the partnership property for safe keeping, or invest it, or give it on pledge, or take a pledge in respect to it, or give or take it on hire;

(6) He may proceed to some other place in order to carry on business.

Article 1415. In an absolute partnership of capital and labour the person supplying the labour may not mix his own property with the partnership property and give it to the partnership solely by virtue of the contract of partnership. If there is a custom of the town, however, for partners to mix their own property with the partnership property, a partner in an absolute partnership of capital and labour may do the same.

Article 1416. If the owner of the capital in an absolute partnership of capital and labour tells the person

JOINT OWNERSHIP

supplying the labour to act as he thinks fit, or has authorized him to act in accordance with his own opinion in the affairs of the partnership, he may in any case mix his own property with the partnership property and can give it to the partnership. He may not, however, unless he is specially authorized, bestow any of the partnership property by way of gift, or give it on loan, or contract debts to an extent greater than the capital, without the express permission of the owner of the capital.

Article 1417. If the person supplying the labour mixes the partnership property with his own property, the profits realized are divided in accordance with the amount of the capital. That is to say, he takes the profit arising out of his own capital, and the profit arising from the partnership property is divided between him and the owner of the capital on the terms agreed upon.

Article 1418. Property bought on credit with the permission of the owner of the capital, and which is in excess of the capital, is jointly owned between the two partners as though it were a partnership on credit.

Article 1419. If the person supplying the labour leaves the town in which he is and proceeds to some other town on the business of the partnership, he may claim such expenses as are customary from the partnership property.

Article 1420. In a limited partnership of capital and labour the person supplying the labour must observe whatever conditions are laid down by the owner of the capital.

Article 1421. If the person supplying the labour exceeds the limits of his authority or acts in contravention of the conditions laid down, he becomes a person

JOINT OWNERSHIP

wrongfully appropriating property, in which case he is entitled to any profit and responsible for any loss arising out of his business transactions. If the partnership property is destroyed, he must make good the loss.

Article 1422. If the owner of the capital forbids the person supplying the labour to go with the partnership property to any particular place, or to sell property on credit, and the latter in contravention of the prohibition proceeds to such place with the partnership property, and such property is destroyed, or if he sells property on credit, and the money is lost, he must make good the loss.

Article 1423. If the owner of the capital fixes the period for the termination of the partnership at some particular date, the partnership is cancelled when such date is passed.

Article 1424. If the owner of the capital dismisses the person who supplies the labour, he must notify such dismissal to him. Any act performed by him up to the time his dismissal was notified to him is valid. He may not deal with any cash assets in his possession after his dismissal has been notified to him. If he has any property in his possession other than cash, he may sell such property and convert it into cash.

Article 1425. The person supplying the labour is only entitled to profit in respect to his work, such work being possessed of value solely by virtue of the contract. Consequently, in a contract of capital and labour, the person supplying the labour is entitled to a share of the profits in accordance with what has been stipulated in the contract.

Article 1426. The owner of the capital is entitled to profit in virtue of the capital subscribed. Consequently,

368 JOINT OWNERSHIP

in a voidable partnership of capital and labour the owner of the capital is entitled to the whole of the profit, and since the portion of the person supplying the labour is equivalent to that of an employee of the owner of the capital, he is entitled to an estimated wage. Such wage may not, however, exceed the amount agreed upon at the time of the conclusion of the contract. If there is no profit, he is not entitled to an estimated wage.

Article 1427. If any of the partnership property be destroyed, the amount thereof is first deducted from the profit and may not be made a charge on the capital. If the quantity destroyed exceeds the amount of the profit and is made a charge on the capital, the person supplying the labour need not make good the loss, and this whether the partnership is valid or voidable.

Article 1428. Any damage or loss must in any case be borne by the owner of the capital. If it has been stipulated that the person supplying the labour shall be jointly liable with him, such stipulation is invalid.

Article 1429. If either the owner of the capital or the person supplying the labour dies, or is afflicted with madness without any lucid interval, the partnership is cancelled.

Article 1430. If the person supplying the labour dies and it is not known what has become of the capital, the loss must be made good from his estate. (See Articles 801 and 1355).

CHAPTER VIII.

PARTNERSHIP IN LAND AND WORK AND PARTNERSHIP IN TREES AND WORK.

SECTION I.

Partnership in land and work.

Article 1431. A partnership in land and work is a type of partnership where one party supplies the land and the other the work, that is to say, cultivates the land, on the terms that the produce is to be divided between them.

Article 1432. The basis of a partnership in land and work is offer and acceptance. Thus, if the owner of the land informs the person supplying the labour, that is, the cultivator, that he has given him the land to be cultivated on condition that he shall receive a certain share of the produce and the latter states that he agrees thereto, or is contented therewith, or makes some statement from which his agreement may be inferred, or if the latter informs the owner of the land that he is ready to cultivate such land on those terms and the owner of the land agrees thereto, a partnership in land and work has been concluded.

Article 1433. In a partnership in land and work the contracting parties must be of sound mind. They need not have reached the age of puberty. Consequently, a minor who has received authority may also enter into a partnership of land and work.

Article 1434. The nature of what is to be sown must be stated, or it must be made known that the cultivator may sow what he likes.

Article 1435. At the time of the conclusion of the contract the share of the cultivator in the produce must be stated, such as an undivided part consisting of a half or a third. If the share is not fixed, or if it is decided that something other than the produce shall be given, or if it is stated that so many *kilés* shall be given from the produce, the partnership in land and work is invalid.

Article 1436. The land must be fit for cultivation and must be handed over to the cultivator.

Article 1437. If any of the conditions mentioned above are absent the partnership in land and work is voidable.

Article 1438. In a valid partnership in land and work the produce shall he divided between the two contracting parties in the manner agreed upon.

Article 1439. In a voidable partnership in land and work the whole of the produce belongs to the owner of the seed. If the other party is the owner of the land, he is entitled to a rent for the land. If he is the cultivator, he is entitled to an estimated wage.

Article 1440. If the owner of the land dies while the crops are green, the cultivator shall continue to work until the crops are ripe. The heirs of the deceased cannot prevent him from so doing. If the cultivator dies, his heir stands in his stead, and may, if he wishes, continue the work of cultivation until the crops are ripe, and the owner of the land may not prevent him from so doing.

SECTION II.

Partnership in trees and work.

Article 1441. A partnership in trees and work is a type of partnership whereby one party supplies the trees and the other tends them on the terms that the fruit produced is to be shared between them.

JOINT OWNERSHIP

Article 1442. The basis of a partnership in trees and work is offer and acceptance. Thus, if the owner of the trees informs the cultivator that he has given him so many trees to tend on the terms that he shall be entitled to a certain share of the fruit and the cultivator, that is, the person who is to tend such trees, agrees thereto, a partnership in trees and work has been concluded.

Article 1443. The two contracting parties must be of sound mind. They need not have reached the age of puberty.

Article 1444. In a partnership in trees and work the shares of the two contracting parties must be stated, that is an individed part, such as a half or a third, as in a partnership in land and work.

Article 1445. The trees must be handed over to the cultivator.

Article 1446. In a valid partnership in trees and work, the fruit must be divided between the two contracting parties as agreed.

Article 1447. In a voidable partnership in trees and work, the fruit produced belongs entirely to the owner of the trees. The cultivator is entitled to an estimated wage.

Article 1448. If the owner of the trees dies while the fruit is unripe, the cultivator may continue to work until the fruit is ripe. The heirs of the deceased cannot prevent him from so doing. If the cultivator dies, his heir stands in his stead and may, if he so wishes, continue to work. The owner of the trees cannot prevent him from so doing.

Promulgated by Royal Iradah 16th Jumadi-ul-akhira 1291.

BOOK XI
AGENCY

BOOK XI.

AGENCY.

INTRODUCTION.

TERMS OF MUHAMMADAN JURISPRUDENCE.

Article 1449. Agency consists of one person empowering some other person to perform some act for him, whereby the latter stands in the stead of the former in regard to such act. The first person is called the principal, the person who stands in his stead is called the agent, and the act is called the authorized act.

Article 1450. Messengership consists of the transmission of information by one person to some other person by means of some third person who is not privy to the matter in question. The person transmitting the information is called the messenger. The person who sends the message is called the person transmitting information. The person to whom the information is transmitted is called the recipient of the information.

CHAPTER I.

FUNDAMENTAL BASIS AND CLASSIFICATION OF AGENCY.

Article 1451. The basis of appointment of a person as agent is offer and acceptance. Thus, if the principal informs the agent that he has appointed him agent for a certain matter and the latter states that he has accepted, or uses some other expression importing acceptance, a contract of agency is concluded. Similarly, if the agent remains silent, but attempts to act in the matter referred to by the principal, he is considered to have accepted the agency by implication and his acts are valid. But if the agent refuses after the offer is made, the offer is of no effect. Consequently, if the principal informs a person that he has appointed him agent for a certain matter, and such person declines, but later begins to deal with the matter, all his acts in that respect are invalid.

Article 1452. Permission and ratification amount to an authority to act as agent.

Article 1453. Subsequent ratification has the same effect as a previous authorization to act as agent.

Example :-

A, without authority, sells property belonging to B, and informs B thereof. B ratifies the sale, and A is considered to have performed the act as though he had previously been appointed agent by B.

Article 1454. Messengership is not of the same nature as agency.

Examples :-

(1) A sends his servant to fetch him money which his banker is going to lend him. The servant is A's messenger, not his agent to borrow money.

(2) A sends B to a horsedealer to buy a horse. B tells the horsedealer that A wishes to buy a certain horse from him. The horsedealer informs B that he has sold A the horse for so much money and asks B to inform A of this fact, and to deliver the horse to him. B does as requested and hands the horse over to A. A accepts forthwith. A sale has been concluded between A and the horsedealer. B has merely been a messenger and intermediary between the two, and not an agent.

(3) A asks the butcher to give his servant who does the marketing so many *okes* of meat every day. The butcher does so. The servant is his master's messenger and not his agent.

AGENCY

Article 1455. An order is sometimes in the nature of agency and sometimes in the nature of messengership.

Example :-

A servant acting on orders from his master, buys property from a merchant. The servant is his master's agent for purchase. But if the master does business with a merchant, and sends his servant to fetch and bring the property purchased, the servant is his master's messenger and not his agent.

Article 1456. The basis of an authority to act as agent is sometimes absolute. That is to say, it is not dependent upon a condition, or made with reference to any particular time or subject to any limitations.

The basis of an authority to act as agent is sometimes conditional.

Example :-

A informs B that he has made him his agent to sell his horse in the event of a certain merchant coming to his place, and B agrees. The authority to act as agent is concluded subject to the merchant coming to such place. If he comes, the agent can sell the horse, but not otherwise.

The basis of an authority to act as agent is sometimes subject to a certain time.

Example :-

A informs B that he has made him his agent to sell his animals in the month of April and B accepts. B can sell the animals as agent when the month of April comes or thereafter, but not before.

The basis of an authority to act as agent is sometimes subject to a limitation.

Example :-

A informs B that he has appointed him his agent to sell his watch for a thousand piastres. B's authority to act as agent is subject to the limitation that he may not sell for less than a thousand piastres.

CHAPTER II.

CONDITIONS ATTACHING TO AGENCY.

Article 1457. The principal must be able to perform the act which is the subject matter of the agency. Consequently, any authority to act as agent conferred by a minor of imperfect understanding, or a lunatic, is invalid A minor of perfect understanding may not confer any power to act as agent upon any other person in such matters as bestowal of property by way of gift, or giving alms, which can only be to the disadvantage of the minor, even though his tutor authorizes him to do so. A minor may, however, authorize some other person to act as agent for him for the purpose of accepting such things as gifts or alms, which can only be for his advantage, even without the permission of his tutor. As regards dispositions of property which may either be to his advantage or disadvantage such as sale and purchase, the minor may authorize some other person to act as agent, if he has been authorized to engage in trade. If not, the authorization to act as agent in dependent upon ratification by the tutor.

Article 1458. The agent must be of sound mind and perfect understanding. He need not have arrived at the age of puberty. Consequently, a minor of perfect understanding, even though not authorized to act on his own behalf, may become an agent. The rights under the contract, however, do not affect him, but his principal.

Article 1459. Any person may appoint any other person his agent to perform any act which he can himself perform, or to fulfil any obligation, or to acquire any right, in respect to any transaction to which he himself is liable or entitled.

Example :-

A. may validly appoint B his agent for buying and selling, giving and taking on hire, giving and taking on pledge, giving and receiving for safe keeping, bestowing and receiving by way of gift, settlement, discharge, admission, instituting an action at law, claiming a right of pre-emption, partition, paying and receiving payment of debts and taking delivery of property.

The subject matter of the agency, however, must be known.

CHAPTER III.

ESSENTIAL ELEMENTS OF AGENCY.

SECTION I.

General.

Article 1460. A contract concluded by an agent must be made by reference to his principal in the case of gift, loan for use, pledge, deposit for safe keeping, lending money, partnership, partnership of capital and labour, and settlement by way of denial. If the matter is not so referred to the principal, it is invalid.

Article 1461. A contract concluded by an agent need not be made by reference to his principal in the case of sale and purchase, hire, and settlement by way of admission. Such contract is valid if merely concluded by the agent alone, without reference to his principal. In either case, however, ownership passes to the principal alone. Should the contract be made without reference to the principal, however, the rights under the contract belong to the contracting party, that is to say, the agent. If the contract is made with reference to the principal, the rights under the contract belong to the principal. In that case, the position of the agent is similar to that of a messenger.

Examples:-

(1) An agent for sale concludes the contract without reference to his principal, but merely with reference to himself, and, upon selling the property of his principal, must deliver the property sold to the purchaser. He may claim and receive the price from the purchaser. Should any person appear who is entitled to the property purchased, obtain judgment therefor, and seize the same, the purchaser may have recourse against the agent for sale, that is to say, may claim the price which he has given to him.

(2) An agent for purchase concludes a contract in this way without reference to his principal. He may take delivery of the property purchased, and, even though he has not received the price of the property purchased from his principal, he is obliged to pay it to the vendor from his own property. Should some defect of long standing appear in the property purchased, the agent has the right of bringing an action to secure its return.

(3) An agent concludes a contract with reference to his principal, as where he states that he has sold or bought as agent for A. In this case, the contractual rights referred to above belong to the principal, the position of the agent being similar to that of a messenger.

Article 1462. In the case of messengership, the rights under the contract belong to the person sending the messenger. The messenger is in no way concerned therewith.

Article 1463. Property in the possession of an agent which he has received in his capacity as agent for sale, or purchase, or paying or receiving payment of debt, or receiving any specific property, is considered to be property deposited with him for safe keeping. If it is destroyed without fault or negligence, the loss need not be made good. Property in the possession of a messenger in virtue of his duties as messenger is also considered to be property deposited for safe keeping.

Article 1464. If a debtor sends the sum of money he is owing to his creditor and it is destroyed while in the possession of the messenger before being received by the creditor, the debtor must bear the loss if the messenger is his. If the messenger is the creditor's, however, it is the creditor's property which is destroyed and the debtor is free from the debt.

Article 1465. If any person appoints two persons simultaneously to be his agent, one of them alone may not act as agent. One of them, however, may act alone in actions at law, or for the return of things deposited for safe keeping, or for paying a debt. But if one person has been appointed agent for any particular matter and the other has also been directly appointed agent for the same matter, either of them may act as agent.

Article 1466. A person who has been appointed agent for any particular matter may not appoint any other person as agent. Nevertheless, if his principal has authorized him to do so, or to act as he thinks fit, the agent can appoint some other person as agent. The person whom the agent authorizes to act as agent in this way becomes the agent of the principal, and not the agent of the agent. Thus, if the first agent is removed or dies, the second agent remains as agent.

Article 1467. If upon the appointment of the agent, it has been agreed that a salary shall be paid to him, the agent is entitled to such salary upon fulfilling the terms of the agency. If no stipulation has been made for payment, and the agent is not one of those persons who work for a wage, his services are free, and he cannot demand payment.

SECTION II.

Agency for purchase.

Article 1468. In accordance with the terms of the last paragraph of Article 1459, the subject matter of the agency must be sufficiently well known to enable it to be carried out. Thus, the principal must state the nature of the thing to be purchased. If there are various sorts of things of that nature, it is not enough merely to state the nature of such thing, but the particular sort or price of such thing must be mentioned. If the nature of the thing to be bought is not stated, or if it is stated, and there are various sorts of that nature and the particular sort or the price thereof is not mentioned, the agency is invalid, unless the authority to act as agent is of a general nature.

Example:-

> A appoints B his agent to purchase a horse. The appointment is valid. A appoints B his agent to purchase cloth for making into clothes. A must state the nature thereof, that is to say, whether he wants striped cloth or cloth of any other nature. He must also state the sort of cloth he wants, such as Damascus or Indian cloth, or state the price thereof, such as so many piastres for the roll. If the nature is not stated, as where the principal merely asks for the purchase of a piece of cloth, or for some cloth, or where, for example, he asks for the purchase of striped cloth without stating the sort or price thereof, the appointment as agent is invalid. But if the principal instructs the agent to buy a roll of cloth to be made into clothes or some striped cloth of whatever nature or sort the agent may think fit, the agency is general and the agent may purchase whatever nature or sort he chooses.

AGENCY

Article 1469. The nature of a thing is changed with any change in the substance of such thing, or the object for which it was intended, or the manufacture thereof.

Example :-

Cotton cloth and linen cloth are of different nature, since the substance from which they are made is different. The wool and skin of a sheep are of a different nature since the object for which they are used is different, the skin being used to make bags, and the wool to make thread to weave carpets, two totally differents things. Sharkot felt differs from Ushak felt, although both are made from wool, since there is a difference in their manufacture.

Article 1470. If the agent acts in contravention of his intructions as to the nature of the thing to be purchased, that is to say, if the principal tells the agent to purchase something of a certain nature, and he buys property of some other nature, the principal is not bound thereby, however much more advantageous the thing may be which the agent has bought. That is to say, the agent is considered to have bought the property for himself and not for his principal.

Article 1471. If the principal instructs the agent to purchase a ram, and he buys a sheep, the principal is not bound thereby, and the sheep belongs to the agent.

Article 1472. If the principal instructs the agent to purchase a certain piece of land, and buildings are erected on such land, the agent cannot thereafter purchase such land on behalf of his principal. But if he instructs him to purchase a certain house, and such house is plastered, or another wall is added thereto, the agent may purchase such house on behalf of his principal.

Article 1473. If the principal instructs the agent to purchase milk, without indicating what milk, the principal shall be understood to mean the milk which it is the custom to use in the district.

Article 1474. If the principal instructs the agent to buy rice, the agent may purchase any sort of rice sold in the market.

Article 1475. If any person intends to appoint some other person as agent to buy a house, he must state the district in which it is situated and the price thereof. If he does not do so, the agency is invalid.

Article 1476. If any person intends to appoint some other person his agent to purchase a pearl or a red ruby, he must state the price he is prepared to pay. If he fails to do so, the agency is invalid.

Article 1477. In the case of things estimated by quantity, the quantity or price of the subject matter of the agency must be stated.

Example :-

> A appoints B his agent to buy corn. A must state the number of *kilés,* or the price thereof, by stating the amount of money to be expended on the corn. If he fails to do so, the agency is invalid.

Article 1478. The subject matter of the agency need not be described.

Example :-

> It need not be stated whether of the best quality or of medium quality, or of the lowest quality.

The description of the subject matter of the agency must, however, correspond to the position of the principal.

Example :-

> A, who lets horses on hire, appoints B his agent to buy a horse. The agent may not purchase an Arab horse at twenty thousand piastres. If he does so, the

principal is not bound thereby. That is to say, the horse is not bought for the principal, but becomes the property of the agent only.

Article 1479. If the appointment as agent is made subject to a limitation, no act may be performed by the agent in contravention thereof. If he does so, the principal is not bound, and any property purchased belongs to the agent. But if the agent acts in contravention of his appointment in a way more advantageous to the principal, such act is not considered to amount to contravention.

Examples :-

(1) A instructs his agent, B, to buy a certain house for ten thousand piastres. If B exceeds this price, A is not bound and the house becomes B's property. If B buys it for less than ten thousand piastres, it is considered to be bought for the principal.

(2) A instructs B, his agent, to buy on credit. B buys and pays cash. The property belongs to the agent. But if A instructs B to buy for ready money and the agent buys on credit, the property is considered to be bought for the principal.

Article 1480. If a person buys half the thing he is appointed agent to purchase, such purchase is not binding upon the principal if such thing will be injured by being divided. If not, he is bound thereby.

Example :-

A instructs B, his agent, to buy a roll of cloth. B buys half a roll. A is not bound thereby, and the cloth becomes the property of the agent. But if A tells B to buy six *kilés* of corn, and B buys three *kilés,* the corn is presumed to have been bought for the principal.

Article 1481. If the principal instructs his agent to buy him cloth to make a cloak, and there is not sufficient cloth in that purchased by the agent to make the cloak, the principal is not bound thereby and the cloth belongs to the agent.

Article 1482. If the price of a thing is not mentioned, the person who is appointed agent to purchase may buy such thing for the estimated value thereof, or at a price subject to minor misrepresentation. Things the price and value of which are fixed, however, such as meat and bread, may not be bought at even subject to minor misrepresentation. If the agent buys such things as a result of flagrant misrepresentation, however, the principal is in no case bound by the purchase, and the property belongs to the agent.

Article 1483. Purchase outright is understood to be purchase for cash. Thus, if a person who has been appointed agent for the purchase of anything purchases such thing by exchanging other property therefor, the principal is not bound thereby, and such thing belongs to the agent.

Article 1484. If a person appoints some other person his agent to purchase something which is necessary for some particular season it is considered to relate to that season.

Example :-

> A appoints B his agent to purchase a cloak made of goat hair in the spring season. B is considered to be appointed agent to purchase such a cloak for use in the summer season. If he buys after the season has passed or buys in the spring of next year, the principal is not bound by such purchase, and the cloak becomes the property of the agent.

Article 1485. A person who is appointed agent to buy some specified thing cannot purchase such thing for himself. If when buying such thing he states that he has purchased it for himself, it nevertheless becomes the property of the principal. Nevertheless, if he buys such thing for a higher price than that fixed by the principal, or, if no price has been fixed and he buys as a result of flagrant misrepresentation, the property in that case belongs to the agent. Again, if the principal is present and the agent states that he has bought such thing for himself, the property belongs to the agent.

Article 1486. If a person appoints some other person his agent to buy a horse, and the latter without making any reply buys such horse, the horse becomes the property of his principal if at the time he made the purchase he stated that he has bought on behalf of his principal. If he states that he has bought for himself, the horse becomes his property. If he merely states that he has purchased the horse without stating for whom, and later states that he has purchased it on behalf of his principal, such statement is effective if made before the horse is destroyed or some defect appears. But if he makes such statement after the horse is destroyed or after some defect appears, such statement is of no effect.

Article 1487. If two persons separately appoint a person as agent to purchase a certain thing, the property belongs to the person for whom the agent intended to effect the purchase.

Article 1488. If an agent for purchase sells his own property to his principal, such sale is invalid.

Article 1489. If the agent becomes aware of a defect in the property purchased before delivering it to his principal, he may himself reject it. He may not reject it after delivery, however, without an order and authority from his principal to do so.

Article 1490. If the agent buys property to be paid for at some future date, the same condition as to payment affects the principal, and the agent may not ask the principal to make payment forthwith. If the agent, however, purchases by an immediate cash payment, and the vendor thereafter adjourns the date for payment, the agent can demand payment forthwith from the principal.

Article 1491. If an agent for purchase pays the price from his own property and takes delivery of the property purchased, he can exercise a right of recourse against his principal, that is to say, he can recover from him the price which he has paid. If he has not already paid the price of the property purchased to the vendor, he may claim the price from his principal, and may exercise a right of retention over the property until such time as the principal has paid.

Article 1492. If property purchased by an agent for purchase is accidentally destroyed or lost while in the possession of the agent, the loss must be borne by the principal, and no reduction is made in the price. If the agent has exercised a right of retention over such property in order to obtain payment of the price, however, and such property is destroyed or lost, the price must be paid by the agent.

Article 1493. An agent for purchase may not rescind a contract of sale without the permission of his principal.

SECTION III.

Agency for sale.

Article 1494. An agent who has been granted an absolute power to conclude contracts of sale may sell his principal's property at any price he thinks fit, whether great or small.

Article 1495. If the principal has fixed the price, that is to say, if he has instructed the agent to sell for so much, the agent may not sell for less than such price. If he does so, the sale is concluded subject to ratification by the principal. If the agent sells it on his own initiative for a price lower than that mentioned, and delivers the property to the purchaser, the principal may call upon him to make good the loss.

Article 1496. If an agent for sale purchases his principal's property for himself, such purchase is invalid.

Article 1497. An agent for sale may not sell the property of his principal to persons whose evidence given on his behalf is invalid. If he sells for more than the value of the property, however, the sale is valid. If the agent is appointed in virtue of a general power, the principal instructing him to sell to whomsoever he may think fit, the agent may validly sell to such persons for an estimated price.

Article 1498. If an agent has been granted an absolute power of sale, he may sell his principal's property for cash or on credit for a period recognized by merchants in respect to such property. He may not, however, sell on credit for a longer period than that recognized by custom. If the agent has been appointed, either expressly or by implication, to sell for cash, he may not sell on credit.

Example :-

A principal instructs his agent to sell certain property for cash or to sell certain property and pay a debt of his with the proceeds. The agent may not sell on credit.

Article 1499. If injury is caused by the separation of a thing, the agent cannot sell half thereof.

Article 1500. An agent may take a pledge or a surety in respect to the price of property which he has sold on credit. If the pledge is destroyed or the surety becomes bankrupt, the agent is not liable to make good the loss.

Article 1501. If a principal instructs his agent to take a pledge or a surety in respect to property sold, the agent may not sell such property without taking a pledge or a surety.

Article 1502. If an agent for sale fails to obtain the price of the property sold from the purchaser, he cannot be forced to pay the price thereof to his principal out of his own property.

Article 1503. The price of the thing sold may validly be received both by the agent and the principal.

Article 1504. If the agent is working without remuneration, he is not obliged to obtain payment of the price of the property sold. If he does not do so of his own accord, however, he must appoint his principal to be his agent to obtain payment of the price. But persons such as brokers and auctioneers who are appointed as agents for sale subject to remuneration, are obliged to obtain payment of the price of the thing sold.

Article 1505. An agent for sale may rescind the sale on his own initiative. The rescission, however, is not executory as regards the principal, and the agent must pay the price thereof to the principal.

SECTION IV.

Instructions given by one person to another.

Article 1506. If one person gives an instruction to another person to pay a sum of money owing by him to some third person, or to the State, and such person pays such sum of money from his own property, he may thereafter exercise a right of recourse against the person who gave the instruction, whether such right of recourse has been agreed upon or not. That is to say, whether he uses expressions which imply a right of recourse, as where he instructs a person to pay a sum of money owing by him and thereafter to recover such sum from him, or where he instructs him to pay and recover from him later, or whether he merely instructs him to pay a sum of money owing by him.

Article 1507. If one person instructs another to pay a sum of money owing by him from his own property in base coin and he pays in sound coin, base coin only can be recovered from the person who gave the instruction. If such person is instructed to pay in sound coin, but pays the debt in base coin, he can recover base coin only. If a person who has been instructed by some other person to pay a sum of money owing by him, sells his own property to the creditor and pays such person's debt therefrom, the person who pays the debt may recover the amount thereof from the person who gave the instruction, whatever that amount may be. If he sells his own property to the creditor for an amount greater than the value thereof, the person who gave the instruction for the debt to be paid cannot deduct the balance from the debt.

Article 1508. If any person instructs any other person to incur expenditure for himself or his relations and family, such person may recover a reasonable amount of expenses from the person who gave the instruction whether the latter has expressly authorized him to do so or not. Again, one person instructs another to have his rhouse repaired and the latter does so. He may recove a reasonable sum from such person, even though no agreement has been made to that effect.

Article 1509. If any person instructs any other person to make a loan of money to some third person, or to make him a present of money, or to give him alms, stating that he will repay him later, and such person does so, he may recover such money from the person who gave the instruction. If the person giving the instruction, however, makes no stipulation as to recourse as by stating that he will give him the money, or that the person paying the money may later recover it from him, but merely gives an instruction to pay, such person has no right of recourse. Nevertheless, if it is customary in such matters to have recourse against the person giving the instruction, as where the person to whom the instruction is given is a member of the family of the person giving the instruction, or is his partner, such person may exercise a right of recourse, even though no stipulation has been made therefor. (See Article 36).

Article 1510. Any instruction given by any particular person is only effective in regard to that person's property.

Example :-

A instructs B to throw certain property into the sea. B does so knowing that the property in question belongs to some one else. The owner of the property can call upon B to make good the loss. The person who gave the instruction is not liable, unless he used compulsion.

Article 1511. If any person instructs any other person to pay a debt owing to him, and amounting to a certain sum, from his own property and such person promises to do so, but fails to pay the sum in question, such person cannot be made to pay the debt by reason merely of his having promised to do so.

Article 1512. If the person to whom an instruction to pay a debt is given owes money to the person giving the instruction, or has money belonging to the latter deposited with him for safe keeping, such person is bound to pay the debt. But if the person giving the instruction orders certain of his property to be sold and the debt to be paid therefrom, the person to whom the instruction is given is not obliged to pay such debt even though he is an unsalaried agent. If he is a salaried agent, however, he is obliged to sell such property and pay the debt of the person who gave the instruction from the proceeds.

Article 1513. If any person gives a sum of money to some other person instructing him to pay it to a creditor of his, the other creditors of the person giving the instruction have no right to claim a share therein and the person to whom the instruction has been given may only pay the money to the creditor mentioned in the instruction.

Article 1514. If any person gives any other person a sum from which to pay a debt owing to some third person, and it is known that the person to whom the money belongs has died before such money has been made over to the creditor, the money in question must be paid to the estate of the person to whom the money belonged, and the creditor must have recourse against the estate.

Article 1515. If any person gives a sum of money to pay to his creditor with instructions that the sum in question shall not be handed over unless an acknowledgment is indorsed on the bill or a receipt given therefor, and such person hands over the money without obtaining

AGENCY

any acknowledgment or receipt, and the creditor later denies having received the money, and the debtor, being unable to prove payment, is obliged to pay the debt a second time, the latter may call upon the person to whom he gave the money to make good the loss.

SECTION V.

Agency for litigation.

Article 1516. Both plaintiff and defendant may authorize any person they may wish to act as their agent for litigation. Neither party need obtain the consent of the other.

Article 1517. Any admission made against his client by the person authorized to act as his agent for litigation is valid if made in Court. If made out of Court, it is invalid and the agent may be dismissed.

Article 1518. Any person who appoints another his agent for litigation may validly forbid him to make any admission against him, in which case an admission made by the agent against his client is invalid. (See last paragraph of Article 1456). Again, if the agent makes an admission in Court, and is not authorized to do so, he shall be dismissed.

Article 1519. An agency for litigation does not include an agency to take delivery. Consequently, if an advocate is not an agent to take delivery, he cannot act as agent to take delivery of the subject matter of the judgment.

Article 1520. An agency to receive does not include an agency for litigation.

AGENCY

SECTION VI.

Dismissal of agents.

Article 1521. The principal may dismiss his agent from his agency. He may not do so, however, if the rights of third parties are affected. Thus, a person owing a sum of money gives his property as a pledge for the debt. At the time the contract of pledge was concluded, or at some later date, he appoints a person as his agent to sell the pledge when the debt falls due. The principal may not dismiss the agent without the consent of the pledgee. Similarly, at the request of the plaintiff, a defendant appoints a person his agent for litigation. He cannot dismiss him in the absence of the plaintiff.

Article 1522. The agent himself may relinquish the agency, but, as stated above, he may not do so if the rights of third persons are affected, but must perform his duties.

Article 1523. Upon a principal dismissing an agent from his agency, the dismissal does not become effective until information thereof has been given to the agent, and any disposition of property made by him up to that time is valid.

Article 1524. Upon the agent giving up the agency, he must inform his principal thereof, and the agent is responsible for performing his duties as agent until the principal has been so informed.

Article 1525. The principal may dismiss a person appointed as agent to receive a debt during the absence of the debtor. If the principal appointed him as agent in the presence of the debtor, any dismissal is invalid if made without the knowledge of the debtor. Thus, if the debtor pays the debt to him while unaware of his dismissal, he is free from liability for the debt.

AGENCY

Article 1526. The agency terminates upon the completion of the duties for which the agent was appointed, and the agent, naturally, is discharged therefrom.

Article 1527. The agent is discharged upon the death of the principal. He is not discharged, however, if the rights of any third party are affected thereby. (See Article 760).

Article 1528. Upon the death of the principal, any agent appointed by the agent is discharged from the agency. (See Article 1466).

Article 1529. Agency is not transmissible by way of inheritance. That is to say, if the agent dies, the validity of the agency expires and consequently the heir of the agent does not stand in his stead.

Article 1530. If the principal or the agent are afflicted with madness, the agency is null and void.

Promulgated by Royal Iradah, 20th Jumudi-ul-Ula, 1291.

BOOK XII.

SETTLEMENT AND RELEASE.

BOOK XII.

SETTLEMENT AND RELEASE.

INTRODUCTION.

TERMS OF MUHAMMADAN JURISPRUDENCE.

Article 1531. A settlement is a contract concluded by offer and acceptance, and consists of settling a dispute by mutual consent.

Article 1532. A person making a settlement is called a settlor.

Article 1533. The price of the settlement is called the consideration.

Article 1534. The subject matter of the settlement is the matter in dispute.

Article 1535. A settlement is divided into three parts: The first part consists of a settlement by way of admission, that is, a settlement brought about by the admission of the defendant. The second part consists of a settlement by way of denial, that is, a settlement brought about by denial of the defendant. The third part consists of a settlement by way of silence, that is, a settlement brought about by the silence of the defendant consequent upon the absence of any admission or denial.

Article 1536. Release consists of two parts: the first part consists of release by way of renunciation of a right: the second consists of release by admission of payment. Release by way of renunciation occurs where one person releases another person by relinquishing the whole of the claims he has against such person, or by subtracting or reducing a certain number of them. It is this form of

SETTLEMENT AND RELEASE

release which is dealt with in this Book. Release by admission of payment is in the nature of an admission and consists of the confession by one person that he has received what was due to him from another person.

Article 1537. A special release is a release of a person from an action instituted in respect to a claim relating to some particular matter, such as a house, or farm, or some other matter.

Article 1538. A general release is a release of a person from all actions.

CHAPTER I.

CONCLUSION OF A CONTRACT OF SETTLEMENT AND RELEASE.

Article 1539. A person making a settlement must be of sound mind. He need not have arrived at the age of puberty. Consequently, a settlement made by a lunatic, or an imbecile, or a minor of imperfect understanding is always invalid. A settlement made by a minor who has been authorized by his tutor is valid, provided that the settlement does not result in a clear loss. Thus, if a person brings an action against a minor who has been authorized, and such minor makes an admission relating thereto, the result is a valid settlement by way of admission. A minor who has been authorized may make a valid contract of settlement to the effect that he will give time for the satisfaction of his claim. If such minor agrees to a settlement in respect to part of his claim and is in possession of evidence to support the same, such settlement is invalid; if he is not in possession of such evidence, however, and his opponent is known to be ready to take an oath, such settlement is

SETTLEMENT AND RELEASE

valid. If he brings an action to recover property from another, and makes a settlement in respect to the value of such claim, such settlement is valid. A settlement by him for an amount considerably smaller than the value of the property is invalid.

Article 1540. A valid settlement of an action brought by a minor may be made by his tutor provided that such settlement does not result in clear loss to the minor. If there is a clear loss, the settlement is invalid. Consequently, if a person brings an action for the recovery of a certain amount of money from a minor and the father of such minor has made a settlement upon the terms that payment shall be made from the property of the minor, such settlement is valid, provided that the plaintiff is in possession of evidence in support of his claim. If the plaintiff is not in possession of such evidence, the settlement is invalid. Should money be due to a minor from another person and the father make a settlement by deducting a part thereof, such settlement is invalid if evidence exists in support of the sum due. If no such evidence exists, however, and the other person is known to be willing to take an oath, the settlement is valid. A settlement made by a tutor in respect of a sum due to the minor, in consideration of property equivalent to the value of the claim, is valid. But if such consideration involves flagrant misrepresentation, the settlement is invalid.

Article 1541. A release by a minor, a lunatic or an imbecile is absolutely invalid.

Article 1542. A power of attorney to carry on litigation does not imply a power of attorney to make a settlement. Consequently, if a person is appointed agent to bring an action against another person and such person settles the action without obtaining the permission of his principal, such settlement is invalid.

402 SETTLEMENT AND RELEASE

Article 1543. If any person appoints any other person his agent to settle an action and the agent accordingly makes a settlement, the principal is bound by such settlement. The agent is in no way responsible for any claim made in connection therewith, unless he has made himself a guarantor therefor, in which case he is liable. Moreover, if an agent makes a settlement by way of admission to the effect that he will give property for property, and he makes such settlement in his own name, such agent becomes liable for any claim made in connection therewith, that is to say, the amount covered by the settlement may be recovered from the agent, the latter preserving a right of recourse against his principal.

Examples :-

(1) An agent, acting in accordance with the terms of his power of attorney, makes a settlement for a certain amount of money. The principal and not the agent will be obliged to pay such sum. But if an agent arranges a settlement for a certain sum of money and he guarantees such sum, the money in that case is recoverable from the agent, who has a right of recourse against his principal.

(2) In the event of a settlement being made by way of admission upon the terms that property shall be exchanged for property, the agent inducing the other party to settle with him in respect to the action of his principal, the sum in respect to which the settlement is made may be recovered from the agent, who has a right of recourse against the principal, owing to the transaction being in the nature of a sale.

Article 1544. If a third person who is not authorized thereunto, that is to say, who acts without permission, intervenes in an action between two persons and makes a settlement with one of them, such settlement is valid in the following cases, but the unauthorized person is held to have acted on his own initiative: if such person guarantees the sum covered by the settlement; if he allows the sum covered by the settlement to attach to his own property; if he allows the sum covered by the settlement to attach to certain specific money or goods present at the time; or if he makes a settlement for a certain sum of money and delivers that sum of money. In the latter case, should such party intervening fail to deliver the sum of money covered by the settlement, such settlement is dependent upon the adoption of the transaction by the defendant. The settlement is valid if adopted by the defendant, who must then pay the sum covered by such settlement. If he does not do so, the settlement is null and void, the action remaining undisturbed.

CHAPTER II.

THE CONSIDERATION AND SUBJECT MATTER OF THE SETTLEMENT.

Article 1545. If the consideration of the settlement is some specific object, such object is considered as an article which has been sold. If it is a debt, it is considered to be the price. Consequently, anything which may be the subject of sale or the price thereof in a contract of sale, may also be the consideration for a settlement.

Article 1546. The consideration of the settlement must be the property of the person making the settlement. Consequently, if the person making the settlement offers some other person's property as the consideration for the settlement, such settlement is invalid.

Article 1547. If it is necessary to take and give delivery of either the consideration of the settlement or the subject matter thereof, such thing must be clearly defined. If not, it need not be clearly defined.

SETTLEMENT AND RELEASE

Examples :-

(1) A brings an action against B with regard to a house in the possession of B. B brings an action against A with regard to a garden in the possession of A. Both agree to a settlement of their actions without defining the nature of the dispute.

(2) A brings an action against B with regard to a house without defining the nature of the dispute, and they come to a settlement on the terms that the defendant shall pay the plaintiff a certain sum of money and that the plaintiff shall drop the action. The settlement is valid. But if a settlement is made whereby the plaintiff gives the defendant a certain sum of money and the defendant in consideration thereof gives up his claim, such settlement is invalid.

CHAPTER III.

THE SUBJECT MATTER OF THE SETTLEMENT.

SECTION I.

Settlement in respect to specific property.

Article 1548. If a settlement by way of admission is made with regard to property in an action relating to specific property, such settlement is in the nature of a sale, and there is an option for defect, an option of inspection, and a contractual option, and, in the event of either the subject matter or the consideration of the settlement being real property, a right of pre-emption attaches thereto. If the whole or part of the subject matter of the settlement is seized by someone who is entitled thereto, the plaintiff may recover the amount of the consideration from the defendant, that is to say, either the whole or a portion thereof. If the whole of the consideration of the settlement or part thereof is seized by someone who is entitled thereto, the plaintiff may recover from the

SETTLEMENT AND RELEASE

defendant the subject matter of the settlement, that is to say, the whole or part thereof.

Example :-

> A brings an action against B claiming a house from him. B admits that the house belongs to A and the two partners agree to a settlement for a certain sum of money. The house is considered to have been sold to the defendant, and, as stated above, the transaction is treated as though it were a sale.

Article 1549. If a settlement by way of admission is made in an action with regard to property in respect to the usufruct thereof, such settlement is in the nature of hire and is treated as though it were a contract of hire.

Example :-

> A brings an action against B claiming a garden from him. B makes a settlement with A on the terms that A is to live in his house for a certain period. A is considered to have taken the house on hire in exchange for the garden in respect to such period.

Article 1550. A settlement by way of denial or silence amounts to receiving satisfaction in the case of the plaintiff, and abstention from swearing the oath by the defendant, whereby the point at issue is decided. Consequently, a right of pre-emption attaches to real property which is the consideration for a settlement, but does not attach to real property which is the subject matter of the settlement. If any person who is entitled thereto seizes the whole or part of such real property, the plaintiff must return to the defendant the amount of the consideration for the settlement, that is to say, the whole or a portion thereof, and may bring an action against the person who claims to be so entitled. If either the whole or part of the consideration is seized by someone entitled thereto, the plaintiff may again bring an action in respect thereto.

406 SETTLEMENT AND RELEASE

Article 1551. If any person brings an action to recover any specific property, as, for example, a garden, and agrees to a settlement in respect to a portion thereof and releases the defendant in respect to the remainder of the action, such person is considered to have received a part of his claim and to have foregone the rest, that is to say, to have relinquished his right to bring an action in respect to the remainder.

SECTION II.

Settlement with regard to debt and other matters.

Article 1552. If any person effects a settlement with any other person in respect to a portion of a claim that he has against such person, the person effecting the settlement is considered to have received payment of part of the claim and to have foregone his right to the balance, that is to say, to have released such person from the remainder.

Article 1553. If any person effects a settlement whereby a debt repayable forthwith is converted into a debt repayable at some future date, he is considered to have relinquished his right to payment forthwith.

Article 1554. If any person effects a settlement whereby a debt repayable in sound coin may be repaid in base coin, such person is considered to have relinquished his right to payment in sound coin.

Article 1555. A settlement may validly be effected in actions relating to the right of taking water, the right of pre-emption and the right of way, whereby a payment is made in order to avoid swearing an oath.

CHAPTER IV.

FUNDAMENTAL CONDITIONS GOVERNING SETTLEMENT AND RELEASE.

SECTION I.

Fundamental conditions governing settlement.

Article 1556. When the settlement is complete, one of the two parties may not go back therefrom. By agreeing to the settlement, the plaintiff becomes entitled to the consideration for the settlement. He no longer possesses any right to bring an action. The defendant may not claim the return of the consideration for the settlement from him.

Article 1557. In the event of the death of one of the two contracting parties, the heirs may not cancel the settlement.

Article 1558. If the settlement takes the form of giving something in satisfaction, the two parties thereto may cancel and rescind the settlement of their own accord. If the settlement does not take such form, but consists of giving up certain rights any cancellation thereof is invalid. (See Article 51.)

Article 1559. If a contract of settlement is concluded whereby a payment is made in order to avoid swearing an oath, the plaintiff is considered to have relinquished his right of bringing an action, and he cannot have the defendant put on his oath.

Article 1560. If the consideration for the settlement is destroyed in whole or in part before it has been handed over to the plaintiff, and such consideration is a thing which is specified, it is considered to be in the nature of a thing seized by someone entitled thereto. That is to say, if a settlement is made by way of admission, the plaintiff

SETTLEMENT AND RELEASE

may claim the whole or part of the subject matter of the settlement from the defendant. If the settlement is made by way of denial or silence, the plaintiff may proceed with his action. (See Articles 1548 and 1550). If the consideration for the settlement is a debt, that is to say, consists of things which are not specified, such as so many piastres, the settlement is not thereby affected, and the plaintiff is entitled to receive from the defendant an amount equivalent to the portion lost.

SECTION II.

Fundamental conditions governing release.

Article 1561. If any person states that he has no claim against or dispute with some other person, or that he is not entitled to anything from him, or that he has finished or given up a claim he had against him, or that he is no longer entitled to anything from him, or that he has received complete satisfaction from him, he is considered to have released such person.

Article 1562. If any person releases any other person from any obligation, such obligation ceases to exist and he can no longer make any claim in connection therewith. (See Article 51).

Article 1563. A release does not extend to anything happening in the future. That is to say, if one person releases another, any rights antecedent to the release cease to exist. Such person may, however, bring an action with regard to rights which accrue after the release.

Article 1564. If any person releases any other person from an action relating to a particular matter, such release is a special release and no action will be heard with regard to that matter. He may, however, bring an action with regard to any other matter.

SETTLEMENT AND RELEASE

Example :-

A releases B from an action with regard to a house. No action will be heard concerning such house. An action, however, will be heard relating to a farm and similar matters.

Article 1565. If any person states that he has released any other person from all actions or that he has no claim in respect to him, such release is general, and he may not bring an action in respect to any right which accrued prior to the release, to the extent that no action relating to a right accruing by reason of a contract of guarantee will be heard. Thus, if a person brings an action alleging that another person was surety for some third person, the action will not be heard. Nor may such person allege that some other person was surety for some person prior to that person's release. (See Article 662).

Article 1566. If a person sells property to some other person and receives the price and releases the purchaser from all actions relating to the thing sold, and the purchaser likewise releases the vendor from all actions with regard to the price and a document is drawn up between them on these lines, and the thing sold is seized by someone entitled thereto, the release ceases to be of any effect and the purchaser may claim the return of the price from the vendor. (See Article 52).

Article 1567. The persons who are released must be known and designated. Consequently. if any person states that he has released all persons who are in his debt or that he has no claim upon any person whatsoever, such release is invalid. But if he states that he has released the people of a certain place and the people of such place and the number thereof are definitely known, the release is valid.

SETTLEMENT AND RELEASE

Article 1568. A release is not dependent upon acceptance. But if the release is disclaimed it is of no effect. Thus, if one person releases another there is no need for the latter to accept. But if at the meeting where the release is made, such person states that he refuses to accept the release, such release is of no effect. If a person disclaims a release after having accepted it, it is of no effect. Again, if a person in whose favour a transfer of debt has been made releases the transferee, or a creditor releases a surety, or the transferee, or the surety disclaims the release, such release continues to be effective.

Article 1569. A person who is dead may validly be released from his debts.

Article 1570. If a person releases one of his heirs from his debts during the course of a mortal sickness, such release is not valid and executory. If he releases a person who is not his heir from his debts, however, such release is effective as regards a third of his property.

Article 1571. If a person whose estate is overwhelmed by debts releases a person who is indebted to him during the course of a mortal sickness, such release is invalid and not executory.

Promulgated by Royal Iradah, 6th Shual, 1291.

BOOK XIII.

ADMISSIONS.

BOOK XIII.

ADMISSIONS.

CHAPTER I.

CONDITIONS GOVERNING ADMISSIONS.

Article 1572. An admission is a statement by one person admitting the claim of some other person against him. The person making the admission is called an admittor. The person in whose favour the admission is made is called the admittee. The subject of the admission is called the thing admitted.

Article 1573. In order to be able to make a valid admission, a person must be of sound mind and have arrived at the age of puberty. Consequently, an admission by a minor, or a lunatic or an imbecile, whether male or female, is invalid An admission made against such persons by their tutors or guardians is equally invalid. A minor, however, who is of perfect understanding and has been authorized is regarded as a person who has reached the age of puberty in respect to all acts performed by him which he has been authorized to do.

Article 1574. A person in whose favour an admission is made need not be of sound mind. Consequently, a person may make a valid admission concerning property in favour of a minor of imperfect understanding and such person will be obliged to give up such property.

Article 1575. A person making an admission must do so of his own free will. Consequently, an admission made as a result of force or constraint is invalid. (See Article 1006).

ADMISSIONS

Article 1576. A person making an admission should not be under interdiction. (See Sections II, III and IV of the Book of Interdiction).

Article 1577. An admission must not be contrary to obvious facts. Consequently, if the body of a minor bears no signs of puberty, he cannot be heard to make an admission that he has arrived at the age of puberty.

Article 1578. A person in whose favour an admission is made must not be absolutely unknown; mere imperfect knowledge of such person, however, does not invalidate an admission.

Example :-

If a person points to certain property in his possession and admits that it is the property of some indeterminate person, or if he admits that the property belongs to one of the inhabitants of a certain town, the inhabitants of such town being indeterminate in number, such person's admission is invalid. On the other hand, if he states that the property belongs to one of two definite persons or to one of the inhabitants of a certain quarter, and the inhabitants of such place are of a determinate number, the admission is valid. In the event of a person stating, as mentioned above, that certain property belongs to one of two determinate persons, such persons may, if they agree to do so, take the property from the person making the admission and thereupon they become joint owners of such property. If they do not so agree, either of them may place the person making the admission upon his oath that such property is not his. If the person making the admission refuses to take the oath in respect to both persons, the property continues to be jointly owned between them. If the person making the admission refuses to take the oath with regard to one of the persons only, the property goes absolutely to the person whose oath he refuses. If the person making the admission takes an oath with regard to both such persons, the former is not liable to any action on the part of the latter, the property belonging to him and remaining in his possession.

CHAPTER II.
VALIDITY OF AN ADMISSION.

Article 1579. A valid admission may be made with regard to a determinate and also with regard to an indeterminate object. The validity of an admission relating to contracts which can only be made with regard to determinate objects, however, such as sale and hire, depends upon the thing with regard to which the admission is made being determinate. Thus, a valid admission may be made by a person that a thing belonging to another person has been entrusted to his safe keeping, or that he has wrongfully appropriated or stolen the property of another and he shall be obliged to make known the nature of such property. But if a person admits that he has sold something to a certain person, or hired something from him, such admission is invalid and he may not be called upon to say what thing he has sold or hired.

Article 1580. The validity of an admission is not dependent upon the acceptance of such admission by the person in whose favour the admission is made. Should such person disclaim the admission, however, such admission is null and void. If the person in whose favour the admission is made disclaims part of such admission only, the admission is null and void in regard to that part only, and is valid in respect to the remainder.

Article 1581. A difference as to the subject of the admission between the person making the admission and the person in whose favour it is made does not invalidate the admission. Thus, if a person brings an action for the recovery of one thousand piastres due under a loan, and the defendant admits one thousand·

piastres is due for the price of a thing sold, the difference is no way invalidates the admission.

Article 1582. A request for a settlement with regard to any property is equivalent to an admission in respect thereto. A request for a settlement of an action, however, in regard to any property is not equivalent to an admission in respect thereto. Thus, if A requests B to repay a debt of one thousand piastres and B requests A to make a settlement for seven hundred piastres in respect to such debt, A admits the thousand piastres claimed. But if A states that he will settle the action in respect to the thousand piastres merely in order to avoid a dispute, there is no admission of the thousand piastres.

Article 1583. If a person seeks to buy, hire or borrow property in the possession of another, or requests such person to bestow such property upon him by way of gift, or to give him such property for safe keeping, or the latter requests the former to take property into his safe keeping, and such person agrees to do so, there is an admission made by such person that the property is not his.

Article 1584. An admission dependent on a condition is null and void. An admission dependent upon the arrival of a generally recognized period of time, however, is equivalent to an admission of a debt repayable at a future definite date.

Example :-

A informs B that he will pay him a certain sum of money if he reaches a certain place or if he undertakes a certain business. The admission is void and the sum of money need not be paid. But if A states that he will repay B a certain sum of money on the first of a certain month, or on the twenty-sixth of October next, such statement is considered to be an admission

ADMISSIONS

of a debt repayable at a future definite date, and upon the arrival of such date, payment of the sum in question must be made. (See Article 40)

Article 1585. An admission may validly be made that a thing is undivided jointly-owned property. Consequently, if one person admits to another that he is in possession of an undivided share of certain immovable property held in absolute ownership belonging to him, such as a half or a third, and the latter confirms such admission, and the person making the admission dies before the division and delivery of such property, the fact that the subject matter of the admission is an undivided share in no way invalidates such admission.

Article 1586. An admission may validly be made by a dumb person using the recognized signs of such persons. An admission by signs cannot validly be made by a person who is able to speak. Thus, if one person asks another who is able to speak whether he is owing some third person a certain sum of money and such person nods his head, there is no admission of the debt.

CHAPTER III.
EFFECT OF AN ADMISSION.

SECTION I.
General.

Article 1587. A person is bound by his admission in accordance with the terms of Article 79, unless the admission is proved to be false by a Judgment of the Court. Thus, a person is legally entitled to a thing in the possession of another, which the latter has obtained by purchase. At the trial, the purchaser, in order to prove his case, states that the thing sold belonged to the vendor and that he sold it to him. The person legally entitled to such thing proves his claim and judgment is given by the Court in his favour. The purchaser may thereupon take action against the vendor and recover from him the price of the thing sold, because although at the trial he opposed the person legally entitled to the thing by admitting that such thing was the property of the vendor, he is not bound by the admission, the Court having found such admission to be devoid of any foundation.

Article 1588. No person may validly retract an admission made with regard to private rights. Thus, if a person admits owing a certain sum of money to another and later retracts his admission, the retraction is invalid and he is bound by his admission.

Article 1589. Should a person allege that he has not been truthful in making an admission, the person in whose favour the admission is made shall swear an oath that such admission is true.

Example :-
A gives a written acknowledgment that he has borrowed a certain sum of money from B. Later, A denies that he has borrowed such money in fact, in spite of his having given the acknowledgement, by reason of his not yet having received the money in question from B. The person in whose favour the admission is made shall then take an oath that such admission is not false.

Article 1590. If one person admits to another that he is in such person's debt to the extent of a certain sum of money, and the latter states that the money to be paid is not his, but belongs to another person, and such person confirms that statement, the money in question becomes the property of the second person in whose favour the admission is made, but the right of receiving it belongs to the first person in whose favour the admission is made. Consequently, if the second person in whose favour the admission is made claims the money from the debtor, the latter is not obliged to pay it to him. If the debtor, however, pays the debt of his own free will to the second person in whose favour the admission is made, he is released from his debt and the first person in whose favour the admission is made cannot claim it again from the debtor.

SECTION II.

Denial of ownership and title to a thing lent.

Article 1591. If a person making an admission makes it in such a manner as to show that the subject matter of the admission belongs to him, the result is a gift to the person in whose favour the admission is made, but such gift does not become absolute until it has been handed over and received. If he does not do so, the result is an admission that the subject matter of the admission was the property of the person in whose favour the admission is made, prior to such admission, which is tantamount to a denial of ownership.

Examples :-

(1) A states that all his property and things in his possession belong to B, and that he has no right to them at all. The result is a gift to B of all property and things in A's possession at that time and delivery and receipt thereof are essential.

(2) A states that all the property and things attributed to him, with the exception of the clothes he is wearing, belong to B and do not concern him in any way. The result is an admission by A that the property in question belongs to B. Such admission, however, does not include property acquired by A after the admission.

(3) A states that all his property and things in his shop belong to his eldest son and that he has no right thereto whatsoever. The result is a gift to his eldest son of

all his property and things in the shop at that time, and such property must be delivered. But if A states that all property and things in a certain shop of his belongs to his eldest son and that he has no right thereto whatsoever, the result is an admission in favour of his son that the property in such shop is the property of his son and he has denied ownership thereof. This admission, however, does not include any property placed in the shop afterwards.

(4) A states that his shop situated in such and such a place belongs to his wife. The result is in the nature of a gift, of which delivery is necessary. But if A states that such and such a shop reputed to be his belongs to his wife, the result is an admission that the shop was his wife's property before such admission and not his own property.

Article 1592. If a person states that the shop which he holds in absolute ownership and by title deed belongs to some other person, that he has no connection therewith of any sort, and that his name inscribed in the deed was lent for convenience only, the result is an admission that the shop belongs to that other person; or if a person states that a shop which he holds in absolute ownership bought by title deed from some other person was purchased on behalf of a third person, that the price was paid out of that person's property, and that the name of the first person was inscribed in the title deed for convenience only, the result is an admission that the shop was in fact the property of the third person.

Article 1593. If a person is in possession of a written acknowledgment admitting a claim for a certain sum of money against some other person and states that such sum belongs to a third person, and that his name on the document has been inscribed for convenience only, the result is an admission that the sum in question belongs to such third person.

Article 1594. If a person while in good health makes an admission disclaiming ownership as set out above, or admits that his name has been used for convenience only, his admission is valid and he his bound by it during his lifetime, and his heirs likewise after his death. The effect of an admission made as above while the person making the admission is suffering from a mortal sickness is governed by the terms of the following Chapter.

SECTION III.

ADMISSION BY A PERSON SUFFERING FROM A MORTAL SICKNESS.

Article 1595. A mortal sickness is a sickness where in the majority of cases death is imminent, and, in the case of a male, where such person is unable to deal with his affairs outside his home, and in the case of a female. where she is unable to deal with her domestic duties, death having occurred before the expiration of one year by reason of such illness, whether the sick person has been confined to bed or not. Should the sickness be of longer duration and the period of one year expire while in the same condition, such person is regarded as being in good health and his transactions as valid, unless the illness increases, and his condition becomes changed for the worse. Should his illness increase, however, and his condition become worse resulting in death before the expiration of one year, he is considered from the time of the change up to his death, to have been suffering from a mortal sickness.

Article 1596. Should a person have no heir at all, or should a man have no heir other than his wife, or should a woman have no heir other than her husband, any admission made during the course of a mortal sickness is regarded as a bequest and will be upheld. Consequently, if a person having no heirs disclaims ownership of his property during a mortal sickness by making an admission that the whole thereof belongs to some other person, such admission is valid, and the estate of the deceased person may not be touched by the representative of the Treasury. Similarly, if a man having no heir other than his wife disclaims ownership of his property during a mortal sickness by making an admission that such property belongs to his wife, or a woman having no heir other than her husband disclaims ownership of all her property by making an admission that such property belongs to her husband, such admission is valid and the estate of neither of the deceased persons may be touched by the representative of the Treasury.

Article 1597. An admission made by a person during an illness from which he recovers that property belongs to one of his heirs, is held to be valid.

Article 1598. If a person after having made an admission during a mortal sickness that certain specific property, or a debt, belongs to one of his heirs, and then dies, the validity of such admission depends upon the ratification of the other heirs. If they agree, the admission is held to be good; if not, it is invalid. Provided that if the other heirs have agreed thereto during the lifetime of the person making the admission, they cannot withdraw their agreement and the admission is held to be valid. An admission with regard to something deposited for safe-keeping, moreover, may always validly be made in favour of an heir. Thus, if a person during a mortal sickness admits that he has received property which he has deposited for safe keeping with his heir, or that he has consumed property belonging to his heir known to have been deposited with him for safe keeping, such admission is valid.

Examples :-
(1) A person admits that he has received property of his deposited for safe keeping with one of his sons. Such admission is valid and executory.

(2) A person admits that one of his sons has received, as agent, money due to him from a certain person and that he has handed it over to him. Such admission is valid.

(3) A person admits that he has sold the property of one of his sons entrusted to him for safe keeping, or his diamond ring worth five thousand piastres lent to him for his use, and has spent the proceeds on his own business. Such admission is valid. The value of the ring must be made good from the estate.

Article 1599. In this connection, by heir is meant a person who was an heir at the time of the sick person's death. Provided that if a right to inherit arises out of a new cause at the time of the death of the person making such admission and not previously, this shall in no way invalidate an admission made while that person was not an heir. Similarly, if a person during the course of a mortal sickness makes an admission in favour of a woman who is a stranger to him in respect to certain property, marries her and then dies, such admission is executory. If the right to inherit is not produced by such a new cause, however, but by an old one, the admission is not executory.

Example :-
A has a son and makes an admission in favour of one of his brothers by the same father and mother. Should the son predecease the father, the admission does not become executory merely because the brother in whose favour the admission was made has become his heir.

Article 1600. An admission made during a mortal sickness but relating to matters concerning a period during which the person making the admission was in good health, is considered to be an admission made during a sickness. Consequently, if a person admits during a mortal sickness that he has been paid a certain number of piastres due from one of his heirs while he was in a state of good health, such admission is not executory unless the other heirs confirm the same. Again, if a person admits during a mortal sickness that he has made a gift of certain property of his to one of his heirs while in a state of good health, and that he has delivered the same, such admission is not executory unless confirmed by the other heirs, or proved by evidence.

Article 1601. An admission made by a person during a mortal sickness to another person who is not one of such person's own heirs is good, even though it includes the whole of his property, whether consisting of some specific object or of some debt. Should it appear that the admission is false, however, it being a matter of common knowledge that at the time the admission was made, the subject matter of such admission had become the property of the person making the admission by way of sale, gift, or transfer on inheritance, such facts must be duly examined. If the admission was not made when drawing up a will, the result is a gift, and delivery of such gift is necessary. If made when drawing up a will, it is taken to be a bequest. In any case, the admission is only valid up to one third of the property of the person making the admission, whether a bequest or a gift.

Article 1602. Debts contracted in good health take priority over debts contracted during ill health, that is to say, in the event of the death of a person whose estate is overwhelmed by debts contracted before his mortal sickness, such debts are paid in priority to those contracted by him by way of admission during his mortal sickness. Consequently, debts contracted while in a state of good health are paid first out of the sick person's estate. If there is any balance remaining over, debts contracted during sickness are paid therefrom. Debts contracted during a mortal sickness and arising out of clearly ascertained causes, such as purchase, loan, or destruction of property are considered to be debts contracted while in a state of good health. If the subject matter of an admission is some specific object, it is dealt with in the same manner. That is to say, if a person admits to some other person during the course of a mortal sickness that certain things are that person's property, such person has no right to the property with regard to which the admission has been made, unless the debts contracted during good health have been paid, or debts which are in the nature of debts contracted during good health and which for reasons as stated above, must be repaid.

Article 1603. If a person admits during the course of a mortal sickness that he has been paid any sum due from any other person, not being a member of his family, such admission is receivable. If the debt was contracted by such person during the course of the illness, the admission is valid. Such admission, however, is not executory as regards persons who became creditors of the sick person while he was in a state of good health. If the debt was contracted by such person while in a state of good health, the admission is valid in any case and this whether there be debts which were contracted while in a state of good health or not.

Example :-

 A while ill admits that he has sold certain property and received the price thereof while sick. Such admission is valid. Persons to whom he became indebted while in a state of good health, however, may refuse to be bound by such admission. If A, however, admits during the course of a mortal sickness that he has sold certain property while in a state of good health and has received the price thereof, such admission is valid in any case, and persons to whom he became indebted while in a state of good health are bound thereby.

Article 1604. A person who pays a debt due to one of his creditors during the course of a mortal sickness may not thereby destroy the right of the other creditors. He may, however, repay a sum of money he borrowed and pay the price of property he bought while sick.

Article 1605. In this connection, a guarantee of property is considered in the same light as the original debt. Consequently, if a person becomes surety for any debt contracted by his heirs or any sum due to him, during the course of a mortal sickness, it is not executory. If such person becomes surety for some other person, not being a member of his family, it is valid up to a third of his property. If such person admits during the course of a mortal sickness that he has become surety for a person, not being a member of his family, while in a state of good health, the admission is valid up to the whole extent of his property. Debts contracted during a state of good health, if any, however, are preferred.

CHAPTER IV.

ADMISSIONS IN WRITING.

Article 1606. An admission in writing is the same as an oral admission. (See Article 69).

Article 1607. If a person causes his own admission to be written down by some other person, it has the force of an admission. Therefore if a person instructs a clerk

ADMISSIONS

to make out a document to the effect that he is owing another person a certain sum of money, and himself signs or seals such document, the document is regarded as though it were written in his own hand and is considered to be a written admission.

Article 1608. The entries made by a merchant in his books which are properly kept are in the nature of written admissions.

Example :-

A, a merchant, makes an entry in his own register that he owes B a certain sum of money. Such entry constitutes an admission of the debt, and, should the occasion arise, is considered as an oral admission.

Article 1609. If a person himself writes or causes a clerk to write an acknowledgment of a debt, which he signs or seals and delivers to some other person, and if such acknowledgment is made out in due form, that is to say, in accordance with the usual practice, it constitutes an admission in writing and has the same force as an oral admission. Receipts which are normally given are of the same category.

Article 1610. If any person as mentioned above writes or causes any other person to write, any acknowledgment of debt, which is signed or sealed, and which he admits to be his and then denies the debt contained therein, such denial is disregarded, and the debt must be paid.

Should he deny that the acknowledgment is his, the handwriting or seal being well known, the denial is disregarded, and action is taken in accordance with the acknowledgment.

If the handwriting and seal are not well known, such person shall be caused to write down specimens of his handwriting, which shall be submitted to experts. If they report that the handwriting in both cases is that of one and the same person, such person shall be ordered to pay the debt in question.

Finally, if the acknowledgment is free from any taint of fraud or forgery, action shall be taken in accordance with the acknowledgment. If it is not free from suspicion however, and should the debtor deny that the acknowledgment is his, and also deny the original debt, he shall, if the plaintiff so demand, be made to swear an oath that neither the debt nor the acknowledgment is his.

Article 1611. Should any person give an acknowledgment of a debt as mentioned above, and then die and the heirs admit that the acknowledgment was made by the deceased, the debt must be paid out of the deceased's estate.

Should the heirs deny that the acknowledgment was made by the deceased, and should his handwriting and seal be well known, action shall be taken in accordance with such acknowledgment.

Article 1612. If a purse full of money is found among the effects of a deceased person, and it is written thereon that the purse is the property of some particular person and has been given to the deceased on trust for safe keeping, the person in question has a right to take the purse from the estate of the deceased and there is no need for any further proof.

Promulgated by Royal Iradah, 9 Jumadi ul Ula, 1293.

BOOK XIV.
ACTIONS.

BOOK XIV.

ACTIONS.

INTRODUCTION.

TERMS OF MUHAMMADAN JURISPRUDENCE.

Article 1613. An action consists of a claim made by one person against another in Court. The person making the claim is called the plaintiff. The person against whom the claim is made is called the defendant.

Article 1614. The thing claimed is the thing about which the action is brought by the plaintiff. It is also called the subject matter of the action.

Article 1615. Estoppel is some statement previously made by the plaintiff which conflicts with the action he has brought, and which causes such action to be declared null and void.

CHAPTER I.

CONDITIONS AND FUNDAMENTAL RULES RELATING TO AN ACTION AND THE DEFENCE THERETO.

SECTION I.

Conditions for the validity of an action.

Article 1616. The plaintiff and the defendant must be of sound mind. A lunatic and a minor of imperfect understanding may not validly bring an action. Their tutors and guardians may act on their behalf in their capacity of plaintiff and defendant.

Article 1617. The defendant must be known. Consequently, if the plaintiff alleges that he is entitled to

ACTIONS

a certain sum of money from one or more persons who are not specified, inhabiting a certain village, the claim is invalid, and the defendant must be specified.

Article 1618. The defendant must be present when the action comes on in Court. If the defendant fails to come to the Court, or to send a representative, action shall be taken as is set forth in the Book on the Administration of Justice by the Court.

Article 1619. The subject matter of the action must be known. If it is not known, the action is invalid.

Article 1620. The subject matter of the action may be made known by pointing it out, or by mentioning its qualities or by describing it. Thus, in the case of some specific piece of movable property, if such property is present in Court, it is sufficient to point it out. If it is not so present, it may be made known by mentioning the qualities, description, and value thereof. If it is real property, it may be designated by mentioning the boundaries thereof. If it is a debt, the nature, variety, description and amount thereof must be stated. These matters will be dealt with in the following Articles.

Article 1621. If the subject matter of the action is some specific movable property and is before the Court, the plaintiff may bring an action and point to the thing claimed, asking for it to be restored to him, since the defendant has wrongfully dispossessed him thereof. If the subject matter of the action is not before the Court, but it can be sent for and produced without expense, it shall be placed before the Court for the purpose of the trial of the action, the giving of evidence, or swearing the oath. If it cannot be brought before the Court without expense, the plaintiff shall give a description and state the value thereof. In actions relating to wrongful appropriation of property, and in the case of pledges, it is not necessary to state the value.

Example :-

An action may validly be brought in which the plaintiff states that his emerald ring has been wrongfully appropriated, but fails to state the value, or even states that he does not know the value thereof.

Article 1622. If the subject matter of the action consists of specific pieces of property, the nature, sort and qualities of which are different the one from the other, it is sufficient if the total value of the whole of them is stated. There is no need to state the value of each of them separately.

Article 1623. If the subject matter of the action is real property, the name of the town and village or quarter and of the street and the four or three boundaries thereof, and the names of the persons, if any, to whom such boundaries belong, together with the names of their fathers and grandfathers must be stated when the action is brought and when giving evidence. In the case of a person who is well known, however, it is sufficient to state his name and description. There is no need to state the names of his father and grandfather. Similarly, if the description of the boundaries may be dispensed with owing to their being so well known, there is no need to state the boundaries either when bringing the action or giving evidence in connection therewith. The plaintiff may also validly bring an action stating that the real property the boundaries of which are set forth in a document he produces to the Court is his property owned in absolute ownership.

Article 1624. The fact that the plaintiff correctly states the boundaries, but incorrectly states the length or area thereof in no way affects the validity of the action.

Article 1625. In an action for the price of real property, it is not essential to state the boundaries thereof.

Article 1626. If the subject matter of the action is a debt, the plaintiff must state the nature, variety, description and amount thereof.

Example :-

> It must be stated as regards the nature of the debt whether it is of gold or silver, or as regards the variety whether it consists of Ottoman or English coin and in respect to the description whether it consists of sound or base coin. The amount must also be stated. If it is stated in general terms, however, to consist of so many piastres, the action is valid, and the amount in dispute will be considered with reference to the custom prevailing in the locality. If there are two types of currency recognized, and the circulation and standard of one is greater than the other, the amount will be construed with reference to the inferior currency. Again, if a person brings an action claiming so many pieces of five, the money is taken to be the black pieces of five, that is base coin, in circulation at the present time.

Article 1627. If the subject matter of the action is some specific piece of property, there is no need to state how the ownership thereof was acquired, but the action may validly be brought by stating that the property in question is owned in absolute ownership. If it consists of a debt, however, the origin thereof must be stated, that is to say, whether it is the price of something sold, or rent, or arising from any other reason.

Article 1628. The effect of an admission is that it bears upon the subject matter of the admission. It does not bear upon the origin thereof and therefore an admission is not a cause of ownership. Consequently, no person may bring an action claiming something merely by reason of the admission of the defendant.

Examples:-

(1) A brings an action alleging that certain property belongs to him, and that B has dispossessed him thereof and in addition has admitted that such property belongs to A. The action will be heard. But if A brings an action alleging that certain property is his because B, who has taken possession thereof, has admitted that it belongs to A, the action will not be heard.

(2) A brings an action alleging that B is owing him a certain sum of money on account of a loan and that B has admitted the debt. The action will be heard. But if A brings an action alleging that B has admitted that he owes A a certain sum of money on account of a loan, and that he consequently claims this sum from him, the action will not be heard.

Article 1629. The subject matter of the action must be capable of proof. Consequently, no action may validly be brought with regard to anything the existence of which can be shown to be impossible either by a process of reasoning or by custom.

Example :-

A alleges that B is his son, B being older than A, and the matter of his birth well known. The action will fail.

Article 1630. If the action is proved, judgment must be given against the defendant in respect to some particular thing.

Examples:-

(1) A gives something to B as loan for use. C then comes forward and claims that he is a relative of A requesting that such thing shall be lent to him. The action will fail.

(2) A appoints B his agent for a certain purpose. C comes forward and alleges that he is A's neighbour and that he is a more suitable person to be appointed agent. The action will fail.

The reason for this is that every person may lend his property for use to whomsoever he wishes, and may appoint whomsoever he pleases as his agent, and even though the matters alleged by the plaintiffs may be true, no judgment can be issued in respect to the defendant.

SECTION II.

The defence to an action.

Article 1631. A defence consists of making an allegation by the defendant in reply to an action brought by the plaintiff.

Examples :-

(1) A brings an action claiming a certain sum of money from B on account of a loan. B replies that he has paid A, or that A has released him from the debt, or that they have come to a settlement, or that the sum in question is not a loan, but is the price of property sold to A, or that he made a transfer to A of a sum of money due to him from C, and that the sum in question was paid by A to him in respect of such transfer. This is B's defence.

(2) A brings an action against B stating that B became surety for the payment of a sum of money due to him from C. B replies that C has paid the sum in question. This is B's defence.

(3) A brings an action against B stating that B is in possession of property belonging to him. B replies that some time ago C brought an action against him in respect to some property and that at the trial of the action A gave evidence in favour of C. This is B's defence

(4) A brings an action against the heirs to the estate of a deceased person, claiming a certain sum of money, which the heirs deny. A proves his claim, and thereupon the heirs allege that the deceased paid the debt in his lifetime. This is the heirs' defence to the action.

Article 1632. Upon the defendant proving his defence, the action brought by the plaintiff is dismissed. If he fails to prove his defence, he may call upon the plaintiff to take the oath. If the plaintiff refuses to take the oath, the defendant's defence is proved. If the plaintiff takes the oath, the action brought by the plaintiff is maintained.

Article 1633. If any person brings an action against some other person claiming a certain sum of money from him and the defendant replies by stating that he has transferred the payment of the debt to some third person and that both parties agreed to such transfer and proves such statement in the presence of the person to whom he transferred the debt, the claim of the plaintiff is rejected and the defendant freed therefrom. If the person to whom the debt has been transferred is not present, the defendant is considered to have answered the claim of the plaintiff pending the arrival of such person.

SECTION III.

Parties to an action.

Article 1634. If any person brings an action in respect to any matter, and the defendant admits the claim, judgment is given on the admission. If he denies the claim, the action is heard, and evidence may be given. If judgment is not given on the admission of the defendant, he does not become a party to the action by reason of his denial.

ACTIONS

Example :-

A brings an action against B alleging that B sent a messenger of his to buy certain property and claims the price. If B admits the claim, he is bound to pay and hand over the price of the thing sold. If he denies, he becomes the defendant to A's claim whose case is then heard and who may produce evidence. If A brings an action alleging that B's agent for purchase bought such property, and the defendant admits the claim, B must pay and hand over the price of the sale. If he denies, however, he does not become defendant to A. In that case the plaintiff's action will not be heard.

Tutors, guardians and trustees of pious foundations are excepted from this rule. Thus, if any person brings an action stating that the property of an orphan or of a pious foundation is his, and the tutor or guardian or trustee admit the claim, the admission is of no effect and no judgment may be issued based thereon. They may, however, make a valid denial and an action brought by the plaintiff as a result of such denial, and the plaintiff's evidence, will be heard. If an action is brought as the result of an admission based upon a contract concluded by a tutor, guardian or trustee of a pious foundation, the action will be heard.

Example :-

A tutor sells property belonging to a minor, having legal justification for so doing. The purchaser brings an action in connection therewith. An admission made by the tutor is valid.

Article 1635. In an action relating to some specific piece of property, the person in possession must be made defendant.

Example :-

A wrongfully appropriates B's horse and sells and delivers it to C. B wishes to get his horse back. He must bring his action against the person in possession of the horse. If he wishes to recover the value of the horse. however, he must bring his action against the person who has wrongfully appropriated the horse.

Article 1636. If a person brings an action claiming that he is entitled to property which has been purchased, it must be ascertained whether the purchaser has taken delivery of such property. If so, the defendant at the trial of the action and hearing of the evidence will be the purchaser only. There is no need for the vendor to be present. If the purchaser has not yet taken delivery of the property from the vendor, both the purchaser of the property, and the vendor as the person in possession of the property, must be present at the trial of the action.

Article 1637. In actions relating to a thing deposited for safe keeping brought against the person with whom it has been deposited, or to a thing lent against the person borrowing it, or a thing hired against the person hiring it, or a pledge against the pledgee, both parties must be present. But if property deposited for safe keeping, or lent, or hired, or pledged has been wrongfully appropriated, the person in possession of such property may bring the action against the person wrongfully appropriating and there is no need for the presence of the owner. If such persons are not present, the owner alone may not bring the action.

Article 1638. A person to whom property has been entrusted for safe keeping may not be made defendant in an action against the purchaser.

Example:-

A brings an action against B alleging that he is in possession of a house which he bought from C for a certain sum of money, claiming that the house be handed over to him. B replies that C handed the house over to him for safe keeping. The plaintiff's claim fails and B is not obliged to prove that C in fact handed the house over to him for safe keeping. If A admits that C handed the house to B for safe keeping, but adds that thereafter C sold it to him and made him his agent to receive it from C, and A proves the sale and his appointment as agent, he is entitled to take the house from the person to whom it has been entrusted for safe keeping.

Article 1639. A person to whom a thing has been entrusted for safe keeping cannot be made defendant in an action brought by the creditor of the person depositing the thing for safe keeping with him. Consequently, if a creditor proves before a person to whom property has been entrusted for safe keeping that a debt is owing to him by the person depositing such property, he cannot satisfy his debt from such property but, as is set forth in Article 799, a person who is entitled to maintenance from some absent person may bring an action claiming that the sum necessary for his maintenance shall be paid to him from money deposited by the absent person for safe keeping.

Article 1640. A creditor may not bring an action against a person in debt to the person owing him money. Consequently, if any person proves before a person in debt to a deceased person that he has a claim against such deceased person, he may not obtain payment from the debtor.

Article 1641. A vendor may not bring an action against a person who purchased something which he has sold to some other person.

Example :-

A sells property to B. B takes delivery thereof and sells it to C. A may not bring an action against C alleging that B has bought the property from him and has taken delivery thereof without paying the price and that he claims the price from C, or that he claims the thing sold in order to exercise a right of retention over such thing until he has received payment of the price.

Article 1642. In the case of a deceased person, one of the heirs alone may become plaintiff, or act as defendant, in actions brought on behalf of or against such deceased person. In the case of an action brought to recover some specific piece of property from the estate, however, the heir in whose possession the property is, must be made defendant. The action may not be brought against an heir who is not in possession of such property.

Examples :-

(1) One of the heirs alone may bring an action to recover a debt owing to the deceased. After proving his claim, judgment is given for all the heirs for the total amount of the claim. The heir acting as plaintiff can obtain his own part alone. He cannot obtain the shares of the other heirs.

(2) A person brings an action to recover a debt owing by the estate of a deceased person. He may bring the action in the presence of one of the heirs only, and this, whether such heir is in possession of property belonging to the estate or not. If the heir in question admits the debt in an action brought in this way, he is only liable to pay his share of the debt, and his admission in no way binds the other heirs. If he does not admit the debt, and the plaintiff proves his case in his presence alone, judgment shall be given against the whole of the heirs. Upon the plaintiff proceeding to collect the amount of the debt from the estate, the other heirs may not call upon him to prove the debt again in their presence. They have the right, however, of defending the action brought by the plaintiff.

(3) If a person brings an action to recover a horse in the possession of one of the heirs only, prior to partition of the estate, and which he claims he deposited

with the deceased for safe keeping, the heir in possession of the horse may be made defendant. No action will be heard against any other of the heirs. If the person in possession admits the claim, judgment shall be given in accordance with such admission, which does not affect the other heirs. His admission is effective in respect to the amount of his own share only and the judgment shall state that his share in the horse belongs to the plaintiff. If the heir in possession denies the claim and the plaintiff proves his case, judgment shall be given against the whole of the heirs. (See Art. 78).

Article 1643. If an action is brought claiming some specific piece of property owned by several joint owners, the ownership arising out of some cause other than inheritance, one of the joint owners may not be made defendant in respect to the share of another.

Example :-

A brings an action claiming as his a house which has been purchased jointly by several persons, and proves his case in the presence of one of the joint purchasers only. If judgment is given in his favour, the judgment relates to such joint owner's share only and does not extend to the others.

Article 1644. In an action brought in respect to places affecting the public interest, such as the public highway, where one member of the public only is plaintiff, the action shall be heard and judgment given against the defendant.

Article 1645. In an action relating to things the benefit of which is jointly owned by two villages, as in the case of a river or grazing ground, the inhabitants of which are indeterminate in number, the presence of a certain number of them is sufficient. If they are determinate in number, however, it is not enough for some of them to be present, but the whole of them must be present either personally, or through their representative.

Article 1646. The inhabitants of a village which are more than a hundred in number are considered to be indeterminate in number.

SECTION IV.

Estoppel.

Article 1647. A statement contradicting a statement previously made with regard to the same matter invalidates an action for ownership.

Examples :-

> (1) If a person arranges to purchase a piece of property, but before completing the purchase brings an action claiming that such property is his own absolutely, such action will not be heard.

> (2) If a person states that he has no right to any particular thing, but, nevertheless, brings an action claiming such thing, such action cannot be heard.

> (3) A brings an action against B asserting that he gave a certain amount of money to B to hand to C. A further states that B retained the money instead of giving it to C as directed, and that he instructed B to fetch the money and pay it over to C. The plaintiff establishes his case by evidence. If the defendant denies such statements but later, while admitting having received the sum of money for delivery to C, states that he has in fact delivered it to C, and seeks to bring an action in rebuttal of the plaintiff's claim, such action cannot be heard.

> (4) A brings an action alleging that a certain shop in the possession of B is his property. B admits that the shop was formerly A's property, but asserts that A sold it to him on a certain date. A completely denies this statement, stating that they had never concluded

a contract of sale and purchase. If B, the person in the possession of the shop, proves his case, the plaintiff cannot later be heard to say that he did in fact sell the shop to B, but the sale was a sale subject to redemption, or subject to a condition making the contract voidable.

Article 1648. If a person admits that certain property belongs to another, he may not later bring an action claiming that such property is his, nor may he bring an action on behalf of any other person, such as his agent or guardian.

Article 1649. If a person releases another from all actions, he may not later bring an action against such person claiming from him property which he asserts to be his own. This, however, will not prevent him from bringing an action on behalf of another person, in the capacity of such person's agent or guardian.

Article 1650. A person who has brought an action claiming property on behalf of another person may not later bring an action claiming such property as his own. But after bringing an action on his own behalf he may bring an action on behalf of some other person in the capacity of such person's agent, the reason being that an advocate sometimes claims property in his own name, but a person who is himself a party to an action does not assert that the property belongs to another.

Article 1651. One claim cannot be paid separately by two persons. Similarly, a claim arising from a single cause cannot be demanded from two persons.

Article 1652. Estoppel operates to prevent two persons claiming the same thing, as in the case of an agent and the person appointing him and an heir and the person from whom he inherits, if estoppel would operate to invalidate a claim in an action by one person. Thus, if in an action an agent introduces a claim in conflict with an action previously instituted by his principal, such claim is invalid.

Article 1653. If one of the parties admits the claim, the estoppel ceases to be operative.

Example :-

A brings an action claiming that he has lent a certain sum of money to B. A later brings an action asserting that the sum of money was by way of guarantee. The defendant admits this, whereupon the estoppel ceases to be operative.

Article 1654. If the Court finds a statement to be false, the estoppel ceases to be operative.

Example :-

A brings an action claiming certain property in the possession of B. The defendant disputes the claim, alleging that the property belongs to C from whom he bought it. If the plaintiff proves his case, he gets judgment. The person against whom judgment is given has a right of recourse against the vendor for the price of the property, because B was estopped from having recourse against the vendor by reason of his admission that such property belonged to the vendor. The estoppel ceases to be operative, since the judgment of the Court has disregarded the admission.

Article 1655. If the matter is subject to doubt, and the plaintiff can offer a satisfactory explanation, the estoppel is removed.

Examples :-

(1) A hires a house, and later brings an action against the lessor asserting that his father bought the house from him when he was a child, adding that at the time he hired the house he was not aware of the facts of the case.

If A can produce documentary evidence of title the case will be heard.

(2) A hires a house and later brings an action against the lessor claiming that he had ascertained that such house had devolved upon him some time previously by way of inheritance from his father. The case will be heard.

Article 1656. The commencement of the division of an estate is an admission that the property divided has been held in common. Consequently, a plaintiff is estopped from bringing an action after the division of the property, alleging that the property divided belongs to him.

Example :-

A, an heir, brings an action after the division of the estate asserting that he bought one of the things divided from the deceased person, or that the deceased person while in good health bestowed such thing upon him by way of gift and gave delivery thereof. Such action will not be heard. But if A asserts that the deceased person gave him the property in question while he was an infant and that at the time of the division of the property he was unaware of such fact, this is regarded as a valid excuse and the case will be heard.

Article 1657. If it is possible to reconcile two apparently contradictory statements, and if the plaintiff does in fact explain away any apparent contradiction, there can be no estoppel.

Examples :-

(1) A admits that he is the lessee of a house. Later, he brings an action alleging that he is the owner of such house. The case will not be heard. But if A explains away the contradiction by stating that he bought the house from the owner after he had hired such house, the case will be heard.

ESTOPPEL

(2) A brings an action claiming the return of a sum of money advanced by way of loan. The defendant by his reply states that he has received nothing from him, or that the two parties had no business transaction together of any sort, or that he does not know the plaintiff. A proves his case. If the defendant later brings an action against A asserting that he has repaid the sum in question, or that A released him from repayment thereof, the defendant is estopped from bringing such action by reason of the contradiction. But if, upon the case being brought by A, the defendant replies that he owes nothing and when the plaintiff proves his case admits owing the sum, but asserts that he has since repaid it, or has been released from repayment thereof by the plaintiff, and proves his case, there is no estoppel.

(3) A brings an action against B alleging that he has deposited something with B for safe keeping and claiming the return thereof. The defendant replies denying the allegation and stating that no such thing was ever deposited with him for safe keeping. A proves his case by evidence and the defendant then seeks to defeat A by alleging that he has returned the thing to A and given delivery thereof. B is estopped from making such a defence. If the thing entrusted to B for safe keeping is in the possession of B, the plaintiff takes the thing itself. If it is no longer in existence, however, B must pay A the price thereof. But if A brings an action and B replies alleging that no such thing belonging to the plaintiff has ever been deposited with him for safe keeping, and A then proves his case by evidence, and B admits that A deposited the thing with him for safe keeping, but that he has returned such thing to A and given A delivery thereof, B is not estopped.

Article 1658. A person who admits being a party to an unconditional and perfectly valid contract, his admission being reduced to writing, is estopped from

ESTOPPEL

alleging later that the contract was entered into subject to a condition as to redemption, or is voidable. (See Article 100).

Examples :-

(1) A sells and delivers his house owned in absolute ownership to B for an agreed price. A then goes into Court and makes an admission to the effect that he has sold his house to B, the boundaries whereof are as stated, such sale being unconditional and perfectly valid, for a certain sum in money. If A later, after his admission has been reduced to writing, brings an action stating that the sale was subject to a condition as to redemption, or that it was made subject to a condition rendering it voidable, such action will not be heard.

(2) If A settles an action which he has brought against B, and makes an admission in Court that the settlement has been validly made, and after such admission has been reduced to writing brings an action alleging that the settlement was made subject to a condition making it voidable, such action will not be heard.

Article 1659. If A in the presence of B sells property held in absolute ownership, which he asserts is his own, to C, and gives delivery thereof to him, and B later brings an action alleging that such property is his or that he has a share therein, although he was present when the sale took place and kept silence without any valid excuse for so doing, it must be ascertained whether B is a relative of the vendor, or his or her husband or wife. If so, the action will not be heard in any case. If he is a stranger, the fact that he was present at the time the sale was concluded, does not of itself prevent the hearing of the action. On the other hand, if, in addition to being present when the sale took place, he keeps silence without any valid excuse for so doing while the purchaser deals with the property as though it were his own, such as by erecting buildings or pulling them down, or planting trees thereon, and then brings an action claiming that such property is his own, or that he has a share therein, such action will not be heard.

CHAPTER II.

Limitation.

Article 1660. Actions relating to a debt, or property deposited for safe-keeping, or real property held in absolute ownership, or inheritance, or actions not relating to the fundamental constitution of a pious foundation, such as actions relating to real property dedicated to pious purposes leased for a single or double rent, or to pious foundations with a condition as to the appointment of a trustee, or the revenue of a pious foundation, or actions not relating to the public, shall not be heard after the expiration of a period of fifteen years since action was last taken in connection therewith.

Article 1661. Actions brought by a trustee of a pious foundation relating to the fundamental constitution thereof or by persons maintained by such foundation may be heard up to a period of thirty-six years. They shall not be heard in any event, however, after the period of thirty-six years has expired.

Example :-
>A has held a piece of real property in absolute ownership for a period of thirty-six years. The trustee of a pious foundation thereupon brings an action claiming that the piece of real property in question is part of the land belonging to his pious foundation. The action will not be heard.

Article 1662. Actions relating to a private road, to a right of flow and to a right of taking water, when relating to real property held in absolute ownership, shall not be heard after the expiration of a period of fifteen years. If they relate to real property which has been dedicated to pious purposes, however, the trustee thereof is entitled to bring an action relating thereto up to a period of thirty-six years. Actions relating to government land and actions relating to private roads, to a right of flow and to a right of taking water, if they concern government land, shall not be heard after the expiration of a period of ten years since action was last taken in connection therewith.

Article 1663. Limitation which is effective in this connection, that is to say, which prevents an action being heard, relates only to a period of time which has been allowed to elapse without any excuse. The effluxion of time which has occurred by reason of some lawful excuse, such as cases where the plaintiff is a minor, or a lunatic, or an imbecile, and that whether he has a guardian or not, or where the plaintiff has gone to some other country for the period of a journey, or where the plaintiff has been in fear of the power of his opponent, is disregarded. Consequently, limitation begins to run from the time of the cessation or removal of the excuse.

Examples :-

(1) No attention is paid to time which has elapsed while a person was a minor. The period of limitation only begins as from the time he reaches the age of puberty.

(2) A has an action against B, a person in authority of whom he stands in fear. If time has elapsed by reason of A's not being able to bring an action against B while in authority, this fact shall not prevent an action being brought. The period of limitation only begins to run from the date of the cessation of the power of B.

Article 1664. The period of a journey is three days at a moderate speed, that is a distance of eighteen hours.

Article 1665. If one of two persons living in places which are separated from each other by the period of a journey, meets the other person in one of such places once during a certain number of years, so that an action pending between them can be brought to trial, but neither of them takes any steps in the matter, no action may be brought by one against the other in respect to any matter which arose before the period of limitation began to run.

Article 1666. If any person brings an action in Court against any other person in respect to some particular matter once in a certain number of years, without the case being finally decided, and in this way fifteen years pass by, the hearing of the action is not barred. But any claim made out of Court does not cause the period of limitation to cease to run. Consequently, if any person makes a claim in respect to any particular matter elsewhere than in Court, and in this way the period of limitation elapses, the hearing of an action by the plaintiff is barred.

Article 1667. The period of limitation begins to run as from the date at which the plaintiff had the right to bring an action in respect to the subject matter of his claim. Consequently, in an action in respect to a debt repayable at some future definite date, the period of limitation only begins to run as from the date on which the debt fell due for payment, since the plaintiff has no right to bring an action in respect to the debt before the due date has arrived.

Examples :-
(1) A brings an action against B claiming from him the price of a thing sold to him fifteen years ago, subject to a period of three years for payment of the

price. The action may be heard, since only twelve years have passed since the date of payment arrived.

(2) An action is brought in regard to property dedicated to pious purposes limited to children from generation to generation. The period for limitation in respect to an action brought by children of the second generation begins to run as from the date of the extinction of the children of the first generation, since the children of the second generation have no right to bring an action while the children of the first generation are alive.

(3) In actions relating to a marriage portion payable at a future date, the period of limitation begins to run from the date of the divorce or death of one of the spouses, since a marriage portion payable at a future date only falls due for payment on divorce or death.

Article 1668. Limitation in respect to a person who is bankrupt only begins to run as from the date of the cessation of the bankruptcy.

Example :-
A brings an action against B, who has been insolvent for fifteen years, and who recently has come into funds, in respect to a debt owing for a period of fifteen years, having refrained from bringing the action previously owing to B's being bankrupt. The action will be heard.

Article 1669. If any person as mentioned above fails to bring an action without any excuse, such action is barred by effluxion of time and will not be heard during his lifetime, nor, on his death, will an action by his heirs be heard.

Article 1670. If a person entitled to bring an action fails during a certain period to do so and on his death his heir likewise fails to do so for a certain period and the total of both periods amounts to the period of limitation, such action will not be heard.

Article 1671. A vendor and purchaser, a person making and a person receiving a gift are like a person leaving property and a person inheriting property.

Examples:-

(1) A owns a piece of land for a period of fifteen years. B who owns a house abutting on to A's land takes no action during this period, and thereafter sells the house to a third person. The purchaser then brings an action against A alleging that A's land comprises a private road leading to his house. The action will not be heard.

(2) The vendor remains silent for a period. and the purchaser similarly remains silent for a period, If the total amount of both periods amounts to the period of limitation, an action brought by the purchaser will not be heard.

Article 1672. If some of a number of heirs in an action brought in respect to property of the deceased in the possession of some third person are barred owing to the period of limitation having elapsed, and others, by reason of some valid excuse, such as that they are minors, are not, and such action is successful, judgment shall be given in their favour for their share of the property, but such judgment shall not include the others.

Article 1673. If any person admits that he has taken certain real property on hire, he may not claim to have become the owner of such property by reason of a period of more than fifteen years having elapsed. But if he denies that he has taken it on hire and the owner states that the real property in question belongs to him absolutely, that he gave it on hire to him a certain number of years ago, and that he has always received the rent, the question will be examined as to whether the lease is generally known among the people, and if so, the action will be heard, but not otherwise.

LIMITATION

Article 1674. A right is not destroyed by the effluxion of time. Consequently, if the defendant explicity admits and confesses in Court in a case in which the period of limitation has elapsed that the plaintiff is entitled to bring his action, the limitation is of no effect and judgment will be given in accordance with the admission of the defendant. If the defendant, however, makes no admission in Court and the plaintiff alleges that he made the admission elsewhere, the plaintiff will fail both on the original action and on the admission. But if the admission which is the subject of the action was reduced to writing at some previous date in a document known to contain the seal or handwriting of the defendant, and the period between the date on which such document was drawn up and the date of bringing the action is less than the period of limitation, an action on the admission will be heard.

Article 1675. No period of limitation applies to actions concerning places appropriated to the use of the public such as the public highway, rivers and pasturing grounds.

Example :-

A has appropriated and held a pasture ground belonging to a particular village for a period of fifty years without his right thereto being disputed. Thereafter the inhabitants of the village bring an action against A in respect to the pasture ground. The action will be heard.

Promulgated by Royal Iradah, 9 Jumadi ul Ukhra, 1293.

BOOK XV.
EVIDENCE.

BOOK XV.

EVIDENCE AND ADMINISTRATION OF OATH.

INTRODUCTION.

TERMS OF MUHAMMDAN JURISPRUDENCE.

Article 1676. Evidence consists of the adduction of reliable testimony.

Article 1677. Conclusively substantiated evidence consists of statements made by a number of persons where it would be contrary to reason to conclude that they had agreed to tell a lie.

Article 1678. Property owned in absolute ownership is property the ownership of which is not limited by a restrictive cause of ownership, such as inheritance or purchase. Ownership which is limited by any such cause is also called indirect ownership.

Article 1679. A person in possession is a person who effectively possesses a specific piece of property, or a person acting as owner of and disposing of property held in absolute ownership,

Article 1680. An outsider is a person who does not exercise possession over or dispose of property as mentioned above.

Article 1681. Tendering the oath consists of administering the oath to one of the parties.

Article 1682. Administration of the oath to both parties consists of putting both parties on oath.

EVIDENCE

Article 1683. By maintaining an existing state of affairs is meant giving judgment for matters to continue as they are. It is in the nature of confirmation. Confirmation also means giving judgment for the continuance of a well ascertained matter, the non-existence of which is not suspected, by which is meant maintaining matters as they were.

CHAPTER I.
NATURE OF EVIDENCE
SECTION I.
Definition of evidence and number of witnesses.

Article 1684. Evidence consists of the giving of information by a person in Court and in the presence of the parties by employing the word "evidence", that is to say, by saying formally: "I give evidence", in order to prove the existence of a right which one person seeks to establish against another. *

Article 1685. In civil cases, evidence is only valid when given by two males, or one male and two females: but in places where males cannot be possessed of the necessary information, the evidence of females alone will be accepted in respect to property.

Article 1686. Evidence of the dumb and the blind is not receivable.

SECTION II.
The manner of giving evidence.

Article 1687. Evidence not given at the trial is invalid.

Article 1688. Witnesses must personally have seen the thing with regard to which they give evidence and must testify accordingly. The giving of hearsay evidence

---

* The translation of certain technical terms has been omitted, as having no meaning for the English reader.

that is to say, evidence of what the witness has heard other people say, is inadmissible. But if a witness states that he has heard from a reliable source that a certain place has been dedicated to pious purposes, or that a certain person is dead, that is to say, if he gives evidence of such fact because he heard it from a reliable source, such evidence is accepted. In matters of state administration, death and paternity, a person may give hearsay evidence without stating that he is giving hearsay evidence, that is to say, without stating that he is saying what he has heard.

Example :-

> A states that he knows that B was governor or judge of the town at a certain date or period, or that B died at a certain time, or that B is the son of C. If A gives such evidence definitely without stating that it is hearsay, even though he has not investigated such matters and his age is such that he could not have examined them, his evidence is accepted. Similarly, if A fails to state that he is giving hearsay evidence and although such evidence has not been the subject of investigation by him, nevertheless, such evidence shall be accepted, if A states that such a thing is common knowledge with his people.

Article 1589. If the witness fails to employ the formula: "I give evidence" and contents himself with saying that he knows a thing to be so, or if he states that he gives information, such statement is not considered to be evidence. Should the Court, however, thereupon ask the witness whether that is his manner of giving evidence and the witness replies in the affirmative, the statement becomes good evidence. Should it be necessary merely to verify or ascertain certain things, as for example in the case of reports furnished by experts, the word "evidence" need not be mentioned, since such reports merely contain information and not legal evidence.

Article 1690. If the person in whose favour or against whom evidence is being given, and the thing about which evidence is being given, are present and if the witness points to the three of them, this shall be considered to be sufficient identification. There is no necessity to state the names of the father and grandfather of the persons for or against whom evidence is given. If the evidence relates to a deceased person, however, or an absent principal, the witness must state the names of such person's father or grandfather. But in the case of a person who is of high repute and is well known, it is sufficient for the witness to state such person's name and description, since the real object is to describe him in such a way as to distinguish him from other persons.

Article 1691. When giving evidence as to real property, the boundaries of such property must be stated. If the witness is unable to mention the boundaries of the real property with regard to which evidence is given, but states that he could indicate them on the spot, he shall proceed to the spot and there indicate the boundaries.

Article 1692. Should the plaintiff bring an action based upon the boundaries set forth in his title deed, in accordance with the terms of Article 1623, witnesses may validly give evidence that such a person is the owner of the property, the boundaries of which are set forth in the title-deed.

Article 1693. If a person brings an action to recover a sum of money owing to the person from whom he has inherited by some other person, it is sufficient if the witnesses give evidence that the sum of money in question was owing to the deceased by such person. There is no necessity to state that such sum has been inherited by the heirs. Should some specific thing be the subject of the claim and not a debt, that is to say, should a definite piece of property belonging to the testator be claimed, which is in the possession of such person, the case will be decided in the same manner.

Article 1694. If a person brings an action to recover a sum of money from the estate of a deceased person, witnesses may validly give evidence that such a sum of money is due to that person by the deceased. There is no necessity to state that the money was owing up to the time of his death. The same rule applies if an action is brought to recover certain property and not a debt, that is to say, when the plaintiff brings an action to recover property of his own in the possession of the deceased.

Article 1695. If a person brings an action to recover a sum of money due from some other person, witnesses may validly give evidence that such a sum is owing by the latter to the plaintiff. If, however, the defendant puts in issue the question as to whether the debt is still due, witnesses may not validly state that they have no information as to whether the debt is still due or not.

SECTION III.

Fundamental conditions as to the giving of evidence.

Article 1696. A condition precedent to giving evidence in civil cases is the institution of an action.

Article 1697. Evidence which is contrary to obvious facts is inadmissible.

Example :-

If A has been seen alive, or a house has been seen to be in good condition, evidence that such person is dead, or that such house has fallen into disrepair is not admissible.

Article 1698. Evidence of facts contrary to what is proved by conclusively substantiated evidence is inadmissible.

Article 1699. The legal object of evidence is to prove a right. Consequently, purely negative evidence is inadmissible, as where someone states that a certain person did not do a certain piece of work, or that a certain thing does not belong to a certain person, or that someone is not in debt to a certain person.

Conclusively substantiated evidence of a purely negative character, however, is admissible.

Example :-
> A brings an action to recover a sum of money advanced as a loan, alleging that he lent a certain sum of money, at a certain time, and at a certain place, to a certain person. If conclusively substantiated evidence is given proving that A was not in that place at that time, but was elsewhere, such evidence is admissible and the plaintiff's case will be dismissed.

Article 1700. It is a condition precedent to giving evidence that the witness should be entirely impartial. Consequently, evidence by an ascendant on behalf of a descendant or of a descendant on behalf of an ascendant, that is to say, the evidence of a father and a grandfather and of a mother and a grandmother on behalf of their children and grandchildren and of children and grandchildren on behalf of their father and grandfather and mother and grandmother, and one of the spouses on behalf of the other, is not admissible. Subject to these exceptions, however, the evidence of relations on behalf of one another is admissible. The evidence of a man who is maintained at some other person's expense, and that of a person in the salaried employment of another on behalf of such person, is inadmissible. The evidence of fellow servants on behalf of one another, however, is admissible. Again, the evidence of partners on behalf of each other in respect to the partnership property, and of a surety in respect to payment by the principal of the sum for which he stood surety, is inadmissible. In other matters, however, the evidence of such persons on behalf of one another is admissible.

Article 1701. The evidence of a person on behalf of his friend is admissible. But if the bonds of friendship uniting them are such that they use each other's property, such evidence is inadmissible.

Article 1702. It is a condition precedent to the validity of the evidence that there should be no enmity of a temporal nature between the witness and the person against whom he gives evidence. Enmity of a temporal nature is ascertained by reference to custom.

Article 1703. A person cannot be both plaintiff and witness. Consequently, the evidence of a guardian on behalf of an orphan and of an agent on behalf of his principal is inadmissible.

Article 1704. A person may not give evidence of his own acts. Consequently, agents and brokers may not give evidence as to any sales effected by them. Similarly, if the judge of a town who has retired gives evidence as to a judgment delivered by him before his retirement, such evidence is inadmissible. But if he gives evidence after his retirement as to an admission made before him prior to his retirement, such evidence is valid.

Article 1705. A witness must be an upright person. An upright person is one whose good qualities are greater than his bad qualities. Consequently, the evidence of persons who habitually behave in a manner inconsistent with honour and dignity, such as dancers and comedians, and persons who are known to be liars, is inadmissible.

SECTION IV.

Relevancy of evidence to the point at issue in the action.

Article 1706. Evidence is admissible if it agrees with the nature of the claim and not otherwise. There is no necessity, however, for mere conformity as to the language employed. It is enough if there is conformity in fact.

Examples :-

(1) The action concerns an object deposited for safe-keeping and witnesses give evidence that the defendant has admitted the deposit; or the action concerns wrongful appropriation of property and witnesses give evidence that the defendant has admitted the wrongful appropriation. The evidence is admissible.

(2) A debtor alleges in Court that he has paid his debt. Witnesses give evidence that the creditor released the the debtor from payment. The evidence is admissible.

Article 1707. The evidence must agree with the claim, whether such evidence goes to the whole or to part only of such claim.

Examples :-

(1) A brings an action alleging that certain property has belonged to him for the last two years. Witnesses give evidence that such property has belonged to A for the last two years. Such evidence is admissible. It is also admissible if they give evidence that such property has belonged to A for one year.

(2) The plaintiff's claim is for one thousand piastres. Witnesses give evidence as to five hundred. Their evidence in regard to the five hundred is valid.

Article 1708. Evidence in respect to more than is claimed is inadmissible. If, however, the divergence between the claim and the evidence is in fact capable of explanation and the plaintiff does so explain such divergence, the evidence is admissible.

Examples:-

(1) A brings an action alleging that certain property has been his for the last two years. Witnesses give evidence that such property has belonged to him for the last three years. The evidence is inadmissible.

(2) The plaintiff's claim is for five hundred piastres. Witnesses give evidence as to one thousand piastres. The evidence is inadmissible. But if the plaintiff, by explaining that at one time one thousand piastres were in fact due to him from the defendant, but that five hundred piastres of that amount have since been repaid, of which the witnesses were unaware, shows that the action is in conformity with the evidence of the witnesses, the evidence of such witnesses is admissible.

Article 1709. If the plaintiff brings an action for absolute ownership without stating how he became possessed of the property, alleging, for example, that a vineyard belongs to him, and witnesses give evidence as to the origin of the ownership, stating from whom the plaintiff bought the vineyard, the evidence is admissible. Thus, if the witnesses give evidence as to ownership arising from a definite cause and the Court asks the plaintiff as to whether his claim to the property arises from that cause or from some other, and the plaintiff replies that he does in fact claim the property by reason of such cause, the Court shall accept the evidence given by the witnesses. If, however, the plaintiff states that his claim is based upon some other cause, or that it is not based on that cause, the Court shall reject the evidence of the witnesses.

EVIDENCE

Article 1710. A plaintiff may validly bring an action claiming ownership arising out of some definite cause, as for example, in the case of a vineyard. If the plaintiff, without mentioning the vendor, states that he has purchased such vineyard, or without stating the details, merely alleges that he has bought such a vineyard from a certain person, such action shall be considered to be an action for absolute ownership; and if the witnesses give evidence that the vineyard in question is the plaintiff's absolute property, such evidence is admissible. If the witnesses, however, give evidence as to absolute ownership of property, stating that the plaintiff bought such property from a certain person and describe the vendor, such evidence is inadmissible. The reason for this is that once an absolute right of ownership is established, the effect thereof is retrospective and will extend to matters incidental to such thing. For example, the fruit formerly produced by the vineyard also becomes the property of the plaintiff. If the right of ownership arises out of some definite cause, however, it can only be effective as from the date upon which such right arose, for example, as from the date of the sale. Consequently, a right of absolute ownership is more extensive than a right of ownership arising out of some definite cause and thus the witnesses have given evidence for more than the plaintiff has demanded.

Article 1711. Evidence given in an action with regard to debt which is contrary to the claim is inadmissible.

Examples :-

(1) The plaintiff claims payment of one thousand piastres alleged to be due to him as the price of a sale. If the witnesses give evidence to the effect that the defendant owes such sum in respect to a loan, their evidence is inadmissible.

(2) The plaintiff claims that certain property has

devolved upon him by way of inheritance from his father. Witnesses give evidence that the property has devolved upon him by way of inheritance from his mother. The evidence is inadmissible.

SECTION V.

Contradictory evidence.

Article 1712. The evidence of witnesses which is contradictory in respect to the matter regarding which the evidence is given, is inadmissible.

Example :-
One witness gives evidence in respect to a thousand piastres gold; another witness gives evidence as to one thousand piastres in silver *mejidies*. Their evidence is inadmissible.

Article 1713. If there is a contradiction in the evidence given by witnesses regarding matters incidental to the subject matter of their evidence and such contradiction extends to the subject matter of the evidence itself, such evidence is inadmissible. If the contradiction with regard to the incidental matter does not affect the subject matter of the evidence, however, the evidence is admissible. Consequently, if the evidence is given with regard to a mere fact, such as wrongful appropriation, or payment of a debt, and one witness gives evidence that the act was performed at a certain fixed time, or at a certain place, and another witness gives evidence that the thing was done at another time or another place, such evidence is admissible, since the conflict of evidence shows a discrepancy to exist concerning the subject matter of the action. As regards matters, however, which are placed on record, such as sale, purchase, hire, suretyship, transfer of debt, gift, pledge, debt, loan, release and testamentary disposition, any contradiction of witnesses as to circumstances of time or place will not affect the validity of the evidence, since such contradiction does not affect the subject matter of the evidence.

Example :-

> A asserts that he has paid a debt due. One witness gives evidence that A paid such debt in his house. Another witness gives evidence that A paid the debt in his shop. The evidence of the witnesses is inadmissible.

> But if a person brings an action in Court claiming property in the possession of some third person, asserting that such person sold him the property for a certain sum of money and claims delivery thereof, and one witness gives evidence that such property was sold in a certain house and the other that it was sold in a certain shop, such evidence is admissible, since an act once performed cannot be repeated, but a matter put on record can be repeated.

Article 1714. Should witnesses contradict each other as regards the colour of property wrongfully appropriated, or whether it is of the male or female sex, their evidence is inadmissible.

Example :-

> Wrongful appropriation of an animal. A witness gives evidence to the effect that the animal is a grey horse. Another witness states that the animal is a dark-brown horse. Another witness states that it is a chestnut horse. Another witness states that it is a horse, while yet another states that it is a mare. The evidence of these witnesses is inadmissible.

Article 1715. Contradictions as to the amount of the price in the evidence of witnesses in an action on a contract renders such evidence inadmissible.

Example :-

> One witness gives evidence stating that certain property was sold for five hundred piastres and another

witness that it was sold for three hundred piastres. Their evidence is inadmissible.

SECTION VI.

Inquiry into the credibility of witnesses.

Article 1716. When witnesses have given evidence, the Court shall ask the person against whom evidence has been given whether he considers that the witnesses told the truth when giving their evidence. If such person states that he considers the witnesses are truthful or straight-forward as regards the evidence they have given, he is taken to have admitted the matter in issue, and judgment is given on his admission. If, however, he states that the witnesses have given false evidence, or that, while being upright persons, they are mistaken in regard to such matters, or have forgotten the matter, or while admitting that the witnesses are upright persons, at the same time denies the matter in issue, judgment shall not be given, but the Court shall take steps to ascertain, both publicly and privately, whether the witnesses are upright or not.

Article 1717. The inquiry as to the credibility of witnesses shall be addressed either publicly or privately to the person having authority over such witnesses.

Thus, if the witnesses are students, the inquiry shall be addressed to the teacher of the school in which they are carrying on their studies, as well as from reliable inhabitants. If they are soldiers, from the officers and clerks of their battalion. If the witness is a clerk, from his superiors and from his fellow clerks in the office. If a merchant, from reliable persons who are also merchants. If a member of a guild, from the warden of such a guild and the members of the committee thereof. If he belongs

EVIDENCE

to any other class, then from reliable inhabitants of the district or village.

Article 1718. A private inquiry as to the credibility of a witness is called in technical legal language a sealed writing and is conducted in writing. The Court shall insert in the document the name of the plaintiff and defendant, the subject matter of the action, the names and descriptions of the witnesses, their profession, their identity, their place of residence, the names of their fathers and their grandfathers, or their names only if they are persons of note, together with their description, adding finally anything which will differentiate the witnesses from any other persons. The document shall then be sealed and placed in an envelope and sent to the persons selected to give information as to the credibility of the witnesses. If such persons, after perusal of the document, consider that the witnesses whose names are written therein are trustworthy, they shall state in writing under the names of the witnesses in question that they consider them to be trustworthy and that their evidence is admissible. If not, they shall state that they do not consider them to be trustworthy. They shall then sign the document and return it to the Court, sealing the envelope without allowing the person who has brought the document, or any other person, to ascertain the contents thereof.

Article 1719. If the persons to whom the document is addressed for the purpose of giving the information fail to certify in writing that the witnesses are upright and that their evidence is admissible, or if in fact they state that they are not upright, or that they do not know them, or that they know nothing of the condition of such persons, or that it is a matter beyond their knowledge, or make some similar statement either directly or by implication,

EVIDENCE 471

the effect of which is that they are unable to certify the uprightness of the witnesses, or if they return the documents to the Court duly sealed, but without having written anything thereon, the Court shall not accept such evidence.

Upon the occurrence of such an event, the Court shall not tell the plaintiff that his witnesses are disqualified from giving evidence, but shall merely instruct him to produce other witnesses if he has any. If the document states, however, that the witnesses are trustworthy and that their evidence is admissible, a public inquiry shall thereupon be instituted as to the credibility of the witnesses.

Article 1720. The public inquiry as to the credibility of witnesses is conducted as follows: the persons called upon to give the information are brought before the Court and the inquiry is made in the presence of the two parties; or the two parties, accompanied by a person specially deputed for that purpose, proceed to the place where the persons called upon to give the information reside, and the inquiry takes place publicly in their presence.

Article 1721. Although in the case of a private inquiry one person may validly be selected to give information as to the credibility of witnesses, at least two should be appointed out of considerations of prudence.

Article 1722. A public inquiry is in the nature of evidence. Consequently, the rules relating to evidence and the number of witnesses are applicable in this case also. It is unnecessary, however, for the persons selected to give information as to the credibility of the witnesses, to use the word evidence.

Article 1723. If, in the opinion of the Court, the credibility of the witnesses has been proved in one particular case, the Court need not again inquire into the credibility of the same witnesses, if they give evidence with regard to some other matter before the expiration of a period of six months from the date on which they last gave evidence. If more than six months have passed however, the Court must again proceed to the inquiry.

Article 1724. If either before or after the inquiry into the credibility of witnesses, the person against whom the evidence is given attacks the witnesses, alleging that they are giving their evidence for some ulterior motive, such as avoiding a loss or realising a gain, the Court shall call upon him to furnish proof of his allegations. If such person is able to prove his case by evidence, the Court shall reject the evidence of such witnesses. If not, the Court shall hold an inquiry into the credibility of the witnesses, if this has not already been done. If an inquiry has in fact been held, the Court shall give judgment in accordance with the evidence.

Article 1725. In the event of some of the persons selected to give information as to the credibility of witneses reporting against them and of others reporting in their favour, the Court shall give preference to the hostile report and shall refrain from giving judgment thereon.

Article 1726. In the event of the decease or disppearance of witnesses who have given evidence in civil matters, the Court may still hold an inquiry into the credibility of their evidence and give judgment accordingly.

APPENDIX.

SWEARING WITNESSES.

Article 1727. Should the person against whom evidence is given ask the Court, before giving judgment, to put the witnesses on their oath that their evidence is not false, the Court may, if it deems it necessary, strengthen their evidence by administering the oath. The Court may inform the witnesses that their evidence will not be accepted unless they swear the oath.

SECTION VII.

Withdrawal of evidence.

Article 1728. Should witnesses after giving their evidence, but before judgment, withdraw the evidence in Court, such evidence is considered not to have been given and the witnesses shall be reprimanded.

Article 1729. Should witnesses who have given evidence in Court withdraw such evidence after judgment has been delivered, the judgment stands, but the witnesses must pay the value of the subject matter of the action to the party against whom judgment has been given. (See Article 80).

Article 1730. Should any of the witnesses withdraw their evidence as mentioned above, the evidence required being given by the others, those who withdraw need not pay the value of the subject matter of the action, but shall be reprimanded only. If the number of witnesses, however, is not enough to give the evidence required, half the value of the subject matter of the action must be paid by the witness who has withdrawn, if there is one only, or if there are more than one, then by them all in equal shares.

Article 1731. A withdrawal of evidence, to be valid, must be made in Court. Any withdrawal made elsewhere is invalid. Consequently, a person against whom evidence is given will not be heard to allege that the witnesses have withdrawn their evidence out of Court. A witness who has given evidence in one Court may validly withdraw his evidence in another Court.

SECTION VIII.

Conclusively substantiated evidence.

Article 1732. No importance is paid to the mere number of witnesses; that is to say, that if one of the parties has more witnesses than the other, he will not be preferred for that reason alone. If the number of witnesses, however, is so large that they conclusively substantiate the evidence, they will be preferred.

Article 1733. Conclusively substantiated evidence is tantamount to positive knowledge.

Article 1734. There is no necessity for the word "evidence" to be used in cases of conclusively substantiated evidence and there is also no need to insist that the witnesses should be of upright character. Consequently, there is no need for an inquiry as to the credibility of such persons.

Article 1735. No definite number of persons is necessary to constitute conclusively substantiated evidence. Their number must be so considerable, however, that it would be contrary to reason to conclude that they had agreed to tell a lie.

CHAPTER II.

DOCUMENTARY EVIDENCE AND PRESUMPTIVE EVIDENCE.

SECTION I.

Documentary Evidence.

Article 1736. No action may be taken on writing or a seal alone. If such writing or seal is free from any taint of fraud or forgery, however, it becomes a valid

OATHS

ground for action, that is to say, judgment may be given thereon. No proof is required in any other way.

Article 1737. The Sultan's rescript, and entries in the land registers are considered to be conclusive, since they are not tainted by fraud.

Article 1738. As is set forth hereinafter in the Book relating to the Administration of Justice by the Courts, registers kept by the Courts in such a way as to be free from any irregular practice or deception are considered to be conclusive.

Article 1739. Documents instituting a pious foundation are not in themselves considered to be conclusive. If registered, however, in Court registers which are reliable as stated above, they are then considered to be conclusive.

SECTION II.
Presumptive Evidence.

Article 1740. A presumption is also a ground for judgment.

Article 1741. A presumption is an inference which amounts to positive knowledge.

Example:-
A is seen leaving an empty house precipitately with a blood-stained knife in his hand. B thereupon enters the house and finds C, who had just had his throat cut. It is certain that A is the murderer of C. No attention is paid to any mere possibility such as the possibility that C killed himself. (See Article 74).

CHAPTER III.
ADMINISTERING THE OATH.

Article 1742. One ground of judgment is taking or refusing to take the oath. Thus, should the plaintiff be unable to prove his case, the defendant shall take an oath at the instance of the plaintiff. If A, however, brings an action against B asserting that B is the agent of some third person, and B joins issue, it is not essential for B to be put on oath. Similarly, should two persons bring an action both asserting that they have bought from C property in the possession of C, and C later admits that he has sold the property of one of them but joins issue with the other, the oath shall not be administered to him. In this connection, hire, and receiving a pledge or a gift, are assimilated to purchase.

Article 1743. Should it be intended to put one of the parties on his oath, he shall be caused to take the oath in the name of God.

Article 1744. The oath may be sworn only before the Court or before some person representing the Court. A refusal to take the oath before any other person is of no effect.

Article 1745. A representative may validly be employed to place a person upon oath, but no substitution is permissible in swearing an oath. Consequently, the advocate of a party in an action may place the other party upon his oath, but when his client is put upon his oath, such client must swear the oath personally and not through his advocate.

Article 1746. The oath is only administered upon the application of the opposite party. In four cases, however, the oath is administered by the Court without any application: —

(1) When a person lays claim to and proves that he has an interest in the estate of a deceased person, the Court shall require the plaintiff to swear an oath that he has not received anything in any way whatsoever in satisfaction of his interest from such deceased person, either directly or indirectly, nor that he has given a release thereof, nor transferred it to any other person, nor received

OATHS

anything in satisfaction thereof from any other person, nor received any pledge by way of security for his interest from the deceased person. Such form of oath is known as *istizhar*.

(2) When a person appears claiming to be entitled to certain property and proves his case, the Court shall require an oath to be taken by such person that he has not sold such property, nor disposed of it by way of gift, nor divested himself in any way of the property therein.

(3) When a person wishes to return a thing purchased on account of defect, the Court shall require him to take an oath that he did not, either expressly or impliedly, by reason of any disposition of such a thing as if it were his own property—as is set forth in Article 344—assent to the defect in the thing purchased.

(4) When the Court is about to give judgment in a case of pre-emption, the Court shall require the person claiming the right of pre-emption to swear an oath that he has not waived the right of pre-emption in any way whatsoever.

Article 1747. If the defendant swears the oath at the instance of the plaintiff without the oath being administered by the Court, such oath is of no effect and must again be administered by the Court.

Article 1748. When a person is about to swear an oath concerning his own act, he must swear such oath positively, stating that the matter is so, or is not so. But when a person is about to swear an oath concerning the act of some other person, he must be made to swear that he has no knowledge of such matter, that is to say, that he does not know such thing.

Article 1749. The oath has reference either to cause or to effect. Thus, an oath that a certain thing has or has not happened is an oath as to cause; and an oath as to whether a thing is still continuing or not is an oath as to effect.

Example :-

An oath in an action for sale and purchase to the effect that the contract of sale was never made at all is an oath as to cause ; but an oath as to whether the contract is still continuing is an oath as to effect.

Article 1750. When different actions are joined together, one oath is sufficient. There is no necessity for a separate oath in each case.

Article 1751. When in a civil action the oath is duly tendered to a person who is called upon to take the oath and such person refuses to take the oath, either expressly by refusing to swear, or impliedly by keeping silence without any excuse, the Court shall give judgment on such refusal. If such person seeks to swear an oath after judgment has been delivered, the Court shall pay no attention thereto, and the judgment shall remain intact.

Article 1752. A dumb man may validly take or refuse to take the oath by the use of generally recognized signs.

Supplement.

Article 1753. A plaintiff who has stated that he has no witnesses will not be heard to say later that he intends to call witnesses. And if he has stated that he intends to call a certain witness and no other, he will not be allowed to call any other witness.

CHAPTER IV.

PREFERRED EVIDENCE AND ADMINISTRATION OF THE OATH TO BOTH PARTIES.

Section I.

Actions regarding possession.

Article 1754. In the case of a dispute relating to real property, possession thereof must be proved by evidence. Judgment will not be given that the defendant is in possession merely as the result of the affirmation of the two parties, that is, an admission made by the defendant in reply to the plaintiff's claim. If the plaintiff, however, brings an action alleging that he has bought certain real property from a certain person, or that a certain person has wrongfully deprived the plaintiff of possession thereof, there is no need for the defendant to prove by evidence that he is in possession of such property. Again, if movable property is in the possession of a person, he is the possessor thereof, and there is no need for proof of that fact by evidence as stated above. The statement of the two parties on this point is sufficient.

Article 1755. In the event of a dispute arising between two persons in respect to real property, each alleging that he is in possession of such property, the parties shall first of all be required to prove by evidence which of them is in possession. Should both parties produce evidence proving that they are in possession, such proof is taken to mean that they are in joint possession. Should one of the parties be unable to prove that he is in possession, while the other produces satisfactory proof thereof, judgment is given for possession in favour of the latter, and the former is considered to be out of possession. If neither party is able to prove that he is in possession, either may demand that the oath be administered to his opponent to the effect that he is not in possession of such real property. If both refuse to take the oath, they are taken to be jointly in possession of such property. If one person takes an oath, the other refusing to do so, judgment shall be given that the person taking the oath is in sole possession of such property and the other is considered to be out of possession. If both persons take the oath, judgment shall be given that neither is in possession, and the real property in question shall be seized until such time as the true facts are established.

EVIDENCE

SECTION II.

Preferred evidence.

Article 1756. If two persons are joint owners of certain property, that is to say, if the two are in joint possession thereof, and bring an action, one party alleging that such property belongs to him alone, the other alleging that he is joint owner thereof, the evidence given of sole ownership shall be preferred. That is to say, if the two parties produce evidence in support of their case, the evidence of the person claiming absolute ownership is preferred to that of the person claiming joint ownership. If both of them claim to be absolute owners and produce evidence in support thereof, judgment shall be given that they are joint owners thereof. If one of the parties can produce no evidence and the other proves his case, judgment shall be given that the latter is sole owner of such property.

Article 1757. In an action for absolute ownership, the evidence of the person not in possession is preferred if no date is mentioned.

Example :-
> A brings an action with regard to a house in the possession of B, alleging that the house is his property and that B is wrongfully in possession thereof and asking that B should be evicted and the house restored to him. If B alleges that the house is his property and that consequently he is lawfully in possession thereof, the evidence of A will be preferred and heard.

Article 1758. Actions relating to ownership arising from causes which are capable of repetition, as for example purchase, are regarded as identical with actions arising out of absolute ownership, if the date is not mentioned. In such cases, also, the evidence of the person who is not in possession is preferred to that of the person in possession. Should both parties, however, claim that their right of ownership is held from one and the same person, the evidence of the person in possession is preferred.

Example :-

A brings an action claiming a shop in the possession of B, alleging that he bought such shop from one *Veli Agha,* and that B in this connection wrongfully took possession of the shop. B comes into Court and alleges that he bought the shop from one *Bakir Effendi,* or that he inherited it from his father, which is the reason for his being in possession. The evidence of A, the person not in possession, is preferred and heard. But if B, the person in possession, alleges that he bought the shop from *Veli Agha,* B's evidence is preferred to that of A, the person not in possession.

Article 1759. In actions relating to ownership arising out of a cause which is incapable of repetition, as in the case of an animal giving birth to young, the evidence of the person in possession is preferred. Consequently, in the event of a dispute relating to a colt between a person not in possession and one who is, and each party alleges that the colt is his property born from his own mare, the evidence of the person in possession is preferred.

Article 1760. In a claim for ownership dependent on date, the evidence of the person giving the earliest date will be preferred.

Example :-

A brings an action relating to a plot of land in the possession of B, alleging that he bought such land a year ago from C. B by his answer states that the land devolved upon him by way of inheritance from his father, who died five years ago. The evidence of the person in possession is preferred. But if B states that he inherited the land from his father who died six months ago, the evidence of the person not in possession is preferred. If each of the two parties alleges that he has bought the subject matter of the action from different persons, and each gives the date at which the person selling to them acquired the thing in question, the evidence given by the person giving the earliest dates will be preferred.

Article 1761. In actions relating to the young of animals, no attention is paid to date, the evidence of the person in possession being preferred, as stated above. But if there is a discrepancy between the age of the animal which is the subject of the action and the date given by the person who is not in possession, the evidence of the latter is preferred. If the age of the animal is unknown, however, or if it is different from either date given, the evidence of neither is accepted, and the animal shall not be taken away from the person in possession.

Article 1762. The greater claim is preferred.

Example :-
> Vendor and purchaser disagree as to the quantity or price of the thing sold. The evidence given by the party claiming most will be preferred.

Article 1763. Evidence as to ownership is preferred to evidence as to loan for use.

Example :-
> A claims the return of property in the possession of B, alleging that he lent the property to B for B's use. B by his reply alleges that A sold the property to him or bestowed it upon him by way of gift. The evidence as to the sale or the gift is preferred.

Article 1764. Evidence as to sale is preferred to evidence as to gift, or pledge, or hire, and the evidence of hire to the evidence of pledge.

Example :-
> A demands payment for certain property from B, which A alleges he sold B. B replies that A made a gift of

such property to him and gave delivery thereof. The evidence of sale is preferred.

Article 1765. In cases of a loan for use, the evidence in favour of a general loan is preferred.

Example :-

A lends his horse to B to use. The horse dies while in the possession of B. A sues B for the value of the horse, alleging that he lent B the horse for a period of four days and on the fifth day it died without having been returned. B by his reply alleges that A did not limit the loan of the horse to a period of four days, but made the loan in general terms. The evidence of the person to whom the horse was lent is preferred.

Article 1766. Evidence given as to good health is preferred to evidence given as to a mortal sickness.

Example :-

A makes a gift to one of his heirs and dies. Another heir alleges that the gift was made during the course of a mortal sickness. The person in whose favour the gift was made alleges that the gift was made while in good health. The evidence of the person in whose favour the gift was made is preferred.

Article 1767. Evidence of soundness of mind is preferred to evidence of madness or imbecility.

Article 1768. In the event of evidence being given concurrently as regards new and old things, the evidence as to the new things is preferred.

Example :-

A possesses a right of flow upon the lands of B held in absolute ownership. A difference of opinion arises between them as to whether such right is of ancient or recent origin. The owner of the house alleges that it is of recent origin and demands the extinction of the right. The owner of the right of flow claims that such right is of ancient origin. The evidence of the owner of house is preferred.

Article 1769. In the event of the person whose evidence is preferred being unable to prove his case by the production of evidence, evidence is asked for from the person whose evidence has not been preferred. If he proves his case, his evidence shall be accepted; if he fails to do so, the oath shall be administered to him.

Article 1770. In the event of the person whose evidence is preferred being unable to prove his case by the production of evidence as stated above, and if the party whose evidence is not preferred produces evidence, judgment shall be given in his favour. If the person whose evidence has been preferred wishes to produce evidence thereafter, such evidence shall not be heard.

SECTION III.

Persons whose evidence is preferred. Judgment based on circumstantial evidence.

Article 1771. If a husband and wife disagree as to the things in the house in which they dwell, the nature of the things must be examined. In the case of things suitable for the husband only, such as a gun or a sword, or of things suitable for both, such as domestic utensils and furniture, the evidence of the wife is preferred. If both are unable to advance any proof, the husband may make a statement on oath. That is to say, if he states on oath that the things in question do not belong to his wife, judgment shall be given in his favour.

The evidence of the husband is preferred as regards things suitable for women only, such as clothing and jewellery. If both are unable to advance any proof, the wife may make a statement on oath. If one of the two makes and sells things which are suitable for the other, that person in any case may make a statement on oath.

Example: -
> An earring is a piece of jewellery suitable for a woman. If the husband is a jeweller, he may make a statement on oath.

Article 1772. Upon the death of one of the spouses, the heir stands in the place of the person from whom he inherits. If the two parties, as stated above, are unable to produce any proof as regards things suitable for both, the surviving spouse may make a statement on oath. Should both spouses have died at the same time, the heir of the husband may make a statement on oath as regards things suitable for both of them.

Article 1773. Should a donor wish to revoke a gift and the beneficiary alleges at the trial of the action that the subject matter of the gift has been destroyed, the beneficiary may make a statement not on oath.

Article 1774. A person to whom a thing has been entrusted for safe-keeping shall make a statement on oath as regards any question of his release from liability. Thus, if a person who has entrusted his property to another for safe-keeping, brings an action against such person, and the latter by his reply alleges that he has returned the thing entrusted to him for safe-keeping, such person shall make a statement on oath. But if he wishes to bring evidence in order not to swear an oath, such evidence shall be heard.

Article 1775. If a person is indebted to another in respect to various sums of money and such person makes a payment to the creditor and an action is brought to

EVIDENCE

determine in respect to which particular debt the payment has been made, the debtor shall make a statement

Article 1776. If a lessee of a mill seeks to deduct a portion of the rent of such mill after the expiration of the term of the lease by reason of the water having been cut off for a certain period during the currency of the lease and the lessor and lessee disagree thereon, and there be no evidence available, the nature of the case must be examined.

If the point at issue is the period of time during which the water was cut off, for example, if the lessee claims that it was ten days and the lessor five only, the lessee may make a statement on oath.

If the point at issue is as to whether the water has been cut off at all, that is to say, if the lessor absolutely denies that the water was cut off, judgment shall be given based on the circumstantial evidence of the case. Thus, if the water is running at the time the action is instituted and heard, the lessor shall make a statement on oath. If the water is not running at the time, the lessee shall make a statement on oath.

Article 1777. If a dispute arises as to whether the channel along which water is flowing to a person's house is old or new, and the owner of the house alleges that it is new and wishes to remove it and neither party can produce any evidence, the nature of the case must be examined. If the water is flowing at the time the case is instituted, or if it is a well-known fact that the water was flowing there formerly, no change shall be made in such channel. The owner of the channel may make a statement on oath, that is to say, he shall be caused to take an oath that the channel is not new.

If at the time the case was instituted there was no water running in the channel and it is not known whether water flowed there formerly, the owner of the house may make a statement on oath.

Section IV.
Administration of the oath to both parties.

Article 1778. If a dispute occurs between vendor and purchaser as to the amount of the price, or the amount of the thing sold, or both, or as to the description or type thereof, judgment is given in favour of whichever of the two produces evidence. If both of them produce evidence, judgment is given in favour of the party who produces evidence for the greater amount.

If neither of the parties can prove their case, they shall be informed that either one party must admit the claim of the other, or the sale will be declared void. If neither party admits the claim of the other, the Court shall put each party upon his oath as to the claim of the other party, beginning with the purchaser. If either party refuses to take the oath, the other is taken to have proved his case. If both parties swear an oath, the Court shall declare the sale void.

Article 1779. If a person taking a thing on hire has a dispute with a person giving a thing on hire with regard to the amount of the rent before taking possession of the thing hired, and an action is instituted in Court in connection therewith, judgment shall be given in favour of the person who produces evidence, as, for example, where the person taking the thing on hire alleges that the rent is so much and the person giving the thing on hire alleges that the rent is so much.

If both produce evidence, judgment shall be given in favour of the person giving the thing on hire.

EVIDENCE

If neither of the parties can prove their case, both of them are put on oath, beginning with the person taking the thing on hire, judgment being given against the person who refuses to take the oath.

If both parties take the oath, the Court shall declare the contract of hire to be void.

Should a dispute arise as to any question of time or distance, the matter shall be dealt with in the same manner. Provided, however, that if both parties produce evidence, judgment shall be given on the evidence of the person taking the thing on hire. If the oath is administered to both parties, the person giving the thing on hire shall first be put on oath.

Article 1780. In the event of a dispute arising between the person giving and the person taking a thing on hire, as is set forth in the preceding Article, after the period of the contract of hire has expired, the oath is not administered to both parties. The person taking the thing on hire alone may make a statement on oath.

Article 1781. If the person giving a thing on hire and the person taking a thing on hire have a dispute as to the amount of the rent during the period of the contract of hire, both parties shall be put on oath, and the contract cancelled as regards the remainder of the period. The person taking the thing on hire may make a statement as to the portion relating to the period which has elapsed.

Article 1782. If a dispute arises between vendor and purchaser as to a thing sold which has been destroyed while in the possession of the purchaser, or if a defect of recent origin has been revealed which prevents such thing being returned, the oath is not administered to both parties, but to the purchaser only.

EVIDENCE 489

Article 1783. If an action is brought with regard to the due date of any particular thing, that is to say, whether the time for the performance of such thing has arrived or not, or with regard to a right of option, or as to whether the whole amount or part only of the price has been received, the oath is not administered to both parties, but in these three cases only to the person who denies.

Promulgated by Royal Iradah, 26th Shaaban, 1293.

BOOK XVI.

ADMINISTRATION OF JUSTICE BY THE COURT.

BOOK XVI

ADMINISTRATION OF JUSTICE BY THE COURT

INTRODUCTION

TERMS OF MUHAMMADAN JURISPRUDENCE

Article 1784. The phrase administration of justice embraces the judgment and the duties of the judge.

Article 1785. The judge is a person appointed by the Sovereign for the purpose of dealing with and settling actions and disputes arising between the people in accordance with the terms of law.

Article 1786. The judgment consists of the stopping and settlement of disputes by the judge. Judgments are of two classes.

The first class consists of the Court giving judgment whereby the person against whom judgment has been given is forced to give up the subject matter of the action as where he orders the thing claimed to be given. This class of judgment is called an obligatory judgment, or a judgment for something which is due.

The second class consists of the Court forbidding the plaintiff to bring an action as where it informs the plaintiff that he has no right to bring an action, and that he is forbidden to do so. This class of judgment is called a judgment by way of dismissal.

Article 1787. The subject matter of the judgment consists of the obligation imposed by the Court upon the party against whom judgment is given. Thus, an obligatory judgment consists of recognizing the right of the plaintiff, and in an action by way of dismissal consists of obliging the plaintiff to give up his action.

Article 1788. The losing party is the person against whom judgment is given.

Article 1789. The successful party is the person in whose favour judgment is given.

Article 1790. Arbitration consists of the parties to an action agreeing together to select some third person to settle the question at issue between them, who is called an arbitrator.

Article 1791. A deputy defendant is an agent appointed by the Court to represent a defendant who fails to appear in Court.

CHAPTER I.
JUDGES.

SECTION I.

Qualities requisite in a judge.

Article 1792. The judge must be intelligent, upright, reliable and firm.

Article 1793. The judge must have a knowledge of Muhammadan law and jurisprudence and of the rules of procedure, and must be able to decide and settle actions in accordance therewith.

Article 1794. The judge must be of perfect understanding. Consequently, any judicial act performed by a minor or an imbecile or a blind man or a person so deaf that he cannot hear the statements of the parties when speaking loudly, is invalid.

JUDGES

SECTION II.

Conduct of judges.

Article 1795. The judge must abstain from any act or deed of a nature injurious to the dignity of the Court, such as engaging in buying or selling, or making jokes while in Court.

Article 1796. The judge may not accept a present from either of the parties.

Article 1797. The judge may not accept the hospitality of either of the parties.

Article 1798. The judge must abstain from any act during the trial likely to arouse suspicion or cause misunderstanding, such as receiving one of the parties alone in his house, or retiring with one of them to consider the judgment, or making signs to one of them with his hand or his eye or his head, or speaking to one of them secretly or in a language not understood by the other.

Article 1799. The judge must be impartial towards the two parties. Consequently, the judge must observe complete impartiality and equality towards the two parties in everything relating to the trial of the action, such as causing them to sit down during the course of the trial, and when looking towards or addressing them and this whether one of the parties is a person of high rank and the other of low estate.

SECTION III.

Duties of judges.

Article 1800. The judge is the representative of the Sovereign for the purpose of carrying on the trial and giving judgment.

JUDGES

Article 1801. The jurisdiction and powers of the judge are limited by time and place and certain matters of exception.

Examples :-

(1) A judge appointed for a period of one year may only give judgment during that year. He may not give judgment before the year commences or after the expiration thereof.

(2) A judge appointed for a certain district may give judgment in any place in such district. He may not, however, give judgment elsewhere. A judge appointed to give judgment in a particular Court may only give judgment in that Court. He may not give judgment elsewhere.

(3) If an order is issued by the soveriegn authority that actions relating to a particular matter shall not be heard in the public interest, the judge may not try such action. Again, the judge may be authorised to hear certain matters only in a particular Court and no other. The judge may only try those cases he is authorised to hear and give judgment thereon.

(4) An order is issued by sovereign authority to the effect that in a certain matter the opinion of a certain jurist is most in the interest of the people, and most suited to the needs of the moment, and that action should be taken in accordance therewith. The judge may not act in such matter in accordance with the opinion of a jurist which is in conflict with that of the jurist in question. If he does so, the judgment will not be executory.

Article 1802. If two judges are appointed jointly to hear and give judgment in an action, one of them alone may not try such action and deliver judgment. If he does so, the judgment is not executory. (See Article 1465).

Article 1803. If there are various judges in one particular place, and one of the parties desires the case to be tried by one judge and the other wishes the case to be tried by another, and a difference of opinion occurs between them in the matter, the judge selected by the defendant shall be preferred.

Article 1804. If a judge is removed from his post, but the news of his removal is not communicated to him for some time, any cases heard and decided by him during that period are valid. A judgment issued by him after the news of his removal has been communiciated to him is invalid.

Article 1805. A judge who is duly authorized may appoint a person as deputy judge and may dismiss him. He may not do so, if he is not duly authorized. If he himself is dismissed or dies, his deputy is not likewise dismissed. (See Article 1466). Consequently, if a judge in a certain district dies, the action in that district shall be tried by the deputy of the deceased judge, until the arrival of a new judge.

Article 1806. The judge may decide a case on evidence heard by his deputy and the deputy on evidence heard by the judge. Thus, if the judge has heard evidence in an action and communicates it to his deputy, the latter may give judgment without rehearing the evidence. Similarly, if the deputy of a judge is authorized to give judgment, he may hear evidence on a certain matter and refer it to the judge, and the latter may give judgment thereon without rehearing the evidence. If a person who is not authorized to give judgment, however, but only to hear evidence for the purpose of investigating and inquiring into a matter, refers a question to the judge, the latter may not give judgment, but must hear the evidence himself.

Article 1807. A judge of the district may hear actions relating to land situated in another district. But as stated in the Book on Actions, the boundaries thereof must be set forth as required by law.

Article 1808. The person in whose favour judgment is given must not be an ascendant or descendant or the wife of the judge, nor his partner, nor a private employee in respect to the property which is the subject matter of the judgment, nor a person who lives at the expense of the judge. Consequently, the judge may not hear a case relating to one of such persons, nor give judgment in his favour.

Article 1809. If the judge of a town or the persons connected with him as stated in the preceding Article, are concerned in an action with any of the inhabitants of such town, the case shall be heard by some other judge in the town, if one is to be found there. If there is no other judge in the town, the case may be tried by an arbitrator to be appointed by the parties, or, if the judge is authorized to appoint a representative, the case shall be heard by him or the case may be tried by the judge of an adjoining district. If the parties do not agree to settle the matter in any one of the ways mentioned above, they may ask the sovereign authority to delegate some person empowered to deal with the question.

Article 1810. In the hearing of actions, the Court shall deal with them in order of priority. The Court may, however, expedite the hearing of an action when it is in the interests of justice to do so.

Article 1811. A judge may, when necessary, ask the opinion of some other person on a point of law.

Article 1812. A judge may not give judgment when in such a condition that he cannot think clearly, as where he is in trouble, or suffering from hunger or sleeplessness.

Article 1813. A judge may not delay a case unduly by reason of investigations as to the facts.

Article 1814. The judge is responsible for keeping a register in Court and recording therein all judgments given and documents issued in such a manner as to be free from any irregularity. In the event of the judge being removed, he must hand over such register to his successor either personally or through some person in whom ne has confidence.

SECTION IV.

The hearing of an action.

Article 1815. The judge must hold the trial in public. He may not, however, reveal the nature of the judgment before it is pronounced.

Article 1816. When the parties are present in Court for the purposes of the trial, the judge shall first of all call upon the plaintiff to state his case. If he has previously reduced his claim to writing it shall be read over and confirmed by the plaintiff. He shall then call upon the defendant to answer. Thus, he shall inform the defendant that the plaintiff makes such and such a claim against him, and shall ask the defendant to reply.

Article 1817. If the defendant admits the claim, the judge shall give judgment on the admission. If he denies, the judge shall call upon the plaintiff for his evidence.

Article 1818. If the plaintiff proves his case by evidence, the judge shall give judgment accordingly. If he cannot prove it, he has a right to the oath, and if he asks to exercise such right, the judge shall accordingly tender the oath to the defendant.

Article 1819. If the defendant swears the oath, or if the plaintiff does not ask for the oath to be administered, the judge shall order the plaintiff to give up his claim upon the defendant.

Article 1820. If the defendant refuses to take the oath, the judge shall deliver judgment based upon such refusal. If the defendant states that he is prepared to swear an oath, after judgment has been so delivered, the judgment shall remain undisturbed.

Article 1821. The contents of a judgment or of a document issued by the judge of a Court in the ordinary way and which is free from any taint of forgery or fraud, may be acted upon and judgment given thereon, without the necessity for any proof by evidence.

Article 1822. If the defendant persists in keeping silence and refuses to answer either in the affirmative or negative, after being questioned as stated above, his silence is considered to amount to a denial.

If he states that he neither confesses nor denies, his answer is considered to amount to a denial.

In both cases the plaintiff shall be called upon to produce evidence.

Article 1823. If the defendant instead of admitting or denying the plaintiff's claim, puts forward a counterclaim, action shall be taken in accordance with the matter mentioned in the Book on Actions and the Book on Evidence.

Article 1824. Neither party may interrupt the other while he is making a statement. If he does so, he shall be prohibited therefrom by the Court.

Article 1825. The Court shall provide a competent and reliable interpreter for the translation of statements made by any person who does not know the language of the parties.

JUDGMENTS

Article 1826. In the case of actions brought by relatives or in cases where there is a possibility of the parties coming to a settlement, the judge shall advise the parties once or twice to come to a settlement. If they agree, a settlement shall be drawn up in accordance with the terms of the Book on Settlements. If they do not so agree, the case shall be tried out.

Article 1827. After the judge has concluded the trial, he shall give judgment and make it known to the parties.

He shall then draw up a formal judgment containing full reasons for the decision and orders given. A copy thereof shall be given to the successful party and, if necessary, a copy to the party losing the action.

Article 1828. Once the judge is fully in possession of the facts and reasons for the judgment, he may not delay promulgation thereof.

CHAPTER II.

JUDGMENTS

Section I.

Conditions attaching to a judgment

Article 1829. No judgment may be issued unless an action has been instituted. Thus, for a judge to give a judgment in any matter where the rights of the public are affected, an action must have been brought by one person against another in respect to that matter. Any judgment issued which is not based upon an action is invalid.

Article 1830. The parties must be present when judgment is given. That is to say, the parties having been present during the hearing of the action, must be present also when judgment is given. But if any person brings an action against some other person and the defendant admits the claim, and leaves the Court before judgment is pronounced, the judge may pronounce judgment in his absence, based upon the admission. Again, if the defendant denies the plaintiff's action, and the plaintiff comes into Court and brings evidence to prove his claim, and the defendant leaves the Court before the enquiry as to the credibility of the witness is commenced and before judgment is given, the judge may proceed to the enquiry as to the credibility of the witnesses, and pronounce judgment in his absence.

Article 1831. If the defendant is personally present in Court after evidence has been given in the presence of his representative, the judge may give judgment against him on such evidence. On the other hand, if the representative of the defendant is present and evidence has been given in the presence of the defendant, the judge may give judgment against the representative after hearing the evidence.

Article 1832. If an action is brought against the whole of the heirs of a deceased person, and evidence has been given in the presence of one of them, and such heir leaves before judgment is pronounced, the judge may give judgment against any other heir who may be summoned to be present on such evidence. There is no need for the evidence to be repeated.

Section II.

Judgment by default.

Article 1833. The defendant shall be summoned to appear before the Court by the judge upon the application of the plaintiff. If he fails to appear, either personally or through a representative, in the absence of any valid excuse, he may be forced to appear.

JUDGMENTS

Article 1834. If the defendant fails to appear, either personally, or through a representative, and it is not possible to bring him into Court, the Court shall, on the application of the plaintiff, issue a summons to him on three separate occasions to appear in Court, and, upon his failing to appear, the judge shall inform him that a representative will be appointed for him, and that the case for the plaintiff together with his evidence, will be heard. If the defendant persists in his refusal to appear, either personally or through a representative, the judge shall appoint a person as his representative in order to safeguard his interests. The case for the plaintiff, together with his evidence, shall then be heard in the presence of the representative. and, if proved, judgment shall be issued accordingly.

Article 1835. A judgment issued by default as mentioned above shall be served upon the defendant.

Article 1836. If a person against whom a judgment has been issued by default appears in Court and shows that he has a defence to the plaintiff's claim, his defence shall be heard and action taken as may be necessary. If he has no defence to the claim, or if he brings a defence which fails, the judgment given shall be put into execution.

CHAPTER III.

RETRIAL.

Article 1837. An action in respect to which a judgment has validly been given, that is to say, a judgment which contains the reasons and grounds therefor, may not be heard again.

Article 1838. If any person against whom judgment has been given alleges that such judgment is contrary to the rules of law and gives the reasons therefor, asking for the case to be heard in appeal, the judgment, if found to be in accordance with law, shall be confirmed. If not, the case will be heard in appeal.

Article 1839. If the person against whom judgment has been given is dissatisfied with such judgment, and asks for the rectification thereof, such judgment shall be examined, and, if it is found to be in accordance with law, shall be confirmed. If not, it shall be reversed.

Article 1840. A defence may be valid before judgment and after judgment. Consequently, if any person against whom judgment has been given, shows that he has a sound defence thereto, and asks for retrial of the action, his defence shall be heard in the presence of the person in whose favour judgment has been given, and the matter tried out.

Example :-

A brings an action against B alleging that a house in B's possession belongs to him, and that he inherited it from his father and proves his case. Judgment is given in his favour. B then sets up the defence that A's father sold the house to his father and produces a valid title-deed. B's defence will be heard, and if proved, the original judgment will be reversed and his action dismissed.

CHAPTER IV.

ARBITRATION.

Article 1841. Actions relating to rights concerning property may be settled by arbitration.

Article 1842. The decision of an arbitrator is valid and executory only in respect to the persons who have appointed him, and the matters he has been appointed to decide. He may not have reference to any person or

ARBITRATION

deal with any matters other than those included in the terms of reference.

Article 1843. More than one arbitrator may be appointed, that is to say, two or more persons may be appointed to give a decision in respect to one matter. Both plaintiff and defendant may each validly appoint an arbitrator.

Article 1844. In the event of several arbitrators being appointed as above, their decision must be unanimous. One alone may not give a decision.

Article 1845. The arbitrators may, if they are duly authorized thereunto by the parties, appoint another person to act as arbitrator. They may not do so otherwise.

Article 1846. If the arbitration is limited as to time it ceases to be of effect after the expiration of such time.

Example :-
> An arbitrator appointed to decide a matter within a period of one month as from a certain date, may only decide such matter within that period. He cannot give a decision after the expiration of that month. If he does so, the judgment will not be executory.

Article 1847. Either of the parties may dismiss the arbitrator before he has given his decision. If the parties have appointed an arbitrator, however, and such appointment has been confirmed by a Court duly authorized thereunto, the arbitrator is considered to be a representative of the Court and cannot be dismissed.

Article 1848. All decisions by arbitrators as regards the persons and matters in respect to which they have been appointed are binding and executory to the same extent as the decisions by the Courts concerning persons within their jurisdiction. Consequently, a decision validly given by the arbitrators in accordance with the rules of law is binding on all parties.

Article 1849. A decision by an arbitrator, upon submission to a properly constituted Court, shall be accepted and confirmed, if given in accordance with law. Otherwise, it shall not be so confirmed.

Article 1850. The parties appointing the arbitrators may authorize the arbitrators, if they think fit, to make a settlement, and such arbitrators may then make a valid settlement. Thus, if each of the parties appoint a person to act as arbitrator with power to dispose of the matter in dispute by way of settlement, and such arbitrators duly arrive at a settlement in conformity with the terms of the Book on Settlements, such settlement and arrangement is binding on both parties.

Article 1851. Should an authorized person act as arbitrator in a dispute and give a decision and the parties later agree to adopt his decision, such decision is executory. (see Article 1453).

Promulgated by Royal Iradah, 26 Shaaban, 1293.

INDEX.

	Page
ACTIONS	431
conditions and fundamental rules relating to,	431
conditions for validity of,	431
defence to,	436
parties to,	437
terms of Muhammadan jurisprudence,	431
ADMINISTRATION OF JUSTICE BY THE COURT	493
action, hearing of,	499
arbitration,	504
judges, conduct of,	495
duties of,	495
qualities requisite in,	494
judgments,	501
by default,	502
conditions attaching to,	501
retrial,	503
terms of Muhammadan Jurisprudence relating to,	493
ADMISSIONS	413
conditions governing,	413
denial of ownership and title,	419
effect of,	417
in writing,	426
mortal sickness, admission by person suffering from,	421
validity of,	415
AGENCY	375
agents, dismissal of,	395
classification of,	375
conditions attaching to,	378
essential elements of,	379
for litigation,	394
for purchase,	382
for sale,	388
fundamental basis of,	375
instructions given by one person to another,	390
terms of Muhammadan jurisprudence relating to,	375
CONSTRAINT	257
terms of Muhammadan jurisprudence relating to,	255
DEPOSIT FOR SAFE KEEPING	188
contract of,	188
effect of,	189
making good loss arising out of,	189
DESTRUCTION OF PROPERTY	232
animals, injury caused by,	238
direct,	232
indirect,	235
public highway, matters occuring in,	236
ESTOPPEL	443
EVIDENCE.—	457
circumstantial evidence, judgment based on,	484
conclusively substantiated,	474
contradictory,	467
credibility of witnesses, enquiry into,	469
definition of,	458
documentary,	474
fundamental conditions as to giving of,	458, 461
manner of giving,	458
nature of,	458
oath, administration of,	475
oath, administration of to both parties,	487
possession, evidence in action regarding,	478

INDEX

	Page
preferred,	480
preferred, persons whose evidence is,	484
presumptive,	475
relevancy of evidence to point at issue,	464
terms of Muhammadan jurisprudence regarding,	457
withdrawal of,	473

GIFT 211
- conditions attaching to, 215
- fundamental basis of, 211
- fundamental rules relating to, 216
- mortal sickness, gifts made during the course of a, 219
- receipt of, 211
- revocation of, 216
- terms of Muhammadan jurisprudence relating to, 211

GUARANTEE 143
- contract of, 144, 148
- conditional, 148
- conditions attaching to a, 145
- for the production of a particular person, 151
- fundamental basis of, 144
- future, 148
- of property, 151, 157
- release from contract of, 156
- to produce a particular person, 151
- terms of Muhammadan Jurisprudence relating to, 143
- unconditional, 148

HIRE 95
- amount of, questions affecting, 106
- animals, hire of, 123
- compensation, 135
  - by the person taking the things on hire, 137
  - in respect to use, 135
- contract of, 100
  - conclusion of, conditions relating to, 103
- delivery of things hired, 123
- essentials to validity of, 103
- execution of conditions relating to, 103
- nullity of, 105
- voidability of, 105
- employees, loss caused by, 139
- fundamental basis of, 100
- general, 97
- lien, right of, of person to whom a thing has been entrusted to work upon, 111
- merchandise, hire of, 123
- options, 114
  - contractual, 114
  - defect, for, 118
  - inspection, of 117
- period of, 112
- person giving on hire rights and obligations of, 132
- person taking on hire, rights and obligations of, 132
- personal services, hire of, 128
- real property, hire of, matters relating to 120
- rent, 106
- rent, necessity for, 107
- rent, right of person giving on hire to take rent, 107
- return of things hired, 134
- rights of contracting parties to deal with things hired, 133
- terms of Muhammadan jurisprudence relating to, 95
- type of things hired and matters relating thereto, 120

INTERDICTION 247
- debtors, interdiction of, 255
- imbeciles, 248
- interdicted persons, classes of, 247
- lunatics, 248
- minors, 248
- prodigals, interdiction of, 254

INDEX

	Page
terms of Muhammadan jurisprudence relating to,	245

JOINT OWNERSHIP — 273
- acquisition of, 232
- dead land, vivification of, 328
- debts jointly owned, 283
- drinking water, right of, 326
- free property jointly owned, 321
- conditions attaching to, 325
- hunting, fundamental conditions affecting, 332
- joint expenses, 335
- expenses connected with repairs to jointly owned property, 335
- repairs to jointly owned property, 335
- rivers, cleaning and improvement of, 339
- watercourses, cleaning and improvement of, 339
- partition, 289
  - by allotment, 297
  - by units, 295
  - cancellation of, 302
  - categories of, 289
  - conditions attaching to, 292
  - effect of, 303
  - method of, 299
  - nature of, 289
  - of usufruct, 306
  - options, 301
  - rescission of, 302
- property owned in absolute ownership, 275, 311
  - classification of, 275
  - description of, 275
  - right of acqueduct, 319
  - right of flow, 319
  - right of way, 319
  - roads, 317
- specific property jointly owned, manner of dealing with, 277
- taking water, right of, 326

terms of Muhammadan jurisprudence relating to, 273
- wells, ownership of land surrounding, 330
- walls and neighbours, 311
- neighbours, relations of to each other, 312

LIMITATION — 449

LOAN FOR USE
- contract of, 199
- effect of, 200

MUHAMMADAN JURISPRUDENCE, DEFINITION AND CLASSIFICATION OF, 15

MAXIMS OF 15

PARTNERSHIP 341
- capital and labour, 362
- classification of, 362
- conditions affecting, 363
- definition of, 362
- effect of, 364
- classification of, 341
- contractual partnership, general conditions affecting, 343
- contractual partnership, rules relating to, 345
- definition of, 341
- for work, 357
- in property, 351
- in property, conditions affecting, 344
- land and work, 369
- on credit, 360
- trees and work, 370
- with equal shares, 349
- with unequal shares, 351

PLEDGES 171
- bailee, deposit of pledge with, 180
- borrowed articles, pledge of, 175
- contracts of, 171
- conditions incidental to, 172
- fundamental basis of, 171

INDEX

	Page
fundamental rules relating to,	176
pledge,	174
change of,	173
expenses connected with preservation of,	174
increase of,	173
matters attached to,	173
preservation of,	174
rights of pledgor and pledgee over,	178
sale of,	181
pledgor,	174
pledgee,	174
terms of Muhammadan jurisprudence relating to,	171

PRE-EMPTION 258
- claim of, 264
- conditions attaching to rights of, 262
- degrees of, 258
- effect of, 268
- terms of Muhammadan jurisprudence relating to, 245

PROPERTY LENT FOR USE 199
- compensation for loss arising out of, 200

REPORT OF DRAFTING COMMISSION 1

SALE 31
- agreement of acceptance with offer, 40
- approval, sale on, 70
- contract of, 37
- delivery, taking and giving, 64
  - expenses connected with, 68
  - giving delivery, 64
  - place of, 42
  - place of delivery, 67
  - procedure connected with, 64
  - taking delivery, 64
- effect of various kinds of, 85
- fundamental basis of, 37
- immediate payment against future delivery, sale by, 87

	Page
manufacture and sale, contract for,	88
matters not explicitly mentioned in the sale,	54
mortal sickness, sale by person suffering from,	90
options,	71
contractual,	71
deceit, for	83
defect, for,	77
inspection, as to,	74
misdescription, for,	72
misrepresentation, for,	83
payment, as to,	73
selection, as to,	74
place where concluded,	42
price,	57
circumstances affecting decrease of,	60
increase of,	60
nature of,	57
power to deal with after sale,	60
right of vendor to dispose of,	60
procedure at the sale,	49
rescission of,	45
right of redemption, sale subject to a,	91
subject matter of,	46
conditions affecting,	46
description of,	46
subject to condition,	44
subject to inspection,	70
subject to payment at a future date,	58
terms of Muhammadan jurisprudence relating to,	31
thing sold,	84
categories of,	84
decrease of,	60
destruction of,	69
increase of,	60
power to deal with, after sale,	60
right of purchaser to dispose of,	60

	Page
right of retention over,	66
things which may and may not be sold,	47
types of,	84

SETTLEMENT AND RELEASE 399

consideration of,	403
contract of,	400
debt and other matters, settlement in regard to,	406
fundamental conditions governing,	407, 408
specific property, settlement in respect to,	404
subject matter of,	403, 404
terms of Muhammadan jurisprudence relating to,	399

TRANSFER OF DEBT 161

conditions relating to,	163
contract of,	161

	Page
effect of,	164
fundamental basis of,	161
terms of Muhammadan jurisprudence relating to,	161

TRUSTS AND TRUSTEESHIP 184

general,	186

WRONGFUL APPROPRIATION 224

general,	224
from a person who has already wrongfully appropriated property,	231
real property,	229

WRONGFUL APPROPRIATION AND DESTRUCTION 223

terms of Muhammadan jurisprudence relating to,	223

Section 2: *The Civil Law of Palestine and Trans-Jordan,* C.A. Hooper. Volume 2

THE CIVIL LAW
OF
PALESTINE
AND
TRANS-JORDAN

BY

C. A. HOOPER

of the Inner Temple, Barrister-at-Law,
Judicial Adviser to the Government of Transjordan.

(Gilchrist Memorial Scholar in Turkish; Ouseley Memorial Scholar in Arabic, in the University of London, 1913—1914).

VOLUME II.

JERUSALEM.
1936.

PREFACE.

The first volume of this work contains a complete translation of the text of the Mejelle, or Ottoman Civil Code. Before making a detailed commentary on those Articles of the Code which call for exposition, there are certain matters affecting the Code as a whole in Palestine and Trans-Jordan which call for explanation and comment, although they do not form an integral part of the Code itself.

I have therefore compiled a short introductory volume serving as an introduction to a more detailed study of the Code itself.

The text of portions of the more important decisions rendered by the Courts of Palestine is given; and in this connection I take the opportunity of acknowledging the kindness of His Honour, the Chief Justice of Palestine, Sir Michael F. J. McDonnell, in allowing me to go through the files containing the judgments of the Supreme Court and to make copies of the more important judgments.

I must express my thanks to Mr. Henry E. Baker for preparing the detailed index and list of cases quoted, etc. and also to Mr. Gaspar Aghajanian who kindly checked the references to the Palestine Decided Cases and to Rashad Effendi Hassan who helped me in many ways; and finally I desire to acknowledge the kindness of Mr. Henry Kantrovitch, Junior Government Advocate of Palestine, in seeing this volume through the press in Jerusalem

C. A. HOOPER

Amman, Trans-Jordan 1936.

Azriel Press, Jerusalem.

TABLE OF CONTENTS.

	Page
Table of Cases	
(1) Cyprus Cases	vii
(2) English Cases	vii
(3) Palestine Cases	vii-xvi
Articles of the Mejelle referred to	xvii-xviii
Chapter I. The origin and development of Muhammadan law	1-16
Sources of Muhammadan law	6-14
(a) The Koran	6-8
(b) The Sunna	8-11
(c) Ijma	11-2
(d) Analogy	12-3
(e) Custom	13-4
Schools of Muhammadan Law	14-6
Chapter II. The Nature of the Civil Code	17-24
Reasons for the compilation of the Mejelle	17
Subject-matter of the Mejelle	18-9
Nature of Examples to the Articles of the Mejelle	19-20
Sources	20-4
Appendix. List of Principal Sources of the Mejelle	25-7
Chapter III. Article 46 of the Palestine Order-in-Council	28-81
(1) Ottoman Law	29-61
(a) Ottoman law as it existed on and before the 1st. November 1914	29-36
Legislative Forms	34-6
Decided Cases	37-57
(1) Ottoman Decisions	37
(2) Cyprus Decisions	37-8
(3) Palestine Decisions	38
(4) English Decisions	55-7
(b) Ottoman laws subsequent in date to 1st November 1914	57-61
(2) Orders-in-Council affecting Palestine and Palestine Ordinances and Regulations	61-3
Statutory Rules and Orders	62-3
(3) The substance of the Common Law and the Doctrines of Equity in force in England	64-71
(a) The substance of the Common Law	65-7
(b) The doctrines of Equity	67-9
(c) The Statute Law	69-71

VIII

	Page
(4) The powers, procedure and practice of the English Courts	71-81
Palestine Decided Cases	72-8
Appendix No. 1. List of the principal Ottoman "Provisional" Enactments	82
Appendix No. 2. List of Ottoman Laws repealed or superseded wholly or in part in Palestine	83-7

Chapter IV. The Law of Contract 88-171

(1) Formation of Contract in Muhammadan law 88-99
    (a) offer and acceptance 88-92
    (b) consideration 92-3
    Palestine Decided Cases 93-8
    Constantinople Cassation Decisions 99

(2) Capacity of parties to a contract 99-108
    (a) minors 99-101
    (b) other persons not possessing full contractual capacity 101-4
        (1) lunatics 101-2
        (2) imbeciles 102
        (3) prodigals 102
        (4) debtors 103
        Palestine Decided Case 103
        Constantinople Cassation Decisions 104
        (5) capacity as dealt with in specific contracts in the Mejelle 104-8
        Palestine Decided Cases 107-8

(3) Consent of parties to a contract 109-14
    (a) constraint 109-11
    Palestine Decided Cases 110-1
    Constantinople Cassation Decision 111
    (b) Deceit 111
    (c) Misrepresentation 111-3
    (d) Options 113-4

(4) The subject-matter of the contract 114-27
Paragraph I of Article 64 of the Ottoman Civil Procedure Code 116-9
    (a) Contracts forbidden by law 116-7
    (b) Contracts contrary to morality 117
    (c) Contracts prejudicial to public order 117-8
    (d) Contracts in conflict with matters of personal status 118
    (e) Contracts in conflict with inheritance and succession 118
    (f) Contracts in conflict with the law of pious foundations (waqf) 118
    (g) Contracts in conflict with the law of immovable property 119
    (n) Contracts the subject-matter of which cannot be produced 119

IX

	Page
Paragraph II of Article 64 of the Ottoman Civil Procedure Code	119-20
(a) matters possessing specific value	119-20
(b) things to be produced in the future	120
Paragraph III of Article 64 of the Ottoman Civil Procedure Code	120-7
Palestine Decided Cases	120-6
Constantinople Cassation Decisions	126-7
(5) Form of Contracts	127-39
(a) Contracts in writing	127-39
(1) when it is customary to reduce them to writing	129-30
(2) when relating to partnership	130
(3) when relating to farming out	130-1
(4) when relating to a loan	131-2
Palestine Decided Cases (Article 80)	132-5
Palestine Decided Cases (Article 82)	135-6
Constantinople Cassation Decisions	136-8, 139
(b) Oral contracts	139
(c) Contracts concluded by conduct	139
(6) Classification of contracts in Muhammadan law	139-41
(1) Contracts for alienation of property	139-40
(2) Contracts for alienation of usufruct	140
(3) Contracts for securing the discharge of an obligation	140
(4) Contracts for representation	141
(1) Valid contracts	140
(2) Voidable contracts	140
(3) Void contracts	141
(7) Breach of Contract: Damages for Breach of Contract	141-158
Article 106 of the Ottoman Civil Procedure Code	141-3
107 ″ ″ ″ ″ ″ ″	143-4
108 ″ ″ ″ ″ ″ ″	144-5
109 ″ ″ ″ ″ ″ ″	145
110 ″ ″ ″ ″ ″ ″	145-6
111 ″ ″ ″ ″ ″ ″	146-9
Palestine Decided Cases	149-55
Constantinople Cassation Decisions	155-7
Article 126 of the Ottoman Civil Procedure Code	158
(8) Interest and Rate of Interest	158-71
Article 112 of the Ottoman Civil Procedure Code	158
Ottoman Regulations	158-9
Palestine Ordinances	159-61
Palestine Decided Cases	161-7
Constantinople Cassation Decisions	167-71
Index	173-197

TABLE OF CASES CITED.

CYPRUS CASES.

Chacalli v Kallourena (CLR III 246) 88.
Jassonides v Kyprioti (CLR VII 83) 1,23.
Joachim v Haji Christofi & anor. (CLR V 77) 56.
Karageordiades v Haji Pavlo & Sons (CLR V 39) 56.
Koukoulli v Hamid Bey (CLR VII 85) 36.
Louka v Nicola (CLR V 82) 1,24.
Mehmet v Kosmo (CLR I 12) 53.
Michailides v Bishop of Papho (CLR IV 76) 88.
Queen's Advocate v Van Milligan (CLR III 211) 56.
R. v Theori (CLR VI 14) 57.
R. v Yallouri (CLR III 41) 57.
Raghib v Gerasimo (CLR III 110) 18,24,56.
Theophilou v Abraam (CLR III 236) 57.

ENGLISH CASES.

Borough of Portsmouth Tramways Co. (1892. 2 Ch. 362) 76.
Carlill v Carbolic Smoke Ball Co. (1893. 1. Q. B. 256) 90.
Currie v Misa (1875 L.R.10. Ex. 162) 93.
Harper v Godsell (1870. 5. Q.B. 422) 75.
Keates v Lord Cadogan (10. C.B. 591) 112.
Kemble v Farren 149.
Ward v Hobbes. (3.Q.B.D.150) 112.

PALESTINE CASES.

Abdel Hadi, Wajih Abdel Karim v. Abdel Hadi, Yusef Abdel Karim (CA 37/32) 108.
Yusuf Abdel Karim v. Abdel Hadi, Wajih Abdul Karim (CA 52/31) 165.
Hafez, Abdullah v. Salman, Abdel Kader Khalil (LA 135/26) 40.
Abdul Kader Haj v. Mohammed el Haj (CA 122/28) 50.
Salam, Mohamed v. Atallah, Mitry Salame (CA 8/24) 162-3.
Abud, Elias Musa v. Triandafilidies, Christo (CA 171/23) 152.

XII

Abu Habib, Ibrahim v. Yasin, Said Mahmoud (LA 20/32) 53.
    Ibrahim Ahmad v. Hamad, Abdul Raham (CA 110/26) 121-2.
Hantash, Abdel Latif Musa v. Qabbani, Rushdieh (CA 107/31) 166.
Hijla, Ahmed Yusef v. Yusef, Darwish Hamed 40.
Jaafar, Kamal v. Bitar, Rajab Mustafa (CA 95/31) 54.
    Rashid v. Bitar, Rajab Mustafa (CA 130/32) 54.
Khadra, Khadijeh Ismail v. Abu Khadra, Amneh Khalil (CA 306/20) 37.
    Laban, Ahmad Hassan & Sons v. Bergman, Fritz (CA 39/32) 54.
        Lieder & Fischer (CA 85/32) 54.
Alpert v. C.E.O. Jerusalem (S.T. 1/28) 56,77.
Anglo-Palestine Bank Ltd., v. Syndic of George Barsky (CA 179/32) 55.
    Co., Jaffa v. Kfar Ganim Co. Ltd. (CA 93/38) 75-6,79.
Armenian Patriarchate v. Daoudi, Muhamed Taher (CA 93/21) 38.
    Jabrieh, Mubarak (CA 393/21) 38.
    Mishaka, Nadra (CA 111/26) 122-3.
Awaida, Abd es Salam, ex parte, (HC 52/27) 52.
Aweidah, Abdul Salam v. Banco di Roma (CA 84/22) 38.
Aydi, Shaban Mustafa v. Khalil, Ibrahim (LA 81/22) 107.
Ayoub, Tawfiq v. Hazboun, Issa (CA 60/29) 51.
    Tewfik v. Imperial Ottoman Bank (CA 319/22) 38.
Ayub, George v. Mayor of Beit Jala (HC 71/31) 36.
Banco di Roma v. Tamimi, Muhammad Ali (CA 69/32) 55.
Banna, Ahmad Zeidan v. Mohammad Mohammad (CA 208/23) 152.
Barghuti, Umar Saleh v. Moslem Supreme Council (HC 48/25) 63.
Bedas, Isa Muhammad v. Bamieh, Abdel Mu'ti (CA 48/33) 154-5.
Berger, Eliezer v. Oriental Touring & Shipping Agency (CA 50/26) 153.
Bishara, Saltie v. Haddad Saleem (CA 72/22) 110.
Blum, Rose v. C.E.O. Jaffa (HC 50/31) 52.
Budairi, Ibrahim v. Budairi, Muhammad Hassan (CA 144/32) 55.
Bushnaq, Othman Salim v. Bonstein, Yehuda Ben Moshe (CA 72/32) 126.
Calaris, Dimitri v. Abu Khadra, Su'ad (CA 28/32) 53.
Central Bank v. Registrar of Companies (CA 74/27) 75, 123-4.
Chedid, Abdullah Bey v. Tenenbaum (PCA 47/32) 72,143.
Coats, J & P Ltd. v. Kirshenbaum & Blumenkrantz (CA 101/26) 74.
Cornue, Fanny v. Ali Ahmed Sheikh Ali (CA 105/32) 54.
Dahdouh, Abdullah v. Execution Officer, Gaza (HC 83/27) 61.
Daher, Tewfik el Haj v. Kadha, Michail (CA 177/23) 161.
Dajani, Muhammad Sa'adat v. Mustakim, Ali (CA 42/31) 52.
Dajjani, Sheikh Mahmoud v. Rahman as Sadiq, Shafiqah Abdur (LA 38/30) 20.

XIII

Darwish, Said ex parte (HC 17/25) 52.
Dinovitz, Jona v. Rosenbaum, Gershon Harris (CA 48/24) 163.
Edelman v. Edelman (HC 31/26) 31.
Egyptian Bonded Warehouses Co. Ltd. v. Wiener, Moshe (CA 93/23) 150.
Eid, Andrawes v. Habayeb, Kustandi Hanna (CA 16/28) 49.
Eliash, Mordekhai v. Director of Lands (HC 77/31) 56,70,76-7.
Estrangin, v. Tynan (O.G. Sept. 16, 1926) 53.
Etkin, Ibrahim Leib v. Shlosberg, Jacob (CA 13/26) 74.
Faghouri, Yusef Issa Hamoud v. Hamoud, Jamileh Mousa (CA 55/31) 98, 117-8, 124-5.
Fakhri Bey, Fatimah Hanem v. Shuqairi, Sheikh Ass'ad (LA 49/32) 38, 53.
Farah, Ibrahim Khoury v. Nazha, Dr. Yacoub (LA 7/32) 2,23,102.
Fares, Fayez v. Commandant of Police (HC 51/32) 71, 78.
Fast v. Abdel Hadi, Ounie (CA 21/31) 53.
Fityani, Jamileh Khanum v. Mizfin, 'Amer ibn Mustafa 'Amer (CA 165/23) 39.
Friedenberg, K. v. Jerusalem Municipality (CADC Jm 212/31) 57.
Friedman, Abraham v. Miller, Miriam (LA 58/30) 111.
　　　　Shlomo v. Abdul Nur, Badi'a bint (LA 96/27) 40-9.
Gesundheit, Jacob v. C.E.O. (HC 13/32) 52-3.
Gluckman, L. v. District Court, Jaffa (CA 52/28) 60.
Guiragossian, Malakeh v. Ghazaleh, Issa Daoud (CA 62/24) 120-1.
Habashi, Ahmed Muhammad v. Omar, Tewfik el Haj (CA 49/28) 49.
Habayeb, Abib ibn Mikhail v. Husseini, Ibrahim Bey (CA 57/23) 149-50.
Habbas v. Sheinfinkel 50.
Hadad, Nasrallah v. Suleiman, Laya (CA 68/31) 165-6.
Haddad, Salim Jiryes v. Tahbub, Fuad Muhammad Said (LA 55/30) 51.
　　　　Tewfik v. Bakeer, Haj Hussein (LA 20/27) 40.
Haifa Municipality v. Khoury, Dr. Caesar (CA 88/30) 2, 23, 51.
Hamanhil Co. v. Jaffa Municipality (CA 130/26) 74.
Hanum, Saadat Kamel v. Palestine Government (LA 70/32) 20.
Hausman, Simon v. C.E.O. Jerusalem (HC 60/27) 40.
Havagimian, Kevork v. Nassarian, Pilpul (CA 106/31) 170-1.
Hazan, Zeiv v. Milstein, Nahum (CA 45/24) 163.
Hazine, Zeev v. N.V.A.Y.S. "Forrostaal" Haag (CA 36/28) 56, 75.
Heifitz, Mordekhai v. Barhum, Nissim Sion (CA 35/28) 91.
Homsi, Habib v. Orthodox Patriarchate Finances Commission (CA 136/33) 98.
Husseini, Fahmi v. C.E.O. Jaffa (HC 3/33) 55.
　　　　Muhammad Shaker v. Hurvitz, Menahem (CA 106/32) 54, 134-5.
Imam, Sheikh Ibrahim v. Benin, Selim Menahem Moshe (CA 52/22) 38.
Isweid, Khalil Mustafa Khalil v. Dajani, Haj Muhammad Ahmad heirs (LA 1/31) 51.

XIV

Jaballi, Abdallah Ahmed v. C.E.O. Jaffa (HC 84/27) 50.
Jarrar, Selim & Tewfik Asad Haj v. Madi, Asad (LA 109/22) 107.
Jibril Muhammad & Yusef v. Jibril, Taha & Khadra (LA 80/24) 40-1.
Kahana, Leib v. Hagis, Joseph Levi (LA 121/25) 39.
Kamal, Sudki v. Rokach, Yusef (CA 43/28) 75.
Karwasarsky, Zipora v. Kaminsky, Bezalel (CA 71/28) 164.
Kassab, Iskandar v. Nassar, Najib (CA 87/26) 74.
Katafago Alphonse v. Avrinos, Germas Khristo (CA 13/22) 90-1.
Kattan, Nakhli v. Zacharia, Joulia (CA 395/21) 161.
Khalil, Samaan Jadoun v. Sqariq, Abdel Raheem (CA 41/28) 164.
Khankin, Joshua v. Mustafa, Qasem Muhammad (CA 58/32 CA 59/32) 54, 103.
Khayat, Selim v. Khayat, Mary (S.T. 1923) 37.
Khoury, Salim Nasrallah v. Shukri, Hassan Bey (CA 147/32) 167.
Kurdieh, Ali Muhammad v. Kialy, Mousa (CA 88/31) 125-6.
Levitsky, A. v. Corn, Zalman (CA 8/33) 128.
Lieber, Israel v. Mirenberg, Jacob (CA 35/31) 76.
Lubin, Lilian v. Wilson, Samuel (CA 219/26) 50, 55, 129, 132-3.
Malfuf, Frizah bint Haj Assad v. Nashef, Halimeh bint Haj Abdullah (CA 29/32) 53.
Masri, Khadijeh bint Sayed v. Idriss, Muhammad Sheikh Abdallah (LA 31/24) 49.
Mikhail, Habib Hanna v. Assife, Jawallah Jiries (CA 146/23) 39.
Morcos, Issa v. Morcos, Emilie (CA 29/29) 136.
Moyal, Daoud v. Calmy, Claire (CA 205/32) 39, 93-5.
  , David v. Salem, Ovadie (CA 161/22) 39,
Muzaffar, Sheikh Abdul Kader v. Dirhalli, Abdul Hamid (CA 15/30) 51.
Nadar, Elias v. Attorney-General (CA 41/24) 39.
Nammour, Muhammad Qasem v. Nammour, Amineh Ahmad (CA 100/25) 135-6.
Nashashibi, Khalil v. Muzhar, Rafat Mohamed (CA 125/21) 38.
Nasr, Ibrahim Elias v. Nasr, Nijmeh Elias (CA 72/31) 136.
  Nicola Elias v. Brakha, Haim (CA 115/28) 50.
Niameh, Hanna Yusef v. Niameh, Yusef (LA 137/25) 39-40.
Ofi, Saleh Ibrahim v. C.E.O. Nablus (HC 25/30) 52.
Oufi, Ibrahim Rehayem v. Keren Kayemeth Leisrael (LA 22/31) 52.
Papoula, Rabbi Bechor v. Nabulsi, Mohammad Said Bey (CA 127/23) 150-2.
Penhas, J. L. v. Falum, Pesach (HC 49/25) 71, 73.
Pinhassovitch, Moussa v. Litvinsky Bros. (LA 58/25) 70, 73-4.
Rahim, Daoud v. Handal, Suleiman (CA 129/23) 39.
Ramadan, Nicola v. Khalil, Hanna (LA 71/23) 39.
Raskowsky v. Raskowsky 50.
Raym, Yitzhaq v. Hadar Hacarmel Coop. Soc. Ltd. (HC 99/32)
Robinson, Henry v. Press, Yeshayahu (CA 62/28) 49-50.
Rokach, Joseph v. Ragheb, Sudki (CA 22/27) 50.
Rosenberg v. Zeidan (CA 2/27) 51.

XV

Saikali, Farha bint Musa v. Khammas, Rida bint Butros (CA 115/25) 136.
Sakija, Mustafa Ismail v. Jacobson, Solomon (CA 98/27) 103.
Salah, Abdul Latif v. Ottoman Bank (CA 58/23) 95-7.
Salahi, Suleiman Musa Darwish v. Salahi, Rida (CA 136/32) 55.
Sarhan, Jamileh bint Muhammad v. Husseini, Ibrahim Muhammad Faraj (CA 78/28) 50, 53.
Savronsky, v. Trachtenberg (CA 38/33) 55.
Shanti, Kamel v. Dellal, Yaqub Saliba (CA 98/31) 166.
Shibel, Saleh Muhammad v. Taha, Haj Khalil (CA 9/31) 97.
Shible, Saleh Muhammed v. Hawa, Assa'd Habib & Sons (CA 129/22) 38.
Shlank, v. Greenberg (LA 38/29) 51.
Skairik, Abdel Halim v. C.E.O. Haifa (HC 70/29) 50-1.
Slonim, Shamuel v. Izzah, Musleh Abdel Latif (CA 54/32) 54,166-7.
Steinberg, Shlomo v. C.E.O. Jerusalem (HC 51/30) 164-5.
Taher, Haj Amin v. Zantut, Shafik (CA 185/22) 161.
Taji, Ibrahim Hakki v. Nakib, Ali (CA 254/23) 51.
Tamari, Wadie v. Karamano (CA 79/25) 39.
Tayyan, Emil v. C.E.O. Nablus (HC 19/29) 76.
Teitelbaum, Moses Isaac v. Gootmann, Jacob (CA 31/28) 154.
Trachtingott, Ishak v. Matross, Elizabeth (CA 67/25) 152-3.
Turjman, Issa v. C.E.O. Jerusalem (HC 49/32) 77-8.
Wahbeh el Haj, Shakib Tanus v. Hankin, Joshua (CA 104/27) 154, 163.
Weizman, Joseph v. Jaffa Waqf Department (CA 116/23) 110.
Yared, Agnes v. Khoury, Kaysar (LA 32/24) 73.
Yasuri, Ribhi v. Abu Ghosh, Sheikh Abdul Hamid (CA 85/26) 147, 153.
Yehudayoff, Eliasha v. Yehudayoff, Yehiel (CA 230/23) 129, 132.
Zaban, Adib v. Altshuler, Meir Shlomo (CA 54/29) 54, 164, 166.
Zachs, Dov & Sons v. Northern Insurance Co. Ltd. (CA 42/50) 51.
Zadeh, Nir Khanum bint Kubar v. Rahil, Michael ibn Francis (LA 132/26) 40.
Zakharia, Spiro Jirius v. Matari, Ali Haj Hassan (LA 175/23) 51.
Zaslevsky v. Goldberg (CA 18/23) 63.
Zeide, Meir v. Alcalay, Salomon (CA 147/26) 153-4.

XVI

CIVIL APPEALS

Abbreviations: PLR Law Reports of Palestine 1920-33.
PP The Palestine Post newspaper.

No.	Year	Report	Page.
306	20	PLR 1	37,50,53,
93	21		38
125	21		38
393	21	PLR 4	38
395	21		161
52	22		38
72	22		110
84	22		38
129	22		38
161	22		39
185	22		161
205	22		39,93-5
319	22		38
18	23		63
57	23		149-50
58	23		95-7
93	23		150
116	23		110
127	23		150-2
129	23		39
146	23		39
165	23		39
172	23		152
177	23		161
208	23.		152
230	23		129-132
254	23		57
264	23		39
8	24	PLR 16	162-3
41	24		39
45	24	PLR 16	163
48	24		163
62	24		120-1
67	25		152-3
79	25		39
93	25		52
100	25	PLR 83	135-6
115	25		136

XVII

CIVIL APPEALS (contd.)

No.	Year	Report	Page.
13	26		74
50	26	PLR 131	153
85	26		147, 153
87	26		74
101	26	PLR 117	74
110	26		121-2
111	26		122-3
130	26		74
147	26	PLR 116	153-4
149	26		154
219	26	PLR 169	50,55,129,132-3
2	27	PLR 229	51
22	27	PLR 154	50
74	27		75, 123-4
98	27	PLR 273; PP 12/12/34	54, 103
104	27		154, 163
16	28	PLR 336	49
31	28		154
35	28		91
36	28	PLR 303	56, 75
41	28	PLR 332	164
43	28		75
49	28	PLR 343; PP 20/11/34	49
52	28		60
62	28		49-50
71	28	PLR 347	164
78	28	PLR 432	50-53
93	28	PLR 357	75-6, 79
115	28	PLR 371	50
122	28	PLR 372	50
29	29	PLR 433	136
54	29	PLR 517	54, 164, 167
60	29		51
68	29		54
15	30	PLR 623	57
42	30	PLR 556	51
88	30	PLR 724	2, 23, 57

XVIII

CIVIL APPEALS (contd.)

No.	Year	Report	Page.
9	31	PLR 593	97
21	31	PLR 709	53
35	31		76
42	31	PLR 577	52
52	31		165
55	31	PLR 608	98, 117-8, 124-5
68	31		165
72	31	PLR 648; PP 19/11/34	53, 136
88	31		125
95	31		54
98	31	PLR 664	166
106	31	PLR 720	170-1
107	31	PLR 783	166
13	32	PLR 718	90-1
28	32		53
29	32		53
37	32		108
39	32	PP 27/6/33	54
54	32	PP 10/2/33	54, 166-7
58	32	PP 8/2/33	54, 103
59	32		54, 103
69	32	PLR 765	55
72	32		126
75	32	PP 28/3/33	133-4
85	32	PP 14/7/33	54
105	32	PLR 810 PP 14/12/32; 8/5/33	54
106	32	PP 1/2/33; 3/2/33	54, 134-5
130	32	PP 23/3/33	54
136	32	PP 14/6/33	55
144	32		55
147	32	PLR 785 PP 31/1/33	167
179	32		55
8	33	PLR 858; PP 4/4/33	128
38	33	PLR 869; PP 13/12/33	55
48	33		154-55
136	33	PP 5/6/34	98

CIVIL APPEAL IN DISTRICT COURT

No.	Year	Report	Page.
212 Jm	31	PP 2/3/33	57

XIX

HIGH COURT.

No.	Year	Report	Page
17	25	PLR 38	52
48	25		63
49	25		71, 73
31	26		31
43	27	PLR 194	40
52	27	PLR 189	52
60	27		40
83	27		61
84	27	PLR 244	50
19	29	PLR 382	76
70	29		50-1
25	30	PLR 471	52
51	30	PLR 538	52, 164-5
50	31	PLR 634	52
71	31		36
77	31	PLR 735	56, 70, 76-7
13	32		52-3
49	32		56, 77-8
51	32	PLR 733	71, 78
74	32	PLR 782	55
99	32	PLR 802 PP 16/4/33	78
3	33	PP 28/4/33	55

LAND APPEALS.

No.	Year	Report	Page
137	20		53
81	22		107
109	22		107
19	23		40
71	23		39
137	23	PLR 41	40
175	23		51
31	24		49
32	24		73
56	24	PLR 41	40
80	24		40-1

XX

LAND APPEALS. (contd.)

No.	Year	Report	Page
81	25	PLR 86	40
121	25		39
137	25		39-40
39	26		40
93	26		40
113	26		40
132	26	PLR 151	40
135	26		40
139	26		40
20	27	PLR 139	40
96	27		40-9
58	28		70, 73-4
38	29	PLR 456	57
39	30		20
55	30	PLR 603	51
58	30		111
1	31		51
2	31		51
22	31	PLR 611	52
7	32		2, 23, 102
20	32		53
49	32	PP 10/5/33	38, 53
70	32	PLR 866 PP 12/12/33	20

LAND COURT.

102 Ja	22		49

PRIVY COUNCIL APPEAL.

47	32	PLR 831	72, 143

SPECIAL TRIBUNAL.

	23		37
1	29	PLR 39	56, 77

XXI

ARTICLES OF THE MEJELLE REFERRED TO.

Article	Page	Article	Page
36	129	739-40	76
69	127	773	88
103	88	776	105
106	140	804	88
108	140	805	89
109	140	809	105
110	141	837	88
127	119	839	89
164	111	840	89
165	112,139	851-3	106
167	88	859	106
175	139	941	100,101
181-5	89	943	100
182	138	944	102
197	92,120	945	23,102
205	92,120	946	102
208	111,113	947	101
237-44	92	948-9	109
300-55	113	957	23,100,101,102
320-5	92	958	23,102
356	112,113	960	100
357	111	963	102
358	113	966	100
361	104	967-8	101
362	104,141	970-1	101
372	140	972	100,101
420	92	973	100
433	88	974-5	100
438	89	977	101
444	104	980	102
447	104	981-4	101
450	92	985	100
458	104	986	99
497-521	113	987-9	100
621	88	990-1	102
629	105	998-1002	103
658	111-2,113	1003-7	109
680	88	1127	112,113
685	105	1160	112,113
706	88	1197-1212	73
731	76	1330	88

XXII

ARTICLES OF THE MEJELLE REFERRED TO (contd.).

Article	Page	Article	Page
1405	88	1576	107
1413	74	1580	89
1432	88	1539	38,167
1433	106	1606	127
1443	106	1610	52
1451	88,99	1660-75	13
1457-8	106	1663-4	53
1531	88	1667 (2)	19,20
1535	89	1667 (3)	19
1539-40	107	1685	8
1568	88	1742-3	11
1573-4	107	1774	74
1575	109	1801 (2)	19,23

To

Lieut. Col. C. H. F. Cox, C. M. G., D. S. O.

BRITISH RESIDENT

AMMAN

TRANS-JORDAN

CHAPTER I.

THE ORIGIN AND DEVELOPMENT OF MUHAMMADAN LAW. (¹)

It is not always realized by practical lawyers that the Ottoman Civil Code, or Mejelle, is no mere collection of arbitrary rules drawn up by a Committee sitting in Constantinople, but is in fact the pure Muhammadan law on civil obligations *(muamelat)* contained in treatises of acknowledged authority, arranged by the Drafting Committee in the form of a Code. (See Report of the Drafting Committee, Vol. I, pp. 1-11). The origin and development of Muhammadan law are of practical importance to persons engaged in the administration of the Code, for, as will be seen later, (see Chapter II, page 21), it is permissible to go outside the Code to ascertain what the precise law on a given point is, in cases where the Code is silent or ambiguous, or where there is room for more than one view of the law to be applied. (See the remarks of Bertram, J. in the case of *Jassonides v. Kyprioti* (C.L.R., Vol. VII, 83); and see the case of *Louka v. Nicola*, (C.L.R., Vol. V, 82),

---

(¹) The reader may consult with advantage the excellent handbook of Muhammadan Law by Mr. Seymour Vesey-Fitzgerald *(Muhammadan Law. An abridgement according to its various schools.* Oxford University Press, 1931.) For full information on questions of Muhammadan jurisprudence, see Abdur Rahim: *Muhammadan Jurisprudence,* being the Tagore Law Lectures, 1907. London, Luzac and Co., 1911; D. B. MacDonald: *Development of Muslim Theology, Jurisprudence and Constitutional Theory,* London, 1907; D. S. Margoliouth: *The Early Development of Muhammadanism,* being the Hibbert lectures, Second Series, 1913, London, Williams and Norgate. For a concise account of the traditions of Islam, see Guillaume: *The Traditions of Islam,* Oxford, Clarendon Press, 1924. One of the sources of the Mejelle has been translated into English. This is the *Hedaya,* translated by Charles Hamilton (second edition by S. G. Grady, H. Allen and Co., London, 1870). It is regarded as an authority by the Indian Courts.

2   MUHAMMADAN LAW

where the Court referred to the *Hedaya* (a standard treatise on Muhammadan Law) for the settlement of a point of law. See also the Palestine cases of *Ibrahim Khoury Farah and another v. Dr. Yacoub Nazha* (L.A. 7/32) and the *Municipality of Haifa v. Dr. Caesar Khoury* (C.A. 88/30).

The following is an attempt to set forth in as concise terms as possible the most salient features of the origin and development of Muhammadan law.

The principles of Muhammadan law are based upon a system of legislation at complete variance with any Western system. The fundamental difference between Muhammadan law and Western systems of law consists in the fact that Muhammadan law, that is, the law common to all Muhammadan countries, is of divine origin in the sense that it is claimed by Muslims to be the will of God himself revealed to mankind for their future and final guidance. Divergences of view, it is true, exist among Muslims as to the correct interpretation to be given to the words and acts by means of which God's will was revealed, and these divergences have given rise to the existence of various schools of law, but the basic principles are common to all Muhammadan countries, that is, to the world of Islam. Islam is the direct government of God, the Kingdom of God for his people on earth. This is the counterpart of the principles of unity and co-ordination, which in the world of Greece and Rome were known as *polis* and *civitas* respectively. The State, in Islam, is personified in God.

This fundamental difference between Western law and Muhammadan law can perhaps best be made clear if the reader will imagine the Christian states of the world, that is, those countries which have adopted the Christian religion, as being all governed by a common *Christian* law based upon and extracted from the will of God, which Christians believe to have been revealed to the world by His Son, Jesus Christ. If this were so, and after making allowance for differences brought about by conflicting interpretation and legal custom, a complete analogy would exist between the law of the Muhammadan and Christian worlds. But every Christian lawyer knows that the law of his country has been made without specific reference to what the will of God, as revealed by Jesus Christ, may have been as to the particular matter determined by the text of the law or by the custom in question. This distinction pervades the domains of both private and public law in the Christian and Muhammadan worlds.

"Muslim law, in the most absolute sense, is the science of all things, human and divine. It tells what we must render to Caesar and what to God, what to ourselves, and what to our fellows. The bounds of the Platonic definition of rendering to each man his due it utterly shatters. While Muslim theology defines everything that a man shall *believe* of things in heaven and in earth and beneath the earth—and this is no flat rhetoric— Muslim law prescribes everything that a man shall *do* to God, to his neighbour, and to himself. It takes all duty for its portion and defines all action in terms of duty. Nothing can escape the narrow meshes of its net." (¹)

Striking evidence of the extent to which one common law, the will of God, governs the world of Islam is available by mere reference to any hand-book of Muhammadan law in use at present. Let us take any book at random—the *Bedayat-ul-Mujtahid*, in two volumes, written by Muhammad ibn Ahmad ibn Rushd al-Qartabi, known as al-Hafid, in Morocco. This handbook — as in the case of the Ottoman Civil Code—is arranged in Books dealing with each subject, and is further sub-divided into Chapters and Sections. The first Book of Volume I of the *Bedayat-ul-Mujtahid* deals with purification; the second with prayer; the third with alms-giving; the sixth with pilgrimage. The first Chapter of Volume II deals with marriage; the second with divorce; the sixth with the law of sale; the seventh with hire; the twelfth with agency, the concluding Chapter dealing with the law of procedure and evidence. Muhammadan law, as we shall see later, is derived from four principal sources, (1) the Koran; (2) the *Sunna,* or sayings and conduct of the Prophet, which have come down to us by means of traditions; (3) *Ijma,* or matters upon

---

(¹) *D. B. MacDonald*: Development of Muslim Theology, Jurisprudence and Constitutional Theory, p. 66.

4 MUHAMMADAN LAW

which the whole world of Islam is agreed; (4) Analogy to which is added (5) Custom, and the author of the *Bedayat-ul-Mujtahid* throughout shows those sections of the law that are derived from the Koran direct; those derived from *Sunna*, and which have been handed down by means of the traditions; those upon which Muslim jurists agree as representing the will of God, when no authority is to be found therefor either in the Koran or the *Sunna*—(*Ijma*); and those based upon analogy (*Qiyas*).

It remains to explain how this situation came into being. Leaving on one side the explanation of how law and religion became divorced in the Christian world, a situation now so plain that it requires no demonstration, we may pass on to consider briefly the origin of the Islamic religion, which is the basis of Muhammadan law.

On the 29th August, 570 A. D., a man was born at Mecca, in Arabia, who was destined to play a *rôle* perhaps second to none in the history of the world. This was none other than *Muhammad ibn Abdullah*, an illiterate Arab of Mecca. The rise of Muhammad to power as the founder of one of the most important religions of the world is intimately connected with the political state of his country at the time. Torn by internecine strife, the tribes, whether sedentary or nomad, stood sorely in need of some form of settled government. These tribes were pagan for the most part, and practised various forms of worship. Influenced by the Christian and Jewish faiths, there can be little doubt that Muhammad realized early the unifying and vitalizing forces exercised by an organized religion over primitive peoples. Dwelling on the political problem of the unification of the Arabs, Muhammad conceived the bold and vast project of uniting them together politically by means of a new religion. The link binding these tribes together had hitherto been that of blood; it now became that of faith. Whoever professed the faith of Islam became a member of the *Ummat-al-islam*, or people of Islam. Thus, ever since its inception, Islam became a great family of brothers with equal rights. Consequently, no separate nationalities can exist in Islam. It is merely a Western conception that has dubbed the Muslim of Egypt an Egyptian Muslim and the Muslim of China a Chinese Muslim. Every Muslim is a member of the state of Islam, the head of which is God, represented on earth by his vicegerent, the successor (*Khalifa*) of Muhammad. There might be a difference of race, but there could be none of nationality.

Muhammad saw visions and dreamed dreams to such an extent that while still a young man he proclaimed himself to be the Prophet of God, claiming that the Deity had specially chosen him as the channel through which His will was to be revealed, and that for the last time, for the guidance of mankind in both temporal and religious affairs. While respecting other Prophets who had revealed God's will to the world on previous occasions, Muhammad proclaimed himself to be the "seal" or last of the Prophets; henceforth God would reveal His will no more, and Muhammad's revelation therefore constituted the final instructions of God for the conduct of man on earth. For this reason there was no longer any need of intermediaries or priests between God and man, the *imams* in the Mosques being merely leaders in prayer, knowing the prayers by heart and being able to recite them well. Consequently, the spiritual element is entirely absent from orthodox Islam. Muhammad stated that at night time during his sleeping hours, God appeared to him through the medium of the angel Gabriel, who spoke God's will to him.[1]

---

[1] The language used by the angel Gabriel is considered by Muslims to have been Arabic. Pious Muslims at the present day not only believe this to be so, but regard the language of the Koran as containing the actual words used by God himself in conversation with Gabriel. The Arabic of the Koran is therefore at once the perfection of language and of style, and cannot be rivalled or improved. This has not prevented nationalist Turks from translating the Koran into Turkish. In striking contrast with the blind belief in the Koran in later years was the disbelief therein while Muhammad was alive: and this is evidenced by his own utterances as recorded in the Koran itself:

"And the infidels say: 'This *Koran* is a mere fraud of his own devising, and others have helped him with it, who had come hither by outrage and lie".

"And they say: 'Tales of the ancients that he hath put in writing and they were dictated to him morn and even." (In *Surah: al Furkan.*)

MUHAMMADAN LAW

Muhammad, in his waking hours, then dictated *verbatim* to his secretary *Zaid ibn Thabit* (2) what the angel had said to him, and these revelations were recorded upon various objects used, in those primitive times, as writing materials, and were afterwards gathered together in the form of a book known as the Koran, (3) which as containing the revealed will of God, was to be henceforth the guide to conduct, both temporal and religious, of all adherents of the new religion. The process of revelation, however, extended over a period of twenty-three years, and by no means found a favourable reception in Mecca. Muhammad found it prudent to leave his native town and flee to *Yathrib*, later known as *Medina* (the town). This flight, known in Arabic as the *Hijrah*, which took place on the night of the 16th July, 622 A. D., is taken as the commencement of the Muhammadan calendar, although Muhammad's religious activities commenced some thirteen years earlier. It was here, however, that he definitely announced himself to be a Prophet. In Medina, Muhammad was well received, and it was in this town that he succeeded in establishing the new religion on a firm foundation. He called it *Islam*, or the religion of the submission to the divine will.

Sources of Muhammadan law.

As mentioned above, Muhammadan law is based upon five sources, which are known in technical language as *usul* or roots.

    (a) The Koran;
    (b) The *Sunna*, or sayings and acts of the Prophet;
    (c) *Ijma*, or matters upon which the whole world of Islam is agreed;
    (d) Analogy;
    (e) Custom.

With these we may deal briefly in their order.

    (a) *The Koran.* An examination of the contents of

---

(2) Muhammad was unable to read or write.
(3) Koran literally means "reading," but to some scholars it means "recitation."

the Koran (¹) shows that it contains precepts defining the conduct of man, both in his religious affairs and in his temporal concerns, and the adherents of the new religion seem never to have paused to consider the practical difficulties attendant upon an absence of distinction in principle between the administration of religious and wordly affairs. Thus, if a point had to be settled about the levying of taxes, the conclusion of a contract, divorce, or the regulation of public worship, it was to the Koran that the early believers in Islam looked for guidance; and if that book did not contain sufficient guidance on the particular point, other supplementary sources of the revelation of God's will were consulted, as will be explained later. Contradictions exist in the Koran itself. The Koran, in its present form, is divided into 114 *surahs,* or chapters. These 114 *surahs* are divided into 6219 verses, of which some 500 refer more or less directly to legal matters. They have not been arranged in chronological order, according to the date of their revelation, but with the exception of the first, according to the number of verses, those containing the largest number coming first (²) These contradictions are largely caused by the failure to classify the *surahs* in chronological order. This difficulty has given rise to the doctrine known as that of the *abrogating and the abrogated,* whereby an earlier text in chronological order is supposed to have been revealed for temporary purposes only, and is abrogated by a later and final text. Thus is the difficulty of contradiction explained away.

---

(1) The Koran did not receive its final form till after Muhammad's death. As mentioned above, the Koran was dictated by Muhammad and recorded in various ways. It was by order of the first Caliph, *Abu Bekr,* that the various fragments of the Koran were collected together. The Koran in its final form was drawn up by the order of *Othman,* the third Caliph, and all other copies were destroyed. It is considered an act of piety to recite the Koran, and persons who learn the Koran by heart are held in high esteem.

(2) A further method of division is used for purposes of ritual, the Koran being divided into thirty parts, called *juz,* and sixty other parts, called *hizb.*

8 MUHAMMADAN LAW

As an example of the actual legislation contained in the Koran, the following extract from the *surah* called "The Cow" is given, dealing with such various matters as evidence, debt, registration of contracts, and pledges.

"O ye who believe! when ye contract a debt (payable) at a fixed date, write it down, and let the notary faithfully note between you: and let not the notary refuse to note, even as God hath taught him; but let him note it down, and let him who oweth the debt dictate, and let him fear God his Lord, and not diminish aught thereof. But if he who oweth the debt be foolish or weak, or be not able to dictate himself, let his friend dictate for him with fairness; and *call to witness two witnesses of your people: but if there be not two men, let there be a man, and two women* of those whom ye shall judge fit for witnesses: if the one of them should mistake, the other may cause her to recollect. And the witnesses shall not refuse, whenever they shall be summoned. And disdain not to put the debt in writing, be it large or small, with its time of payment: this will be more just for you in the sight of God, better suited for witnessing, and the best for avoiding doubt. But if the goods be there present, and ye pass them from hand to hand, then it shall be no fault in you not to write it down. And have witnesses when ye sell, and harm not writer or witness: it will be a crime in you to do this. But fear God and God will give you knowledge, for God hath knowledge of all things.

"And if ye be on a journey and shall find no notary, let pledges be taken: but if one of you trust the other, let him who is trusted restore what he is trusted with, and fear God his Lord. And refuse not to give evidence. He who refuseth is surely wicked at heart: and God knoweth your deeds."

If the reader will turn to Article 1685 of the Civil Code, he will there find reproduced the provisions of the Koran as to evidence set out in italics above.

(b) The *Sunna*. The foundation, then, of all Muhammadan law is the Koran. But the actual amount of law contained in the 500 verses referred to above is small; and at an early stage in the development of Islam, the necessity was felt of amplifying the purely Koranic law. The Prophet himself began expounding the Koran to those of his adherents who came into immediate contact with him, the Koran containing injunctions to obey the Prophet, setting him forth as the best example for the believer (Koran III, 29; IV, 62; XXXIII, 21) and references are implicitly made to expositions given by him (Koran XVI, 46). There was obvious need for this. Thus, the Koran institutes prayer, pilgrimage, fasting, ablution, and levying of the tithe (*zakah*) without prescribing how it is to be done. Those adherents of Muhammad who were in touch with him naturally enquired from him on these points, taking note of his replies and observing his conduct. This combination of words and acts is known as *Sunna*. The *Sunna*, since its source was the Prophet himself, the chosen mouthpiece of God, is second only to the Koran as a source of law. The *Sunna* is divided into :

(1) *Sunnat-ul-qual* or the verbal expositions given by the Prophet;

(2) *Sunnat-ul-f'il*, or the acts of the Prophet in respect to these matters;

(3) *Sunnat as-suqut* or *at-taqrir* or tacit assent of the Prophet. This tacit assent was said to be given when the Prophet, hearing or observing certain things said or done, refrained from expressing disapproval.

(4) *Hadiths*. (Traditions). Writing was not common in the days when Muhammad lived, but, deprived of the support of the written word, memories were correspondingly tenacious. Everything the Prophet said or did was carefully remembered by his adherents, and preserved in the form of a tradition called *hadith*, or story, handed down from mouth to mouth. The *hadiths*, then are the means by which the *Sunna* referred to above was preserved and handed down to posterity. A *hadith* is technically the narration of a saying or act of the Prophet, narrated by the person who was present to some other person, who in turn narrated it to some other person, and so on until it was finally written down by persons known as traditionists, who collected these traditions in authentic collections.

Every *hadith* is composed of two parts: (a) the text (*matn*) of the tradition; (b) the authority (*isnad* or *sanad*) for the tradition. This is sometimes known as the *sillsilah*, or chain of witnesses supporting the tradition, and through whom it has been transmitted. This chain goes back from the narrator down to the person who saw the Prophet act or heard him speak.

The *Sunna* of the Prophet, and consequently the *hadiths*, did not relate exclusively to legal matters, but the majority are of a legal nature. The number of traditions is great and their importance as a source of Muhammadan law cannot be exaggerated. They are not all of uniform value or importance and the validity of many of them, indeed, is contested, in the sense that they do not correctly represent the acts or words of Muhammad, being inaccurate or even forged. Those containing all the requisites for a valid tradition are known as *sahih*, or authentic, and constitute thereby a source of law *(hujjah or delil)*.

Several collections of traditions exist. The oldest collection is that of *Malik* known as the *Muwatta*. The corpus of the traditions, however, exists in six collections, known as the *Kuttub as-sittah*, or the six books. They are the following:—

(1) *Bukhari* } known as *as-sahihain* or
(2) *Abu Muslim* } *Jami' as-sahih*
(3) *Ibn Majah*
(4) *Abu Daud* } known as the *Sunnan*
(5) *At-Tirmidhi* } (plural of *Sunnah*)
(6) *An-Nasai*

The following are examples of *hadiths* applying to the law of evidence:

From *Tirmidhi*:

Ibn Amru ibn As stated that the Prophet said to him, *"Evidence is for the plaintiff and the oath for the defendant."*

From *Abu Daud:*

Ibn Abbas stated that the Prophet said to a man when administering an oath to him *"Swear in the name of God,* than whom there is no other, that you owe him nothing, that is to say, the plaintiff".

From *Abu Daud*:

Amru ibn Shuaib stated that his father told him, who in turn heard it from his grandfather, that the Prophet said to him: "The evidence of a traitor or a traitress, of an adulterer or an adultress, or of a man at enmity with another shall not be received".

If the reader will turn to Articles 1742 and 1743 of the Civil Code, he will there find reproduced the provisions of the traditions printed in italics above.

The value of the *Sunna* as a source of law is great. The positive law in it is equal with that of the Koran. The *Sunna* completes the Koran when it is silent, interprets it when it is ambiguous or incomplete, and even replaces it, when the text of the *hadith* and the circumstances of the case justify the presumption that the legislator intended to abrogate the terms of the Koran on the subject.

Those Muslims who accept the above two sources of law as furnishing the basis upon which the faith and the ordinary conduct of life are to be regulated are called *ahl-as-sunna* — people of the *Sunna,* and consequently "*Sunnites*." The Muslims of the former Ottoman Empire, and consequently of Palestine where the Ottoman Civil Code is now applied, are *Sunnis.* (See page 14, Muhammadan Schools of Law.)

(c) *Ijma'*. Ijma is the consensus of opinion of the community of the believers: in other words, the manner in which Muslims have understood and practised the law as revealed to them. This is a source of law equal in value to a text of the *Koran* or of a *hadith*. This *ijma'* must be unanimous and uninterrupted.

Ijma' has three forms:

(a) *Ijma' ul qual* verbal consensus of opinion.
(b) *Ijma' ul f'ili* consensus of acts *i.e.* the acts which the believers of any school habitually perform.
(c) *Ijma' sukuti* or *Ijma' at-taqrir* tacit consent *i.e.* tacit approval of acts not contradicted by anyone.

12 MUHAMMADAN LAW

The doctrine of *Ijma'* is based upon various traditions of the Prophet who is reported in one of them to have said. "My community will never agree to what is wrong". According to Ibn Rushd, while the agreement of all Muslims is necessary to constitute *Ijma'*, a distinction must be made between two categories of *Ijma'* as follows:

(1) *Ijma'* relating to the elementary duties of all Muslims, such as ablution, prayer, fasting.

(2) *Ijma'* relating to rules of worship aud positive law *e.g.* matrimony, divorce, criminal law, which the faithful leave to the consensus of opinion of the doctors of Muhammadan law (*mujtahidun*). This authority belongs first to the companions (*sahaba*) of the Prophet and is called *Ijma-as-sahaba*. A tradition states: "My companions are like the stars. Whichever of them you follow you will find the right path." Another states: "My companions are to my community what salt is to food: without the salt, the food is worth nothing". After the companions, who had all passed away by the year *A.H.* 100, those who knew them, known as followers (*tabiun*), come next in authority.

Ijma' is most important in the historical development of Muhammadan law, and in doctrine it is a conclusive argument when it is a question of proving the existence of a law, of interpreting it, or of showing that it has been abrogated.

(d) *Qiyas* or deduction by analogy. This is a deductive process, not based on any theory of divine revelation, but of logical reasoning. In the absence of any rule applicable to special cases, the Court sought to ascertain the rule applicable to *similar* cases, and decided accordingly. This system has been attacked by certain Muslim jurists.

All the Sunni jurists agree that in all matters which have not been settled by the Koran, the traditions, or by consensus of opinion (*Ijma'*) the law may be deduced from what has been laid down by these three authorities by the means of *qiyas*, or deduction by analogy. Rules of law analogically deduced do not stand so high in authority as those laid down by a text of the Koran, or a tradition, or by consensus of opinion, the reason for this being that they rest upon the application of human intelligence. Several conditions must be satisfied for *qiyas* to be applicable. The five following are the most important.

(1) The law enunciated in the text to which analogy is sought to be applied must not have been intended to have been confined to a particular state of facts.

(2) The law of the text must not be such that the reason for its existence cannot be understood by human intelligence, nor must it be in the nature of an exception to a general rule.

(3) The rule deduced must not be opposed to a text of law already in existence. It must be in the nature of a corollary to the text.

(4) The deduction must not be such as to involve a change in the law embodied in the text.

(5) It must not be a deduction based merely on the general policy of the law.

A development of *qiyas* is *istihsan*, or equity. Where for any reason the law analogically deduced fails to commend itself to the jurist owing to its narrowness and unsuitability to the habits and usages of the people, the jurist is at liberty to refuse to adopt the law to which analogy points and to accept instead a rule which in his opinion will better serve the interests of men and of justice. *Istihsan* means considering a thing to be good, or juristic preference. An example of *istihsan* is to be found in the rules in the Civil Code relating to limitation of actions (see Articles 1660-1675)

(*e*) Custom—*Urf, ta'amul, adah*. A tradition states: "What appears good to the Muslims is also good in the sight of God". It is in virtue of this tradition that custom has been admitted as a source of law.

Custom is divided into:
    (1) *'urf 'am*—general custom.
    (2) *'urf khass*—special custom.

To be validly recognized, it must be proved that:—
    (1) The custom is recognized by jurists;
    (2) It is attested by persons worthy of credence;

(3) It is not at variance with the fundamental provisions of the *sharia*.

Custom is important as a source of law, and frequent references will be found to it in the Civil Code.

The whole of Muhammadan legislation is known collectively as the *sharia*, or divine legislation, and the Courts which administer it as the *Sharia* Courts.

Schools of Muhammadan Law.

We have now seen in briefest outline how the world of Islam came into being, and how a great system of law based on the supposed will of God was established by the adherents of the new religion, and have also seen that the sources of this system are all based on the Islamic religion. As time went on, the administration and study of the law inevitably fell into the hands of persons who devoted most of their time to the subject, and thus arose a class of professional jurists. It was not long before divergences of opinion on points of administration and interpretation began to manifest themselves, and this gave rise to the establishment of various schools of law. To understand how these schools came into being, reference must be made to the political expansion and internecine quarrels of the Muslims after the foundation of Islam by Muhammad. Upon the death of Muhammad, the prophet of God, the selection of his successor became a matter of first importance. Muhammad left no precise instructions on the point, and the first successor, — *Khalifa* — (Caliph) of Muhammad was one Abu Bakr, who in turn was followed by Omar, Othman and Ali. These four are known as the *Khulafa-ar-rashidun*, or rightly-minded Caliphs. Disputes too numerous and complicated to mention here arose among the Muslims concerning the fourth Caliph, Ali, which produced a complete breach in the world of Islam and divided it into two parts. Those who were in favour of Ali, became known as *Shiahs* or partisans, the bulk of Islam being known as *Sunnis*, a term used to denote those who are guided by the conduct and words (*Sunna*) of the prophet. This schism had its influence on law and Shiah Muhammadan law to-day differs on some essential points from Sunni Muhammadan law. It is with the latter that we are concerned in the Civil Code.

Some time after the establishment of Islam, the political centre of Islam shifted from Arabia to Syria and later to Baghdad, which became the seat of the Caliphate and under the relative tranquillity that prevailed, considerable progress was made in the arts and sciences. Attention was naturally paid to law and in the great *Sunni* branch, four separate schools of law came into being which are named after their founders, who are known as the four Imams. These are known respectively as the Hanifite, the Malikite, the Shafeite and the Hanbalite schools of law. The principles of these schools are substantially the same. They differ in points of detail only.

(1) The Hanifite school is the most important school of law and was founded by *Abul-Hanifa en-Numan ibn Thabit*, commonly known as the Imam Abu Hanifa who was born in 80 *A.H.* He relied more upon deduction and less upon traditions than other jurists. His chief work was the formulation of the theories and principles of Muhammadan jurisprudence. He drew attention to the importance of the doctrine of *qiyas*, or analogical deduction, and became the principal exponent of the doctrine of *istihsan* or equity, whereby the actual theory of law is modified in its application to actual facts when it would result in real hardship to apply the letter of the law. He recognized the authority of local customs and usages as guiding the application of laws. He is said to have set up a committee of forty of his followers to undertake the codification of laws. This took thirty years to complete, but the whole Code has been lost. Abu Yusif, his principal follower was Qadhi of Baghdad. Abu Hanifa was flogged for refusing the post of Qadhi of Baghdad and the Caliph Al-Mansur had him cast into prison, where he died. The adherents of the Hanifite school are to be found in parts of the former Ottoman Empire, India, Turkey, Afghanistan, and in large numbers in Egypt, Arabia and China.

(2) The founder of the Malikite school of law was the Imam *Malik ibn Anas* who was born at Medina in

MUHAMMADAN LAW

A.H. 95. Malik was the highest authority on tradition (*hadith*) in Northern Africa, and depended for his work largely on the traditions and usages of the Prophet. He was the author of the *al-Muwatta*, a collection of some 300 traditions.

(3) The founder of the Shafeite school of law was a pupil of Malik, by name *Muhammad Ibn Idris Ash-Shafi'i*, and attained greater experience as a jurist than his master. He took up a position mid-way between that of *Abu Hanifa* and *Malik ibn Anas* in the use of tradition and analogy, (*qiyas*). He wrote a treatise on jurisprudence.

(4) The founder of the Hanbalite school was *Abu Abdullah Ahmed Ibn Hanbal,* known as the Imam Hanbal. A pupil of *Ash-Shafi'i,* he was born at Baghdad in A. H. 164. He was a great traditionist and interpreted the traditions literally. He was the author of *Masnad-ul-Imam Hanbal,* a collection of some 50,000 traditions.

The result of the labours of the Muhammadan jurists as shown in treatises written by them is known by the technical name of *fiqh*. A jurist himself is known as a *faqih*.

CHAPTER II.

THE NATURE OF THE CIVIL CODE.

Reasons for the Compilation of the Mejelle.

The Ottoman Civil Code or Mejelle, as we have seen, was compiled by a Commission of Ottoman jurists sitting in Constantinople and published in parts called Books between the years 1867 and 1877, and for the most is itself little more than a translation from the Arabic authorities on Muhammadan law. Until the compilation of the Code, Muhammadan law had been scattered throughout treatises on the subject, almost all of which were written in Arabic and of varying authority, not always easily accessible, and sometimes not even comprehensible to Ottoman judges, whose native language was Turkish. (For a concise statement of the nature of Muhammadan law, see Chapter I). At the time the Drafting Commission began their labours, the Ottoman Empire was already in possession of a Commercial Code written in Turkish (translated and adapted from French) dealing with such matters as commercial companies, bills of exchange, and bankruptcy. In deciding commercial actions, however, the judges were frequently obliged to deal with such matters as the contract of sale, agency, pledges and similar matters, the law of which was hidden away in the Arabic treatises referred to above. Moreover, the Ottoman Government had undertaken a reorganization of the whole judicial system of the Empire, whereby the activities of the *Qadhis*, hitherto administering almost the whole of the law, were restricted to little more than matters of personal status. It was consequently necessary to place at the disposal of the new judges, trained on more or less modern lines, the Civil law arranged in the convenient form of a Code and written in Turkish. Thus the Code came into being. (See also the Report of the Commission appointed to draft the Mejelle; Vol. I, pp. 1-11).

18 NATURE OF CIVIL CODE

Subject matter of the Mejelle.

The Mejelle itself deals principally with the substantive law of that branch of Muhammadan law known as *muamelat*, or civil transactions. It is divided into Books, each Book dealing with a specific branch of law as follows: (1) Sale; (2) Hire; (3) Guarantee; (4) Transfer of Debt; (5) Pledges; (6) Trusts and Trusteeship; (by which is not meant the trusts of English law, but the law relating to property deposited for safe keeping and property lent for use); (7) Gift; (8) Wrongful Appropriation and destruction of property; (9) Interdiction, Constraint and Pre-emption; (10) Joint Ownership; (11) Agency; (12) Settlement and Release; (13) Admissions. There are also three books dealing with adjective law and comprise (14) Actions; (15) the law of evidence and administration of the oath; and (16) Administration of justice by the Court.

Each book is sub-divided into an Introduction, in which the relevant terms of Muhammadan jurisprudence are defined, and into Chapters dealing with specific portions of the subject, which in turn are divided into Sections. This arrangement of the subject matter is that generally followed in the corresponding portions of the treatises on Muhammadan Law (or *Fiqh* books). Prefixed to the whole are ninety-nine maxims of Muhammadan jurisprudence. (Compare the maxims of the English law of equity, and the maxims of Roman law). In the language of the Drafting Commission, "The preliminary study of these rules facilitates the comprehension of the questions and serves to fix them in the mind": (Vol. I, page 16).

The question as to whether the headings to the Chapters or Sections are to be considered as forming part of the law contained in the Mejelle was considered in the Cyprus case of *Raghib v. Gerasimo* (C.L.R., Vol. 3, p. 128) where the Court decided that:

"The headings of the Chapters in the Mejelle (whether they are to be considered as part of the Chapters or not) are indications of the contents of the Chapters and may be looked at with a view to their construction". (*Digest*, page 86).

The importance of the matter resides in the fact that it might be possible by a process of argument to attach a meaning to an isolated Article, which in the absence of any proof to the contrary, could not reasonably bear such a meaning in view of its being part of the specific portion of law dealt with by the Book, Chapter or Section.

Chapters 6 and 7 of Book 10 (Joint Ownership) dealing with partnerships have been replaced in Palestine by the Partnership Ordinance, 1930; and Chapter 6 of Book 16 (Arbitration) by the Arbitration Ordinance 1926.

Nature of examples to the Articles of the Mejelle.

A question which does not appear to have been the subject of judicial decision in either Palestine or Cyprus is that of whether the examples attached to many of the Articles are to be considered as parts of the particular Article itself and consequently as containing substantive law, or as illustrations merely of the principle contained in the Article itself. In certain cases it is clear that the example is nothing more than a mere illustration of the principle set forth in the Article. In other cases, however, (of which Article 1667, examples 2 and 3, and Article 1801, example 4, are cases in point,) the examples themselves, while illustrating the principle contained in the Article, also contain substantive law not specifically set forth elsewhere in the Code. The examples are usually taken from the *Mesail* or "questions" to be found in the *Fiqh* Books. The Drafting Commission, in its report (see Vol. I, page 6), stated that:

" In order to explain the fundamental points, however, a large number of questions have been added by way of illustration taken from the *fetwa* books"; the Commission defining *fetwa* books as being "those compilations which contain *fetwas* issued regarding the application of the rules of Muhammadan jurisprudence to any given set of facts". (Vol. I, page 4)

It therefore appears that the examples are principally merely illustrative of the law contained in the Article itself, but that occasionally they contain substantive law not to be found in the Code elsewhere. It would consequently appear that the correct view is that the examples must be looked at in the light of the Article they illust-

20 NATURE OF CIVIL CODE

rate. Where the example is obviously merely illustrative of the principle contained in the Article, any decision or judgment should be based on the Article; but where an example makes a definite statement of law supplementary to that contained in the Article itself, a decision or judgment could, it is submitted, be based on the law contained in the example. See the Palestine case of *Sheikh Mahmoud el Dajjani and another v. Shafiqah Abdur Rahman as Sadiq and others* (L.A. 38/30) where the Court, *semble*, relied on the second example to Article 1667 of the Mejelle. The following is from the text of the judgment:

"The ground of this appeal is that the Waqf is *moratab*, a Waqf for children "from generation to generation" within Article 1667 of the Mejelle and Article 142 of the Laws of Waqf edited by Omar Hilmi Effendi; that is to say, it is a Waqf in which descendants of the dedicator of one generation have no right to participate while any descendants of the preceding generation are still alive".

A further example is the case of *Saadat Kamel Hanum, Mutawalli of Ali Pasha Waqf v. the Governmeut of Palestine* (L.A. 70/32—see List of Palestine Decided Cases set out under Article 1667).

Sources.

The Mejelle, representing as it does, the Hanifite School of law (see Chapter I) is based upon the writings of the leading jurists (*Fuqaha*) of that school. The list given as an appendix at the end of this Chapter shows the principal works from which the Mejelle is extracted.

The most important of these works, as sources of the Mejelle, is the *Radd-al-Muhtar,* the *Durr-al-Mukhtar* and the *Majma-al-Anhur,* though this statement should not be taken as in any way derogating from the authority of the others.

In printing the works of Muslim jurists a curious habit has sprung up of including a separate and generally smaller work of some other jurist on the margin. Thus, on the margin of the edition of the *Majma-al-Anhur* printed by authority of the Ministry of Education in Constantinople dated 25th June, 1317, the *Badr-al-Muntaka,* being a commentary on the *Multaka-al-Abhur,* is set out.

NATURE OF CIVIL CODE 21

The *Majma-al-Anhur* is itself a commentary on the *Multaka-al-Abhur*. These works are usually given high-sounding titles such as "Confluence of the Seas" (*Multaka-al-Abhur*), this being a complimentary reference to the all-embracing nature of Muhammadan jurisprudence, since it is based on the will of God.

A knowledge of the sources of the Mejelle is of definite practical value in deciding questions upon which the Mejelle is silent, or ambiguous, or leaves room for more than one opinion. A reference to the terms of the report of the Commission appointed to draft the Mejelle (Vol. I, pp. 1—11) will show that Muslim jurists (*Fuqaha*), whose views are authoritative and upon which the Mejelle is based, differ on many points of law with which the Mejelle deals. These considerations bring up the broad question of the interpretation of the Mejelle. This question will be dealt with in detail in Chapter IV, but it may be stated here in general terms that in cases where the Drafting Commission have laid down the law in positive and unequivocal terms, there can be no room for interpretation as to the fundamental meaning of the text; but where the Mejelle is ambiguous, there is room for interpretation and where it is silent the law on the point may be ascertained by reference to the original authorities.

The Drafting Commission in their report (Vol. I. p. 9) referred to the Great Imam and the two Imams. The Great Imam is *Abu Hanifa*, and the two Imams are *Muhammad* and *Abu Yusif*, respectively. These persons were the founders of the *Hanifite* School of law and their opinions are considered to be authoritative.

The following is an extract from an authoritative handbook of Muhammadan law as applied in India:

"The primary authorities for the doctrines of the Hanafi school are the writings, or recorded opinions, of
 (1) Abu Hanifa (d. 767 A. D.), from whom the school derives its name,
 (2) Abu Yusuf (d. 798 A. D.), Chief *Kazi* under the Khalifa Haroun Ar-Rashid,
 (3) Imam Muhammad (d. 802 A. D.).

22 NATURE OF CIVIL CODE

The two last are commonly spoken of as "the two disciples".

The relative weight of these authorities in Anglo-Muhammadan law is unsettled, except that the opinion of Muhammad will in general be outweighed by that of either of the other two—Abu Hanifa's, because he was the founder of the School, and Abu Yusuf's because of the very important judicial office which he held.

But the scale may be turned in favour of any one of them by proof that his opinion was preferred by the compiler of some standard Digest, such as the Hedaya or the Fatawa Alamgiri, or the Court may adopt the view which in its opinion is most in accordance with justice in the particular circumstances of the case before it.

All the authorities referred to in the preceding section profess to base their opinions on (1) some text of the Koran directly in point, or (2) some duly authenticated tradition as to what the Prophet said or did, or (3) some evidence as to the unanimous opinion of the companions of the Prophet, or (4) some inference, by way of analogy or otherwise, from one or other of these primary sources. But for the purpose of ascertaining the proper rule for determining a civil suit in British India, the primary sources are of less weight than the secondary; in other words, the Courts have held themselves bound to accept the inferences drawn from the Koran and the traditions in the standard medieval text-books in preference to what might appear to the judges a more correct inference.

But again, these secondary medieval sources are of less weight (for the purpose aforesaid) than the practice of the Courts of British India. In other words, a judge is not at liberty to decide a point of law according to his own reading of a medieval Muhammadan treatise (the Hedaya, for instance) in opposition to a single decision of the Privy Council, or in opposition to a series of decisions of the High Court which he represents or to which he is subordinate." [1]

It should be borne in mind that these remarks are made with regard to the position of Muhammadan law in India, where the Courts were dealing largely with personal status law which has not been codified as in the case of the Mejelle; but the extract sets forth authoritatively the view taken by the Courts on the general question of interpretation where the texts are ambiguous or there is room for more than one opinion, and which,

---

[1] Wilson's Anglo-Muhammadan Law, 6th. Edition, 1930, by A. Yusuf Ali, page 89.

NATURE OF CIVIL CODE

it is submitted, apply in Palestine. (See the terms of Article 1801, Example 4).

As regards points where the Code is silent, it is submitted that it is the obvious duty of Courts to examine the sources in order to ascertain what the law is. The Drafting Commission, indeed, have stated in their Report: (Vol. I, p. 5) "We collected together those matters of Muhammadan jurisprudence which...... are of frequent occurrence and of the greatest necessity at the present day", from which it seems clear that the Code itself is not exhaustive. مرجع الطلاب

The Courts of Palestine have themselves on occasion gone behind the terms of the Mejelle and in the case of *Ibrahim Khoury Farah and another v. Dr. Yacoub Nazha* (L.A. 7/32) the Court referred to the *Majma-al-Anhur* for a definition of an imbecile:

"An imbecile is a person of slight comprehension, confused speech, and uncertain action, although he does not strike or insult persons as a lunatic does" (see Majma-al-Anhur, Vol. II, page 564, Chapter on Interdiction). The Mejelle contains a similar definition in Article 945 which provides:

"Ma'tuh is the person who is so deranged in mind that his understanding is small, his speech confused and his plan of action bad".

It further places such a person on the same level with infants and lunatics who are under a *natural* inhibition (Article 957), while as regards his actions, such a person is similar to an infant capable of transacting business (Article 978).

It may be thus concluded that an insane person (ma'tuh) is a person seized of a kind of lunacy devoid of violence."

In the case of the *Municipality of Haifa v. Dr. Caesar Khoury*, (C.A. 88/30), the Court held that:

"The Mejelle is a digest of opinion rather than a formulation of the law, the compilers thereof stating for the clearer understanding of the fundamental principles, "We have added many examples which have been taken from the ancient fetwas"; and the form the sections take is of enunciating a well established principle followed by one or more illustrative cases modifying or explaining the principle stated" (per Corrie, J.).

The question of reference to the sources of the Mejelle has also been the subject of judicial decision in Cyprus. In *Jassonides v Kyprioti* (C.L.R. Vol. VII, page 83) the Court held as follows:

NATURE OF CIVIL CODE

"The Mejelle was not intended to supersede the early authorities. The utterances of the Prophet, as recorded in the Koran and elsewhere and those of his earliest exponents the Imams, are still part of the law of Cyprus and the Articles of the Mejelle are to be construed in the light of those utterances" (per Bertram J.). (*Digest*, page 102).

In *Louka v. Nicola*, (C.L.R., Vol 5, page 82), the Court considered the authority of the *Hedaya*, and came to the following conclusion:—

"We are not sure how far the rules laid down in the Hedaya are binding in a case in which we have to administer Ottoman Law. The Hedaya or "guide" is a work which has long had a very high reputation in India, it consists of extracts from the most approved works of the early writers on Muhammadan Law, and was composed in the latter half of the 12th. century. It is referred to and its ruling on one point is mentioned with approval in the Report prefixed to the Mejelle. It follows mainly the doctrines of the Hanifa School, which the Ottoman Turks also follow. The version of it which we have is an English translation made by order of Warren Hastings, the Governor-General of Bengal. It has been a text book for the examination of the students who are seeking to be called to the English Bar with a view of practising in India. And we find that it is referred to in judgments of the Privy Council as an authority on Muhammadan Law." (*Digest*, p. 101).

In *Raghib v. Gerasimo*, (C.L.R. Vol. 3, page 124), the Court considered the authority of the *Miraat-al-Mejelle*, and held that it was:

"An Arabic work, which gives under each section of the Mejelle, the sources whence the law contained in the Mejelle is derived" (*Digest*, page 102)

In the same case the Court considered the *Multaka-al-Abhur* and held that it was:

"A collection in Arabic of the deductions from decisions given by Abu Hanifa". (*Digest*, page 102).

APPENDIX TO CHAPTER II.

LIST OF PRINCIPAL SOURCES OF THE MEJELLE.

Title of Work	Name of Author
(1) The Ankarawi	Muhammad ibn al Husain el Ankarawi
(2) The Ashbah wa an-Nazair (including the following Commentaries): (a) Commentary of Abdul Ghani (b) Commentary of Muhammad Effendi (c) Commentary of Piri Zada (d) Commentary Nuzhat an Nawazir (e) Commentary Zawaher al Jawahir	Sheikh Zain ibn Nujaim
(3) The Badaia	Ala Eddin Kasafi
(4) The Badaya	Ala Eddin (Melik al Ulama) Abu Bekr ibn Mesoud ibn Ahmad Samarkandi.
(5) The Bazazia	Hafiz Eddin Muhammad ibn Muhammad ibn Shehab (known as Ibn al Bazaz al Kurdi)
(6) The Durer-al-Hukam	Muhammad Ibn Qaramiz al Qadhi (known as Mulla Khosrau)
(7) The Durr-al-Mukhtar	Muhammad Ala Eddin al Haskafi
(8) The Fatawa Alamgiriya	Composed by a Committee of jurists by order of the Sultan Aurungzib
(9) The Fatawa Ali Effendi	Sheikh-Al-Islam Ali Effendi (known as Chataljali)
(10) The Fatawa Ibn Nujaim	Ibn Nujaim
(11) The Fath-ul-Qadir	Kemal Eddin Muhammad Abdul Wahid
(12) The Feiziya	Sheikh Feizi Effendi
(13) The Hashiyat-al-Ashbah	Ahmad ibn Muhammad al Hamawi
(14) The Hedaya	Burhan Eddin Ali Abu Bakr al-Marghinani
(15) The Hindiya (a name for the Fatawa Alamgiriya. See No. 8 above).	Composed by a Committee of jurists by order of the Sultan Aurungzib

SOURCES OF MEJELLE

Title of Work	Name of Author
(16) The Iddet Erbab al Fatawa	Abou Saoud
(17) The Inaya	Muhammad ibn Muhammad Mahmud
(18) The Jamia ar-Ramuz	Al-Kahastani
(19) The Jauhira	Abdul Ghani el-Maidani
(20) The Kanz	Abdul Barakat Abdullah ibn Ahmad ibn Mahmud al Nasafi
(20a) (Commentary on the Kanz, usually cited as al-Zilai)	Fakhr Eddin Osman ibn Ali al-Zilai
(21) The Kazikhan	Fakhr Eddin Hassan ibn Mansur al Ausjandi al Farghani
(22) The Khairiya	Khair al-Ramli
(23) The Khulasat al-Fatawa	Sheikh-al-Islam Tahır Ibn Abdul Rashid Bukhari
(24) The Kifaya	Imam Eddin Amir
(25) The Kulliat	Abu'l Baka
(26) The Mabsut	Shams-al-Aima Sarkhasi
(27) The Majamia	Al-Khadimi
(28) The Majma-al-Anhur	Abdullah al Rahman ibn al Sheikh Muhammad ibn Sulaiman (known as Daud Effendi)
(29) The Muin-al-Hukam	Ala Eddin Abul Hassan Ali ibn Khalil al-Tarablusi (Qadhi of Jerusalem)
(30) The Multaka-al-Abhur	Ibrahim ibn Muhammad ibn Ibrahim al-Halabi
(31) The Qaniya	Nejm Eddin Mukhtar ibn Mahmud al-Zahidi
(32)* The Radd-al-Muhtar	Muhammad Amin (known as Ibn Abidin)

* ("The *Radd-ul-Muhtar* is an extremely valuable and authoritative work on Mahommadan Law....It purports to be a commentary on the *Durr-ul-Mukhtar*, which again is a gloss on the *Tanwir-ul-Absar*. The texts quoted in the *Rad-ul-Muhtar* are chiefly from the latter, whose author is referred to as *the* author, whilst the author of the *Durr-ul-*

SOURCES OF MEJELLE 27

Title of Work	Name of Author
Mukhtar is referred to as the Commentator (*Sharih*). The *Radd* represents to a large extent the developed Hanafi principles. At the same time it must not be supposed that the doctrines it expounds are accepted in their entirety". (Syed Ameer Ali, Mahommedan Law, Vol. II, (fifth edition), page 249, Note 1.)	
(32a) Takmila Radd-al-Muhtar	
(33) The Tahtawi	Seyyed Ahmad al-Tahtawi
(34) The Tanwir-al-Absar	Shems Eddin Muhammad al-Ghuzi
(35) The Tatarkhaniyah	Alim ibn Alai
(36) The Tenqih	Muhammad Amim (known as Ibn Abidin)
(37) The Zakhira	Sheikh-al-Islam Muhammad ibn Hassan al-Bukhari

CHAPTER III.

ARTICLE 46 OF THE PALESTINE ORDER-IN-COUNCIL.

The terms of Article 46 of the Palestine Order-in-Council, 1922, are of considerable importance in determining the future development of the interpretation of the Code where, as is sometimes the case, the Code itself is silent, or ambiguous, or deficient on certain points with regard to which the substance of the common law, and the doctrines of equity in force in England make provision. The terms of Article 46 are as follows:—

"The jurisdiction of the Civil Courts shall be exercised in conformity with the Ottoman Law in force in Palestine on November 1st, 1914, and such later Ottoman Laws as have been or may be declared to be in force by Public Notice, and such Orders-in-Council, Ordinances and Regulations as are in force in Palestine at the date of the commencement of this Order, or may hereafter be applied or enacted; and subject thereto and so far as the same shall not extend or apply, shall be exercised in conformity with the substance of the common law, and the doctrines of equity in force in England, and with the powers vested in and according to the procedure and practice observed by or before Courts of Justice and Justices of the Peace in England, according to their respective jurisdictions and authorities at that date, save in so far as the said powers, procedure and practice may have been or may hereafter be modified, amended, or replaced by any other provisions. Provided always that the said common law and doctrines of equity shall be in force in Palestine so far only as the circumstances of Palestine and its inhabitants and the limits of His Majesty's jurisdiction permit and subject to such qualification as local circumstances render necessary."

An examination of this Article, which defines and determines the law to be applied in Palestine, shows that it deals with four main classes of legislation. These four classes of legislation are as follows:

(1) Ottoman Law;
(2) Orders-in-Council affecting Palestine and Palestine Ordinances and regulations;
(3) The substance of the common law and doctrines of equity in force in England;

(4) The Powers, Procedure and Practice of English Courts.

It will be convenient to deal with each of these four classes in detail.

(1) Ottoman Law:

(a) *Ottoman Law as it existed on and before the 1st. November, 1914.*

It is clear that the Ottoman Law brought into force in Palestine by the Order-in-Council is the whole corpus of the Ottoman Law as it stood on the 1st of November, 1914. The reason for this is not far to seek. This was the law actually in force in Palestine before the commencement of hostilities on the 1st. November, 1914, between the Allied Powers and Turkey, of which Palestine was then a part, and which continued to be applied, so far as the Courts functioned at all, during the period of hostilities. It is consequently desirable to study the nature and sources of Ottoman Law. It is not surprising to find a proviso of this type in the Article, since the inhabitants of Palestine understood and were used to the Ottoman Law and it would have been a matter of political unwisdom and practical impossibility for the Mandatory Power to draft and enforce a whole series of new laws and regulations.

As with other nations having a long history behind them, the history of the development of the legal system of the former Ottoman Empire is bound up indissolubly with the history of the development of the Empire itself. The Turks, it is well known, were originally virile and independent inhabitants of Central Asia whence from time to time they made incursions into such remote regions as China and Finland. One particular branch or tribe of the Turks, known later as the Ottomans, (or *Osmanlis*), in the course of one of these incursions, descended into a fertile and beautiful tract of territory in North Western Asia, now known as Anatolia. Here they found various groups of inhabitants, mostly Christians, who were rapidly subjugated and absorbed into the rough administrative system elaborated by the conqueror.

The Turkish conquerors had been converted to Islam before their invasion of Anatolia, but prior to that conversion, already had a loosely organised legal system of their own. Of the details of this system little is known, but the brief accounts of the Arab traveller *Ibn Batuta*, who visited Anatolia in the fifteenth century, show that the Ottomans had a system of law, administered by judges bearing not an Islamic, but a purely Turkish designation, that of *yarghouji*. A concurrent jurisdiction administered pure Islamic Law, known as *Sharia*, or that legislation which is based upon the will of God. (For a brief statement of the origin and sources of Muhammadan Law, see Chapter I). The Ottomans, therefore, upon their arrival in Anatolia, were in possession of two separate and distinct systems of law: the *Sharia* or pure Islamic law: the temporal system administered by the *yarghoujis* brought by the Ottomans from the steppes of Central Asia.

The Ottoman invaders, however, found and subjugated various Christian populations in Anatolia. These consisted of Greeks, Armenians and others, possessors of that famous Byzantine civilization and administrative ability which was to make them for centuries to come the controllers and guiders of the administrative machine of the Ottomans. Devoid of those great military qualities possessed in such striking measure by their masters, the Greeks combined surprising diplomatic ability with remarkable commercial and administrative gifts. These gifts the Ottomans were quick to perceive and to use for their own ends. Contrary to common belief, the Ottomans, as Muslims, have never shown religious fanaticism on an organized scale; and their toleration was displayed to a remarkable degree on the occasion of the final conquest of Anatolia, by their allowing their new subjects to maintain intact almost the whole of their institutions affecting their personal relations.

It is well known that in medieval times religion was the dominating factor in the family life of Christian communities. Matters affecting family relationships were settled by the priest, who had a special legal jurisdiction based on divine precept. The Ottomans allowed these jurisdictions to be maintained intact, and solemnly confirmed them from time to time by the issue of imperial edicts. Such communities were given the generic name of *millets*(¹) by the Ottomans. Thus, a system of religious law, administered in separate Courts, was allowed to survive in the newly founded Ottoman Empire; and this system was applied wherever Ottoman conquests extended.

While maintaining and confirming the special jurisdictions of the Christian communities, the Ottomans found other strangers, if not in their midst, at least at their gates, to whom they found it convenient and politic to grant privileges analogous to the rights confirmed in the case of their Christian subjects. These were the numerous traders of the Mediterranean seaboard who carried on a brisk commerce with Anatolia. Of their own free will, the Ottoman Sultans were pleased to grant to these foreign traders extensive privileges, which became known as Capitulations,(²) for the same spirit of toleration and laisser-faire which actuated the Ottomans in their relations with their Christian subjects animated them when dealing with foreigners in non-military matters. The Capitulations, so freely granted by the Ottomans to foreigners as concessions at the outset, were later used by the latter as precedents to obtain fresh concessions as of right.

Thus we find that the Ottomans, at the beginning of their domination of Anatolia and of certain parts of Europe, recognized three distinct systems of law: one

---

(¹) *Millet* literally means "nation". This designation seems to show that the Ottomans regarded their new subjects as independent in so far as their special religious non-Islamic position made such compatible with political submission. The Christian communities were in fact so many nations within a nation.

(²) The capitulations as between Turkey and the Allied Powers are now definitely and entirely abolished by the Treaty of Lausanne, dated the 24th. July, 1923, Article 28 of which reads as follows: "Each of the High Contracting Parties hereby accept, in so far as it is concerned, the complete abolition of the Capitulations in Turkey in every respect".

The capitulations in Palestine, however, are in suspense; but see the Palestine Decided Case of *Edelman v. Edelman*. (H. C. No. 31/26).

32 PALESTINE ORDER-IN-COUNCIL

based on the principles of Muhammadan law; the second a kind of common law administered by the *yarghoujis*, of the details of which we know little; and the third a *régime d'exception*, consisting of the law governing the personal status of the Christian communities of the Empire, and the legal privileges attaching to the Capitulatory régime. It is therefore a matter of small surprise that when the Ottoman Empire, expanding with such rapidity that the normal and inelastic procedure of Muhammadan legislation proved insufficient to meet the ever-growing needs of the State, the Sultans found it natural to legislate directly themselves. This they did by a series of laws and regulations known as *qanuns* and *nizams* (Turkish: *qanun* or *qanun-namé* — law; *nizam* or *nizam-namé* — regulation), to which they added a series of imperial rescripts known as *iradés* (Turkish: *iradé-i-seniyé*—imperial will). Thus a fourth system of law based on temporal legislation by the Ottoman Sultans made its appearance in the Empire.

With the first three elements the Ottoman legal system had proved sufficient to meet all the needs of the moment. Even after the failure of the Ottoman arms against Vienna, no change of any moment was made in the legal system. But a political change of the first importance took place. The European Powers, and particularly Russia, instead of fearing the redoubtable Ottoman, now began to cast covetous eyes upon the vast Empire he had brought under his sway. The eighteenth century saw the Sultans compelled to give way at all points: the nineteenth saw them practically at the mercy of Europe. And Europe insisted upon reforms being carried out which would assure what she called equality of treatment for the Christian subjects of the Porte. Turkey, in common with other countries of the Near East, had to some extent come under the influence of the intellectual currents radiated from France at the time of the French Revolution. Certain of her statesmen had been to France and had conceived a genuine admiration for the products of the French mind. It was therefore inevitable that when the European powers insisted with the Porte upon the necessity of new laws, Turkey, seeking to give what satisfaction she could, should turn to French legislative models. This process of borrowing from France was inaugurated for the first time on a large scale by the promulgation of a charter of reform in 1839 known as the *Khat-i-sherif* of *Gulkhané*, and consolidated in 1856 by the promulgation of another imperial edict known as the *Khat-i-humayoun*. These two documents, and the laws promulgated as a result of the promises contained therein, are known collectively as the *Tanzimat-i-Khairiyé*, or benevolent reforms. In drafting these new laws, the Turkish legislator—there was then no Parliament in Turkey, and consequently the Sultan was the supreme legislative power—thought that time and trouble could be saved by borrowing almost *en bloc* from France the principal legal codes of that country. It was at this time also that she codified the Muhammadan law relating to obligations into a Civil Code. Moreover, she borrowed large parts of the French legal system and French judicial methods almost without change, and this process continued almost without interruption down to 1914, when Turkey entered the World War as a belligerent on the side of the Central Powers.

It is therefore clear that, apart from the Muhammadan element, French influence reigned supreme in the old Ottoman legal system, and it is this system of law which has been taken over by the present mandated territories which were formerly parts of the Ottoman Empire. This influence is so strong that it is impossible to understand fully Ottoman legal principles without a study of French law.

Muhammadan law, however, still plays a *rôle* of first importance—it should be the only law in an ideal Muhammadan state—but in practice it is limited to the law governing civil transactions, (codified in the Civil Code), the law relating to the personal status of Muslims (marriage, divorce, alimony etc.), the land laws — adapted to suit the peculiar needs of the Ottoman Empire—and certain other laws to which allusion need not be made here.

Briefly, then, Ottoman law now consists of three large and entirely dissimilar elements:

(1) Muhammadan law which has survived in the Ottoman Empire;

(2) French law adopted by the Ottomans and adapted to their own needs;

(3) The personal law of the non-Muslim communities.

The classification of Ottoman law consequently follows that of France, subject to the incorporation of the Muhammadan element.

Legislative Forms.

Legislation in the former Ottoman Empire took place by means of the Sultan and Parliament which consisted of the Chamber of Deputies and the Senate.([1]) Ottoman legislation may be roughly divided into two categories:

(1) Legislation by the Sultan with the advice of the Council of Ministers prior to the introduction of the Constitution of 1876 (7 Zul Hijja, 1293).

(2) Legislation by the Sultan and Parliament after the introduction of the Constitution. The Constitution of 1876, however, was suspended by order of the Sultan a few months after its introduction and it was not until the restoration of the Constitution as a result of the Young Turk Revolution of 1908 that legislation by the Sultan and Parliament was reintroduced. Even so, Parliament sat at comparatively rare intervals between this date and the entry of the Ottoman Empire on the side of the Central Powers during the world war. The result is that Ottoman legislative forms are not of a uniform character and one of the principal results of this state of affairs is the existence of a number of enactments passed in the form of "decisions" or "regulations" which would normally have been a subject for legislation by Parliament. Laws sometimes modified Regulations and vice versa. For an example of a law modifying a Regulation, see Destur, 2nd. series, Vol. 4, page 421.

([1]) For the text of the Ottoman Constitution, see Destur, 1st. Series, Vol. 4, page 4, and principal amendments thereto, Destur, 2nd. Series, Vol. I, page 638.

PALESTINE ORDER-IN-COUNCIL 35

The following is a list of the principal legislative forms in use in the former Ottoman Empire:

Title of enactment	Principal Function
1. Law (*Qanun*)	To designate an enactment of importance which has been or would be submitted to Parliament.
2. Regulation (*Nizam*)	To implement the terms of a law.
3. Instructions (*taalimat*)	To regulate some matter of departmental importance.
4. Royal Irada (*Iradé-i-Senié*)	To express the royal will.
5. *Khat-i-Humayoun*	To express the royal will on some specially solemn occasion.
6. *Beyan-namé-i-Humayoun*	To give effect to a royal announcement where the prerogative was concerned.
7. *Firman-i-ali*	To bestow a concession or privilege.
8. *Berat-i-ali*	To confer an investiture or patent of office.
9. *Kararnamé*	A decision (of the Council of Ministers) having the force of law.
10. *Emrnamé*	To make known an order of the Sultan.

A peculiar feature of Ottoman legislation is the enactment of a considerable number of "provisional" laws, by which term was meant laws assented to by the Sultan while Parliament was not in session, and ordered by him to be added to the laws of the Empire, and acted upon until such time as they were submitted to the legislature for ratification. The following is a translation of the last Article of the provisional law of salvage:

"I order that this draft shall be put into force provisionally, and shall be added to the laws of the State; and Parliament, upon being opened, shall be asked to confirm it".

Provisional laws were signed in the ordinary way by the Sultan, and countersigned by the Ministers concerned. This exercise of the royal prerogative was of frequent occurrence in the Ottoman Empire, even after 1908, owing to the long intervals during which Parliament stood adjourned. There can be no doubt that until the law provisionally put into force and added to the corpus of laws of the Empire, was submitted to Parliament, any action taken in accordance with the terms thereof was considered by the Ottoman Courts to be strictly legal, and it is submitted that these laws, a list of the most important of which is set out at the end of this Chapter, are consequently part of the corpus of Ottoman legislation taken over under the terms of Article 46 of the Order-in-Council. A contrary view has been taken by the High Court in Palestine, however, which in the case of *George Ayub v. The Mayor of Beit Jala* (H. C. No. 71/31), dealt with an application to set aside an order issued under the terms of the provisional Ottoman Law relating to Primary Schools, when the following judgment was given:

"The Ottoman Law of Primary Schools of 23rd. September, 1329, was only a provisional law which never received Parliamentary approval in conformity with the Ottoman Law: and in consequence is not validated by Section 46 of the Palestine Order-in-Council, 1922.

The refusal of the licence by the Municipality according to the Mayor's letter of 18th. November, 1931, was therefore not based upon legal grounds and the Rule must be made absolute."

An interesting side-light is thrown upon the subject by the Cyprus case of *Koukoulli v. Hamid Bey* (C. L. R. Vol. VII, page 85, *Digest*, p. 102,) in which the Court came to the conclusion that all laws of general application appearing by the Destur to have been in force in the Ottoman Empire on the 13th. July, 1878, are presumed to have been in force in Cyprus on that date, unless the contrary is proved.

The bulk of Ottoman legislation is collected together in two series of volumes usually referred to by the technical name of *Destur* (compilation). The first consists of four volumes, and four supplements, together with an additional volume known as the *Mutemmim*, extending up to 1906. The second series consists of eleven volumes, extending up to the year 1920. They are not quite complete, however, and some enactments have only been published in the Ottoman Official Gazette, known as the *Tekvim-i-veqayi*.

Decided Cases.

A series of volumes containing Ottoman Court of Cassation decisions testify to the importance attached to these decisions in the former Ottoman Empire. Many of them, it is true, state the obvious, but some are of importance as being declaratory of the law and it is submitted that these decisions, to the extent that they are declaratory of the law, form part of the corpus of legislation taken over under the terms of Article 46 of the Order-in-Council.

It is convenient at this point to deal with the general question of the extent to which the Courts of Palestine consider themselves to be bound by previous decisions; and these decisions are of four categories: (1) Ottoman; (2) Cyprus; (3) Palestine; (4) English.

(1) *Ottoman decisions.* It has been submitted above that the decisions of the Ottoman Court of Cassation are binding on the Palestine Courts in so far as they are declaratory of the law in force. These are the decisions of the highest Court in the Ottoman Empire.

The Palestine Court of Appeal approved decisions of the Ottoman Court of Cassation in *Khadijeh Ismail Abu Khadra v. Amneh Khalil Abu Khadra* (C. A. 306/20); but in *Selim Khayat v. Mary Khayat* (Special Tribunal, 1923) the Court refused to be bound by an isolated decision of, *semble*, the Ottoman Court of Cassation:

"I am informed by the advocate of the petitioner that there is a decision of the Court of Cassation which goes so far as to declare that a decision of alimony has no further effect against a man who was married to a Christian, but has since become a Moslem. I do not consider myself bound to be guided by an isolated decision which purports to allow a person who has become liable under a judgment valid at the time it was made, to defeat that judgment by subsequently changing his religion."

(2) *Cyprus decisions.* The decisions of the Supreme Court of Cyprus are of undoubted value to the Palestine Courts, since in many branches of law, and notably in the case of the Mejelle and the Land Law, the Cyprus Courts have, over a number of years, applied the same law in

similar circumstances. The Palestine Court of Appeal has adopted this view, and in the cases of *Tewfik Effendi Ayoub v. Imperial Ottoman Bank,* (C. A. No. 319/22), has even gone further and, by implication, has felt itself to be bound by a Cyprus decision. See also the case of *Fatimah Hanem Fakhri Bey v. Sheikh Ass'ad Shuqairi* (L. A. No. 49/32).

(3) *Palestine decisions.* There is a marked tendency on the part of the Supreme Court of Palestine to be bound by its own previous decisions on the same point. In many cases the Court, without going into details as to the merits of the case in the judgment, has been content to cite a previous decision and to be bound by it. The following Palestine Decided Cases are examples of this type of judgment:

(1) "It has repeatedly been held by this Court that where a Defendant in such a case was unable to produce documentary evidence in support of his allegation, and such documentary evidence must necessarily be of a kind binding upon the other party, the only course open to the Defendant was to ask in accordance with Article 1589 of the Mejelle, that the Plaintiff should take an oath that the Defendant's admission in the document in question was not false. With regard to this contention, it is enough to say that this point was decided by this Court in the case of *Armenian Patriarchate v. Muhamed Taher Daoudi* C. A. No. 93/21." (*The Armenian Patriarchate v. Mubarak Jabrieh.* C. A. 393/21).

(2) "Apart from any authority expressly enabling the Magistrate to hear a particular form of action, jurisdiction must be held to lie with the District Court; and actions for *Muhaya* have been so heard since the date of the ordinance. (See the judgment of the Court of Appeal in *Khalil Nashashibi v. Rafat Mohamed Muzhar and others;* Civil Appeal No. 125/21 confirming with amendment a judgment of the District Court of Jerusalem.)" (*Sheikh Ibrahim Imam v. Selim Menahem Moshe Benin,* C. A. 52/22.)

(3) "And whereas the Court of Appeal is bound by its previous judgments in this respect, the judgment is therefore confirmed by a majority with costs." (*Abdul Salam 'Aweidah v. Banco di Roma* C. A. No. 84/22).

(4) "It has been held in several previous cases in this Court that the amendments to Articles 139 to 150 of the Ottoman Penal Code made by rules of Court dated 10th. December, 1918, are applicable on appeal to this Court" (*Saleh Muhammed Shible v. Assa'd Habib Hawa and Sons and others.* C. A. No. 129/22).

(5) "The facts of this case are up to a certain point identica with those in *Moyal v. Calmy*, C. A. No. 205/22. The difference between the two cases arises from the fact that the promissory note which is the subject of this action has been endorsed by Mme Calmy in favour of the respondent. In accordance with the judgment in *Moyal v. Calmy*, Mme Calmy could have obtained judgment on this promissory note had she not endorsed it." (*David Moyal v. Ovadie Salem*, C. A. No. 161/22).

(6) "Whereas this action arises out of a current account and is not based solely on the bills given in settlement thereof this Court, in accordance with its decision in the appeal of *Rahim v. Handal*, (Court of Appeal, Civil Appeal No. 129/23) holds that Article 146 of the Commercial Code does not apply and the Appellant's claim is not barred by lapse of time: it therefore sets aside the judgment of the District Court and remits the case for completion of the hearing." (*Habib Hanna Mikhail v. Jawallah Jiries Assife*. C. A. No. 146/23).

(7) "It has been held by the Court that when a person adjudged against desires to appeal without waiting for a copy of the judgment to be served upon him, he can do so, provided that he serves a copy of the judgment on the other party. It does not follow, however, that time begins to run against him from the date of service of such copy. The wording of Article 22 is clear. We hold that this appeal is not out of time." (*Jamileh Khanum Fityani v. 'Amer Ibn Mustafa 'Amer Mizfin*, C. A. No. 165/23).

(8) "Appeal dismissed with costs in accordance with the judgment of this Court in Civil Appeal No. 264/23". (*Elias Nadar v. The Attorney General* C. A. No. 41/24).

(9) "There was however no issue of fact to be decided, and the only point raised is a single question of law. In accordance with the Judgment of this Court in *Daoud Rahim v. Suleiman Handal*, Civil Appeal No. 129/23, we hold that the Respondent can sue on the admission of debt." (*Wadie Tamari v. Mr. Karamano*. C. A. No. 79/25).

(10) "If the Respondent applies for the proceedings to be cancelled, the effect of the judgment is merely to annul the proceedings in Court and in accordance with the judgment of this Court in L. A. 71/23 (*Nicola Ramadan and others v. Hanna el Khalil*), it is open to the Appellant to renew his appeal on payment of the prescribed fee within the period allowed for opposition; without it being necessary for him to lodge a fresh appeal or fresh pleadings". (*Leib Kahana v. Joseph Levi Hagis and others*. L. A. No. 121/25).

(11) "It has been decided by Judgments of the Court of Appeal that a Magistrate is a proper person to appoint with reference to the verification of handwriting and seals within the meaning of Article 97 of the Code of Civil Procedure where such

Article states that the Court shall appoint one of its own members to conduct the proceeding". (*Hanna Yusef Niameh v. Yusef, Nicola and Jubraeil sons of Elyas Niameh.* L. A. No. 137/25).

(12) "Following the judgment of this Court in Land Appeal No. 79 of 1926, the appeal is dismissed with costs". (*Nir Khanum Bint Kubar Zadeh etc. v. Michael ibn Francis Rahil,* L. A. No. 132/26).

(13) "It thus appears that while in a series of judgments the Court has refused to order the registration of a plaintiff whose claim was based solely upon ten years possession, no case has been cited in which such possession unsupported by evidence of title has been held to be sufficient ground for registration against the holder of a Kushan; and to hold this, would, in my opinion, be inconsistent with those judgments, especially that in *Ahmed Yusef Abu Hijla and others v. Darwish Hamed el Yusef and others,* which seems to me to be indistinguishable from the present case". (per Corrie J.)

(The following cases were considered in this case: L. A. 56/24; L.A. 137/23; L. A. 81/25; L.A. 113/26; L. A. 19/23; L. A. 93/26). (*Abdullah el Abd el Hafez and another v. Abdel Kader Khalil Salman.* L. A. 135/26).

(14) "The Appellant in his original action before the Land Court of Haifa applied, inter alia, that the Respondent be prevented from passing over a certain road. Respondent alleged that Appellant did not possess the road or alternatively that the Respondent had a right of way over the said road, thereby disclosing an action of title to a right of way. The Land Court dismissed the action on the grounds that the cause of action was not within their jurisdiction. However, by a decision of the Court of Appeal in Land Appeal No. 139/26 it was decided that Article 2 (D) of the Land Courts Ordinance 1921 must be construed to include "rights of way" and that therefore such claims are within the jurisdiction of the Land Courts". (*Tewfik Haddad v. Haj Hussein Bakeer.* L. A. No. 20/27).

(15) "In deciding this cause we are guided by the decision given by this Court in H. C. No. 43/27". (*Simon Hausman v. C.E.O. Jerusalem and another.* H. C. No. 60/27).

(16) "The Land Court, however, has given judgment for the respondent in reliance upon certain judgments of this Court and we have therefore to consider the effect of the judgments.

The first judgment relied upon by the Land Court is in *Mohammad and Yusef sons of Jibril Taha Jibril v. Taha and Khadra children of Abdel Fattah Taha Jibril,* Land Appeal 80/24 delivered on 29th. May, 1924. In that case certain of the heirs of Jibril Taha, the plaintiffs, proved that the land had in fact been held in partnership between Jibril and his brother Abdel

[Note: error in original numbering. Page 49 follows page 40 with no loss of information.]

Fattah, their ancestor, and the Court set aside sales as regards the shares to which the plaintiffs were entitled as heirs of Abdel Fattah. In that case, however, the purchasers being themselves heirs of Jibril could not be regarded as purchasers in good faith without notice of the plaintiffs rights; and the judgment is thus not authority for the present case.

The other judgment relied upon by the Land Court is that given in *Khadijeh Bint Sayed el-Masri and another v. Muhammed Sheikh Abdallah Idriss*, Land Appeal No. 31/24. delivered on 22nd. September, 1924, setting aside the judgment of the Land Court of Jaffa in action No. 102/22 delivered on 17th. February, 1926. In that case twelve out of twenty-four shares in certain land were registered in the name of Sheikh Abdallah Idriss, and on his death were transferred into the names of these three sons by whom they were sold to Said Abu Ghazalle. The plaintiffs, other heirs of Sheikh Abdallah, claimed to have the sale declared void as regards the shares to which they were entitled by inheritance. Their action was dismissed. On appeal, this Court allowed the plaintiffs' claim and declared the sale void as regards the plaintiffs' shares. In that case, however, the questions raised in the appeal were (a) Whether or not the plaintiffs' action was barred by time and (b) Whether or not the plaintiffs had knowledge of, and acquiesced in the sale. The defence that the purchaser had bought in good faith without knowledge of the plaintiffs' right, was not raised, and it may be inferred that such a plea could not have been sustained in view of the fact that Said Ghazalle, the purchaser, was owner of other twelve out of twenty four shares in the land in co-ownership with Sheikh Abdallah. The decision in that case therefore does not govern the present case, where the purchaser has bought in good faith without notice of any right vested in the respondents. The appeal must therefore be allowed, the judgment of the Land Court set aside and the respondent's action dismissed with costs here and below". (*Shlomo Friedman v. Badi'a bint Abdul Nur.* L. A. No. 96/27).

(17) "The offer of Appellant (Plaintiff) to take the oath now on appeal is of no avail, as it has already been held by this Court that it is only when a party in the Court below has specifically reserved his right to take the oath on appeal that he may do so. This was not the case in the present action". (*Andrawes Eid v. Kustandi Hanna Habayeb and others* C. A. No. 16/28).

(18) "The question before the Court has on previous occasions been decided by the Court of Appeal, the Court having decided that evidence may be heard as to the authority of one person to sign the name of another to a sanad". (*Ahmed Muhammad el Habashi v. Tewfik el Haj Omar.* C. A. No. 49/28).

(19) "The judgment of February 20th. 1925 remitted the case for proof of the fact that the date of death of I. J. Lewis preceded the date on which his wife was naturalised, and laid it

down that if it were proved to be so, this case would be governed by the decision in *Habbas v. Sheinfinkel.* The District Court after hearing evidence found as a fact that Lewis did die at a date earlier than that on which his widow acquired Ottoman nationality. Since the date of the decision of 20th. February, 1925, in this Court, the Court has had before it the case of *Raskowsky v. Raskowsky* with reference to the naturalisation of a French subject during the war under the same Ottoman Law. It has been argued that the judgment in that case is binding on the Court in this case. All we need to say as to that, is that in Raskowsky's case a distinction was to be drawn, on the facts, between it and *Habbas and Sheinfinkel.* In this case the Court of Appeal has held that Habbas and Sheinfinkel governs the facts and there is no more to be said for that argument". (*Henry Robinson v. Yeshayahu Press and others.* C. A. No. 62/28).

(20) "The question has been decided by the decision in Appeal No. 306 of 1920, the Court giving judgment "that an allegation of a false admission cannot be heard as against admission made before the Land Registrar". (*Jamileh Bint Muhammad Sarhan v. Ibrahim Muhammad Faraj el Husseini.* C. A. No. 78/28).

(21) "This Court has held in the case of *Joseph Rokach and others v. Sudki Ragheb and others*, (Civil Appeal No. 22 of 1927) that where a contract contains a stipulation that there shall be no necessity for Notarial protest, the fact that the wording of the contract differs from that of Article 107 of the Code of Civil Procedure does not necessarily make the stipulation inoperative". (*Nicola Elias Nasr v. Haim Brakha and others.* C. A. No. 115/28).

(22) "Following the judgment of this Court in *Lubin v. Wilson*, Civil Appeal No. 219/26, the Court holds that the words "judgment in presence appealable", do not constitute an exercise by the District Court of its discretion under Section 15 (2) of the Arbitration Ordinance, 1926, as amended by the Arbitration Amendment Ordinance, 1928, Section 3". (*Abdul Kader Haj v. Mohammad Eff. el Haj.* C. A. No. 122/28).

(23) "By virtue of a decision of this Court, H. C. No. 84 of 1927, dated 31st. January, 1928, in the case of *Abdallah Ahmed Jaballi v. The C. E. O. Jaffa and Solomon Jacobson* it was ordered that upon the sale of land by an execution office where there is a dispute as to the estimated value of the property offered for sale an inspection must be made by three persons, one appointed by each party, *i. e.* the judgment creditor and the judgment debtor, and one by the Chief Execution Officer, the last of whom shall draw up a report of their proceedings and of their opinion for the information of the Chief Execution Officer. Therefore the above mentioned procedure must now be carried out with regard to the valuation of the property subsequent to such valuation

having been made". (*Abdel Halim Skairik v. C. E. O. Haifa.* H. C. No. 70/29).

(24) "The Appellant relies on the decision of this Court in *Tawfiq Ayoub v. Issa Hazboun*, Civil Appeal No. 60/29. In that case also the fees were paid on the last date for appeal, a Friday, and the Cash Registers were not open. The Chief Clerk, however, was in the office and received the fees. The Court held that the appeal was made within the legal period. In the present case, however, there is one important distinction to be noted. Not only were the Cash Registers closed, but there was no one in the office who had authority to receive payment of fees. So far as payment of fees was concerned the office was closed on the 31st. January, 1930; and hence the rule laid down in *Ibrahim Hakki el Taji v. Ali el Nakib*, Civil Appeal 254/23, applies, and the appeal is not made within time". (*Sheikh Abdul Kader el Muzaffar v. Abdul Hamid Dirhalli.* C. A. No. 15/30).

(25) "The appeal having been made to the wrong Court, and no correction having been made until after the time for appeal had expired, the Court holds, in accordance with the principle laid down in Land Appeal No. 38/29, *Shlank v. Greenberg and others*, that it is not properly seised of the Appeal". (*Dov Zachs and Son v. The Northern Insurance Co. Ltd.*, C. A. No. 42/30).

(26) "The Land Court, when giving judgment on title to land, may make the order dependent upon the fulfilment by the successful party of a condition; which may be the re-payment of money received in respect of the land. And in *Spiro Jirius Zakharia and another v. Ali Haj Hassan el Matari and others* (Land Appeal No. 175/23), this Court held that where the Land Court declared a sale to be invalid the order for retransfer of the land ought to be made conditional upon repayment of the purchase money. But that is a totally different matter from a claim for repayment of purchase money made independently of any question of title". (*Salim Iiryes Haddad v. Fuad Muhammad Said Tahbub* L. A. No. 55/30).

(27) *Municipality of Haifa v. Dr. Caesar Khoury.* (C. A. No. 88/30). In this case the Court refused to be guided by a former decision on the same point in *Rosenberg v. Zeidan* (C. A. No. 2/27).

(28) "The Registration of Land Ordinance, 1929, was not in force when the Settlement Officer heard this claim; therefore the Settlement Officer was not bound to hear witnesses whom deceased Respondent (who claimed by possession) desired to call: which Section 2 of the said Ordinance provides for. This principle has been clearly settled in Land Appeal No. 2/31. We hold, therefore, that the Settlement Officer was right in refusing to hear witnesses whom the deceased Respondent desired to call". (*Khalil Mustafa Khalil el 'Isweid and others v. The heirs of Haj Muhammad Ahmed al Dajani.* L. A. No. 1/31).

(29) "The judgment under appeal was given by the Land Court of Nablus in accordance with the judgment of the High Court in *Saleh Ibrahim Ofi and others v. Chief Execution Officer, Nablus, and others.* H. C. No. 25/30. The Appellant argues that decisions of the High Court do not bind the Land Court or the Court of Appeal. This is a view that cannot be accepted. The judgments of the Supreme Court sitting as a High Court of Justice bind the Supreme Court sitting as a Court of Appeal and all inferior Courts." (*Ibrahim Rehayem el Oufi v. Keren Kayemeth Le-Israel.* L. A. No. 22/31).

(30) "With regard to the plea that deceased was of unsound mind when he signed the said documents, the District Court decided that this was a contradictory plea and was inadmissible in law having regard to Article 1610 of the Mejelle and the decision in Civil Appeal No. 93/25 and heard no evidence in support of the contention: nevertheless the Court did say in their judgment "the allegation of insanity is not supported by any reliable evidence." (*Muhammad Sa'adat Dajani v. Ali Mustakim.* C. A. No. 42/31.)

(31) "The petitioner relies on the order made by this Court in *ex-parte Abd es Salam Awaida.* (H. C. No. 52/27). In that case the order of the Chief Execution Officer for the registration of immovable property in the name of a purchaser at a sale by the Execution Office was set aside upon a petition filed after registration in the name of the purchaser had actually been effected. It is, however, to be noted that in that case the ground of the petition was that Article 91 of the Law of Execution does not allow the sale of immovable properties the annual income of which is sufficient to pay the debt: and that the annual income of the properties sold exceeded the balance of the debt remaining due; so that the Chief Execution Officer had not jurisdiction to order the registration: and that an application to that effect had been presented to the Chief Execution Officer before the order for registration was made. From that petition the present case is distinguishable by the fact that the petition is not based on an alleged excess of jurisdiction by the Chief Execution Officer, but upon a claim that the Improvement Tax in respect of which execution was levied was imposed by the Local Council illegally.

"Further, there seems to be no ground for distinguishing this case from *ex parte Said Darwish and others* (High Court No. 17/25) in which a petition for an order restraining the District Officer, Jerusalem, from taking the land of the petitioners for the construction of a public road was dismissed on the ground: — "that the application should have been brought when the land was taken for the road and not after the road was made." (*Mrs. Rose Blum v. Chief Execution Officer, Jaffa and another.* H. C. No. 50/31).

(32) "In view of the authority of High Court No. 51/30,

there having been a stipulation as to payment of interest in this case, we make the Order absolute." (*Jacob Gesundheit v. C. E. O. and others.* H. C. No. 13/32).

(33) "Following the judgments in Civil Appeal No. 78/28, Civil Appeal No. 306/20, and Land Appeal No. 137/20, wherein it was decided that a person once having made an admission before the Land Registry in a land transaction, the person making the admission cannot subsequently set up the defence that such an admission was a false admission and request the oath to be taken by the person in whose favour the admission was made, neither can an allegation of a false admission be heard as against admissions made before the Land Registry." (*Ibrahim Abu Habib v. Said Mahmoud Yasin and others.* L. A. No. 20/32).

(34) "The first day's hearing of this case was taken in the Court below by their Honours Judges Daoudi and Mani. The subsequent hearings of this case were taken by Judges Izzat and Said Toukan. In accordance with the decision of this Court in Civil Appeal No. 21/31 —*Fast v. Ounie Abdel Hadi,*— the judgment of the lower Court must be set aside and the case remitted to the District Court for re-hearing and for judgment to be given accordingly." (*Dimitri Calaris v. Su'ad Abu Khadra and others.* C. A. No. 28/32).

(35) "On the authority of Civil Appeal No. 72/31 the appeal is dismissed." (*Frizah Bint Haj Assad Malfuf etc. v. Halimeh bint Haj Abdullah Nashef.* C. A. No. 29/32).

(36) "I am aware that under Article 1663 of the Mejelle it is arguable that the time during which a Plaintiff was "a long way off" (*Muddet Safar*) does not count in estimating the period, within which a Plaintiff is required to bring his action and that Article 1664 defines *Muddet Safar* as a distance of three day's journey or eighteen hours at a moderate rate of travelling; also that the Cyprus Courts have held that residence in a foreign country was not absence on a journey (*Muddet Safar*) for the purpose of prescription — see *Mehmet v. Kosmo* — C. L. R. I. 12. This Court, however, in the case of *Estrangin v. Tyan* (Official Gazette 16th. September, 1926), has held that where the Defendant was living in a foreign country such absence was a cause for suspension of the running of the period of prescription, even though the person against whom the plea was put forward had a duly authorized agent in Palestine and that actual presence in Palestine of the Plaintiff during the whole period was required if the period was to run against him. In accordance with the above decision the judgment of the lower Court must be quashed and the case remitted to enable the Appellant to produce evidence as to the dates he was absent from and his return to Palestine, and to give a fresh judgment following the law laid down in the above— quoted case." (*Fatimah Hanem Fakhri Bey v. Sheikh Ass'ad Shuqairi.* L. A. No. 49/32).

(37) "In accordance with the judgment of this Court in *Adib el Zaban and another v. Meir Shlomo Altshuler* (C. A. No. 54/29), the Court holds that where a Plaintiff claims that he has been charged interest at a rate in excess of that allowed by Law, he cannot avail himself of the provisions of the Usurious Loans (Evidence) Ordinance, 1922, which is restricted to the case of a plea by a Defendant." (*Shamuel Slonim v. Musleh Abdel Latif el Izzah.* C. A. No. 54/32).

(38) "In accordance with the decision of the Supreme Court in Civil Appeal 98/27, the appeal is allowed and the judgment of the District Court is set aside and the case is remitted to the District Court for completion." (*Joshua Khankin v. Qasem Muhammad Mustafa.* C. A. Nos. 58-59/32).

(39) "The Jaffa District Court in a civil case between Fritz Bergman and present Appellants, when the same issue was raised, awarded judgment to Plaintiff, for a sum therein mentioned to be paid in Palestine currency, at the rate of exchange prevailing on the day of payment, and the judgment, on appeal, was upheld. (See *Ahmad Abu Laban and Sons,* Civil Appeal No. 39/32). There is nothing in the present appeal at variance with the facts upon which the before-mentioned appellate judgment was based, or to distinguish it therefrom. Accordingly, the appeal must be allowed." (*Ahmad Hassan Abu Laban and Sons v. Lieder and Fischer.* C. A. No. 85/32).

(40) "This lease was never registered or in the words of the law (Transfer of Land Ordinance, 1920, Section 9) the consent of Government was never obtained to it, and is therefore governed by Civil Appeal No. 68/29." (per Frumkin J.) (*Mrs. Fanny Cornue v. Ali Ahmed Sheikh Ali and others.* C. A. No. 105/32).

(41) "Now, the Law of Evidence Amendment Ordinance, 1924, Section 12, enables either party to give evidence on his own behalf or be summoned to give evidence for the other party; and this Court has previously decided that such evidence may be called by Defendant even in the case where a written document within the meaning of Section 80 of the Civil Procedure Code is the subject matter of the action. See Civil Appeal No. 77/32." (per Baker J.) (*Muhammad Shaker Husseini v. Menahem Hurvitz and others.* C. A. No. 106/32).

(42) "While if the question of the validity of the agreement dated 16th. January, 1931, were left to this Court for determination, we should undoubtedly hold that it was valid as an agreement for sale, which is not a disposition of land within the meaning of Section 2 of the Transfer of Land Ordinance, 1920, we are bound to follow the judgment of this Court in *Kamal Abu Jaafar and another v. Rajab Mustafa Bitar and another* (C. A. No. 95/31) in which the agreement was held to be void". (*Rashid Abu Jaafar v. Rajab Mustafa Bitar and another.* C. A. No. 130/32.)

(43) "The Appellants then applied to amend their statement of claim and to sue the Respondents in a personal capacity. They rely upon the judgment of this Court in *Ibrahim el Budairi v. Muhammad Hassan Budairi,* C. A. No. 144/32. In that case, however, the claim was framed against the Defendant in a personal capacity, and not as *mutawalli,* and the Plaintiff was thus entitled to continue his action although the Defendant had ceased to be *mutawalli* of the *waqf* from which the sum claimed arose; the Plaintiff alleging that the Defendant had retained in his own hands the amount claimed. The present case is clearly distinguishable, and the Appellants, having sued the Respondents as *mutawallis,* are not now entitled to amend their claim so as to continue the action against the Respondent in their personal capacity." (*Suleiman Musa Darwish Salahi and others v. Rida Salahi and others.* C. A. No. 136/32).

(44) "There is nothing in the Commercial Code which prevents the Court from fixing the date of cessation of payments by judgment given after the order of adjudication. Under Article 151, the date may be fixed by the Court of its own motion: and it is clear that this power is not removed from the Court by the fact of a Report having been made to it by the Judge Commissaire. The date when the bankrupt ceased to pay his debts is a question of fact. All the facts were before the District Court and it is not suggested that there was not evidence before them upon which they could make their finding. In accordance, therefore, with the judgment of this Court in C. A. No. 69/32, *Banco di Roma v. Muhammad Ali Tamimi and others,* the appeal must be dismissed." (*The Anglo-Palestine Bank, Ltd. v. The Syndic of the Bankruptcy of George Barsky.* C. A. No. 179/32).

(45) "We are also of opinion that, inasmuch as Respondents have been registered as owners in the Land Registry, we are bound by the decision in High Court No. 74/32, the facts of which were very similar and which laid down that the Court had no jurisdiction to set aside a registration of ownership in the Land Registry, it being a cause or matter in accordance with Article 43 of the Palestine Order-in-Council 1922, in which the Land Court has jurisdiction". (*Fahmi el Husseini v. C. E. O. Jaffa and another.* H. C. No. 3/33).

(46) "We hold that it was not within the competence of the learned judges thus to interpret the expression used by them in their judgment; and further that in view of the judgment of this Court in *Lubin v. Wilson* C. A. 219/26, the words "subject to appeal" cannot be interpreted to mean that the Court has exercised the discretion which a grant of leave to appeal under Section 15 (2) of the Arbitration Ordinance, 1926, implies." (*Savronsky v. Trachtenberg.* C. A. No. 38/33).

(4) *English decisions.* It will be seen later that Article 46 of the Order-in-Council incorporates a certain amount

of English Law into Palestine and it seems almost obvious that English case law must be incorporated with it, and that the Courts will be bound by precedent to the same extent as the English Courts, subject, however, it is submitted, to the dates mentioned in the Article. English case law, based on the common law, is in fact part of the common law itself. The case is slightly different as regards Palestine legislation based on English law and legal principles, but which can nevertheless be claimed as purely local legislation. It is submitted in this case that English case law, even if it cannot be held to be binding on the Courts, at least plays a *role* of first importance in helping and guiding the Court to a right conclusion. The High Court of Palestine itself—by implication—appears to have come to this conclusion in the Palestine Decided Cases of *Mordekhai Eliash v. Director of Lands*, (H. C. No. 77/31), and *Alpert v. Chief Execution Officer* (Special Tribunal No. 1/28; see also H. C. No. 49/32), and cases are frequently cited from the English Law Reports in judgments of the Palestine Courts, of which the case of *Zeev Hazine v. N. V. Algemine Yzer Stalmaashappy "Forrostaal" Haag* (C. A. No. 36/28) is an example.

In Cyprus, where English law and legal principles have to a certain extent applied, the following decisions show the view adopted by the Courts.

(1) "These decisions of the Courts in England are decisions on the meaning to be placed upon the general principle, and the fact that they are decisions of Courts of Law in England does not disentitle us from taking the same view of the same general principles as the many learned judges in England have done in the cases we have cited." (*Queen's Advocate v. Van Milligan*, C. L. R., Vol. 3, p. 211, Digest, p. 37).

(2) "We can find nothing in the Ottoman Law to serve as a guide in this matter; and we think, therefore, that we may rightly adopt the principle acted upon in such cases by the English Courts." *Karageordiades v. Haji Pavlo and Sons*, C. L. R. Vol. 5, p. 39, Digest, p. 37).

(3) "Where no Ottoman or Cypriote legislative authority exists the Court will avail itself of the principles acted on in the English Courts." (*Joachim v. Haji Christofi and another*, C. L. R. Vol. 5, p. 77, Digest, p. 37).

(4) "The Court will consider English decisions on points of practice but is not bound by them." (*Raghib v. Gerasimo, Abbot of Kykko*. C. L. R. Vol. 3, p. 110, Digest, p. 37).

(5) "Clause 153 of the Cyprus Courts of Justice Order, 1882, enabling an accused person to plead that he has been previously acquitted or convicted, as the case may be, of the same offence, was no doubt framed with regard to the English practice and principles regulating the matter; as, so far as we are aware, nothing is to be found in the Ottoman Law in force in Cyprus touching the question. The decisions of the English Courts, though not binding upon us here, are of great value as decisions upon the same state of facts." (*R. v. Yallouri,* C. L. R. Vol. 3, p. 41, Digest, p. 37).

(6) "The Order in Council is to a great extent based on English practice, and in seeking to determine what was the intention of the enacting power, where it is not clearly expressed, we are of opinion that regard should be had to the rules in force in England in regard to the matter in question." (*R. v. Theori,* C. L. R. Vol. 6. p. 14, Digest, p. 37).

(7) "Semble, in determining the obligations of a person, who in English Law is in the position of a trustee, the Court will apply the principles of the English law of trusts." (*Theophilou v. Abraam,* C. L. R. Vol. 3, p. 236, Digest, p. 37).

(b) *Ottoman Laws subsequent in date to 1st November, 1914.*

The Article makes it a condition that for any such laws to be in force a public notice must be issued declaring them to be in force. This public notice, if published, would appear in the Palestine Gazette. In *K. Friedenberg v. the Municipality of Jerusalem* (C. A. No. 212/31, District Court, Jerusalem), the following judgment was given:

"The Municipal Tax Law of 26th. February, 1330, came into force after November 1st. 1914, and has never been declared by Public Notice to be in force in Palestine.

Therefore in accordance with the provisions of Article 46 of the Palestine Order-in-Council, 1922, the Tax cannot legally be collected.

The judgment of the Magistrate is set aside and judgment for the Plaintiff (Appellant) must be entered with costs in this Court and in the Court below."

Article 46 is silent as to the last date within which such later Ottoman Laws are comprised. Upon reference to Articles 58 and 59 of the Organic Law of Transjordan, where similar provision is made, steps have been taken to fix the two dates, which are the 1st. of November, 1914, (Article 58) and the 23rd. September, 1918, (Article 59). It is understood that the latter date marks the effective occupation of Trans-Jordan by the occupying Forces of the

58 PALESTINE ORDER-IN-COUNCIL

Allies and the effective cessation of all Ottoman authority, whether actual or expressed by means of legislative enactments. It therefore seems reasonable, in view of the silence of Article 46 of the Palestine Order-in-Council, to assume that the category of Ottoman Law which may be declared by public notice to be in force in Palestine ceases at the date when Ottoman authority as referred to above ceased to be effective. This, it is submitted, is a point which must be decided by the Government of Palestine. Reference, however, should be made to the terms of Article 73 of the Order-in-Council.

The reason why the Article gives power to the Government of Palestine to accept or reject any Ottoman Legislation subsequent in date to the 1st. November, 1914, appears to be that certain of these Ottoman enactments represent legislation which was already in force and presumably acceptable to the people. These can be taken over by the mere publication of a notice, thus saving the Palestine Government the necessity of passing fresh enactments. It also gives power to reject certain Ottoman enactments which were aimed at and intended to be prejudicial and were in fact inimical to the Allied Powers.

A point arises here which requires careful examination. The Article refers to "such later Ottoman Laws" subsequent in date to the 1st. of November, 1914, as distinct from "the Ottoman Law" in force on and before the 1st. of November, 1914. This seems, on a strictly literal interpretation, to refer to those Ottoman enactments to which the name law (*qanun*) was given and to exclude Regulations (*nizams*), Instructions (*taalimat*) and Decisions (*qararat*) etc. It is submitted, however, from the internal evidence contained in the Article itself, that this was not the intention, and that the use of the word "laws" is a drafting error and that "law" was intended, *i. e.* the whole corpus of Ottoman legislative enactments of whatever nature and called by whatever name. The reasons for this view are the following: —

(1) The Article itself refers to "the Ottoman Law" in force in Palestine on the 1st. of November, 1914. This clearly refers to the whole body of Ottoman legislative

enactments as mentioned above. This being the case, it is not reasonable to suppose that the draftsman of the Article would have singled out only Ottoman laws later in date than the 1st. of November, 1914, and rejected all legislative enactments not bearing the title "law" *(qanun)*. In support of this view, reference may be made to the terms of Article 52 of the Order-in-Council. Here we find a reference to "the law of procedure of the Moslem Religious Courts of the 25th October, 1333 A. H." Upon a reference to the Turkish text of this enactment (rightly styled a law by the draftsman of the Article, since it deals with a matter which, if a Legislative Assembly existed, should be submitted to that body), we find that it is in fact called a "decision" *(qarar)*. This enactment is to be found in the *Destur* (second series) Vol. 9, page 783. A further proof in support of this submission is the Ottoman Family Law Ordinance, 1919 (See Bentwich, Vol. I, page 58). This Ordinance provides that the provisions of the "Ottoman Family Law of the 25th. October, 1333" shall be applied in the Moslem Religious Courts in Palestine. This Ottoman enactment is not, however, a law, but is in fact also called a "decision" *(qarar)*. The Turkish text of this enactment which, has all the attributes of a law, is to be found in the *Destur* (Second Series) Vol. 9, page 762.

(2) The Article itself goes on to declare Orders-in-Council, Ordinances and Regulations to be in force. These are Palestine enactments, it is true, but it does not seem reasonable to suppose that the draftsman of the Article would have been at pains to refer specifically to Palestine Regulations and exclude Ottoman Regulations. Moreover, it is submitted that, in general, the normal function of Regulations and Instructions is to implement the terms of laws passed by the Legislature. It would appear unreasonable to suppose that the draftsman of the Article was admitting the adoption of laws, and rejecting Regulations and instructions which may prove essential for implementing the terms of an Ottoman law taken over under the terms of the Article.

Allusion is made here to a point upon which the Article is silent, but which appears to be of importance. It is clear that owing to the altered circumstances of Palestine, brought about by the change of administration since the war, many of the terms of Ottoman Laws cannot be applied, since the altered circumstances do not allow of their application, or if they were applied, would at once come into conflict with the terms of some other enactment passed by the Palestine Government. An interesting Palestine Decided Case in this connection is *L. Gluckmann v. The District Court of Jaffa.* (C. A. No. 52/28) where the Court gave the following judgment:

"The Ottoman Stamp Law of 1906 did not provide for an appeal from judgments of Courts of First Instance in questions relating to fines, imposed under Section 60 of the said law, the only provision was an appeal to the Court of Cassation at Constantinople. The appeal must therefore be dismissed for lack of jurisdiction."

Article 58 of the Transjordan Organic Law and Article 113 of the Iraq Organic Law, which were designed to meet exactly similar circumstances as those dealt with by Article 46 of the Palestine Order-in-Council, both contain a provision to the effect that Ottoman laws taken over by the Transjordan and Iraq Governments respectively shall only remain in force "so far as circumstances permit". At the end of Article 46 of the Palestine Order-in-Council a provision is made of this nature, but it is restricted to "the said Common Law and Doctrines of Equity". It is true that another matter besides Ottoman Law is dealt with in the Article, namely English practice and procedure, which have also been excepted from the terms of the proviso at the end of the Article, and this gives cause for some hesitation in the submission which is now made that the failure to include Ottoman law in the proviso arose either from an oversight or from the fact that the matter was taken for granted. It may be that the intention of the draftsman of the Article was that English Practice and Procedure should only be modified by express enactment; but even here there are several points in direct conflict with Ottoman Practice and Procedure as contained in the Ottoman law taken over and prior in date to the 1st. of November, 1914. In spite of this double omission, however, it is submitted that any interpretation other than one which admits that the intention was that Ottoman Law should only be applied so far as circumstances permit, is bound to result in hardship, if indeed it does not render the administration of the law, in many cases, impossible.

A certain portion of the Ottoman judicial organisation has been taken over in Palestine. In *Abdullah Dahdouh and another v. Execution Officer, Gaza and another.* (H. C. No. 83/27), the Court issued the following judgment:

"The judgment the execution of which is in question is a judgment of the Ottoman Court of First Instance, which is now represented by the District Court.

The Chief Execution Officer is therefore the President of the District Court having jurisdiction in the area, to whom applications with regard to execution of the judgment should be made." (See also the Chapter on Judicial Organisation).

(2) Orders-in-Council affecting Palestine and Palestine Ordinances and Regulations.

An Order-in-Council is a means of legislation which is employed for two distinct purposes:

(1) In the first place it is the means by which the Crown legislates through the Privy Council in virtue of powers conferred upon it by Statute. An example of the conferment of such powers is to be found in the Copyright Act, 1911. By section 29 of that Act it is stated that "(1) His Majesty may, by Order-in-Council, direct that this Act (except such parts, if any, thereof as may be specified in the Order) shall apply:

(a) to works first published in a foreign country to which the Order relates..................... ..."

A further example is legislation for certain mandated territories under the powers conferred by the Foreign Jurisdiction Act, 1890, e. g. the Palestine Order-in-Council, 1922.

The last part of the preamble to the Palestine Order-in-Council reads as follows:

"Now therefore, His Majesty, by virtue and in exercise of the powers in this behalf by the Foreign Jurisdiction Act, 1890, or otherwise, in His Majesty vested, is pleased by and with the advice of His Privy Council, to order, and it is hereby ordered, as follows:"

The Order-in-Council is also used for making regulations with regard to trade and commerce in time of war. During the Great War this prerogative power was largely

62 PALESTINE ORDER-IN-COUNCIL

superseded by the powers conferred upon Executive Departments by Emergency Acts.

The Crown legislates in the case of protectorates exclusively by Order-in-Council. The reason for this is that the Foreign Jurisdiction Act, 1890, which consolidated all pre-existing enactments relating to protectorates, provides that "by treaty, capitulation, grant, usage, sufferance, and other lawful means Her Majesty the Queen has jurisdiction within divers foreign countries". Section 1 of the Act states that "It is and shall be lawful for Her Majesty the Queen to hold, exercise, and enjoy any jurisdiction which Her Majesty now has, or may at any time hereafter have, within a foreign country in the same and as ample a manner as if Her Majesty had acquired that jurisdiction by cession or conquest of territory".

The expression "foreign country" means "any country or place out of Her Majesty's Dominions", (Section 16 of the Foreign Jurisdiction Act, 1890), and consequently applies to mandated territories, *e. g.* Palestine.

Statutory Rules and Orders. The modern tendency is more and more to fix general principles in enactments and to delegate powers as regards the execution thereof to the Executive Authorities. The rules, regulations and orders made in virtue of these powers, of which there are an enormous number, are collectively known as "Statutory Rules and Orders" (S. R. O.). Orders-in-Council therefore form part of the Statutory Rules and orders when issued under powers conferred by statute, but it is a question whether they do so, when issued in virtue of the prerogative without any statutory authorization.

(2) In the second place, it is the means by which the Crown legislates, through the Privy Council, with regard to matters coming within its power by virtue of the prerogative.

The principal employment of the Order-in-Council in exercise of the prerogative is for legislation for Crown Colonies in whole or in part, so far as the Crown has not relinquished the right. Under this power, a large amount of legislation of great importance is performed direct by the Council.

PALESTINE ORDER-IN-COUNCIL

The terms of Article 46 are amplified as regards these matters by the terms of Articles 73 and 74, as amended, of the Order-in-Council. Attention may be drawn to the fact that the date referred to in Article 46, *i. e.* the date of the commencement of the Order, is the 1st. September, 1922, and not the date of the Order itself, *i. e.* the 10th. August, 1922.

"When the British Army took possession of Palestine there began that Military Occupation which continued until the day when the Palestine Order-in-Council, 1922, came into effect on the 1st. September, 1922, and it was declared that His Majesty 'by treaty, capitulation, grant, usage, sufferance and other lawful means has power and jurisdiction within Palestine'". (per Haycraft, C. J., in *Zaslevsky v. Goldberg*, C. A. No. 18/23).

Paragraph 2 of Article 74 refers to "Proclamations, Ordinances, Orders, Rules of Court and other legislative acts" done on or before the 1st. of September, 1922.

Palestine legislation, then, consists of:

(a) Orders-in-Council affecting Palestine issued or to be issued at any date;

(b) Proclamations, Ordinances, Orders, Rules of Court and other legislative acts done by the Commander-in-Chief of the Egyptian Expeditionary Force; the Proclamations, Ordinances, Orders, Rules of Court, etc. done by Military Governors in Palestine, or any other officer of the administration between October the 1st. 1917 and June the 30th. 1920; (In the Palestine Decided Case of *Umar Saleh Barghuti v. Moslem Supreme Council* (H. C. No. 48/25) an ordinance was referred to as "a term which implies the highest form of local legislation");

(c) Similar Proclamations, Ordinances, Orders, Rules of Court etc. done by the High Commissioner or any Department of the Government of Palestine on or after the 1st. July, 1920, to the 1st. of September, 1922, (Article 74(2) of the Order-in-Council);

(d) Proclamations, Ordinances, Orders, Rules of Court and other legislative acts issued on or after the 1st. of September, 1922, and the 1st of April, 1923;

(e) Proclamations, Ordinances, Orders, Rules of Court and other legislative acts issued since the 1st. of April, 1923.

(3) *The substance of the Common Law and the Doctrines of Equity in force in England.*

It is important here to consider the effect of the words "subject thereto" on the preceding clauses of the Article. It appears to be that they include all the preceding enactments referred to, that is to say, Ottoman Laws prior to and later than the 1st. of November, 1914, so far as they have been declared to be in force by public notice, and Orders-in-Council, Ordinances and Regulations, which, in the light of the terms of Articles 73 and 74 should, it seems, be taken to include Proclamations, Orders, Rules of Court and other legislative acts.

It is also important to study the effect and presumed intention of the words "so far as the same shall not extend or apply". It is submitted that the meaning and intention here is the introduction and incorporation in the corpus of Ottoman law and jurisprudence, of certain portions of Common Law and the Law of Equity of England. It is a matter of local ascertainment as to what this law is, but the object of the draftsman of the Article appears to have been to provide a ready remedy where none existed in Ottoman law. In other words, it appears to have been thought that the corpus of Ottoman Law supplemented by Palestine legislation was not enough to meet the rapidly changing conditions brought about by the institution of the new Government and it was, therefore, thought desirable and convenient to place at the disposal of the Courts ready-made English Law when they found Ottoman Law and Palestine Legislation insufficient or defective. The terms of the Article are imperative and do not confer an option: the words are *"shall* be exercised", not *"may* be exercised".

The date as from which the English Law is to come into force appears to be the date of the commencement of the Order-in-Council, *i. e.* the 1st. September, 1922. This seems to refer to the law as it stood on that date. It appears to be static and not to include any English Law passed after that date, since the words "any other provisions" seem to refer to Palestine amendments.

Two expressions in the Article require careful examination and they are "the substance of the Common Law" and "the doctrines of equity" in force in England at that date, *i. e.* the 1st. September, 1922.

(a) *The Substance of the Common Law.*

The term "common law" is an elusive expression, elusive because it is used to designate a body of law which is the outcome of a process of slow and complicated historical development.

The common law of England was originally the whole of that body of rules of law commonly accepted in England and administered in the Courts. Based on custom and precedent, it was what the people and the Courts found to be acceptable and right. To be sure, it was often harsh and primitive, in accordance with the times in which it had its origin and in which it slowly developed; and two other bodies of law were to originate and be applied at a later date, the object of which was to temper the harshness of the common law and to remedy its vagueness owing to its unwritten character. These two systems are known as equity and statute law respectively. With equity we will deal later; but statute law must be considered now, since it is very largely common law formally enacted—and often expanded — in the form of a legislative enactment, known as a statute, passed by the legislature of England. The tendency of English legislation has been to give effect to what the people and the Courts have found to be acceptable and right, and not to impose upon them theories of which they may not stand in need, although in modern times, much statute law, *i. e.* legislative enactments of Parliament, breaks new ground and, since it does not formally give effect to common law hitherto applied but not written down in the form of a law, cannot be claimed in any sense as part of the common law. There are many examples of common law, subsequently codified in the form of statute law to be found in the Commercial law of England. It was not till 1882 that the common law relating to bills of exchange and cheques was incorporated in a formal document known as the Bills of Exchange Act, which thus made the common law on the subject part of the statute law of England. Thus it will be seen that

PALESTINE ORDER-IN-COUNCIL

common law and statute law are closely connected and in many cases one and the same thing.

Sir John Salmond, in a work of authority (¹) neatly sums up the nature of the common law in the following words: "The common law is the entire body of English law — the total *corpus juris Angliae* — with three exceptions, namely (1) statute law, (2) equity, (3) special law in its various forms. When, therefore, it is said that a certain rule is a rule of common law, the precise significance of the statement depends on the particular branch of law which for the purpose in hand is thus contrasted with the common law. We may mean that it is a rule of common law as opposed to a rule established by statute; or as opposed to a rule of equity; or as opposed to a rule of special law—for example, a local custom, or a rule of foreign law applied in exclusion of the law of England, or a rule of military or prize law, or a conventional rule established by the parties in derogation of the common law. It is not correct, however, to regard the term common law as possessing a number of different meanings and applications. It always denotes the same thing, namely the residue of the law after excepting statute law, equity, and special law. It is not true that common law sometimes means the whole law of England except statute law, and at other times means the whole law of England except equity. If it was used in the first of these senses, it would include equity; and if it was used in the second, it would include statute law. But this is not so. The term always, in its proper sense, excludes statute law, equity, and all the forms of special law; but sometimes the particular contrast intended to be expressed is that between common law and statute law: sometimes it is that between common law and special law.

As opposed to equity the common law is not infrequently called law *simpliciter* We speak of law and equity, rather than of common law and equity, notwithstanding the fact that equity is just as truly a branch of law as the common law itself. For in its origin equity was not law at all, but was *justitia naturalis* administered in Chancery to correct the defects or supply the deficiencies of that *strictum jus* which was administered in the King's Courts of law".

"In modern times, however, it is no longer possible in any proper scheme of legal classification or arrangement to take this ancient view of the relation between statute and common law. The immense development of statute law in modern times and its invasion of almost every portion of the old common law has made it impossible now to treat the common law as possessing

---

(¹) Salmond, Jurisprudence, 7th Edition, London, 1924, page 105.

any independent existence as a special and central portion of the *corpus juris*, subject merely to the exceptional interference of special statutory provisions possessing the same relation to it as local custom does. Common law and statute law must now be regarded as fused into a single system of general law, just as in the case of common law and equity. Indeed, a very large portion of the general law has its sole source in statute, and the residue of the common law is undergoing a slow transformation into statute law by the process known as codification. Yet although statute law must now be recognised in any logical and practicable scheme of legal classification as being part of the general law of the land, the older mode of thought is still to be traced in the persistence of the ancient usage of legal speech. Statute law, although it is part of the general law of the land, is still distinguished in name from the common law, just as equity is still distinguished from it".

(b) *The doctrines of Equity.*

Reference was made above to the fact that the harshness of the common law of England was tempered by the creation of another system of law known as equity. Equity in its ordinary sense means nothing more than that which is just and proper in the circumstances. But it acquired a special legal sense when invoked to temper the vigour of the rules of the common law which had become fixed and inflexible and consequently took no account of the special circumstances of a case, or the development or progress of the times. The system of law now known as equity has its origin deep down in English history: it is the second great system of English law, coming midway between common law and statute law. People complained to the King of the harshness of the treatment they had received at the hands of the common law Courts. The King referred the matter to his Chancellor to deal with, who gave a judgment on the matter in accordance with the equity of the case, *i. e.* the merits of the case as distinct from the strict legal rights of the parties at law. Over the course of many years this granting of special justice by the King through his Chancellor became hardened into a system, and special Courts known as Courts of Equity arose, which dispensed justice based on those rules or doctrines which, as opposed to the harsh rules or doctrines of the common law, became known as the doctrines of equity, which in their turn likewise became a fixed system of practice and precedent. Thus, two separate and distinct systems of law were administered in England by two distinct and separate sets of Courts known as the Courts of Common Law and the Courts of the King's Chancellor, or the Courts of Chancery. This state of affairs continued till the year 1873, when an Act of Parliament known as the Judicature Act was passed which brought about what is known as "the fusion of law and equity". By this Act all points of conflict between common law and equity were abolished, and the whole 'fused' into one uniform system. The terms "common law" and "equity", however, were maintained as differentiating the two systems of law and the rights and remedies they embrace.

"Until the year 1873, England presented the extremely curious spectacle of two distinct and rival systems of law, administered at the same time by different tribunals. These systems were distinguished as common law and equity, or merely as law and equity (using the term law in a narrow sense as including only one of the two systems). The common law was the older, being coeval with the rise of royal justice in England, and it was administered in the older courts, namely, the King's Bench, the Court of Common Pleas and the Exchequer. Equity was the more modern body of legal doctrine, developed and administered by the Chancellor in the Court of Chancery as supplementary to, and corrective of, the older law. To a large extent the two systems were identical and harmonious, for it was a maxim of the Chancery that equity follows the law (*Aequitas sequitur legem*); that is to say, the rules already established in the older courts were adopted by the Chancellors and incorporated into the system of equity; unless there was some sufficient reason for their rejection or modification. In no small measure, however, law and equity were discordant, applying different rules to the same subject matter. The same case would be decided in one way, if brought before the Court of King's Bench, and in another, if adjudged in Chancery. The Judicature Act, 1873, put an end to this anomalous state of things, by the abolition of all portions of the common law which conflicted with equity, and by the consequent fusion of the two systems into a single and self-consistent body of law administered in a single court called the High Court of Justice and substituted for the old courts of common law and the Court of Chancery.

Although the distinction between common law and equity has thus become to a large extent historical merely, it has not ceased to demand attention, for it is still valid and operative for many purposes. The so-called fusion of law and equity effected by the Judicature Act has abolished only such rules of the common law as were in conflict with the rules of equity in the sense that both rules will not be recognised and applied in one and the same court of justice. So far as common law and equity are consistent with each other and so capable of being administered concurrently in a single court, these two systems still subsist, and the distinction between them is still in force. Thus the distinction between legal and equitable ownership, legal and equitable rights, legal and equitable remedies, remains an essential part of the modern system. It is still the case that one person may be the legal owner of property and another the equitable owner of the same property, as in the case of a trustee and his beneficiary. Similarly, a mortgage or charge may still be either legal or equitable. These distinctions between law and equity are not conflicts between two irreconcilable systems of law, but are such as to be capable of recognition as part of one and the same system. A legal right and an equitable right, legal ownership and equitable ownership, although as a matter of history they originated in different courts and in different legal systems, are now two different kinds of rights and of ownership recognised in the same court administering a single and harmonious legal system. [1]

(c) *Statute Law.*

Statute law, the third system of English law, though not explicitly mentioned in Article 46 is of considerable importance, since as we have seen, much of the common law of England has, at different times, been codified and incorporated into a statute. The question therefore arises as to whether the "substance" of the Common law mentioned in the Article may be taken to include Statute law which was formerly common law. It is submitted that this is the case, for the reason that statutes have, for the most part, left the law almost entirely unchanged. The presumed object of the draftsman of the Article in incorporating the substance of the English common law and the doctrines of equity, was to place at the disposal of the people and the Courts ready-made laws and remedies where none existed. Statute law which does not incorporate or codify common law does not come within the scope of the Article.

The reference in the Article to the common law and the doctrines of equity of England really necessitates a

---

[1] Salmond: Jurisprudence, page 89.

70 PALESTINE ORDER-IN-COUNCIL

careful comparison of the terms of Ottoman and English Law, as the latter stood on the 1st. September, 1922, in order to discover to what extent Ottoman Law does not extend or apply in Palestine, and to the extent English law would extend or apply were it in force in Palestine in its entirety. The balance between the two systems found to exist as a result of the examination would represent the amount of English law, which in theory at least, is in force in Palestine.

It is not possible here to make the exhaustive comparison referred to above, but some essential points may be referred to affecting common law and equity. An attempt will be made in the following chapters at a comparison of the subject matter of the Code with the corresponding sections of English Law.

(1) *The Common Law*. The Courts have at their disposal in the common law of England a body of rights and remedies some of which are not available in Ottoman law. Important examples are the law of contract and the law of torts so far as they find no counterpart either in the Ottoman law or the legislation of Palestine.

The principles of the Common law of England will have considerable influence upon the terms of Article 64 of the Ottoman Code of Civil Procedure which establishes freedom of contract.

(2) *Equity*. It is well known that the Ottoman Courts rarely, if ever, granted specific performance, (it has been held by the Supreme Court of Palestine that specific performance of a contract for the sale of land cannot be enforced: *Moussa Pinhassovitch v. Litvinsky Bros. and others*, L. A. No. 58/25); nor did they give relief against forfeitures or oppressive transactions, as where a man transfers the whole of his immovable property to a man of straw in a collusive agreement in fraud of creditors, taking a secret written admission from the transferee that the immovable property is not his. Moreover, the law of Trusts as understood in English Law is entirely lacking in Ottoman Law. (See the case of *Mordekhai Eliash v. The Director of Lands*, H. C. 77/31). Again, certain of the maxims of Equity are not to be found among the

ninety-nine maxims of Muhammadan jurisprudence contained in the Mejelle (See Articles 2-100). A point of considerable importance is the effect of Equity on the law of Personal Status, though this point may be affected by the proviso as to the limit of jurisdiction.

There are, however, several limitations imposed upon the application of the substance of the Common Law and the doctrines of Equity. Article 46 provides that this law shall only be in force subject to four qualifications which are as follows: This law shall not apply to the extent that:

(1) The circumstances of Palestine do not permit;

(2) The circumstances of the Palestinians do not permit;

(3) The limits of His Majesty's jurisdiction do not permit;

(4) Local circumstances render some qualification of the law imperative.

(4) *The powers, procedure and practice of the English Courts.*

The Article provides that where the Ottoman Law prior to or later in date than the 1st. November, 1914, and the Ordinances and Regulations of the Palestine Government do not extend or apply, the powers vested in and the procedure and practice observed by or before Courts of Justice and Justices of the Peace in England shall be applied. (See the Palestine Decided case of *Fayez el Fares v. The Commandant of Police,* H. C. 51/32, and *J. L. Penhas v. Pesach Falum and another.* H. C. 49/25).

This provision as to the application of the practice and procedure of the Courts of Justice and Justices of the Peace is a concomitant of the same provision regarding substantive law. By powers presumably is meant the general powers to administer justice inherent in any judge or bench of judges, and all matters ancillary thereto. By Courts of Justice presumably is meant the High Court of Justice including the various divisions of the High Court, the Court of Appeal, County Courts and the Courts of Justices of the Peace. Obviously it cannot mean the House of Lords, the Privy Council, or Courts of special jurisdiction *e. g.* the Salford Court in Manchester or the Court of Passage in Liverpool.

The date at which this law of procedure is to be incorporated in the Law of Palestine is the date of the commencement of the Order-in-Council, *i. e.* the 1st. September, 1922.

The provision following as to modification, amendment or repeal obviously applies to legislative or other acts in Palestine and not in England.

It is a moot point as to whether there is any reasonable ground for saying that the draftsman of the Article had in view any definite development of the Palestine legal system along the lines of English Law and procedure. The references to English Law and procedure are, indeed, of so far-reaching a nature as to appear to justify the conclusion that this was the intention, subject, however, to what now appears to be a well-established principle of British legislation for the Crown Colonies, that the foundation upon which the law and institutions of any particular territory rest shall not be disturbed. In Palestine there is still a large Islamic majority and it therefore appears that it is not the intention to disturb the salient features of Muhammadan jurisprudence.

The question of the application of English Law was considered by the Lords of the Judicial Committee of the Privy Council in the case of *Abdullah Bey Chedid and others v. Tenenbaum* (Privy Council Appeal, 47/32). In delivering judgment, Tomlin, L. J., after citing the terms of Article 46 of the Order-in-Council said:

"Their Lordships' attention has not been directed to any provision of the Turkish law or any local ordinance which deals with the question whether in an action to recover damages for breach of contract the plaintiff is bound to establish his readiness and willingness to perform his part. In the absence of any such provision their Lordships are of opinion that regard must be had to the English law applicable in the case of concurrent obligations".

Palestine Decided Cases: The terms of Article 46 of the Order-in-Council, as regards the application of English law, have either explicitly or by implication been the subject of judicial consideration and decision as is shown by the following cases:

(1) "We are by Clause 46 of the Palestine Order-in-Council, 1922, authorised to apply rules of equity to be found in English Law when not inconsistent with the Ottoman Law. There is a rule of equity that prescription cannot be successfuly pleaded in bar to an action to recover land of which the Plaintiff has been deprived by fraud unless the Plaintiff has allowed the time of prescription to run since he had knowledge of the fraud. But to avail herself of this equitable rule the Plaintiff must prove either that the Defendant was a party to the fraud or has purchased with knowledge of it." (*Agnes Yared v. Kaysar and Nasrallah Khoury.* L. A. No. 32/24).

(2) "For the Respondents to the Petition, Messrs Felman and Weiman, in whose favour the judgment of the District Court was given, it is argued that the order was an injunction: a form of order unknown to the Ottoman Code of Procedure, and with regard to which it was therefore necessary under Article 46 of the Palestine Order-in-Council 1922, to apply the English Procedure and practice. This argument might be accepted if it were the fact that in Ottoman Law a Court could not make an order prohibiting a party from doing a specific act. Such, however, is not the case. The Ottoman Law does empower the Courts to give such orders. The general authority to issue orders in the nature of injunctions as regards uses of Mulk property is contained in Section 1197 of the Mejelle: and the Articles 1198 to 1212 contain specific instances in which this power is to be applied as between neighbouring owners. Such being the fact, there is no occasion to import any procedure of English Law." (*J. L. Penhas v. Pesach Falum and another.* H. C. No. 49/25).

(3) "There is no law whereby specific performance of an agreement for sale of land can be enforced in Palestine, nor does it affect the position that the agreement should have been expressed to be in the form of a sale to be perfected by registration at a later date. If the vendor fails to register the land in the name of the purchaser at the agreed date, the purchaser cannot compel him to do so. The remedy is in damages. It is true that Section 7 (1) of the Land Courts Ordinance, 1921, provides that: "The Courts shall have regard to equitable as well as to legal rights in land and shall not be bound by any rule of the Ottoman Law prohibiting the Courts from hearing actions based on unregistered documents." This provision has been applied by the Courts to unregistered transactions which took place before the British Occupation, in which it appeared from the circumstances, such as delivery of possession and payment of purchase money, that the parties intended the transaction to take effect as a sale without registration. In spite of the Ottoman Law as to registration, a considerable part of the land of Palestine remains unregistered and was habitually dealt with by unregistered deed. It was held that under such circumstances it would be inequitable to refuse

to recognise the validity of a sale of land by unregistered deed, merely for lack of registration; and in a number of cases judgment has been given upholding the validity of the unregistered sale and declaring that as against the vendor, the purchaser is entitled to registration. That principle however can only be applied to a case in which the sale took place before the British Occupation, as the Proclamation of the 18th. November, 1918, rendered all dispositions of immovable property made after the Occupation invalid." *Moussa Pinhassovitch v. Litvinsky Bros. and others.* L. A. 58/25).

(4) "We assume in the absence of any known law to the contrary that the English Rule prevails and that a month begins to run from the end of the day of the contract, and ends at the end of the corresponding day of the next month. The Jewish day ends at sunset, the Christian day at midnight." (*Ibrahim Leib Etkin v. Jacob Shlosberg.* C. A. No. 13/26).

(5) "The question in this case is whether the partners in a *Mudaribe* partnership who have received the capital of the partnership are bound to render an account of the manner in which they have dealt with it to the partner who supplied it or are they entitled to refuse to submit an account and to rely on the provisions of Articles 1413 and 1774 of Mejelle. The Mejelle is silent on the question of accounts and Article 1774 does not say at what stage of the proceedings the oath of the person who is entrusted is to be accepted. If when the accounts have been submitted the other party disputes them he cannot call upon the accounting party to prove that they are correct but he must be given an opportunity to prove the contrary himself. If he fails to do so his only cause is to demand the oath." (*Iskandar Kassab v. Najib Nassar and another.* C. A. No. 87/26).

(6) "There is no such general rule in Ottoman Law that when the infringement of a law creates damage to a person, that person has a right to a civil action for damages against the infringer. We must in every case where damages are sought enquire whether a right to such civil remedy exists either under a rule of the Common Law or by statute." (*Messrs. J. and P. Coats Ltd. v. Messrs Kirshenbaum and Blumenkrantz.* C. A. No. 101/26).

(7) "As regards the Appellant's claim that the Respondents have no lien on the goods for payment of their charges; it is clear that in Ottoman Law there is no such lien in favour of a warehouseman and that such a right must therefore be based on express agreement." (*Hamanhil Company v. Municipality of Jaffa.* C. A. No. 130/26).

(8) "A company has now *(19th. December, 1927)* no power to create an equitable charge, other than a floating charge upon its whole assets, unless such a charge can validly be created in accordance with the general law applicable to persons as well

as to Companies. The District Court basing itself on the provisions of the Mejelle has held that no such power exists. There can, in our opinion, be no doubt that if the position is governed by the Mejelle, the District Court's judgment is right. The Appellant, however, has argued that the provisions of the Mejelle in this respect are over-ruled by the law of the 28th April, 1330 (4th. May, 1914), which amended Article 64 of the Code of Civil procedure. The provisions of the law are as follows: (Here the Court sets out the text of the Article). It is argued that this law enables one person to give another an equitable charge upon future crops. The words to which our attention has been directed are: "agreements contracted on what will come into existence in the future are also recognised." The effect of this provision is, in my opinion, merely to bring "agreements contracted on what will come into existence in the future" within the first paragraph of the law, and to render such agreements enforcible and effective "as between the contracting parties." The first paragraph of the law practically re-enacts the former Article 64, and I hold that neither under the old Article nor under the first paragraph of the amending law, is it possible for one person to charge his property in favour of another, otherwise than by a specific mortgage, in such a manner as to give the chargees any rights against a third party, though the charge may be valid against the chargor." (*Central Bank and another v. The Registrar of Companies.* C. A. No. 74/27).

(9) "If the question were to be determined according to English Law, I hold that it would be governed by the judgment in *Harper v. Godsell* (1870), 5 Q. B., p. 422." (*Zeev Hazine v. N. V. Algemine Yzer Stalmaashappy "Forrostaal" Haag.* C. A. No. 36/28).

(10) "There being no law in this country to enforce specific performance of a contract, it has been an established practice to include in all contracts for the sale of land a penalty clause rendering each party liable to a specific sum of money, should one or the other fail to carry out his part of the contract and the contract of sale in this case was no exception to the practice." (*Sudki Kamal and others v. Yusef Rokach and others.* C. A. No. 43/28).

(11) "We do not think that this view can be supported. Section 94 of the Companies (Winding-Up) Ordinance directs that "This Ordinance shall be interpreted by reference to the law of England relating to Companies". Moreover, except for the substitution of "Egyptian Pounds" for "Pounds", the Sub-section is taken verbatim from sub-section (1) of Section 130 of the Companies (Consolidation) Act, 1908, which re-enacted Section 80 of the Act of 1862.

"Now it is clear that by the Law of England, a secured creditor of a Company can petition for the winding up of the

Company even though he may have attempted to recover the amount due to him by the exercise of a remedy conferred upon him by his security, *(Borough of Portsmouth Tramways Company,* [1892] 2 Ch. 362). Hence we have no doubt that the secured creditor of a Company registered under the Companies Ordinance, 1920, can petition for the Company to be wound up." (*The Anglo-Palestine Co., Jaffa v. Kfar Ganim Co. Ltd.* C. A. No. 93/28).

(12) "It is well settled that however small may be the interest in the mortgaged property of a person who seeks redemption, he must pay to the mortgagee all that is due on the mortgage as a condition of being allowed to redeem (Halsbury, XXI, p. 279). The Ottoman law appears to be the same — see Mejelle, Articles 731, 739 and 740." *Emil Tayyan v. Chief Execution Officer, Nablus and others.* H. C. No. 19/29).

(13) "In their judgment the District Court stated that: "the Defendant has given security which in our opinion is sufficient to cover any claim against him". The judgment proceeds: "We continue the security and also the arrangement by which Mr. Rojansky is in charge of all books of the Defendant. Complete liberty of access to these books to be given to all parties, in addition to the security the Defendant is constituted as Trustee for all parties. In view of the security and of the nature of the business we are of opinion that to appoint a Receiver would not be a proper remedy, and we refuse to make such an order. Neither do we think it proper to restrain the Defendant from the management."

"The Defendant is appealing against that portion of the judgment whereby he is constituted a Trustee.

" We know of no power either under English or Ottoman Law whereby such an appointment can be made, nor, indeed, do we understand the effect of such an appointment. If the Plaintiffs are successful in the arbitration proceedings now pending, the Defendant will obviously have to account to them for his management of the business, and he has given security for his liability in that event. Accordingly, we hold that the Defendant's appeal on this point must succeed." (*Israel Lieber v. Jacob Mirenberg and another.* C. A. No. 35/31).

(14) "This is a return to the Rule Nisi calling upon the Director of Lands to show cause why a disposition of lands of the nature of a private trust should not be registered in the Land Registry. The Petitioner admits that the Ottoman Law is silent as to the creation of private trusts but claims that while it does not allow them it does not forbid them and he argues, because certain sections of the Companies Ordinance, 1929, No. 98 of 1929, namely Section 29 (2), 78 (1) (2) and (3), 79 (1) and (3), 98 (1) (b), 119 (3), 124 (1), 180 and sub-sections (O) and (W) of Schedule II thereof refer to Trusts and Trustees, while Section 29 (2) of the

Partnership Ordinance No. 19 of 1930 refers to trusts that therefore the legislator has introduced the doctrine of private trusts into the law of Palestine. The Companies Ordinance of 1929 and the Partnership Ordinance of 1930 are very lengthy enactments based upon English Statutes which have been if one may use the expression swallowed virtually holus bolus by the legislator of Palestine with comparatively small alterations. Now there is a presumption that the legislator does not intend to make any substantial alteration in the Law beyond what it explicitly declares either in express terms or by clear implication; or, in other words, beyond the immediate scope and object of the statute. (Maxwell on the Interpretation of Statutes, Sixth Edition, page 149). The same authority states that it is more reasonable to hold that the legislature expressed its intention in a slovenly manner, than that a meaning should be given to its enactment which could not have been intended. I do not think one can seriously hold, knowing the nature of the Legislation with which we are dealing, that the Legislature intended by a mere side-wind to introduce a new principle of law such as the doctrine of private trusts into Palestine." (*Mordekhai Eliash v. Director of Lands.* H. C. No. 77/31).

(15) "As regards the second point, the Petitioners' argument is based upon the judgment of the Special Tribunal constituted under Article 55 of the Palestine Order-in-Council 1922, in the case of *Alpert v. the Chief Execution Officer, Jerusalem and others* (Special Tribunal No. 1/28). In his judgment in that case, in which the other members of the Tribunal concurred, the Chief Justice said: —

"The word alimony as we have seen, is used in section 53 (a) of the Palestine Order-in-Council and it is there enumerated as one of the matters within the exclusive cognizance of a Rabbinical Court, and must, in my opinion, there be interpreted in the sense which it bears in English Law, for there is nothing to show that the legislative authority—in this case His Majesty in Council—intended it to be used in any other sense".

"The Petitioners' argument is that the same principle must be applied in ascertaining the meaning of the term maintenance in Article 54 of the same Order-in-Council: that in the English Law the maintenance of an infant means an obligation incumbent upon the parents or grand-parents of such infants and upon no other persons; and consequently that it is this restricted meaning which must be given to the term maintenance of minors in the Order-in-Council. This argument might be of substance if it were the fact that in English Law the term maintenance were applicable solely to a liability imposed upon the parents and grand-parents of a minor for his support. Such, however, is not the position. Apart from its special meaning of the maintenance of an action, the term maintenance in English Law is one of wide application relating not only to persons but also to "corporeal things and documents". See Stroud's Judicial Dictionary, 2nd. edition p. 1139. Thus the term maintenance of minors means simply provision for their support. It is true that English Law imposes no liability upon an uncle for the maintenance of his nephews, but that is not a question with which we are concerned. It is only for the purpose of ascertaining the meaning in which the term maintenance is used in the Order-in-Council that we have to refer to English Law." (*Issa Turjman and another v. C.E.O. Jerusalem and another.* H. C. No. 49/32).

(16) "The Attorney General impugns the Order Nisi on the ground that it does not tally with a Rule Nisi for the grant of a mandamus as employed in the High Court of Justice in England, but the order follows the precedents established during the last eight years in respect of orders directed to public officers under Section 6(b) of the Courts Ordinance No. 21 of 1924 which is concerned with a procedure which in the absence of petitions of right has been built up in this territory as regards orders not only in the nature of mandamus and prohibition as contemplated in that subsection, but also as regards orders on petitions and applications as contemplated in the second paragraph of Article 43 of the Palestine Order-in-Council." *Fayez el Fares v. The Commandant of Police.* H. C. No. 51/32).

(17) "There is no power under this Article (Article 1197 of the Mejelle, *q. v.* to issue an order in respect to threatened injury; and in so far as the Courts of Palestine have power to issue such an order, it can only be by virtue of Article 46 of the Palestine Order-in-Council 1922." (*Yitzhaq Raym and others v. Hadar Hacarmel Cooperative Society Ltd.* H. C. No. 99/32).

(This was an application for an order to issue to the Respondents directing them to show cause why they should not be restrained from cutting off or threatening to cut off water from certain houses).

The Article is silent as to legal interpretation. This is an important point and one which may well have considerable influence on the future of the judicial system of Palestine. Allusion has been made above to the fact that a portion of the non-Muhammadan Ottoman legislation taken over in virtue of the Article is based on French Law. The Ottoman Courts, when deciding any disputed or difficult points, frequently referred to the decisions of the French Courts of Appeal or Cassation. This process has been continued by the Courts in Cyprus where such laws, *e. g.* the Ottoman Commercial Code, have been in force.

The question of the interpretation of texts of Muhammadan law, *e. g.* the Civil Code itself, should obviously be made with reference to the views of authoritative writers on Muhammadan law. The decisions of the Indian Courts and especially of the Judicial Committee of the Privy Council on such points are of great importance and help where they deal with the same law as in force in Palestine, *e. g.* the law of pre-emption, gift, waqf. This point is dealt with in detail in Chapter 5 (*q. v.*).

Palestine Ordinances based on English law should, it is submitted, be interpreted with reference to English law. Sometimes an Ordinance contains an express stipulation to this effect, *e. g.* The Companies (Winding-up) Ordinance, 1922. (See *The Anglo-Palestine Co., Jaffa v. Kfar Ganim Co. Ltd.* C. A. No. 93/28).

In the case of English law incorporated under the terms of the Article, the interpretation thereof must obviously be made by reference to the decisions and methods of interpretation obtaining in the English Courts.

The following table gives a summary of the Section:

The jurisdiction of the Civil Courts is to be exercised in accordance with:

(a) Ottoman law in force in Palestine on November, 1st. 1914;

(b) Ottoman laws later in date than the 1st. of November, 1914; provided that

(1) They have already been declared by public notice to be in force;

(2) They are in future, *i. e.* since the date of the commencement of the Order-in-Council (1st. September, 1922) declared by public notice to be in force.

(c) Orders-in-Council, Ordinances and Regulations in force in Palestine at the date of the commencement of the Order-in-Council, *i. e.* 1st. September, 1922.

(d) Orders-in-Council, Ordinances and Regulations enacted or applied in Palestine after the date referred to in (c) above.

(e) The substance of the common law and the doctrines of equity in force in England on the date of the commencement of the Order-in-Council (i. e. the 1st. September, 1922) where any case cannot be brought within the terms of the enactments referred to in (a) to (d) above, but only so far as

(1) The circumstances of Palestine;
(2) The circumstances of its inhabitants;
(3) The limits of His Majesty's jurisdiction;
(4) Local circumstances,

permit of such a course being adopted.

(f) The powers vested in and the procedure and practice of the Courts of Justice and of Justices of the Peace in England in cases where any cases cannot be brought within the terms of the enactments referred to in (a) to (d) above on the date of the commencement of the Order-in-Council, i. e. the 1st September, 1922, subject to any subsequent amendment or repeal of such powers, procedure, or practice.

From the text of the Article it appears that the provision as to the application of the Common law and equity of England stop at the date of the commencement of the Order-in-Council, i. e. 1st. September, 1922. It is not limited as to date, however, in the case of powers, procedure and practice, save as to modification, amendment or repeal in Palestine.

The provision as to the circumstances of Palestine and its inhabitants, the limits of His Majesty's jurisdiction and local circumstances apply only to the common law and equity of England and not to the case of powers, procedure and practice.

In short, therefore, it appears that wherever it can be proved to the Court that Ottoman law and Palestine legislation do not contain any provision of substantive law,—meaning by that term the substance of the common law and the doctrines of equity in force in England,—or of procedure, or do not provide a remedy or relief, but that such law or procedure or remedy or relief, are available in the law of England, the Courts are bound to apply such law or procedure, or to grant such remedy. In deciding whether to apply English law or grant a remedy or relief, the Court, it is submitted, must first satisfy itself that the circumstances of Palestine and its inhabitants and the limits of His Majesty's jurisdiction permit of such law being applied, and that local circumstances do not render some qualification thereof imperative.

APPENDIX No. 1 TO CHAPTER III.
LIST OF THE PRINCIPAL OTTOMAN "PROVISIONAL" ENACTMENTS.

(1) Execution Law
(2) Code of Civil Procedure
(3) Law governing the disposition of immovable property
(4) Law governing the inheritance of immovable property
(5) Law governing the partition of immovable property
(6) Law governing the mortgage of immovable property
(7) The Magistrates Law
(8) The Law of the Notary Public
(9) The Public Demonstrations Law
(10) The Law of Criminal Procedure.

PALESTINE ORDER-IN-COUNCIL

APPENDIX NO. 2 TO CHAPTER III.

LIST OF OTTOMAN LAWS REPEALED OR SUPERSEDED WHOLLY OR IN PART IN PALESTINE.

Title of Ottoman enactment	Repealed by
Law of 27 Ramadan, 1294, relating to Municipalities (Articles 43 and 66 no longer in force)	Trial of Contraventions against Municipal Regulations Ordinance, 1918.
Law of Mortgage of 25th February, 1328 (superseded in certain particulars)	See Articles 7 (2) and 8 (1) of Credit Banks Ordinance, 1920-1922.
Law of 13 December, 1329, (Articles 2—5; 17—22; 38—40) superseded in so far as they concern animals intended for import or export.	Animals, (Export and Import) Ordinance, 1920.
Law for mortgage of immovable property of 16 Rebi ul Thani, 1331, (Articles 2, 3, 4, 8 and 11 modified or repealed.)	Mortgage Law Amendment Ordinance, 1920.
Ottoman Land Law, Article 103.	Mewat Land Ordinance, 1921.
All Ottoman Laws on the exercise of pharmacy and trade in drugs and poisons declared out of force.	Public Health Ordinance, 1921.
All Ottoman laws relating to the registration and protection of Trade Marks	Trade Marks Ordinance, 1921—1923.
Ottoman Penal Code (Article 40).	Young Offenders Ordinance, 1922.
Law of hunting of 18 Safar, 1299, Articles 32—46	Game Preservation Ordinance, 1924.
Articles 24—40 and 43—49 of the Ottoman Code of Criminal Procedure superseded.	Arrest of Offenders and Searches Ordinance 1924.
Ottoman Magistrates Law and Amendments thereto, in so far as they are inconsistent with the Magistrates Courts Jurisdiction Ordinance, 1924.	Magistrates Courts Jurisdiction Ordinance, 1924.
Code of Criminal Procedure, Articles 404—408 superseded.	Contempt of Court Ordinance, 1924.
Ottoman Civil Code	Law of Evidence Amendment Ordinance, 1924.
Ottoman Code of Civil Procedure (All Articles on evidence inconsistent with the terms of the Law of Evidence Amendment Ordinance, 1924).	

84 PALESTINE ORDER-IN-COUNCIL

Title of Ottoman Enactment	Repealed by
Copyright Law	Copyright Ordinance, 1924,
Law dealing with wireless telegraphy of 6th August, 1330	Wireless Telegraphy Ordinance, 1924.
Code of Criminal Procedure, Articles 9—19; 50—57; 64—107; 122—348; 371—403; 409; 417—462.	Trial upon Information Ordinances, 1924-1925.
Ottoman Penal Code, Articles 23, 24, 25, 26, 28, 35 and 47.	Ditto
Law concerning prosecution of Government Officials of 4th February, 1329.	Ditto
Ottoman Code of Criminal Procedure. (Remaining Articles to be read in the light of Article 74(2) of the Trial Upon Information Ordinance).	Ditto
Law of 14th Muharram, 1332, concerning exemption from customs enjoyed by industrial establishments.	Customs Duties Exemption Ordinance, 1924.
Decree of 14 Safar, 1297 (and Amendments thereto) regarding exemption of agricultural instruments.	
Law of 23 October, 1300 (immunities enjoyed by railways and public works).	
Decree issued by Director General of Customs of 17 July 1900 (immunities enjoyed by Municipalities)	
Law of 24 Rebi-ul-Thani, 1309, Article 8, (immunities to commercial samples and passengers baggage)	
Code of Civil Procedure, Article 112.	Modified by Bills of Exchange (Protest) Ordinance, 1924.
Commercial Code, Article 141.	
Ottoman Patents Law	Patent and Design Ordinance, 1924.
Law of Muuicipalities, Article 41, and Articles 50—55 (as from the British Occupation).	Municipal Councils Validation Ordinance, 1925.
(1) Law of Mines, 14 Safar, 1324	Mining Ordinance, 1925.
(2) Law of Transport in Mines of 24 Muharram 1327 (as amended by law of 16 Jamad el Akhir, 1332).	

PALESTINE ORDER-IN-COUNCIL 85

Title of Ottoman Enactment	Repealed by
(3) Law amending law of Mines of 7 Rejeb, 1933.	Mining Ordinance, 1925
(4) Law amending law of Mines of 14th Muharram, 1332.	ditto
(5) Ottoman Land Code, Article 107.	ditto
All Ottoman Laws, Regulations and decrees concerning the monopoly of Salt	Salt Ordinance, 1925.
Ottoman Penal Code, Articles 156 and 157.	Passport Ordinance, 1925.
Any Ottoman Regulation regarding boilers	No. 1 of 1926.
Provisional law concerning diseases of animals of 1332.	No. 3 of 1926.
Law concerning hunting of 1299 (Articles 1—31) superseded	No. 4 of 1926.
Ottoman Civil Code Articles 1841—1851 superseded. Article 60 amended.	No. 9 of 1926.
Law regarding quarries superseded.	No. 10 of 1926.
Law concerning theft of animals (1332) (Article 11 repealed)	No. 17 of 1926.
Law regarding village watchmen (1330)	No. 17 of 1926.
Decrees and Regulations relating to Religious Communities (Superseded).	No. 19 of 1926.
Regulations of 1286 concerning the construction and alignment of roads, (Articles 1—6 of Chapter I, superseded).	No. 24 of 1926.
Regulations of 1309 concerning construction and alignment of roads, Articles 1, 2, 3, 4, and 9 superseded.	No. 24 of 1926.
Regulations of 1296 (as amended by the law of 1330) superseded.	No. 28 of 1926.
Law of 1332 relating to expropriation for municipalities superseded.	No. 28 of 1926.
Ottoman Penal Code (Article 37 superseded)	No. 29 of 1926.
Magistrate's Law of 1331 (paragraph 2 of Article 61 superseded).	No. 29 of 1926.
Commercial Code (Land and Sea). All Articles relating to carriage of goods by sea repealed and superseded.	No. 43 of 1926.
Law of Municipalities of 1294. Chapter III superseded.	No. 45 of 1926.
Regulations of 1286 and law of 1332 relating to village roads and works superseded.	No. 1 of 1927.

86 PALESTINE ORDER-IN-COUNCIL

Title of Ottoman Enactment	Repealed by
Ottoman Penal Code (Articles 197, 198, 199, 200 and 202 superseded).	No. 2 of 1927.
Law relating to Guides of 1312 superseded.	No. 18 of 1927.
Ottoman Penal Code (Article 139 repealed).	No. 22 of 1927.
Ottoman Press Law (Article 20 repealed).	No. 22 of 1927.
Stamp Law of 1323 superseded	No. 31 of 1927.
Tariff of Hejaz stamp duty superseded	No. 31 of 1927.
Ottoman Penal Code, Art. 155 superseded	No. 32 of 1927.
Ottoman Criminal Procedure Code, Articles 108—121 superseded	No. 35 of 1927.
Ottoman Magistrates Law, 1329, Article 59 superseded	No. 35 of 1927.
All Ottoman laws, regulations and decrees relating to manufacture, sale etc. of intoxicating liquors superseded.	No. 42 of 1927.
All regulations regarding change of religious community superseded	No. 43 of 1927.
Ottoman Penal Code, Articles 143, 144, 145, 146 and 147 superseded subject to proviso that all laws repealed by these Articles are not revived.	No. 48 of 1927.
Ottoman Penal Code, Articles 45, 46, 81, 121, 180 and 184 superseded : Article 230 superseded, together with amendments thereto in so far as they prescribe penalties for persons thieves or stolen property etc.	No. 50 of 1927.
Decree of 1285 relating to Customs Exemptions for Consuls cancelled.	No. 7 of 1928.
Law of 1329 relating to Cadastral Survey superseded.	No. 9 of 1928.
Customs Law of 1863, (1309) superseded.	No. 11 of 1929.
Ottoman Penal Code (Articles 207—213 superseded).	No. 15 of 1929.
Commercial Code, Articles 154—160 and 249—262.	No. 18 of 1929.
Law of 1325 relating to collection of taxes superseded.	No. 26 of 1929.
Ottoman Penal Code, Articles 48—66 and any addenda thereto superseded.	No. 41 of 1929.

PALESTINE ORDER-IN-COUNCIL 87

Title of Ottoman Enactment	Repealed by
Law of 26 Rebi-ul-Awwal, 1330, relating to illegal assemblies superseded.	No. 41 of 1929.
Commercial Code, Articles 70—146 superseded. Supplement to Commercial Code Articles 84—90 superseded.	No. 47 of 1929.
Law of Cheques of 1330, superseded.	No. 47 of 1929.
Commercial Code, Articles 10—19, 24, 26, 30, 32, 33, and 35—52 repealed.	No. 19 of 1930.
All laws and regulations relating to the Postal and Telegraph services repealed	No. 20 of 1930.
Ottoman Penal Code, Articles 129, 134, 135, and 136 repealed.	No. 20 of 1930.
Ottoman Law of Census of 14 August, 1330 repealed.	Census Ordinance, 1931
Ottoman Law of Execution of Judgments of 28th Nissan, 1330, Articles 131—142	Imprisonment for Debt Ordinance, 1931.
Ottoman Provisional Law of 1st November, 1328 relating to the destruction of locusts repealed.	Locusts Destruction Ordinance, 1932.
Ottoman Land Law, Articles 109, 110, 111 and 126 repealed.	Land Law (Amendment Ordinance) 1933.
Ottoman Penal Code, Addendum to Article 99 repealed.	Unlawful Instigation Ordinance, 1933.
Ottoman Law for Printing of Books of 20th Safar 1292 repealed.	
Ottoman Law of Printing Presses of 11th Rajab 1327 repealed.	
Ottoman Press Law of 11th Rajab, 1327.	Press Ordinance, 1933.
Ottoman Penal Code, Articles 137 and 138	
Ottoman Code of Criminal Procedure of the 5th Rajab 1296. Addendum of 3rd Ramadan 1332 repealed.	
Ottoman Law of Primary Education, 1332	Education Ordinance, 1933.
Ottoman Regulations concerning Primary Education.	Education Ordinance, 1933.
Ottoman Penal Code, Articles 140 and 141 repealed.	Education Ordinance, 1933.

CHAPTER IV.

THE LAW OF CONTRACT.

(1) *The formation of contract in Muhammadan Law.*

Muhammadan law, and consequently the Civil Code, does not deal specifically with contract as a branch of law; and indeed there is only one formal definition of a contract (*aqd*) in the whole Code, Article 103, which defines contract as being "What the parties bind themselves and undertake to do with reference to a particular matter. It is composed of the combination of offer and acceptance". (See also notes to Article 103, and the Cyprus Case of *Chacalli v. Kallourena*, C. L. R. Vol. III, page 246. (*Digest*, page 20) and *Michailides v. Bishop of Papho*, C. L. R., Vol. IV, page 76. (*Digest*, page 20). The different rules governing the subject are scattered throughout the various books of the Code, and many are to be found in the Book of Sale which apply to every class of contract. These rules have been considerably affected and amplified by Articles 64, 80-82 and 106-112 of the Ottoman Code of Civil Procedure, which will be considered later. Muhammadan law contemplates contract as the means by which one person divests himself of his ownership in a particular thing and transfers such ownership to another person.

(a) *Offer and acceptance.*

A contract is concluded by means of offer (*ijab*) and acceptance (*kabul*). If either of these elements is lacking, there can be no contract, with the exception, however, of the contract of guarantee. As regards offer and acceptance, see Articles 167, 433, 680, 706, 773, 804, 837, 1330, 1405, 1432, 1442, 1451 and 1531. In the case of guarantee, the offer of the guarantor is considered to be sufficient (see Article 621), and in the case of release there is no need for acceptance, though the release may be formally disclaimed. (see Article 1568). A similar provision applies in the case of an admission. (see Article 1580). The formation of contract requires no special formality. The contract may, at the option of the parties, be in writing, or by word of mouth. It may also be by conduct.

The offer and acceptance must be made at the same place or rather on the same occasion. This is known as the meeting or *majlis* of the parties. This rule of law has now been modified by Article 64 of the Code of Civil Procedure. (see *post*). It should be noted that in a contract of hire silence is considered to indicate assent and acceptance. (see Article 438, and notes thereto, and compare the terms of Article 1451 and the last paragraph of Article 1535). Article 438 is precisely the contrary of Article 805 (*q.v.*).

Before the passing of Article 64 (as amended) of the Code of Civil Procedure, the question of the *majlis*, or meeting place of the parties, was one of some difficulty, since Muhammadan law appears to have contemplated every contract, whether made by word of mouth, or reduced to writing, or concluded by conduct, as being made in the actual physical presence of the parties. (see Articles 181-185). For what appears to be an exception to the general rule, see the terms of Article 840, which is, in effect, no more than an example of the principle laid down in Article 839. In this case there could not normally be a *majlis*, or meeting place of the parties. An authoritative writer on Muhammadan law,[1] however, has gone further and has stated that offer and acceptance must be made at the same meeting "or what the law considers as such", though no authority is cited for this latter statement.

"The proposal and acceptance must be made at the same meeting (*majlis*) either in fact or what the law considers as such. Suppose a man proposes face to face with another to sell his horse to him, if the person addressed leaves the place without signifying his acceptance, the offer comes to an end, because there is no obligation on the owner of the horse to keep his offer open. But if the offer is communicated by means of a messenger or a letter, the meeting for the purpose of acceptance is held to be at the place and time the message reaches the person for whom the

---

[1] Abdur Rahim: Muhammadan Jurisprudence, page 284.

offer was intended. If the promisee then signifies his acceptance the contract is concluded. The acceptance must be in terms of the proposal, that is to say, the two minds must be in agreement, otherwise there is no real consent"; but however that may be, Article 64 of the Code of Civil Procedure, it is submitted, has done away with any necessity for an actual meeting of the parties, and it is sufficient if the minds of the parties are *ad idem* on the subject matter of the contract. Thus, if A advertises in the press or by means of a special pamphlet that he will pay a reward to any person who supplies information required by him, and B, a member of the public, supplies such information, there has been a complete offer and acceptance. (see also the English Leading Case of *Carlill v. Carbolic Smoke Ball Co.* 1893. I. Q. B. 256). The following is the text of the judgment in the Palestine Decided Case of *Alphonse Katafago v. Germas Khristo Avrinos* (C. A. No. 13/22.)

"The Respondent Germas Avrinos has sued the Appellant Alphonse Katafago, the representative at Acre of the Regie Company, in his representative capacity, for a sum of 53534 ps. alleged to be due under a contract for the sale and purchase of 8236 kilos of tobacco at 6½ ps. a kilo. In support of his claim he has put in a letter from himself dated 19th. September, 1921, and a reply by the Appellant dated 7th. October, 1921, and has asked to be allowed to call witnesses in confirmation of the letters.

The District Court has held that the letters constitute a valid contract and have given judgment in favour of the Respondent.

From the opening sentence of the judgment, it is clear that the District Court regarded the Regie Company as the actual defendant in the case.

It is not alleged by the Respondent that the contract upon which the action is founded was entered into by the Appellant Katafago and it has been objected on behalf of the Appellant that under these circumstances, even if there is a valid contract it is not enforceable either against him or against the Regie Company, in view of the fact that it is outside the authority of the Company's local representative to contract on behalf of the Company for the purchase of tobacco.

Previous, however, to the issue of the order which made it clear that corporations could sue and be sued in their own names, the usual form in which to bring an action against a corporation was to sue an agent for the corporation in his representative capacity and there is no rule providing that an action cannot still be brought against a corporation in this form. The Court therefore holds that this objection fails.

LAW OF CONTRACT

This point having been disposed of, the next point to be determined is the main issue in the case, namely, whether the letters from the Respondent dated 19th. September, 1921, and the reply of the Appellant dated 7th. October, 1921, are evidence of the existence of a contract between the parties for the sale and purchase of tobacco.

The District Court has held that the fact of such a contract having been entered into is proved and that in the absence of any agreement by the Respondent to rescind such contract the Appellant is bound by it.

The first paragraph of the respondent's letter, however, makes it clear that no agreement had been reached between the parties, because in fact they had not been able to agree as to the liability for the payment of tithes on the tobacco and the following paragraphs of the letter contain an offer to the company of two alternatives: either that they should buy the tobacco at $6^1/_2$ P. T. a kilo, the tithes to be paid by the Respondent, or that the negotiations should be abandoned, the tobacco—then in bonded warehouse—be delivered to the Respondent. The Appellant's reply is to the effect that his Company do not propose to proceed with the transaction and that Respondent is at liberty to remove the tobacco on payment of the prescribed dues.

The Court holds that these two letters prove that no agreement was ever arrived at between the parties and further that even if, contrary to the first paragraph of Respondent's letter, an agreement was in fact entered into, the last paragraph of the letter contains an offer to annul the contract of which offer the Appellants letter is an acceptance. In the face of these letters it is useless to consider whether the Respondent is at liberty to call witnesses to prove that the tobacco was weighed by the Company's agent, or any other fact in corroboration of the contract alleged to be contained in the letters.

The Court therefore holds that there is no agreement existing between the parties and the judgment of the District Court is reversed with costs here and below."

The Palestine Decided Case of *Mordekhai Heifitz v. Nissim Sion Barhum,* (C. A. No. 35/28) is an example of acceptance of rescission of a contract by conduct. The following is from the judgment of the Court of Appeal:

"Respondent duly received the notice from Appellant cancelling the agreement to which he made no reply. It is also admitted that subsequent to the receipt of the said notice Respondent refrained from doing any work in connection with the trees in the orchard. Some nine months subsequent to the receipt of the Appellant's notice, *i. e.* in the late spring of 1925, at the time of the harvest of the second year's crop, Respondent served a Public

92	LAW OF CONTRACT

Notary Notice on Appellant demanding the fruit of the second year otherwise he would hold Appellant liable for damages for breach of contract.

Appellant in the meantime had entered into a contract with another cultivator for the crop, and we are of opinion that Appellant was justified in doing so, and that Respondent having raised no objection to Appellant's notice and his failure to perform any of the work stipulated to be done on the trees in the orchard subsequent to the receipt of Appellant's notice amounted to an acceptance of the cancellation of the contract and a waiver or abandonment thereof, and accordingly that there was no breach on the part of appellant."

The basic idea underlying alienation of ownership in the view of Muhammadan jurists is physical transfer from one owner to another. Thus, contracts of lease and hire are regarded as being the sale of future usufruct. Muhammadan jurists contemplated not merely the abstract state of mind of the purchaser, but also the state of his mind with reference to the subject-matter. This explains the general rule of law, now practically repealed by the terms of Article 64 of the Code of Civil Procedure, that there can be no contract of sale concluded with reference to a thing not in existence (see Articles 197 and 205). This theory, again, explains the existence of certain options, such as an option for inspection or an option for defect. (see Articles 320—355).

(b) Consideration.

It is nowhere specifically stated in the text-books of Muhammadan jurisprudence that consideration, as understood in English law, is an essential element of a valid contract. The word consideration in Arabic is *'awaz* which means "something in return", or "instead of", and is commonly employed in such phrases as *hiba bil 'awaz* (gift for something in return); *hiba bi shart ul 'awaz* (gift subject to a condition for something in return). In the Mejelle *'awaz* is usually replaced by *semen*, price, (see Articles 237—244, 450, (rent), and cf. Article 420), but it seems that these are merely particular forms of *'awaz,* or consideration.

In the leading English case of *Currie v. Misa* (1875), L.R. 10 Ex. 162, the following definition was given of consideration:

"A valuable consideration in the sense of the law may consist either in some right, interest, profit, or benefit accruing to one party, or some forbearance, detriment, loss or responsibility given, suffered, or undertaken by the other."

The consideration for a contract is contemplated by Muhammadan law as *valuable* consideration, in the sense of something possessing some real intrinsic value, however small. It will thus be seen that the consideration of Muhammadan law differs considerably from that of English law as defined above. The definition given in *Currie v. Misa* seems to cover almost every conceivable type of contract. There are certain contracts in Muhammadan law, however, to which valuable consideration in the sense of something possessing some specific material value does not apply, such as an absolute gift.

Contracts in Muhammadan law are therefore divided into two classes in respect to consideration:

(1) Contracts importing valuable consideration (*uqud muawaza*). (Art 658). These are contracts which are based upon and are consequently made binding by reason of some valuable consideration forming the basis for the contract, as in the contract of sale or hire. This is usually called in Muhammadan law *bedel* or *semen*.

(2) Contracts which do not import valuable consideration. These are divided into two categories:

(a) Where the benefit accrues to the person taking delivery of the subject matter of the contract *e. g.* gift, alms, loan for use;

(b) Where the benefit accrues to the person giving delivery *e. g.* deposit for safe keeping.

Palestine Decided Cases.

(1) "This is an action on a promissory note for 1000 Napoleons drawn in Alexandria on the 30th. June, 1920, by the appellant Daoud Moyal in favour of the Respondent Mme. Claire who was at that time his wife. The consideration for the note is stated in it to be "Valeur en Compte". It is common ground

LAW OF CONTRACT

between the parties that the note was given in pursuance of and part performance of an agreement between them dated the same day, made in Alexandria. The parties were both of the Jewish religion and the agreement was made in anticipation of a divorce between the parties expected to be subsequently pronounced by the Chief Rabbi of Alexandria; and was intended to ensure the validity of that divorce and to govern the rights of the parties after divorce, both as to dowry and other financial matters, and to custody of their child.

In Clause 3 of the agreement the appellant, while declaring that his Spanish nationality is doubtful, binds himself to acquire the Ottoman or such other nationality as would render the divorce valid. The divorce was pronounced shortly afterwards, but no steps were at any time taken by the appellant to alter his national status.

Clause 4 of the agreement begins as follows: "Monsieur David Moyal reconnait devoir a Madame Claire Calmy une somme de livres Egyptiennes deux mille (LE. 2000) qui constitue en partie la restitution de sa dot et de sa contredot et en partie une somme convenue à forfait en réglement de tous droits revenant a Madame Claire Calmy en dépendance d'une situation patrimoniale qui a été réglée anterieurement à ce jour.

The remainder of the clause contains provisions as to the manner of payment of this sum of LE.2000. It is in fulfilment of these provisions that the promissory note which is the subject of this action was given. The Appellant has based his appeal on the ground that he was at the time when the agreement and promissory note were made a Spanish subject: that Spanish Law recognises no possibility of divorce between Spanish subjects: that any agreement made in contemplation of or for the purpose of rendering valid a divorce was in consequence absolutely void *ab initio,* and the provisions in it with regard to payments by the Appellant, being ancillary to and dependent upon the main agreement as to obtaining an effectual divorce, were also void. The appellant argues that it follows that there is total failure of consideration for the promissory note. It is to be noted that this argument was not put forward in the District Court where the appellant pleaded that the question at issue was one of personal status and that the case lay within the jurisdiction not of the civil but the Rabbinical Court. His advocate also admitted in the District Court that the divorce was valid, though the appellant now states that this is to be taken as an admission of the validity of the divorce in its religious and not in its civil aspect. Apart from this admission, however, it is difficult to see how this defence can be sustained. The course of events contemplated by the parties when the note was made has taken place. The Respondent has consented to the religious divorce and has ceased to be dependent upon the appellant for support; and if that divorce is not valid from a civil point of view, this is only because of difficulties which were known to the Appellant at the time, and which he has not taken steps to remove in accordance with his intention declared in Clause 3 of the Agreement. In fact the Appellant's argument reduces itself to this, that as he has failed to carry out his intention as declared in Clause 3, he is relieved from the necessity of fulfilling Clause 1.

I cannot accept this reasoning. I hold that the Agreement establishes the fact that the consideration for which the appellant gave the bills was the concurrence of the Respondent in the arrangements mentioned in Clauses 1 and 2, namely the divorce by the Rabbinical Court of Alexandria and surrender of custody of the child: and further that on payment of the bills the appellant obtains a defence against any claim that may at any time be made in respect of dowry or the situation patrimoniale mentioned in Clause 4 of the Agreement. The judgment of the Court is that the appeal is dismissed with costs". (*Daoud Moyal v. Claire Moyal (nee Calmy)*, C. A. 205/22).

(2). "On the 22nd. September, 1922, the Plaintiff, Said Kemal, paid to defendant, the Imperial Ottoman Bank at Nablus, LE.250 to be sent to Abdul Latif Salah at the Post Office, Berlin. He signed a memorandum stating that the amount was to be sent to Herrn Abdul Latif Salah, Berlin, Postliegend, through the London Branch, which was to change the sum into marks according to the rate of exchange. The defendant bank telegraphed to its office in London: "Remit by telegram to Abdul Latif Salah Berlin Postliegend the equivalent of L.251-12 for account Said Kemal. "Speedalow". The telegram was answered by a letter of 23rd. May acknowledging and repeating the telegram and containing these words: "We have therefore passed to your debit the sum of L.251-12 the equivalent of which at 6100 namely marks 1.534.760 we have remitted by telegram to Abdul Latif Salah Berlin Postliegend for account of Said Kemal in accordance with your instructions."

Meanwhile on the 22nd. the Plaintiff telegraphed to Abdul Latif Salah *"Automobile vendu touchez Deutsch Bank Berlin 251 sterling 12 shillings Said."* Abdul Latif who gave evidence swore that on the 23rd. he called at the Deutsche Bank, asked for his money, and was told that none had been "advised" for him. He called on the 25th., 26th., 27th. with the same result. On the 29th. September meeting with a similar reply on his enquiry at the Bank, he produced the telegram of the 22nd. and a clerk marked upon it a note that the money had not been received, with the date 29/9 and the stamp *"Uebersee Abteilung"*. Abdul Latif continued calling for his money till the 13th. October and on the 11th. obtained a similar note made on the same telegram dated 11/10 but apparently initialled by a different clerk. The second

LAW OF CONTRACT

stamp contained the words "Deutsche Bank." After 13th. October Abdul Latif left Berlin and returned to Palestine. On 17th. October a letter was written by Defendant's London agents to the Nablus Bank stating that they were "advised by the Deutsche Bank Berlin, that the beneficiary has not yet called at their office." The plaintiff brought action against defendant for a return of the L.E.250 and an equal sum in damages. Abdul Latif intervened as a third party claiming the damages from both parties alternatively. His claim against the plaintiff was that he had instructed him to forward the money to him at Berlin and that he was responsible for the negligence of the agent he employed.

The District Court dismissed the action of the third party against the Plaintiff. With that we agree. The plaintiff had sent the money in the ordinary way employed by careful business people, by employing a well known and reliable Bank, and he was not responsible if owing to some mistake in Berlin the money did not reach the third party in time. The District Court was of opinion that if the plaintiff was not liable to the third party the defendant could not be liable to him and they gave judgment for the defendants as against plaintiff. In the claim by the third party against defendants the Court gave judgment in favour of the latter on the ground that all the defendant had to do was to send the money to the Deutsche Bank and that having done that they were not responsible for what happened if the Deutsche Bank made a mistake and the money never reached the third party. From the judgment of the District Court the plaintiff appealed and so did the third party, but against the judgment given against him in favour of the plaintiff, not against the other judgment given against him in favour of the defendant. He said in the Court of Appeal "I confirm my claim to Haj Said." This being the case of the third party we have no difficulty in dealing with it. The judgment of the District Court was perfectly right in dismissing his case against the plaintiff and we confirm it on the ground already stated. But the Plaintiff's case is quite different. He was agent of the third party as between those two, but he dealt with the Bank as a principal and handed to them money for a specific purpose, namely, to arrange for the payment of a corresponding amount in German marks to Abdul Latif Salah, Post Office, Berlin. It is not asserted that Abdul Latif ever received at the Post Office an advice that money was awaiting him at any bank. Now the agreement of the defendant Bank was to send to the Deutsche Bank to his account. The Deutsche Bank was the agent of the defendant in this transaction and through some mistake the Bank denied the receipt of money for Abdul Latif notwithstanding his repeated applications during a period of three weeks. The District Court seems to have been of opinion that as there was no specific agreement by the Bank to deliver the money within a reasonable period of time they were not necessarily in fault, although they failed to deliver the money from the 23rd. September to the 13th. of October. If this view of the Bank's responsibility were correct, few people would send money through its agency. It is, however, of common knowledge and no banker will deny that when money is given to a Bank to forward, it is part of the agreement that it shall be forwarded with reasonable rapidity, and with the telegraph at its service it was clearly a failure of performance if the money was not delivered at Berlin within 21 days of its receipt at Nablus. It must be borne in mind that a transaction of this kind although called "forwarding money" is really paying money to a banker at one place in consideration of his agreement to arrange for the payment of a corresponding sum to a named person at another place. The arrangement between a banker and his agent or agents is generally made by telegram as was done in this case. After 21 days it was natural for Abdul Latif to abandon hope and return to Palestine treating the forwarding arrangement as having failed. This is in our opinion clearly a case of failure of consideration. The sum of L.E.250 was paid to the defendant Bank for a purpose which was not carried out and the money must be returned with interest from the date of protest. When the money has been recovered it will be received by the plaintiff on account of the third party." *(Abdul Latif Salah v. The Ottoman Bank and another,* C.A. 58/23)

(3). "The Appellant is suing on an undertaking by the Respondent given in a letter dated 22nd. July, 1929. There is, however, no evidence before the Court that any consideration was given for the undertaking, which consequently is unenforceable.

Further, the letter does not specify that the buildings already constructed upon the land at the date when the letter was written were to be removed forthwith. Even, therefore, if the undertaking were enforceable, no action for damages for non-removal of such buildings would lie until the termination of the Respondent's term of occupation of the land."

The following is a copy of the letter referred to in the judgment:

"Whereas I have started to erect buildings on the land of "Jilmi" which I purchased from you by virtue of a contract dated 9th. February, 1929, in which contract it is provided in clause 10 that I shall return the subject matter sold to you, if the sum determined in the said clause is paid by you and relying on your resolution to pay the principal together with the commission fixed, you find that the buildings do not suit your interest now, therefore I have now given up building and I leave the land in the state in which I had taken it over from you I undertake to you that if I commit a breach of this undertaking or erect any buildings or plant anything or make any alteration therein, I shall be bound to pay to you the penalty of LP. 7000 as liquidated damages in the same way as provided in clause 14 of the contract in question". *(Saleh Muhammad Shibel v. Haj Khalil Taha,* C. A. No. 9/31).

(4) "It is clear that the consideration for the promise by the Respondent to pay L.P. 20 to the Appellant upon her remarriage was the agreement by the Appellant to divorce the Respondent. Hence it cannot be maintained that there was no consideration for the bill. As regards the application to this case of Article 64 of the Code of Civil Procedure as amended, we must infer that the District Court was of opinion that the bill was not in accordance with the provisions of that Article because it was contrary to public policy that a woman should agree to pay money for her divorce and further should make such payment dependent upon her remarriage. With regard to this we hold that the parties being Muslims, are entitled by Sharia Law to make an agreement whereby the wife undertakes to pay a sum of money to her husband in consideration of his agreeing to her divorce. Further, it does not render such an agreement void that the payment of such sum is, under the agreement, deferred to the date when the woman remarries. The Respondent has remarried, and it cannot be maintained that the bill constituted an illegal restraint upon marriage."

The following is from the judgment of the Court below.

"Upon consideration the Court holds that the contract entered into between appellant and respondent in order that appellant could get a divorce from the respondent is void. The Court does not agree with the views of the Magistrate;

(1) That there was consideration to the undertaking made by appellant to pay to respondent in accordance with the English Law;

(2) We do not hold that such a contract is in accordance with Article 64 of the Civil Procedure Code.

Therefore it has been decided to set aside the judgment of the Court below, and dismissal of the claim of the respondent, with costs". (*Yusef Issa Hamoud el Faghouri v. Jamileh Mousa Hamoud*, C. A. 55/31).

(5) "To deal now first with the question of the pension. The Appellant was unable to quote to us any authority in the law of Palestine relating to the question of the consideration for the promise by the Synod to continue the pension of the deceased to his family after his death. The only consideration which one can find in the resolution refers to the past services of the deceased, as Turkish Secretary to the Patriarchate, and we know of nothing which can take the case out of the general rule of English law to the effect that acts done by the promisee before the promise was made may constitute a motive for the promise but are not true consideration. For this reason we agree with the District Court that the resolution was a *nudum pactum* and dismiss the appeal on this point." *(Habib Homsi v. Commission on the Finances of the Orthodox Patriarchate*, C.A. 136/33).

Constantinople Cassation Decisions.

(1) "Any obligation undertaken in pursuance of a condition which is contrary to law is not binding. It is laid down by Article 76 of the Mejelle that the oath may at no time be administered to the plaintiff. An undertaking entered into provided that the plaintiff swears an oath is contrary to law and therefore not binding. Any action brought on the undertaking should therefore be dismissed." (C.C.D. No. 71, dated 30th. April, 1327 Vol. I, page 171).

(In this case A undertook to pay B L.12 French money in the event of C. swearing an oath that certain animals had in fact been stolen).

(2) "An undertaking to perform an act which a person is not obliged himself to perform, and which is not based upon any legal grounds, such as a contract of guarantee, by the very nature of which the guarantor is bound, is invalid." (C.C.D. No. 21, dated 29th. March, 1328, Vol. 2, page 44).

(3) "If a person undertakes in writing to secure the return of bonds on behalf of a person who has himself deposited them as a pledge with some third person, he is obliged to return either the identical bonds, if they are still in existence, or to give the value thereof if they have been destroyed. The action may not be dismissed on the grounds that the undertaking in writing contains only a mere promise." (C. C. D. No. 31, dated 22nd. April, 1330, Vol. 4, p. 62).

(4) "Judgment may not be given on a contract which contains a mere promise. A was granted a permit to quarry stones and sand in a village and in this connection drew up a contract whereby he undertook to pay a certain sum to the village mosque. A later refused to pay the sum and an action was brought against him to enforce payment thereof. *Held*, that no judgment could validly be given. since contracts of this sort, which only contained a mere promise, imposed no obligation upon any one and the case should therefore be dismissed (C.C.D. No. 64 dated 30th. June, 1330, Vol. 4, page 128).

(2) *Capacity of parties to a contract*

(a) *Minors.*

The time at which full legal capacity is obtained by both males and females in Muhammadan law is upon the completion of the age of puberty, *i. e.* upon completing the fifteenth year (*sin-al-bulugh*). (Article 986). Puberty (*bulugh*) begins upon the completion of the twelfth year of age in the case of males and upon the completion of the ninth year of age in the case of females. (Article 986). Persons below the age of puberty are minors (*sabi* or *saghir*) and are under the control of their tutors (*weli*) or guardians (*wasi*). As to who these persons are, see Article 974 and notes thereto. The Ottoman Commercial Code (Article 2) made an exception as regards the power of persons to engage in commerce, *i. e.* as merchants, fixing the age at twenty-one years completed, or eighteen years completed subject to the consent of their tutors or guardians and the permission of the Commercial Court. As to how puberty is proved, see Articles 985, 988 and 989 and notes thereto, and see also Article 987.

All persons not having completed the age of puberty are considered to be in a state of interdiction (*hajr*) (see Article 941) which, however, may be removed by a grant of permission (*izn*) by the tutor (*weli*) or guardian (*wasi*). They are then known as persons to whom permission to dispose of their property has been given (*mazoun*).

Muhammadan law divides minors into two categories:

(a) minors of imperfect understanding (*saghir ghair mumayiz*) ;

(b) minors of perfect understanding (*saghir mumayiz*)

A minor of imperfect understanding is a young person who cannot understand buying and selling and who cannot distinguish flagrant misrepresentation (*ghubn fahish*) which is misrepresentation amounting to five in ten, from minor misrepresentation (*ghubn yasir*) (see Article 943). As to how these points are to be proved to the satisfaction of the Court, see notes to Article 943.

A minor of perfect understanding is a young person who can distinguish between these matters. (Article 943). Such a person is also said to be *akil*, of sound mind.

A minor is *ipso facto* interdicted (Article 957) which means that any disposition of property by him, unless he has been granted permission by his tutor or guardian, (Article 972) or the Court (Article 975) is invalid (see Article 960), subject, however, to the following exceptions and conditions :

(1) A minor of imperfect understanding cannot make any valid disposition of his property, even though his tutor assents thereto ; (Article 966).

(2) (*a*) A minor of perfect understanding may, without his tutor's assent, enter into any disposition of property which is purely for his own benefit ;

(b) If the disposition of property is purely for his own disadvantage, it is invalid even if his tutor agrees;

(c) In cases where it is not certain whether the disposition of property will be for his advantage or disadvantage, the transaction can only be valid if the permission of the tutor has been obtained. (Article 967).

Permission given by a tutor to a minor of perfect understanding to enter into dispositions of his property may be either express or implied. (Article 971). It may not, however, be made subject to any limitation as to time, place, or the type of business. (Article 970).

The result of the grant of permission is that the minor is considered to have arrived at the age of puberty in respect to the matters included in the permission. (Article 972).

A tutor may hand over to a minor a portion of his property on trial with which to engage in business. If the trial shows that the minor is fully capable of looking after his own property, in which case he is said to be *rashid*, or of mature mind (Article 947), he may hand him over the rest of his property (Article 968).

A minor who has been granted permission by his tutor may be interdicted by him, in accordance with the terms of Article 973. The same provision of law applies when the minor has been granted permission by the Court (Article 977).

As regards the circumstances in which the property of minors should be handed over to them on attaining the age of puberty, see Articles 981, 982, 983 and 984.

(b) *Other persons not possessing full contractual capacity.*

In addition to minors, lunatics and imbeciles are *ipso facto* interdicted; and prodigals and persons who are in debt may also be interdicted by the Court.

1. *Lunatics.* A lunatic (*majnun*) is *ipso facto* interdicted (*mahjur*). (Article 957 and see Article 941). Muhammadan law divides lunatics into two classes:

(a) Persons who are continuously mad and whose madness lasts the whole time (*majnun mutbik*);

LAW OF CONTRACT

(b) Persons whose madness is intermittent *i. e.* persons who are sometimes mad and sometimes have lucid intervals. (*majnun ghair mutbik*) (Article 944). Any disposition of property by a lunatic who is continuously mad is null and void, for they are considered to be minors of imperfect understanding. (Article 979 and see Article 960).

Any disposition of property by a lunatic who is not continuously mad and made during a lucid interval is valid, since his acts are like the acts of a sane person. (Article 980).

2. *Imbeciles.* An imbecile (*matuh*) is defined by Muhammadan law as being a person whose mind is so deranged that his comprehension is extremely limited, his speech confused, and his actions imperfect (Article 945 and see also the Palestine Decided Case of *Ibrahim Khoury Farah v. Dr. Yacoub Nazha*, (L. A. 7/32). Such a person is *ipso facto* interdicted (Article 957). An imbecile, however, is considered to be a minor of perfect understanding (*saghir mumayiz*), and is consequently able to dispose of property within the limits laid down by Article 967.

(3) *Prodigals.* Muhammadan law divides prodigals into two classes:

(*a*) Those who by reckless expenditure waste and destroy their property to no purpose. (Article 946). Mere dissolute conduct is not a sufficient reason for interdiction. (Article 963);

(*b*) Those who are so stupid and simple-minded that they are deceived in their business. (Article 946).

Such persons may be interdicted upon application made to the Court, the Court alone having the power to act as tutor. (Articles 958 and 990).

An interdicted prodigal is, as regards his civil transactions, like a minor of perfect understanding (*saghir mumayiz*) (Article 990) and consequently able to dispose of property within the limits laid down by Article 967. Any other disposition of property by him after interdiction is null and void. (Article 991). Any expenditure necessary for the maintenance of the interdicted person and those dependent upon him for support may be made from his own property. (Article 992 and see Article 996).

LAW OF CONTRACT

(4) *Debtors*. A person who is in debt may be interdicted upon application made to the Court by the creditors. (Article 959). For the purpose of interdiction, by being in debt is meant putting off paying creditors, although the debtor is able to pay; and the Court has power to sell the debtor's property and pay his debts therefrom (Article 998). The interdiction only applies to property in existence at the time the interdiction was declared, (Article 1001), but extends to everything likely to prejudice the rights of creditors. (Article 1002). A debtor who is bankrupt may be interdicted, for the reasons referred to in Article 999— but see notes to this Article and the effect thereon of the law relating to bankruptcy. Any expenditure necessary for the maintenance of an interdicted debtor and for persons dependent upon him for support may be paid from the debtor's property (Article 1000).

The matters referred to above represent, as has been stated, the Muhammadan law, and are, subject to certain exceptions (see notes to Articles 998 and 999), within the jurisdiction of the Muhammadan Sharia courts. (See the Palestine Decided Cases of *Mustafa Ismail Sakija v. Solomon Jacobson* for the estate of *Joseph Bey Moyal*, C.A. 98/27 and *Joshua Khankin v. Qasem Muhammad Mustafa*, C. A. 58 and 59/32).

Non-Muslims are within the jurisdiction of the Personal Status Courts of the Community to which they belong. Thus, wherever questions of minority, madness, prodigals, debtors or imbeciles are before the Civil Courts, a certificate should normally be produced from a Sharia or personal Status Court having jurisdiction proving the point of personal status in question.

Palestine Decided Case.

"Although civil bankruptcy amounts to interdiction and is, in accordance with the Palestine Order-in-Council, a matter of personal status falling within the jurisdiction of the Sharia Court, yet Article 52 limits the jurisdiction of this Tribunal to matters between Muslims, while allowing jurisdiction in cases such as this to the Civil Courts under Article 47." (*Mustafa Ismail Sakija v. Solomon Jacobson for the estate of Joseph Bey Moyal*, C. A. 98/27).

Constantinople Cassation Decisions.

(1) "If a guardian is appointed by the Sharia Courts for a plaintiff who is suddenly afflicted with madness during the course of an action, and the trial is carried on through the guardian, and a medical certificate is later submitted to the effect that the plaintiff has recovered his sanity, and the plaintiff obtains a certificate from the Sharia Court that there is no longer any need for his remaining under the supervision of the guardian, and produces the same to the Civil Court, such Court may go on with the trial. The Court may not, however, go on with the trial, merely relying on the medical certificate. (C.C.D., dated 27th July, 1327, No. 125, Vol. 1, page 289.)

(2) "The Civil Courts are not entitled to form an opinion and take a decision as to whether a document issued by a Sharia Court appointing a mother guardian of her son for the purpose of dealing with his affairs and keeping his property on account of his being unable to look after his personal affairs, prohibits him from disposing of his property by contract. Consequently, if a defence is made in reliance upon such a document that the son in question is interdicted and that any disposition of his property is void, the Court may not enter into the merits of the case relying on the text of the document and take a decision accordingly, but the defence must be adjourned until a document (on the point) has been obtained from the Sharia Court and a decision should be given based thereon. (C.C.D. No. 148, dated 27th. November, 1330, Vol. 4, page 307).

(5) *Capacity as dealt with in specific contracts in the Mejelle.*

In addition to the general rules laid down as to capacity in Chapter I of Book IX of the Code, special Articles are devoted to the subject in each of the Books or Chapters dealing with the various contracts and transactions contained in the Code; and the requirements of law are not all uniform. They are as follows:

(1) *Sale.* The parties must be of sound mind (*akil*) and perfect understanding (*mumayiz*). (Article 361). A sale which is defective in any essential condition, such as a sale by a lunatic, is void. (Article 362, and see notes thereto).

(2) *Hire.* The parties must be of sound mind (*akil*) and perfect understanding (*mumayiz*). (Article 444). If the owner of hired premises is a minor, or is mad and a contract of hire has been concluded for an estimated rent, (*ejr misl*), the contract is dependent upon the ratification of the tutor (*weli*) or guardian (*wasi*). (Article 447, and see example to Article 458).

(3) *Guarantee.* The surety or guarantor (*kefil*) must be of sound mind (*akil*) and have arrived at the age of puberty (*baligh*). A lunatic (*majnun*), an imbecile (*matuh*), or a minor cannot make a valid contract of guarantee; and if a minor does in fact become a guarantor and ratifies the contract after arriving at the age of puberty, he is not bound thereby. (Article 628). The person guaranteed (*makful anhu*) need not be of sound mind (*akil*) nor have arrived at the age of puberty (*baligh*). (Article 629).

(4) *Transfer of debt.* The transferor (*muhil*) and the person in whose favour the transfer is made (*muhal lahu*) must be of sound mind (*akil*) and the transferee (*muhal alieh*) must be of sound mind (*akil*) and have reached the age of puberty (*baligh*). Any breach of these conditions makes the contract void (Article 684). For the contract to be executory the transferor (*muhil*) and the person in whose favour the transfer is made (*muhal lahu*) must have reached the age of puberty. Consequently, a transfer or acceptance of a transfer by a minor of perfect understanding is dependent upon ratification by the tutor (Article 685).

(5) *Pledge.* The pledgor (*rahin*) and pledgee (*murtehin*) must be of sound mind (*akil*) but they need not have reached the age of puberty (*baligh*). Consequently, a minor of perfect understanding (*sebi mumayiz*) may be either pledgor or pledgee (Article 708).

(6) *Deposit for safe keeping.* The person making the deposit (*muwaddi*) and the person receiving it (*mustawdi*) must be of sound mind (*akil*) and perfect understanding (*mumayiz*). They need not have arrived at the age of puberty (*baligh*). Consequently, a lunatic and a minor of imperfect understanding (*sebi ghair mumayiz*) cannot validly make or receive a deposit for safe keeping. (Article 776).

(7) *Loan for use.* The person giving a thing on loan for use (*muir*) and the person taking a thing on loan for use (*musteir*) must be of sound mind (*akil*) and perfect understanding (*mumayiz*). They need not have arrived at the age of puberty (*baligh*). Consequently, a lunatic (*majnun*) or a minor of imperfect understanding (*sebi ghair mumayiz*) cannot conclude a valid contract of loan for use. (Article 809).

LAW OF CONTRACT

(8) *Gift*. The donor (*wahib*) must be of sound mind (*akil*) and have arrived at the age of puberty (*baligh*). A gift by a minor (*saghir*), a lunatic (*majnun*) or an imbecile (*matuh*) is invalid. These persons, however, may be the beneficiaries of a gift (Article 859; and see Articles 851, 852 and 853).

(9) *Partnership in land and work.* (*muzaria*). The contracting parties must be of sound mind (*akil*). They need not have reached the age of puberty (*baligh*).(Article 1433).

(10) *Partnership in trees and work.* (*musakat*). The contracting parties must be of sound mind (*akil*). They need not have reached the age of puberty(*baligh*).(Article 1443).

(11) *Agency*. The following rules are laid down by Articles 1457 and 1458:

(a) *Principal*.

(1) Any authority to act as agent conferred by a minor of imperfect understanding (*sebi ghair mumayiz*) or a lunatic (*majnun*) is invalid;

(2) A minor of perfect understanding (*sebi mumayiz*) may not confer any authority to act as agent in any matter which can only be for his disadvantage;

(3) A minor may confer authority to act as agent in matters which can only be for his advantage;

(4) As regards matters which may be for his advantage or disadvantage, a minor may appoint an agent if he has been authorized to engage in trade, *i. e.* buying and selling. If not, any such appointment depends upon ratification by the tutor (Article 1457).

(b) *Agent*.

The agent must be of sound mind (*akil*) and perfect understanding (*mumayiz*). He need not have arrived at the age of puberty (*baligh*). Consequently, a minor of perfect understanding, even though not authorized to act on his own behalf, may become an agent (Article 1458).

(12) *Settlement*. The person making the settlement (*musalih*) must be of sound mind (*akil*). He need not have arrived at the age of puberty (*baligh*). Consequently, a settlement made by a lunatic (*majnun*), an imbecile (*matuh*) or a minor of imperfect understanding (*sebi ghair mumayiz*) is always invalid. A settlement made by a minor

who has been authorized by his tutor is valid, provided the settlement does not result in a clear loss. (Article 1539 and see terms of Article 1540).

(13) *Release.* A release by a minor, a lunatic or an imbecile is absolutely invalid (Article 1541).

(14) *Admissions.*

(a) *Person making the admission.* To make a valid admission, a person must be of sound mind (*akil*) and have arrived at the age of puberty (*baligh*). Consequently an admission made by a minor, (*sebi*), a lunatic (*majnun*) or an imbecile (*matuh*) is invalid. (Article 1573). A person making an admission must not be interdicted. (Article 1576).

(b) *Person in whose favour the admission is made* A person in whose favour an admission is made need not be of sound mind (*akil*). (Article 1574).

Palestine Decided Cases:

(1) "On 21st. June, 1919, the Appellants, who are the heirs of the transferor, signed a written acknowledgement that the transfer was an absolute sale, and that the attempts which they had previously made to have the transaction annulled were made in error, and they thereby released the Respondents from any claim in respect of the transfer. In view of the undertaking admittedly given by Respondent at the time of the transfer and notwithstanding the admission by the Appellants dated 21st. June, 1919, (which admission cannot be accepted against such of the Appellants as were then minors) the transaction was not an absolute sale but was by way of mortgage." *(Shaban Mustafa el Aydi and others v. Ibrahim and Tewfik el Khalil,* L. A. 81/22).

(2) "In this case the Appellant seeks to set aside a sale of land on the ground that the seller through whom he claims by right of succession sold to a purchaser who was an infant and unable to enter into a contract of sale. An infant who is not of an age to understand business is not bound by his contract either as seller or as purchaser, and he may repudiate such a transaction either during infancy or on his becoming of age. But this is not a plea to be set up by a seller who has sold to an infant and who wishes afterwards to avoid the transaction. The Appellants, who are the heirs of the seller, are in the same position as their ancestor. It is alleged that the seller, after the sale, sold some of the trees to third persons. This, if proved, would go to show only that the seller believed that he could avoid the sale. The appeal must be dismissed." *(Selim and Tewfik children of Asad Haj Jarrar v. Asad el Madi, guardian of Mukhtar Madi, his son,* L. A. 109/22).

LAW OF CONTRACT

(3) "There was no evidence before the Court below that Appellant, or his guardian, during the period of his minority, at any time authorized Respondent to spend any money for and on behalf of Appellant. The appeal is therefore allowed, the judgment of the Land Court quashed, and the Respondent's action dismissed."

The following is from the judgment of the Court below:

"The Plaintiff sues the Defendant, who is his younger brother, for LP. 397, being moneys expended by the Plaintiff for the support, maintenance and education of the Defendant between the years 1335 and 1339 (1917—1921). The Defendant put in no written defence, but in Court, when called as a witness by the Plaintiff, he denied having received any money from the Plaintiff, or that the Plaintiff had expended any money on his behalf. The Plaintiff gave evidence in support of his claim and in addition produced an account kept, save for a few entries, by Ahmed el Qadi, his former clerk. The latter does not claim to have had any personal knowledge of the payments recorded, but the account appears to be genuine and to have been regularly kept, and we are of opinion that it may be regarded as corroboration of the evidence of the Plaintiff under Article 5 of the Evidence Ordinance, 1924.

There is another matter that should be referred to. There have been numerous law-suits between the parties with reference to the distribution of their father's estate and the receipt of the rents and profits thereof by the Plaintiff. At the last sitting the Defendant's advocate raised, for the first time, the defence that the amount now sued for had been taken into account by way of set-off in a case brought by the Defendant against the Plaintiff in reference to the profits of the lands of Keshdah, which was settled by agreement. The written agreement was not filed or served on the Plaintiff as required by the Code of Civil Procedure, and we are of opinion that if the amount now claimed had really been taken into account in the settlement of that case, this would have been the first fact to have been mentioned by the Defendant."

The following is from the pleadings of the appellant:

"The order given by an infant is invalid, because under Article 967 of the Mejelle the dispositions of an infant without the permission of his curator are invalid. Wajih Eff. had no curator, but his mother was his guardian and she used to incur expenditure for him. In accordance with the Mejelle and other laws, expenditure incurred on behalf of an infant without the permission of his guardian is a gift." *(Wajih Abd el Karim Abd el Hadi v. Yusef Abd el Karim Abd el Hadi,* C. A. 37/32).

LAW OF CONTRACT

(3) *Consent of parties to a contract.*

(a) *Constraint: Chapter II of Book IX of the Mejelle.*

It is an essential condition to the validity of contracts dealt with in the Mejelle that the parties should freely consent thereto. If either of the parties does not consent to the contract for any reason on any essential point, the contract entered into is voidable (*fasid*), though mere failure to agree on subsidiary points will not invalidate a contract (see *post*, paragraph 3 of Article 64 of Code of Civil Procedure). Constraint is dealt with in Chapter II of Book IX of the Mejelle. (Articles 948, 949 and 1003-1007).

Any contract entered into as a result of constraint or force, (*ikrah*) is consequently invalid. (Article 1006). Not all the contracts of Muhammadan law are subject to this rule, however, some contracts relating to matters of personal status being an exception. (see the notes to Article 1006). Constraint should be distinguished from undue influence. It should be noted that any unilateral act performed as a result of force or constraint is invalid. (see Article 1575).

Constraint is divided into two categories in Muhammadan law:

(1) Major constraint (*ikrah mulji*) whereby the death of a person or the loss of a limb is caused. (Article 949);

(2) Minor constraint (*ikrah ghair mulji*), whereby grief or pain alone is caused, such as assault or imprisonment. (Article 949).

For constraint to be effective, the following conditions must be fulfilled:

(*a*) The person who causes the constraint must be capable of carrying out his threat. (Article 1003);

(*b*) The person who is the subject of the constraint must be afraid of the occurrence of the event with which he is threatened. (Article 1004);

(3) The person who is the subject of the constraint must perform the act he has been forced to do in the presence of the person causing the constraint, or of his representative. (Article 1005).

LAW OF CONTRACT

Palestine Decided Cases.

(1) "In the year 1917 the Defendant was indebted to the Plaintiff in the sum of L. T. 200 paid in gold with interest on a promissory note not yet due. The Defendant offered to pay in Turkish notes of the nominal amount. These notes were legal tender but the Plaintiff was not bound to accept them because the debt was not due. The notes were much depreciated in value and he refused to accept them. Finally he accepted and gave a receipt in gold. The Plaintiff stated that he was induced to receive the money by a threat that if he refused the notes he would be reported to the Government and would run the very serious risk of being deported to Anatolia. In 1920 the Plaintiff sued the Defendant for the difference between the amount due in gold and the amount which he had been induced to receive under compulsion and threat. The District Court refused to hear evidence of compulsion and gave judgment for the defendant. The judgment was appealed and the case sent back to the District Court to find two issues of fact:

(a) Was the payment made in gold or in Turkish notes?

(b) If made in Turkish notes was the Plaintiff induced to accept them in payment by fear of the treatment he might receive from the Government officials if he refused, a fear induced by the Defendant?

When the case was sent back for the trial of these issues it was considered that the answers would be conclusive that it was of common notoriety that in 1917 under the rule of Jamal Pasha the fear of deportation and the risk even to life involved was so general that threats of the kind put forward by the Plaintiff would be sufficient to render the agreement to receive the amount of the debt before it was due in Turkish notes a void agreement. The District Court heard evidence on both sides and found in the affirmative on both issues, giving judgment for the Plaintiff for the difference between the amount due in gold and the value of the Turkish notes received under compulsion. There was nothing more to be done in the case than to have those issues decided. There was evidence on which the District Court could find as it did find and the judgment should be confirmed." (*Saltie Bishara v. Saleem Haddad,* C. A. 72/22).

(2) "There is a civil right to set aside a contract on the ground of violence (Mejelle, Article 1006) quite independent of a criminal action, and an action may be brought to declare such a contract void and to set it aside, without recourse to the criminal Courts. The judgment of the District Court dismissing the action will be set aside and the case returned to be tried on the merits. Costs to be paid by the losing party." (*Joseph Weizman v. Waqf Department of Jaffa,* C.A. 116/23).

(3) A Magistrate having held that a mortgage, the subject of the appeal, had been obtained by threats, and the Court below (the Land Court) having accepted the judgment of the Magistrate as proof of the constraint, *held*, that the Land Court was wrong in not considering whether the threats were of such a nature as, under the Civil Law, to render the mortgage void. (*Abraham Friedman v. Mrs. Miriam Miller*, L.A. 58/30).

Constantinople Cassation Decision:

"If it is alleged by the defendant during the hearing of the action that when he delivered the document produced he did so under the influence of compulsion and constraint, he must be called upon to prove this defence. The plaintiff may not be called upon to prove that the defendant consented".

(C. C. D. 24th. September, 1327, No. 152, Vol. I, page 347).

[In this case the defendant pleaded that the plaintiff had threatened to murder him and destroy his sheep and other property and that he had entered into the contracts in question in order to save his life].

(b) *Deceit (taghrir).*

Deceit, or fraud, is defined by Article 164 of the Mejelle as cheating, (see notes to Article 164). If the conclusion of a contract, *e. g.* of sale, has been brought about by the exercise of actual deceit, together with flagrant misrepresentation *(ghubn fahish)* the party to the contract who has been the victim of such deceit may cancel the contract: that is to say, the contract is voidable at the option of the party deceived. (see Article 357 and notes thereto). Thus, if the vendor sells a piece of glass stating it to be a diamond, the sale is void (see Article 208 and notes thereto). The person who has been the victim of deceit may, in addition to cancelling the contract, claim to have made good any loss which he may have suffered by reason of the deceit, provided that the contract is of the class of contracts of which valuable consideration is a part. (See Article 658 and notes thereto).

(c) *Misrepresentation (ghubn)*

Misrepresentation, in Muhammadan law, is of two kinds

(*a*) flagrant misrepresentation (*ghubn fahish*);

(*b*) minor misrepresentation (*ghubn yasir*).

LAW OF CONTRACT

The maxim of English law, *caveat emptor,* (let the buyer look out) it is submitted, applies to Muhammadan law, for minor misrepresentation does not give rise to any remedy at law, and flagrant misrepresentation (see Article 165) only in the cases set forth in Article 356. Muhammadan jurists, while not expressly laying it down in terms, seem to consider it to be the duty of the contracting parties to be prudent men of business, and if one person allows another to get the better of him in a bargain, without being actually deceived by him, he must abide by the results of his own lack of prudence (see the terms of Article 65 and compare the English leading cases of *Ward v. Hobbes,* 3 Q.B.D., 150, and *Keates v. Lord Cadogan,* 10 C.B., 591). The law, however, will protect the orphan, pious foundations and the Treasury from being imposed upon. Thus, by the terms of Article 356, if the sale of the property of orphans is tainted by flagrant misrepresentation although unaccompanied by actual deceit, the sale is invalid, and property belonging to pious foundations and the Treasury is treated on the same basis as the property of orphans. (See notes to Article 356). An action for flagrant misrepresentation will also lie in the case of an inequitable partition of jointly-owned property (see Articles 1127 and 1160). The rigour of this rule is, however, tempered by the existence of certain other options referred to in paragraph 3 (d) below.

The misrepresentation (*ghubn*) referred to here is a passive rather than an active misrepresentation. An example is where a person, knowing the true value of his property, allows it to be thought that it is of far greater value than it is in fact, or fails to disclose the true facts, and sells the same at a price far in excess of the true value. The victim is said to be *maghbun,* or one who has suffered something to his great disadvantage. Where the misrepresentation is active, it becomes changed to actual deceit or fraud (*taghrir*) as where one person takes active and effective steps, as by telling falsehoods, to deceive another. (see example 2 to Article 658). As to the propriety of translating the word *ghubn* by misrepresentation, see the translation note to Article 356. Deceit and misrepresentation are classified as one of the options of the Muhammadan law of contract. (see paragraph 3(d) below). Finally, an action of deceit is not transmissible to heirs (Article 358), and a purchaser who is the victim of deceit and knows that the sale is tainted by flagrant misrepresentation and who deals with the thing sold in any manner indicative of a right of ownership loses the right to cancel the sale. Misrepresentation and deceit are dealt with generally in Articles 208, 356-360, 658, 1127 and 1160.

(d) *Options*.

In addition to the option for deceit and misrepresentation, there are certain other options available to the contracting parties. They apply chiefly to contracts of sale and hire. The options are divisible into two classes:

(1) *Options conferred by the contract itself by the agreement of the parties.*

These are :

(*a*) an option of cancellation or ratification within a fixed period (see Articles 300-309 and 497-506);

(*b*) an option as to payment by a certain time, failing which a contract of sale need not be carried out (see Articles 313-315);

(*c*) an option as to selection in the case of sale (see Articles 316-319).

The terms of Article 64 (as amended) of the Code of Civil Procedure have virtually made these options superfluous. (see paragraph 4 *post*).

(2) *Options conferred by operation of law.*

These are :

(*a*) an option for misdescription, whereby if a vendor sells property as possessing a certain desirable quality, and the property proves to be devoid of such quality, the purchaser may cancel the sale if he wishes. If he does not wish to do so, he must take the thing sold and pay the whole of the fixed price (see Articles 310-312);

(*b*) an option of inspection, whereby if a person buys, or hires any property without seeing it, he has an option upon inspection thereof of either cancelling or ratifying the contract. (Articles 320-335; 507-512);

LAW OF CONTRACT

(c) an option for defect, whereby in an unconditional contract of sale or hire, the purchaser or the person taking the property on hire may cancel the contract if the property is found to be unsound or defective, even though no stipulation is made to that effect in the contract, for in such a contract there is an implied warranty that the thing sold or given on hire is free from defect. (Articles 336-355; 513-521).

These options are dealt with in detail in the Chapters dealing with Sale and Hire.

(4) *The subject matter of the contract.*

Freedom of contract is considerably limited by the terms of Muhammadan law as reproduced in the Civil Code; and to remedy this defect, and, it appears, in order to avoid the reproach of seeking to change the terms of the Code, the origin and nature of which have already been seen, the Ottoman legislative authorities introduced modifications to Article 64 of the Code of Civil Procedure, dated the 10th. May, 1914, which, in effect, have had the desired result.

The following are the terms of the preamble to the amendment to Article 64.

"The freedom and certainty of contractual undertaking exercise the same influence upon economic evolution as does the freedom of disposing of the rights of ownership. The contracts of the Civil Code are subject to such conditions as to nullity and voidability that contracts at the present time depend more upon the straightforwardness of the contracting parties than upon any guarantees afforded by law. Unfortunately, in many cases the parties to a contract who wish to refuse to carry out their contractual obligations are certain of being able to cancel their contracts in the present state of the Civil law, since, being secured from the dangers of voidability by reason of present conditions, the question of drawing up a contract is a matter of difficulty. The task of completely modifying the Civil Code in such a manner as to make it conform to the necessities of the moment and more in agreement with the transactions of the people is a vast undertaking for the execution of which, no doubt, the principles of Muhammadan jurisprudence are a sufficient guarantee. Nevertheless, the necessity of overcoming the difficulties caused by economic progress as mentioned above is a matter of extreme urgency which admits of no delay, and it was consequently decided to take certain legislative action with a view to guaranteeing freedom of contract. With this object in view, Article 64 of the Code of Civil Procedure has been modified, and it has been amended so as to include certain general conditions relating to contractual obligations as recognized in progressive countries. All contracts drawn up by the parties thereto subject to these conditions are executory and valid, and are to be regarded as a special law governing the parties. Need for reform is daily growing greater, and business relations are daily becoming more varied and more extensive to such an extent that it is impossible for the legislator to foresee all the conditions and agreements in an age of progress such as ours, and it is certain that the parties to a contract are best able to express their own wishes; and in making this new amendment we have had in mind that the wishes of the two contracting parties shall be safeguarded and have provided that all contracts shall be executory and valid in respect to the contracting parties, providing that they are not contrary to laws and regulations laid down with a view to maintaining public order, and in respect to the subject matter of the contract and custom relating thereto. We have included all specific interests and rights which possess some specific value in relation to the subject matter of the contract, and in this manner we have saved bilateral contracts from doubt and complication, and have given greater reliability and fixity to civil and commercial transactions."

The following are the terms of Article 64.

(1) "The terms of all contracts and agreements which are not forbidden by special laws and regulations and which are not contrary to morality and which do not disturb public order nor conflict with matters of personal status, such as the capacity of the contracting parties, and the rules of law relating to inheritance and succession, and to any disposition of money or real property dedicated to pious purposes and immovable property, are valid as regards the contracting parties. Provided, however, that if the subject matter of the contract cannot be produced, such contract may be declared null and void.

(2) "Any matter which possesses some specific value ([1]) may be the subject of contract. Any determinate object, interest, or right which is generally recognized as being capable of transmission is regarded as possessing some specific value. Agreements relating to things to be produced in the future are also valid.

(3) "Should the parties have agreed as to the fundamental points of a contract, such contract shall be regarded as being

---

([1]) For a definition of an object possessing some specific value, see Article 127 of the Code. cf. this definition with the definition given in paragraph 2 above.

completely concluded, even though subsidiary matters may have been passed over in silence. In cases where the parties have not been able to arrive at an agreement concerning subsidiary matters, the Court shall give a decision thereon, bearing in mind the nature of the business."

The terms of Article 64 of the Code are of the first importance, since they affect, and in some cases modify, the terms of the Mejelle. Indeed, every Article of the Mejelle affecting the right to enter into contractual relationship should be construed with reference to the terms of Article 64. It has been said, moreover, that the terms of this Article are so far-reaching that they repeal whole sections of the Mejelle *en bloc*. This extreme view does not seem to be justified and it is submitted that the correct way of construing the Articles of the Code dealing with contractual relationship is to read into them a qualifying clause such as "unless otherwise provided by the clauses of any contract valid under the terms of Article 64 of the Code of Civil Procedure."

The result is that any person called upon to pronounce as to the validity of a contract may safely say that any contract or agreement placed before him is valid, provided it is not contrary to any of the matters excepted by the terms of Article 64, which are either forbidden or are subject to certain restrictions. These matters are the following:

Paragraph I of Article 64.

(a) *Contracts forbidden by law.* The Article refers to contracts which are "forbidden by special laws and regulations." This makes it essential to distinguish between "special" and "general" laws. By a "general" law is meant any law of general application which lays down certain rules applying generally to all the branches of the subject with which it deals. The Civil Code itself is a law of this nature, for it lays down certain rules of general application to matters affecting contract or tort. On the other hand, matters of detail or special import may require to be regulated by special terms of law which are not of general application; and viewed from this angle such laws or regulations are "special laws or regulations" since they regulate special, distinct and separate matters. The contract of insurance, in Ottoman law, was subject to special rules contained in the Ottoman law of Insurance, and any contract of insurance drawn up contrary to its terms would have been invalid. Again, the Ottoman Commercial Code is a law of a general nature regulating commercial transactions in general. It was silent as to contracts of a speculative nature. This matter was later dealt with by the Addendum to Article 28 of the Ottoman Commercial Code, whereby all such contracts are stated to be invalid. By Article 3 of the Ottoman Maritime Code, the sale of a ship is made subject to certain formalities, and in the event of these formalities not being observed, the sale, it is submitted, would be invalid, for this is a special law governing maritime matters. Again, the Ottoman Regulations governing the rate of interest forbid any contract for interest where the rate exceeds 9% per annum.

It would consequently be of no avail for any of the parties to any of these contracts to plead the terms of Article 64 in support, for, while the Article does affect the terms of the Civil Code itself, it is of no effect upon the terms of these "special" laws and regulations.

(b) *Contracts contrary to morality (adab).* These are contracts similar to contracts contrary to morality as contemplated by the terms of English law. That is to say, sexual immorality of any nature and any contracts in furtherance thereof. Examples are contracts in connection with prostitution or the white slave traffic.

(c) *Contracts prejudicial to public order. (intizam umumi).* By public order here is meant civil well-being from the point of view of social conduct and the municipal discipline of the State. It seems to follow as a consequence that it includes matters of public policy, subject, however, to the important qualification that in deciding what are matters contrary to public policy, the peculiar social institutions of Palestine must be taken into account. Thus, a contract in which a sum of money was to be paid by a wife to a husband as consideration for his divorcing her, was held by the Court of Appeal in Palestine to be valid, since contracts of this type are sanctioned by the Muhammadan law of personal status. (*Yusef Issa Hamoud el Faghouri v. Jamileh Mousa Hamoud*, C. A. 55/31). A contract made in furtherance of a public meeting prohibited under powers contained in any law or regulation would also appear to be illegal, as being prejudicial to public order.

(d) *Contracts in conflict with matters of personal status.* These contracts include all matters of contractual capacity dealt with by the Code, *e. g.* minority, lunacy, imbecility, interdiction generally, death-bed gifts or bequests. The language of the Article is "matters of personal status, *such as* the capacity of the contracting parties". It therefore seems to include also all matters of personal status peculiar to any religious sect in Palestine in the sense that any contract in conflict with the terms of any Article of law affecting the matters set forth in Article 51 of the Palestine Order-in-Council would be invalid. (see also paragraph (e) below).

(e) *Contracts in conflict with the law of inheritance and succession.* Inheritance and succession are both parts of the law of personal status as regards Muslims, Jews and most Christians in Palestine. The law with regard to Muslims can be consulted in almost any handbook of Muhammadan law; and as regards Jews and Christians in the special laws and regulations issued by the Ecclesiastical authorities (see paragraph (d) above).

(f) *Contracts in conflict with the law of pious foundations* (waqf).

Pious foundations, or *waqf*, (plural *awqaf*) are common to the whole world of Islam and are extremely numerous. The law governing their constitution and administration forms an important branch of Muhammadan law. There are also Christian *waqfs* in Palestine. A comprehensive outline of the Muhammadan law dealing with pious foundations will be found in the Chapter dealing with the law of real property.

LAW OF CONTRACT

(g) *Contracts in conflict with the law relating to immovable property.* A comprehensive outline of the law relating to immovable property will be found in the Chapter dealing with real property.

(h) *Contracts the subject matter of which cannot be produced.* By this term of law is meant, it would appear, that if the matter with reference to which the contract has been concluded cannot be produced in the physical sense, the Court will, upon application being made, declare the contract null and void. This stipulation seems to be irreconcilable with the provisions of English law and might work hardship. Thus, an oil company, acting on the reports of experts, obtains a concession, or concludes a contract with land-owners for the extraction of oil from the ground. It turns out, however, that the oil, for technical reasons, cannot be extracted from the land with reference to which the contract has been made. Or a contract for the salvage of a sunken vessel or the cargo is made. Upon salvage operations being carried out, the vessel breaks up, or it turns out that the cargo cannot be raised owing to the position of the vessel. In both these cases any contract must, it is submitted, be declared null and void by the Court, upon application being made by one of the parties, and any expenditure incurred cannot be recovered. The condition refers to production in the physical sense only; not in the abstract sense. Thus, a contract relating to a reversionary interest, or an interest in a life insurance would be valid.

Paragraph II of Article 64.

(a) *Matters possessing specific value.* In Muhammadan law property which possesses specific value (*mal mutaqqawim*) is defined as being:

(1) a thing the benefit of which it is lawful to enjoy;
(2) acquired property (see Article 127 and notes thereto).

This definition has been extended by the second paragraph of Article 64 so as to include interests or rights which are capable of transmission. The word used for "interest" (*menfaa*, plural *menafi*') is not to be understood in its strict legal sense in Muhammadan law, which relates to some advantage arising out of the use of some specific object *e.g.* hire of a house.

(b) *Things to be produced in the future.*

This term of law virtually cancels certain of the provisions of the Mejelle whereby a contract, the subject matter of which is not in existence at the time of the conclusion thereof, is null and void. (see for example, the terms of Articles 197 and 205 and notes thereto). Such contracts are now perfectly valid. Thus, A concludes a contract with B for the sale of next year's orange crop. The sale is valid.

Paragraph III of Article 64.

The object of this paragraph is to do away with some of the effects of the formalism of the Muhammadan law of contract. Thus, an otherwise valid contract might have been held to be voidable owing to some subsidiary matter having been passed over in silence through mere inadvertence. Thus, the parties may have omitted to state in the contract who is to pay the cost of transport. The Court will in the circumstances decide which party is to pay the cost of transport; or if dispute has arisen on the point, it will give a decision.

Palestine Decided Cases.

(1) "The dispute in this case arose from an undertaking which one of the sellers made to the effect that in case she is unable to deliver the house to the purchaser at the beginning of the Hejira year she will pay a certain amount of money as rent. Part of the property sold had been occupied by the seller and co-owners and part let to a tenant. At the expiration of the year the maker of the said undertaking delivered the part of the house she occupied, but was unable to deliver the leased part. The seller had, however, brought an action in which she sued the tenant for ejection, but her claim was dismissed in virtue of the Rent Ordinance. The party to whom the undertaking was made refused to take delivery of the part of the house which the seller and co-owners occupied and sued for the sum which the seller undertook to pay. The undertaker now argues that causes outside her control prevent

her from carrying out her undertaking and that under Article 108 of the Civil Procedure Code she is not liable. The Respondent on the other hand states that the reason why the vendor was required to give the undertaking was to avoid the possibility of any such excuse, and that she is not entitled under the circumstances to take it as a basis for argument. The view I take, having regard to the Rent Ordinance which was a temporary measure, the effect of which terminated at the time fixed for delivery under the contract, is that the parties hoped that delivery of the whole house would be possible and that the person giving the undertaking hoped to deliver when the effect of the Rents Ordinance came to an end, and that Respondents entertained the same hope. It is not therefore possible to hold that the contract was made in this form because the parties had anticipated the impossibility of delivery only, but the presumptions of possibility and impossibility are equal. In case therefore it is held that the parties expected the possibility of the issue of another Ordinance extending the provisions of the Rent Ordinance to a date subsequent to the contract, constitutes, in my opinion, a circumstance which it is outside the power of the person giving the undertaking to avoid. But if the contract is held to have been made in anticipation of impossibility, it was originally invalid in virtue of paragraph I of Article 64 of the Code of Civil Procedure. If it is held that the contract was based on impossibility, I hold that Respondent i. e. Plaintiff is not entitled to demand all the rent (LE.200), but is entitled to claim rent for the part, delivery of which could not be effected, the Appellant having given up the part she occupied and Respondent having refused to take delivery." (per Ali Effendi Jarallah, J. majority judgment).

The following is the text of the undertaking referred to in the judgment:

"We, on the undermentioned date, have undertaken to sell our house and the land belonging to it which is situated in the land of the Armenians, near Chamberlain garage, near Jaffa Gate (*Bab el Khalil*), to Mr. Eisa Daoud el Ghazaleh. One of the terms is that we should stay in the house freely without having to pay rent up to the first of Moharram next.

We now undertake that in case it be not possible for us to deliver the house at that time, we shall be liable for payment of its rent to the purchaser in question, its amount being £.200 annually by virtue of a formal Quoshan No. 154 of the month of August, 1327." (*Malakeh Guiragossian v. Issa Daoud el Ghazaleh*, C. A. No. 62/24).

(2) "On the 19. 9. 25 a contract was entered into between both parties according to which the Defendants leased their orchard to the Plaintiff for the period of three years only at a rent of

LAW OF CONTRACT

L.E.900 which was paid to them. Definite terms were stipulated as regards Plaintiff that should he fail to comply with any of these terms, he would not have the right to claim the rent (Mousakat) and the Defendants would not be liable for any expenses. The Defendants brought an action against the Plaintiff in this Court, file No. 218/925 by which they complained that the Plaintiff failed to comply with certain conditions of the contract, and claimed the crops of the Defendants. The Court entered judgment in favour of the Defendants ordering the Plaintiff to return the orchard. On 1.10.25 the Plaintiff brought this action against the Defendants in which he shows that he abided by that judgment and asks for judgment against the Defendants for the return of the rent of the three years amounting to L.E.300 plus the expenses which he spent during the said period equal to P.T.35642 with costs.

There arose a difference between both parties as regards the interpretation of the following expression in the contract, viz: — "If the Plaintiff should fail to comply with the terms of the contract, he would not be entitled to claim the rent and the Mousakat." The Plaintiff alleges that the meaning of this expression is that he will not have the right to claim the leased property and the Mousakat, but this does not cancel his right to claim the rent. Defendant's advocate alleges that the meaning of it is that he is not entitled to claim the rent. Upon consideration the Court finds that the contract entered into between both parties, as the Court has held in its previous judgment, to which the Plaintiff has objected and submitted, is in accordance with Article 64 of the Code of Civil Procedure. And whereas it has been proved in the said judgment that the Plaintiff has failed to comply with certain conditions of the said contract, therefore he has no right to claim any part of the expenses which he had incurred."

The judgment was appealed, but the appeal was dismissed. *(Ibrahim Ahmad Abu Habib v. Abdul Raham and Halimeh, children of Mahmoud Hamad, C. A. 110/26).*

(3) "This is not a promissory note valid as a negotiable instrument under Article 145 of the Ottoman Commercial Code because the name of the promisee is not in the document. Promissory notes payable to bearer were made lawful by Article 28 of the Appendix to the Code of 14th. Shaban 1284, but was later invalidated by an Amendment of 6th. Rajab, 1296. If regarded as an admission of a debt it may be that such a document is evidence of such an admission, if supported and completed by proof of the person who advanced the money and to whom the promise was originally made, but we are not required to decide that question because the Plaintiff in the case does not pretend to be the creditor of the Convent, but a mere holder. An alternative would be to treat it as a contract valid under Article 64 of the

Ottoman Code of Civil Procedure. That Article was apparently intended to sanction contracts not recognised by the Mejelle, provided they are not repugnant to customary morality or law. The document is not objectionable on moral grounds, but it is of a kind expressly excluded from the Commercial Code on grounds of public policy (14 Rajab 1296). So clearly is the law opposed to this sort of document, which is of the nature of paper money which is a promise to an unascertained bearer and may be sold for money or any other consideration, that there is a law expressly forbidding any but the Government and the Imperial Ottoman Bank to issue such documents. (16 Shaban 1299, Article 9). The Convent is not a body possessing any such privilege."

This was an appeal from the judgment of the District Court, Jerusalem, for the payment by the Appellant of the sum of 1000 gold Napoleons in pursuance of a bill made payable to bearer, and bearing the seal of the Appellant.

The following is from the dissenting judgment of Frumkin J.

"The Mejelle does not deal with notes of this kind, but we have Article 64 of the Ottoman Code of Civil Procedure as amended on the 21st. Nissan 1330, which has, to a very large extent, modified the Law of Contract of the Ottoman Empire. This Article inter alia provides:

"All contracts and undertakings are binding upon the parties unless such contracts or undertakings are:
(1) prohibited by special law ;
(2) prejudicial to morals and public security;
(3) contrary to established principles relating to capacity of parties, inheritance, the disposal of waqf money and waqf land, and disposal of 'Immovable property'".

Consequently, as long as any contract or undertaking does not fall under any of the restrictions of the said Article, it is binding and enforceable by law. As it is not alleged that the note in question is prejudicial to morals and public security or contrary to any of the principles mentioned, we have only to see if it is prohibited by special law.

In my opinion it is not............................ In his note the appellant in this case undertook to pay on a certain date a certain sum of money to any person who will at that time be in possession of the document. Under Article 64 of the Code of Civil Procedure this undertaking is binding and the judgment of the District Court should be confirmed." (*The Armenian Patriarch v. Nadra Eff. Mishaka*, C. A. 111/26).

(4) "A Company has now no power to create an equitable charge, other than a floating charge upon its whole assets, unless

124   LAW OF CONTRACT

such a charge can validly be created in accordance with the general law applicable to persons as well as to Companies.

The District Court basing itself on the provisions of the Mejelle has held that no such power exists.

There can, in our opinion, be no doubt that if the position is governed by the Mejelle, the District Court's judgment is right. The Appellant, however, has argued that the provisions of the Mejelle in this respect are over-ruled by the Law of the 28th. April, 1330 (4th. May, 1914) which amended Article 64 of the Code of Civil Procedure. The provisions of the Law are as follows:- (Here the Court sets out the text of the Article).

It is argued that this law enables one person to give another an equitable charge upon future crops. The words to which our attention has been directed are "agreements contracted on what will come into existence in the future are also recognised."

The effect of this provision is, in my opinion, merely to bring "agreements contracted on what will come into existence in the "future" within the first paragraph of the law, and to render such agreements enforcible and effective" as between the contracting parties.

The first paragraph of the law practically re-enacts the former Article 64, and I hold that neither under the old Article nor under the first paragraph of the amending law, is it possible for one person to charge his property in favour of another, otherwise than by a specific mortgage, in such a manner as to give the chargee any rights against a third party, though the charge may be valid against the chargor". (*Central Bank and another v. The Registrar of Companies,* C. A. 74/27).

(5) "It is clear that the consideration for the promise by the Respondent to pay LP.20 to the Appellant upon her re-marriage was the agreement by the Appellant to divorce the Respondent. Hence it cannot be maintained that there was no consideration for the bill. As regards the application to this case of Article 64 of the Code of Civil Procedure, as amended, we must infer that the District Court was of opinion that the bill was not in accordance with the provisions of that article because it was contrary to public policy that a woman should agree to pay money for her divorce and further should make such payment dependent upon her remarriage. With regard to this we hold that the parties being Muslims, are entitled by Sharia Law to make an agreement whereby the wife undertakes to pay a sum of money to her husband in consideration of his agreeing to her divorce. Further, it does not render such an agreement void that the payment of such sum is, under the agreement, deferred to the date when the woman remarries. The Respondent has remarried, and it cannot be maintained that the bill constituted an illegal restraint upon marriage."

LAW OF CONTRACT

The following is the judgment of the District Court reversing the judgment of a Civil Magistrate:

"Upon consideration the Court holds that the contract entered into between appellant and respondent in order that appellant could get a divorce from the respondent is void. The Court does not agree with the views of the Magistrate:

1. That there was consideration to the undertaking made by appellant to pay to respondent in accordance with the English law.
2. We do not hold that such a contract is in accordance with Article 64 of the Civil Procedure Code.

Therefore it has been decided to set aside the judgment of the Court below, and to dismiss the claim of the respondent with costs." (*Yusef Issa Hamoud el Faghouri v. Jamileh Mousa Hamoud*, C. A. 55/31).

Note: As to the validity under Muhammadan law of a cash payment as consideration for a divorce, see *Mohammad Kadri Pasha:* Code of Muhammadan Personal Law, translated by Sir Wasey Sterry; and the *Hedaya*, translated by Charles Hamilton, 2nd. Edition by Grady, page 112 (of *Khoola*).

(6). (Judgment of the Court below) "Plaintiff Mousa Kiali sued Defendant Ali Muhammad Hasan el Kurdieh claiming from him LP.500 as compensation for breach of the contract entered into between them dated the 21-1-28, in that he had failed and refused to put Plaintiff in charge of the grove the subject matter of the contract made for 'musakat' lease. It was due to the fact of refusal by Defendant to put plaintiff in charge of this grove that the latter served on him a notarial notice dated the 6-10-28 whereby he had asked him to put him (Plaintiff) in charge of the grove. Defendant contended that the contract being contrary to the provisions of Article 1444 of the Mejelle was void; that he had put Plaintiff in charge of the grove; and that he had not committed the breach of the terms of the contract. Further the Defendant alleged that the fact that Plaintiff was put in charge of the said grove is supported by the terms of the contract where it is laid down that he was put in charge thereof. Plaintiff's Counsel pleaded that the expression mentioned in the contract 'delivery and acceptance' is but a formal one inserted in every contract, but that it has been proved before the Court that Plaintiff was never put in charge of the grove as Defendant refused to deliver the grove to him and that in fact he turned the Plaintiff out when he went to take charge of it. Further, Plaintiff called Defendant as a witness and on hearing him as witness his replies were 'I don't know' to nearly every question put to him The parties entered into a certain contract whereby they held the party committing any breach of the terms thereof liable to pay compensation to the other party.

LAW OF CONTRACT

It has been proved in this Court that Defendant failed to perform his obligations laid down in the said contract in that he refused to deliver the grove to Plaintiff. Although Defendant contended that the contract was void, yet the question of the invalidity of the contract does not bar a claim to compensation. The claim is not made regarding the invalidity of the contract, and therefore the Court did not deal with the question of validity or invalidity of the contract. The contract was entered into in respect of things allowed by law. The Court therefore unanimously passes judgment in pursuance of Article 64 of the Civil Procedure Code, in favour of Plaintiff Mousa el Kiali against Defendant Ali Muhammad Hasan el Kurdieh for £500 as compensation for breach of the contract entered into between the parties."

Judgment of the Court of Appeal.

"After hearing both parties, the Court sees no reason to interfere with the judgment of the District Court." (*Ali Muhammad Kurdieh v. Mousa el Kialy*, C. A. 88/31).

(7) "In the contract between them dated the 7th. of September, 1929, the parties agreed that notice of breach of contract need not be served. This is an agreement which is valid and enforceable under the amendment dated 21 Nissan 1330, to the Code of Civil Procedure, Article 64. We hold that under the terms of that contract the Appellant was entitled to sue without serving notice upon the Respondent. The Respondent now alleges that the agreement between the parties was subsequently annulled but he has not brought any evidence before the District Court to prove it. The appeal is allowed, the judgment of the District Court is set aside and the case is remitted for completion. The Respondent will be at liberty to submit evidence to prove his allegation that the agreement between the parties was annulled". (*Othman Salim Bushnaq v. Yehuda Ben Moshe Bonstein*, C. A. 72/32).

Constantinople Cassation Decisions.

(1) "An action arising out of a lottery established with the approval of the Government for the benefit of public schools may be entertained and must be heard. Consequently, no decision may be given dismissing such actions on the ground that they are not legal contracts and consequently may not be heard (C. C. D. No. 95 dated 20th. September, 1330, Vol 4, p 192).

(In this case the Court below had dismissed the action, since they had not been able to find any term of law validating a lottery in either the Mejelle, or the Commercial Code, or the *fiqh* books (treatises on Muhammadan Law), nor bringing it within the scope of any contract recognized by law. The Court of Cassation recognized the validity of the action owing to the lottery having been established "with the special permission of the Imperial Government").

(2) "Contracts relating to the sale of a thing not yet in existence which were concluded prior to the modification of Article 64 of the Code of Civil Procedure dated 28th. April, 1330, must be dealt with in accordance with the terms of the Mejelle. Where a contract is concluded for the daily supply of milk, and the contract is not carried out, it must be ascertained, upon an action being brought, whether the contract was concluded prior to the passing of the amendment to Article 64 of the Code of Civil Procedure, and if so, the question must be settled in accordance with the terms of the Mejelle, bearing in mind that the subject of the sale was not in existence." (C. C. D. No. 109 dated 4th. October, 1330, Vol 4, p 224).

(3) "Companies such as *Mukhtarlik*" companies are null and void. Consequently, any action brought in connection therewith may not be heard and must be dismissed." (C. C. D. No. 207 dated 22nd. February, 1330, Vol 4, p 434).

(4) (1) An undertaking may be proved by the evidence of witnesses.

(2) A contract of agency is not a binding contract and the principal may, — provided the rights of third parties are not affected — dismiss the agent, or the agent may retire, at any moment he likes." (C. C. D. No. 38 dated 16th. May, 1331, Vol 5, p 85).

(5) *Form of Contracts.*

Contracts may be made:
    (a) by writing;
    (b) by word of mouth;
    (c) by conduct.

(a) *Contracts in writing.*

The Civil Code does not insist upon any contract being reduced to writing. (see Articles 69 and 1606 of the Mejelle). This liberty, however, has been considerably restricted by Article 80 of the Code of Civil Procedure (which should be read with Articles 81 and 82) the text of which is as follows:

80. Claims relating to undertakings and contracts of any nature whatsoever, which it is customary to reduce to writing, and claims relating to partnerships, farming out and loans, which exceed one thousand piastres, must be proved by a document. Any action brought in respect to a document relating to the matters mentioned above, must be proved by a document or by

LAW OF CONTRACT

the admission of the defendant or by an entry in a register, even though it does not exceed one thousand piastres.

81. The procedure set forth in Article 80 shall be in force and apply in cases where interest added to the principal sum, or where the amount obtained by adding a number of items together which are actually claimed, exceeds one thousand piastres.

82. The procedure set forth in Article 80 shall not apply in the following circumstances, but the subject matter of the claim may be proved by the evidence of witnesses. The circumstances referred to above consist of the following matters:

(1) Transactions between husband and wife, ascendants and descendants, brother and sister or their children, or father and mother and her sister, and father-in-law and mother-in-law; (see the Palestine Decided Case of *Mr. Levitsky as Syndic of the Bankruptcy of Haim Lederberg v. Zalman Corn* (C. A. 8/33).

(2) Claims which could not be reduced to writing on account of *force majeure* or for any reason which is legally acceptable;

(3) Where the document in the possession of the creditor has been lost accidentally;

(4) Where the parties are in a village and there is no person in that village able to write out a document.

The reason for putting the stipulation as to writing in the Code of Civil Procedure was, according to both *Ahmed Zia* (page 391) and *Baz:* (Commentary on the Code of Civil Procedure, (page 283), to guard against the danger of lying evidence, which, at the time, had been greatly on the increase. It was thought that the temptation to procure lying witnesses was slight where the amount at issue was less than five thousand piastres. The limit was formerly five thousand piastres, but was reduced later (4th October, 1330) to one thousand piastres. This provision of law, it is submitted, has not been affected by the terms of the Law of Evidence Amendment Ordinance, 1924, (Bentwich, Volume I, page 384).

On analysis, the Article is seen to contain the following stipulations:

All claims relating to contracts the value of which exceeds 1000 piastres must, in the following cases, be evidenced by writing. It follows that in such case, the contract itself must be in writing, though this need not be a formal contract: an exchange of correspondence or some note or memorandum agreed to by the parties as embodying the basis of the contract would be sufficient, though any note or memorandum, or any account of monies spent or received on account of the contract by one of the parties only, will not bring the contract within the rule. There are four cases where contracts must be evidenced by writing.

(1) *When it is customary to reduce them to writing.*

This rule relates to contracts of any nature whatsoever. What amounts to a custom is a question for the Court which must be strictly proved by the evidence of witnesses who have special knowledge, *i. e.* experts (see Chapter VI, and notes to Article 36). The following have been held to be contracts which it is customary to reduce to writing:

(a) Submissions to arbitration [Palestine Decided Cases of *Eliasha Yehudayoff v. Yehiel Yehudayoff* (C. A. 230/23.) *Lilian Lubin v. Samuel Wilson* (C.A. 219/26)].

(b) All contracts of hire (Constantinople Cassation Decision No. 169, Volume IV, page 352).

Experience shows that in a country where there is a low degree of literacy, the custom of the people is to take particular care to reduce their agreements and contracts to writing: and in the territories forming part of the former Ottoman Empire this is particularly the case, owing to the facilities afforded by the institution of the Notary Public, of which advantage is taken by all classes of the people. Experience in the Courts also shows that it is very rarely that the parties fail to reduce their contracts to writing. One reason for this is that the creditor will insist upon having clear evidence in writing upon which to sue wherever money is concerned, before parting with his money, either in the form of a formal contract, or of an acknowledgment (*ikrar*) of the debt.

It is therefore submitted that there are grounds for holding that it is an established general custom for the parties to reduce to writing all contracts involving any payment of money which, while not being a loan, involves an advance of money. The rule, however, is not absolute

LAW OF CONTRACT

and in contracts which are of their nature not of frequent occurrence, oral evidence is clearly admissible.

The rule applies not only to any claim on the original contract, but to any matter arising out of or incidental to the contract. Thus, A concludes a contract with B to the value of £.100 which it is customary to reduce to writing. A sues B for non-fulfilment of the contract. A must produce a contract in writing to the Court. But if B has paid, for example, £.50 in part performance of the contract, B must produce documentary evidence of this fact to the Court, other than the actual contract upon which A relies and to which B is a party. He cannot produce oral evidence to prove payment if A does not admit the payment. Again, A brings B and C together, who contract for a large sum, the contract being by custom in writing. B promises A 1% commission for his services on the capital value of the contract. The commission amounts to more than 1000 piastres. B fails to pay. A must submit documentary evidence to prove his claim. The original contract between B and C will not do.

The reason for the apparent harshness of this rule is, as we have seen, that experience has shown the utter unreliability of oral evidence in the territories formerly forming part of the Ottoman Empire. On the other hand, this does not mean that persons who are unable to produce documentary evidence to prove their claims cannot come into Court. They still have the right to the oath.

(2) *When relating to partnership.* The partnerships referred to here are ordinary partnerships and not commercial partnerships. The bulk of the law relating to partnerships in the Mejelle has now been repealed by the Palestine Partnership Ordinance, 1930, which imposes an obligation as to registration.

(3) *When relating to farming out* (iltizam). Contracts of farming out relate to the collection of taxes, and dues and rents due to the Government, to Municipalities, or even to a private individual. A person known as a *multazim* undertakes to collect the dues himself (and employs persons to assist him) and usually pays to the Government,

Municipality or private person a lump sum representing what the normal revenue is expected to be. Examples are the collection of dues from the public for passing over a bridge, or by a person to whom a concession has been granted by the Government.

(4) *When relating to a loan.* This provision embraces a large proportion of the contracts with which the Courts are normally called upon to deal. A point arises here as to whether it can reasonably be held that a contract not on the face of it a specific contract for a loan of money, but which nevertheless involves a loan, or payment of an advance, comes within the rule. (see paragraph (1) above).

Article 81 shows how the minimum of one thousand piastres is arrived at. If the value of a contract amounts to exactly one thousand piastres it does not come within the rule. If it amounts to one thousand and one piastres and upwards, it does.

If the principal sum expressed in the contract amounts to less than one thousand piastres, but exceeds that amount where interest legally payable is added, the contract comes within the rule. This stipulation applies, it is submitted, whether there is a contract as to the amount of interest or not.

Where the action relates to several heads of claim, and the total amount exceeds one thousand piastres, with the addition of interest, the cases come within the rule. These items may relate to one contract, or, it would appear, to several separate contracts for small sums in respect to which one action is brought. It seems that the rule could be defeated here if the plaintiff is content to bring separate actions.

Thus, A brings an action claiming 900 piastres from B, plus interest amounting to 300. The total amount claimed exceeds one thousand piastres. A must produce written evidence to prove his case.

The reason for the terms of the first paragraph to Article 82 seems to be that the legislator presumes a far greater degree of honesty between relatives.

A definition of *force majeure* (*sebeb iztirari*) is given in Article 108 of the Code of Civil Procedure. What constitutes a reason for not complying with the rule, which is legally acceptable, is a matter for the Court itself to decide; but any wide interpretation of the provision would obviously result in the terms of Article 80 itself being defeated.

The loss of a document here implies its destruction also, e. g. by fire. This fact must be strictly proved to the Court. The provision of law relates to "ordinary" documents, i. e. not certified by the Notary Public, since if the document is certified by the Notary Public and the original is lost or destroyed, a certified copy can be obtained.

As regards the fourth paragraph, it seems that the parties must be in the village itself at the time the contract is concluded. The mere fact that the parties are villagers who are unable to read and write and the other inhabitants of the village are in the same position will not take them out of the rule if it can be proved that the contract was entered into elsewhere, i. e. a place where there are persons able to write.

Palestine Decided Cases. (Article 80)

(1) In the Palestine Decided Case of *Eliasha Yehudayoff v. Yehiel Yehudayoff* (C. A. 230/23) it was held that a submission to arbitration was one of those contracts which it is customary to reduce to writing:

"When we come to Article 80 of the Civil Procedure Code we have to consider whether a submission to arbitration is one of the contracts which it is customary to reduce into writing and we have no hesitation in deciding that it is so. We have never in the practice of this Court had to do with any award not in writing or not based on a written submission being relied on as the basis of a judgment, nor as being used for the purpose of establishing any legal liabilities. We therefore decide that as a matter of law a submission to arbitration must be in writing if it is to be enforced in a Court of Justice."

(2) A similar conclusion regarding a submission to arbitration was reached in the case of *Lilian Lubin v. Samuel Wilson* (C. A. 219/26). The following is from the judgment of the Court below:

"We come now to the difficult question as to whether or

not Article 80, C. P. C. applies to this case. The Defendant is endeavouring to prove a contract, involving the sum of L.E.2000, by personal evidence. This is possible if such a contract is not usually committed to writing. We hold that such an agreement must be in writing and is one which is usually committed to writing, and as such we cannot admit personal evidence."

(3) What amounts to an admission under the terms of Article 80 was considered in the case of *Benza Rein v. Abraham Flint* (C. A. 75/32) where the following judgment was given:

"The Appellant, Mrs. Rein, sued the Respondent Abraham Flint, in the Magistrate's Court, Jerusalem, on an undertaking in writing to deliver a house by a specified date. The Respondent's defence was that an agreement had been made between the parties for the settlement of their mutual claims against one another, which included the Appellant's claim under the undertaking. After hearing evidence, the Magistrate was satisfied that the defence was proved and dismissed the action.

On appeal, the Magistrate's Court's judgment was confirmed. The President of the District Court has, however, granted leave to appeal to this Court on the points of law set out in para. 10 of the Appellant's application, which reads as follows: —

"Whereas the judgment affects the lawful interests of my client, and whereas neither the judgment of the Magistrate's Court nor that of the District Court in its appellate capacity contains any reason for the provisions of the said Article 80 being disregarded, and whereas by virtue of the said Article 80 any claim against a written document can only be proved by evidence in writing, and whereas even supposing for a moment that verbal evidence was admissible in this case (which is denied), the evidence given by Mr. Barshira did not prove anything against my client, and whereas alternatively it is at any rate evidence given by a single witness without any corroboration:

I now pray on behalf of my client and in accordance with Articles 5 and 6 of the Magistrates Courts Jurisdiction Ordinance, 1924, for leave to appeal to be granted to her on the following point of law, viz: whether judgment could be given in this case or in any other case on the evidence of a single witness not corroborated by some other material evidence, and especially whether the clear provisions of Article 80 of the Code of Civil Procedure could be set aside in this case (or in any other similar case) and verbal evidence admitted against a written document confirmed by Defendant himself.

The general rule under the Civil Procedure Code, Article 80, is clear: namely that an agreement varying an agreement in writing must be proved by evidence in writing; "or by the admission of the Defendant, or by his account books." In the absence

LAW OF CONTRACT

of written evidence, therefore, we have to see whether there was before the Court an admission by the Appellant. Now the Appellant gave evidence in the course of which she said:—

"An agreement was arrived at on 17.3.1929. I do not know what they said therein. I know the advocate to whom I entrusted the matter. Only the advocate knows the details of the agreement. I did not discuss the details of the agreement."

This amounts to an admission that there was an agreement and an authority to the advocate concerned, Mr. Barshira, to make admissions on the Appellant's behalf as to the terms of the agreement.

Mr. Barshira stated in evidence:—

"I arranged the agreement with Flint on behalf of Rein. Madame Binze (the Appellant) knows very little and asked that the affair be dealt with. I apprised her of the gist of the agreement and she paid some money. She was satisfied with the agreement to reduce the amount she had to pay. This agreement covered all the disputes between the parties excepting a debt which Madame Rein remained owing to Flint, and in accordance with the said agreement I told Madame Rein that she would have to pay LP.24 to Flint."

This statement is an admission on behalf of the Appellant that her claim against the Respondent on the undertaking was included in the agreement.

The appeal, therefore, fails and must be dismissed."

(4) "This is an appeal against a judgment of the Jerusalem District Court of the 4th. July, 1932. The action was upon a promissory note and the District Court at the request of the Respondent heard the evidence of the two Respondents and Plaintiff in order to contradict the contents of the promissory note. The Plaintiff denied the allegation against the truth of the document set up by Defendants. The Court, however, in their judgment stated they did not believe the Plaintiff and gave judgment in Respondent's favour.

Now, the Law of Evidence Amendment Ordinance, 1924, Section 12, enables either party to give evidence on his own behalf or be summoned to give evidence for the other party; and this Court has previously decided that such evidence may be called by Defendant even in a case where a written document within the meaning of Section 80 of the Civil Procedure Code is the subject matter of the action — (See Civil Appeal 77/32).

It is, however, clear that a document of this nature can only be contradicted by the evidence of the person who is setting the document up and suing upon it and not by the evidence of the person being sued on the document.

Defendants may give evidence contradicting a written document of the nature set out in Article 80 of the Civil Procedure

Code, but such evidence cannot be of any avail unless the same is materially corroborated by the evidence of the other party.

The appeal is allowed with costs and the judgment of the lower Court must be quashed and judgment entered for the Plaintiffs for the sum claimed — £.635. — together with interest from the date of action as claimed.

The note runs "we promise to pay" and is signed by two or more persons. Accordingly, the note is deemed to be a joint note only and not joint and several.—See Pearson on Bills, Vol. I, page 247". (Per *Baker J.*)

"No verbal evidence is admissible against documentary evidence".

This rule, which is laid down in Article 80 of the Ottoman Code of Civil Procedure, has not been overruled by Sections 2 or 12 of the Law of Evidence Amendment Ordinance. The provisions of these sections go only so far as to make parties to a civil case competent to give evidence, and their evidence to be relied upon in all such cases where oral evidence is otherwise admissible.

Hence, the evidence of the defendants in this case is not legal evidence against the document. On the other hand there is nothing definite in the evidence of the plaintiff which could be taken against him in contradiction of the document given in his favour.

The appeal is therefore allowed, and the judgment of the District Court set aside and judgment entered for Appellant against Respondents jointly for the amount of LP.635 with interest from date of maturity and costs here and below including LP.2 advocate fees". (Per *Frumkin J.*) *(Muhammad Shaker Husseini v. Menahem Hurvitz and others, C. A. 106/32).*

Palestine Decided Cases (Article 82)

(1) "The Court below heard the alleged witnesses to the Promissory Note, also the person who, at the deceased debtors request, signed for him, which in accordance with Article 82 of the Civil Code of Procedure they were justified in doing.

The Court state in their judgment that they were not satisfied with the evidence of these witnesses and dismissed Plaintiff's claim. This can only mean that the Court did not believe these witnesses. Now where a lower Court has made a finding that they believe or do not believe witnesses, I am of opinion that the Appellate Court is debarred from interfering with such a finding unless it be a finding which there is no evidence to support.

There was evidence in the case which the Court did not believe. Therefore the judgment of the District Court must be confirmed and the appeal dismissed". (*Muhammad Qasem Nammour v. Amineh Ahmad Nammour and another*, C.A. 100/25).

(2) "The transaction alleged is one between husband and wife and therefore was within the terms of Article 82 of the Code of Civil Procedure. The evidence of witnesses on oath is therefore admissible to prove the Respondent's claim. There was evidence before the District Court upon which it could find that £ 200 was due to the Respondent from her husband, and it is not for the Court to go into the credibility of that evidence". (*Farha bint Musa Saikali v. Rida bint Butros Khammas*, C.A. 115/25).

(3) "Finally it is argued that the transaction was really one between husband and wife, and that evidence is admissible under the Code of Civil Procedure, Article 82 and should have been heard by the District Court to prove the real nature of the transaction.

The answer to this contention is that, though the present action is one between husband and wife, the original transaction, as to which it is sought to give evidence, was between the Defendant and *Habib Samaan*. The law has seen fit to provide that where the terms of the transaction have been put in writing, oral evidence shall not be admissible. It is not necesssary for us to decide how far the Code of Civil Procedure, Article 82, creates an exception to this Rule in the case of transactions between relatives, but it is clear that to admit oral testimony in this case would mean that oral testimony must be admitted in every case in which the maker of a document alleges that the transaction was not really between himself and the other party, but between himself and some relative of his. Where a person has deliberately availed himself of a certain provision of the law, he must abide by the consequences." (*Issa Morcos v. Emilie Morcos*, C.A. 29/29).

(4) "In this case the husband and wife reduced their agreement to writing, and we hold that relations such as contemplated in Section 82 of the Civil Procedure Code who, *inter se*, have reduced their agreements to writing, cannot be held to come within the exemption which Section 82 gives to such relatives in normal circumstances when they are assumed to conduct their affairs on a basis of mutual confidence, and that in consequence oral evidence is not admissible to rebut the terms of the written document which can only be rebutted by documentary evidence as prescribed by Section 80." (*Ibrahim Elias Nasr v. Nijmeh Elias Nasr*, C.A. 72/31).

Constantinople Cassation Decisions.

(1) All contracts of hire, of any nature whatsoever, must, in accordance with custom, be proved by documentary evidence, and this whether the contract relates to the period of hire or to

LAW OF CONTRACT

the amount of the rent. The evidence of witnesses may not be heard in such matters (C. C. D. No. 169, dated 24th December 1330, Vol 4, page 352).

(2) If the matter concerning which the action is brought has not been reduced to writing, any defence as to payment may be proved by the evidence of witnesses. A register produced to show the claims which have been made is not considered to be a document within the meaning of Article 80 of the Code of Civil Procedure (C. C. D. dated 18th May, 1327, No. 82, Vol I, page 195)

(3) An action the value of which exceeds five thousand piastres can only be proved by the evidence of witnesses provided that the document relating to the debt has been lost. (C. C. D. Dated 31st August, 1329, J. A. page 5359.)

(4) Payments alleged to have been made in respect to a debt evidenced by a document may only be proved by a document. They may not be proved by the evidence of witnesses. (C. C. D. Dated 1st September, 1329 J. A. page 5542)

(5) If the sum claimed by the plaintiff exceeds 5000 piastres. being the price of a contract for whitewashing by way of transfer and the transfer is proved, the plaintiff may be called upon to prove by evidence the amount of work which he alleges he has performed. A decision that the evidence of witnesses cannot be heard on the point owing to the terms of Article 80 of the Civil Procedure Code is wrong. (C. C. D. dated 19th. June, 1330. No. 58, Vol 4, p 118).

(6) A claim to payment made in respect to an action brought on a document may only be entertained if it is based on a document. It is contrary to law to hear the evidence of witnesses on this matter. (C. C. D. of the 5th. March, 1328, No. 4, Vol 2, p 9)

(7) If a guarantee given in respect to the carrying out of an undertaking is certified by the Notary Public, the contents thereof may not be proved by witnesses but must be proved by official documents also. Consequently, if it is alleged that the guarantor who has entered into a contract of guarantee certified by a Notary Public has died before the contract comes into force, no judgment may be issued based on the evidence of witnesses unless the truth of the matter has been ascertained officially by investigation and enquiry as to the date of his death from the Census and Public Health Department and other Departments concerned. (C.C.D. dated 4th August, 1328, No. 102, Vol 2, p 229)

(8) Actions relating to the farming out of taxes can only be proved by documentary evidence. Such actions may not be proved by the evidence of witnesses. Consequently when no documentary evidence is available the matter must be settled by the oath. (C. C. D. dated 8th September, 1328, No. 124, Vol 2, p 279)

LAW OF CONTRACT

(9) If the debt alleged to have been assigned has been reduced to writing, it may not be proved by the evidence of witnesses. (C. C. D. dated 4th February, 1329, No. 160, Vol 3, p 377).

Article 80 of the Code of Civil Procedure should also be read in the light of Article 72 of that Code. This Article divides written contracts into two categories.

(1) Agreements and contracts legalized by certification by the Notary-Public of the place at which they have been drawn up, which are known as official documents;

(2) Agreements and contracts not so legalized, which are known as ordinary documents.

The terms of Article 72 — which should be read in the light of the terms of Articles 61-73 of the Law of the Notary-Public — are as follows:

"Documents embracing undertakings and contracts are of two kinds:

(1) Documents which have been certified officially and according to regulation by the competent officials in the place in which they were drawn up. These are called "Official documents";

(2) Documents which have not been certified by the competent official but which merely bear a signature or seal. These are called "ordinary documents".

The officials authorized to "legalize documents" are the various Notaries-Public appointed under the terms of the law of the Notary-Public. The advantage of having an agreement or contract attested by a Notary-Public, is that an official document is conclusive in respect to any party thereto bound by the undertaking, his heirs or assigns, and need not be proved, unless forgery or fraud is alleged. (Article 74 of the Code of Civil Procedure, and compare terms of Article 1321 of the Mejelle). It has the additional advantage of disposing of any doubt as to the place in which the contract or agreement was drawn up, since a Notary-Public may only attest documents drawn up in the place in which he has jurisdiction (see also Articles 73-75 and 76 of the Code of Civil Procedure). In practice the Notary-Public actually draws up the contract or agreement in the majority of cases, in accordance with the wishes of the parties. It should be noted that a written contract or agreement certified by the Notary-Public is only conclusive in respect to the matters mentioned in the contract.

If the Notary-Public certifies that the parties were in good health or in full possession of their mental faculties, this is no bar to an action to prove that one or more of the parties were not in full possession of their mental or physical faculties (see *Baz*, Code of Civil Procedure, page 278). The same thing applies to an action on the contract or agreement claiming excessive interest, or flagrant misrepresentation (*ghubn fahish*), (see Mejelle, Article 165). Again, it is open to proof that one or more of the parties to a contract or agreement certified by a Notary-Public is a minor of imperfect understanding, or has been interdicted for debt or prodigality, or has entered into the contract as a result of constraint.

Constantinaple Cassation Decisions.

(1) Contracts of hire certified by a Municipality only and which are not certified by the Notary-Public are not considered to be official documents. (C.C.D. dated 14th. February, 1325, J.A. page 406)

(2) If the signature and seal placed on a guarantee given in respect to tithes are not certified in the ordinary way, the guarantee will be considered to be an ordinary document. Consequently, if it is proved as a result of enquiries made by a committee of experts that the signature and seal are not those of the person who denies, the other party has a right to the oath. (C.C.D. dated 1st April, 1325, J.A. page 117).

(3) Documents containing contracts for interest are considered to be ordinary documents. (C.C.D. dated 1st March, J.A. page 3491).

(b) *Oral Contracts.*

A contract may be made by word of mouth. This is the type of contract which is usually entered into in the every-day transactions of the people.

(c) *Contracts concluded by conduct.*

A valid contract may also be concluded by any conduct of the parties which takes the place of offer and acceptance (see Article 175 and notes thereto).

(6) *Classification of contracts in Muhammadan law.*

Contracts in Muhammadan law may be classified thus:

(1) *Contracts for the alienation of property.*

(a) Alienation of property by way of exchange. This is the contract of sale;

LAW OF CONTRACT

(b) Alienation of property without exchange. This is gift;

(c) Alienation of property by dedicating it to pious purposes. This is *waqf*, or pious foundations;

(d) Alienation with a view to succession. This is bequest.

(2) *Contracts for the alienation of usufruct.*

(a) Alienation of usufruct in exchange for property. This is hire, which includes letting things immovable for hire; contracts for service (*e. g.* carriage of goods, domestic and professional services);

(b) Alienation of usufruct not being in exchange for property *e. g.* a loan for use, or deposit for safe keeping.

(3) *Contracts for securing the discharge of an obligation,* (*e.g.* pledge or suretyship).

(4) *Contracts for representation.* (e. g. agency and partnership). [1]

Contracts are divided into three main classes:
(1) valid; (*sahih*)
(2) voidable; (*fasid*)
(3) void; (*batil*)

(1) *Valid Contracts.* A valid contract is a contract which is lawful both in itself and as regards matters incidental thereto. (Article 108 and see notes thereto). Valid contracts are also referred to as concluded (*munakid*) contracts. (Article 106 and see notes thereto).

(2) *Voidable Contracts.* A voidable contract is one which, while valid in itself, is invalid as regards matters incidental to it. (Article 109 and see notes thereto).

The word used for voidable (*fasid*) is sometimes used by writers on Muhammadan law in the sense of void. (Ali Haidar, Vol. I, page 218). In the event of the conclusion of a voidable contract each of the parties has, in general, the right of cancelling the contract (see Article 372 and notes thereto).

---

[1] Abdur Rahim: Muhammadan Jurisprudence, page 288.

(3) *Void contracts.* A void contract is a contract which is invalid in itself (see Article 110 and notes thereto). If a contract is defective in any essential condition it is void (see Article 362 and notes thereto). A void contract has no legal effect and consequently is unenforceable at law.

(7) *Breach of Contract: Damages for breach of contract.*

Articles 106-111 of the Code of Civil Procedure deal with the circumstances under which damages for breach of contract may be awarded. The terms of these Articles provide as follows:

(1) No damages can normally be awarded unless the party claiming them has drawn what is known as a "protest" upon the party alleged to have failed in the performance of his obligations, (Article 106);

(2) A protest is not essential if a special condition to that effect has been inserted in the contract, (Article 107);

(3) Damages may be awarded where:

(*a*) the party in default has acted in good faith (Article 108), when only the actual loss suffered may be awarded in damages (Article 109);

(*b*) the party in default has acted in bad faith. In this case damages may include actual and consequential loss. (Article 110)

(4) A liquidated sum of money may be awarded as damages where a clause is inserted in the contract to this effect and stating the sum, (Article 111);

(5) *Force majeure, i. e.* any cause of failure or delay outside the control of the party upon whom the obligation falls or which cannot be attributed to him, is a valid defence to a claim for damages, (Article 108).

It is not essential that a claim for damages should be decided at the same time as the original action (Article 126).

The following is the text of the Articles:

Article 106.

"Damages claimed on account of non-performance or delay in the performance of the terms of any special contract drawn up with a view to the doing of any particular thing or the delivery of any specific quantity of things at any fixed place by one party to the contract from the party upon whom the obligation falls shall not be awarded unless the party making the claim has officially served upon the other party, in accordance with the usual procedure, a protest, *i. e.* a warning, served through the official channel, calling upon such other party to carry out the obligation which he has undertaken to perform."

Notes:

The word used for protest (*protesto*) is of Italian origin, and is used textually in Turkish, though it is sometimes used in translation, when it becomes *ikhtar*. This explains the use of the phrase "protest *i. e.* warning" in the text of the Article. "The word "*protesto*" is taken from Italian and is used literally in our tongue. The word warning (*ikhtar*) is also sometimes used instead" (*Ahmed Zia*, Commentary on the Ottoman Code of Civil Procedure, page 446). The object of the protest is to give a warning to the party who is under an obligation to perform all or any of the terms of the contract that the other party intends to hold him to his undertaking and to give him an opportunity to fulfil the same. It possesses the additional advantage of being proof that such party has failed to carry out the terms of the contract. The protest also constitutes a valuable piece of evidence, in the event of the case coming before the Court, that such party has failed to carry out his obligations under the contract as agreed. It is essential that the protest should be drawn through the Notary-Public, who is the official channel referred to in the Article. For particulars as to the duties of the Notary Public in general, see the terms of the law of the Notary-Public dated the 28th October, 1913.

It should be noted that an essential condition to a claim for damages for breach of contract is that the contract should not be contrary to the terms of Article 64 of the Code of Civil Procedure, (*Ahmed Zia*, page 447; *Baz*, page 333). The injury must be one which has happened in fact and must be a material injury. Injury to the feelings or reputation will not sustain a claim to damages. The Court must satisfy itself as to the validity of the claim to damages and if necessary must refer the matter to experts to determine the actual extent and amount of the damage suffered in view of all the circumstances of the case. The amount claimed by the plaintiff in the protest is not conclusive.

Damages do not apply in the case of a contract of debt. (see Article 112).

The Article is silent as to time, and appears to presume that a time-limit will be fixed in every contract. This is frequently not the case. In the case of the majority of simple contracts no time limit is expressly stated, though it is an implied condition that there will be no avoidable delay. Thus A asks his tailor to make a suit of clothes, or concludes a contract to buy a horse or a motor-car without stipulating any specific date for delivery in the contract. If the subject-matter of the contract is not delivered, or there be delay in delivery, the question arises as to what is to be the determining factor as to when failure or delay to perform the contract becomes an accomplished fact. It is submitted that a reasonable time in view of all the circumstances must be the test. A further point of difficulty is the moment at which a protest is to be served where a time-limit for performance of the contract has been fixed. It is clear that the party upon whom the obligation falls is fully within his rights up to the last hour agreed upon, and the other contracting party would be justified in strict law in not serving a protest upon him until the moment at which the time for completion expired. But if he does this he is almost certain to be out of time with his protest and thus deprived of his right to claim damages. A reasonable view seems to be that a protest may be served where the one party has grounds for believing that the other party does not intend to fulfil the terms of the contract. The weak point in this view is that one party may generally be under the impression that the other party intends to perform his part of the contract in due time and so not draw a protest on him.

It should be noted that the Article refers to the party upon whom the obligation falls. It is therefore open to one party upon whom, for example, an obligation to deliver goods is imposed, to allege that the other will not pay the price; and such person would be as much entitled to draw a protest as the other, since an obligation to pay is as much an obligation as delivering goods. In any case, a party claiming damages for breach of contract is bound to establish his readiness to perform his part of the contract, and this point was definitely decided by the Privy Council in the case of *Abdullah Bey Chedid and others v. Tenenbaum* (Privy Council Appeal, 47/32). In this case Tomlin L. J. said "Their Lordships' attention has not been directed to any provision of the Turkish law or any local ordinance which deals with the question whether in an action to recover damages for breach of contract, the plaintiff is bound to establish his readiness and willingness to perform his part. In the absence of any such provision, their Lordships are of opinion that regard must be had to the English law applicable in the case of concurrent obligations".

Article 107.

"If a stipulation be inserted in the contract itself to the effect that if, at the expiration of the period of the contract, the person upon whom an obligation falls fails to carry out the same, notice shall be dispensed with, and the expiration of the prescribed period shall be considered to take the place of a notice, such stipulation shall take the place of a protest, *i. e.* warning, at the expiration of the period."

Notes:

This Article includes all contracts, whether they are official or ordinary contracts — see the terms of Article 72 of the Code of Civil Procedure. The Article is silent as to delay, but it is clear that the intention is to include delay, since this Article is obviously a counterpart of Article 106. It has been stated (*e. g. Baz*, page 334) that the actual words of the Article should be included in the contract. The contention seems to be absurd, since had the draftsman of the Article intended this to be the case, he would have said so. Moreover, the language of the Article is "If a stipulation be inserted in a contract *to the effect that* (dair) ...." which strengthens the view that any stipulation which fairly meets the requirements of the Article is sufficient.

Article 108.

"Judgment may be given that a contracting party who has failed to carry out or has delayed in carrying out what he has undertaken to do, is to make good the loss sustained by the payment of damages, although he may not in any way have acted in bad faith. If his failure to carry out, or his delay in carrying out, his undertaking arose out of *force majeure, i. e.* from some cause which cannot be attributed to him or which is not within his control, judgment may not be given against him."

Notes:

In this case the damages are actual, that is to say, they are intended to compensate the party who has suffered from the breach for the actual amount of the loss he has suffered.

It is for the Court to decide as to what constitutes *force majeure* and the existence of *force majeure* should be proved by the evidence of witnesses, unless judicial notice may be taken thereof, as in the case of an earthquake. The fact that the failure to carry out the contract was due to *force majeure* must also be established by the evidence of witnesses, or any other evidence the Court may decide to receive. The following examples of *force majeure* are taken from the commentary of *Ahmed Zia*, page 450.

(1) Goods destroyed by chance;
(2) Goods burnt in a fire;
(3) Means of communication stopped as a result of war;
(4) Destruction of crops by locusts, droughts or floods;
(5) Theft of goods en route to consignee.

The following two cases are taken from the commentary of *Baz*, page 335:

(1) Illness of such a nature as to prevent the carrying out of a personal undertaking, e. g. in a contract of employment.
(2) A river is frozen over and a ship intended to convey goods cannot proceed on her journey.

This is the view of the Ottoman commentators as to some of the cases which constitute *force majeure* and are based upon the terms of the Article which define *force majeure* as being:

(1) Some cause which cannot be attributed to the party upon whom the obligation falls;
(2) Some cause which is outside his control.

It is therefore clear that negligence or incompetence is not an excuse, as where a person who undertakes to deliver goods by steamer fails to find a steamer, for here the presumption is that he would not have undertaken the transport of the goods had he been aware that there was no reasonable opportunity of being able to find means of transport.

Article 109.

"If the failure to carry out an undertaking is not due to bad faith on the part of the person who has undertaken to perform it, the loss to be made good by him shall consist of the ascertained amount of injury suffered by the other party owing to such failure."

Article 110.

"If the failure to carry out the contract is due to bad faith on the part of the person upon whom the obligation falls, the loss to be made good by such person on account of failure to carry out his obligation shall consist of the direct injury sustained by the other party and the profit of which he has been deprived."

Notes: (Articles 109 and 110)

"Bad faith" has been used to translate *hila* and *dasisa*, lit. "tricks and subterfuges". The rule is that if the party upon whom an obligation falls fails to carry out or delays in carrying out the same, and the failure or delay is due to mere inability, or incompetence, or laziness, or any other cause not amounting to *force majeure*, the measure of damages is an amount sufficient to compensate the other party for the actual amount of injury or loss which he has suffered and no more. Where delay has been due to bad faith, *e. g.* failure to deliver goods owing to a rise in prices, the vendor having found a more favourable market, the measure of damages is the actual amount of injury or loss, plus any consequential injury or loss, arising out of the breach of contract, *e. g.* loss of rents, profits, etc. Thus, A makes a contract with B, whereby B undertakes to build a shop for A, the material to be supplied by A, the work to be finished within a period of six months. A delivers the materials to B who, through negligence, or laziness, or incompetence, fails to carry out the contract within the stipulated period, and the materials, lying out in the sun and rain, are rendered useless for the purpose for which they were supplied. In this case, the measure of damages is the actual amount of injury suffered by A and no more. But if B in collusion with C, a competitor of A, intentionally fails to complete, or delays in completing the contract, as where he builds a shop for C in priority to A so that C may be in a position to compete more easily with A in business, A may be awarded damages to an amount sufficient to indemnify him for the loss actually sustained, and in addition he may claim for loss of profits which he could have made had he been able to carry on business in the shop, or for loss of rent which he could have obtained had he intended to let the shop on hire. A, however, must strictly prove to the Court that he would have made profits or have obtained the rents but for B's failure in bad faith. The Court, it is submitted, would be wrong in accepting any mere conjectural statement of profits or rents which *might* have been obtained. There can be no room here for a mere opinion or forecast, however probable it may appear. An example is the case of purchase for resale. Thus A buys goods from B for LP.100 and contracts to sell them to C for LP.150. B sells to another customer for a higher price, this being clearly a breach in bad faith of the contract with A. A is entitled to be awarded the LP.50 he could have made out of his contract with C. A must produce the contract with C to the Court and satisfy the Court that it was entered into in good faith.

Article III.

"If the contract contains a clause to the effect that whoever of the two parties fails to carry out his undertaking shall pay to the other party a definite fixed sum by way of indemnity, that sum and no more and no less is payable."

LAW OF CONTRACT

Notes:

This appears to be the penalty of English law: but in any case, it is submitted that the English rule of law regarding equitable relief against penalties will apply under the terms of Article 46 of the Order-in-Council (see Chapter 3). It is obvious that a penalty clause in a contract is open to abuse. A shrewd person may well know that a party to a contract will probably be unable to carry out its terms; or he may make it his business to see that the contract is not carried out. In either case, under the very explicit and absolute terms of the Article he is entitled to claim the penalty in the event of the other party failing to do his part. This rule of law is bound to result in hardship. Cases are not uncommon where penalty clauses for very large sums have been inserted in contracts. A case in point is *Ribhi el Yasuri v. Sheikh Abdul Hamid Abu Ghosh*, (C. A. 85/26) where judgment was given to enforce a penalty clause for £ 5000.

The following extracts show the English doctrine of equity on the point, which is unknown to Ottoman law, and which consequently does not extend or apply in the sense of Article 46 of the Palestine Order-in-Council:

"Equity relieves against penalties when the intention of the penalty is to secure the payment of a sum of money or the attainment of some other object, and when the event upon which the penalty is made payable can be adequately compensated by payment of interest or otherwise. Thus relief is granted in equity against the penalty in a money bond, and also against penal sums made payable on breach of bonds, covenants, and agreements for payment of money by instalments, or for doing or omitting to do a particular act. But the relief is only granted where compensation can be made for the breach. And by statute similar relief was introduced into the practice of the common law courts. Before relief can be given it has to be ascertained whether the specified sum is in fact a penalty or liquidated damages. If it is a penalty, then the actual damages only are payable, not exceeding the amount of the penalty. On the other hand, the fact that a sum is made payable by way of penalty for breach of a negative covenant does not in general deprive the covenantee of his right to an injunction". (Halsbury: Laws of England, Vol. 13, p. 150).

"Where the terms of a contract specify a sum payable for non-performance, it is a question of construction whether this sum is to be treated as a penalty, or as "liquidated damages". The difference in effect is this. The amount recoverable in case of a penalty is not the sum named, but the damage actually incurred. The amount recoverable as liquidated damages is the sum named as such. In construing these terms a judge will not be bound by the phraseology of the parties: they may call the sum specified "liquidated damages", but if the judge finds it to be a penalty, it will be treated as such.

We find a good illustration of the rule in the clause commonly inserted in charter-parties: "penalty for non-performance of this agreement, estimated amount of freight". Only the actual damage suffered can be recovered, irrespective of the amount of freight; and the clause has hence been described as a *brutum fulmen*. In one case the clause ran: 'penalty for non-performance of this agreement, proved damages not exceeding estimated amount of freight.' It was held that, the clause being a penalty clause, the damage in fact suffered could be recovered, even though they actually exceeded the estimated amount of freight.

A bond is in form a promise to pay a penal sum, generally on the non-performance of a covenant or agreement contained or recited in the bond. It may, however, take the form of a promise to pay a sum in compensation for damages arising from an act or acts specified in the bond. In the case of bonds or contracts containing provisions of this nature it has been laid down that the Court must look to all the circumstances of each contract — to what the parties did as well as to the language used — and must say from them what the intention of the parties was, but the following rules may be stated:

(1) If a contract is for a matter of uncertain value, and a fixed sum is to be paid for the breach of one or more of its provisions, this sum may be recovered as liquidated damages. But the sum fixed must not be unreasonable or extravagant, having regard to all the circumstances of the case. If it is, it will be a penalty.

(2) If a contract is for a matter of certain value, and on breach of it a sum is to be paid in excess of that value, that is a penalty and not liquidated damages.

(3) If a contract contains a number of terms, some of certain and some of uncertain value, or some of great and some of trifling value, and a fixed sum is to be paid for the breach of any of them, there is a presumption that this is a penalty.

An illustration of (1) is afforded by clauses in building contracts to pay a fixed sum weekly or per diem for delay; or, in the case of a tenant of a public-house, to pay to the landlord a fixed sum as penalty on conviction for a breach of the licensing laws.

An illustration of (2) is a promise to pay a larger sum if a smaller were not paid by a fixed day. The rule is harsh, for a man might suffer serious loss by the non-receipt of an expected payment: yet he can only recover the smaller sum.

On the other hand, it is no penalty to provide that if a debt is to be paid by instalments the entire balance of unpaid instalments is to fall due on default of any one payment, or that a deposit of purchase money should be forfeited on breach of any one of several stipulations, some important, some trifling.

An illustration of (3) is offered by *Kemble v. Farren*. Farren agreed to act at Covent Garden Theatre for four consecutive seasons and to conform to all the regulations of the theatre; Kemble promised to pay him £3. 6s. 8d. for every night during those seasons that the theatre should be open for performance, and to give him one benefit night in each season. For a breach of any term of this agreement by either party, the one in default promised to pay the other £1000, and this sum was declared by the said parties to be "liquidated and ascertained damages and not a penalty or penal sum or in the nature thereof." Farren broke the contract, the jury put the damages at £750, and the Court refused to allow the entire sum of £1000 to be recovered:

If on the one hand, the plaintiff had neglected to make a single payment of £3. 6s. 8d per day, or on the other hand the defendant had refused to conform to any usual regulation of the theatre, however minute or unimportant, it must have been contended that the clause in question, in either case, would have given the stipulated damages of £1000. But that a very large sum should become immediately payable, in consequence of the non-payment of a very small sum, and that the former should not be considered as a penalty appears to be a contradiction in terms.'

But these rules are no more than presumptions as to the intention of the parties; which may be rebutted by evidence of a contrary intention, appearing from a consideration of the contract as a whole". (Anson, Law of Contract, 16th Edition, 1923, p. 330).

Palestine Decided Cases.

(1) "In this case the Appellant has been ordered by the District Court to pay compensation at the amount of LE.1250 for non-delivery of certain quantities of wood which he had to deliver under a contract entered into between him and the Respondent. According to this contract Appellant undertook to pay 5 pounds for each ton not delivered in due time. Appellant argues that non-delivery is due to the withdrawal by the Forest Authorities of the licence granted to him by the same authority to cut trees from his own lands. The Forest Department had no legal power to withdraw the licence, non-performance of the contract is due to a cause beyond his control, and he is therefore to be released from liability under Article 108 of the Civil Procedure Code.

For our judgment it is not material to find out whether or not the land of the plaintiff has been declared to be forest land under the protection and control of the Government and consequently if it was necessary to obtain a licence from the Forest Department at all, as long as it is clear from the Wood and Forest Ordinance that the Forest Department had no authority whatsoever to withdraw a licence already given. Appellant has therefore to succeed in his appeal as to the wood not delivered after being prevented from delivery through the withdrawal of the licence. But there is no excuse for not delivering the due portion before that date. Under his contract he had to deliver 40 tons a week. He delivered wood in the first three weeks of the contract. During these weeks he only delivered 57 tons. Appellant has therefore to pay Respondent 5 pounds for each of the sixty-three tons not delivered, namely three hundred and sixty five pounds. Judgment amended accordingly, each party to pay his own costs." (*Adib Ibn Mikhail Habayeb v. Ibrahim Bey el Husseini*, C. A. No. 57/23).

(2) It is not disputed that the Respondent Moise Wiener was convicted under Articles 236 and 45 as an accomplice of one Sturlezi in embezzlement of the property of the Appellant Co. It is clear that had the Respondent and Sturlezi been put on trial together and convicted together, it would have been open to Appellant to obtain judgment against them jointly and severally for civil damages. The fact that Sturlezi was tried and convicted alone and a judgment given against him in favour of Appellant for damages, before the respondent was tried and convicted, does not in my opinion relieve the respondent of his civil liability, though in so far as the appellant recovers damages against Sturlezi for an amount in excess of that for which he is solely liable, its civil claim against the Respondent is to that extent satisfied. I hold that the Respondent is liable to Appellant jointly with Sturlezi for the damages caused by the wrongful act of Respondent and Sturlezi.

The judgment of the District Court must be set aside and judgment entered for the Appellant for L.200 and costs, subject to the proviso that any sum recovered by the Appellant from Sturlezi by way of damages in excess of that for which he is solely liable shall be accounted a satisfaction to that extent of the amount recoverable by the Appellant from the Respondent". (*Egyptian Bonded Warehouses Co. Ltd. v. Moise Wiener*, C. A. No. 93/23).

"This appeal arises out of an action for damages for non-fulfilment of a contract for the sale of land which contains stipulations for payment of damages in the case of refusal by either party to complete, and also a proviso that "if the sale is stopped or delayed by the Government for whatever cause neither of the parties would be liable for damages".

The Registrar has refused to register a transfer of more than 70 out of the 500 dunoms to which the contract relates, basing his refusal on the fact that the respondent has no right over the remainder of the land. The District Court has inferred that the meaning of this refusal is that the remainder of the land is mahlul and has held that this is such interference by Government as is included in the proviso and hence that damages as provided by the contract are not payable. The District Court has, however, ordered that interest on the purchase money paid by the purchasers shall be paid from the date of the contract.

Against this judgment the purchaser has appealed, alleging that damages as stipulated in the contract are payable by the vendor, on the ground that the Registrar's refusal is due to the fact that the vendor contracted to sell land that did not belong to him but to the Government, and hence that the Registrar's refusal is not interference by the Government such as was contemplated in the proviso quoted, which applies only to refusal to sanction a transfer under Article 4 of the Transfer of Land Ordinance. The vendor has lodged a counter appeal to the effect that no damages are payable, and hence that the District Court was wrong in ordering payment of interest. It was known to both parties when making the contract that the land was not registered in the vendor's name but in that of other persons. There is no evidence to show whether either party was aware at the time of making the contract that any claim that the land was mahlul had been or would be made. The vendor admits that if refusal of permission to register the transfer were due solely to his failure to pay transfer fees, he would not be protected by the proviso, but would be liable in damages.

The same would appear to be the case if the refusal to register were due to the existence of rights in the land in favour of owners or mortgagees whose interests had not been acquired or extinguished by the vendor, for when a man agrees to sell land as owner, it is his duty to take all necessary steps to place himself in a position to fulfil his agreement and for this purpose to obtain the concurrence of all persons having or claiming interests in the land adverse to his own. If he failed to do so, the purchaser would be entitled to damages for non-fulfilment of the contract. Apart from agreement to the contrary, it would not affect the position that the party claiming a right adverse to that of the vendor was the Government. It would be the duty of the vendor to place himself in a position to transfer the land either by establishing that the claim of the Government was without foundation, or by paying the tapu value of the land in accordance with the Land Code. It would be in accordance with this general principle that the proviso on which the vendor relies in this case should be read as referring only to interference by the Government based on some ground which the vendor is unable to remove.

On the other hand, if such were the intention, it would have been easy for the parties to give expression to it in the contract, and this they have not done. Moreover, the proviso in the form in which it stands, may have been inserted by parties aware that a claim to the land might possibly be put forward by

152   LAW OF CONTRACT

the Government and agreed that if such claim were made the sale should be abandoned without either party being entitled to damages.

The judgment of the District Court is set aside and the case remitted for the Court to ascertain whether the refusal of the Registrar to register the sale was due to a claim by the Government that the land is mahlul or to the fact that the Respondent has failed to obtain from the registered owners a proper authority to make him to transfer the land, and to give judgment accordingly". (*Rabbi Bechor Papoula and others v. Mohammad Said Bey Nabulsi and others*, C. A. No. 127/23).

(3) "The Court holds: that in the absence of any evidence that the Respondent would not have been allowed by the authorities to build and lease any building other than that specified in his original permit, the compensation payable to the Respondent for loss of rent due to stoppage of building work by the Appellants is to be estimated on the basis of the rent obtainable for the building which the Respondent was in course of erecting at the time when the work was stopped and has since actually completed". (*Elias Musa Abud and another v. Christo Triandafilidies*, C. A. No. 171/23).

(4) "The measure of damages is the sum that would be required to make good the work that has already been done and to complete the building. There was no evidence before the District Court upon which to assess the amount of damages". (*Ahmad Zeidan al Banna v. Mohammad Mohammad*, C. A. 208/23.

(5) "The claim on which the action was based was a breach of promise of marriage. The Judges who heard the evidence and read the documents found that the promise had not been proved. It was thus the duty of the Judges to give judgment on that finding and dismiss the action. That is the opinion of the majority of the Court. If the Court was then entitled to consider the question of damages as arising from invitation only (as finally found) they could not have given judgment otherwise than for the Defendant because they were divided in opinion. If the Law permits of the introduction of a third judge, which we do not decide, in such cases he would not be entitled to give judgment on the facts without hearing the evidence except by consent of the parties.

The result is that the Appeal is allowed and the judgment of the District Court set aside and judgment directed to be entered for the Defendant by judgment of the majority of the Court. The dissenting judge will write his own judgment. The question whether an action for breach of promise of marriage can be heard in this country by a Civil Court has not been raised in this case, and we express no opinion". (*Ishak Trachtingott v. Elizabeth Matross*, C. A. No. 67/25).

(6) "This action was based on an alleged breach of contract. The District Court has held, in our view rightly, that no evidence of breach of contract was before them. The Appellants now argue that nevertheless they are entitled to refuse to complete: and in that event, are entitled to repayment of the purchase money they have paid. They do not deny that they may be subject to a claim for damages in respect of losses incurred by the Respondents owing to non-completion, but they argue as no such claim is before the Court, judgment should be given in their favour for repayment of the purchase money without deduction. In our opinion, however, it is not open to the Appellants to vary the nature of their claim in this manner. The action was based on breach of contract, and must be decided on that ground: the defence has been directed to the question whether or not a breach has been committed by the Respondents; it has not been concerned with the question what damages are payable by the Appellants in the event of their refusal without justification to complete. If the Appellants desire to claim repayment of the purchase money on the ground of their own refusal to complete, they must commence an action based on this ground when it will be open to the Respondents to make a counter claim". (*Eliezer Berger and another v. Oriental Touring and Shipping Agency*, C. A. No. 50/26).

(7) "The Ottoman Law allows penalties to be agreed and enforced for breach of contracts. Had it been proved that the Plaintiff had contracted to sell lands that he would be unable to transfer within the period allowed by the contract then it might well be said that the Defendant was not obliged to pay a deposit on a contract which the Plaintiff had no power to perform. But there is no evidence of this, and the defendant broke the contract without being able to justify that proceeding. It is very unfortunate that we should have to confirm the judgment for the Plaintiff on this reckless agreement, but we see no alternative but to dismiss the appeal subject to an amendment, that the money already paid is to be deducted from the LP.5000". (*Ribhi el Yasuri v. Sheikh Abdul Hamid Abu Ghosh*, C. A. No. 85/26).

(8) "If the agreement purported to be a disposition of ownership it was so far invalid, but that so far as it contained an agreement to make a transfer in the Land Registry Office, it was a lawful contract of the kind that is generally made by persons who contemplate a sale of land. If such a contract is broken the injured party in the absence of a stipulation for a penalty, has a right to be compensated in damages to be estimated by the Court, and the measure will be the difference between the agreed price

and the estimated market price of the land at the time when the contract was broken, or in this case, when the contract was repudiated by an action brought for return of the purchase money". (*Meir Zeide v. Salomon Alcalay,* C. A. No. 147/26).

(9) "The Appellant is entitled to damages for breach of contract. The only question that remains therefore is that of the measure of damages. Under the agreement between the parties, the sugar was to be delivered at Haifa in 3 consignments in January, February and March, 1925, respectively. On 5th. February, 1925, after the first consignment had reached Haifa but before the arrival of the second consignment the Respondent served a Notarial Notice upon the Appellant's agent repudiating the contract. Upon receipt of that notice the Appellant was free from the contractual obligation to deliver the sugar to the Respondent.

We hold that he should have disposed of the sugar for the best price reasonably obtainable, and that the measure of damages to which he is entitled is the amount, if any, by which the price thus obtainable fell short of the contract price.

The Court must therefore ascertain:

(a) the price CIF Haifa obtainable in Haifa for 15 tons of Hungarian Sugar on 5th. February, 1925;

(b) the price CIF Haifa obtainable in Haifa for 15 tons of Czechoslovakian sugar on the date of arrival at Haifa of the second consignment in February, 1925;

(c) the price CIF Haifa obtainable in Haifa for 15 tons of Czechoslovakian sugar on the date of arrival of the third consignment in March, 1925.

The amount, if any, by which the total of these sums fall short of the contract price, L.990 Sterling, is the measure of damages to which the Appellant is entitled. (*George Afenduli v. Jad Sweidan,* C. A. No. 149/26).

(10) "Judgment of the Court below is confirmed with the modification that the interest provided for on the sums of L.310 and L.600 respectively shall be omitted, since such interest cannot be added as damages to the fixed damages provided for by the contract even though the contract purported to allow such interest". (*Shakib Janus Wahbeh el Haj v. Joshua Hankin,* C.A. No. 104/27).

(11) "The Court, after hearing Mr. B. Benaharon on behalf of Appellants, and Respondent in person, holds that both parties failed to fulfil their obligations contained in the contract. Therefore, the question of damages does not arise". (*Moses Isaac Teitelbaum and another v. Jacob Gootmann,* C. A. No. 31/28.

(12) "There is but one question arising out of this appeal which we are called upon to decide and that is whether the

Lower Court when arriving at the measure of damages flowing from the breach of contract by Appellant were correct in estimating the price of 1000 boxes of oranges (the nondelivery thereof being the original cause of action) at the market price of oranges on the 30th. January, 1932.

The Lower Court appears to have arrived at the above mentioned date by reference to the first part of clause 4 of a contract entered into between the two parties and dated the 7th. day of February, 1931, which reads as follows:

> "The 1st. party (the Appellant) undertakes to deliver to the second party (the Respondent) the 1000 boxes of oranges up to the 30th. January".

It is quite clear that the said clause in its ordinary and proper meaning does not lay down a specific date for delivery but limits the time by prescribing that oranges should be delivered at any time before that date and therefore the Court was wrong in estimating the price of the 1000 boxes of oranges at the market price on the 30th. day of January, 1932. The judgment of the Lower Court is accordingly quashed and the case remitted for a fresh estimate to be made and a new judgment to be given". (*Isa Muhammad Bedas v. Abdel Mu'ti Bamieh*, C. A. No. 48/33.)

Constantinople Cassation Decisions.

(1) If it is proved that the failure of the defendant to carry out the terms of the contract does not arise out of bad faith, the sum estimated and fixed must consist of damages. Judgment may not be given for interest.
(C.C.D. No. 5, dated 7th March, 1327, Vol. I, page 16).

(2) In actions for damages full enquiries must first be made as to whether the loss alleged has in fact been suffered and a decision must be taken in accordance with the result of such investigations, which must be set forth in the reasons for the judgment.
(C.C.D. No. 31, dated 3rd April, 1327, Vol. I, page 74).

(3) The protests which are drawn in accordance with Article 119 of the Commercial Code relate to bills of exchange. The stipulations as to time mentioned therein may not be taken as a basis for protests which are served in connection with a claim for damages arising out of failure or delay in carrying out the terms of a contract. Consequently, if one of the parties to a contract serves a protest on the other party in circumstances such as these, his rights are preserved, provided he does so before the other party has applied to the Courts.
(C.C.D. No. 141, dated 25th August, 1327, Vol. I, page 324).

(4) No judgment may be given in actions for damages for the amount claimed, unless the reasons and proofs relied upon as establishing the injury sustained are set forth.

(C.C.D. No. 147, dated 17th September, 1327, Vol. I, page 336).

(5) (a) If a claim is made for damages in a civil court arising out of a judgment of acquittal in a penal matter, enquiries must be made as to whether the defendant has brought an action as a civil claimant in the Criminal Court and has been granted the status of a Civil Claimant or not.

(b) In the event of there being more than one civil claimant, judgment may not be given that payment of the whole of the damages asked for may be obtained from one of them only by an accused person who has been acquitted, since there is no rule of law authorizing the giving of judgment to the effect that the defendants are jointly and severally liable in respect to such claims.

(C.C.D. No. 157, dated 3rd October, 1327, Vol. I, page 357).

(6) (a) If a purchaser draws a protest but fails to claim the delivery of the property as specified in the contract, he is not entitled to claim damages.

(b) If the vendor is obliged in accordance with the contract to obtain the subject-matter of the contract and hand it over gradually, but keeps silent until the expiration of the period, and the purchaser fails to serve a protest within such period calling upon him to carry out the terms of the contract, he is considered to have renounced his right to claim damages.

(C.C.D. No. 72, dated 9th June, 1328 Vol. II, page 161).

(7) If it appears from the terms of the contract produced in an action brought claiming damages for failure to deliver the property agreed upon within the stipulated period that the plaintiff has the right to claim damages without drawing a protest, the amount of damages must be estimated by experts on the basis laid down in the contract and judgment given accordingly. The Court is wrong if it fails to take into consideration the terms of the contract.

(C.C.D. No. 3, dated 5th August, 1328, Vol. II, page 232).

(8) In view of the fact that a protest does not give rise to the creation of a non-existent right, there is no justification in making a claim for damages by reason of no actual result having appeared consequent upon an incomplete attempt, not considered to be a contract.

(C.C.D. No. 180, dated 12th November, 1320).

(9) In view of the fact that the right of a private employee to his wages depends upon his being in a position to perform the work, and being capable thereof, he is not entitled to any

wage if he is prevented from performing the work. If it is proved that the employee who demands wages from a person was in fact not in a position to perform the work on account of being prevented therefrom by some other person, the employee may not bring an action against such person claiming from him his wages as damages, since such person is not bound to pay the wages of the employee, and is not liable to damages in law on that account.

(C.C.D, No. 108 dated 6th December, 1328).

(10) Article 106 of the Code of Civil Procedure lays down that in order that one of the contracting parties may make a claim for damages he must have drawn a protest containing a request for carrying out the terms of the contract as they stand. If no statement to that effect is made in the protest, the Courts may not hear any actions for damages which are brought before them.

(C.C.D. No. 19, dated 1st April 1329).

(11) If a waterpipe to a garden which has been hired has been broken, and the person giving the garden on hire fails to repair it, the person taking the garden on hire may, for this reason, cancel the contract of hire. He may not, however, claim damages which is contrary to law.

(C.C.D. No. 30 dated 21st April, 1330).

(12) Any claim for damages which is not based upon a valid contract must be dismissed.

(C.C.D. No. 109 dated 4th October, 1330).

(13) If the defendant claims the price of milk produced by animals during the period in which they have been attached without any legal justification for so doing, the claim must be proved by witnesses, for any judgment to be given for damages. No judgment may be issued upon the reports of experts.

(C.C.D. No. 109 dated 4th October, 1330).

(14) If the respondent states that he has suffered injury owing to his not having been able to deal with his land for a period of three years on account of the action having been appealed, and makes a claim to have the loss made good by the appellant, the respondent must be called upon to prove the amount of damage which he has actually suffered. Failure to do so and a subsequent issue of a judgment is contrary to law.

(C.C.D. No. 141 dated 9th November, 1330).

(15) If a person widens a channel from the dam of a river to his factory and thereby cuts off the water of the channel leading from the dam to the factory of another person, the latter may not claim damages from the owner on the grounds that his factory has been brought to a standstill, since such a state of affairs does not give rise to a claim to have the loss made good, either in accordance with the terms of the Mejelle or of the Code of Civil Procedure.

(C.C.D. No. 180, dated the 19th January, 1330).

158   LAW OF CONTRACT

Article 126.

"If a claim is made for damages for loss or injury sustained, and it has not been possible to determine how the same was incurred and to investigate the details thereof and to give a judgment thereon at the same time as the original action, the applicant shall be called upon to supply details of the claim to the Court in order that a separate judgment may be issued in respect thereto."

(8) Interest and Rate of Interest.

Article 112. If the contract be for the payment of a sum of money, and there be delay in making such payment, damages may be awarded at the rate of one per cent. per month on the principal amount, and the creditor shall not be required to prove that he has suffered any loss. If no stipulation for the payment of interest be included in the contract, it shall be payable from the date of the protest, if it was claimed in the protest, and otherwise from the date of presentation of the statement of claim.

The rate of one per cent per month mentioned in the Article, i. e. 12% per annum, was the amount allowed under the old Ottoman Regulations governing the rate of interest dated the 16th Shewal, 1280. These have now been repealed and replaced by the Ottoman Regulations dated 9 Rajab, 1304/22nd March, 1303/3rd April, 1887, whereby the rate of interest was decreased to 9% per annum. The text of these Regulations is as follows:

Article 1. As from the date of the publication of these regulations, the maximum rate of interest shall be fixed at nine per cent. per annum in respect to all ordinary and commercial debts.

Article 2. Contracts as to interest concluded at a rate of twelve per cent per annum before the date of the publication of these regulations shall remain in force until the date of publication of these regulations.

Article 3. If it can be proved that contracts for interest have been concluded between lender and creditor for an amount in excess of the legal limit, or has been mentioned in documents, or has been added to capital, the amount of interest shall be reduced to nine per cent.

Article 4. Interest on loans shall not exceed the amount of the capital, however many years the loan may last. All judges are forbidden to give judgment for interest which exceeds the capital.

Article 5. Compound interest may not be applied to loans. If, however, (1) during a period of three years the debtor has not paid any money on account of the sum borrowed; (2) an agreement has been concluded between the debtor and the creditor to add the interest accrued during three years to the capital, compound interest may be counted for a period of three years only. Operations of compound interest arising out of current accounts between merchants under the terms of the Commercial Code are exempted from the provisions of this Article.

Article 6. So long as lending and borrowing transactions are in progress between creditor and debtor, whether there has been a transfer or whether the note of the debt has been renewed or changed, all demands for reduction of excessive interest to the legal amount shall be entertained. If the debt has been entirely paid, however, and if operations have been finally concluded as between creditor and debtor, any claim for reimbursement of excessive interest shall not be entertained.

Article 7. The Regulations regarding the rate of interest dated 16th Shaul, 1280, shall be abrogated as from the date of the publication of these Regulations.

The position as regards evidence was materially altered by the Palestine Usurious Loans Ordinance 1934 dated the 17th August, 1934. Articles 2 and 3 of the Ordinance prescribe that:

(1) Where proceedings are taken in any Court for the recovery of money lent and there is evidence which satisfies the Court that the interest charged in respect of the sum actually lent, whether such interest was described in the contract as interest or as capital or was made payable in any other way, is at a higher rate than allowed by law, the court may re-open the transaction and take an account between the lender and the person sued and may, notwithstanding any statement or settlement of account or

LAW OF CONTRACT

any agreement purporting to close previous dealings and create a new obligation, re-open any account already taken between them and relieve the person sued from payment of any sum in excess of the sum adjudged by the Court to be due; and if any excess has been paid or allowed in account by the debtor, may order the creditor to repay it.

(2) Any Court in which proceedings might be taken for the recovery of money lent by any person shall have and may at the instance of the borrower or surety or other person liable exercise the like powers as may be exercised under sub-section (1) hereof where proceedings are taken for the recovery of money lent, notwithstanding any provision or agreement to the contrary and notwithstanding that the time of the repayment of the loan or any instalment thereof may not have arrived.

(3) The foregoing provisions of this section shall apply to any transaction which whatever the form may be is substantially one of money lending.

(4) Nothing in the foregoing provisions of this section shall effect the right of any *bona fide* assignee or holder for value without notice.

In any proceedings for the recovery of money lent and in any proceedings under sub-section (2) of section 2 of this Ordinance, a Court may receive any evidence whether parol or written by any person in regard to the rate of interest charged notwithstanding any provision of the law relating to the admissibility of evidence or the competency of witnesses.

The stipulations of Article 5 of the Ottoman Regulations relating to compound interest charged by a bank to a customer was modified by the Legal Rate of Interest Ordinance, 1929, Article 2 of which reads as follows:

"Notwithstanding anything in the Ottoman Law dated 9th Rajab, 1304 A. H., concerning the legal rate of interest, a bank may charge a customer compound interest in respect of any loan or overdraft at such rate, not exceeding 9%, and with such rests as may be agreed between the bank and the customer".

The effect of these enactments seems to be as follows:

(1) The maximum rate of interest which can be legally enforced is 9% per annum simple interest;

(2) The Courts will reduce any sum agreed upon by the parties in excess of 9% to that amount; unless the debt has been entirely paid;

(3) The total amount of interest payable may never exceed the amount of the principal sum;

LAW OF CONTRACT

(4) Compound interest is not allowed, subject to a period of three years if the debtor has paid nothing in respect to the sum borrowed. As regards accounts outstanding between merchants under the terms of the Commercial Code, however, compound interest is allowed. Compound interest is also allowed under the Legal Rate of Interest Ordinance, 1929, in respect to any loan or overdraft made by a bank at a rate not exceeding 9%;

(5) Any person may give oral or written evidence under the terms of the Usurious Loans Ordinance, 1934, for or against any plea made by a defendant that the claim includes interest at a higher rate than that allowed by law.

There is no specific legislation in force in Palestine with regard to money lenders.

Palestine Decided Cases.

(1) "The judgment of this Court is that the L.T.300 shall be repaid at the rate of 7% from 1st November, 1916, to the 24th of June, 1918, when the Moratorium ended, and at the rate of 9% from that date to payment, provided that the sum due for interest does not exceed the capital". *(Nakhli Kattan v. Joulia widow of George Zacharia,* C. A. No. 395/21).

(2) "The Court holds: (a) That the transaction which gives rise to the action was a bei bil wafa and not a bei bil Istighlal.

(b) That it follows that apart from any special circumstances the mortgagee would not be entitled to receive interest on the loan but would be entitled to possession of the property and to have the same sold upon default by the borrower in repayment of the loan.

(c) That as the mortgagee was never in possession of the property, he could not obtain judgment for possession and hence the prohibition of sale in satisfaction of a mortgage debt suspended the only right which the mortgagee could exercise in enforcement of his security.

(d) That accordingly under Article 22 of Proclamation No. 42, interest (is payable) on the amount lent and remained unpaid from the date of that Proclamation, namely 24th June, 1918, at a rate to be fixed by the Court". *(Haj Amin el Taher v. Shafik Zantut,* C. A. No. 185/22).

(3) "The District Court was right in deducting the excessive interest leaving legal interest on these notes. Judgment confirmed on this point". *(Tewfik el Haj Daher v. Michail el Kadha,* C. A. No. 177/23).

LAW OF CONTRACT

(4) "The Court holds: (a) That the Usurious Loans (Evidence) Ordinance 1922 being a Law of Procedure applies in the case of loans made before the passing of the Ordinance, where action was not commenced until the Ordinance was in force.

(b) That the nature of the acknowledgement gives rise to the presumption that the sum made payable after a delay of six months included interest on the sum lent, and hence that the District Court should have admitted oral evidence to prove whether in fact the sum payable did or did not include interest at a rate in excess of the legal rate: and the fact that the acknowledgment was given before the Notary-Public is immaterial.

(c) In the event of the Appellants being unable to establish their claim by evidence, they are entitled to have an oath administered to the Respondent.

(d) The judgment of the District Court is set aside and the case remitted.

The following is a copy of the acknowledgment:

"On Saturday June......, there came to the office of the Notary-Public of the Magistrate's Court of Ramallah, Mohamed Abdul Salame and his brother Mousa of Anata village and were identified by true witnesses and identifiers Hanna Zaron and Said Lalash. They then stated that they owe Mitry Salameh Atallah, the sum of LE.115 payable in six months and that they are jointly and severally responsible for it, and that at the date of maturity the creditor is free to demand payment by one or both. They also asked me to draw up this deed which I have drawn and certified by the debtors under their own signatures in my presence and in the presence of the said undersigned identifiers. Then it was registered in its special register by me Abd Rahman Hassan Danaf Ansary, Notary-Public of Ramallah".

The following is a copy of the decision and judgment in this case: —

"The Court cannot find from the circumstances of this case anything that leads to the least suspicion as to the existence of the excessive interest claimed. The original debt was admitted before the Notary-Public and a deed was drawn by them to that effect in which Plaintiffs admitted that they owe the said sum. Whereas the said debt is not due to a matter which creates doubts or suspicions as to the admission, and whereas the deed which is alleged to contain excessive interest was made before the promulgation of the Usurious Loans Ordinance, and whereas there is no provision in the said Ordinance that it is retroactive, and whereas the said Ordinance allows but does not bind the Court to hear evidence of witnesses, we therefore dismiss the request of Plaintiffs for lack to prove, by evidence of witnesses excessive interest. Nevertheless in order to prevent injustice being done and to remove doubts and suspicions the Court decides to ask

LAW OF CONTRACT

Plaintiffs whether they wish to ask Defendant to take the oath that their admission is not false". *(Mohamed Abdul Salam and another v. Mitry Salame Atallah,* C. A. No. 8/24).

(5)   "The agreement between the parties was that the Appellant should repay to the Respondent in April, 1916, the sum of 15000 francs gold with interest at 9% for the two years for which the loan was made. It is argued for the Respondent that under this agreement he is entitled to interest at that rate reserved until the date of payment. Had this been the intention, however, it would have been simpler to have expressed it in the agreement. The agreement, however, provided payment of interest at maturity, the Respondent should thereupon become entitled to recover the principal sum and interest for the two years by a sale of the Appellant's vineyard as provided in the agreement. At the date of maturity however, the moratorium laws were in force. Under these laws a creditor could not obtain payment of the whole of the principal sum due to him, but was entitled to interest on the part postponed, which interest in a case such as this where no rate of interest until payment was fixed, was payable at 7% interest without the necessity of protest and the Respondent is entitled to interest accordingly. Such provisions ceased to be in force on 31st December, 1917.

As protest was not made within the extended period allowed by the Proclamation, interest ceased to be payable after the 31st December, 1917, on any part of the principal until the date of commencement of action from which date interest is payable on the whole of the principal sum at 9%. Subject to this amendment the Judgment of the District Court is affirmed". *(Jona Dinovitz v. Gershon Harris Rosenbaum,* C. A. 48/24).

(6)   "As regards the plea of usurious interest: it is to be noted that the agreement does not specify any date upon which the L.600 sterling was to be credited to the Respondent. Indeed the transaction, though expressed to be a loan, appears in reality to have been a transaction in exchange; and in view of the absence of any agreed date for payment the transaction appears to have been purely speculative in character and it cannot be proved that the sum of L.600 sterling was not a fair equivalent of 1,140,000 roubles, or that any question of interest was involved. Accordingly, the claim to prove usurious interest fails". *(Zeiv Hazan v. Nahum Milstein,* C. A. 45/24).

(7)   "Judgment of the Court below is confirmed with the modification that the interest provided for on the sums of L.310 and L.600 respectively shall be omitted, since such interest cannot be added as damages to the fixed damages provided for by the contract even though the contract purported to allow such interest". *(Shakib Tanus Wahabeh el Haj v. Joshua Hankin,* C. A. 104/27).

LAW OF CONTRACT

(8) "Article 112 of the Code of Civil Procedure (Turkish Text) prescribes that interest shall be paid without the creditor having to prove that he has suffered loss. It would, therefore, appear that the Court has no discretion with regard to awarding interest and that the award should follow the judgment. Accordingly, the appeal is allowed and the judgment of the Haifa District Court amended by the inclusion of an award of interest at the legal rate from the time of action until payment". (*Samaan Jadoun Khalil v. Abdel Raheem Sqariq and others*, C. A. 41/28).

(9) "By virtue of Section 6 of the Law concerning the rate of interest of 9th Rajab, 1304, it is prescribed that claims for the reduction of interest to the legal rate may be heard so long as there is an account outstanding between the parties. This Article has not been over-ruled by the Usurious Loans Ordinance 1922. The case is therefore remitted for Plaintiff's claim to be heard and tried on its merits and if Plaintiff satisfies the Court that he has actually paid monies in excess of 9% then he will be entitled to a return of those monies. The Court confirms the dicta of the Lower Court that Appellant cannot claim on bills which have not yet become due". (*Zipora Karwasarsky v. Bezalel Kaminsky*, C. A. 71/28).

(10) "I am of opinion that the Turkish Law concerning the rate of interest should not have been applied in this case. On the other hand, I cannot agree with my brother Khayat, whose judgment I have read, that the Court below erred in not allowing oral evidence on behalf of the Plaintiff under section 1 (section 2 in Bentwich) of Ordinance No. 11 of 1922, the Usurious Loan (Evidence) Ordinance 1922. That section expressly provides that where the defendant pleads usurious interest, written or oral evidence may be received to support or rebut such plea. I cannot agree that as my learned brother says, we must take it "that the intention of law is to give the right to every debtor claiming the existence of excessive interest to prove his claim by personal evidence."

When the meaning of a statute is unambiguous its intention must be gathered from the words used. In the present case the ordinary law is varied in cases where the Defendant pleads usurious interest: The Courts have no power to extend it also to cases in which the Plaintiff puts forward that plea". (*Adeeb Zaban and another v. Meir S. Altshuler*, C. A. 54/29).

(11) "The Respondent, Kaufman, is the owner of property which he has mortgaged to the Petitioner Steinberg as security for L.500 by registered Deeds of Mortgage the particulars of which are: —

Date	No.	Amount secured.
15th August, 1922	672	L.300
1st October, 1923	968	L.100
1st June, 1925	804	L.100

Subsequently the Respondent Kaufman mortgaged the property to the Respondent Meshiah. The Petitioner has obtained an order for sale of the property in satisfaction of his mortgage debt, and the question has been raised whether he is entitled to have interest upon his loans paid out of the proceeds of sale in priority to the debt due to the second mortgagee. The three Deeds of Mortgage in favour of the Petitioner all contain an agreement by the mortgagor to pay interest at the rate of 9% and the second mortgagee must be held to have notice of this agreement, whether he in fact inspected the register or not before the mortgage in his favour was executed. In our view, therefore, the Petitioner is entitled to have interest on his loans paid out of the proceeds of sale before any payment is made to the Respondent Meshiah". (*Shlomo Steinberg v. Chief Execution Officer, Jerusalem and others*, H. C. 51/30).

(12) "We are satisfied that the judgment of the Lower Court must be affirmed, other than that part which refers to the payment of interest from the 2nd of May, 1924. We are satisfied that "Ejr Misl" is in the nature of compensation or damages and that therefore no interest can be paid on an award of this nature". (*Yusuf Abdul Karim Abdel Hadi v. Wajih Abdul Karim Abdel Hadi*, C. A. 52/31).

(13) "The heirs of Khalil Suleiman claimed against Nasrallah Hadad their guardian a sum of L.E.825 Egyptian. The Defendant did not deny the principal claim neither that accounts had been taken. He however pleaded that there was excessive interest and that payments were made after the accounts had been taken. Counsel for Plaintiff admitted both the excessive interest and the payments in question. The Court below entered judgment in the said sum with interest from the date of the action. Both parties have appealed against the said judgment. The Defendant bases his appeal on the following grounds: —

1. The action cannot be sustained inasmuch as the respective shares of the Plaintiffs have not been specified.

2. The money was in his hands by way of trust and as a trustee he could not be charged interest at all in accordance with the Moslem Sharia Law.

3. The Court deducted the excessive interest only from the date of the making of the accounts in 1924, whereas it should have been deducted as from 1920.

The Plaintiff appeals on the following grounds: —

1. The share of the Defendant's mother was deducted by the Court from the amount claimed while in fact his share was not included in the statement of account which was limited to their share and to the shares of their sisters and the daughter of one of them Elen and that his mother's share had already been paid.

LAW OF CONTRACT

2. The Appellant had from the outset undertaken to pay interest and the Court should have given judgment for interest from the date of the transaction and not from the date of action.

3. There was an error in calculating the excessive interest and the amount of the judgment should have been L.573.050.

On consideration of the appellate grounds of both parties, we hold that: —

1. The Defendant's contention regarding the date as from which the excessive interest should be deducted must be upheld in that once usurious interest has been proved it should be deducted from the date of its commencement.

2. As regards the allegation that he should not be ordered to pay interest at all, being a guardian, he cannot go back on his undertaking to pay interest once he had undertaken to do so.

As regards the cross-appeal of the Plaintiffs, all the grounds are relevant and must be considered and examined. Whereas the judgment of the Court does not give details to show how the sum awarded in the judgment was arrived at, we are of opinion that the judgment must be set aside and the case remitted to the District Court for examination and a fresh judgment to be given in compliance with this judgment". (*Nasrallah Hadad v. Laya, widow of Khalil Suleiman and others,* C. A. 68/31).

(14) "In view of the oath taken by Respondent before us, we are satisfied that the document was properly admitted in evidence by the lower Court, and the judgment of the said Court, in so far as it relates to the payment of interest, must be affirmed.

With regard to the second part of the appeal, the mortgage deed, not containing any provision for the payment of interest, the interest payable under the document of the 5th. December, 1927, cannot and is not a privileged debt secured by the property the subject of the mortgage and accordingly Appellant must succeed in this part of his appeal. The provisional attachment is hereby removed: and subject to this amendment, the judgment of the lower Court is affirmed". (*Kamel esh - Shanti v. Yaqub Saliba Dellal and another,* C. A. 98/31).

(15) "The Respondent Rushdieh bint Saleh Arnaout has lodged a cross-appeal claiming interest on the amount due from the date of action. To this she is clearly entitled, and the judgment of the District Court must be amended accordingly". (*Abd el Latif Musa Abu Hantash v. Rushdieh widow of Mustafa Qabbani,* C. A. 107/31).

(16) "In accordance with the judgment of this Court in *Adeeb Zaban and another v. Meir Shlomo Altshuler,* (C. A. 54/29), the Court holds that where a Plaintiff claims that he has been charged interest at a rate in excess of that allowed by Law, he cannot avail himself of the provisions of the Usurious Loans

(Evidence) Ordinance, 1922, which is restricted to the case of a plea by a Defendant". (*Shamuel Slonim v. Musleh Abdel Latif el Izzah,* C. A. 54/32).

(17) "The bills given by Nasrallah were a renewal of the debt owing by Yusef. Accordingly, Section 6 of the Law of Interest is applicable, and the claim that excessive interest was included can be extended to the bills given by Yusef Khuri". (*Salim Nasrallah Khoury and others v. Hassan Bey Shukri,* C. A. 147/32).

Constantinople Cassation Decisions.

No. (2) "Interest does not cease to run owing to the death of the debtor and must consequently be levied in regard to the heir also up to the time of payment.
(C.C.D. No. 177 dated 16th. November, 1327)
(C.C.D. No. 144 dated 25th. November, 1330)

No. (3) "Judgment may be given for interest which exceeds the amount of the principal sum and which accumulated in respect to a period prior to the promulgation of the new Regulations — 9 Rajab, 1304. — It is contrary to law, however, to regard the sum claimed as having earned no interest at the date of the New Regulations and to amend two rates of interest, one in respect to the period prior to the passing of the new Regulations, which exceeded the amount of the principal sum, and one in respect to the later period".
(C.C.D. No. 21 dated 2nd. April, 1328)
(C.C.D. No. 223 dated 21st. January, 1328)

No. (4) "If in an action there is no agreement as to interest in accordance with the terms of Article 112 of the Code of Civil Procedure, and no protest has been made in connection therewith, judgment must be given for interest beginning from the date of the statement of claim. Judgment for interest as from the date the bill fell due for payment is contrary to law". (C.C.D. No. 38, dated 9th. April 1328).

No. (5) "If the subject-matter of the claim is corn, it is obvious that judgment cannot be given for interest in such a case, and consequently any judgment for interest is contrary to law". (C.C.D. No. 104 dated 6th. August, 1328).

No. (6) "If there is nothing in the contents of the note produced with regard to a sum of L.T.100 borrowed for a period of five years, to substantiate the allegation of the plaintiff that the capital is L.T.60 and the rest interest, the Court must administer the oath to the defendant in accordance with the terms of Article 1589 of the Mejelle, that the amount in excess of L.T. 60 contained in the note does not consist of interest, and thereafter the amount of the principal and interest must be fixed. If the interest is found to be in excess of the amount allowed by law, it must

LAW OF CONTRACT

be reduced to its legal limit, and judgment given accordingly".
(C.C.D. No. 106 dated 7th. August, 1328).

No. (7) "If the debt is owing by a deceased person, the agreement as to interest must be considered to be of no effect as from the date of such person's death".
(C.C.D. No. 143, dated 29th. September, 1328)
(C.C.D. No. 7, dated 4th. March, 1330)

No. (8) "If judgment has been passed by a Sharia Court for the original sum claimed, *i. e.* the capital, no action may be heard in the Civil Courts in respect to any interest in connection therewith". (C.C.D. No. 151, dated 4th. October, 1328).

No. (9) "In view of the fact that interest ceases with the death of the debtor, the date of his death must be ascertained, and interest must be calculated accordingly. If not, the judgment will be quashed".
(C.C.D. No. 161 dated 7th. October, 1328).

Note: See decisions No. 992—997 above.

No. (10) "If the defendant pleads that the amount claimed contains excessive interest (*faiz fahish*) he must be called upon to state the amount thereof, and the oath must be administered to the Plaintiff (upon request) that the amount does not contain excessive interest to the amount stated, or any smaller sum".
(C.C.D. No. 177, dated 3rd. November, 1328).

No. (11) "Excessive interest (*faiz fahish*) claimed in respect to a note produced may not be proved by the evidence of witnesses, but an oath must be administered in accordance with Article 1589 of the Mejelle".
(C.C.D. No 186, dated 21st. November, 1328).

No. (12) Judgment may be given up to the date of the promulgation of the new Regulations regarding the rate of interest, for interest to an amount exceeding the principal sum, in respect to debts relating to any period preceding the date of the publication of the New Regulations".
(C.C.D. No. 223, dated 21st. November, 1328).

No. (13) If a person brings an action to recover money owing to him by some other person and his claim fails from lack of prosecution, and his heirs after his death renew the action and claim interest on the sum in question, such interest must be considered to run from the date of the renewal of the action. The date of the statement of claim of the action which was so presented, may not be taken as the date from which interest begins to run".
(C.C.D. No. 4, dated 6th. March, 1329).

No. (14) "Interest may not be awarded on expenses in connection with an attachment (*Hajz*). Consequently, judgment for the sum claimed together with expenses occasioned by attachment is contrary to law".
(C.C.D. No. 21, dated 25th. March, 1329).

No. (15) "The addition of interest to rent (*ujret*) (e. g. of a house) is contrary to law.

(C.C.D. No. 31, dated 25th. April, 1329).

No. (16) "The addition of interest to any sum considered to be an indemnity, such as the amount paid upon expropriation, is contrary to law".

(C.C.D. No. 58, dated 28th. May, 1329).

No. (17) "If the sum claimed is payment for services rendered, such as the fee of a broker, awarding interest thereon is contrary to law.

(C.C.D. No. 125, dated 18th. November, 1329).

No. (18) "An estimated rent is in the nature of an indemnity and consequently interest may not be awarded thereon".

(C.C.D. No. 155, dated 23rd. January, 1329).

No. (19) "Interest may not be awarded on the cost of destruction which is in the nature of an indemnity".

(C.C.D. No. 2, dated 7th. March, 1330).

No. (20) "If it is not stated in the note evidencing the debt that interest will be given in respect to more than one year, calculating the interest until the time of payment of the sum awarded in the judgment is contrary to law. Consequently, any sums paid by means of a note in respect of the principal sum together with interest must be set off from the capital sum together with interest at the time of payment and deducted therefrom. Any decision given for the reduction from the interest which has accrued at the time of payment of the sum awarded in the judgment is contrary to law".

(C.C.D. No. 77, dated 16th. August, 1332).

No. (21) "If in an agreement for the transfer of immoveable property in which a sum of L.40 is paid in advance, there is a provision for the payment of an indemnity of L.40 in the event of failure to transfer, interest cannot be claimed on the money paid in advance, the return of which is claimed, together with the L.40 stipulated for as damages".

(C.C.D. No. 95, dated 21st. September, 1332).

In three of the Constantinople Cassation Decisions referred to above (Nos. 2, 7 and 9) conflicting decisions have been given as to whether interest is payable by the heirs of a deceased debtor; and this brings up the question as to whether debts fall due for payment by reason of the death of the debtor, which would not normally fall due for payment until some later date, the creditor having a right to demand payment forthwith from the heirs who have succeeded to the estate. The question was considered, though not in all its aspects, in the Palestine

LAW OF CONTRACT

Decided Case of *Kevork Havagimian v. Mrs. Pilpul Nassarian*, (C. A. 106/31), where the following judgment was delivered:

"The Court holds that in view of the date of the Promissory Notes in this case, the Bills of Exchange Ordinance, 1929, and not the Mejelle must be consulted to see whether such Promissory Notes mature on the death of the debtor.

There being no such provision in the Ordinance, we need not concern ourselves to interpret the provisions of the Mejelle, and no authority under the Law of England having been cited to us under Section 2 (2) of the Bills of Exchange Ordinance, 1929, the appeal is dismissed".

The District Court on 9/9/1931 had dismissed the Appellant's action on the ground that there is no law which lays down that a debt matures upon the death of the debtor.

From the Judgment of the District Court:

"Whereas two bills produced in connection with the case have not yet fallen due for payment".

"Whereas the Court fails to find any Article of law whereby they should hold that the bills are deemed matured in case of the debtor's death".

It is submitted, however, that according to Muhammadan law debts do in fact fall due for payment upon the death of the debtor and the creditor has a right of claiming payment forthwith from the heirs as soon as they have succeded to the estate. The reason for this appears to be that the creditor, by reason of the death of the debtor, finds himself in a different contractual relationship from that of the original debtor, and it may be that the new parties, *i. e.* the heirs, may waste the property of the succession, so that when the date for payment of the debt arrives, the creditor may be unable to recover the loan. The question arises in a practical form as regards a contract whereby payment is effected by instalments. According to Muhammadan law, the whole of any unpaid instalments become payable forthwith from the estate upon the death of the debtor.

"Upon the death of the debtor the instalments, *i. e.* deferred payment, become void and payment must at once be made from the estate" (Ali Haidar, Volume I, page 396).

"If the debtor, for example, a purchaser, dies, the instalments (deferred payments) become void and the money is payable forthwith from the estate. But the instalments do not become void with the death of the creditor. The heirs of the vendor, or in the event of there being no heirs, the Treasury, may not claim the price from the purchaser and debtor before the due date. (Ali Haidar, Volume I, page 401).

"If the purchaser dies before the due date, the debt falls due for payment; but if the vendor dies it does not, because deferred payments become void with the death of the debtor, but not with that of the creditor" (Baz, Majelle, page 124).

"This rule applies, moreover, to any debt of any nature, *e. g.* an overdraft by a Bank on a trading or private account for a specific period. The most common form of acknowledgement of a debt is the *sened deyn* (loosely translated as "promissory note"). There is no special enactment affecting the matter in either Ottoman or Palestine legislation and consequently the general rule of Muhammadan law, it is submitted, must prevail. (See the notes to Article 245 where the whole question is discussed exhaustively).

INDEX.

Abrogating and the abrogated doctrine 7
Abu Abdullah Ahmed ibn Hanbal 16
Abu Daud 10-11
Abul Hanifa en Numan ibn Thabit 15,21
Abu Muslim 10
Abu Yusif 21
Acceptance
    of admission, unnecessary 89
        offer, when necessary 88
        rescission of contract, by conduct 91-2
Accounts
    when corroboration 108
Acknowledgment before Notary Public
    oral evidence against, to prove excessive interest 162-3
Adab 117
Adah 13
Admission
    before Land Registrar, allegation of falsity against 50,53
    by imbecile, invalid 107
        lunatic, invalid 107
        minor, invalid 107
    capacity to make 107
    need not be accepted 89
    what amounts to, under Art. 80 C.C.P. 133-4
Agency
    capacity of parties to 106
    contract of, not binding 127
Agent
    authority by lunatic to, invalid 106
    capacity to act as 106
    may retire at will 127
Ahl-as-Sunna 11
Akil (See Minor of Perfect Understanding)
Al-Hafid 3
Alimony
    meaning of 77
Al-Muwatta (See Muwatta)
Al-Qartabi, Muhammad ibn Ahmed ibn Rushd (See Al-Hafid)
Ambiguous texts
    interpretation of, 1-2, 21-3
Analogy 3,4,12,13

174

An-Nasai 10
Appeal
    claim for loss pending 157
    time for lodging 39, 51
        payment of fees on, 51
    to Ottoman Court of Cassation, in stamp cases 60
Aqd (See Contract)
Arbitration
    in Mejelle 19
    submission to, customarily in writing 129, 132-3
Arbitration Ordinance, 1926
    s. 15 (2) 50, 55
As-sahihain 10
Attachment
    expenses of, no interest claimable on 168
At-tirmidhi 10
Awaz (See Consideration)

Bad Faith
    breach of contract in, measure of damages for 141, 145-6
Badr-al-Muntaka 20
Baligh 106, 107
Batil (See Void)
Bearer
    promissory note payable to, validity of 122-3
Bedayat-ul-Mujtahid 3
Bei bil Wafa
    rights of mortgagee under 161
Belief of Witnesses
    finding as to, when Court of Appeal will interfere with 135-6
Benevolent Reforms 33
Berat-i-ali 35
Beyan-namé-i-Humayoun 35
Bills of Exchange Act 65
Breach of Contract (See Contract)
Breach of Promise to Marry 152-3
British India
    practice of Courts in 22
Bukhari 10
Bulugh (See Puberty)

Caliph (See Khalifa)
Cancellation
    option of, 113

Capacity of parties
    to admissions 107
        agency 106
        contract generally 99-104
            Musakat 106
            Muzaria 106
        deposit for safe keeping 105
        gift 106
        guarantee 105
        hire 104
        loan for use 105
        partnership in land and work 106
            trees and work 106
        pledge 105
        release 107
        sale 104
        settlement 106-7
        transfer of debt. 105
Capitulations 31, 32
Caveat Emptor
    rule of Muhammadan law 112
Cessation of Payments
    date of 55
Chapters
    of Mejelle, headings to, whether law 18-9
Chief Execution Officer
    order for registration by, when set aside 52
    President of District Court is 61
Christian communities
    jurisdiction of priests of 30-1
    law of 31
Common Law
    application of, limitation on 71, 80
    distinguished from Equity 68-9
    statute law, when included in 69
    substance of, 28, 64-9, 70
Companies (Consolidation) Act 1908
    S. 130 75
Companies Ordinance, 1920 76
              , 1929 76
Companies (Winding up) Ordinance, 1922 79
    s. 94 75
Composition of Court
    change in, effect of 53
Compound interest
    when payable 159, 160, 161
Conduct
    acceptance of rescission of contract by 91-2

Consent
>   of parties to contract essential for validity   109

Consideration
>   agreement to divorce, when good   93-5, 98, 124-5
>   division of contracts with respect to   93
>   past, not good   98
>   valuable, defined   93
>   want of, renders undertaking unenforceable   97

Constraint
>   defendant must prove   111
>   effectiveness of, conditions for   109
>   invalidates any nnilateral act   109
>   major, defined   109
>   minor, defined   110
>   when, invalidates contract   109

Contract
>   breach of, damages for (See Damages)
>   capacity to, generally   99-104
>   classification of, in Muhammadan law   139-41
>   conflicting with immovable property law   119
>   inheritance law   118
>   matters of personal status.   118
>   succession law   118
>   waqf law   118
>   consent of parties to   109-114
>   contrary to morality   117
>   customarily in writing   129-30, 136-7
>   definition of, in Mejelle   88
>   division of, with respect to consideration   93
>   effect of deceit on,   111
>   farming out, in writing   130-1
>   forbidden by law   116-7
>   formalities unnecessary for   89
>   form of   127-39
>   for sale of non-existing things   92
>   impossibility of performance of   120-1
>   in Muhammadan law   88
>   invalidity of, declaration of   110
>   for constraint   109
>   not bar to damages claim   126
>   of agency, not binding   127
>   guarantee, capacity of parties to   105
>   hire (See Hire)
>   insurance   117
>   loan, in writing   131
>   which subject matter cannot be produced   119
>   partnership, in writing   130

      performance of, impossibility of, 120-1
                  time for 142-3
      prejudicial to public order 117-8
      rescission of, acceptance of, by conduct 91-2
      speculative, invalid 117
      subject matter of 114-27
      valid 109, 140
      void 109, 141
      voidable 140
      written, categories of 138
Contradictory plea 52
Copyright Act, 1911
      s. 29 61
Corporation
      action against, how brought 90
Corroboration
      when accounts are 108
Court of Appeal
      bound by High Court decisions 38
                its own decisions 38
      credibility of evidence, not matter for 135-6
      when, will interfere with finding as to belief of witnesses 135-6
Courts of Justice
      meaning of, in Art. 46 of P.O.i.C. 71-2
      powers of, 71
Courts Ordinance, 1924
      s. 6 (b) 78
Credibility of Evidence
      not matter for Court of Appeal 135-6
Custom 3, 13, 14
Cyprus Courts
      decisions of, when binding on Palestine Courts 37, 38
      law applied by 36, 37

Damages
      claim for, against embezzler 151
                necessity of protest for 141-3
      fixed, interest not claimable on 154, 163
      for breach of contract, claim for, condition precedent to 142
                              not barred by invalidity of contract 126
                              when decided 141
                              not variable 153
                      measure of 145-6, 152, 153-5
                      not payable when both parties in default 154
                      of debt, not claimable 142
                      when awarded 141
      in Ottoman law 74
      when not recoverable for cutting off of water 157

178

Dasisa and Hila (See Bad Faith)
Day
    end of 74
Death
    of debtor, debt matures on 170-1
            instalments mature on 170-1
Debt
    matures on debtor's death 170-1
    payment of, before maturity, creditor can refuse 110
    renewal of, Art. 6 of Ottoman Interest Law applies to 167
Debtor
    death of, debt matures on 170-1
            instalments mature on 170-1
    interdiction of 103-4
    jurisdiction of Sharia Court over 103
Deceit
    action for, not transmissible to heirs 113
    definition of 111
    effect of, on contract 111
    misrepresentation when becomes 112
    remedies of victim of 111
    sale by, when purchaser cannot cancel 113
Decision
    meaning of 58-9
Defect
    option for 92, 114
Delil 10
Deposit for safe keeping
    capacity of parties to 105
Destur 34, 36, 59
    contents of 36
    definition of 36
    laws in, presumption as to in Cyprus 36
Disposition
    by imbecile 102
        lunatic 103
        minor, validity of 100-1
        prodigal 102
Divorce
    agreement to, when good consideration 93-5, 98, 124-5
Document
    legalisation of, by Notary Public, effect of 138-9
    meaning of, in Art. 80 C.C.P. 137
    official, definition of, 138
    ordinary (See Ordinary document)
Doctrines of Equity (See Equity)
Drafting Commission,
    Report of 1, 19, 21, 23

Durr-al-Mukhtar 20, 25

Ejr Misl (See Estimated Rent)
Embezzler
    liability of, to pay damages 151
Emrname 35
English decisions
    role of, in Cyprus 56
              Palestine 56
English law
    amount of, in force in Palestine 70
    application of, in Palestine 72, 80-1
    date for coming into force in Palestine 64
    equity in 28, 64, 66, 67-9, 70, 73
    interpretation of 79
    of penalty, 147-9
        procedure, date for coming into force in Palestine 72, 80
        trusts, when applicable in Cyprus 57
    when not imported into Palestine law 73
Equitable charge
    upon future crops, not creatable 74-5, 123-4
Equity
    application of, limitations on 71, 80
    distinguished from Common law 68-9
    fusion with Common law 68-9
    in English law 28, 64, 66, 67-9, 70, 73
        Muhammadan law 13
    maxims of 70
Estimated Rent
    contract of hire, when ratification necessary 104
    interest not payable on 165, 169
Evidence
    as to force majeure 144
    credibility of, not matter for Court of Appeal 135-6
    oral, against acknowledgment before Notary Public, to
                    prove excessive interest 162-3
        as to transaction between spouses 136
        when admissible against written document 54, 134-5
Examples
    in Mejelle, nature of 19-20
Excessive interest
    Court may deduct 161
    date from which deducted 165-6
    oath as to, 162-3, 167, 168
Execution proceedings
    sale in, valuation of property on 50
Expenses
    of attachment, interest on, not claimable 168

Faqih 16
Farming out
    contract for, in writing 130-1
Fasid (See Voidable)
Fatawa Alamgiri 22, 25
Fees
    on appeal, time for payment of 51
Fetwa books 19
Fiqh 16
Firman-l-ali 35
Flagrant misrepresentation 100, 111
    definition of, 100
    when remedy for, 112
Force majeure
    definition of, 131, 141, 145
    evidence as to, 144
    examples of, 145, 149-52
    what constitutes, Court decides 144
Foreign country
    meaning of, in Foreign Jurisdiction Act, 1890 62
Foreign Jurisdiction Act, 1890
    meaning of foreign country in 62
Forfeitures
    relief against, not granted in Palestine 70
Fraud
    effect of, on prescription 73
French law
    influence of, on Ottoman law 32-3
Fuqaha 20, 21
Future crops
    equitable charge on, not creatable in Palestine 74-5, 123-4
General law
    meaning of 116-7
    Ottoman Commercial Code is a, 117
Ghubn fahish (See Flagrant Misrepresentation)
    yasi (See Minor Misrepresentation)
Gift
    by imbecile, void 106
        lunatic, void 106
        minor, void 106
    capacity of parties to 106
Great Imam (See Abu Hanifa)
Guarantee
    contract of, capacity of parties to 105
Guarantor
    minor, when bound 105
Guardian
    decision of Sharia Court regarding 104
    powers of 99-101

Hadith 9, 11, 16
Hajr (See Interdiction)
Hanbalite School 15, 16
Handwriting
    verification of, 39
Hanifite School 15, 20, 21
Headings
    to Mejelle chapters, whether part of law 18-9
Hedaya 1, 2, 22, 24
Heirs
    liability of, for interest 167, 168, 169-71
High Court
    decisions of, bind Court of Appeal 52
                   inferior Courts 52
Hijra 6
Hila and Dasira (See Bad Faith)
Hire
    contract of, capacity of parties to 104
                customarily in writing 129, 136-7
                documentary evidence to prove 136-7
                when official document 139
Hizb 7
Hujja 10
Husband and wife
    transactions between, oral evidence as to 136

Ibn Majah 10
Ijab (See Offer)
Ijma 3, 11, 12
    as-sahaba 12
    at-taqrir 11
    sukuti 11
    ul l'ili 11
    ul qual 11
Ikhtar (See Protest)
Ikra (See Constraint)
    ghair mulji (See Minor Constraint)
    mulji (See Major Constraint)
Ikrar 129
Iltizan (See Farming out)
Imam 5
    abu Hanifa 15, 21
    Great (See Abu Hanifa)
    Hanbal 16
    Muhammad 21, 22
    the two 21

Imbecile
> admission by, invalid 107
> considered minor of perfect understanding 102
> definition of 23, 102
> dispositions by 102
> gift by, void 106
> interdiction of 102
> release by, invalid 107
> settlement by, invalid 106

Immovable property
> law of, contracts conflicting with 119

Imperial rescripts 32

Impossibility of performance
> of contract, damages in case of 120-1

Indemnity
> interest not claimable on, 169

Indian Courts
> decisions of 79

Inheritance
> law of, contracts conflicting with 118

Injunction
> in Ottoman law 73

Insane person,
> definition of 23

Insanity
> proof of cessation of 104

Inspection
> option for 92, 113

Instalments
> maturity of, on debtor's death 170-1

Instructions 35, 58
> function of 59

Insurance
> contract of 117
> Ottoman law of 117

Interdiction
> jurisdiction in 103-4
> of debtors 103-4
>> imbeciles 102
>> lunatics 101, 102
>> minor 100
>> prodigals 102

Interest
> compound, when payable 159, 160, 161
> excessive, Court may deduct 161
>> date from which deducted 165-6
> from date of action, Court must award 164, 166-7, 168
> liability of heirs for 167, 168, 169-71

            may not exceed capital   159, 160, 161
            not claimable on cost of destruction   169
                        estimated rent   165, 169
                        expenses of attachment   168
                        fixed damages   154, 163
                        indemnity   169
                        payment for services   169
                        rent   169
            on first mortgage payable before second mortgage   164-5
            Ottoman law of   117, 158-9
            when not claimable on money paid in advance   169
Interpretation
      of ambiguous texts   1-2, 21-3
            English law   79
            Mejelle   21
            Muhammadan law   79
            non-Muhammadan Ottoman law   78
            Ottoman Commercial Code   78
            Palestine Ordinances   79
Intizam umumi (See Public Order)
Irade-i-seniye   32, 35
Islam   2, 4, 6
Isnad   9
Istihsan   13, 15

Jami as-sahih   10
Joint note
      when promissory note signed by two persons is   135
Joint ownership
      in Mejelle   19
Judgment in presence appealable
      effect of use of words   50
Judgment subject to appeal
      effect of use of words   55
Judicature Act, 1873   68-9
Jurisdiction
      in interdiction   103-4
      of Land Court   40
Juz   7

Kabul (See Acceptanee)
Kararname   35
Kefil (See Guarantor)
Khalifa   5, 14
Khat-i-humayoun   33, 35
      sherif of Gulkhane   33

184

Khulafa-ar-rashidun 14
Koran 3, 5, 6, 7, 8
    III 29; 8
    IV 62; 8
    XVI 46; 9
    XXXIII 21; 8

Land Court
    judgment on title by, conditions in 51
    jurisdiction of 40
Land Courts Ordinance, 1921
    s. 2 (b) 40
    s. 7 (1) 73
Land Registrar
    admission before, allegation of falsity of 50, 53
Land Settlement Officer
    hearing of witnesses by, when unnecessary 51
Lapse of time
    when claim not barred by 39
Law 35, 58, 59
Law of Evidence (Amendment) Ordinance, 1924
    s. 12 effect of, on Art. 80 C.C.P. 54, 128, 134-5
Legalisation of document
    by Notary Public, effect of, 138-9
Legal Rate of Interest Ordinance, 1929 160, 161
Legislation
    by Sultans 32
    in protectorate 62
    Ottoman Empire, forms of 34-6
    Palestine, what constitutes 63
Lien
    of warehouseman no, in Ottoman law 74
Limitation of actions 13
Loan
    contracts relating to, in writing 131
    for use, capacity of parties to 105
Lottery
    action arising out of, when entertainable 126, 127
Lunatic
    admission by, invalid 107
    authority by, to agent invalid 106
    classes of 101-2
    dispositions by 103
    gift by, void 106
    interdiction of, 101, 102
    release by, invalid 107
    sale by, void 104
    settlement by, invalid 106

Maghbun 112
Mahjur (See Interdiction)
Maintenance
    meaning of 77-8
    of interdicted prodigal 102
Majlis 89
    modification of rule of 89-90
Majma-al-Anhur 20, 21, 23, 24, 26
Majnum (See Lunatic)
    ghair mutbik 102
    mutbik 101
Makful anhu 105
Malik ibn Anas 10, 15-6
Malikite School 15-6
Mal mutaqqawim
    meaning of 119
Masnad-ul-Imam Hanbal 16
Matu 9
Matuh (See Imbecile)
Maxims
    of Equity 70
        Mejelle 18, 71
Mazoun 100
Medical certificate
    insufficient to prove recovery of sanity 104
Mejelle
    arbitration in, 19
    contract in, definition of 88
    examples in, nature of 19-20
    headings to chapters of, whether law 18-9
    interpretation of 21
    joint ownership in 19
    maxims of 18, 71
    modified by Art. 64 of C.C.P. 116
    nature of 1, 17-24
    not exhaustive 23
    silence of, duty of Courts in case of 23
    sources of 20-4, 25-7
    subject matter of 18-9
Menfaa
    meaning of 119
Mesail 19
Millet
    meaning of 119

186

Minor 99-101
    admission by, invalid 107
    capacity of, to act as agent 106
                  appoint agent 106
                  let on hire 104
                  make a gift 106
    categories of, in Muhammadan law 100
    dispositions by 100-1
    guarantor, when bound 105
    interdiction of 100
    of imperfect understanding 100, 106
        perfect understanding 100, 106
    release by, invalid 107
    sale to, binds vendor 107
    settlement by, validity of 106-7
    transfer of debt by, when executory 105
                  to, when executory 105
    when, needs tutor's permission 100-1
Minor misrepresentation 100
    no remedy at law for 112
Miraat-al-Mejelle 24
Misdescription
    option for, 113
Misrepresentation 111-3
    flagrant, definition of, 100
            when remedy for 112
    minor 100
        no remedy at law for 112
    when, becomes deceit 112
Moneylenders
    no specific Palestine law regarding 161
Month
    commencement of 74
    end of 74
Morality
    contract contrary to 117
Moratab Waqf 20
Moratorium
    effect of 163
Mortgage
    interest on first, payable before second, 164-5
    obtained by threats, when valid 110
Mortgagee
    rights of, under bei bil wafa 161
Mortgagor
    duty of, on redemption 76
Muamelat 1, 18

Mudaribe partner
    accounting by 74
    when may demand oath 74
Muddet safar
    what constitutes 53
Muhal alieh 105
        lahu 105
Muhammadan law 1-16, 17, 24, 32, 33
    caveat emptor rule of 112
    categories of minors in 100
    contract in, 88
            classification of, 139-41
    equity in, 13
    in India 22
    interpretation of 79
    of alienation of ownership 92
        maturity of debt on debtor's death 170-71
    schools of, 2, 14-6
Muhammad ibn Abdullah 4-6
Muhammad ibn Idris ash-Shafi'i 16
Muhaya
    action for 38
Muhil 105
Muir 105
Mujtahidun 12
Mukhtarlik companies
    null and void 127
Multaka-al-Abhur 20, 23, 26
Multazim 130
Mumayiz (See Minor of Perfect Understanding)
Munakid 140
Murtehin 105
Musakat
    capacity to contract 106
Musalih (See Settlement)
Mustawdi 105
Musteir 105
Mutawalli
    claim as, when continuable in personal capacity 55
Mutemmim 36
Muwaddi 105
Muzaria
    capacity to contract 106

Nationalities 4, 5
Nizam 32, 35, 58
    function of 59
    name 32

188

Non-existing things
    contract for sale of 92
Notarial Notice (See also Protest)
    waiver of, form of, immaterial 50, 144
        valid 126
Notary Public
    acknowledgment before, oral evidence against to prove excessive interest 162-3
    duties of 142
    legalisation of document by, effect of 138-9
Notary Public Law
    Arts. 61-73 138

Oath
    as to excessive interest 162-3, 167, 168
    in absence of documentary evidence 130
    when Mudaribe partner may demand 74
        plaintiff may take, on appeal 49
Offer and acceptance
    necessity for, in contract 88-92
    where made 89
Official documents
    definition of 138
Option
    classes of 113
    effect of Art. 64 of C.C.P. on 113
    for cancellation 113
        defect 92, 114
        inspection 92, 113
        misdescription 113
        payment 113
        ratification 113
        selection 113
Oral Evidence (See Evidence)
Order
    directed to public officer 78
    with regard to threatened injury 78
Order-in-Council
    purposes of 61
    when part of Statutory Rules and Orders 62
Ordinance
    highest form of Palestine legislation 63
    Palestine, interpretation 79
Ordinary documents
    definition of 132, 138
    what are 139
Organic Law of Iraq
    Art. 113 60

Organic Law of Transjordan
    Art. 58 57, 60
    Art. 59 57
Orphan
    sale to, invalidated by flagrant misrepresentation 112
Osmanlis (See Ottomans)
Ottoman Civil Code (See Mejelle)
Ottoman Civil Procedure Code
    Art. 64 70, 75, 89, 92, 98, 109, 113, 114-27, 142
        dispenses with majlis 90
        effect of, on option 113
        modifies Mejelle 116
        para. 1. 116-9
             2. 119-20
             3. 120
        preamble to 114
    72. 138-9, 144
    73. 138
    74. 138
    75. 138
    76. 138
    80. 54, 127-31, 132-5, 137
    81. 128, 131-2
    82. 128, 131, 135-6
    97. 39
    106. 141-3
    107. 50, 141, 143-4
    108. 121, 141, 144-5, 149-52
    109. 141, 145
    110. 141, 145
    111. 141, 146-9
    112. 142, 158, 164
    126. 141, 158
Ottoman Commercial Code, 17
    a "general law" 117
    Art. 2. 100
        28. (Addendum) 117
        146. 39
        151. 55
    interpretation of 78
Ottoman Constitution of 1876 34
Ottoman Court of Cassation
    appeal to, in stamp cases 60
    decisions of, when binding on Palestine Courts 37
        taken over by Art. 46 of P.O.I.C. 37
Ottoman Empire
    legislation of, forms of, 34-6
    systems of law in 31-2

Ottoman Execution Law
    Art. 91. 52
Ottoman judicial organisation
    part of, taken over in Palestine 61
Ottoman Insurance Law 117
Ottoman Interest Regulations of Rajab 1304 A.H. 158-9
    Art. 5. modified by Legal Rate of Interest
                                Ordinance 1929 160
                     Usurious Loans Ordinance, 1934 159-60
      6. applies to renewal of debts 167
        not overruled by Usurious Loans (Evidence)
                                Ordinance, 1922 164
          retroactive 167, 168
Ottoman law 28-39
    applicability of, in Palestine 60-1
    classification of 34
    damages in 74
    elements of 33
    influence of French law on 32-3
    injunction in 73
    interpretation of 78
    no lien of warehouseman in 74
    non-Muhammadan, interpretation of 78
    of interest 117, 158-9
Ottoman laws
    applied to Palestine by Public Notice 57
    date of last 57-8
    modification of 34
    repealed or superseded 83-7
    subsequent to Nov. 1, 1914 57-61
    "such later", meaning of 58-61
Ottoman Maritime Code
    Art. 3 117
Ottoman Municipal Tax Law of Feb. 26, 1330
    not in force in Palestine 57
Ottoman Official Gazette 56
Ottoman Penal Code
    Arts. 139-50 amendments to 38
Ottomans 29
    legal system of 30-4
    legislative forms of 34-6
Ottoman Stamp Law of 1906
    Art. 60 60
Ownership
    alienation of, in Muhammadan law 92
    joint, in Mejelle 19

Palestine Courts
   when bound by decisions of Cyprus Courts   37, 38
                               Ottoman Court of
                                     Cassation   37
                        previous decisions   39-57
Palestine legislation
   what constitutes   63
Palestine Order in Council
   date of commencement of   63
   Art. 43   55
       46   28, 36, 57, 71-8, 147
           "any other provisions"   64
           Courts of Justice   71-2
           "Orders in Council, Ordinances, and Regulations
                              in force in Palestine"   61-3
           "Ottoman Law as it existed on and before
                              Nov. 1, 1914"   29-37
           "Ottoman laws subsequent to Nov. 1, 1914   57-61
           "Powers, Procedure and Practice" of English
                              Courts   71-2, 80
           "so far as the same shall not extend or apply"   64
           "subject thereto"   64
           "substance of Common Law and doctrines of
                              Equity"   64-71
           summary of   79-80
           when, takes over decisions of Ottoman Court of
                              Cassation   37
       47   103
       51   118
       52   59, 103
       53(a)   77
       54   77-8
       73   58-63
       74   63
Palestine Ordinances
   interpretation of,   79
Partner
   mudaribe (See Mudaribe partner)
Partnership
   contracts relating to, in writing   130
   in land and work (See Muzaria)
       trees and work (See Musakat)
   obligation to register   130
Past consideration
   not good consideration   98
Payment
   cessation of, date of   55
   for services, interest not claimable on   169
   of debt before maturity, creditor can refuse   110
   option for,   113

192

Penalty
    English law as to 147-9
        applicability of, 147
    Ottoman law allows 153
Performance
    of contract, impossibility of 120-1
        time for 142-3
Personal status 17
    contract conflicting with matters of 118
    law governing 32, 33
Pious foundation
    sale to, invalidated by flagrant misrepresentation 112
Pledge
    capacity of parties to 105
Possession
    witnesses as to, when Land Settlement Officer need not hear 51
Powers
    of Courts of Justice 71
Prerogative 61, 62
    of Sultans 35
Prescription
    effect of fraud on 73
        residence abroad on 53
President of District Court
    is Chief Execution Officer 61
Previous decisions
    when binding on Palestine Courts 39-57
Price 92
Privileges
    granted by Sultans 31
Privy Council 22, 24, 61, 62, 71
Procedure
    English law of, date of commencement of, in Palestine 72, 80
Proclamation of Nov. 18, 1918. 74
Prodigals
    classes of 102
    dispositions by 102
    interdicted, maintenance of 102
    interdiction of 102
Promise
    to marry, breach of 152-3
    when not binding 99
Promissory note
    payable to bearer, validity of 122-3
Protectorate
    legislation in 62

Protest (See also Notarial Notice)
    object of 142
    origin of word 142
    time for service of 143
    waiver of, form of 50, 144
    when necessary for damages claim 141-3
Provisional Law of Salvage 35
Provisional Law relating to Primary Schools 36
Provisional laws 35-6
    list of principal Ottoman 82
Puberty 99-100, 101
Public Notice
    applying Ottoman law to Palestine 57
Public Officer
    order directed to 78
Public Order
    contracts prejudicial to 117-8
    meaning of 117-8
Public Policy 98, 117, 123, 124
Purchasers in good faith 49

Qadhis 17
Qanun 32, 35, 58, 59
    name 32
Qarar 58, 59
Qiyas 4, 12, 13, 15, 16

Radd-al-Mukhtar 20, 26
Rahin 105
Rashid 101
Rate of Exchange
    date on which calculated 54
Ratification
    of contract of hire, when necessary 104
    option for, 113
Readiness and willingness to perform 72, 143
Redemption
    mortgagor's duty on 76
Registrar of Lands
    refusal of, to register transfer, when defence to damages claim 150-2
Registration
    Chief Execution Officer's order for, when set aside 52
Regulation (See Nizam)
Regulations
    modification of 34

194

Release 88
    by imbecile, invalid 107
        lunatic, invalid 107
        minor, invalid 107
    capacity to grant 107

Rent
    estimated (See Estimated Rent)
    interest not claimable on, 169

Rescission
    acceptance of, by conduct 91-2

Residence
    abroad. effect of, on prescription 53

Right of way 40

Royal Irade 88

Rules of Court of Dec. 10, 1918 38

Sabi (See Minor)

Safe Keeping
    deposit for, capacity of parties to 105

Saghir (See Minor)
    ghair mumayiz 100
    mumayiz 100

Sahaba 12

Sahih 10, 140

Sale
    by deceit, when purchaser cannot cancel 113
        lunatic, void 104
    capacity of parties to 104
    in execution proceedings, valuation of property on 50
    of non-existing things, contract for 92
        ship, formalities for 117
    to minor, binds vendor 107
        orphan invalidated by flagrant misrepresentation 112
        pious foundation, invalidated by flagrant misrepresentation 112
        Treasury, invalidated by flagrant misrepresentation 112

Schools of Muhammadan law 2, 14-6

Sebeb iztirari (See Force Majeure)

Secured creditor
    when, can petition for winding up 75-6

Selection
    option for 113

Semen (See Price)

Sened Deyn 171

Services
    payment for, interest not claimable on 169

Settlement
>by imbecile, invalid 106
>>lunatic, invalid 106
>>minor, validity of 106-7
>capacity to make 106

Shafeite school 16

Sharia 14, 30

Sharia Court
>decision of, as to guardian 104
>jurisdiction of, over debtors 103

Shiahs 14

Ship
>formalities for sale of 117

Sign
>authority to, for another 49

Silence
>of Mejelle, duty of Courts in case of 23

Sillsilah 9

Sources
>of Mejelle 20-4, 25-7

Special laws
>meaning of 116-7

Specific performance
>when not granted in Palestine 70, 73, 75

Speculative contracts
>invalidity of 117

Spouses
>transaction between, oral evidence as to 136

Statute law 65, 66, 67, 69
>when included in substance of Common Law 69

Statutory Rules and Orders 62

Subsidiary matters
>meaning of 120

Succession,
>law of, contract conflicting with 118

Such latter Ottoman laws
>meaning of, in Art. 46 of P.O.i.C. 58-61

Sultans
>legislation by 32
>prerogative of 35
>privileges granted by 31

Sunna 3, 8, 9, 10, 11

Sunnat-at-suqut 9
>-at-taqrir 9
>-ul-f'il 9
>-ul-qual 9

Sunnites 11, 14, 15

Supreme Court of Palestine
    tendency of, to be bound by its own decisions 38
Surah 7
Surety (See Guarantor)

Ta'alimat 35, 58
    function of 59
Ta'amul 13
Tabiun 12
Taghrir (See Deceit)
Tanzimat-i-Khairiye 33
Tekvim-i-veqayi 36
Threatened injury
    order with regard to 78
Title
    judgment of Land Court on, conditions in 51
Tradition (See Hadith)
Transfer of debt
    by minor, when executory 105
    capacity of parties to 105
    to minor, when executory 105
    when executory 105
        void 105
Transfer of land
    refusal of Registrar of Lands to register, when defence to damages claim 150-2
Transfer of Land Ordinance, 1920
    s. 2 54
       9 54
Treasury
    sale to, invalidated by flagrant misrepresentation 112
Trustee
    appointment of 76
Trusts
    English law of, when applicable in Cyprus 57
    private, lacking in Palestine 70, 76-7
Tutor
    permission of, when minor needs 100-1

Ummat al Islam 4
Undertaking
    provable by witnesses' evidence 127
    unenforceable for want of consideration 97
Unregistered land transaction
    effect of 93-4
Uqud Muaza (See Valuable consideration)

Urf 13
    am 13
    khan 13
Usul 6
Usurious Interest (See Excessive Interest)
Usurious Loans (Evidence) Ordinance, 1922
    does not overrule Art. 6 of Ottoman Interest Regulations 164
    is a law of procedure 162
        restricted to plea by defendant 54, 164, 166-7
        retroactive 162
Usurious Loans Ordinance, 1934 159-60

Valuable consideration
    defined 93
Valuation of property on sale
    procedure for, in execution 50
Verification of handwriting 39
Void
    when contract is 109, 141
Voidable
    when contract is 109, 140

Wages
    when employee cannot claim 156-7
Wahib 106
Waiver
    of notarial notice, form of, immaterial 50, 144
                    valid 126
Waqf
    law of, contracts conflicting with 118
    moratab 20
Warehouseman
    has no lien in Ottoman law 74
Wasi (See Guardian)
Water
    cutting off of, when damages not recoverable for 157
Weli (See Tutor)
We promise to pay
    note signed, by two persons, joint note 135
Winding up
    when secured creditor can petition for 75-6
Witnesses
    credibility of, not matter for Court of Appeal 135-6
    evidence of, to prove undertaking 127
    when Land Settlement Officer need not hear 51
Written Document
    admissibility of oral evidence against 54, 134-5

Yarghouji 30, 32

Zakah 9.